Seventh Edition

Writing Themes About Literature

EDGAR V. ROBERTS

Lehman College
of
The City University of New York

PRENTICE HALL, *Englewood Cliffs, New Jersey 07632*

Library of Congress Cataloging-in-Publication Data

Roberts, Edgar V.
  Writing themes about literature / Edgar V. Roberts.
    p.   cm.
  Includes index.
  ISBN 0-13-971052-3

  1. English language—Rhetoric. 2. Literature—History and
criticism—Theory, etc. 3. Criticism—Authorship. 4. Report
writing. I. Title.
PE1479.C7R59 1991
808'.0668—dc20   90-7350
                                                      CIP

Editorial/production supervision: Patricia V. Amoroso
Cover design: 20/20 Services Inc.
Prepress buyers: Mary Ann Gloriande and Herb Klein
Manufacturing buyer: David Dickey

 © 1991, 1988, 1983, 1977, 1973, 1969, 1964 by Prentice-Hall, Inc.
A Division of Simon & Schuster
Englewood Cliffs, New Jersey 07632

Printed in the United States of America

10 9 8 7 6 5 4 3 2 1

ISBN 0-13-971052-3

PRENTICE-HALL INTERNATIONAL (UK) LIMITED, *London*
PRENTICE-HALL OF AUSTRALIA PTY. LIMITED, *Sydney*
PRENTICE-HALL CANADA INC., *Toronto*
PRENTICE-HALL HISPANOAMERICANA, S.A., *Mexico*
PRENTICE-HALL OF INDIA PRIVATE LIMITED, *New Delhi*
PRENTICE-HALL OF JAPAN, INC., *Tokyo*
SIMON & SCHUSTER ASIA PTE. LTD., *Singapore*
EDITORA PRENTICE-HALL DO BRASIL, LTDA., *Rio de Janeiro*

Contents

6 WRITING ABOUT POINT OF VIEW: THE POSITION AND STANCE OF THE WORK'S SPEAKER OR NARRATOR

85

7 WRITING ABOUT AN IDEA OR THEME: THE MEANING AND THE MESSAGE IN LITERATURE

98

8 WRITING ABOUT IMAGERY: THE WORK'S LINK TO THE SENSES

108

16 WRITING AN EVALUATION: DECIDING ON LITERARY QUALITY   235

17 WRITING ABOUT FILM: VISUAL AND AUDITORY LITERATURE   243

18 WRITING THE RESEARCH THEME: EXTRA RESOURCES FOR UNDERSTANDING   255

APPENDIX A: TAKING EXAMINATIONS ON LITERATURE

APPENDIX B: A NOTE ON DOCUMENTATION

APPENDIX C: WORKS USED FOR SAMPLE THEMES AND REFERENCES

Plays:

To the Instructor

In the seventh edition of *Writing Themes About Literature* I have kept and strengthened those features that so many of you have valued over the years. As always, I base my approach not on genres, with specific assignments to be determined, but rather on topics for full-length themes on texts in any genre. The chapters may also be used as starting points for classroom study and discussion and may be adapted for shorter writing assignments. The result is that the seventh edition offers great scope and variety, either for a one-semester course or for a two- or three-semester sequence with the possibility of complete or near complete use.

As in each past edition of *Writing Themes About Literature*, the chapters consist of two parts. The first is a discussion of a literary approach, and the second is one or more sample themes showing how the approach may be applied in a theme-length assignment.

A major characteristic preserved in this edition is that, after the preliminary discussion in Chapter 1, the chapters are arranged in order of increasing difficulty. Commencing with Chapter 2, which helps students connect their reading with their responses, the chapters progress from topics relevant to all the genres. The comparison-contrast chapter (13), for example, illustrates in its two parts the ways in which the earlier techniques may be focused on any of the topics in the book; in addition, the theme of extended comparison may serve as a longer assignment for a one-semester course. The later chapters, such as prosody, evaluation, film, and research, are increasingly technical and sophisticated, but they also combine and build on the various techniques of analysis presented in the earlier chapters.

Although you might assign the chapters in sequence throughout your course, you may choose them according to need and objective. One instructor, for example, might pass over the earlier, more general chapters and go directly to the later and more technical ones. Another might omit the longer comparison-contrast theme but might repeat the shorter one for separate assignments such as comparative studies of imagery, structure, character, and point of view. Still another might use just a few of the chapters, assigning them two or more times until students have overcome initial difficulties. No matter how the chapters are used, the two parts— discussion and illustration—enable students to improve the quality of their analytical writing.

The illustrative parts of the chapters—the sample themes—are presented in the belief that the word *imitation* need not be preceded by adjectives like *slavish* and *mere*. Their purpose is to show what *might* be done— not what *must* be done—on particular assignments. Without the samples as guides, students must add the task of creating their own thematic form to the already complex task of understanding new concepts and new works of literature. Some students may follow the samples closely while others may adapt them or else use them as points of departure. My assumption is that students will become free to go their own way as they become more experienced.

Because the sample themes are guides, they represent a full treatment of each of the topics. Nevertheless, in this edition they have been kept within the approximate length of most assignments. If students are writing outside of class, they can readily create themes as full as the samples. Even though the samples treat three or more aspects of particular topics, there is nothing to prevent assigning only one aspect, either for an impromptu or for an outside-class theme. Thus, using the chapter on setting, you might assign a paragraph about the use of setting in only the first scene of a story, or a paragraph about interior settings, colors, or shades of light.

Following each sample essay is a commentary—which my students recommended that I include in the fourth edition and which I have kept ever since—designed to connect the precepts in the first part of the chapter to the example in the second. New in the seventh edition is the "close look" at one of the paragraphs in each theme. My hope is that this additional analysis will help students understand possible methods of paragraph development.

I have designed all changes in the seventh edition of *Writing Themes About Literature*, as in earlier editions, to guide students in reading, studying, thinking, planning, drafting, organizing, and writing. Many chapters are extensively revised; some are almost entirely rewritten. In making the many revisions, alterations, repositionings, and additions (and subtractions), I have tried to improve, sharpen, and freshen the underlying information and examples. With all the changes, the seventh edition of *Writing Themes About Literature* is comprehensive for composition courses in which literature is introduced, and also for literature courses at any level.

A particular word seems in order about the number of works in Appendix C, some of which are newly included in the seventh edition. At one time I believed that clarifying references could be drawn from a pool of works commonly known by advanced high school and college students, and I, therefore, thought that no reference anthology was necessary. I presented a small number of works in the second edition, keyed to some but not all of the sample themes, but reviewers recommended against it for the next editions. Recent commentary, however, has emphasized that references to unknown works, even complete and self-explanatory ones, do not fully explain and clarify. Therefore, after the fifth edition I made the book almost completely self-contained, with an increased number of works in Appendix C (for the chapter on problems, however, I have continued to assume acquaintance with Shakespeare's *Hamlet*, and for the theme on film I have assumed that students might be shown Welles's *Citizen Kane*). The result is that both references and sample essays may be easily verified by a reading of the accompanying works. Thus the student preparing to write about plot and structure can compare the sample themes on that topic with the complete text of Welty's "A Worn Path." This story is also one of the subjects in the sample extended comparison-contrast theme of Chapter 13, in addition to the references made to it elsewhere in the test. The other included works are used similarly. I believe that the unity and coherence provided by these works give students great help in understanding their own assignments.

An innovation of the sixth edition, continued in the seventh, is the glossary based on the terms set in bold face in the text. The increasing number of students taking entrance examinations and GREs has justified this continuation. A student may consult the glossary, which contains definitions and page numbers for further reference, and thereby develop full and systematic knowledge of important concepts in the text.

Finally, the seventh edition brings into focus something that has been true of *Writing Themes About Literature* since its first appearance in 1964. The book is to be used in the classroom as a practical guide for writing; the stress throughout is on writing. This emphasis is made to help students not only in composition and literature, but in most of their classes. In other subjects such as psychology, economics, sociology, biology, and political science, instructors use texts and ask students to develop raw data, and they assign writing on this basis. Writing is on external, written materials, not on descriptions of the student's own experiences or on opinions. Writing is about reading.

Yet we instructors of composition face the problems we have always faced. On the one hand the needs of other departments, recently thrown into renewed focus by studies about writing-across-the-curriculum, cause wide diversification of subject matter, straining the general knowledge of the staff and also creating a certain topical and thematic disunity. On the other, programs stressing internalized subject matter, such as personal experiences or occasional topic materials, have little bearing on writing for other courses. We as English faculty, with a background in literature, have the task of meeting the service needs of the institution without compromising our own disciplinary commitment.

The approach in this book is aimed at these dilemmas. Teachers can work with their own discipline—literature—while also fulfilling their primary and often required responsibility of teaching writing that is externally, not internally, directed. The book thus keeps the following issues in perspective:

- The requirement of the institution for composition.
- The need of students to develop writing skills based on written texts.
- The responsibility of the English faculty to teach writing while still working within their own expertise.

It is, therefore, gratifying to claim that the approach in *Writing Themes About Literature* has been tested for many years. It is no longer new, but it is still novel. It works. It gives coherence to the sometimes fragmented composition course. It also provides for adaptation and, as I have stressed, variety. Using the book, you can develop a virtually endless number of new topics for themes. One obvious benefit is the possibility of eliminating not only the traditional "theme barrels" of infamous memory in fraternity and sorority houses, but also the newer interference from business "enterprises" that provide themes to order.

While *Writing Themes About Literature* is designed as a rhetoric of practical criticism for students, it is based on profoundly held convictions. I believe that true liberation in a liberal arts curriculum is achieved only through clearly defined goals. Just to make assignments and let students do with them what they can is to encourage frustration and mental enslavement. But if students develop a deep knowledge of specific approaches to subject material, they can begin to develop some of that expertness which is essential to freedom. As Pope said:

> True ease in writing comes from art, not chance,
> As those move easiest who have learned to dance.

It is almost axiomatic that the development of writing skill in one area—in this instance the interpretation of literature—has an enabling effect on skill in other areas. The search for information with a particular goal in mind, the asking of pointed questions, the testing, rephrasing, and developing of ideas—all these and more are transferable skills for students to build on throughout their college years and beyond.

I have one concluding article of faith. Those of us whose careers have been established in the study of literature have made commitments to our belief in its value. The study of literature is valid in and for itself. But literature as an art form employs techniques and creates problems for readers that can be dealt with only through analysis, and analysis means work. Thus the immediate aim of *Writing Themes About Literature* is to help students to read and write about individual literary works. But the ultimate objective (in the past I wrote *"primary* objective") is to promote the pleasurable study and, finally, the love, of literature.

ACKNOWLEDGMENTS

As I complete my preparation of the seventh edition of *Writing Themes About Literature,* I express my deepest thanks to those who have been loyal to all the earlier editions. Your approval of the book makes me thankful at the same time that it has challenged me to create an acceptable new edition. The changes in the following pages are based on my own experiences and thought and also on my continued work with my students at Lehman College. But as I think about the revisions I am impressed with how much my book has been influenced by the collective wisdom of many other people. Those who have been particularly helpful for the seventh edition are William T. Cotton, Loyola University of the South; Betty Gipson, Southwest Baptist University; Joseph LaBriola, Sinclair Community College; Rene Morrissette, Central New England College of Technology; and Albert E. Wilhelm, Tennessee Technological University. Conversations and discussions with others have influenced my changes in innumerable and immeasurable ways. I am grateful to Phil Miller of Prentice Hall, who has given me firm and friendly support over a number of years. I should also like to thank Kate Morgan of Prentice Hall for her thoughtful, creative, and thorough assistance. Pattie Amoroso of Prentice Hall was the production editor for the seventh edition, and for her skill and hard work I am thankful. I should particularly like to thank Ilene McGrath, who copyedited the manuscript and who offered many improvements. Finally, I thank Jonathan Roberts for his skilled and unfailing help in preparing the manuscripts of the many halting and tentative drafts leading to the final copy.

EDGAR V. ROBERTS

chapter 1

Preliminary:

The Process of Writing Themes About Literature

The following chapters introduce a number of analytical approaches important in the study of literature, along with guidance for writing informative and well-focused themes based on these approaches. The chapters should help you fulfill two goals of composition and English courses: (1) to write good themes, and (2) to assimilate great works of literature into the imagination.

The premise of the book is that no educational process is complete until you can *apply* what you study. That is, you have not learned something—really *learned* it—until you talk or write about it. This does not mean that you retell a story, state an undeveloped opinion, or describe an author's life, but rather that you deal directly with topical and artistic issues about individual works. The need to write requires you to strengthen your understanding and knowledge through the recognition of where your original study might have fallen short. Thus, it is easy for you to read the chapter on Point of View (Chapter 6), and it is also easy to read, say, Jackson's story "The Lottery," but your grasp of point of view as a concept will not be complete—nor will your appreciation of the technical artistry of "The Lottery" be complete—until you have *written* about the technique. As you prepare your theme, you need to reread parts of the work, study your notes, and apply your knowledge to the problem at hand; you must check facts, grasp relationships, develop insights, and express yourself with as much exactness and certainty as possible.

Primarily, then, this book aims to help you improve your writing skills through the use of literature as subject matter. After you have finished a number of themes derived from the following chapters, you will be able to approach just about any literary work with the confidence that you can understand it and deal with it well, if not expertly.

WHAT IS LITERATURE AND WHY DO WE STUDY IT?

Although the word **literature** broadly includes just about everything that is written, we use it more specifically to mean written compositions that tell stories, dramatize situations, express emotions, and analyze and advocate ideas. Most literary works during recorded history were designed only for the printed page, and we read them silently. Works composed before history began, however, were originally *oral,* and, fortunately, many of these have been preserved and now exist as printed texts. Also a great deal of literature is designed to be read aloud (many poems), and much is designed to be spoken and acted out by live actors (plays).

Whatever the form, literature has many things to offer, almost as many things as there are people. In fact, people often cannot explain why they enjoy reading, for goals and ideals are not easily articulated. There are, however, areas of general agreement about some of the things that the systematic and extensive reading of literature can do.

Literature helps us grow, both personally and intellectually; it provides an objective base for knowledge and understanding; it links us with the broader cultural, philosophic, and religious world of which we are a part; it enables us to recognize human dreams and struggles in different places and times that we would never otherwise know; it helps us develop mature sensibility and compassion for the condition of *all* living things—human, animal, and vegetable; it gives us the knowledge and perception to appreciate the beauty of order and arrangement, just as a well-structured song or a beautifully painted canvas can; it provides the comparative basis from which we can see worthiness in the aims of all people, and it therefore helps us see beauty in the world around us; it exercises our emotions through interest, concern, tension, excitement, hope, fear, regret, laughter, and sympathy. Through cumulative experience in reading, literature shapes goals and values by clarifying our own identities, both positively, through acceptance of the admirable in human beings, and negatively, through rejection of the sinister. It helps us shape our judgments through the comparison of the good and the bad. Both in our everyday activities and in the decisions we make as individuals and as citizens, it enables us to develop a perspective on events occurring locally and globally, and thereby it gives us understanding and control. It encourages us to assist creative, talented people who need recognition and support. It is one of the shaping influences of life. It makes us human.

TYPES OF LITERATURE: THE GENRES

Literature may be classified into four categories or *genres:* (1) prose fiction, (2) poetry, (3) drama, and (4) nonfiction prose. While all are art forms, each with its own requirements of structure and style, usually the first three are classed as **imaginative literature.**

The genres of imaginative literature have much in common, but they also have distinguishing characteristics. **Prose fiction, or narrative fiction,** includes **novels, short stories, myths, parables, romances,** and **epics.** *Fiction* originally meant anything made up, crafted, or shaped, but as we understand the word today, it means a prose story based in the imagination of the author. While fiction, like all imaginative literature, may introduce true historical details, it is not real history, for its purpose is primarily to interest, divert, stimulate, and instruct. The essence of fiction is **narration,** the relating or recounting of a sequence of events or actions. Works of fiction usually focus on one or a few major characters and deal with problems. **Poetry** is more economical than prose fiction in the use of words, and it relies heavily on **imagery, figurative language,** and **sound. Drama** is literature designed to be performed by actors. Like fiction, drama may focus on a single character or a small number of characters, and it presents fictional events as if they were happening in the present, to be witnessed by an audience. Although most modern plays present dialogue in prose, on the ground that dramatic speech is to be as lifelike as possible, many plays from the past, like those of ancient Greece and Renaissance England, are in poetic form.

Imaginative literature differs from **nonfiction prose,** the fourth genre, which consists of news reports, feature articles, themes, editorials, textbooks, historical and biographical works, and the like, all of which describe or interpret facts and present judgments and opinions. A major goal of nonfiction prose is truth in reporting and logic in reasoning. It bears repeating that the truth in imaginative literature, unlike that in nonfiction prose, is truth to life and human nature, not to the factual world of news, science, and history.

READING LITERATURE
AND RESPONDING TO IT ACTIVELY

Do not expect a cursory reading to produce full understanding. After a quick reading of a work, it may be embarrassingly difficult to answer pointed questions or to say anything intelligent about it at all. A more careful, active reading gives us the understanding to make well-considered answers. Obviously, we must first follow the work and understand its details, but more importantly we must respond to the words, get at the ideas, and understand the implications of what is happening. We must apply our own experiences to verify the accuracy and truth of the situation and incidents, and we must articulate our own emotional responses to the characters and their problems.

To illustrate such active responding, the following story, "The Necklace" (1884), by the French writer Guy de Maupassant, is printed with the sorts of marginal annotations that any reader might make when reading. These are broad and general, and are not directed toward specific analytical approaches such as setting, point of view, and character. Many of the observations, particularly at the beginning, are *assimilative;* that is, they do no more than record details and turning points in the action. But as the story progresses, the comments increasingly reflect responses to the story's developing meaning. Toward the story's end, the comments are full rather than minimal, for they result not only from a first reading, but also from a second and third. Here, then, is Maupassant's "The Necklace":

Guy de Maupassant (1850–1893)

The Necklace   1884

Translated by Edgar V. Roberts

She was one of those pretty and charming women, born, as if by an error of destiny, into a family of clerks and copyists. She had no dowry, no prospects, no way of getting known, courted, loved, married by a rich and distinguished man. She finally settled for a marriage with a minor clerk in the Ministry of Education.

> "She" is pretty but poor. Apparently there is no other life for her than marriage. Without connections, she has no entry into high society and marries an insignificant clerk.

She was a simple person, without the money to dress well, but she was as unhappy as if she had gone through bankruptcy, for women have neither rank nor race. In place of high birth or important family connections, they can rely only on their beauty, their grace, and their charm. Their inborn finesse, their elegant taste, their engaging personalities, which are their only power, make working-class women the equals of the grandest ladies.

> She is unhappy.
>
> A view of women that excludes the possibility of a career. In 1884 women had little else than their personalities to get ahead.

She suffered constantly, feeling herself destined for all delicacies and luxuries. She suffered because of her grim apartment with its drab walls, threadbare furniture, ugly curtains. All such things, which most other women in her situation would not even have noticed, tortured her and filled her with despair. The sight of the young country girl who did her simple housework awakened in her only a sense of desolation and lost hopes. She daydreamed of large, silent anterooms, decorated with oriental tapestries and lighted by high bronze floor lamps, with two elegant valets in short culottes dozing in large armchairs under the effects of forced-air heaters. She visualized large drawing rooms draped in the most expensive silks, with fine end tables on which were placed knick-knacks of inestimable value. She dreamed of the perfume of dainty private rooms, which were designed only for intimate tête-à-têtes with the closest friends, who because of their achievements and fame would make her the envy of all other women.

> She suffers because of her cheap belongings, wanting expensive things. She dreams of wealth and of how other women would envy her if she had all these fine things. But these luxuries are unrealistic and unattainable for her.

When she sat down to dinner at her round little table covered with a cloth that had not been washed for three days, in front of her husband who opened the kettle while declaring ecstatically, "Ah, good old boiled beef! I don't know anything better," she dreamed of expensive banquets with shining place-settings, and wall hangings depicting ancient heroes and exotic birds in an enchanted forest. She imagined a gourmet-prepared main course carried on the most exquisite trays and served on the most beautiful dishes, with whispered gallantries which she would hear with a sphinxlike smile as she dined on the pink meat of a trout or the delicate wing of a quail.

> Her husband's taste is for plain things, while she dreams of expensive gourmet food. He has adjusted to his status. She has not.

5 She had no decent dresses, no jewels, nothing. And she loved nothing but these; she believed herself born only for these. She burned with the desire to please, to be envied, to be attractive and sought after.

> She lives for her unrealistic dreams, and these increase her frustration.

She had a rich friend, a comrade from convent days, whom she did not want to see anymore because she suffered so much when she returned home. She would weep for the entire day afterward with sorrow, regret, despair, and misery.

> She even thinks of giving up a rich friend because she is so depressed after visiting her.

Well, one evening, her husband came home glowing and carrying a large envelope.
"Here," he said, "this is something for you."

> A new section in the story.

She quickly tore open the envelope and took out a card engraved with these words:

> The Chancellor of Education and Mrs. George Ramponneau request that Mr. and Mrs. Loisel do them the honor of coming to dinner at the Ministry of Education on the evening of January 8.

An invitation to dinner at the Ministry of Education. A big plum.

10   Instead of being delighted, as her husband had hoped, she threw the invitation spitefully on the table, muttering:

"What do you expect me to do with this?"

It only upsets her.

"But honey, I thought you'd be glad. You never get to go out, and this is a special occasion! I had a lot of trouble getting the invitation. Everyone wants one; the demand is high and not many clerks get invited. Everyone important will be there."

She looked at him angrily and stated impatiently:

"What do you want me to wear to go there?"

She declares that she hasn't anything to wear. He tries to persuade her that her theater dress might do for the occasion.

15   He had not thought of that. He stammered:

"But your theater dress. That seems nice to me . . ."

He stopped, amazed and bewildered, as his wife began to cry. Large tears fell slowly from the corners of her eyes to her mouth. He said falteringly:

"What's wrong? What's the matter?"

But with a strong effort she had recovered, and she answered calmly as she wiped her damp cheeks:

20   "Nothing, except that I have nothing to wear and therefore can't go to the party. Give your invitation to someone else at the office whose wife will have nicer clothes than mine."

Distressed, he responded:

"Well, all right, Mathilde. How much would a new dress cost, something you could use at other times, but not anything fancy?"

Her name is Mathilde.
He volunteers to pay for a new dress.

She thought for a few moments, adding things up and thinking also of an amount that she could ask without getting an immediate refusal and a frightened outcry from the frugal clerk.

Finally she responded tentatively:

She is manipulating him.

25   "I don't know exactly, but it seems to me that I could get by on four hundred francs."

He blanched slightly at this, because he had set aside just that amount to buy a shotgun for Sunday lark-hunts the next summer with a few friends in the Plain of Nanterre.

However, he said:

"All right, you've got four hundred francs, but make it a pretty dress."

> The dress will cost him his next summer's vacation. (He doesn't seem to have included her in his plans.)

As the day of the party drew near, Mrs. Loisel seemed sad, uneasy, anxious, even though her gown was all ready. One evening her husband said to her:

> A new section, the third in the story. The day of the party is near.

30 "What's the matter? You've been acting funny for several days."

She answered:

"It's awful, but I don't have any jewels to wear, not a single gem, nothing to dress up my outfit. I'll look like a beggar. I'd almost rather not go to the party."

> Now she complains that she doesn't have any nice jewelry. She is manipulating him again.

He responded:

"You can wear a corsage of cut flowers. This year it's all the rage. For only ten francs you can get two or three gorgeous roses."

35 She was not convinced.

"No . . . there's nothing more humiliating than looking shabby in the company of rich women."

> She has a very good point, but there seems to be no way out.

But her husband exclaimed:

"God, but you're silly! Go to your friend Mrs. Forrestier, and ask her to lend you some jewelry. You know her well enough to do that."

> He proposes a solution: borrow jewelry from Mrs. Forrestier, who is apparently the rich friend mentioned earlier.

She uttered a cry of joy:

40 "That's right. I hadn't thought of that."

The next day she went to her friend's house and described her problem.

Mrs. Forrestier went to her mirrored wardrobe, took out a large jewel box, opened it, and said to Mrs. Loisel:

"Choose, my dear."

> Mathilde will have her choice of jewels.

She saw bracelets, then a pearl necklace, then a Venetian cross of finely worked gold and gems. She tried on the jewelry in front of a mirror, and hesitated, unable to make up her mind about each one. She kept asking:

45 "Do you have anything else?"

"Certainly. Look to your heart's content. I don't know what will please you most."

Suddenly she found, in a black satin box, a

> A "superb" diamond necklace.

superb diamond necklace, and her heart throbbed
with desire for it. Her hands shook as she picked
it up. She fastened it around her neck, watched it
gleam at her throat, and looked at herself ecstatically.

Then she asked, haltingly and anxiously:

"Could you lend me this, nothing but this?"   **This is what she wants, just this.**

50   "Why yes, certainly."

She jumped up, hugged her friend joyfully,   **She leaves with the "treasure."**
then hurried away with her treasure.

The day of the party came. Mrs. Loisel was a   **A new section.**
success. She was prettier than anyone else, styl-   **The Party. Mathilde is a huge**
ish, graceful, smiling and wild with joy. All the   **success.**
men saw her, asked her name, sought to be intro-
duced. All the important administrators stood in
line to waltz with her. The Chancellor himself eyed
her.

She danced joyfully, passionately, intoxi-   **Another judgment about women.**
cated with pleasure, thinking of nothing but the   **Don't men want admiration, too?**
moment, in the triumph of her beauty, in the glory
of her success, on cloud nine with happiness made
up of all the admiration, of all the aroused desire,
of this victory so complete and so sweet to the
heart of any woman.

She did not leave until four o'clock in the   **Loisel, with other husbands, is**
morning. Her husband, since midnight, had been   **bored, while the wives are hav-**
sleeping in a little empty room with three other   **ing a ball.**
men whose wives had also been enjoying them-
selves.

55   He threw over her shoulders the shawl that   **Ashamed of her wrap, she rushes**
he had brought for the trip home, a modest every-   **away to avoid being seen.**
day wrap, the poverty of which contrasted sharply
with the elegance of her evening gown. She felt it
and hurried away to avoid being noticed by the
other women who luxuriated in rich furs.

Loisel tried to hold her back:

"Wait a minute. You'll catch cold outdoors.
I'll call a cab."

But she paid no attention and hurried down
the stairs. When they reached the street they
found no carriages. They began to look for one,
shouting at cabmen passing by at a distance.

They walked toward the Seine, desperate,   **A comedown after the nice**
shivering. Finally, on a quay, they found one of   **evening. They take a wretched-**
those old night-going buggies that are seen in Paris **looking buggy home.**
only after dark, as if they were ashamed of their
wretched appearance in daylight.

60   It took them to their door, on the Street of Martyrs, and they sadly climbed the stairs to their flat. For her, it was finished. As for him, he could think only that he had to begin work at the Ministry of Education at ten o'clock.

      She took the shawl off her shoulders, in front of the mirror, to see herself once more in her glory. But suddenly she cried out. The necklace was no longer around her neck!

      Her husband, already half undressed, asked: "What's wrong?"

      She turned toward him frantically:

65   "I . . . I . . . I no longer have Mrs. Forrestier's necklace."

      He stood up, bewildered:

      "What! . . . How! . . . It's not possible!"

      And they looked in the folds of the gown, in the folds of the shawl, in the pockets, everywhere. They found nothing.

      He asked:

70   "You're sure you still had it when you left the party?"

      "Yes. I checked it in the vestibule of the Ministry."

      "But if you had lost it in the street, we would have heard it fall. It must be in the cab."

      "Yes, probably. Did you notice the number?"

      "No. Did you see it?"

75   "No."

      Overwhelmed, they looked at each other. Finally, Loisel got dressed again:

      "I'm going out to retrace all our steps," he said, "to see if I can find the necklace that way."

      And he went out. She stayed in her evening dress, without the energy to get ready for bed, stretched out in a chair, drained of strength and thought.

      Her husband came back at about seven o'clock. He had found nothing.

80   He went to Police Headquarters and to the newspapers to announce a reward. He went to the small cab companies, and finally he followed up even the slightest hopeful lead.

      She waited the entire day, in the same enervated state, in the face of this frightful disaster.

      Loisel came back in the evening, his face pale and haggard. He had found nothing.

"Street of Martyrs." Is this name significant?

Loisel is down-to-earth.

SHE HAS LOST THE NECKLACE!

They can't find it.

He goes out to search for the necklace.

But is unsuccessful.

He really tries. He is doing his best.

"You'll have to write to your friend," he said, "that you broke a clasp on her necklace and that you are having it fixed. That will give us time to look around."

She wrote as he dictated.

85   At the end of a week they had lost all hope.

And Loisel, looking five years older, declared:

"We'll have to see about replacing the jewels."

The next day they took the case which had contained the necklace and went to the jeweler whose name was inside. He looked at his books:

"I wasn't the one, Madam, who sold the necklace. I only made the case."

90   Then they went from jeweler to jeweler, searching for a necklace like the other one, racking their memories, both of them sick with worry and anguish.

In a shop in the Palais-Royal, they found a necklace of diamonds that seemed to them exactly like the one they were looking for. It was priced at forty thousand francs. They could buy it for thirty-six thousand.

They got the jeweler to promise not to sell it for three days. And they made an agreement that he would buy it back for thirty-four thousand francs if the original was recovered before the end of February.

Loisel had saved eighteen thousand francs that his father had left him. He would have to borrow the rest.

He borrowed, asking a thousand francs from one, five hundred from another, five louis° here, three louis there. He wrote promissory notes, undertook ruinous obligations, did business with finance companies and the whole tribe of loan sharks. He compromised himself for the remainder of his days, risked his signature without knowing whether he would be able to honor it, and, terrified by anguish over the future, by the black misery that was about to descend on him, by the prospect of all kinds of physical deprivations and moral tortures, he went to get the new necklace, and put down thirty-six thousand francs on the jeweler's counter.

Loisel's plan to explain delaying the return. He takes charge, is resourceful.

Things are hopeless.

They hunt for a replacement.

A new diamond necklace will cost 36,000 francs.

They make a deal with the jeweler. (Is Maupassant hinting that things might work out for them?)

It will take all of Loisel's inheritance plus another 18,000 francs. He borrows at enormous rates of interest.

louis: a gold coin worth twenty francs.

95   Mrs. Loisel took the necklace back to Mrs. Forrestier, who said with an offended tone:

"You should have brought it back sooner; I might have needed it."

Mrs. Forrestier complains about the delay.

She did not open the case, as her friend feared she might. If she had noticed the substitution, what would she have thought? What would she have said? Would she not have taken her for a thief?

Is this enough justification for not telling the truth? It seems to be for the Loisels.

Mrs. Loisel soon discovered the horrible life of the needy. She did her share, however, completely, heroically. That horrifying debt had to be paid. She would pay. They dismissed the maid; they changed their address; they rented an attic flat.

A new section, the fifth.

She learned to do the heavy housework, dirty kitchen jobs. She washed the dishes, wearing away her manicured fingernails on greasy pots and encrusted baking dishes. She handwashed dirty linen, shirts, and dish towels that she hung out on the line to dry. Each morning, she took the garbage down to the street, and she carried up water, stopping at each floor to catch her breath. And, dressed in cheap house dresses, she went to the fruit dealer, the grocer, the butcher, with her basket under her arms, haggling, insulting, defending her measly cash penny by penny.

They suffer to repay their debts. Loisel works late at night. Mathilde accepts a cheap attic flat and does all the heavy housework herself to save on domestic help.

She pinches pennies and haggles with the local tradesmen.

100   They had to make installment payments every month, and, to buy more time, to refinance loans.

They struggle to meet payments.

The husband worked evenings to make fair copies of tradesmen's accounts, and late into the night he made copies at five cents a page.

Mr. Loisel moonlights to make extra money.

And this life lasted ten years.

For ten years they endure.

At the end of ten years, they had paid back everything—everything—including the extra charges imposed by loan sharks and the accumulation of compound interest.

The last section. They have finally paid back the entire debt.

Mrs. Loisel looked old now. She had become the strong, hard, and rude woman of poor households. Her hair unkempt, with uneven skirts and rough, red hands, she spoke loudly, washed floors with large buckets of water. But sometimes, when her husband was at work, she sat down near the window, and she dreamed of that evening so long ago, of that party, where she had been so beautiful and so admired.

Mrs. Loisel (how come the narrator does not say "Mathilde"?) is roughened and aged by the work. But she has behaved "heroically" (¶ 98), and has shown her mettle.

105   What would life have been like if she had not lost that necklace? Who knows? Who knows? Life is so peculiar, so uncertain. How little a thing it takes to destroy you or to save you!

A moral? Our lives are shaped by small, uncertain things; we hang by a thread.

        Well, one Sunday, when she had gone for a stroll along the Champs-Elysées to relax from the cares of the week, she suddenly noticed a woman walking with a child. It was Mrs. Forrestier, still youthful, still beautiful, still attractive.

A scene on the Champs-Elysées. She sees Jeanne Forrestier, after ten years.

        Mrs. Loisel felt moved. Would she speak to her? Yes, certainly. And now that she had paid, she could tell all. Why not?

        She walked closer.

        "Hello, Jeanne."

110   The other gave no sign of recognition and was astonished to be addressed so familiarly by this working-class woman. She stammered:

        "But . . . Madam! . . . I don't know. . . . You must have made a mistake."

        "No. I'm Mathilde Loisel."

        Her friend cried out:

        "Oh! . . . My poor Mathilde, you've changed so much."

Jeanne notes Mathilde's changed appearance.

115   "Yes. I've had some tough times since I saw you last; in fact hardships . . . and all because of you! . . ."

        "Of me . . . how so?"

        "You remember the diamond necklace that you lent me to go to the party at the Ministry of Education?"

        "Yes. What then?"

        "Well, I lost it."

Mathilde tells Jeanne everything.

120   "How since you gave it back to me?"

        "I returned another exactly like it. And for ten years we've been paying for it. You understand that this wasn't easy for us, who have nothing. . . . Finally it's over, and I'm damned glad."

        Mrs. Forrestier stopped her.

        "You say that you bought a diamond necklace to replace mine?"

        "Yes, you didn't notice it, eh? It was exactly like yours."

125   And she smiled with proud and childish joy.

        Mrs. Forrestier, deeply moved, took both her hands.

        "Oh, my poor Mathilde! But mine was only costume jewelry. At most, it was worth only five hundred francs! . . ."

SURPRISE! The lost necklace was *not* real diamonds, and the Loisels slaved for no reason at all. But hard work and sacrifice probably brought out better qualities in Mathilde than she otherwise might have shown. Is this the moral of the story?

STUDYING BY USING A NOTEBOOK

The marginal comments demonstrate the active reading–responding process you should apply with everything you read as a student. You may freely use your text margins as the places where you may record your responses. In addition, you should also keep a notebook, either the one for your class, or a separate one for all your reading.

The things to record are not difficult or unusual in light of your primary objective, which should be to learn an assigned work inside and out, and then to say perceptive things about it. If you have developed note-taking methods that work well for you, just keep following these. If you have not, you should create a note-taking pattern of first observations followed by more searching ones, as in the study plan to be suggested here. The idea is that you should use the notebook systematically to supply yourself with a "memory bank" of your own knowledge about a work, which you can use as a fund of your own ideas and from which you can draw when you begin the processes of writing.

Whether you are preparing a particular assignment or not, you should use your notebook in the ways described below. Follow the *Guidelines for the First Reading of a Work* to make secure your first impressions and basic understanding. Follow the *Guidelines for Further Study* for a more searching examination of the work.

Guidelines for the First Reading of a Work

1. Observations for Basic Understanding

   a. Determine what is happening in the work. For a story or play, where do the actions take place? What do they show? Who is involved? Who is the major figure? Why is he or she major? What relationships do the characters have with each other? What concerns do the characters have? What do they do? Who says what to whom? What do the speeches do to advance the action, and to advance your understanding of the characters? For a poem, who is talking, and to whom? What is the situation, and what does the speaker say about it? Why does the poem end as it does and where it does?

   b. Record things that you think need explaining. Write down words that are new or not immediately clear. Whenever you run across a passage that you do not quickly understand, decide whether the problem arises from unknown words. If so, use your dictionary and write the relevant meanings in your notebook, but be sure that these meanings clarify your understanding. Make note of special difficulties so that you may ask your instructor about them.

2. Notes on First Impressions

a. Make a record of your reactions and responses, which you may derive from your marginal notations. Is there anything funny, memorable, noteworthy, or otherwise striking? Did you laugh, smile, worry, get scared, feel a thrill, learn a great deal, feel proud, find a lot to think about?

b. Make notes on interesting characterizations, events, techniques, and ideas. If you like a character or idea, describe what you like, and do the same for characters and ideas you don't like. Is there anything else in the work that you especially like or dislike? Any parts easy or difficult to understand? Why? Are there any surprises? What was your reaction to them? Be sure to use *your own* words in these notes.

Guidelines for Further Study

3. Development of Ideas and Enlargement of Responses

a. In your notebook, or on separate cards if that is more convenient, write out in full some of the passages that you think are interesting, well written, and important. Keep these passages within easy reach, and when riding public transportation, walking to class, or otherwise not occupying your time, memorize sentences, lines, and phrases.

b. Write expanded notes on things needing special emphasis. What explanations need to be made about the characters? Which actions, scenes, and situations invite interpretation? Why so? What assumptions do the characters and speakers reveal about life and humanity generally, about themselves, the people around them, their families, their friends, and about work, the economy, religion, politics, and the state of the world? What manners or customs do they exhibit? What sort of language do they use: formal or informal words, slang or profanity? What literary conventions and devices have you discovered, and how do these add to the work? (If an author addresses readers directly, for example, that is a **convention;** if a comparison is used, this is a **device** which might be either a **metaphor** or a **simile.**)

c. Trace developing patterns. Make an outline or scheme for the story or main idea: What conflicts appear? Do these conflicts exist between people, groups, or ideas? How does the author resolve them? Is one force, idea, or side the winner? Why? How do you respond to the winner, or loser?

d. Make a practice of writing a paragraph, or several paragraphs, describing your reactions and thoughts after reading and considering the work. If you are reading to prepare for a specific type of theme, your paragraphs may be useful later, for you might transfer them directly as early drafts. Even if you are making only a general preparation, however, always continue the practice of writing down your thoughts.

e. Always, whenever questions occur to you, make a note of them for use in class and also in your own further study.

Specimen Notebook Entries

Following are some sample notes on "The Necklace," which follow the suggestions for notebook entries listed under Guidelines 1 and 2 for a first reading and are related to the marginal responses placed beside the story (pp. 4–13). Since the notebook is not to be a composition, however, the order of the observations follows the general progress of reading. What is important is that the notebook record enough observations and responses to be useful later, both for additional study and for a developing essay.

Notes on Maupassant's "The Necklace"

Early in the story, Mathilde seems spoiled. She is poor, or at least lower middle class, but is unable to face her own situation.

As a dreamer, she seems harmless. Her daydreams about a fancy home, with all the expensive belongings, are not unusual. Most people dream of being well off, and therefore they indulge their wishes for better things.

She seems not to like her husband, and is embarrassed by his taste for plain food. The story contrasts her taste for trout and quail with Loisel's cheaper favorites.

Only when the Loisels get the invitation does Mathilde seem difficult. Her wish for an expensive dress (the cost of Loisel's entire vacation), and then her wanting the jewelry, make real difficulty for her husband.

Her success at the party shows that she has the charm the speaker talks about in paragraph 2. She seems never to have had any other chances in life to exert her power.

The worst part of her personality is her hurrying away from the party because she is ashamed of her everyday shawl. Therefore, it is Mathilde's unhappiness and unwillingness to adjust to her modest means that cause the financial downfall of the Loisels. It is her fault.

Borrowing the money to replace the necklace shows that both Loisel and Mathilde have a strong sense of honor. Making up for the loss is good, even if it destroys them financially.

There are some nice touches, like Loisel's seeming to be 5 years older (paragraph 86), and his staying with the other husbands of women enjoying themselves (paragraph 54). These are done quickly but tellingly.

It's too bad that Loisel and Mathilde don't tell Jeanne that the jewels are lost. Their pride stops them—or perhaps a fear of being accused of theft.

Their ten years of slavish work (paragraphs 98–102) show how they have come down in life. Mathilde's work must all be done by hand, without any labor-saving machines, so she really does pitch in, and is heroic.

The attic flat (paragraph 98) shows Mathilde's strength as it also shows her becoming loud and frumpy. She does what she has to. The earlier apartment and the elegance of her imaginary rooms brings out her limitations.

The setting of the Champs-Élysées also reflects her character, for she feels free there to confess the disastrous loss and sacrifice to Jeanne (paragraph 107), and it is this that produces the surprise ending.

The narrator's thought about how "little a thing it takes to destroy you or save you" (paragraph 105) is full of thought. The necklace is little, but it makes a huge problem. This makes for the story's irony.

Questions: Is this story more about the surprise ending or about the character of Mathilde? Is she to be condemned or admired? Does the outcome stem from the little things that make us or break us, as the speaker suggests, or on the difficulty of rising above one's economic class, which seems true, or both? What do the speaker's remarks about women's status mean? (Remember, the story was published in 1884.) This probably isn't relevant, but wouldn't Jeanne, after hearing about the substitution, give the full value of the necklace to the Loisels, and wouldn't they then be pretty well off?

These are reasonable, if fairly full, notebook responses and observations to "The Necklace." You should use your notebook similarly for *all* assignments. If your assignment is simply to learn about a work, general notes like those taken here should be enough. If you are preparing for a test, you might write pointed observations more in line with what is happening in your class, and also write and answer your own questions (see Appendix A, pp. 281–91). If you have a writing assignment, your notes should be focused directly on your topic, such as character, idea, setting, and so on. Whatever your purpose, you should always use a notebook as you read, and put into it as many details and responses as you can. Your notebook will then be invaluable in helping you refresh your memory and develop ideas.

How Much Time for Study with the Notebook?

An obvious practical question concerns the amount of time you need for the marginal observation and note-taking process. There is no way around it: Studying takes time. Two hours out of class for every hour in class is a rough rule of thumb. This number may seem arbitrary, but if you average that much time in sensitive reading and careful note taking, you will be able not only to do your assignments and take your tests, but to conquer them.

WRITING THEMES ON LITERARY TOPICS

Writing is the sharpened, focused expression of thought and study. As you develop your writing skills, you also improve your perceptions and increase your critical faculties. Although few people ever achieve perfection in writing—a state in which words and ideas blend perfectly together—everyone can improve.

The development of your ability to think and to write about literature will also prepare you to write about other topics. Because literature itself contains the subject material, though not in a systematic way, of philosophy, religion, psychology, sociology, and politics, learning to analyze literature and to write about it will also improve your capacity to deal with these and other disciplines.

Writing begins with the search for something to say—an idea. Not all ideas are equal; some are better than others, and getting good ideas is an ability that you develop the more you think and write. Your thinking will improve the longer you engage in the analysis of literature (or of any topic). In the same way, the quality of your thought will improve as you originate ideas, see the flaws in some of your thinking processes, propose new avenues of development, secure new data to support ideas, and create new ideas in the course of diligent and applied thought. Your objective always will be to persuade your reader that your details are correct and that your conclusions are both valid and interesting.

Unlike ordinary conversation and classroom discussion, writing must stick with great determination to a specific point. Ordinary conversation is usually random and disorganized; it shifts from topic to topic, often without any apparent cause, and it is repetitive. Classroom discussion is a form of deliberately structured talk, but it is free and spontaneous, and digressions may sometimes occur. By contrast, writing is the most concise and highly organized form of expression that you will ever create.

When you see a complete, polished, well-formed piece of writing, you may believe that it was always perfect, right from the beginning. Nothing could be further from the truth, for writing usually, if not always, begins in uncertainty and vagueness, and it gets into a presentable form not by magic but only by much thought and work. If you could see the early drafts of writing you admire, you would be surprised (maybe even shocked), but you might also be encouraged to see that good writers are also human, and that their first versions are messy, uncertain, unfinished, and generally incomplete. In final drafts, early ideas are discarded and others added; new facts are introduced; early paragraphs are cut in half and assembled elsewhere with parts of other paragraphs; words are changed and misspellings corrected; much paper is wadded up and thrown into waste baskets; sentences are revised or completely rewritten; and new writing is added to tie together the reassembled materials and make them flow smoothly together.

All this is normal. In fact, for your own purposes, you should think of your finished, final, polished theme not as something to begin with, but rather as *something to achieve.* How you reach your goal is up to you, because everyone has unique work habits. But you should always remember that *writing is, above all, a process*—a process in which you try to overcome not only the difficulties of reading and interpretation, but also the natural lethargy and resistance of the human mind.

Because writing is a process, you may take heart if your pathway toward a finished theme sometimes seems halting, digressive, and purposeless. Many of these ordinary difficulties in writing can be overcome if you stress to yourself that writing cannot be perfect the first time. *It is important just to start*—no matter how unacceptable the first products seem—to create a beginning, to force yourself to lock horns with the materials. You are not committed to anything you first put down on paper or on the screen of a word processor. You may throw it out and write something else, or you may write over it, or move it around, as you wish. But if you keep it locked in your mind by not beginning to write anything at all, you will have nothing to work with. In fact, the thing to do is to accept the uncertainties in the writing process and use them to work *for* you rather than *against* you.

Invention and Prewriting

The intentional, systematic, and also accidental processes that take place in the development of writing have been called **invention** and **prewriting.** Invention is the process of uncovering, discovering, and dragging out of your mind some of the things to say about a particular topic. Prewriting is the process of studying, thinking, raising and answering questions, planning, developing tentative ideas and first drafts, crossing out, erasing, changing, rearranging, and adding. In a way, "prewriting" and "invention" are different words for thinking, planning, and drafting. Both words acknowledge the mysterious and uncertain but also the exciting and stimulating ways in which minds work, and also the fact that ideas are not known and shaped until they take written form. *Writing, at any stage, should always be thought of as a process of discovery as well as creation.*

The following description of the invention and prewriting process, with the topic being "The Character of Mathilde in Maupassant's 'The Necklace,' " is presented as an approximation of general writing processes.

As you go about your own assignments, you may take leaps and shortcuts if you can. In the entire process, however, you will probably not vary the stages widely.

Not every step in the writing process can be detailed here. Although there is an early draft of the theme on pages 27–28, there is not enough space to show the development of all the early drafts. If you compare the original notes and marginal observations, however, (see pages 15–16, 22–27) with early drafts of observations and paragraphs, you can see that many changes take place and that one step really merges with another.

Reading and Thinking About the Work

1. TAKE NOTES FOCUSED ON YOUR ASSIGNMENT. Because our subject is the character of Mathilde in "The Necklace," our notes will be about her—her traits as shown by her actions, thoughts, speeches, and reactions. The same focus would apply if your assignment were to be on metaphor, or ideas, and so on. By focusing your notes and excluding other approaches to the work, you are already concentrating on your writing assignment.

2. USE THE STUDY QUESTIONS IN YOUR TEXT, IF IT HAS SUCH QUESTIONS. Your answers to these questions, together with your notes and ideas, can often be used directly in parts of your developing theme.

3. USE A PEN, PENCIL, TYPEWRITER, OR WORD PROCESSOR AS AN EXTENSION OF YOUR THOUGHT. *Seeing* your thoughts is vital in thinking; therefore you will need to get thoughts into a visible form so that you may ponder them and develop them further. For many people, handwriting is a psychological necessity in this process. In noting, sketching out, and drafting the things to go into the developing theme, be sure to use *only one side* of your paper or notecards. With everything on only one side, you may spread your materials out, and in this way may get an overview as you plan and write.

A special word is in order about word processors, which are important for many students. Once you can handle the keyboard—the same as for a typewriter—the word processor can help you in developing ideas, for you can eliminate unworkable thoughts and put others in their places. You may move sentences and paragraphs tentatively into new contexts, test out how they look, and move them somewhere else if you do not like them. If you see spellings that are questionable, you may check them out with a dictionary and make corrections on the screen. (Because spelling, among other things, may be an element of grading, be sure that you reach an agreement with your instructor about whether to use a spell-check program.) Studies have shown that the lower parts of pages prepared by hand or with a conventional typewriter contain many errors and awkward sentences. The reason is that writers hesitate to make improvements when they get near the end of a page because they do not want to bother starting the page over. Word processors eliminate this difficulty completely. Changes can be made anywhere in the draft, at any time, without damage to the appearance of the final draft.

In addition, with the rapid printers available today, you can print drafts, even in the initial and tentative stages. With a complete draft, you can use your pen or pencil to make additional notes, marginal corrections, arrowed lines indicating new spots for particular passages, and suggestions for further development. With the marked-up draft for guidance, you can go back on the word processor and carry out your own instructions for change and improvement. You may repeat this process as often as is necessary. The result is that the machine is an additional incentive for improvement, right up to your final draft.

Indeed, no matter what method of writing you use, it is important to realize that *unwritten thought is incomplete thought.* Therefore, somewhere in the composing process, it is vital to prepare a complete draft of what you have written. Even with the word processor's screen, you cannot lay everything out at once but can see only a small part. A clean, readable draft permits you to gather everything together and make even more improvements.

4. ONCE YOU HAVE PUT EVERYTHING TOGETHER IN THIS WAY, DEVELOP A CENTRAL IDEA, which will help you focus your planning and writing.

Developing a Central Idea

The first requirement of a finished theme—although it is *not* the first requirement in the writing *process*—is that it have a **central idea.** In fact, a theme may be defined as *a fully developed and organized set of paragraphs that are directly connected to a central idea.* Everything in a theme should expand upon and contribute to the reader's understanding of the idea. The idea helps the writer control and shape the theme, and it provides guidance and understanding to the reader.

Let us consider how this definition applies to themes about literature. A successful theme is a brief but thorough (not exhaustive) examination of a literary work in the light of a particular approach, such as *point of view, imagery,* or *symbolism.* Unity is achieved through the consistent reference to the central idea, and completeness is achieved through the demonstration of how a selected number of details relate to and support the idea. Typical central ideas might be (1) that a character is strong and tenacious, or (2) that the point of view makes the action seem "distant and objective," or (3) that one work is different from or better than another. All details included in themes on these topics must be tied to these ideas. Thus, it is a fact that Mathilde Loisel in "The Necklace" spends ten years of slavish work and sacrifice; this fact is not relevant to a theme on her character, however, unless you *connect* it by showing how it shows one of her major traits—in this case, her strength and tenacity.

You cannot find a central idea in a hat. It comes about as a result of the steps just described. In a way, you might think of discovering a central idea as one of the major goals in prewriting. Once you can formulate the idea, you have a guide for accepting some of your materials, rejecting others, rearranging, changing, and rewording.

BRAINSTORMING IDEAS FROM YOUR NOTES. You can use a full set of notes as the basis for "brainstorming"; that is, a concentration of your mind to fit details from the work to the subject of your theme. Not everything will be relevant, for notes by definition are disorganized and unfocused. However, the notes are a starting point. Since our assignment concerns character, you should sift the notes for observations about Mathilde's character traits. Be sure to rewrite them to focus directly on her character, and guard against leading yourself astray into a plot summary or some other digression. Sentences formulated during brainstorming about Mathilde's character might look like this:

> Mathilde begins the story as a fish out of water. She dreams of wealth but is confined to a drab existence with her ordinary husband.
>
> Her fantasies about lavish rooms make her even more dissatisfied. She is almost punishing herself.
>
> Her character can be related to the real places where she lives and moves (the first place on the Street of Martyrs, the scene of the dinner, the attic flat), and also the imaginary place which she fills with the most expensive things she can dream up.
>
> Her first response to the invitation causes discomfort to her husband, but no real harm. She is pouty, whiny, and cranky, however, and she manipulates Loisel into buying her an expensive party dress.
>
> Her dream world hurts her real life when her desire for wealth causes the borrowing of the necklace. The loss of the necklace is just bad luck.
>
> The attic flat brings out her potential coarseness, but it also develops her potential for sacrifice and cooperation. That she is a loser makes her, in effect, a winner.

These are all observations focusing on Mathilde's character. With slight modifications, they might all find a place in your developing theme, although their final use depends on further thought and organization. What is clear, however, is that the brainstorming producing these sentences represents an essential stage of composition. The rough notes are no longer rough but are in a state that can, with additional substantiating details, lead directly to further development.

DEVELOPING YOUR OBSERVATIONS. As a continuation of your brain-storming, you should begin writing paragraphs, all the time checking both the work and your original notebook entries. The object is to explore what you know and therefore to catch and imprison important ideas. Until you write things down, you will not know which way your mind is directing you. Here are a few such "brainstorming" paragraphs:

1. Mathilde comes to life as a character. She is a dreamer, but that is not at all unusual. Her thoughts of unreachable wealth are like those that cause people to make bets and buy lottery tickets. She really thinks of a life better than the one she is living.

2. The original apartment in the Street of Martyrs, and the dream world of wealthy places, both show negative sides of her character. The real-life apartment, though livable, is shabby. The furnishings all bring out her discontentment. The shabbiness makes her think only of luxuri-ousness, and her one servant girl makes her dream of many servants. The luxury of her dream life thus heightens her unhappiness with what she has.

3. Mathilde is coarsened during the ten years of repayment. She gives up her domestic help and does all the heavy housework herself. She climbs stairs carrying heavy buckets of water, and throws water around to clean floors. She washes greasy and encrusted pots and pans, takes out the garbage, and does the clothes and dishes by hand. She gives up caring for her hair and hands and wears the cheapest cloth-ing possible. She becomes loud and argumentative and spends much time haggling with shopkeepers to save as much money as she can. Whatever delicacy and attractiveness she has, she loses.

4. Her Sunday walk to the Champs-Élysées is in character. This is a fashionable street, and her walk to it is similar to her earlier daydreams about wealth, for it is on this wide street that the wealthy stroll and flaunt themselves. Her meeting with Jeanne there is accidental, but it also brings out her sense of pride; that is, she confesses to the loss of the necklace, having seen things through to the complete repayment of all indebtedness. The Champs-Élysées thus brings out the surprise and irony of the story, and Mathilde's going there is totally in character, in keeping with her earlier dreams of a luxurious life.

DETERMINING YOUR CENTRAL IDEA. Once you have written such para-graphs, you are ready to form your central idea. Look for a common thread in your notes and paragraphs. In the materials we have been developing here, a common thread is the relationship of various settings to Mathilde's character. Both her weaknesses and her strengths may be connected to *the real and imaginary places in the story.* Once you have found such a common thread, you can use it as your central idea to accelerate your thinking further.

Make your central idea into a sentence. Because the central idea is so vital in shaping a theme, you should formulate it *as a complete sentence.* Just the topic of setting and character alone (or any other topic) cannot shape thoughts as much as a sentence, which will move the topic toward new exploration and discovery. You might tinker with the topic and make several different sentences, such as these:

1. The setting is related to Mathilde's character.
2. The settings determine Mathilde's character.
3. Mathilde is fated not to rise above her shabby surroundings.
4. If she had been truthful, Mathilde could have overcome her bad luck.

Each of these sentences would give unique guidance for a theme. The first is the simplest, for it would require no more than an exemplification of how the setting relates to Mathilde's character. The second would do the same and would also stress how Mathilde is a prisoner of economic circumstances. The third is like the second, but it also suggests an economic-political argument about the condition of people like Mathilde. The fourth suggests an analysis of Mathilde's weaknesses and an argument about how her own limitations hold her down.

Once you pick out your central idea (let us use the first one), you can use it to bring your observations and conclusions into deeper focus. Let us see what we may do with the third of our brainstorming paragraphs:

Original Paragraph	**Reshaped Paragraph**
Mathilde is coarsened during the ten years of repayment. She gives up her domestic help and does all the heavy housework herself. She climbs stairs carrying heavy buckets of water, and throws water around to clean floors. She washes greasy and encrusted pots and pans, takes out the garbage, and does the clothes and dishes by hand. She gives up caring for her hair and hands and wears the cheapest clothing possible. She becomes loud and argumentative and spends much time haggling with shopkeepers to save as much money as she can. Whatever delicacy and attractiveness she had, she loses.	The attic flat reflects the coarsening of Mathilde's character. Maupassant emphasizes the strain she endures to keep up the flat, such as throwing around heavy buckets of water to wash the floors, cleaning greasy and encrusted pots and pans, taking out the garbage, and washing clothes and dishes by hand. This makes her rough and coarse, a fact also shown by her giving up care of her hair and hands, her wearing of the cheapest dresses possible, and her becoming loud and penny-pinching in haggling with the local shopkeepers. If at the beginning she is delicate and attractive, at the end she is unpleasant and coarse.

Notice that details from the story are almost the same in each paragraph, but while the left-hand paragraph is unfocused, the right-hand one connects the details to Mathilde's housework in the attic flat. The right-hand paragraph thus leads to a discovery: It shows how details from a work may substantiate a unifying central idea—how the work may be linked to interpretation. When we first read the story, we follow the details and appreciate the story's movement. When we think about the story, however, and begin to write about it, we uncover ways of seeing and assimilating it. The process of writing thus leads us to broaden our understanding and appreciation of the author's thoughts.

Creating a Thesis Statement

Using the central idea for guidance, we can now go back to our earlier notes and paragraphs to select additional materials for development. Our goal is to establish a number of major topics to support the central idea. The paragraph we have just shaped will serve us substantially as it is. Going on, we might select from the second paragraph, which has two topics that we may entitle "real-life apartment" and "dream surroundings." Let us then list our topics:

1. Real-life apartment
2. Dream surroundings
3. Attic flat

We may use this list as the order of topics for the development of our theme.

For our reader's benefit, however, we should also use this ordering for the writing of our **thesis sentence** or **thesis statement.** This sentence is operative in the first part of the following general plan for most themes: (1) Say what you are going to say. (2) Say it. (3) Say what you've said. The thesis sentence says what you are going to say. It is a plan or groundwork for your theme; it connects the central idea and the list of topics in the order of presentation. Thus, if we put the central idea at the left and our list of topics at the right, we have the shape of our thesis statement:

Central Idea	**Topics**
The setting of "The Necklace" reflects Mathilde's character.	1. Real-life apartment 2. Dream surroundings 3. Attic flat

From this arrangement we can write the following thesis statement, which should usually be placed at the end of a theme's introductory paragraph (and thus tell the reader what to expect in the developmental part of the theme):

Mathilde's character development is related to her first apartment, her dream-life mansion rooms, and her attic flat.

With changes that may seem necessary during the finishing touches of the theme, this thesis sentence, along with the central idea, can go directly into our introduction. The central idea, as we have seen, is the glue. The thesis sentence lists the parts to be fastened together—that is, the topics in which the central idea is to be demonstrated and argued.

Drafting the Theme

In the drafting stage, you fit together the points of the thesis sentence with related prewriting materials. You may alter, reject, and rearrange things, as you wish, as long as you change your thesis sentence to account for your changes (a major reason why the introduction is usually the last part of a theme to be completed). Our proposed thesis statement contains three topics (it could be two, or four, or more), which we will use in forming the body of the theme.

Just as the organization of the entire theme is based on the thesis, the form of each paragraph is based on its **topic sentence.** A topic sentence is an assertion about how a topic from the predicate of the thesis sentence supports the central idea. The first topic in our example is the relationship of Mathilde's character to her first apartment, and the resulting paragraph should emphasize this relationship. Suppose we choose her trait of being constantly dissatisfied. We can then form a topic sentence by connecting the trait with the location, as follows:

> Details about the first apartment explain her dissatisfaction and depression.

Beginning with this sentence, the paragraph should show how things in the apartment, such as the furniture, the curtains, and the unwashed tablecloth, feed Mathilde's capacity for dissatisfaction.

You should follow the same process in forming other topic sentences, so that when you finish them you can use them to develop other paragraphs for the body.

Developing an Outline

All along we have been developing an **outline**—that is, a skeletal plan of organization for the theme. Some writers never use formal outlines at all, while others rely on them constantly. Still other writers insist that they cannot write an outline until they have finished their theme. All these views can be reconciled if you realize that finished themes should have a tight structure. At some point, therefore, you should create a guiding outline for use either in the developing or final shaping of your theme. Whatever works best for you, it is vital that your finished theme follow an outline form.

The outline we have been developing here is the **analytical sentence outline.** This type is easier to create than it sounds, for it is nothing more than a graphic form, a skeleton, of the theme. It consists of the following:

TITLE: How Setting in "The Necklace" Is Related to the Character of Mathilde

1. INTRODUCTION

a. *Central Idea:* Setting is used to bring out the change and development of Mathilde.

b. *Thesis Sentence:* Her character development is related to her first apartment, her dream-life mansion rooms, and her attic flat.

2. BODY: *Topic sentences a, b, and c (and d, e, f, if necessary)*

a. Details about her first apartment explain her dissatisfaction and depression.

b. Her dream-life images of wealth are like the apartment because they too make her unhappy.

c. The attic flat reflects the coarsening of her character.

3. CONCLUSION

Topic sentence: Everything in the story, particularly the setting, is focused on the character of Mathilde.

The **conclusion** is technically independent of the body, but it is part of the thematic organization and hence should be tied to the central idea. It may be a summary of the body (i.e., "Say what you've said."); it may evaluate the main idea; it may briefly suggest further points of discussion; or it may be a reflection on the details of the body.

By the time you create an outline, you will have been planning and drafting your theme for a number of hours. The outline should thus be a guide for *organizing, finishing,* and *polishing* the results of your note taking and brainstorming. However, throughout the discussion of the writing process, we have seen that much of writing is discovery. At the right point, therefore, your outline can lead you to new ideas and can help you to adapt materials that you have not originally planned to use. In short, the needs of filling out the outline form itself can be an incentive to further discovery and development.

USING THE OUTLINE. The sample themes to be developed here are organized according to the principles of the analytical sentence outline. To emphasize the shaping presence of these outlines, all central ideas, thesis sentences, and topic sentences are underlined. In the concluding stages of your own writing, you might wish similarly to underline these "skeletal" sentences as a check on your organization. Unless your instructor requires that you continue the underlines, however, you may remove them in your final drafts.

Briefly, here is how to use the outline:

1. Include both the central idea and the thesis statement in your introduction. (Some instructors require a fusion of the two in the final draft.

Therefore, make sure you ask what your instructor expects.) Use the suggestions in the writing sections to determine what else to put in the introduction.

2. Include your topic sentences at the beginning of your paragraphs, changing them as necessary to provide transitions. It is also acceptable to include the topic sentence elsewhere in the paragraph, but if you re-locate it be sure that your details make it follow naturally and logically. Usually you may devote a single paragraph to each topic. However, if your topic is difficult, long, and heavily detailed, you may divide it into two or more subtopics, each devoted to single paragraphs. Should you make this division, your topic then is really a **section,** and each paragraph in the section should have its own topic sentence.

THE SAMPLE THEME

To show the process of writing in operation, the two following themes, on the relationship of setting to Mathilde's character, represent *two stages of the same assignment.* Though the first draft might be considered complete, it omits a topic and some details that are included in the second draft. The first draft therefore shows how even working from an outline leaves much yet to do in the writing of a finished, polished theme. Both themes have been subjected to the prewriting process, in which much is accepted and discarded, changed and rearranged, and moved around from place to place. The outline for the final draft has been modified for the second, and as a result, new materials are included in the newly shaped context. The first draft, then, represents a relatively advanced but not yet completed stage of composition, which we all go through in the process of developing an acceptable piece of writing.

Sample Theme, Draft 1

*How Setting in "The Necklace" Is Related to the Character of Mathilde Loisel**

[1]   In "The Necklace" Maupassant does not give much detail about the setting. He does not even describe the necklace itself, which is the central object in his plot, but he says only that it is "superb" (paragraph 47). Rather, he uses the setting to reflect the character of the central figure, Mathilde Loisel.° All

---

* For the text of this story, see pages 4–13.
° Central idea

[1] his details are presented to bring out her traits. Her character development is related to her first apartment, her dream-life mansion rooms, and her attic flat.°

[2] Details about her first apartment explain her dissatisfaction and depression. The walls are "drab," the furniture "threadbare," and the curtains "ugly" (paragraph 3). There is only a single country girl to do the housework. The tablecloth is not cleaned daily, and the best dinner dish is beef and vegetables boiled in a pot. Mathilde has no pretty dresses, but only a theater dress which she does not like. The details show her dissatisfaction about life with her low-salaried husband.

[3] Her dream-life images of wealth are like the apartment because they too make her unhappy. In her daydreams, the rooms are large, filled with expensive furniture and bric-a-brac, and draped in silk. She imagines private rooms for intimate talks, and big dinners with delicacies like trout and quail. With dreams of such a rich home, she feels even more despair about her modest apartment on the Street of Martyrs in Paris.

[4] The attic flat reflects the coarsening of Mathilde's character. Maupassant emphasizes the strain she endures to keep up the flat, such as throwing around heavy buckets of water to clean the floors, cleaning greasy and encrusted pots and pans, taking out the garbage, and doing dishes and washing clothes by hand. This makes her rough and coarse, a fact also shown by her giving up care of her hair and hands, her wearing of the cheapest dresses possible, and her becoming loud and penny-pinching in haggling with the local shopkeepers. If at the beginning she is delicate and attractive, at the end she is unpleasant and coarse.

[5] In summary, Maupassant focuses everything in the story, including the setting, on the character of Mathilde. Anything extra is not needed, and he does not include it. Thus he says little about the big party scene, but emphasizes the necessary detail that Mathilde was a great "success" (paragraph 52), because this detail brings out some of her early attractiveness and charm (despite her more usual unhappiness). In "The Necklace," Maupassant uses setting as a means to his end—the story of Mathilde and her needless sacrifice.

The following advanced draft, a revision and a rewriting, is an improvement on the first because changes have been made to create greater emphasis and unity. Some of the details in the early draft, while relevant, are not tied clearly enough to the central idea. The second draft, on the other hand, creates more introductory detail, includes another topic, and reshapes each of the paragraphs to stress the relationship of central idea to topic. Within the limits of a short assignment, the theme illustrates all the principles of organization and unity that we have been discussing.

° Thesis sentence

Sample Theme, Draft 2

Maupassant's Use of Setting in "The Necklace" to Show the Character of Mathilde

[1]   In "The Necklace" Maupassant uses setting to reflect the character and development in the major figure, Mathilde Loisel.° As a result, his setting is not particularly vivid or detailed. He does not even provide a description of the ill-fated necklace—the central object in the story—but states only that it is "superb" (paragraph 47). He includes only enough description to illuminate his central character, Mathilde. Her traits and her change may be related to the first apartment, the dream-life mansion rooms, the attic flat, and the public street.°

[2]   Details about the modest apartment of the Loisels on the Street of Martyrs (Rue des Martyrs) indicate Mathilde's peevish lack of adjustment to life. Though everything is serviceable, she is unhappy with the "drab" walls, "threadbare" furniture, and "ugly" curtains (paragraph 3). She has domestic help, but wants more servants than the simple country girl who does the household chores. Her dissatisfaction is also shown by details of her irregularly cleaned tablecloth and the plain and inelegant boiled beef that her husband adores. Even her best dress, which she wears for the theater, provokes her unhappiness. All these details of the apartment establish that Mathilde's dominant character trait at the start of the story is maladjustment. She therefore seems unpleasant and unsympathetic.

[3]   Like the real-life apartment, the impossibly expensive setting of her daydreams strengthens her unhappiness and her avoidance of reality. As she indulges herself, all the rooms of her fantasies are large and expensive, being draped in silk and filled with nothing but the best furniture and bric-a-brac. Maupassant gives us the following description of her imaginings:

> She imagined a gourmet-prepared main course carried on the most exquisite trays and served on the most beautiful dishes, with whispered gallantries which she would hear with a sphinxlike smile asshe dined on the pink meat of a trout or the delicate wing of a quail. (paragraph 4)

With dreams like this filling her mind, her despair is even greater. Ironically, this despair, together with her inability to live with reality, causes her economic and social undoing. It makes her agree to borrow the necklace (which is just as unreal as her daydreams of wealth), and losing the necklace drives her into the reality of giving up her apartment and moving into the attic flat.

[4]   Also ironically, the attic flat is related to the coarsening of her character while at the same time it brings out her best qualities of cooperativeness and honesty. Maupassant emphasizes the drudgery of the work she endures to maintain the flat, such as walking up many stairs, washing floors with large

° Central idea
° Thesis sentence

buckets of water, cleaning greasy and encrusted pots and pans, taking out the garbage, handwashing clothes, and haggling loudly with local tradespeople. All this reflects her coarsening and loss of sensibility, also shown by her giving up hair and hand care, and wearing the cheapest dresses. The things she does, however, make her heroic (paragraph 98). As she cooperates to help her [4] husband pay back the loans, her dreams of a mansion fade and all she has left is the memory of that one happy evening at the Minister of Education's reception. Thus the attic flat brings out her physical change for the worse at the same time that it also brings out her psychological and moral change for the better.

Her walk on the Champs-Élysées illustrates another combination of traits—self-indulgence and frankness. The Champs-Élysées is the most fashionable street in Paris, and her walk to it is similar to her earlier indulgences in her dreams of wealth; she is, in effect, seeing how the upper-class people are [5] living. But it is on this street where she meets Jeanne, and it is her frankness in confessing the loss and replacement to Jeanne that makes her, finally, completely honest. While the walk thus serves as the occasion for the story's concluding surprise and irony, Mathilde's being on the Champs-Élysées is totally in character, in keeping with her earlier reveries about luxury.

Other details in the story also have a similar bearing on Mathilde's character. For example, the story mentions little about the party scene, but emphasizes only that she was a great "success" (paragraph 52)—a judgment that shows her ability to shine if given the chance. After she and Loisel decide that the necklace cannot be found, Maupassant includes details about the Parisian [6] streets, the visits to loan sharks, and the jewelry and jewelry-case shops, in order to bring out Mathilde's sense of honesty and pride as she "heroically" prepares to live the life of the poor. Thus, in the "The Necklace," Maupassant uses setting to highlight Mathilde's maladjustment, her needless misfortune, her loss of youth and beauty, and finally her growth as a responsible human being.

Theme Commentaries

Throughout this book, the sample themes are followed by short commentaries which show how the themes embody the chapter's instruction and guidelines. For each theme in which a number of possible approaches are suggested, the commentary points out which one is employed, and when a sample theme uses two or more approaches, the commentary makes this fact clear. In addition, each commentary singles out one of the paragraphs for detailed analysis of its strategy and use of detail. It is hoped that the commentaries will help you develop the insight necessary to use the sample themes as aids in your own study and writing.

AVOIDING SOME COMMON PROBLEMS IN WRITING THEMES

The fact that you understand the early stages of the composing process, and can develop a central idea and organize with an outline, does not mean that you will have no problems in writing. It is not hard to recognize good writing when you see it, but explaining what makes writing good is another matter.

The most difficult and perplexing questions that students usually ask are these:

1. "How can I improve my writing?"
2. "I got a *C* on my last theme, but why wasn't the grade a *B* or an *A*? How can I get higher grades?"

These are really different versions of the same question. Still another version of the question is:

3. "When I first read a work, I have a hard time following it. Yet when my instructor explains it, my understanding is increased. How can I develop my own ability to understand the work and write about it well without my instructor's help? How can I become an independent, confident reader and writer?

The best way to begin an answer is to observe that one of the major mistakes writers make when writing about literature is to do no more than retell a story or reword an idea. Retelling a story shows only that you have *read* it, not that you have *thought about* it. You are always to be judged on what *you* yourself say and think, and you should therefore try to produce the results of your own thinking. Writing a good theme requires that you arrange your responses and thoughts into a pattern that can be followed by a perceptive reader.

Using Your Own Order of References

There are many ways to break the pattern of summarizing stories and to set up your own pattern of development. One is to stress *your own* order when referring to parts of the work. Do not treat things as they occur in the work, but change them to suit your own thematic plans. Rarely, if ever, should you begin by speaking about a work's opening; it is better to talk about the conclusion or middle first. Beginning your theme by referring to later parts of the work helps you stress your own central idea rather than get caught up in the work's chronological order. If you refer again to paragraph 4 of the second draft theme on "The Necklace" (pp. 29–30), you will see that this technique is used. The references there are used only to stress the writer's thoughts, and hence they do not follow the story's order. The principle is that you, also, *should introduce references only to support your points*—the ones that *you* wish to make.

Considering Your Audience: A Student Who Has Read but Not Thought

In preparing to write, you need to consider how much detail to select and discuss. This task is made easy if you assume that your **audience,** or **mythical reader,** is another student, like yourself, who has read the work but has not thought about it. Such a reader knows the events and knows who says what and when. This reader should not expect you to retell everything but looks to you rather as an *explainer or interpreter*. Thus, you should introduce details from the work only if they exemplify and support your central idea, and you may omit details that have no bearing, even if they are important in the work itself.

To look at your writing situation in still another way, you might remember that Sherlock Holmes, from A. Conan Doyle's famous detective stories, always points out to Dr. Watson that all important facts are available to both of them. Watson, however, does not *observe* things as Holmes does, and therefore he cannot produce solutions to the mysteries the two men go about solving. If you look back to the sample theme on "The Necklace," you will notice that everywhere *the assumption has been made that readers already know the story*, just as Watson knows the facts as well as Holmes. In these themes, references are introduced only as part of the arguments brought out in the themes themselves; the idea is to help readers follow the central idea and draw those conclusions that follow from the presentation. There is no other reason for bringing in references from the story, for the reader, like Watson, does not need to be *told* as much as to be *guided*.

Using Literary Material as Evidence

The comparison with Sherlock Holmes should remind you that whenever you write, your position is like that of a detective using clues as evidence for building a case, or of a lawyer using evidence as support for arguments. For practical purposes only, when you write, you may conveniently regard the work as a part of your own discourse. Your goal should be to convince your readers of your own knowledge and the reasonableness of your conclusions.

It is vital to use evidence convincingly so that your readers may follow your ideas. Let us look briefly at two new examples to see how writing may be improved by the pointed use of details. These are from longer themes on the character of Mathilde:

1	2
The major extenuating thing about Mathilde is that she seems to be iso-	The major flaw of Mathlide's character is that she is withdrawn and uncom-

lated, locked away from other people. She and her husband do not speak to each other much, except about things. He speaks about his liking for boiled beef in a pot, and she states that she cannot accept the big invitation because she has no nice dresses. Once she gets the dress, she complains because she has no jewelry. Even when borrowing the necklace from Jeanne Forrestier, she does not say much. When she and her husband discover that the necklace is lost, they simply go over the details, and Loisel dictates a letter of explanation, which she writes in her own hand. Even when she meets Jeanne on the Champs-Elysées, she does not say a great deal about her life, but only goes through enough details about the loss and replacement of the necklace to make Jeanne exclaim about the needlessness of the ten-year sacrifice.

municative, apparently unwilling or unable to form an intimate relationship. For example, she and her husband do not speak to each other much, except about things, such as his taste for boiled beef in a pot and her lack of a party dress and jewelry. With such a marriage, one might suppose that she might be more open with her close friend, Jeanne Forrestier, but even here Mathilde does not say much. This flaw hurts her greatly, because if she were more open she might have explained the loss and avoided the horrible sacrifice. This lack of openness, along with her self-indulgent dreaminess, is her biggest defect.

The answer to that difficult question of how to turn a *C* into an *A* is to be found in a comparison of these two passages. In general, superior writers always allow their minds to play on the materials. They give readers the results of their thoughts. They dare to trust their responses and are not afraid to make judgments about the work they are considering. Their principal aim in referring to actions, scenes, and characters is to develop *their own* thematic pattern. Inferior writers do none of these things.

A close comparison of the two paragraphs bears out these assertions. Although the first paragraph has more words than the second (158 to 119), it is not adequate, for the writer is doing little more than retelling the story. The paragraph is cluttered with details that do not support any conclusions. If you judge it for what you might learn about Maupassant's actual *use* of Mathilde's withdrawn, solitary traits in "The Necklace," you cannot avoid concluding that it gives you no help at all. The writer did not have to think much to write the paragraph.

On the other hand, the details in the second paragraph all support the declared topic. Phrases like "for example," "but even here," and "this lack" show that the writer of paragraph 2 has assumed that the audience knows the story and now wants help in interpretation. Paragraph 2 therefore guides readers *by connecting the details to the topic*. It uses these details *as evidence*, not as a retelling of actions. By contrast, paragraph 1 recounts a number of clearly relevant actions but does not *connect* them to the topic.

More details, of course, could have been added to paragraph 2, but they are unnecessary because the paragraph demonstrates the point with the details used. There are many things that make good writing good, but one of the most important is evident here: *In good writing, details are used only as evidence in an original pattern of thought.*

Keeping to Your Point

To show distinctions between good and inferior writing, let us consider a third example. The following paragraph is drawn from an essay on "The Idea of Economic Determinism in 'The Necklace.' " In this paragraph the writer discusses the theme as it is brought out in a number of incidents. The idea is to assert that Mathilde's difficulties result not from character but rather from financial restrictions:

> More important than chance in governing life is the idea that people are controlled by economic circumstances. Mathilde, as is shown right at the start, is born poor. Therefore she doesn't get the right doors opened for her, and her marriage is to a minor clerk. With a vivid imagination and a burning desire for luxury, seeming to be born only for the wealthy life, her poor home brings out her daydreams of expensive surroundings. She taunts her husband, Loisel, when he brings the big invitation, because she does not have a suitable (read "expensive") dress. Once she gets the dress it is jewelry that she lacks, and she borrows that and loses it. The loss of the necklace is the greatest trouble, because it forces the Loisels to borrow deeply and to lead an impoverished life for ten years.

This paragraph shows how easily writers may be diverted from their objective. The first sentence is an effective topic sentence, indicating that the writer begins with a good plan. The remaining part, however, does not follow through. The flaw is that the material of the paragraph, while an accurate account of what happens in the story, is not tied to the topic. Once the second sentence is under way, the paragraph gets lost in a retelling of events, and the fine opening sentence is left behind. From the example of this paragraph, we may conclude that writers cannot assume that detail alone will make an intended meaning clear. Instead they must do the connecting themselves, to make sure that all relationships are *explicitly* clear. This point cannot be overstressed.

Let us see how the problem in this paragraph may be addressed. If the ideal paragraph can be schematized with line drawings, we might say that the paragraph's topic should be a straight line, moving toward and reaching a specific goal (explicit meaning), with an exemplifying line moving away from the straight line briefly to bring in evidence but returning to the line after each new fact to demonstrate the relevance of the fact. Thus the ideal scheme looks like this, with a straight line touched a number of times by an undulating line:

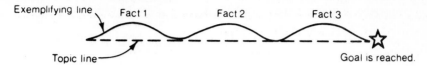

Notice that the exemplifying line, waving to illustrate how documentation or exemplification is to be used, always returns to the topic line. A scheme for the faulty paragraph on "The Necklace," however, would look like this, with the line never returning but flying out into space:

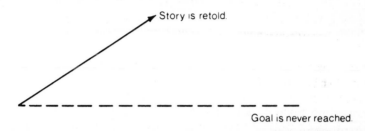

How might the faulty paragraph be improved? The best way is to remind the reader again and again of the topic and to use examples from the text to support the topic. Consistently with our diagram, each time the topic is mentioned, the undulating line merges with the straight, or central-idea line. This relationship of topic to illustrative examples should prevail no matter what subject you write about. If you are analyzing *point of view*, for example, you should keep connecting your material to the speaker, or narrator, and the same applies to a topics like character, setting, and whatever other aspect of literature you are studying. According to the principle, we might revise the paragraph on the idea of economic determinism in "The Necklace" as follows, keeping as much of the original wording as we can. (The parts of sentences stressing the relationship of the examples to the topic of the paragraph are underlined.)

> More important than chance in governing life is the idea that people are controlled by economic circumstances. As illustration, the speaker begins by emphasizing that Mathilde, the major character, is born poor. Therefore she doesn't get the right doors opened for her, and her marriage is to a minor clerk. In keeping with the idea, her vivid imagination and burning desire for luxury (she seems to have been born only for the wealthy life) feed on her weakness of character as she feels deep unhappiness and depression because of the contrast between her daydreams of expensive surroundings and the poor home she actually has. The straitened economic circumstances inhibit her relationship with her

husband, and she taunts him when he brings the big invitation, because she does not have a suitable (read "expensive") dress. As a merging of her unrealistic dream life with actual reality, her borrowing of the necklace suggests the impossibility, according to the idea, of overcoming economic restrictions. In the context of the idea, the ten-year sacrifice to pay for the lost necklace demonstrates that lack of money keeps people in place, destroying their dreams and hopes of a better life.

The original paragraph has been improved so that now it reaches the goal of the topic sentence. While it has also been lengthened, the length has been caused not by inessential detail but by phrases and sentences that give form and direction. You might object that if you lengthened all your paragraphs in this way, your themes would grow too bulky. The answer is to reduce the number of major points and paragraphs, on the theory that *it is better to develop a few topics pointedly than many pointlessly*. Revision done to strengthen central topic ideas requires that you throw out some topics or else incorporate them as subpoints in the topics you keep. This assertion of your own control can result only in improvement.

Providing Insight, Newness, and Growth

Sticking to a point is therefore one of the first requirements of a good theme, for you will not be successful unless you thoroughly exemplify and support your central idea. Another major quality of excellence is to make your central idea expand and grow. The word *growth* is a metaphor for *development*—the creation of new insights, the disclosure of ideas that were not at first noticeable, and the expression of new, fresh, and original interpretations.

An argument here might be that you cannot be original when you are writing about someone else's work. "The author has said everything," might go the argument, "and therefore I can do little more than follow the story." This claim assumes that you have no choice in selecting material, and no opportunity to make individual thoughts and original contributions. But you have. The author has presented the work to you, and, if you look hard, you can find layer upon layer of meaning. One obvious area of originality is the development and formulation of your central idea. For example, a natural first response to "The Necklace" is that "It is about a woman who loses a borrowed necklace and endures hardship to help pay for it." Because this response refers only to the story and not to any idea, an area of thought might be introduced if the hardship is called "needless." Though better, this idea is not very original either. But an original insight can result if the topic is connected to the relationship between the dreamy, withdrawn traits of the major character and her misfortune. Thus, an idea might be that "People themselves bring about their own misfortunes." With such an idea, it is possible to do more in creating a fresh, original theme analyzing the story's development than the first response could do.

You can also develop your ability to treat your subject freshly and originally if you plan the body of the theme to build up to what you think is your most important, incisive, and well-conceived idea. As examples of such planning, the following arrangements of brief topic outlines suggest how a central idea may be widened and expanded:

A. Mathilde as a growing character (*Character*, Chapter 4)

1. Mathilde is at first a person with normal daydreams.
2. Mathilde takes a risk to make her daydreams seem real.
3. Mathilde develops by facing her mistake and working hard to right it.

B. The idea of economic determination (*Idea or Theme*, Chapter 7)

1. Mathilde's economic class inhibits her wishes.
2. Her economically poor married life is a damper on her character.
3. The ten-year hardship is her punishment for trying to live beyond her means.

C. The development of irony in the story (*Tone*, Chapter 11)

1. Mathilde's dissatisfaction is heightened by her dreams.
2. The loss of the necklace ironically makes the Loisels seem poorer than they really are.
3. Mathilde's failure to confess the loss to Jeanne makes the sacrifice needless.

D. The symbolic value of the necklace (*Symbolism and Allegory*, Chapter 10)

1. The necklace symbolizes economic wealth and ease.
2. That the necklace was false symbolizes the discrepancy between appearance and reality.
3. Restoring the necklace symbolizes the value of sacrifice and work.

These lists indicate how a subject may be enlarged if the exemplifying topics are treated in an increasing order of importance. Both the first and last outlines, for example, move toward ideas about moral values, while the second moves toward a broad consideration of the story, and the third suggests a climax based on the story's situational irony. Details in themes derived from the lists would all be included as a part of the developing pattern of growth; in no way would they be introduced to retell the story. These suggested patterns show how two primary standards of excellence in writing—organization and growth—can be met.

It should be clear that whenever you write, an important goal should be the development of your central idea. Constantly adhere to your topic, and constantly develop it. Nurture it and make it grow. Admittedly, in a short theme you will be able to move only a short distance with an idea, but you *should never be satisfied to leave the idea exactly where you found it*. To the degree that you can learn to develop your ideas, you will receive recognition for increasingly superior writing. Your grades, in short, will go higher.

Using Accurate and Forceful Language

In addition to being organized and well developed, the best writing is *accurate, insightful,* and *forceful*. The first sentences and paragraphs we write are usually weak, and they need to be rethought, recast, and reworded. Sometimes we cannot carry out this process immediately, for it may take days or even weeks for us to gain objectivity about what we say (if we ever do). As a student you usually do not have that kind of time, and thus you must acquire the habit of challenging your own statements almost as soon as you write them. Ask yourself whether they really *mean* what you intend and whether you can make them stronger.

As an example, consider the following sentence, which was written in a student theme as a central idea about "The Necklace":

> The central idea in this story is how Mathilde and her husband respond to the loss of the necklace.

This sentence could not help the development of a theme. Because it promises no more than the retelling of the story, it needs more thought and rephrasing. Here are two revisions of the sentence that would be more helpful:

> In the story Guy de Maupassant exemplifies the idea that hard work and responsibility are basic and necessary in life.

> Guy de Maupassant makes the surprise ending of the story a symbol of the need for always being truthful.

Although both new sentences deal with the same story materials, they point toward different treatments. The first would be built up out of the virtue shown by the Loisels in their sacrifice. Since the second sentence contains the word *symbol*, any theme to be developed from it would stress the mistake the Loisels make in not confessing the loss. In dealing with the symbolic meaning of their failure, such a theme would focus on the negative aspects of their characters, while the theme developed from the first sentence would stress their positive aspects. Whatever the final theme, however, either of the two revised sentences is more accurate than the original sentence and would move a theme writer toward a superior composition.

Equally vital—and equally challenging and important—is to make sure to say *exactly* what you mean. If you do not keep your eyes steadily on your subjects, you may wind up saying nothing. For example, consider these two sentences from themes about "The Necklace":

1. It seems as though the major character's dreams of luxury cause her to respond as she does in the story.

2. This incident, although it may seem trivial or unimportant, has substantial significance in the creation of the story; by this I mean the incident which occurred is essentially what the story is all about.

These sentences are vague and unhelpful; neither of them goes anywhere. The first sentence is satisfactory up to the verb "cause," but then it falls apart because the writer has lost sight of the meaning. It is best to describe *what* that response is, rather than to be satisfied with nothing more than that there *is* a response. To make the sentence more specific, we might make the following revision:

Mathilde's dreams of luxury make it impossible for her to accept her own possessions, and therefore she goes beyond her means to attend the party.

With this revision, the writer could consider the meaning of the story's early pages and could contrast the ideas there with those in the latter part. Without the revision, it is not clear where the writer might go.

The second sentence is so vague that it confuses rather than informs. The cause, again, is that the writer has lost sight of the topic. If we adopt the principle of making things more specific, however, we may bring the dead sentence to life:

The accidental loss of the necklace, which is trivial though costly, supports the narrator's claim that major turns in life are produced not by earthshaking events, but rather by minor ones.

When you write your own sentences, you might test them: Are you referring to an idea? State the idea directly. Are you mentioning a response or impression? Do not say simply, "The story's ending left me with a definite impression," but *state* what the impression is, like this: "The story's ending surprised me and also made me sympathetic to Mathilde's condition." Similarly, do not rest with a statement such as "I found 'The Necklace' interesting," but try to describe *what* was interesting and *why* it was interesting: "I found 'The Necklace' interesting because it shows how chance may either make or destroy people's lives." If you always name and pin down your impressions and responses, no matter how elusive they seem, your sentences will be exact and forceful. Naturally, your instructor will tell you how you are doing—both what is good and what needs improving. Good writing habits that you develop from these criticisms of your work, and also from discussions with your instructor, will help you to write more accurately and forcefully.

To sum up, follow these guidelines whenever you do any kind of writing: (1) Keep returning to your points. (2) Use material from the work you are studying as evidence supporting your argument; do not retell stories or summarize major arguments. (3) Let no details from the work stay in your theme unless you have clearly connected them to your main points. (4) Try to develop your topic; make it bigger than it was when you began. (5) Constantly try to make your statements specific, accurate, and forceful. If you always observe these guidelines, you will have a head start with all writing assignments.

chapter 2

Writing About Likes and Dislikes:
Responding to Literature

The act of reading is accompanied by emotional responses which, at their simplest level, take the form of pleasure or displeasure: You either like or dislike a poem, story, or play. You have not said much, however, if all you say is that you have liked or disliked something. Writing about likes and dislikes should require you to explain the reasons for your responses. In short, your discussion should be *informed* and *informative*.

Sometimes a first response is that a work is "boring." This reaction is usually a mask covering an incomplete and superficial first reading; it is neither informed nor informative. As you study most works, however, you will invariably get drawn into them. One common word that describes this process is *interest*; to be interested in a work is to be taken into it emotionally. Another word is *involvement*; it suggests that one's emotions become almost enfolded in the characters, problems, and outcomes of a work. Sometimes both words are used defensively, just like the word *boring*. It is easy to say that something is "interesting," or that you get "involved" in it, and you might say just these things while hoping that no one will ask what you mean. Both *interest* and *involvement* do indeed describe genuine responses to reading, however. Once you get interested, your reading ceases to be a task or assignment and grows into a pleasure.

USING YOUR NOTEBOOK
TO RECORD RESPONSES

No one can tell you what you should or should not like; liking is your own concern. While your experience of reading is still fresh, therefore, you should use your notebook (discussed earlier, pp. 13–17) to record not only your observations about a work, but also your responses. Be frank in your judgment. Write down your likes and dislikes, and try to explain the reasons for your response, even if these are brief and incomplete. If you change or modify your first impressions following later thought and fuller understanding, record these changes too. Here is a notebook entry that explains a favorable response to Guy de Maupassant's "The Necklace":

> I like "The Necklace" because of the surprise ending. It isn't that I like Mathilde's bad luck, but I like the way Maupassant hides the most important fact in the story until the end. Mathilde does all that work and sacrifice for no reason at all, and the surprise ending makes this point strongly.

This paragraph could be expanded as a part of a developing essay. It is a clear statement of liking, followed by references to likable things in the work. This response pattern, which can be simply phrased as "I like [or dislike] this work *because* . . .," is a useful way to begin notebook entries because it always requires that a response be followed with an explanation. If at first you cannot write any full sentences detailing the causes of your responses, at least make a brief list of the things you like or dislike. If you write nothing, you are likely to forget your reactions; recovering them later, either for discussion or writing, will be difficult.

Responding Favorably

Usually you can equate your interest in a work with liking it. You can be more specific about favorable responses by citing one or more of the following:

> You like and admire the characters and what they do and stand for.
>
> You learn something new—something you had never known or thought before.
>
> You gain new insights into things you already knew.
>
> You learn about characters and customs of different places, times, and ways of life.
>
> You get interested and involved in the outcome of the action or ideas and do not want to put the work down until you have finished it.
>
> You feel happy or thrilled because of reading the work.

You are amused and laugh often as you read.

You like the author's presentation.

You find that some of the ideas and expressions are beautiful and worth remembering.

Obviously, if you find none of these things, or find something that is distasteful, you will not like the work.

Responding Unfavorably

Although so far we have dismissed *boring* and stressed *interest, involvement*, and *liking*, it is important to know that disliking all or part of a work is normal and acceptable. You do not need to hide this response. Here, for example, are two short notebook responses expressing dislike for "The Necklace":

1. I do not like "The Necklace" because Mathilde seems spoiled, and I don't think she is worth reading about.
2. "The Necklace" is not an adventure story, and I like reading only adventure stories.

These are both legitimate responses because they are based on a clear standard of judgment. The first stems from a distaste for one of the main character's unlikable traits; the second, from a preference for rapidly moving stories which evoke interest in the dangers faced and overcome by main characters.

Here is a notebook-type entry that might be developed from the first response. What is important is that the reasons for dislike are explained. They would need only slightly more development for use in a theme:

I do not like "The Necklace" because Mathilde seems spoiled, and I do not think she is worth reading about. She is a phony. She nags her husband because he is not rich. She never tells the truth. I dislike her for hurrying away from the party because she is afraid of being seen in her shabby coat. She is foolish and dishonest for not telling Jeanne Forrestier about losing the necklace. It is true that she works hard to pay the debt, but she also puts her husband through ten years of hardship. If Mathilde had faced facts, she might have had a better life. I do not like her and cannot like the story because of her.

As long as you include reasons for your dislike, as in this model notebook paragraph, you can use them again when developing your theme. After further consideration, you will expand your thoughts, include new details, pick new topics for development and paragraphs, and otherwise modify your notebook entry. You might even change your mind. However, even if you do not change your mind, it is better to record your original responses and reasons honestly than to force yourself to say you like something that you do not.

PUTTING DISLIKES INTO A LARGER CONTEXT

While it is important to be honest about disliking a work, it is more important to broaden your perspective and expand your taste. For example, a dislike based on preference for only mystery or adventure stories, if it is applied generally, would cause a person to dislike most works of literature. This seems unnecessarily self-limiting.

By putting negative responses into a larger context, it is possible to expand the ability of liking and appreciation. Some readers might be deeply involved in personal concerns and therefore be uninterested in remote or "irrelevant" literary figures. However, if by reading about literary characters they can gain insight into general problems of life, and therefore their own concerns, they can find something to like in just about any work of literature. Other readers might like sports and therefore not read anything but sports magazines. But what probably interests them about sports is competition, so if competition or conflict can be found in a literary work, they can like that work.

As an example, let us consider again the dislike based on a preference for adventure stories and see if this preference can be widened. Here are some reasons for liking adventures:

1. Adventure has fast action.
2. Adventure has danger and tension, and therefore interest.
3. Adventure has daring, active, and successful characters.
4. Adventure has obstacles which the characters work hard to overcome.

No one could claim that the first three points apply to "The Necklace," but the fourth point is promising. Mathilde, the major character, works hard to overcome an obstacle: she pitches in to help her husband pay the large debt. If our student likes adventures because the characters try to gain worthy goals, then he or she can also like "The Necklace" for the same reason. The principle here is clear: If a reason for liking a favorite work or type of work can be found in another work, then there is reason to like that new work. The problem is that the student must first be able to articulate responses to the favorite work. Thought and analogy will then do the rest, and therefore such a comparative method can become the basis for analyzing and developing responses to newly encountered works.

The following paragraph shows a possible operation of this "bridging" process of extending preferences. (The sample essay [pp. 47–48] is also developed along these lines.)

> I usually like only adventure stories, and therefore I disliked "The Necklace" at first because it is not adventure. But one of my reasons for liking adventure is that the characters work hard to overcome difficult obstacles, like finding buried treasure or exploring new places. Mathilde, Maupassant's main character in "The Necklace," also works hard to overcome an obstacle—helping to pay back the money and interest for the borrowed 18,000 francs used as part of the payment for the replacement necklace. I like adventure characters because they stick to things and win out. I see the same toughness in Mathilde. Her problems get more interesting as the story moves on after a slow beginning. I came to like the story.

In this way, an accepted principle of liking can be applied to another work where it also applies. A person who adapts principles in this open-minded way can redefine dislikes, no matter how slowly, and may consequently expand the ability to like and appreciate many kinds of literature.

An equally open-minded way to develop understanding and widen taste is to put dislikes in the following light: An author's creation of an unlikable character, situation, attitude, or expression may be deliberate. Your dislike might then result from the author's *intentions*. A first task of study is therefore to understand and explain the intention or plan. As you put the plan into your own words, you may find that you can like a work with unlikable things in it. Here is a paragraph that traces this pattern of thinking, based again on "The Necklace":

> Maupassant apparently wants the reader to dislike Mathilde, and I do. At first, he shows her being unrealistic and spoiled. She lies to everyone and nags her husband. Her rushing away from the party so that no one can see her shabby coat is a form of lying. But I like the story itself because Maupassant makes another kind of point. He does not hide her bad qualities but makes it clear that she herself is the cause of her trouble. If people like Mathilde never face the truth, they will get into bad situations. This is a good point, and I like the way Maupassant makes it. The entire story is therefore worth liking even though I still do not like Mathilde.

Neither of these two ways of broadening the contexts of response is dishonest to the original negative reactions. In the first paragraph, the writer applies one of his principles of liking to include "The Necklace." In the second, the writer considers her initial dislike in the context of the work, and discovers a basis of liking the story as a whole while still disliking the main character. The main concern in both responses is to keep an open mind despite initial dislike, and then to see if the unfavorable response can be more fully and broadly considered.

However, if you decide that your dislike overbalances any reasons you can find for liking, then you should explain your dislike. As long as you relate your response accurately to the work, and measure it by a clear standard of judgment, your dislike of even a commonly liked work is not unacceptable. What is important here is not so much that you like or dislike a particular work (you will eventually find hundreds or even thousands of works to like) as *that you develop your own abilities to analyze and express your ideas.*

WRITING ABOUT RESPONSES: LIKES AND DISLIKES

In writing about your responses, you should rely on your initial informed reactions. It is not easy to reconstruct your first responses after a lapse of time, so you will need your notebook observations as a guide in the pre-writing stage. Develop your essay by stressing what interests you (or does not interest you) in the work.

A major challenge is to relate the details of the work to the point you are making about your ongoing responses. That is, it might be easy to begin by indicating that you like the work, and then, in describing what it is that you like, you might forget your responses as you enumerate details. You should therefore stress your involvement in the work as you bring out evidence from it. You can show your attitudes by indicating approval (or disapproval), by commenting favorably (or unfavorably) on the details, by indicating things that seem new (or shopworn) and particularly instructive (or wrong), and by giving assent to (or dissent from) ideas or expressions of feeling.

Introduction

Begin by describing briefly the conditions that influence your response. Your central idea should be why you like or dislike the work. The thesis sentence should list the major causes of your response, which are to be developed in the body.

Body

The most common approach is to consider specific things about the work that you like or dislike. The list on pages 42–43 may help you articulate your responses. For example, you may have admired a particular character, or maybe you got so interested in the story that you could not put it down. Also, it may be that a major idea, or a new or fresh insight, or a particular outcome, is the major point that you wish to develop. The sample notebook-paragraph on page 42 shows a surprise ending as the cause of a favorable response.

A second approach (see pp. 44–46) is to explain any changes in your responses about the work (i.e., negative to positive and vice versa). This approach requires that you isolate the cause of the change, but it does *not* require you to follow the text from beginning to end. One way to deal with such a change—the "bridge" method of transferring preference from one type of work to another—is shown in the sample theme (pp. 47–48). Another way is to explain a change in terms of a new awareness or understanding that you did not have on a first reading. Thus a first response to Poe's "The Masque of the Red Death" might have been unfavorable or neutral because, say, the story seems unnecessarily sensational and lurid. But further consideration may have led you to discover new insights that might have changed your mind, like the futility of challenging death, or the impossibility of stopping an epidemic. The theme would then demonstrate how these new insights figure into the process of your changed attitude.

Conclusion

Here you might summarize the reasons for your major response. You might also face any issues brought up by a change or modification of your first reactions. For example, if you have always held certain assumptions about your taste but like the work despite these assumptions, you may wish to talk about your own change or development. This topic is personal, but in an essay about likes or dislikes, discovery about yourself is something you should aim for.

Sample Theme

*Some Reasons for Liking Maupassant's "The Necklace"**

---

[1]
To me, the most likable kind of reading is adventure. Although there are many reasons for my preference, an important one is that adventure characters work hard to overcome obstacles. Because Guy de Maupassant's "The Necklace" is not adventure, I did not like it at first. But in one respect the story is <u>like</u> adventure: The major character Mathilde, with her husband Loisel, works <u>hard</u> for ten years to overcome a difficult obstacle. <u>Thus, because Mathilde does what adventure characters also do, the story is likable.°</u> <u>Mathilde's appeal results from her hard work, strong character, sad fate, and also from the way our view of her changes.</u>°

* For the text of this story, see pages 4–13.
° Central idea
° Thesis sentence

[2]   <u>Mathilde's hard work makes her seem good.</u> Once she and her husband are faced with the huge debt of 18,000 francs, she works like a slave to pay it back. She gives up her servant and moves to a cheaper place. She does the household drudgery, wears cheap clothes, and bargains with shopkeepers for the lowest prices. Just like the characters in adventure stories, who do hard and unpleasant things, she does what she has to do, and this makes her admirable.

[3]   <u>Her strong character shows her endurance, a likable trait.</u> At first she is nagging and fussy, and she always dreams about wealth and tells lies, but she changes and gets better. She recognizes her blame in losing the necklace, and she has the toughness to help her husband redeem the debt. She sacrifices "heroically" (paragraph 98) by giving up her comfortable way of life, even though in the process she also loses her youth and beauty. Her jobs are not the exotic and glamorous ones of adventure stories, but her force of character makes her as likable as an adventure heroine.

[4]   <u>Her sad fate also makes her likable.</u> In adventure stories the characters often suffer as they do their jobs. Mathilde also suffers, but in a different way, because her suffering is permanent while the hardships of adventure characters are temporary. This fact makes her pitiable, and even more so because all her sacrifices are not necessary. This unfairness about her life invites the reader to take her side.

[5]   <u>The most important quality promoting admiration is the way in which Maupassant shifts our view of Mathilde.</u> As she goes deeper into her hard life, Maupassant stresses her work and not the innermost thoughts he reveals at the beginning. In other words, the view into her character at the start, when she dreams about wealth, invites dislike, while the focus at the end is on her achievements, with never a complaint—even though she still has golden memories, as the narrator tells us (paragraph 104):

        But sometimes, when her husband was at work, she sat down near
        the window, and she dreamed of that evening so long ago, of that
        party, where she had been so beautiful and so admired.

A major quality of Maupassant's changed emphasis is that these recollections do not lead to anything unfortunate. Thus his shift in focus, from Mathilde's dissatisfaction to her willingness to accept responsibility and sacrifice, encourages the reader to like her.

[6]   "The Necklace" is not an adventure story, but some of the good qualities of adventure characters are present in Mathilde. Also, the surprise revelation that the lost necklace was false is an unforgettable twist which makes her more deserving than she seems at first. Maupassant has arranged the story so that the reader finally admires Mathilde. <u>"The Necklace" is a skillful and likable story.</u>

COMMENTARY ON THE THEME

This theme demonstrates how a reader may develop appreciation through the transferring or "bridging" of a preference for one type of work to a work that does not belong to that type (described earlier in this chapter, pp. 44–46). In the theme, the bridge is an already established taste for adventure stories, and the reason for liking "The Necklace" is that Mathilde, the major character, shares the admirable qualities of adventure heroes and heroines.

In paragraph 1, the introduction, the grounds for transferring preference are established, and the concluding thesis sentence lists the four topics to be developed in the body.

The body first stresses how admiration is brought out by the character of Mathilde. Paragraph 2 deals with her capacity to work hard, while paragraph 3 considers the equally admirable quality of endurance. The fourth paragraph describes how Mathilde's condition evokes sympathy and pity. These paragraphs hence explain the story's appeal by asserting that the major character is similar to admirable characters from works of adventure. (Paragraph 5, which marks a new direction by describing an aspect of the author's skill, is given detailed discussion below.)

Paragraph 6, the conclusion, restates the comparison and also introduces the surprise ending as an additional reason for liking "The Necklace." With the body and conclusion together, therefore, the theme establishes five separate reasons for approval. Three of these, which are derived directly from the major character, constitute the major grounds for liking the story, while two are related to Maupassant's techniques as an author.

Throughout the essay, the central idea is brought out in words and expressions such as "likable," "Mathilde's appeal," "strong character," "she does what she has to," "pitiable," and "take her side." These expressions, mixed as they are with references to many details from the story, help shape continuity in the theme. It is this thematic development, together with details from the story as supporting evidence, that shows how an essay on the responses of liking and disliking may be both informed and informative.

A Close Look at Paragraph 5

The fifth paragraph is derived from notes pointing out that harm comes from Mathilde's early and unadmirable dream world but that her later memory of the big party does not have any unfortunate results. The quotation from the story is selected to underline this shift of emphasis, for it shows that Mathilde's later dreaming occurs only "sometimes," while Maupassant earlier gives the impression that she daydreams all the time. With this observation as a base, the paragraph is constructed to demonstrate that Maupassant, as the story unfolds, alters the reader's perceptions of Mathilde, from bad to good. For this reason paragraph 5 marks a new direction from paragraph 2, 3, and 4, because it moves away from the topic material itself—Mathilde's character—to Maupassant's *technique* in handling the topic material. The paragraph also reflects a somewhat advanced way of determining a work's quality, for *explaining* how something is done requires more understanding than just *following* it. In addition, appreciation and deeper liking will result from such increased perception and analysis.

chapter 3

Writing About Plot and Structure:

The Organization of Narratives and Drama

I. PLOT

Fictional and dramatic characters are derived from life, and so are the things that they do. These things are the **actions** or **incidents,** which occur in chronological order. Once we have established a *narrative* or sequential order, however, there is still more to be considered. This is **plot,** or the plan of development of the actions.

WHAT IS PLOT?

Without a plot, we do not have a story or drama. A plot is a plan or groundwork of human motivations, with the actions resulting from believable and realistic human responses. In a well-plotted work, nothing is irrelevant; everything is related. The British novelist E. M. Forster, in *Aspects of the Novel*, presents a memorable illustration of plot. As a minimum narration of actions, in contrast to a story with a plot, he uses the following: "The king died, and then the queen died" (p. 130). This sentence describes a sequence, a chronological order, but no more. To have a plot, a sequence must be integrated with human motivation. Thus Forster's following sentence contains a plot: "The king died, and then the queen died of grief." With the phrase "of grief," which shows that one thing (grief over the king's death) produces or overcomes another (the normal human desire to live), there is a plot. Thus the use of chronological order is important not because one thing happens *after* another, but because it happens *because of* another. It is response, interaction, causation, and conflict that make a plot out of a series of actions.

CONFLICT.   **Conflict,** the last word on this list, is the most significant element of plot. In fact, it is the essence of plot because in conflict, human energy is brought out to the highest degree. In its most elemental form, a conflict is the opposition of two people. They may fight, argue, enlist help, and otherwise oppose each other. Conflicts may also exist between groups, although conflicts between individuals are more identifiable and therefore more interesting. A more abstract kind of conflict is one in which an individual opposes larger forces such as natural objects, ideas, modes of behavior, public opinion, and the like. A difficult choice may be presented as a conflict, or **dilemma.** In addition, a conflict may not be the opposition of characters, but rather the contrasts between ideas or opinions. There are many ways, in short, to bring out conflict.

DOUBT, TENSION, AND INTEREST.   Conflict is the major element of plot because opposing forces arouse curiosity, cause doubt, and create tension. The same responses are the lifeblood of athletic competition. Consider which kind of game is more interesting: (1) one in which the score is so close that the outcome is in doubt to the last moment, or (2) one in which one team gets so far ahead that the game is no longer competitive. Obviously the first would be more interesting, as a game should be a genuine contest between teams of comparable strength. The same applies to conflict in a literary work. The protagonist should be exerting great energy to win, and there should be uncertainty about ultimate success, for unless there is doubt about the outcome there is no tension, and without tension there is no interest.

PLOT IN OPERATION.   To see a plot in operation, let us build on Forster's description. Here is a bare plot for a story: "John and Jane meet, fall in love, and get married." This plot has no conflict and would attract few readers. However, let us introduce conflicting elements in this common "boy meets girl" story:

> John and Jane meet at school and fall in love. They go together for two years and plan to marry, but a problem arises. Jane wants a career first, and after marriage she wants to be an equal contributor to the family. John understands Jane's wishes, but he wants to marry first and let her finish her career studies afterward. Jane believes that this solution will not work but is a trap from which she will never escape. This conflict interrupts their plans, and they part in regret and anger. Even though they still love each other, both marry other people and build separate lives and

careers. Neither is happy even though they like and respect their spouses. The years pass, and, after children and grandchildren, Jane and John meet again. He is now a widower and she has divorced. Because their earlier conflict is no longer a barrier, they marry and try to make up for the past. Even their newly found happiness, however, is tinged with regret and reproach because of their earlier conflict, their unhappy solution, their lost years, and their increasing age.

Here we have a true plot because our story contains a major conflict together with related conflicts. The (1) initial difference in plans and hopes is resolved by (2) a parting of the characters, leading to choices that are (3) not totally happy. The later marriage produces (4) not unqualified happiness, but regret and (5) a sense of time irretrievably lost. These conflicting attitudes and choices account for the interest our short-short story causes. The situation is lifelike; the conflict rises out of realistic aims and hopes; the outcome is true to life. The imposition of the various conflicts and contrasts has made an interesting plot out of our original "boy meets girl" sequence.

WRITING ABOUT PLOT

A theme about plot is an analysis of the conflict and its routes and developments. The organization should not be derived from sequential sections and principal events, because these invite no more than a chronological retelling of the story. Instead, the organization should be developed out of the important elements of conflict.

Introduction

The things to bring out are brief references to the principal characters, circumstances, and issues of the plot. The theme's central idea should be a sentence describing the plot, or principal conflict. The thesis sentence lists those topics to be developed in the body.

Body

The body should focus on the major elements of the plot, brought out to emphasize the plan of conflict in the story or play. In developing your ideas, try to answer questions like these: What is the conflict? How is it embodied in the work? What person or persons are the antagonists, and how do their characteristics and interests involve them in the conflict? If the conflict stems out of contrasting ideas or values, what are these, and how are they brought out? Does the major character face a difficult decision of any sort? (In our model short-short story, for example, Jane faces the decision of choosing a career and losing John, or accepting John on his terms and losing her career.) Do the characters reach their goals? Why or why not? As a result of the outcome, are the characters successful or unsuccessful, happy or dissatisfied?

To keep your theme reasonably brief, you will need to be selective about what you discuss. Rather than detailing everything that a character does, for example, stress the major elements in his or her conflict. Such a theme on Eudora Welty's "A Worn Path" might emphasize Phoenix as she encounters the various obstacles both in the wood and in town. Similarly, an essay about the plot of Maupassant's "The Necklace" might emphasize the major character, Mathilde, as she changes from a spoiled and petulant woman, as a result of her frustration about not being rich, to one who becomes coarse and loud, as a result of her hardship and sacrifice.

When there is a conflict between two major characters, the most obvious approach is to focus equally on both. For brevity, however, you might also stress just one of them. Thus in Chekhov's *The Bear*, Mrs. Popov, whose conflict is between old love of her dead husband, on the one hand, and new love of the very alive Smirnov, on the other, might be the major focus, even though Smirnov is equally major and important.

In addition, the plot may be analyzed more broadly in terms of impulses, goals, ideas, values, issues, and historical perspectives. Thus you might emphasize the elements of chance working against Mathilde, as a contrast to her dreams about wealth. Discussing the plot of Poe's "The Masque of Red Death" might stress the haughty pride of Prospero, the major character, for the plot could not develop without his egotism. In short, when you sketch out your ideas for the body, you have liberty of choice.

Conclusion

The conclusion may contain a brief summary of the points in the body. Also, a study of plot often leaves out one of the most important reasons for reading, and that is the interest and *impact* produced by the conflict. Thus the conclusion is a fitting location for a brief consideration of effect. Additional comments might focus on whether the author has arranged things so far as to direct your favor toward one side or the other, or whether the plot is realistic, true to life, fair, and impartial.

Sample Theme

*The Plot of Eudora Welty's "A Worn Path"** *

[1] At first, the complexity of Eudora Welty's plot in "A Worn Path" is not clear. The main character is Phoenix Jackson, an old, poor, and frail woman; the story seems to be no more than a record of her walk to Natchez through the woods from her rural home. By the story's end, however, the plot is clear: It consists of the brave attempts of a courageous, valiant woman to carry on against overwhelming forces.° Her determination despite the great odds against her gives the story its impact. The powers ranged against her are old age, poverty, environment, and illness.▫

[2] Old age as a silent but overpowering antagonist is shown in signs of Phoenix's increasing senility. Not her mind but her feet tell her where to find the medical office in Natchez. Despite her inner strength, she is unable to explain her errand to the nursing attendant. Instead she sits dumbly and unknowingly for a time, until "a flame of comprehension" comes across her face (paragraph 87). Against the power of advancing age, Phoenix is slowly losing. The implication is that she soon will lose entirely.

[3] An equally crushing opponent is her poverty. She cannot afford to ride to town, but must walk. She has no money, and acquires her ten cents for the paper windmill by theft and begging. The "soothing medicine" she gets for her grandson (paragraph 92) is given to her out of charity. Despite the boy's need for advanced medical care, she has no money to provide it, and the story therefore shows that her guardianship is doomed.

[4] Closely connected to her poverty is the way through the woods, which during her walk seems to be an almost active opponent. Thus the long hill obviously tires her, the thornbush catches her clothes, the log endangers her balance as she crosses the creek, and the barbed-wire fence threatens to puncture her skin. Another danger on her way is the hunter's dog, which topples her over. Apparently not afraid, however, Phoenix carries on a cheerful monologue:

> "Out of my way, all you foxes, owls, beetles, jack rabbits, coons and wild animals! . . . Keep out from under these feet, little bob-whites. . . . Keep the big wild hogs out of my path. Don't let none of these come running my direction. I got a long way." (paragraph 3)

She prevails for the moment as she enters Natchez, but all the hazards of her walk are still there, waiting for her.

[5] The force against Phoenix creating the greatest pathos is her grandson's incurable illness. His condition highlights her helplessness, for she is his only support. Her difficulties would be enough for one person alone, but with the grandson the odds against her are doubled. Despite her care, there is nothing

---

* For the text of this story, see Appendix C, pages 322–28.
° Central idea
▫ Thesis sentence

[5] anyone can do for the grandson but take the long worn path to get something to make him easy during his flaring pain.

This brief description of the conflicts in "A Worn Path" only hints at the story's great power. Welty layers the details to bring out the full range of the conditions against Phoenix, who cannot win despite her dogged determination and devotion. The most hopeless fact, the condition of the invalid grandson, is

[6] not revealed until she reaches the medical office, and this delayed final revelation makes one's heart go out to her. <u>The plot is strong because it is so real, and Phoenix is a pathetic but memorable protagonist struggling against overwhelming odds.</u>

COMMENTARY ON THE THEME

The strategy of this theme is to explain the elements of plot in "A Worn Path" selectively, without duplicating the story's narrative order. Thus the third aspect of conflict, the woods, might be introduced first if the story's narrative order were to be followed, but it is deferred while the more personal elements of old age and poverty are considered first. It is important to note that the theme does not consider the other characters as part of Phoenix's conflict, for other persons are helpful. Rather the antagonist takes the shape of impersonal and unconquerable forces, such as the grandson's illness.

(Paragraph 1 is discussed in the next section.) Paragraph 2 concerns old age; paragraph 3 her poverty; paragraph 4 the woods; and paragraph 5 the grandson's illness. The concluding paragraph (6) points out that in this set of conflicts the protagonist cannot win, except as she lives out her duty and her devotion to help her grandson. Continuing the theme of the introduction, the last paragraph also accounts for the power of the plot: By building up to Phoenix's personal affirmation against unbeatable forces, the story evokes sympathy and admiration.

A Close Look at Paragraph 1

The strategy of this paragraph, as the introduction, is to prepare the way for the major points to be covered in the body. Ironically, then, even though the paragraph begins the theme, it is not written until the body is substantially completed. Because the story itself does not reveal the major detail about the invalid grandson until the end, this paragraph begins by treating the effect of this revelation on the reader's final perception of the forces opposing the protagonist. Thus the opening briefly describes how the first impression changes by the story's end. Because the goal is to deal with the elements of plot, the thesis sentence anticipates the body by listing the four topics about to be treated.

II. STRUCTURE

Structure describes the arrangement and placement of materials within a narrative or drama. While *plot* concerns conflict, *structure* concerns layout—the way the work is shaped to bring out the conflict. The study of structure in fiction and drama deals with the causes and reasons for matters such as placement, balance, recurring themes, juxtapositions, true and misleading conclusions, suspense, and the imitation of models or forms such as letters, conversations, confessions, and the like. Thus a story may be divided into parts, or it might move from countryside to city, or a play might develop relationships between two people from their first introduction to their falling in love. The study of structure is about these arrangements and the purposes for which they are made.

Formal Categories of Structure

Many aspects of structure are common to all genres of literature. Particularly for drama and narratives, however, the following aspects form the backbone, skeleton, or pattern of development.

1 EXPOSITION. The **exposition** is the laying out, the putting forth, of the materials in the work: the main characters, their backgrounds, their characteristics, basic assumptions about life, goals, limitations, and potentials. It may not be limited to the beginning of the work, where it is most expected, but may be found anywhere. Thus, intricacies, twists, turns, false leads, blind alleys, surprises, and other quirks may be introduced to perplex, intrigue, please, and otherwise interest readers. Whenever something new arises, to the degree that it is new it is a part of exposition. Eventually, however, the introduction of new materials stops, and the story proceeds to a conclusion with only the exposition that has already been included.

2. COMPLICATION. The **complication** is the onset of the major conflict—the plot. The participants are the **protagonist** and **antagonist**, together with whatever ideas and values they represent, such as good and evil, freedom and suppression, childhood and age, love and hate, intelligence and stupidity, knowledge and ignorance, and the like.

3. CRISIS. The **crisis** (Greek for *turning point*) is the separation between what has gone before and what will come after, usually a decision or action undertaken to resolve the conflict. The crisis is that point in the structure in which uncertainty and tension are greatest.

4. CLIMAX. The **climax** (Greek for *ladder*) is the fulfillment of the action undertaken in the crisis, and it is hence the *high point* in the structure. It is the logical conclusion of all the previous tension and uncertainty, when all doubts and mysteries are ended. In most works, the climax occurs close to or at the end. In Chekhov's play *The Bear*, for example, the climax is that Smirnov, after touching and holding Mrs. Popov when instructing her in the use of the dueling pistol, declares his impetuous love. This brings their hostility to an unexpected height and also to a sudden reversal. In Lowell's "Patterns," the climax is the very last sentence, "Christ, what are patterns for?" This outburst summarizes the speaker's developing sorrow, frustration, and anger.

   5. RESOLUTION OR DENOUEMENT.   The **resolution** (a releasing or untying) or **denouement** (untying) is the finishing of things after the climax. Once the "untying" begins, there is no more tension and uncertainty, and most authors conclude as quickly as possible. Chekhov ends *The Bear* with his two major characters kissing while servants enter dumbfoundedly. Welty ends "A Worn Path" with her major character beginning her long walk home; Poe ends "The Masque of the Red Death" by asserting the "illimitable dominion" of the Red Death itself; and Twain ends "Luck" with the simple statement that the major character is a fool.

Formal and Actual Structure

   The formal structure just described is an ideal one, a pattern that takes place in straightforward, chronological order and that is almost identical to the plot. In practice, however, most narratives and dramas vary this structure. Mystery stories, for example, leave crucial details of exposition unexplained (because the goal is to mystify), while a suspense story may provide all the details for the reader but withhold them from the protagonist so as to create concern and doubt about his or her discovery and success.
   More realistic, less "artificial" stories might also contain structural variations. For example, Welty's "A Worn Path" produces a double take because of a detail of exposition introduced at the very end. During most of the story, the complication seems to be that Phoenix's major conflict is with age, poverty, and environment. At the end, however, we learn that she is the sole guardian and caretaker of her invalid grandson. This new detail also introduces an entirely new element of conflict—that Phoenix is also fighting hopeless illness—and our response enlarges to include anguish and pity. The structure of the story, in other words, is designed to withhold an essential detail to maximize impact.
   There are numerous other possible variants in structure. There might be a **flashback** method, for example: The moment at which the flashback is introduced may be a part of the resolution of the plot, and the flashback might lead you into a moment of climax but then go from there to develop the details that are more properly part of the exposition. Let us again

consider our brief plot about John and Jane and develop a flashback way of structuring the story.

> Jane is now old, and a noise outside causes her to think of the argument that forced her to part with John many years before. Then she thinks of the years she and John have spent happily together after they married. She then contrasts her happiness with her earlier, less happy marriage, and from there she reflects on her years of courtship with John before their conflict over career plans developed. Then she looks over at John, reading in a chair, and smiles. John smiles back, and the story ends.

This method is only one way of structuring the actions. There might be others. Let us suppose that John is terminally ill, or perhaps even dead in his coffin. Flashbacks in each instance would produce a different story. We might also suppose that Jane, now quite old, is giving advice to a grandchild and tells her story in the process. Then, too, we might select that point when she and John have just met again, with the final action being their wedding. The years of happiness might then be introduced as anticipation, or as a resolution described by a narrator, who might have heard about things later from a friend. In short, the possibilities of structuring our little story are great. Using the flashback method such as the one demonstrated here, we would necessarily bring out all the formal elements of plot, but the actual arrangement—the *real* structure—would be unique.

There are many other ways to structure works. A plot might be developed by a group of persons, each one knowing no more than a part of the details, as with Orson Welles's film *Citizen Kane*. Once all the separate stories have been told, all the elements of structure for the total story will be clear. If a work is structured as though demonstrating a process of discovery, elements of exposition and complication might appear not in chronological but in accidental order. An example is Glaspell's *Trifles*, which develops from discoveries that Mrs. Peters and Mrs. Hale make in the farmhouse kitchen while their husbands search for clues in other rooms. Additionally, parts of a story might be set out as fragments of conversation, as in "A Worn Path," or as a ceremony, as in "Young Goodman Brown," or as an announcement of a party, as in "The Necklace." The possible variations are extensive.

WRITING ABOUT STRUCTURE

Your theme will be concerned with arrangement and shape. In form, the theme should not follow the part-by-part unfolding of the narrative or argument. Rather it should explain why things are where they are: "Why is this here and not there?" is the fundamental question to be answered. Thus it is possible to begin with a consideration of a work's crisis, and then to consider how the exposition and complication have built up to this crisis. A vital piece of information, for example, might have been withheld in the earlier exposition (as in "The Lottery" and "A Worn Path") but delayed until the crisis; thus the crisis might be heightened because there would have been less suspense if the detail had been introduced earlier.

Introduction

The introduction should center on the issues of structure to be explored specifically in the body. The central idea is a succinct statement about the structure, such as that it is arranged to reveal the nature of a character's structure, or to create surprise, or to bring out maximum humor. The thesis sentence presents a plan of development for the remainder of the theme.

Body

The body is best developed in concert or agreement with what the work contains. The locations of scenes is an obvious organizing element. Thus an essay on the structure of "A Worn Path" might be based on the countryside, the town, and the building, where the actions of the story occur. Both "Young Goodman Brown" and "Miss Brill" take place outside (a dark forest and a sunny public park). "The Necklace" begins in interiors and concludes outdoors. The locations of "A & P" are the aisles and the checkout counter of a supermarket. A structural study of any of these works might be based on these locations and their effect on the plot.

Other ways to consider structure may also be derived from a work's notable aspects. Donne's "A Valediction: Forbidding Mourning" develops as a set of fanciful images introduced to soothe the listener's feelings. Shakespeare's "That Time of Year" presents three related but different images of aging. "The Lottery" could be fruitfully studied for the means by which it achieves suspense.

It is also possible to study not the entire work, but a major part or an important action. You might, for example, choose the climax of a story. Questions to explore are these: Where does the climax begin? When does it end? How is it related to the crisis? Is the climax an action, a realization, or a decision? To what degree does it relieve the work's tension? What is the effect of the climax on your understanding of the character involved in it? How is this effect related to the arrangement of the climax? Somewhat similar questions would be relevant if you chose, say, the complication, or the crisis.

Conclusion

Here you may highlight the main parts of your theme. Also you may wish to deal briefly with the relationship of structure to the plot. If the work you have analyzed departs from chronological order, you might stress the effects of this departure. Your aim should be to focus on the success of the work as it has been brought about by the author's choices in development.

Sample Theme

The Structure of Eudora Welty's "A Worn Path"*

---

[1]   On the surface, Eudora Welty's "A Worn Path" is structured simply. The narrative is not difficult to follow, and things go forward in straight chronology. The main character is Phoenix Jackson, an old, poor woman. She walks from her rural home in Mississippi through the woods to Natchez to get a free bottle of medicine for her grandson, who is a hopeless invalid. Everything takes place in just a few hours. This action is only the frame, however, for a skillfully and powerfully structured plot.° The masterly control of structure is shown in the story's locations, and in the way in which the delayed revelation produces both mystery and complexity.▫

[2]   The locations in the story coincide with the increasing difficulties faced by Phoenix. The first and most obvious worn path is the rural woods with all its physical difficulties. For most people the obstacles would not be especially challenging, but for an old woman they are formidable. In Natchez, the location of the next part of the story, Phoenix's inability to bend over to tie her shoe demonstrates the lack of flexibility of old age. In the medical office, where the final scene takes place, two major difficulties of the plot are brought out. One is Phoenix's increasing senility, and the other is the disclosure that her grandson is an incurable invalid. This set of oppositions, the major conflicts in the plot, thus coincide with locations or scenes, and demonstrate the power against Phoenix.

[3]   The most powerful of these conditions, the revelation about the grandson, makes the story something like a mystery. Because this detail is not known until the end, the reader wonders for most of the story what might happen next to Phoenix. In fact, some parts of the story are false leads. For example, the episode with the hunter's dog is threatening, but it leads nowhere; Phoenix, with the aid of the hunter, is unharmed. That she picks up and keeps the nickel might seem at first to be cause for punishment. In fact, she thinks it does, as this scene with the hunter shows:

---

* For the text of this story, see Appendix C, pages 322–28.
° Central idea
▫ Thesis sentence

> . . . he laughed and lifted his gun and pointed it at Phoenix.
>
> She stood straight and faced him.
>
> "Doesn't the gun scare you?" he said, still pointing it.
>
> "No, sir, I seen plenty go off closer by, in my day, and for less than what I done," she said, holding utterly still. (paragraphs 53–55)

[3]

But the young hunter does not notice that the coin is missing, and he does not accuse her. Right up to the moment of her entering the medical building, therefore, the reader is still wondering what might happen.

Hence the details about the grandson, carefully concealed until the end, make the story more complex than it at first seems. Because of this concluding revelation, the reader must do a double take, a reconsideration of what has gone on before. Phoenix's difficult walk into town must be seen not as an ordinary errand but as a hopeless mission of mercy. Her character also bears re-evaluation: She is not just a funny old woman who speaks to the woods and animals, but she is a brave and pathetic woman carrying on against crushing odds. These conclusions are not apparent for most of the story, and the bringing out of the carefully concealed details makes "A Worn Path" both forceful and powerful.

[4]

Thus the parts of "A Worn Path," while seemingly simple, are skillfully arranged. The key to the double take and reevaluation is Welty's withholding of the crucial detail of exposition until the very end. The result is that parts of the exposition and complication, through the speeches of the attendant and the nurse, merge with the climax near the story's end. In some respects, the detail makes it seem as though Phoenix's entire existence is a crisis, although she is not aware of this condition as she leaves the office to buy the paper windmill. It is this complex buildup and emotional peak that make the structure of "A Worn Path" the creation of a master writer.

[5]

COMMENTARY ON THE THEME

To highlight the differences between themes on plot and on structure, the topic of this sample essay is Welty's "A Worn Path," also analyzed in the sample essay on plot. Both essays are concerned with the conflicts of the story, but the essay on plot concentrates on the opposing forces while the essay on structure focuses on the placement and arrangement of the plot elements. Note that neither theme retells the story, event by event. Instead, these are analytical essays which explain the conflict (for plot) and the arrangement and layout (for structure). In both themes, the assumption is that the reader has read "A Worn Path"; hence there is no need in the theme to tell the story again.

The introduction of the theme points out that the masterly structure accounts for the story's power. The second paragraph develops the topic that the geographical locations are arranged climactically to demonstrate the forces against the major character. (For paragraph 3, see below.) The fourth paragraph deals with the complexity brought about by the delayed information: the necessary reevaluation of Phoenix's character and her mission to town. The concluding paragraph also considers this complexity, accounting for the story's power by pointing out how a number of plot elements merge near the end to bring things out swiftly and powerfully.

A Close Look at Paragraph 3

Paragraph 3 considers how the exposition about the grandson creates uncertainty about the issues and direction of the story. The early absence of this detail is thus vital structurally. As supporting evidence for this topic, the paragraph cites two important details—the danger from the hunter's dog and the theft of his nickel—as structural false leads about Phoenix's troubles. Other structurally important but misleading details could also be used as evidence for the argument, such as the dangers of the woods and the height of the stairs (both of which might cause fatigue or illness). The two conflicts cited in the paragraph, however, are enough to make the point about Welty's control of structure, and further exemplification is not needed. The quoted passage is selected to show how the reader's concern is directed toward serious conflicts for Phoenix, but not the major conflict brought out at the end by disclosure of the grandson's condition.

chapter 4

Writing About Character:
The People in Literature

Character in literature is an extended verbal representation of a human being—the inner self that determines thought, speech, and behavior. Through dialogue, action, and commentary, authors portray characters who are worth caring about, rooting for, and even loving, although there are also characters at whom you may laugh or whom you may dislike or even hate.

In stories and plays, you may expect that each action or speech, no matter how small, is part of a total portrait. Whereas in life things may "just happen," in literature all actions, interactions, speeches, and observations are deliberately selected and designed. Thus you read about important events such as a long period of work and sacrifice (Maupassant's "The Necklace"), the taking of a regular journey of mercy (Welty's "A Worn Path"), the murder of a husband by a wife (Glaspell's *Trifles*), or a series of blunders elevating a fool to great fame (Twain's "Luck"). Although these major events are designed to be interesting, they are also shaped to give you an understanding of character.

MAJOR CHARACTER TRAITS

In studying a literary character, you should determine the character's major **trait** or **traits.** A trait is a mode of behavior or quality of mind, such as acting first and thinking later, or looking into a person's eyes or avoiding eye contact completely, or borrowing money and not repaying it, or thinking oneself the constant center of attention. Often, traits are minor and therefore negligible, but sometimes a particular trait may be the primary characteristic of a person (not only in literature but also in life). Thus, characters may be lazy or ambitious, anxious or serene, aggressive or fearful, assertive or bashful, open or secretive, confident or self-doubting, adventurous or timid, noisy or quiet, visionary or practical, reasonable or hot-headed, careful or careless, even-handed or biased, straightforward or underhanded, "winners" or "losers," and so on.

With this sort of list, to which you may add at will, you can analyze and develop conclusions about character. For example, in preparing to write about Mathilde Loisel, the main character in Maupassant's "The Necklace" (pp. 4–13), you would note that at the beginning she dreams of unattainable wealth and comfort and that she is so swept up in her visions that she scorns her comparatively good life with her reliable but dull husband. It is fair to say that this aversion to reality is her major trait. It is also a major weakness, because Maupassant shows how her dream life destroys her real life. By contrast, the narrator of Amy Lowell's poem "Patterns" (pp. 347–50) considers the destruction of her hopes for happiness because of the news of her fiancé's death. Because she faces her difficulties directly, she exhibits strength. By similarly analyzing the thoughts, speeches, and actions in all the characters you encounter, you can draw conclusions about their qualities and strengths.

APPEARANCE, ACTION, AND CHARACTER

When you assemble materials for a theme on character, be sure to connect physical appearance with mental or psychological states. Suppose your author stresses the neatness of one character and the sloppiness of another. If you accept the premise that external appearance represents choice—and that choices indicate character—you can use these details. The same applies to your examination of what a character *does*, assuming, once again, that your characters are free to act according to their will. You must go beyond the actions themselves and discuss what they *show about* the character. Always try to get from the outside to the inside, for it is on the inside that character resides.

TYPES OF CHARACTERS: ROUND AND FLAT

Loosely, there are two kinds of literary characters, which E. M. Forster (in *Aspects of the Novel*) calls "round" and "flat."

ROUND CHARACTERS. The basic trait of **round characters** is that they *recognize, change with,* or *adjust to* circumstances—a quality that in real life is a major element in mental health. The round character profits from experience and undergoes an alteration, which may be the realization of new strength, the decision to perform a particular action, the acceptance of a new condition, or the recognition of previously unrecognized truths. Round characters are relatively fully developed. For this reason they are often given the names **hero** or **heroine.** Because many major characters are anything but heroic, however, it is preferable to use the more neutral word **protagonist,** which implies only that a character is a center of attention, not a moral or physical giant. The protagonist is central to the action, moves against an **antagonist,** and exhibits the same qualities of living and adapting characters.

To the degree that round characters are both individual and unpredictable, and because they undergo change or growth, they are **dynamic.** In Glaspell's *Trifles* (pp. 363–73), for example, Minnie Wright is a dynamic, round character (she is the subject of the sample theme in this chapter). We learn that she was, when younger, a vibrant, happy, and musical person, but we also learn that her married life has been blighted and deprived. Finally, however, after submitting patiently to her husband for thirty years, she strangles him when he is asleep. At the play's end, even though we recognize that she is likely guilty of first-degree murder, we understand why she has changed from subservience to violent self-assertion. Because of her change, she is dynamic.

Obviously, round characters are central to serious literature, for they are the focal points of conflict and interest. They may lead no more than ordinary lives, and they may face no more than the common problems of living, but they are real and human because they grow and develop as they win or lose their struggles. Admittedly, in brief stories or plays we cannot learn everything there is to know about round characters, but skillful authors give us enough details to clarify issues and enable us to understand the dynamic processes by which round characters develop and grow.

FLAT CHARACTERS. In contrast to the round character, the **flat character** does not grow, no matter what the circumstances. Flat characters are flat because they may be stupid or insensitive, or because they may lack knowledge or insight. They end where they begin, and they are **static,** not dynamic. Flat characters are not worthless, however, for their inability to change may highlight the development of the round characters. Usually flat characters are relegated to minor positions (e.g., relatives, acquaintances, service people, functionaries), although not all minor characters are automatically flat.

Sometimes flat characters are prominent in certain types of literature, such as cowboy, police, and detective stories, where the focus is less on character than on performance. Such characters should be lively and engaging, even though they do not develop or change. They should also be strong, tough, and clever enough to perform recurring tasks such as solving a crime, overcoming a villain, or finding treasure. The term **stock character** refers to characters in these repeating situations, and, to the degree that stock characters have many common traits, they are **representative** of their class, or stock group. Such characters, with variations in names, ages, sexes, places, and locations, have been constant in literature almost from the beginnings of culture. Some regular stock characters are the foolish boss, the obtuse or greedy politician, the wiseacre, the resourceful cowboy or detective, the bewildered parent, the overbearing or henpecked husband, the submissive or henpecking wife, the angry police captain, the lovable drunk, the younger or older sister or brother, and the town do-gooder.

Stock characters stay flat as long as they perform only their functions and exhibit conventional and unindividual traits. When they possess no attitudes except those of their class, they are given the label **stereotype,** because they all seem to have been cast in the same mold.

Complications occur when stock characters go beyond stereotypical behavior. John Wright, the murdered husband in Glaspell's *Trifles,* has been insensitive, overbearing and cruel—a flat, stock, domineering husband. From the same kind of mold, his wife, Minnie, has been a stereotypically self-effacing wife. The play develops, however, with the disclosures that Minnie has emerged from her stock role to murder her oppresser, her husband. Because of this emergence, she is round. Mrs. Popov of *The Bear* (pp. 354–63) is another round character who emerges from a stock role. She gives up her grieving widow's role to respond to the love of her outrageous visitor, Smirnov.

HOW IS CHARACTER DISCLOSED IN LITERATURE?

In preparing your theme, you should consider that authors use four distinct ways to present information about characters. Remember that you must use your own knowledge and experience to make judgments about the qualities—the flatness or roundness—of the characters being revealed.

1. *What the characters themselves say (and think, if the author expresses their thoughts).* On the whole, speeches may be accepted at face value to indicate the character of a speaker. Sometimes, however, words may reflect temporary emotional or intellectual states, particularly when the speaker is dynamically changing. Thus, if characters in deep despair say that life is worthless, you must balance this speech with what the same characters say when they are happy. You must also consider the situation

or total context of a statement. Shakespeare's Macbeth voices hatred for life near the end of *Macbeth*, but he speaks in this way after he has spent the play as a terrorist tyrant. Because he is a dynamic, round character, his brooding self-condemnation indicates his change from the person full of "the milk of human kindness" at the play's beginning to the bleakly evil person at the end.

2. *What the characters do.* You have heard that "actions speak louder than words," and you should interpret actions as signs of character. Thus you might consider Phoenix's trip through the woods (Welty's "A Worn Path") as an expression of a loving, responsible character, even though Phoenix nowhere makes such a claim herself. The difficulty and hardship she goes through, however, justifies this conclusion.

Often, action is inconsistent with logic or expectation. Such behavior may signal naiveté, weakness, deceit, a scheming personality, a change or realization of some sort, or strong inner conflicts. Here is an inconsistency: Smirnov, in *The Bear*, would be crazy to teach Mrs. Popov how to use her dueling pistol, because she has threatened to kill him with it. But his change is his realization that he loves her, and his cooperative if potentially self-destructive act shows that his loving nature has overwhelmed his sense of self-preservation. A strong inner conflict is seen in the two on-stage women in Glaspell's *Trifles*. They have an obligation to the law, but they feel a stronger obligation to the accused killer, Minnie Wright. Hence they remain silent even though they know beyond doubt that she is the murderer. That they in effect form a jury for acquittal, after drawing their own conclusions that Minnie's action was justifiable, indicates their roundness and depth.

3. *What other characters say about them.* In stories and plays, as in life, people always talk and gossip about other people. Such speeches require you to evaluate both the speakers and the context of their remarks. If the speakers are straightforward and honest, their speeches are likely accurate, as with the two women who tell us about Phoenix's condition in "A Worn Path," or the women discovering the circumstances of the murder in *Trifles*. However, words may also ironically indicate something other than what the speaker intends, perhaps because of prejudice, self-interest, stupidity, or foolishness. Mrs. Popov of *The Bear* tells about her dead husband, to whose memory she has declared everlasting devotion. Unwittingly, she reveals that he was a total, worthless scoundrel and, also unwittingly, she reveals that she is foolish to waste her life for him. In the light of her situation, the abandonment of her mourning, along with her sudden love for Smirnov, is totally within her character.

4. *What the author says about them, speaking as storyteller or observer.* What the author, speaking with the authorial voice, says about a character is usually accurate, and the authorial voice is naturally to be accepted factually. However, when the authorial voice *interprets* actions and char-

acteristics, as in Hawthorne's "Young Goodman Brown," the author himself or herself assumes the role of a reader or critic, and any opinions may be questioned. For this reason, authors frequently avoid interpretations and devote their skill to arranging events and speeches so that readers may draw their own conclusions.

REALITY AND PROBABILITY: VERISIMILITUDE

You are entitled to expect characters in literature to be true to life. That is, their actions, statements, and thoughts must all be what human beings are *likely* to do, say, and think under the conditions presented in the work. This expectation is often called the standard of **verisimilitude, probability,** or **plausibility.** In other words, there are persons *in life* who do seemingly impossible tasks (such as giving away large sums of money, or always finding a parking space). Such characters *in literature* would not be true to life, however, because they do not fit within *normal* or *usual* behavior.

One should therefore distinguish between what can *possibly* happen and what would frequently or *usually* happen. Thus, in Maupassant's "The Necklace," it is possible that Mathilde could be truthful and tell her friend Jeanne Forrestier about the lost necklace. In light of her pride, honor, shame, and respectability, however, it is more in character for her and her husband to hide the fact, borrow money to buy a replacement necklace, and endure the ten-year penance to pay back the loans. Granted the possibilities of the story (self-sacrifice or the admission of a fault), the decision she makes with her husband is the more *probable* one she could choose.

Nevertheless, probability does not rule out surprise or even exaggeration. In *The Bear*, the main characters, who are strangers when the play opens, fall suddenly and surprisingly in love just as they become so angry that they are threatening to fight a duel. The change, however, is not impossible if we consider that Chekhov shows that both Mrs. Popov and Smirnov are emotional, somewhat foolish, and impulsive. These qualities of character preserve the condition of probability, even in the face of their sudden embraces that close the play.

There are many ways of rendering probability in character. Works that attempt to mirror life—realistic, naturalistic, or "slice-of-life" stories like Welty's "A Worn Path"—set up the expectation that life is played out within the limits of everyday probability. Less realistic conditions establish different frameworks of probability, in which characters are *expected* to be unusual. Such an example may be seen in Hawthorne's "Young Goodman Brown." Because the premise of this story is that Brown is undergoing some kind of nightmarish psychotic trance, his bizarre and unnatural responses are probable, just as Phoenix Jackson's speeches, influenced as they are by her approaching senility, are probable in "A Worn Path."

You might also encounter works containing *supernatural* figures, such as Brown's woodland guide in "Young Goodman Brown." You may wonder whether such characters are probable or improbable. Usually, gods and goddesses embody qualities of the best and most moral human beings, and devils like Hawthorne's guide take on attributes of the worst. However, you might remember that the devil is often given dashing and engaging qualities so that he may deceive gullible sinners and lead them into hell. The friendliness of Brown's guide is therefore a probable trait.

WRITING ABOUT CHARACTER

Usually you will write about a major character, although you might also study a minor character or characters. After your customary overview, begin taking notes. List as many traits as you can, and also determine how the author presents details about the character. Determine the reliability of comments made by other characters or by the authorial voice. When characters go into action, consider what these actions tell about their natures. If there are unusual traits, determine what they show.

Try to answer questions such as these: Does the character come to life? Is he or she round or flat, lifelike or wooden? What admirable qualities or shortcomings do you find? Is the character central to the action, and therefore the hero or protagonist? What traits make the character genuinely major? Do you like him or her? Why? Who or what is the antagonist? How does reaction to the antagonist bring out qualities in your character? Is the character in a stock situation? Does he or she show stereotypical qualities? If so, how does he or she rise above them? What is the relationship of the character to the other characters? What do the others say or think about him? How accurate are their observations?

Introduction

The introduction may begin with a brief identification of the character to be analyzed, which may be followed by reference to noteworthy problems in determining the character's qualities. The central idea is a statement about the character's major trait or quality. The thesis sentence links the central idea to the main sections of the body.

Body

The organization should be designed to illustrate the central idea and make it convincing. You might select one of the following approaches:

1. *Organization around central traits or major characteristics,* such as "unquestioning devotion and service" ("A Worn Path") or "the habit of seeing

the world only on one's own terms" ("Miss Brill"). This kind of structure would show how the work embodies the trait. For example, a trait may be brought out, in one part, through speeches that characters make about the major character (as at the end of "Miss Brill,") and in another part through that character's own speeches and actions. Studying the trait thus enables you to focus on the different ways in which the author presents the character, and it also enables you to focus on separate parts of the work.

2. *Organization around a character's growth or change.* The beginning of such a body would describe a character's beginning traits and then analyze changes or developments. *It is important to avoid retelling a narrative or dramatic action,* and to stress the actual alterations as they emerge, being sure to analyze how they are brought out within the work (such as the dream of Goodman Brown, or Minnie Wright's long suffering).

3. *Organization around central incidents, objects, or quotations that reveal primary characteristics, bring them out, or cause them.* Certain key incidents may stand out, along with objects closely associated with the character being analyzed, together with several key quotations spoken by the character or by someone else in the work. It is important to show how the things you choose serve as signposts, keys, or wedges to understanding the character, for these guides are not to be separate topics in their own right. See the sample theme for an illustration of this type of development.

4. *Organization around qualities of a flat character or characters.* If the character is flat, the body might develop topics such as the function and relative significance of the character, the group of which the character is representative, the relationship of the flat character to the round ones and the importance of this relationship, and any additional qualities or traits. Of major interest will be your discussion of the defects that prevent the character from developing, and the importance of these shortcomings in the author's presentation of human character.

Conclusion

Beyond a summary, you might indicate here how the character's traits are related to the work as a whole. If the person was good but came to a bad end, does this misfortune elevate him or her to tragic stature? If the person suffers, does this fact suggest any attitudes about the class or type of which he or she is a part? Or does it illustrate the author's general view of human life? Or both? Do the characteristics explain why the person helps or hinders other characters? How does your theme help in clearing up first-reading misunderstandings? These and similar questions are appropriate for your conclusion.

Sample Theme

The Character of Minnie Wright of Glaspell's Trifles*

[1]   Minnie Wright is Susan Glaspell's major character in <u>Trifles.</u> We learn about her, however, not from seeing and hearing her, for she does not appear or speak, but only from secondhand evidence and observation. The major speaking characters tell much about her, and their evidence is augmented by the condition of her kitchen, which has been uncared for after her arrest the day before. Lewis Hale, the neighboring farmer, tells about Minnie's behavior on the morning when her husband, John, was found strangled in his bed. Martha Hale, Hale's wife, tells about Minnie's young womanhood and about how she became alienated from her nearest neighbors because of John's stingy and unfriendly ways. The many objects in the kitchen highlight her emotional upset before the murder. <u>From this information we get a full portrait of Minnie, who has changed from passivity to destructive assertiveness.°</u> Her change in character is indicated by her clothing, her dead canary, and her unfinished patchwork quilt.°

[2]   <u>The clothes that Minnie has worn in the past and in the present indicate her character as a person of charm who has withered under neglect and contempt.</u> Martha mentions Minnie's attractive and colorful dresses as a young woman, even recalling a white dress with blue ribbons (speech 135). Martha also recalls that Minnie when young was "sweet and pretty, but kind of timid and—fluttery" (speech 108). In the light of these recollections, Martha observes that Minnie had changed, and changed for the worse, during her thirty years of marriage with John Wright, who is likened to a "raw wind that gets to the bone" (speech 104). As more evidence for Minnie's acceptance of her drab life, Mrs. Peters says that Minnie asked for no more than an apron and shawl as extra clothing for her stay under arrest in the sheriff's home. This modest clothing, as contrasted with the colorful dresses of her youth, suggests the suppression of her spirit.

[3]   <u>Minnie's dead canary, however, while indicating her love of music, also shows the emergence of her rage.</u> For twenty-nine years of marriage Minnie has endured her cheerless farm home, the contempt of her husband, her life of solitude, the abandonment of her early enjoyment of singing, a general lack of pretty things, and the recognition that she could not share the social life of the local farm women as an equal. But her buying the canary (speech 87) suggests the reemergence of her love of song, just as it also suggests her growth toward self-assertion. That her husband has wrung the bird's neck may thus be seen as the cause not only of immediate grief (shown by the dead bird in a "pretty box" [speech 110]), but also of the anger that marks her change from a stock, obedient wife to a person angry enough to kill.

[4]   <u>Like her love of song, her unfinished quilt indicates her creativity.</u> In thirty years on the farm, never having had children, she has had no chance to be creative except for needlework, like the quilt. Mrs. Hale comments on the beauty

---

* For the text of this play, see Appendix C, pages 363–73.
° Central idea
□ Thesis sentence

of Minnie's log-cabin design (speech 73), and a stage direction draws attention to the "bright pieces" in the sewing basket (speech 72 S.D.). The inference is
[4] that even though Minnie's life has been bleak, she has been able to indulge her characteristic love of color and form—and also of warmth, granted the purpose of a quilt.

Ironically, the quilt also shows Minnie's creativity in the murder of her husband. Both Mrs. Hale and Mrs. Peters interpret the breakdown of her stitching on the quilt as signs of distress about the dead canary and also of her nervousness in planning revenge. Further, even though nowhere in the play is it said that John is strangled with a quilting knot, no other conclusion is possible. Both Mrs. Hale and Mrs. Peters agree that Minnie probably intended to knot the quilt rather than sew it in a quilt stitch, and Glaspell pointedly causes the men to learn this detail also, even though they scoff at it. In other words, we learn
[5] that Minnie's only outlet for creativity—needlework—has enabled her to perform the murder in the only way she can: She quietly puts a rope under John's neck, makes a slip-proof quilting knot, and then strangles him by drawing the knot tight. Even though her plan for the murder is deliberate (Mrs. Peters reports that the arrangement of the rope was "crafty" [speech 65]), Minnie is by no means cold or remorseless. Her passivity after the crime demonstrates that planning to evade guilt, beyond simple denial, is not in her character. She is not so diabolically creative that she plans or even understands the irony of strangling her husband just as he killed the bird by wringing its neck. Glaspell, however, has made the irony plain.

It is important to emphasize again that Minnie is not a speaking character in the play and that everything that we know about her comes from others. Nevertheless, the picture that Glaspell draws is fully realized, round, and poignant. For the greater part of her adult life, Minnie has been representative of women whose capacities for growth and expression have been stunted by the grind of life and the cruelty and insensitivity of others. She has patiently accepted her drab and colorless marriage that is so different from her youthful
[6] expectations. Amid the dreary farm surroundings, Minnie has suppressed hurts and grudges, just as she has suppressed her prettiness, colorfulness, and creativity. In short, she has been nothing more than a stock, flat character. But the killing of the canary has caused Minnie to change and to destroy her husband in an assertive rejection of her stock role as the suffering wife. She is a woman who is slow to anger and who is concerned about household matters even when in jail, but whose patience finally reaches the breaking point.

COMMENTARY ON THE THEME

The strategy of this theme is to use details from the play as evidence for the central idea that Minnie Wright is a round, developing character. The theme illustrates one of the types in the third approach described on page 71. Other organizations could also have been chosen, such as the qualities of acquiescence, fortitude, and potential for anger (approach 1), the change in Minnie from submission to vengefulness (approach 2), or the reported actions of Minnie's singing, knotting quilts, and sitting in the kitchen on the morning after the murder (another type of approach 3).

Because of the unusual fact that Minnie does not appear onstage during the play, the introductory paragraph deals with the information about her. The theme thus highlights how Glaspell in *Trifles* uses approaches 2 and 3 (p. 68) as the ways of rendering the play's main character, while not choosing approach 1.

The body is developed through inferences made from details in the play, the major ones being Minnie's clothing (paragraph 2), her canary (3), and her quilt (4 and 5). The last paragraph, 6, summarizes a number of these details, and it also considers how Minnie transcends the stock, representative qualities of many other women in her position, and gains roundness as a result of this outbreak.

A Close Look at Paragraph 3

Paragraph 3 indicates how a specific character trait, together with related details, may support the central idea. The trait is Minnie's love of music (shown by her canary). The connecting details, selected from study notes, are the 29-year absence of music from Minnie's life, her isolation, her lack of pretty clothing, the contemptibility of her husband, and her grief when putting the dead bird into the box. In short, the paragraph weaves together enough material to show the relationship between Minnie's trait of loving music and the crisis of her developing anger—a change that marks her as a round character. Other details might have been woven into the paragraph, such as Minnie's irregular stitching of her quilt (indicating her distress after the killing of the bird) and the broken hinge of the birdcage door (showing John's cruelty), but these details are omitted from the discussion because the conclusions about Minnie have already been sufficiently supported.

chapter 5

Writing About Setting:
The Background of Place,
Objects, and Culture in Literature

Setting in literature is important because literary characters, like human beings generally, do not exist in isolation. Just as they interact with other characters in the process of becoming human, they gain identity because of their cultural and political allegiances, their jobs, their possessions, and the locations where they work and love. Literature must therefore necessarily include descriptions of places, things, and backgrounds—the *setting*. Broadly, setting is the natural, manufactured, and cultural environment in which characters live and move, including all the artifacts they use in their lives. As characters go about their activities, the scenes and artifacts change according to the aims of individual authors. The location of an action, for example, may be a countryside or a house, or the speaker of a poem may be seated on a rock while looking at a tree. Further, as characters speak with each other and reveal their thoughts, they also reveal the degree to which they share the customs and ideas of their times.

SETTING AND STATEMENT

Setting is not only the background for action, it is also one of the means by which authors create meaning, just as painters include backgrounds and objects to render ideas. For example, in Welty's "A Worn Path" (pp. 322–28) and Hawthorne's "Young Goodman Brown" (pp. 302–11), paths through woods are a major topographical feature. These are of course to be expected, granted the time and economic circumstances of the stories, but as they are used they also convey the idea that life is tenuous and uncertain. Similarly, in Glaspell's *Trifles*, the objects in the kitchen of the Wright farm suggest that midwest homesteads early in the twentieth century were colorless and harsh.

At a certain point, the setting of a work might reach the level of symbolism (see Chapter 10, pp. 129–40), in which the author employs a detail of setting to stand for a condition of life. The horse Toby in Chekhov's *The Bear* is such a symbol. Mrs. Popov has made caring for the horse, which was her dead husband's favorite, a major part of her memorial obligations. When Mrs. Popov tells the servants not to give oats to the horse, Chekhov is using this ordinary barnyard animal to indicate that new commitments may entail the abandonment of past obligations. Updike, in "A & P," refers to a Congregational Church in the middle of the town in which the story takes place. On a symbolic level, the church indicates the decorum and restraint that people of the town are expected to exercise.

TYPES OF SETTINGS

Nature and the Outdoors

The outdoors often provides the substance for the development of an author's meaning. It therefore is important to note the presence of natural conditions, such as times of day, sun or clouds, lightness or darkness, calm or storm, and also to hills and valleys, streams and banks, trees and animals, and waves breaking or winds blowing—all of which may be shaping influences on the characters or on the speaker's views.

Things Made by Human Beings

Authors must necessarily bring in references to constructed things (*"infrastructure"* and *artifacts*) like castles, apartments, streets, pathways, walking sticks, paper windmills, pistols, birdcages, canning jars, necklaces, park benches, cash registers, hair ribbons, and medicine. All such things may enter directly into the evolution of actions and ideas. Welty's Phoenix Jackson ("A Worn Path"), for example, takes her walk from country to town to receive a bottle of medicine for her grandson, and by this action Welty demonstrates the beauty of her devotion. Guy de Maupassant ("The Necklace") demonstrates the economic deterioration of his characters by moving them from a modest apartment to an attic flat, and thereby he shows how life may be unpredictable. Like life, literature includes all the forces that may be generated among people by places and objects of value.

STUDYING THE USES OF SETTING

In studying setting, you should first discover all the important details and then determine how the author has used them. *Use* is most important, for setting is usually integral to the author's development of character and theme. At times a setting may involve no more than a reference to an object, as in Keats's poem "Bright Star." Some works may require a more extensive use of setting, such as Coleridge's "Kubla Khan," while in other works the setting may be so extensive that it may be considered as a virtual participant in the action. An instance of such "participation" is Welty's "A Worn Path," where woods and byways are almost active antagonists against Phoenix as she follows the path toward Natchez.

Setting and Credibility

One of the major purposes of setting is to lend **realism,** or **verisimilitude.** As the description of location and objects is more particular and detailed, the events of the work become more believable. Langston Hughes locates the speaker of "Theme for English B" (pp. 352–53) in the area near Columbia University in New York City, and for this reason the speaker's assertions have a close connection with the real world. Even unrealistic and symbolic works seem more believable if they include places and objects from everyday experience, whether past, present, or future. Thus, the historic town and surrounding woods of colonial Salem, Massachusetts, form the setting of Hawthorne's "Young Goodman Brown," in which the protagonist confronts the devil worship that destroys his love and trust. Such admittedly fanciful and dreamlike works would lose credibility without realistic settings.

Setting and Character

Setting may intersect with character as a means by which authors underscore the importance of place, circumstance, and time on human growth and change. The freezing, lonely, impoverished, dreary kitchen of Glaspell's *Trifles* enables us to understand at least partly why Minnie Wright has killed her husband. (Another blending of setting and character, as seen in Maupassant's "The Necklace," is explored in the sample essays in Chapter 1 [pp. 27–30]).

A major aspect of setting may be found in the ways in which characters respond to social, political, and religious circumstances. How they adjust is the measure of their strengths or weaknesses. While some of the townspeople in Jackson's "The Lottery," for example, have doubted the value of the custom of the lottery, they are still acquiescent enough to engage in the ritual execution. Their acceptance indicates their lack of thought and sensitivity. Young Goodman Brown's Calvinistic religious conviction that people are sinful and hypocritical, which not reality but his nightmarish encounter confirms, indicates the weakness of his character because it alienates him from family and community. In Updike's "A & P," Sammy's strength of character is made clear by his decision to defy the arbitrary and straightlaced dress code imposed by the store manager.

Setting and Organization

Authors frequently use setting as one of their methods of organization. The various actions in Jackson's "The Lottery" are all related to the place of the lottery drawing in the village square, "between the post office and the bank" (paragraph 1), and the story begins at ten o'clock in the morning and ends almost exactly at noon—in other words, according to a pattern of before, during, and immediately after the drawing. In Maupassant's "The Necklace," the action removes Mathilde and her husband from an acceptable though not lavish apartment on the Rue des Martyrs in Paris to a cheap attic flat. The story's final scene is believable because Mathilde takes a nostalgic walk on the most fashionable street in Paris, the Champs Élysées. Without this organizational shift of setting, she could not have met Jeanne Forrestier again, for their ways of life would otherwise never intersect.

Another organizational application of place, time, and object is the **framing** or **enclosing setting.** An author opens with a particular description and then encloses the work by returning to the same setting at the end. Like a picture frame, the setting affects the reader's thoughts. An example of a frame is Welty's "A Worn Path," which begins with the major character's walk to Natchez and ends with the start of her walk away from it. The use of objects as a frame may be seen in Mansfield's "Miss Brill," which opens and closes with references to the heroine's shabby little fur-piece. The stones at the beginning of "The Lottery" create an ironic frame, for at the end these same stones are being thrown. Framing in this way creates a sense of roundness and completeness, just as it may underscore the author's ideas about life and the human condition.

Setting and Atmosphere

Setting also helps to create **atmosphere** or **mood.** You will agree that an action usually *requires* no more than a functional description of setting. Thus, an action in a forest *needs* just the statement that there are trees.

However, if you read descriptions of shapes, lights and shadows, animals, wind, and sounds, you may be sure that the author is working to create an atmosphere or mood for the action (as in Hawthorne's "Young Goodman Brown"). There are many ways of creating moods. Descriptions of bright colors (red, orange, yellow) may contribute to a mood of happiness. Darker colors, like some of those in Poe's "The Masque of the Red Death," may suggest gloom. References to smells and sounds bring the setting even more to life by asking additional sensory responses from the reader. The setting of a story in a small town or large city, or on open plains, or on a mountain top, may evoke responses to these places that contribute to the work's atmosphere.

Setting and Irony

Just as setting may reinforce character and theme, so may it work ironically to establish expectations that are opposite to what occurs. At the beginning of "The Lottery," for example, Jackson describes the folksiness of the assembling townspeople—details which make the conclusion of the story doubly ironic, for it is just these real, everyday folks who cast the stones of ritual execution. Another ironic use of setting is in "Miss Brill," where the location, musical background, and sunlight are all appropriate to goodwill and happiness. However, the young man and woman insult the heroine cruelly, and even though her external circumstances are ironically unchanged, her joy is shattered.

WRITING ABOUT SETTING

In preparing to write about setting, take notes on important locations, artifacts, and customs. Determine if there is one location of action or more. Raise questions about how much detail is included: Are things described visually so that you can make a sketch or draw a plan (such a sketch might help you to organize your essay), or are the locations left vague? Why? What influence do the locations have upon the characters in the story, if any? Do the locations bring characters together, push them apart, make it easy for them to be private, make intimacy and conversation difficult? What artifacts are important in the action, and how important are they? Are they well described? Are they vital to the action? Are things like shapes, colors, times of day, locations of the sun, conditions of light, seasons of the year, and conditions of vegetation described? Do characters respect or mistreat the environment around them? What cultural assumptions do the characters make about themselves? How do these assumptions affect their judgments and actions? What conclusions do you think the author expects you to draw as a result of the world and the culture that he or she has created?

Remember to build a strong central idea so that you may avoid simply redescribing scenes, objects, and stories. Emphasize the connection between setting and whatever aspect or aspects you choose about the work. A possible central idea might thus be, "The normal, everyday setting (of "The Lottery") not only is plainly described, but in retrospect it demonstrates that human evil is also common and ordinary," or "The dreary kitchen underscores the long-suffering ordeal of Minnie Wright (of *Trifles*) and helps readers understand her murderous anger against her husband." Emphasis on such ideas would encourage you to consider setting as illustration and evidence, not as an end in itself.

Introduction

The introduction should give a brief description of the setting or scenes of the work, with reference to the amount of detail, such as a little, a lot, important, unimportant, and so on. The sample theme on Poe's "The Masque of the Red Death" notes, for example, that Poe includes many details of setting and that these details are vital to the story. The central idea explains the relationship to be explored in the essay, and the thesis sentence determines the major topics in which the central idea will be traced.

Body

Following are five possible approaches to themes on setting. You are free to choose the one you want, but you may find that some works invite one approach rather than others. As you develop your theme, however, you may find it necessary to introduce one or more of the other approaches.

1. SETTING AND ACTION. Here you explore the importance of setting in the various actions. How extensively is the setting described? Are locations essential or incidental to the actions? Does the setting serve as part of the action (e.g., places of flight or concealment; public places where people meet openly or out-of-the-way places where they meet privately; natural or environmental conditions; seasonal conditions such as searing heat or numbing cold; customs and conventions)? Do any objects cause inspiration, difficulty, or conflict (for example, a star, a rose, a verse translation, a walking stick, a pretty necklace, a coin, a horse, a toy windmill, a dead bird)? How strongly do these objects influence the action?

2. SETTING AND ORGANIZATION. The aim here is to analyze how setting is connected to the organization of the work. How does the setting figure into the various parts of the work? Does it undergo any expected or unexpected changes as the action changes? Are some parts of the set more important in shaping the action than other parts? Is the setting apparently used as a frame or enclosure? Do any objects, such as money or property, figure into the developing or changing motivation of the characters? Do descriptions made at the start become important in the action or later on? If so, in what order?

3. SETTING AND CHARACTER. The major issue is the degree to which setting influences and seems to interact with character. Are the characters happy or unhappy where they live? Do they express their feelings, or get into discussions or arguments about their home environment? Do they seem adjusted? Do they want to stay or leave? Do the economic, philosophical, religious, or ethnic aspects of the setting make the characters respond or undergo changes? What jobs do the characters perform because of their ways of life? What freedoms or restraints do these jobs cause? How does the setting influence their decisions, transportation, speech habits, eating habits, attitudes about love and honor, and general behavior?

4. SETTING AND ATMOSPHERE. To what extent does the setting contribute to moods, such as happiness or gloom? Does the setting go beyond the minimum needed for action or character? Are descriptive words used mainly to paint verbal pictures, to evoke moods through references to colors, shapes, sounds, smells, or tastes? Does the setting establish a mood, say, of joy or hopelessness, lushness or spareness? Do things happen in daylight or at night? Do the movements of the characters suggest permanence, or do the locations emphasize the impermanence (like footsteps on a stairway, or snow falling on a field)? If temperatures are mentioned, are things warm and pleasant, or cold and harsh? Does the atmosphere suggest that life, too, is this way?

5. SETTING AND OTHER ASPECTS. Earlier in this chapter, "Setting and Statement" and "Setting and Irony" are listed as important uses of setting (pp. 75 and 79). If the author has used setting either to reinforce or to make ironic the circumstances and ideas in the work, you might consult either of these sections as guides for the body of your theme. If you perceive a contrast between setting and content, that too could be the basis of an essay such as those described in the paragraph on "Setting and Irony." If you wish to explore the symbolic implications of a setting, you might wish to consult the discussions of symbolism in Chapter 10.

Conclusion

When concluding, you may summarize your major points or may also write about related aspects of setting that you have not considered. Thus, you might have been treating the relationship of setting and action and

ın connections that the setting has with character or
.night also point out whether your central idea about
.s to other major aspects of the work.

Sample Theme

Poe's Use of Interior Setting to Augment the Eeriness of "The Masque of the Red Death"**

[1] In "The Masque of the Red Death," Edgar Allan Poe uses many details of setting to create an eerie atmosphere.° The story is about the foolishness and impossibility of trying to evade death. Poe's Prince Prospero is the example of this idea. He believes that he can lock himself away in his castle, with a thousand followers, and avoid the plague of the red death raging outside. At the end, however, Death invades the castle in person and destroys all the people. Poe uses interior setting to underscore this irony, and also to make Prospero's pride seem pointless and insane. The prevailing eerie mood is brought out through Poe's use of graphic description, geographical direction, evocative color, and sepulchral sound.□

[2] The extensive fourth paragraph of the story contains Poe's graphic description of Prospero's bizarre suite of seven rooms. The reader may follow the moods accompanying the changing colors, from normal, to brightly garish, to somber: The blue room is in the east, and going west in order of increasing depressiveness, the next six rooms are purple, green, orange, white, violet, and finally black. The narrator explains that each room is lighted by a "brazier of fire" throwing light through a stained glass window which provokes awe by casting a glaring, grisly light.

[3] These rooms are not only vividly described, but they are spatially arranged to complement the certainty of death. The direction of east to west suggests a movement away from life. One might observe that the blue room, in the east, is on the side of the sun rising—an optimistic idea of blue skies and new beginnings of new days. On the other hand the westernmost room, the black one, is the direction of the setting sun and the end of the day at midnight, when Death takes over. If one doubts that Poe intended this geographical direction to have meaning, it is important to note that Prospero's charge against the ghostly figure of the Red Death takes him directly from east to west—from blue to black, from life to death—on his insane rush toward doom.

[4] The most weird and garish room is the black one, on which Poe devotes the most evocative of his visual descriptions. The room is hung with black velvet tapestries, but its darkness is made flamboyant by the scarlet, "deep blood" light (Poe avoids the more neutral word "red" here). The narrator states that the room is "ghastly in the extreme" and that it produces a look of wildness (paragraph 4). Visually, this room evokes feelings of wildness, evil, and an almost

---

* For the text of this story, see Appendix C, pages 311–15.
° Central idea
□ Thesis sentence

ghoulish delight in blood. It is a sinister room, designed not to relax but to
[4]   disturb and distress.

To these ominous locations, Poe adds the eeriness of sepulchral sounds
by including a "gigantic clock of ebony" in the black room. He devotes an entire
paragraph (the fifth) to this weird clock, and this paragraph is the high point of
the story's setting. Poe's words hint that the clock is vaguely alive. It is not
placed or set against the west wall but is standing there (Poe's word is "stood"),
as though living, and its massive pendulum is in constant, "monotonous" motion (like the beating of a ghostly heart?). Poe's implication is that the clock
[5]   represents the dismal world of death, for every hour the "clang" from its "brazen
lungs" announces the chilling end of another period of life. Poe's narrator points
out that the clock's musical but eerie sounds stop all revelry and create a
distressed silence among the merrymakers (Poe uses the word "disconcert"
twice in the paragraph to describe the clock's effect). This use of sound, having
its source in this mysteriously living clock, is designed to make readers as
uneasy, unsettled, and anxious as Prospero's companions.

Thus Poe's interior setting is both descriptive and evocative. The major
action takes place in the rooms—the costume party attended by all Prospero's
friends, except the one uninvited guest, the Red Death himself, who instantly
kills all the partygoers. Prospero's last movement takes him through all the
[6]   rooms, in a ritual passage from morning to midnight, from life to death. In this
way, Poe employs his setting to show the folly of trying to escape death, and
also to suggest that the attempt is not only foolish but also bizarre and insane.
The events of the story, the sustained mood, the consistent idea, are all tied
together by Poe's masterly control of setting.

COMMENTARY ON THE THEME

Because it treats the relationship of setting to mood or atmosphere, this
theme illustrates the fourth approach described above. (For an example of
the third approach, relating setting to character, see Chapter 1, pp. 27–30.)
The theme considers those aspects of setting needed for the story and then
stresses how Poe's descriptions build the eerie mood, the irony of the
major character's pretentions, and the folly of his pride. The thesis sentence announces four topics for further development.

In the body, paragraph 2 describes the physical layout of Prospero's
suite of rooms, and it also points out the eerie suggestiveness of Poe's
descriptions of color and light. Paragraph 3 treats Poe's geographical arrangement of the rooms, the idea being that this arrangement complements the story's movement from life to death. Paragraphs 4 and 5 treat the
last and most sinister of the rooms. Paragraph 4 stresses the mood brought
out by the colors black and scarlet or "deep blood," and paragraph 5
stresses the somber sounds of the huge clock in the room. The conclusion
summarizes the central idea, stressing once again that Poe goes beyond
simple description to heighten the eerie, macabre atmosphere of his story.

A Close Look at Paragraph 5

In keeping with the topic sentence that Poe's description of the great clock is the high point of his setting for "The Masque of the Red Death," paragraph 5 is placed as the final and most important part of the theme's body. The paragraph mentions Poe's major references to the size, color, and location of the clock (thus including some of Poe's detail) and then stresses Poe's descriptions of the clock's sounds (thus analyzing how Poe gains his effect). Original words conveying impressions of the clock's effects are "ominous," "sepulchral," "weird," "massive," "chilling," "uneasy," "unsettled," and "anxious." Most important, the paragraph considers how Poe's words "brazen lungs," "monotonous," and "stood" convey the suggestion that the clock has a malevolent, ghostly animation. Throughout the paragraph, the topic idea is that the clock, because of this seemingly living connection with the malign world of death, is Poe's major means of achieving an atmosphere complementary to the story's eerie action. The paragraph hence demonstrates a way in which theme writers may develop their central idea within a unified paragraph that stresses the hints and suggestions to be found in an author's descriptive diction about setting.

chapter 6

___

Writing About Point of View:

The Position and Stance
of the Work's Speaker
or Narrator

Point of View refers to the **voice** that authors use when presenting their work. You might also think of point of view as a work's **speaker, persona** or **narrator**—a living personality who tells stories, presents arguments, or expresses attitudes such as love, anger, or excitement. To write about point of view is to describe the effect of the speaker on the literary work.

It is most important to recognize not only that authors try to create stories, poems, and plays that are vital and interesting, but also that they try to bring their *presentations* to life as well. You may be sure that authors devote care and skill to their speaking voices—their points of view. The situation is like that of actors performing a play: The actors are always themselves, but in their speaking roles they *impersonate* characters (like Smirnov and Mrs. Popov in Chekhov's *The Bear*) and temporarily become them.

Authors, too, impersonate the characters who do the talking, with the difference that authors also *create* these impersonations, like the speakers of Updike's "A & P" and Hawthorne's "Young Goodman Brown" (pp. 334, 311). Updike's narrator, Sammy, is visualized as a real person, a young man, telling about an incident leading up to his suddenly quitting his job as a grocery store cash-register clerk. He is therefore the major participant, or **major mover,** with his own identity that is totally separate from that of the writer, Updike. Unlike Sammy, Hawthorne's speaker is telling a story about someone else and, for this reason, is distant from the action and objective about it. Because of this distance, Hawthorne's speaker is not easily separated from the author, even though the words we read may be different in many respects from those that Hawthorne himself might have used in speaking for himself personally. For this reason we may conclude that the speaker is Hawthorne's special *authorial* creation or impersonation for "Young Goodman Brown."

AN EXERCISE IN POINT OF VIEW:
REPORTING AN ACCIDENT

As an exercise to show that point of view is derived from lifelike situations, let us imagine that there has been an accident; two cars, driven by Alice and Bill, have collided. How might this accident be reported by a number of people?

    a. What would Alice say?
    b. What would Bill say?

Let us now assume that Frank, who is Bill's best friend, and Mary, who knows neither Bill nor Alice, were witnesses.

    c. What might Frank say about who was responsible?
    d. What might Mary say about who was responsible?

Let us finally assume that you are a reporter for a local newspaper and are sent to report the accident. You know none of the people involved.

    e. How will your report differ from other reports?

A question that applies to all the persons in our hypothetical situation is, "To what degree is each of these reports designed to persuade listeners and readers of the correctness and justness of the details and claims made in it?"

    The differences in the accident reports may be explained in terms of *point of view.* Obviously, because both Alice and Bill are deeply involved, they will arrange their words to make themselves seem blameless. Frank, because he is Bill's best friend, will likely report things in Bill's favor. Mary will favor neither Alice nor Bill, but let us assume that she did not look at the colliding cars until she heard the crash; therefore her report will be restricted because she did not *actually see* everything. Most likely, *you* as an impartial reporter will have the most reliable and objective account of all, because your major interest is to learn all the details and report the truth accurately, with no concern about the personal interests of either Alice or Bill.

Above all, however, each person's report will have the "hidden agenda" of making its author seem honest, objective, intelligent, impartial, and thorough. You might also consider what the various individuals might say to a friend in ordinary conversation, or to a judge and jury when under oath. It seems clear that the ramifications of telling a story are far reaching, and the consideration of the various interests and situations can become quite subtle. Some of these relationships may be clarified in the sketch shown on page 87.

CONDITIONS THAT AFFECT POINT OF VIEW

From this hypothetical situation, which is like many situations in real life, we may conclude that point of view depends on a number of things: (1) position while observing, (2) completeness and accuracy of observation, (3) personal involvement, (4) partiality or impartiality, (5) desire to draw conclusions about an action, (6) situation, at the time of the narration or monologue, of the speaker and listener, audience, or reader. These are the more obvious elements that enter into ways in which people, whether in personal or public life, speak about things happening in the world around them.

In a story or a poem, the author develops point of view in light of these same considerations. Amy Lowell's speaker in "Patterns" is a woman responding with sorrow and indignation to the news of her lover's death, and Donne's speaker in "A Valediction: Forbidding Mourning" is a lover consoling his sweetheart before going on a trip. Both these speakers are personally involved in their own situations. A totally uninvolved speaker is the one in Jackson's "The Lottery," who listens, sees, and reports, but gives no sign of being moved by the cruel actions in the little country village. It is fair to say that this speaker is about as impartial as it is possible to be.

KINDS OF POINTS OF VIEW

In the various works you read you will encounter a wide variety of points of view. As a convenient way to begin your analysis, you should first determine the grammatical voice used in the work. Then you should study the ways in which the subject, characterization, dialogue, and form of the work are interlocked with the point of view.

First-Person Point of View

If the voice of the work is an *I*, the author is using the **first-person point of view**—the impression of a fictional narrator or speaker. In our hypothetical accident, both Alice and Bill are first-person speakers. In literature, Sammy of Updike's "A & P" and the unnamed speaker of Arnold's "Dover Beach" are also first-person speakers, while in Twain's "Luck" there are two separate first-person speakers (the first *I* introduces the second *I*). Of all the points of view, the first person is the most independent of the author, for such a speaker is often given a unique identity, with name, job, and economic and social positions.

First-person speakers report (1) what they have done, said, heard, and thought (first-hand experience), (2) what they have observed others do and say (first-hand witness), and (3) what others have told them (second-hand testimony and hearsay). Their abilities, position while observing, attitudes, possible prejudices or self-interest, and judgment of their readers or listeners are to be considered in everything they say. Their own involvement, and sometimes their own growth, are primary subjects in their statements and narrations. When they describe their own experiences, they have great authority and sometimes great power. Thus, the speaker of Amy Lowell's "Patterns" is considering the consequences of the letter informing her that her fiancé has been killed. As she speaks we recognize her strength, and we sympathize with her indignation because her loss is so immediately personal and grievous.

Second-Person Point of View

Although the **second-person point of view** (in which the narrator tells a listener what he or she has done and said, using the *you* personal pronoun), is possible, it is rare because in effect the second-person requires a first-person speaker who tells the listener—the *you* of the narration—what he or she did at a past time. Thus a parent might tell a child what the child did during infancy, or a doctor might tell a patient with amnesia about events before the injury, or a prosecuting attorney might describe a crime to a defendant. Recently a series of "do your own" adventure books have become popular, in which readers pick out their own actions in a developing story. In practice, however, the second-person point of view is almost negligible. A. A. Milne uses it for a time at the beginning of *Winnie the Pooh* but drops it as soon as the events of Pooh Bear and the rest of the animals get under way. Jay MacInerny, in *Bright Lights, Big City*, uses the second person, but in fact the *you* of the story means *I* and *me*. Hence MacInerny's second person is really first person.

Third-Person Point of View

If things in the work are in the third person, (*he, she, it, they*), the author is using the **third-person point of view.** It is not always easy to characterize the voice in this point of view. Sometimes the speaker may use an *I* (as in Poe's "The Masque of the Red Death") and be seemingly identical with the author him or herself, but at other times the author may create a distinct **authorial voice,** as in Mansfield's "Miss Brill." There are three variants of the third-person point of view: **dramatic** or **objective, omniscient,** and **limited** or **limited omniscient.**

DRAMATIC OR OBJECTIVE.   The basic mode of presenting action and dialogue is the **dramatic** or **objective point of view** (also called **third-person objective**). The narrator in the dramatic point of view reports things in a way that is analogous to a hovering or tracking motion-picture camera, or to what some critics have called "a fly on the wall (or tree)." Thus, characters outdoors may be seen and heard at a distance, or up close, and when they go into an interior, such as a car or a house, the speaker continues to follow their speeches and actions. Authors using the dramatic point of view avoid interpretive statements, stressing instead only the details of the work. A dramatic presentation is as complete and impartial as can be allowed by the speaker's position as an observer. Let us remember that Mary, of our hypothetical accident situation, would give an objective description because of her impartiality, but also that her report would be incomplete because she did not see things before the accident. You, as the reporter, would also describe things objectively, but your report would be more detailed because you would include the results of additional observations and interviews.

In stories and poems, the dramatic point of view is like your report and Mary's, the idea being that readers, somewhat like a jury, can form their own interpretations if they are given the right evidence. Thus Jackson's "The Lottery" (the subject of the sample theme, pp. 94–96)—a powerful example of the dramatic point of view—is an objective story about a bizarre small-town lottery. We the readers draw conclusions about this story (such as that the people are tradition bound, insensitive, cruel, and so on), but Jackson does not explicitly state any of these things for us.

OMNISCIENT.   The third-person point of view is **omniscient** (all-knowing), with the speaker not only presenting the action and dialogue of the work, but also, godlike, reporting what the characters are thinking. Our hypothetical accident does not offer the possibility of an omniscient point of view, because no human being can know the unspoken thoughts of others. Authors, however, by delving into the minds of their characters, assume a stance that enables them to add dimension to the development of character and action.

LIMITED OR LIMITED OMNISCIENT.   More common than the omniscient point of view, in which the inner workings of every character may be described, is the **limited third-person,** or **limited omniscient third-person point of view,** in which the author confines or *limits* attention to a major character. In our accident case, Frank, being Bill's friend, would be sympathetic to Bill, and thus his account would likely be third-person limited, with Bill as the center of interest. In a literary work, the central figure on whom things are focused is called the **point-of-view character,** as in Mansfied's "Miss Brill" (pp. 319–22) and Maupassant's "The Necklace" (pp. 4–13). Everything in these stories is there because the point-of-view characters—Miss Brill and Mathilde—see it, hear it, respond to it, think about it, do it or share in it, try to control it, or are controlled by it. Obviously there are differences in how fully authors reveal their point-of-view characters. Thus we get more deeply into the mind of Miss Brill than that of Mathilde, because Mansfield presents more responses and thoughts than does Maupassant.

MINGLING POINTS OF VIEW

In some works, an author may shift the point of view in order to sustain interest, create suspense, or put the burden of response entirely upon readers. For example, Mansfield in "Miss Brill" interrupts the limited omniscient focus on Miss Brill's thoughts and reactions immediately after she is insulted. The last paragraphs are objective until the last sentence, when the limited omniscient point of view is resumed. The result is that Miss Brill is made totally alone in her grief, cut apart; readers can no longer share her sorrow as they earlier share her observations about the characters in the park. A similar shift occurs at the end of Hawthorne's "Young Goodman Brown," where the narrator objectively and almost brutally summarizes Brown's gloomy, loveless life after his nightmare about evil.

A Table of Points of View

The following table summarizes and further classifies the types of points of view. With this table you should be able to distinguish differences and shades of variation in stories and poems.

1. *First Person* (*I* and *me*). First-person speakers are involved to at least some degree in the actions of the work. Such narrators may have (1) a complete understanding, (2) partial or incorrect understanding, or (3) no understanding at all.
   a. *Major participant*
      i. telling his or her own story and thoughts as a major mover
      ii. telling a story about others and also about her or himself as one of the major movers
      iii. telling a story mainly about others, and about him or herself only tangentially

     b. *Minor participant, telling a story about events experienced and witnessed*

     c. *Nonparticipating but identifiable speaker who learns about events in other ways (e.g., listening to participants, examining documents, hearing news reports) and then tells the story.*

2. *Second person (you).* Occurs only when the speaker knows more about a character's actions than the character him or herself—for example, parent, psychologist, lawyer. This point of view cannot be sustained easily and usually is found only in brief passages.

3. *Third person (she, he, it, they).* The speaker is outside the action and is mainly a reporter of actions and speeches. Some speakers may have unique and distinguishing traits even though no separate identity is claimed for them ("the unnamed third-person narrator"). Other third-person speakers who are not separately identifiable may represent the words and views of the authors themselves (the authorial voice).

     a. *Dramatic or third-person objective.* Speaker reports only actions and speeches. Thoughts of characters can be expressed only as dialogue.

     b. *Omniscient.* Omniscient speaker sees all, reports all, knows and explains the inner workings of the minds of any or all characters.

     c. *Limited or limited omniscient.* The focus is on the actions, responses, thoughts, and feelings of a single major character.

WRITING ABOUT POINT OF VIEW

Your goal will be to explain how point of view contributes to making the work exactly as it is. In prewriting activity, therefore, consider things like language, authority and opportunity for observation, the involvement or detachment of the speaker, the selection of detail, interpretive commentaries, and narrative development. A major purpose should be to determine ways in which the narration is made to seem real and probable: Are the actions and speeches reported authentically, as they might be seen and reported in life? When you take notes and write preliminary drafts, try to apply this question to various parts of the work, so that you can determine whether the point of view is as "true" as the work itself.

Introduction

In your introduction you should set out the idea and major points of your theme. Briefly state the major influence of the point of view on the work. (For example, "The omniscient point of view causes full, leisurely insights into the many facets of the major character," or "The first-person point of view enables the work to resemble an exposé of back-room political deals.") To what extent does the point of view make the work interesting and effective, or uninteresting and ineffective? How will the analysis of particular aspects of the work (action, dialogue, characters, description, narration, diction) support your central idea?

Body

Your object is to develop your analysis of how the point of view determines such aspects as situation, form, general content, and language. If you have a first-person point of view, what is the situation prompting the speaker to tell her story or explain her situation (assuming, for the moment, a woman)? Is the speaker identifiable? What is her background? Is she talking to a listener, to herself, or to the reader? How does her audience affect what she is saying? Is the level of language appropriate to her and to the situation? How much does she tell about herself? To what degree is she involved in the action (i.e., as a major mover, minor participant, or non-participating observer?) Does she make herself the center of humor or admiration? How? Does she seem aware or unaware of any changes she might undergo? Does she criticize other characters? Why? Does she seem to report fairly and accurately what others have told her?

If you have any of the third-person points of view, does it seem that the author is speaking in an authorial voice, or that he or she has adopted a special but unnamed voice for the work? What is the speaker's level of language? Are actions, speeches, and explanations made fully or sparsely? Does the speaker assume that the reader or listener has any special kinds of knowledge (e.g., of history, art, technology, philosophy, religion)? From what apparent vantage point does the speaker report action and speeches? Does this vantage point make the characters seem distant or up close? How much sympathy does the speaker express for the characters? To what degree is your interest centered on a particular character? Does the speaker give you thoughts and responses of this character (limited third-person)? If the work is in the third-person omniscient, how extensive is this omniscience (e.g., all the characters, or just a few)? Generally, what limitations or freedoms can be attributed to the point of view?

An excellent way to strengthen your argument is to explore how some other point of view might affect the work you are considering (see paragraph 4 of the sample theme [p. 95]). Hardy's poem "Channel Firing" (pp. 346–47), for example, uses a first person speaker—a corpse long buried in a churchyard cemetery near the ocean who has been wakened by the noise of naval guns. This unusual situation, which prompts ironic humor, could not be duplicated with a third-person point of view; indeed, as it stands the poem absolutely depends on the first person. In contrast, Mansfield's "Miss Brill" employs the third-person limited point of view, with the speaker presenting an intimate portrait of the major character but also preserving an objective and ironic distance. If Miss Brill herself were the narrator, we would get the intimacy but not the distance, and hence the story could not work. It might be a similar story, but not the one that Mansfield has given us.

You can see that this approach requires creative imagination, for you must speculate about a point of view that is not present. If you consider alternative points of view deeply, however, you will find that your analytical and critical abilities will be greatly enhanced.

Conclusion

In your conclusion you should evaluate the success of the point of view: Is it consistent, effective, truthful? What does the writer gain or lose (if anything) by the selection of point of view?

Hint: Distinguish Point of View from Opinion

Be careful to distinguish between *point of view* and *opinions* or *beliefs*. Point of view refers to the dramatic situation occasioning the speaking of a work, including language, listeners or audience, and perspective on events and characters, while an opinion is a thought about something. In examining point of view, then, you should draw conclusions about how the speaking situation of the work actually *creates* the work. Opinions and philosophical and religious judgments belong to the consideration of ideas but have little bearing on point of view.

Sample Theme

*Shirley Jackson's Dramatic Point of View in "The Lottery"**

---

[1]   The dramatic point of view in Shirley Jackson's "The Lottery" is essential to her success in rendering horror in the midst of the ordinary.° The story, however, is not only one of horror: It may also be called a surprise story, an allegory, or a portrayal of human insensitivity and cruelty. But the validity of all other claims for "The Lottery" hinges on the author's control over point of view to make events develop out of a seemingly everyday, matter-of-fact situation—a control that could not be easily maintained with another point of view. The success of Jackson's point of view is achieved through her characterization, selection of details, and diction.°

[2]   Because of the dramatic point of view, Jackson succeeds in presenting the villagers as ordinary folks attending a normal, festive event—in contrast to

---

* For the text of this story, see Appendix C, pages 328–34.
° Central Idea
□ Thesis sentence

horal of their real purpose. The contrast depends on Jackson's speaker, who is emotionally uninvolved and who tells only enough about the 300 townsfolk and their customs to permit the conclusion that they are ordinary, common people. The principal character is a local housewife, Tessie Hutchinson, but the speaker presents little about her except that she is just as ordinary and common as everyone else—an important characteristic when she, like any other ordinary [2] person being singled out for punishment, objects not to the lottery itself but to the "unfairness" of the drawing. So is it also with the other characters, whose brief conversations are recorded but not analyzed. This detached, reportorial method of making the villagers seem common and one-dimensional is fundamental to Jackson's dramatic point of view, and the cruel twist of the ending depends on the method.

While there could be much description, Jackson's speaker presents details only partially in order to conceal the lottery's horrible purpose. For example, the speaker presents enough information about the lottery to permit readers to understand its rules, but does not disclose that the winning prize is instant [3] death. The short saying "Lottery in June, corn be heavy soon" is mentioned as a remnant of a long-forgotten ritual, but the speaker does not explain anything more about this connection with scapegoatism and human sacrifice (paragraph 32). All such references do not seem unusual as the narrator first presents them, and it is only the conclusion that reveals, in reconsideration, their shocking ghastliness.

Without doubt, a point of view other than the dramatic would spoil Jackson's concluding horror, because it would require more explanatory detail. A first-person speaker, for example, would not be credible without explaining the situation and revealing feelings that would give away the ending. Such an "I" speaker would need to say something like "The little boys gathered rocks but seemed not to be thinking about their forthcoming use in the execution." But how would such detail affect the reader's response to the horrifying conclusion? Similarly, an omniscient narrator would need to include details about people's [4] reactions (how could he or she be omniscient otherwise?). A more suitable alternative might be a limited omniscient point of view confined to, say, a stranger in town, or to one of the local children. But any intelligent stranger would be asking "giveaway" questions, and any child but a tiny tot would know about the lottery's horrible purpose. Either point-of-view character would therefore require revealing the information too soon. The only possible conclusion is that the point of view that Jackson chose—the dramatic—is best for this story. Because it permits her naturally to hold back crucial details, it is essential for the suspenseful delay of horror.

Appropriate both to the suspenseful ending and also to the simple character of the villagers is the speaker's language. The words are accurate and descriptive but not elaborate. When Tessie Hutchinson appears, for example, she dries "her hands on her apron" (paragraph 8)—words that define her everyday household status. Most of these simple, bare words may be seen as [5] part of Jackson's similar technique of withholding detail to delay the reader's understanding. A prime example is the pile of stones, which is in truth a thoughtless and cruel preparation for the stoning, yet this conclusion cannot be drawn from the easy words describing it (paragraph 2):

> Bobby Martin had already stuffed his pockets full of stones, and the
> other boys soon followed his example, selecting the smoothest and
> roundest stones; Bobby and Harry Jones and Dickie Delacroix—

the villagers pronounced this name "Dellacroy"—eventually made a great pile of stones in one corner of the square and guarded it against the raids of the other boys.

[5] Both the nicknames and the connotation of boyhood games divert attention andobscure the horrible purpose of the stones. Even at the end, the speaker uses the word "pebbles" to describe the stones given to Tessie's son Davy (paragraph 76). The implication is that Davy is playing a game, not helping to kill his own mother!

Such masterly control over point of view is a major cause of Jackson's success in "The Lottery." Her narrative method is to establish the appearance of everyday, harmless reality, which she maintains up to the beginning of the last ominous scene. She is so successful that a reader's first response to the stoning is that "such a killing could not take place among such common, earthy [6] folks." Yet it this reality that validates Jackson's vision. Horror is not to be found on moors and in haunted castles, but among everyday people like Jackson's 300 villagers. Without her control of the dramatic point of view, there could be little of this power of suggestion, and it would not be possible to claim such success for the story.

COMMENTARY ON THE THEME

The strategy of this theme is to describe how Jackson's dramatic point of view is fundamental to her success in building up to the shocking horror of the ending. Words of tribute throughout the theme are "success," "control," "essential," "appropriate," and "masterly." The introductory paragraph sets out three areas for exploration in the body: character, detail, and diction. In your theme on point of view, you might well devote all your analysis to any one of these points, but for illustration here they are all included.

The body begins with Paragraph 2, in which the aim is *not* to present a full character study (since the theme is not about character but point of view), but rather to discuss the ways in which the dramatic point of view *enables* the characters to be rendered. The topic of the paragraph is that the villagers are to be judged not as complete human beings but as "ordinary folks." Once this idea is established, the thrust of the paragraph is to show how the point of view keeps readers at a distance sufficient to sustain this conclusion.

The second part of the body (paragraphs 3 and 4) emphasizes the sparseness of detail as an essential part of Jackson's purpose of delaying conclusions about the real horror of the drawing.

The third section of the body (paragraph 5) emphasizes the idea that the flat, colorless diction defers awareness of what is happening; therefore the point of view is vital in the story's surprise and horror. The concluding paragraph (6) emphasizes the way in which general response to the story, the and also its success, are conditioned by the detached, dramatic point of view.

A Close Look at Paragraph 4

Paragraph 4, which continues the topic of paragraph 3, shows how assertions about alternative points of view may reinforce ideas about the actual point of view chosen by the author (see pp. 93–94). The material for the paragraph is derived from notes speculating about whether Jackson's technique of withholding detail to build toward the concluding horror (the topic of paragraph 3) could be maintained with different points of view. A combination of analysis, thought, and imagination is therefore at work in the paragraph. In effect, the supporting details in the paragraph demonstrate a negative: Other points of view would *not* allow for the withholding technique. (The first-person and the omniscient points of view would require giving a way the ending. Even the more congenial limited omniscient point of view would be ineffective because most point-of-view characters would uncover information rather than withhold it.) In the light of the less suitable alternatives, therefore, paragraph 4 concludes by confirming the superiority of Jackson's use of the dramatic point of view.

chapter 7

Writing About an Idea or Theme:
The Meaning and the Message
in Literature

The word **idea** refers to the result or results of general and abstract thinking. Synonymous words are *concept, thought, opinion,* and *principle.* In literary study the consideration of ideas gets us involved in *meaning, interpretation, explanation,* and *significance.* Though ideas are usually extensive and complex, separate ideas may be named by a single word, such as *justice, right and good, love, piety, causation,* and, not surprisingly, *idea* itself.

IDEAS NEED THE FORM OF ASSERTIONS

Although a single word may give us the name of an idea, an idea is not operative until we phrase it as a sentence or **assertion.** In other words, an idea needs a subject and a predicate to get it moving so that we can use it as the basis for discussion. It is important to understand that an *assertion* of an idea is not the same as an ordinary sentence, such as "It's a nice day." This observation may be correct (depending on the weather), but it cannot be called an idea. Rather, an idea should indicate *thought* about the day's quality, such as "A nice day requires blue sky, a warm sun, and light breezes." Because this latter sentence deals with an assertion about "nice," it lends itself to the development of a theme on the idea of a nice day.

In studying literature, you should always phrase ideas as assertions. For example, you might claim that an idea in Chekhov's *The Bear* is "love," but it would be difficult to begin writing unless you make an assertion, such as *"The Bear* demonstrates the idea that love is both irresistible and irrational."* With this assertion you could explain the sudden and apparently impossible love between Smirnov and Mrs. Popov. Similarly, for Eudora Welty's "A Worn Path" you might make the following assertion based on the character Phoenix Jackson: "Phoenix embodies the idea that caring for others gives no reward but the continuation of the duty itself."

Although we have noted only one idea in these works, there are usually many separate ideas. When one of the ideas seems to be the major one, it is sometimes also called the **theme.** Loosely, the words *theme* and *major idea* or *central idea* are the same.

IDEAS IN LITERATURE: VALUES
AND THE HUMAN SIDE OF THINGS

In literature, ideas are of interest because they concern people in their lives—the ways in which they *actually* lead them, *should* lead them, or *ought to be allowed to* lead them. This means that ideas are not ends in themselves. Rather they apply to the human side of things, and usually they are presented along with the expression or implication that certain things should be highly valued.

As a general rule, **values** are embodied in literary works coincidentally with ideas. For example, the idea of justice may be considered abstractly and broadly, as Plato does in his *Republic* when developing his concept of a just government. In comparison, justice is also considered by Langston Hughes in "Theme for English B," but Hughes is not abstract and speculative, like Plato, but rather personal. Hughes's idea is that human beings are equal regardless of race, and he asserts the need for equal treatment by showing that his young black speaker shares many traits with other human beings. In short, to talk about Hughes's idea is also to talk about his values. Another poem dealing with justice is Lowell's "Patterns," in which the speaker, in despair because of her lover's death in battle, questions the justice of "the pattern called war." Lowell's values clearly place individuals higher than the politics of state warfare.

THE PLACE OF IDEAS IN LITERATURE

Because writers of poems, plays, and stories are usually not systematic philosophers, it would be a mistake to go "message hunting" as though their works contained nothing but ideas. Indeed, there is much benefit and pleasure to be derived from savoring a work, from being taken up in the developing pattern of story and conflict, from following its implications and suggestions, and from listening to the sounds of its words—to name only a few of the things for which literature is treasured.

All these reservations aside, ideas are vital to understanding and appreciation, for it is indisputable that writers have ideas and want to communicate them. For example, in *The Bear* Chekhov's purpose is to make his audience laugh at two unlikely people falling suddenly in love. The play is funny, however, not only because it is preposterous, but also because it is based on the idea that love takes precedence over other resolutions that people might make. Eudora Welty in "A Worn Path" tells the poignant *story* of an aging woman on a hopeless quest, but the story embodies *ideas* about the strength of human character and the beauty of loving duty. Other ideas to be found in literary works, in addition to these, may be *happiness, impermanence, taste, maturity, pain,* and many more.

DISTINGUISHING IDEAS FROM SUMMARIES

As you make assertions about ideas in a work, it is important to avoid the trap of retelling plots or main actions. Such a trap is contained in the following sentence about Updike's "A & P": "The major character, Sammy, quits his job to protest the way his boss mistreats the girls." This sentence successfully describes the story's major action, but it does not express an *idea*. Indeed, it *obstructs* understanding because it focuses only on what happens and does not introduce an idea to connect characters and events. The necessary connection might be achieved with a sentence such as " 'A & P' illustrates the idea that making a protest involves severe costs," or " 'A & P' embodies the thought that individual rights are more important than arbitrary regulations." Themes based on these connecting formulations could be focused on ideas and would not be sidetracked by the retelling of Updike's story.

In a similar way, you should maintain the distinction between ideas and situations. For example, in Donne's "A Valediction: Forbidding Mourning," the speaker is saying goodbye to his sweetheart, who is apparently about to cry because he is going away. That is the *situation* of the poem. But in consolation the speaker cleverly develops the idea that true lovers (like themselves) are never apart but are always connected by their bond of love. This assertion, which the speaker exemplifies in the last four stanzas of the poem, is one of Donne's unique ideas above love.

HOW DO YOU FIND IDEAS?

Ideas do not just leap out from the page and announce their presence. To determine an idea, you need to look carefully and to consider the meaning of what you have read, and then you need to develop explanatory and comprehensive assertions. There is no rule requiring that your assertions must be the same as those that others might make; people notice different things, and individual formulations vary. A study of Hughes's "Theme for English B" might produce any of the following assertions: (1) Young people are ambitious, regardless of color. (2) Similarities in taste demonstrate the similarity of persons of all races. (3) Despite many breakdowns of color barriers, whites are still freer than blacks. (4) People become human through common experiences. Any of these assertions would be useful in a theme about ideas in "Theme for English B," and it follows that if one were chosen, the others would need to be either set aside or incorporated into the growing fabric of the theme. In studying for ideas, you should follow a similar process—making a number of formulations for an idea and then selecting one for further development.

As you study, you should be alert to the various ways in which authors convey ideas. Thus one author might prefer an indirect way through a character's speeches, while another may prefer direct statement. In practice, authors may employ all the following methods within the same work.

Direct Statements by the Authorial Voice

Although authors are interested mainly in rendering action, dialogue, and situation, they sometimes, through their authorial voice, state ideas to guide us and deepen our understanding. Such authorial ideas are usually brief but are nevertheless crucial. In the second paragraph of "The Necklace," for example, Maupassant's authorial voice presents the idea that women have only charm and beauty to get on in the world. Ironically, however, Maupassant uses the story to show that for Mathilde, the major character, nothing works, for her charm cannot prevent disaster for her. Poe, in "The Masque of the Red Death," asserts a key idea that "there are matters of which no jest can be made" (paragraph 9). This idea is expressed as authorial commentary just as the Red Death has invaded the party, and it demonstrates the futility of Prospero's attempts to overcome death.

Direct Statements by the First-Person Speaker

First-person narrators or speakers frequently express ideas along with their descriptions. (See also Chapter 6, "Writing about Point of View," pp. 85–97). Because they are part of a dramatic presentation, the ideas may be right or wrong, well-considered or thoughtless, brilliant or half-baked, depending on the speaker. An example of brilliant ideas may be seen in Donne's "A Valediction: Forbidding Mourning," a short poem but nevertheless one in which the speaker develops many perspectives on the nature of love. Less well-considered ideas are expressed by Sammy, of Updike's

"A & P," who seems engulfed in intellectual commonplaces, particularly in his insinuation about the intelligence of women (paragraph 2). In his defense, however, Sammy *acts* upon a worthy idea about rights of expression and dress.

Dramatic Statements Made by Characters

In many works, characters express their own views, which may be admirable or contemptible. Through such dramatic speeches, you may encounter thirteen ways of looking at a blackbird, and must do considerable interpreting and evaluating yourself. For example, Old Man Warner in "The Lottery" states that the lottery is valuable even though we learn from the narrator that the beliefs underlying it have long been forgotten. Because Warner is a zealous and noisy supporter, however, his words show that outdated ideas continue to do harm even when there is strong reason to abandon them and develop new ideas. In Chekhov's *The Bear*, both Smirnov and Mrs. Popov express many silly thoughts as they begin speaking to each other, and it is their sudden love that reveals how wrongheaded their ideas have been.

Figurative Language

Authors often use figurative language to express and reinforce ideas. In the poem "Bright Star," for example, Keats uses a fixed star, presumably the North Star, as a symbol of constancy. Writers of fiction and drama also freely use figurative language. At the opening of "Miss Brill," Mansfield compares a sunny day to gold and white wine—lovely suggestions of beauty and happiness which contrast ironically with the pain that Miss Brill is to experience. In Glaspell's *Trifles*, a character compares John Wright, the murdered man, to "a raw wind that gets to the bone" (speech 104). With this figurative language Glaspell conveys the idea of bluntness, cruelty, and indifference that this character so completely embodies.

Characters Who Stand for Ideas

Quite often, characters engage in actions that are so typical that they stand out as representatives of certain ideas and values. Thus Mathilde's story in Maupassant's "The Necklace" is so powerful that she comes to stand for the idea that unrealizable dreams may invade and damage the real world. Two diverse or opposed characters may represent contrasting ideas, as with Sammy and Lengel of Updike's "A & P," who stand for opposing views about rights of expression.

In effect, characters who stand for ideas may assume symbolic status, as in Hawthorne's "Young Goodman Brown," where the protagonist symbolizes the alienation accompanying overzealousness. The speaker of Frost's "Desert Places" invites identification as a symbol of the frightening qualities of emptiness and unconcern within individual human beings. Hughes's speaker in "Theme for English B" stands for individuals who by virtue of common humanity deserve equality. In this way, such characters may be equated directly with particular ideas, and to talk about them is a shorthand way of talking about the ideas.

The Work Itself as It Represents Ideas

One of the most important ways in which authors express ideas is to make them an inseparable part of a work's total impression. All the events and characters may point toward an idea that the work itself makes forceful. For example, in "Theme for English B," Hughes makes objective the idea that the urgency of ending racial barriers overrides the socially convenient reasons for which they have been established. Although he does not use these exact words, the poem effectively makes the idea clear. Similarly, Shakespeare's tragedy *Hamlet* dramatizes the idea that an evil person (Claudius) originates destructive forces that cannot be stopped until they destroy everything in their path. Even "escape literature," which ostensibly enables readers to forget their immediate concerns, embodies conflicts between good and evil, love and hate, good spies and bad, earthlings and aliens, and so on. Thereby, such stories *do* embody ideas and themes, even though their reason for existence is not thought but forgetfulness.

WRITING ABOUT AN IDEA

Most likely you will wish to write about a major idea or theme, but you may also get interested in one of the many other ideas you find. In Hardy's "Channel Firing," for example, a major idea is that destructive warfare is an inescapable condition of human history. The poem also contains other challenging ideas, such as that no civilization is permanent, that the concept of the afterlife may be nothing more than fancy, and that life is synonymous with disturbance. If your assignment were on "Channel Firing," you could reasonably take any of these for your theme topic.

If you choose a major idea, such as that on warfare in Hardy's poem, remember that in a well-written story, poem, or play, things are introduced only as they have a bearing on the idea. In this sense, the idea is like a key in music, or like a continuous thread tying together actions, characters, statements, symbols, and dialogue. As readers, we can trace such a thread, with all the variations that writers work upon them. Thus in Amy Lowell's "Patterns," the details can be related to the idea that an abstraction such as service in warfare has no meaning when compared with life and love.

As you take notes and sketch your plan of attack, you should explore all the methods of expressing ideas described above (pp. 100–103) and use as many as you think will best give you useful information. You might rely most heavily on the direct statements of the authorial voice, or on a combination of these and your interpretation of characters and actions. Or you might focus exclusively on a first-person speaker and use his or her ideas to develop your analysis.

In developing preliminary drafts, try to answer questions such as these: What is your best wording of the idea? Is the idea personal, social, political, economic, scientific, ethical, esthetic, or religious? How pervasive in the work is the idea (throughout for a major idea; intermittently, or just once, for a secondary idea)? How can character, action, dialogue, statement, description, scene, structure, and development be related to the idea? Are there contradictory statements? Implications? Images? Symbols? Is the idea asserted directly, dramatically, ironically? How? What value or values are embodied in the idea?

Introduction

In your introduction you might state any special circumstances in the work that affect ideas generally or your idea specifically. Your statement of the idea will serve as the central idea for your essay. Your thesis sentence should indicate the particular parts or aspects of the story that you will examine.

Body

In the body, your general goal should be (1) to define the idea, and (2) to show its importance in the work. Each separate story, poem, or play will invite its own approach, but here are a number of strategies for development:

1. ANALYZING THE IDEA AS IT APPLIES TO CHARACTER. Example: "Minnie Wright is an embodiment of the idea that a life lived amid cruelty and insensitivity will lead to alienation, unhappiness, despair, and also even to violence."

2. SHOWING HOW ACTION BRINGS OUT THE IDEA. Example: "That Mrs. Popov and Smirnov fall in love rather than fight a duel indicates Chekhov's idea that love is so strong that it literally rescues human lives."

3. SHOWING THE IDEA OPERATING IN DIALOGUE. Example: "The speeches of Mrs. Popov to Luka, to Smirnov, and to the entering servants illustrate the idea that the poses people adopt may mask and contradict their true self-interest."

4. Demonstrating how the structure is determined by the idea. Example: "The idea that horror may exist in ordinary things leads to a structure in which Jackson introduces seemingly commonplace people, builds suspense about an impending misfortune, and develops a conclusion of mob destructiveness."

5. Treating variations or differing manifestations of the idea. Example: "The idea that overzealousness leads to destruction is shown in Brown's nightmarish distortion of reality, his rejection of others, and his dying gloom."

6. Dealing with a combination of these (together with any other significant aspect). Example: "Chekhov's idea that love is complex and contradictory is shown in Smirnov's initial scornfulness of Mrs. Popov, his self-declared independence of character, and his concluding embrace." [Here the idea is to be traced through speech, character, and action.]

Conclusion

In your conclusion you might begin with a summary, together with your evaluation of the validity or force of the idea. If you have been convinced by the author's ideas, you might say that the author has expressed the idea forcefully and convincingly, or else you might show the relevance of the idea to current conditions. If you do not like the idea, it is never enough just to state your disagreement; you should include reasons and should demonstrate the shortcomings or limitations of the idea. If you wish to mention a related idea, whether in the work you have studied or in some other work, you might introduce that here, but be sure to stress the connections.

Sample Theme
The Idea of the Strength of Love in Chekhov's The Bear*

---

[1] In the one-act farce The Bear, Anton Chekhov shows a man and woman, who have never met before, falling suddenly in love. With such an unlikely main action, ideas may seem unimportant, but one can nevertheless find a number of ideas in the play. Some of these are that responsibility to life is stronger than responsibility to death, that people may justify even the most stupid and contradictory actions, that love makes people do foolish things, and that lifelong commitments may be made with hardly any thought at all. One of the play's

* For the text of this play, see Appendix C, pages 354–63.

major ideas is that love and desire are powerful enough to overcome even the strongest obstacles.° This idea is shown as the force of love conquers com-
[1]   mitment to the dead, renunciation of womankind, unfamiliarity, and anger.▫

        Commitment to her dead husband is the obstacle to love shown in Mrs. Popov. She states that she has made a vow never to see daylight because of her mourning (speech 4), and she spends her time staring at her husband's picture and being self-satisfied with her faithfulness. Her devotion to the dead is so intense that she claims to be virtually dead herself out of sympathy for her
[2]   husband:

>   My life is already ended. *He* lies in his grave; I have buried myself
>   in these four walls . . . we are both dead. (speech 2)

In her, Chekhov, has created a strong obstacle so that he might illustrate the power of all-conquering love. By the play's end, Mrs. Popov's embracing Smirnov is a visual example of the idea (speech 151, S.D.).

        Renunciation of women is the obstacle for Smirnov. He tells Mrs. Popov that women have made him bitter and that he no longer gives "a good goddamn" about them (speech 69). His disillusioned words apparently make him an impossible candidate for love. But, in keeping with Chekhov's idea, Smirnov
[3]   soon confesses his sudden and uncontrollable love at the peak of his anger against Mrs. Popov. Within him, the force of love operates so stongly that he would even claim happiness at being shot by the "little velvet hands" of Mrs. Popov (speech 140).

        As if these personal causes were not enough to stop love, a genuinely real obstacle is that the two people are strangers. Not only have they never met, but they have never heard of each other. According to the main idea, however,
[4]   this unfamiliarity is no major problem. Chekhov is dramatizing the power of love, and shows that it is strong enough to overcome even the lack of familiarity or friendship. Indeed, that Smirnov and Mrs. Popov are total strangers may be irrelevant to the idea about love's strength.

        Anger and the threat of violence, however, make the greatest obstacle. The two characters become so irritated about Smirnov's demand for payment that, as an improbable climax of their heated words, Smirnov challenges Mrs. Popov, a woman, to a duel! He shouts:

>   And do you think just because you're one of those romantic cre-
[5]   >   ations, that you have the right to insult me with impunity? Yes? I
>   challenge you! (speech 105)

Along with their own personal barriers against loving, it would seem that the threat of shooting each other, even if poor Luka could stop them, would cause lifelong hatred. And yet love knocks down all these obstacles, in line with Chekhov's idea that love's power is, like a flood, irresistible.

        The idea is not new or surprising. It is the subject of popular songs, stories, and other plays, movies, and TV shows. What is surprising about Chek
[6]   hov's use of the idea is that love in <u>The Bear</u> overcomes such unlikelyconditions, and wins so suddenly. These conditions bring up an interesting and

---

° Central idea
▫ Thesis sentence

closely related idea: Chekhov is showing that intensely negative feeling may lead not to hatred but rather to love. In the speeches of Smirnov and Mrs. Popov, one can see hurt, disappointment, regret, frustration, annoyance, anger, rage, and potential self-destructiveness. Yet at the high point of these negative [6] feelings, love takes over. It is as though hostility finally collapses because it is the nature of people to prefer loving to hating. The Bear <u>is an uproarious</u> <u>dramatization of the power of love, and it is made better because it is founded</u> <u>on a truthful judgment of the way people really are.</u>

COMMENTARY ON THE THEME

This theme follows the sixth strategy (p. 105) by showing how separate components from the play exhibit the idea's pervasiveness. Throughout, instances of dialogue, situations, soliloquies, and actions are evidence for the various conclusions. Transitions between paragraphs are effected by phrases like "these personal causes" (4), "greatest obstacle" (5), and "The idea" (6), all of which emphasize the continuity of the topic.

The introduction notes that the play is a farce but even so that it contains a number of ideas. The major idea is that love has the power to surmount great obstacles. The thesis sentence lists the four obstacles to be explored in the body.

As the operative aspects of Chekhov's idea, paragraphs 2 through 5 detail the nature of each of the obstacles. The obstacle of paragraph 2, Mrs. Popov's commitment to her husband's memory, is "strong." The one in paragraph 3, Smirnov's dislike of women, is seemingly "impossible." The one in paragraph 4, their being total strangers, is a "genuinely real" difficulty. In paragraph 5, the obstacle of anger is more likely to produce "hatred" than love.

A Close Look at Paragraph 6

There are two objectives in the concluding paragraph. One is to reassert the central idea—a brief summary, as it were. The second is to build on the idea by suggesting another related and important idea. The conclusion therefore demonstrates a major quality of reading literature, namely that a consequence of one idea is the exploration of other ideas. In the paragraph, the topic moves from the idea of love's power to the idea that normal human beings cannot long sustain potentially destructive anger. Obviously, this second idea is a broad generalization which could bear extensive treatment in its own right. Even though the topic would require great development if it came at the beginning, it is effective as a part of the conclusion. The final sentence blends the two ideas, thereby looking both inwardly into the theme and outwardly to the consideration of new ideas.

chapter 8

Writing About Imagery:
The Work's Link to the Senses

In literature, imagery refers to words that trigger your **imagination** to recall and recombine **images**—memories or mental pictures of sights, sounds, tastes, smells, sensations of touch, and motions. The process is active, and even vigorous, for when particular words or descriptions produce images, you are applying your own experiences with life and language to your understanding of the works you are reading. In effect, *you are re-creating the work in your own way through the controlled stimulation produced by the author's words.* Imagery, in short, is a channel to your active imagination, and along this channel, writers—poets, dramatists, and writers of fiction—bring their works directly into your consciousness.

For example, the word "lake" may cause you to imagine or visualize a particular lake that you remember vividly. Your mental picture or image may be a distant view of calm waters reflecting blue sky, a nearby view of gentle waves rippled by the wind, a view of the lake bottom from a boat, or an overhead view of a sandy and sunlit shoreline. Similarly, the words *rose, apple, hot dog, malted milk,* and *pizza* all cause you to visualize these things, and, in addition, may cause you to recall their smells and tastes. Active and graphic words like *row, swim,* and *dive* stimulate you to picture moving images of someone performing these actions.

RESPONSES AND THE WRITER'S USE OF DETAIL

In studying imagery we describe and interpret our imaginative reconstruction of the pictures and impressions evoked by the work's images. We let the writer's words simmer and percolate in our minds. To get our imaginations stirring, we might follow Coleridge in this description from "Kubla Khan" (lines 37–41):

> A damsel with a dulcimer
> In a vision once I saw:
> It was an Abyssinian maid,
> And on her dulcimer she played,
> Singing of Mount Abora.

We do not read about the color of the young woman's clothing, or anything else about her appearance except that she is playing a stringed instrument, a dulcimer, and that she is singing a song about a mountain in a foreign, remote land. But Coleridge's image is enough. From it we can imagine a vivid, exotic picture of a young woman from a distant land singing, together with the loveliness of her song (even though we never hear it or understand it). The image lives.

IMAGERY, IDEAS, AND ATTITUDES

In using images, writers do more than prompt you to re-create sensory impressions with your active imagination. They also transfer their own ideas by the *authenticating* effects of the vision and perceptions underlying them; in this way the help you to widen your understanding, to receive new ways of seeing the world, or to strengthen your old ways of seeing it. Langston Hughes, in "Theme for English B," for example (pp. 352–53), develops the idea that human beings are equal—an idea basic to our Declaration of Independence. Rather than stating the idea directly, he uses a number of images of everyday, ordinary activities that his speaker shares in common with most human beings (line 21):

> . . . I like to eat, sleep, drink, and be in love.

These simple images form an equalizing link that is not only true, but unarguable. Such uses of imagery are one of the strongest means by which literature reinforces ideas.

In addition, as you form mental pictures from a writer's images, you will also respond with appropriate attitudes and feelings. Thus the phrase "beside a lake, beneath the trees," from Wordsworth's poem "Daffodils," prompts both the visualization of a wooded lakeshore and also the related pleasantness of outdoor relaxation and happiness. In contrast, Masefield in "Cargoes" triggers unpleasant responses through the images of "pig lead" and "cheap tin trays." By such a use of imagery, writers not only create sensory vividness and express thoughts, but also influence if not control the reader's attitudes.

CLASSIFICATION OF IMAGERY

SIGHT.   Sight is the most significant of our senses, for it is the key to our remembrance of other impressions. Therefore, the most frequently occurring literary imagery is to things that we can visualize either exactly or approximately—**visual images.** John Masefield, in his poem "Cargoes" (the subject of the sample theme, pp. 114–15), asks us to re-create mental pictures or images of ocean-going merchant vessels from three periods of human history. He speaks about a "quinquereme" (a ship with rows of five men pulling three tiers of oars) from the ancient Near East, associated with the Biblical King Solomon; then he turns to a "stately Spanish galleon" at the time of the Renaissance; finally he refers to a modern British ship caked with salt, carrying grubby and cheap things over the English Channel. His images are vivid as they stand, without the need for more detailed amplification. In order to reconstruct them imaginatively, we do not need ever to have seen the ancient Biblical lands or waters, or to have seen or handled the cheap commodities on a modern merchantship. We have seen enough in our lives both in reality and in pictures to *imagine* places and objects like these, and hence Masefield is successful in implanting his visual images into our minds.

SOUND.   **Auditory images** are images appealing to our experiences with sound. In Owen's poem "Anthem for Doomed Youth" (p. 352), which is about death in warfare, the speaker asks what "passing bells" may be tolled for "those who die as cattle." He is referring to the traditional tolling of a parish church bell to announce to the community that a parishioner has died. Such a ceremonial ringing suggests a period of peace and order, when there is time to pay ceremonial respect to the dead. But the poem then points out that the only sound for those who have fallen in battle is the "rapid rattle" of "stuttering" rifles—in other words, not the solemn, dignified sounds of peace, but the horrifying noises of war. Owen's auditory images evoke corresponding sounds in our imaginations, and help us experience the poem and hate the uncivilized depravity of war.

SMELL, TASTE, AND TOUCH.   In addition to sight and sound, you will also find images from the other senses. An **olfactory image** refers to smell, a **gustatory image** to taste, and a **tactile image** to touch. A great deal of love poetry, for example, includes observations about the fragrances of flowers. As a twist on this common olfactory imagery, Shakespeare's speaker in Sonnet 130, "My Mistress' Eyes," candidly admits that the breath of his woman friend is not the same as the scent of roses (lines 7–8).

Images derived from and referring to taste—gustatory images—are also common, though less frequent than those to sight and sound. In Masefield's "Cargoes," for example, there are references in line 5 to "sweet white wine," and in line 10 to "cinnamon." Although the poem includes these things as cargoes, the words themselves also register in our minds as gustatory images because they appear to our sense of taste.

Tactile images of touch and texture are not as common because touch is difficult to render except in terms of effects. The speaker of Lowell's "Patterns," for example, uses tactile imagery when imagining a never-to-happen embrace with her fiancé who, we learn, has been killed in war. Her imagery records the effect of the embrace ("bruised"), while her internalized feelings are expressed in metaphors ("aching, melting"):

> And the buttons of his waistcoat bruised my body as he clasped me
> Aching, melting, unafraid. (lines 51–52)

Tactile images are not uncommon in love poetry, where references to touch and feeling are natural. Because references to erotic love might easily verge on pornography, however, love poetry usually deals with yearning and hope (as in Keats's "Bright Star," p. 345) rather than actual sensuous fulfillment.

IMAGES OF MOTION AND ACTIVITY.   References to movement are also images. Images of general motion are **kinetic** (remember that *motion pictures* are also called *cinema*), while the term **kinesthetic** is applied to human or animal movement. Imagery of motion is closely related to visual images, for motion is most often seen. Masefield's British coaster, for example, is a visual image, but when it goes "Butting through the Channel," the motion makes it also kinetic. When Hardy's corpses sit upright at the beginning of "Channel Firing," the image is kinesthetic, as is the action of Amy Lowell's speaker walking in the garden after hearing about her fiancé's death. Whatever the topic of the visual image—a person in a woods, a prince in a room, a pounding surf, a window blind—to the degree that there is motion, the visual image is also kinetic or kinesthetic.

IMAGERY OF LORE AND IMAGINATION

Because there are few restrictions upon the human imagination, the references of imagery may be not only real, but also imagined. Hawthorne in

"Young Goodman Brown" describes the protagonist's walk into the woods, an area that seems realistic but which turns into imagined regions of fantasy and nightmare. Coleridge in "Kubla Khan" gives us both reality and unreality in a single line about a "woman [real] wailing for her demon lover [unreal]."

WRITING ABOUT IMAGERY

In preparing to write, you should work with a thoughtfully developed set of notes, dealing with issues such as the following: Is the imagery primarily visual (shapes, colors), auditory (sounds), olfactory (smells), tactile (touch and texture), gustatory (taste), kinetic or kinesthetic (motion), or a combination of these? Do the images stand out in detail? Are they vivid? How is this vividness achieved? Within a group of images, say visual or auditory, do the images pertain to one location or area rather than another (natural scenes rather than interiors, snowy scenes rather than grassy ones, loud and harsh words rather than quiet and civilized ones)? Are the images derived from reality or imagination? What characteristics of either world are observable? What responses and ideas are produced by the images? How are they integrated within the respective works? With answers to questions like these, you will have virtually ready-made material to be turned directly into the body of your theme.

Introduction

Here you set our your plan for the body, such as that writer uses images to strengthen ideas about war, character, love, and so on, or that the writer relies predominantly on images of sight, sound, action, and so on. Your central idea should delineate your objective, and your thesis sentence should outline the aspects you will cover in the body.

Body

You might choose to deal exclusively with one of the following aspects, or you may combine your approaches, as you wish.

1. IMAGES SUGGESTING IDEAS AND / OR MOODS. The emphasis in such a theme is to be on the results of the imagery. What ideas or moods are evoked by the images? (The auditory images beginning "Anthem for Doomed Youth," for example, all point toward a condemnation of war's brutal cruelty. The visual and auditory images of Kubla Khan's pleasure dome all suggest the idea that the world can be a fertile, magical place.) Do the images promote approval or disapproval? Cheerfulness? Melancholy?

Are the images drab, exciting, vivid? How? Why? Are they conducive to humor, or surprise? How does the writer achieve these effects? Are the images consistent, or are they ambiguous? (For example, the images in Masefield's "Cargoes" indicate first approval and then disapproval, with no ambiguity. By contrast, Shakespeare's images in "My Mistress' Eyes" might be construed as insults, but in context, they may be seen as compliments.)

2. THE TYPE OF IMAGES.   Here the emphasis is on the categories of images themselves. Is there a predominance of a particular type of image, such as references to sight, or is there a blending? Is there a bunching of types at particular points in the poem or story? If so, why? Is there any shifting as the work develops (as, for example, in Owen's "Anthem for Doomed Youth," where the auditory images first evoke loudness and harshness but later bring out quietness and sorrow)? Are the images appropriate, given the nature and apparent intent of the work? Do they assist in making the ideas seem convincing? If there seems to be any inappropriateness, what is its effect?

3. SYSTEMS OF IMAGES.   Here the emphasis should be on the areas from which the images are drawn. This is another way of considering the appropriateness of the imagery, whether in a poem, story, or play. Is there a pattern of similar or consistent images, such as darkness (Hawthorne's "Young Goodman Brown") or brightness to darkness (Mansfield's "Miss Brill")? Do all the images adhere consistently to a particular frame of reference, such as a sunlit garden (Lowell's "Patterns"), an extensive recreational forest and garden (Coleridge's "Kubla Khan"), a kitchen (Glaspell's *Trifles*), a graveyard (Hardy's "Channel Firing"), or a group of seagoing vessels (Masefield's "Cargoes")? Is there anything unusual or unique about the set of images? Do they produce unexpected or new responses?

Conclusion

Beyond a recapitulation of your major points, the conclusion is the place for additional insights. It would not be proper to go too far in new directions here, but you might briefly take up one or more of the conclusions you do not develop in the body. In short, what have you learned from your study of imagery in the work about which you have written?

Sample Theme

*The Images of John Masefield's Poem "Cargoes"**

[1] In the three-stanza poem "Cargoes," John Masefield develops imagery to create a negative impression of modern commercial life.° There is a contrast between the first two stanzas and the third, with the first two idealizing the romantic, distant past and the third demeaning the modern, gritty, grimy present. Masefield's images are thus both positive and lush, on the one hand, and negative and stark, on the other.□

The most evocative and pleasant images in the poem are in the first stanza. The speaker asks that we imagine a "Quinquereme of Nineveh from distant Ophir" (line 1), an ocean-going, many-oared vessel loaded with treasure for the Biblical King Solomon. As Masefield identifies the cargo, quoting the King James Bible directly, the visual images are rich and romantic (lines 3–5):

[2]
With a cargo of ivory,
And apes and peacocks,
Sandalwood, cedarwood, and sweet white wine.

Ivory suggests richness, which is augmented by the exotic "apes and peacocks" in all their exciting strangeness. The "sandalwood, cedarwood, and sweet white wine" evoke pungent smells and tastes. The "sunny" light of ancient Palestine (line 2) not only illuminates the imaginative scene (visual), but invites readers to imagine the sun's warming touch (tactile). The references to animals and birds also suggest the sounds that these creatures would make (auditory). Thus, in this lush first stanza, images derived from all the senses are introduced to create impressions of a glorious past.

[3] Almost equally lush are the images of the second stanza, which completes the poem's first part. Here the visual imagery evokes the royal splendor of a tall-masted, full-sailed galleon (line 6) at the height of Spain's commercial power in the sixteenth century. The galleon's cargo suggests great wealth, with sparkling diamonds and amethysts, and Portugese "gold moidores" gleaming in open chests (line 10). With cinnamon in the second stanza's bill of lading (line 10), Masefield includes the gustatory image of a pleasant-tasting spice.

[4] The negative imagery of the third stanza is in stark contrast to the first two stanzas. Here the poem draws the visual image of a modern "Dirty British coaster" (line 11) to focus on the griminess and suffocation of modern civilization. This spray-swept ship is loadedwith materials that pollute the earth with noise and smoke. The smoke-stack of the coaster (line 11) and the firewood it is carrying suggest the creation of choking smog. The Tyne Coal (line 13) and road rails (line 14) suggest the noise and smoke of puffing railroad engines. As

* For the text of this poem, see Appendix C, page 351.
° Central idea
□ Thesis sentence

[4] if this were not enough, the "pig lead" (line 14) to be used in various industrial processes indicates not just more unpleasantness, but also something more poisonous and deadly. In contrast to the lush and stately imagery of the first two stanzas, the images in the third stanza invite the conclusion that people now, when the "Dirty British coaster" butts through the English Channel, are surrounded and threatened by visual, olfactory, and auditory pollution.

[5] The poem thus establishes a romantic past and ugly present through images of sight, smell, and sound. The images of motion are also directed to agree with this view: In stanzas one and two the quinquereme is "rowing" and the galleon is "dipping." These kinetic images suggest dignity and lightness. The British coaster, however, is "butting," an image indicating bull-like hostility and stupid force. These, together with all the other images, focus the poem's negative views of today's consumer-oriented society. The facts that life for both the ancient Palestinians and the Renaissance Spaniards included slavery (of those men rowing the quinquereme) and piracy (by those Spanish "explorers" who robbed and killed the natives of the isthmus) should probably not be emphasized as a protest against Masefield's otherwise valid contrasts in images. His final commentary may hence be thought of as the banging of his "cheap tin trays" (line 15), which makes a percussive climax of the oppressive images filling too large a portion of modern lives.

COMMENTARY ON THE THEME

The method illustrated in this sample theme is the first (pp. 112–13), the use of images to develop ideas and moods. All the examples—derived directly from the poem—emphasize the qualities of Masefield's images. This method permits the introduction of imagery drawn from all the senses in order to demonstrate Masefield's ideas about the past and the present. Other approaches might have concentrated exclusively on Masefield's visual images, or upon his images drawn from trade and commerce. Because Masefield uses auditory and gustatory images but does not develop them extensively, these images might be appropriately devoted to single paragraphs.

The introductory paragraph of the theme presents the central idea that Masefield uses his images climactically to lead to his negative view of modern commercialism. The thesis sentence indicates that the topics to be developed are those of [1] lushness, and [2] starkness.

Paragraphs 2 and 3 form a unit stressing the lushness and exoticism of stanza 1 and the wealth and colorfulness of stanza 2 (see the detailed close look at paragraph 2, below).

Paragraph 4 stresses the contrast of Masefield's images in stanza 3 with those of stanzas 1 and 2. To this end the paragraph illustrates the imaginative reconstruction needed to develop an understanding of this contrast. The unpleasantness, annoyance, and even the danger of the cargoes mentioned in stanza 3 are therefore emphasized as the qualities evoked by the images.

The last paragraph demonstrates that the imagery of motion—not much stressed in the poem—is in agreement with the rest of Masefield's imagery. As a demonstration of the need for fair, impartial judgment, the conclusion introduces the possible objection that Masefield's imagistic portraits may be slanted because they include not a full but rather a partial view of their respective historical periods. Thus the concluding paragraph adds balance to the analysis illustrated in paragraphs 2, 3, and 4.

A Close Look at Paragraph 2

Paragraph 2 contains fairly full responses to the images in Masefield's first stanza. The paragraph uses words such as "lush," "evocative," "rich," "exotic," "pungent," and "romantic" to characterize the pleasing mental pictures the images invoke. Another goal of the paragraph is to point out the extent of Masefield's images: While many refer to sight, the imagery touches upon all the senses. Although the paragraph indicates enthusiastic responses to the images, however, it does not go beyond the limits of the images themselves. For example, it is tempting to draw attention to the bright, arresting colors that peacocks would have in real life, but Masefield does not refer to colors in the poem, and the paragraph correspondingly does not mention the colors. Ivory would unquestionably have been sculpted into statues and ornaments, but because Masefield does not mention statuary, the paragraph does not go beyond his general reference to "ivory." Masefield's images, in short, are considered only as they evoke an impression of lushness and richness, not as they might be further imaginatively amplified. The illustrative value of this paragraph is that readers should not go farther in interpretation than writers invite them to go.

chapter 9

Writing About Metaphor and Simile:

A Source of Depth and Range in Literature

One way in which writers make their works interesting, enlarging, and forceful is to use **figurative language**—that is, replicating patterns of words and expressions (also called **rhetorical figures** or **rhetorical devices**). Although these devices may be used in any kind of work, they are most commonly found in poetry because they facilitate the compactness and economy so essential in poems.

There are many rhetorical figures, but the two most important are **metaphor** and **simile.** Both devices clarify, illuminate, and vitalize one thing (unknown, or to be explained) by showing that it is similar to or identical with another (known).

1. METAPHOR. A **metaphor** (a "carrying out of a change") is *the direct verbal equation of two things.* The sentence "All the arts are sisters," for example, is a metaphor emphasizing the close relationship between poetry, music, sculpture, painting, architecture, and acting, to name the major arts. Notice that the metaphor does not claim that the arts are *like* sisters, but rather that the arts *are* sisters.

2. SIMILE. While a metaphor merges identities, a **simile** (the "showing of similarity or oneness") is a figure, using "like" with nouns and "as" (also "as if" and "as though") with clauses, *that draws attention to similarities between two things.* Thus the sentence "Come with . . . eyes as bright / As sunlight on a stream" (from Christina Rossetti's poem "Echo," page 206) makes a comparison of the listener's eyes with a natural scene. Because the simile is introduced by "as," the speaker's emphasis is on the *similarity* of the listener's eyes to sunlight on a stream, not on the *identification* or *equation* of the two.

IMAGERY, METAPHOR, AND SIMILE

To see the relationship of metaphor and simile to imagery (the subject of Chapter 8) you might recall that imagery stimulates readers to form mental pictures evoked by a writer's words and descriptions. Images arise in each work more or less functionally and expectedly from the topic material. Readers bring the work alive to themselves by reconstructing the images to the best of their knowledge and experience.

Metaphors and similes go a step beyond imagery by introducing references that may not normally be expected within the subject matter of a given work. A topic—an observation, attitude, idea, feeling, or action—is granted new life by the comparison of a simile or the equation of a metaphor. For example, to communicate a character's joy and excitement, the sentence "She was happy" is accurate, but it is also ordinary. A better way to get excitement across is to cause the reader to *share* the emotion, and for this there is nothing better than figurative language. Let us then try the following simile: "She felt as if she had just found an inexhaustible diamond mine in her backyard." Because readers can easily understand and reconstruct for themselves the combined disbelief, exhilaration, and joy of such an experience, they also imaginatively share the character's happiness. No ordinary description can create the same response.

Even though the diamond-mine simile is not unusual, you can see that it demonstrates a powerful means of enlarging a work's content. When metaphorical language is used by a skilled writer, there is virtually no limit to its capacity to present insights that are different, unusual, original, unpredictable, and surprising. Indeed, the originality and mental power of authors is shown by the skill with which they demonstrate the aptness of the metaphorical links they establish in their works. Similes and metaphors are therefore an inseparable part of the way of seeing the world anew that is the special contribution of great literature.

METAPHORICAL LANGUAGE IN OPERATION

As a poetic example dealing with joy and excitement, like our diamond-mine simile, let us briefly consider John Keats's sonnet "On First Looking into Chapman's Homer." Keats (1795–1821) wrote the poem after he read the Elizabethan writer John Chapman's translation of Homer's ancient

Greek epics *The Iliad* and *The Odyssey*. Keats's idea is that Chapman not only translated Homer's words but also transmitted his greatness. A brief paraphrase of the poem is this:

> I have enjoyed much art and read much European literature, and have been told that Homer is the best writer of all, but not knowing Greek, I could not genuinely appreciate his works until I discovered them in Chapman's translation. To me, this experience was exciting and awe-inspiring.

This paraphrase also destroys the poem's sense of exhilaration and discovery. Contrast the second sentence of the paraphrase with the last six lines of the sonnet:

> Then felt I like some watcher of the skies
> When a new planet swims into his ken;
> Or like stout Cortez when with eagle eyes
> He star'd at the Pacific—and all his men
> Look'd at each other with a wild surmise—
> Silent, upon a peak in Darien.

If all we had of the poem were our paraphrase, we would pay little attention to it. But in Keats's lines there are two powerful similes ("like some watcher" and "like stout Cortez"). These deserve special care. In reading, we should not just read them and pass them by, but should use our imaginations to *experience* them. We should read them again, hear them, mull them over, feel them, and dream about them. We should imagine what it would be like to be an astronomer discovering a new planet, and to be the first people to see the Pacific Ocean. As we imagine ourselves in these roles, we also imagine our accompanying amazement, wonder, excitement, anticipation, joy, and sense of accomplishment. If we succeed in realizing these feelings, then Keats has unlocked experiences that his unpromising title does not suggest. He has given us something new. He has enlarged us.

VEHICLE AND TENOR

To describe the relationship between a writer's ideas and the metaphors and similes chosen to objectify them, two useful terms have been coined by I. A. Richards (in *The Philosophy of Rhetoric*). First is the **tenor,** which is the totality of ideas and attitudes not only of the literary speaker but also of the author. Second is the **vehicle,** or the details that carry the tenor. The vehicle of the diamond-mine simile is the discovery of the mine, while the tenor is unbounded joy and excitement. Similarly, the tenor of the similes in the last six lines of Keats's sonnet is awe and wonder; the vehicle is the reference to astronomical and geographical discovery.

CHARACTERISTICS
OF METAPHORICAL LANGUAGE

It would be difficult to find any good piece of writing that does not employ metaphorical language. Such language is most vital, however, in imaginative writing, particularly poetry, where it compresses thought, promotes understanding, and shapes response.

POSITIVE AND NEGATIVE ASSOCIATIONS.   As was described in Chapter 8 on Imagery, images are embodied in words or descriptions that denote sense experience that leads to many associations. A single word naming a flower, say *rose*, evokes a positive response. A person might think of the color of a rose, recall its smell, associate it with the summer sun and pleasant days, and recognize the love and respect that a bouquet of roses means as a gift. But the word *rose* is not a metaphor or simile until its associations are used in comparative or analogical way, as in the opening lines of "A Red, Red Rose" by Robert Burns:

> O my Luve's like a red, red rose,
>   That's newly sprung in June:

We realize that the speaker would probably like to continue praising his woman friend forever, but Burns is too good a poet to let the praise drag on. He therefore creates interest by using a simile comparing the "Luve" to a rose, in this way drawing on our own knowledge, associations, and feelings about this most beautiful flower. We recognize that after winter's drabness and leaflessness, the lush growth of June marks a new beginning, an entirely new, beautiful, colorful, and fragrant earth. Thus the rose suggests loveliness, colorfulness, fertility, love, and the end of dreariness. Once we have let the simile work on us in this way (and in other ways that may draw on our own individual experiences with spring and flowers), we have come to an appreciation of the speaker's enthusiasm. That a rose may have unpleasant associations, perhaps because of its thorns, should not be considered. Such an extension of meaning, although truthful, would likely be a misreading.

It would, that is, unless the writer deliberately called some of these less happy ideas to mind. In one of the most famous poems about a rose, by Edmund Waller ("Go Lovely Rose," in which the speaker addresses a rose that he is about to send to his sweetheart), the speaker observes that roses, when cut, die:

> Then die—that she
> The common fate of all things rare
>   May read in thee:
> How small a part of time they share
> That are so wondrous sweet and fair.

Here the speaker is directing the reader's responses to his similes comparing the rose with his woman friend. The structure of the poem is the full development of the simile (the speaker uses the phrase "resemble her to thee" in reference to this figure). In these lines, the tenor is an awareness that life is lovely but also fragile and short.

COMPRESSION.   As has already been suggested, a major characteristic of poetry is brevity and compactness. Metaphors and similes are essential to this quality, as may be seen in Shakespeare's Sonnet 30 (this poem is the subject of the sample theme at the end of this chapter and is printed on page 125). Shakespeare's opening metaphor equates the business of a law-court with personal reverie and self-evaluation:

> When to the sessions of sweet silent thought
> I summon up remembrance of things past, . . .

A *session* is the time in which judges, juries, lawyers, and witnesses carry out the legal business of a court (i.e., "the court is now in session"; think also of "school is now in session"). Also, to *summon* is a legal commandment for a person to appear before a court. Through the metaphor, the speaker asks us to visualize his "sweet silent thought" as though he is sitting as a lawyer–judge over his memories, which he has summoned from the past. The implication is that all experiences, whether good or bad, are alive and present; that personal judgment and reassessment are ongoing processes; and that individual consciousness is not stable and unchanging but is instead a series of conflicting and contrasting impulses.

This development of Shakespeare's metaphor may seem much more than Shakespeare intended, because we use more words in prose than he uses in the two lines of verse. Once we have understood his language, however, our minds are unlocked, and we may then allow ourselves this kind of expansion as we consider the full ramifications of his similes and metaphors.

DEGREES OF DEVELOPMENT

Some metaphors and similes are fuller than others. Often a single word creates a metaphorical context. Shakespeare's word *tell* in line 10 of Sonnet 30, for example, indicates a counting of past sorrows just as a bank teller counts ("tells") money. In Burns's "A Red, Red Rose," the speaker declares that roses are "newly sprung in June," in this way focusing on the association of his sweetheart with fertility and growth. Sometimes a single word stretches out to incorporate nearby words into a metaphorical system, as in line 4 of Keats's "On First Looking into Chapman's Homer," where Keats uses the word *fealty*. This metaphor refers to the medieval feudal system of land ownership dependent on the permission of a powerful lord or baron. The landholder, who was a person of considerable power, gave a portion of his proceeds to the lord and also provided the lord with military service. This arrangement was called holding the land in *fealty*. Thus Keats's metaphor, which equates writers with landholders and Apollo as the principal lord, states that writers derive their literary power from God.

EXPLANATORY NOTES AND DICTIONARIES

Often a full response to metaphors and similes is not easy at first reading. You can deepen your understanding, however, if you use your time and ingenuity, and also if you use explanatory notes (if they are available), or a dictionary, to clarify passages. Thus, in Shakespeare's line "And heavily from woe to woe tell o'er," the meaning of the word *tell* has been replaced in today's usage (it commonly means *to speak* or *to relate*), and you may therefore miss its metaphorical meaning unless you consult an explanatory note or a dictionary. Similarly, you will need an explanation of *fealty*, such as the one above, or *demesne*, from Keats's "On First Looking into Chapman's Homer." So be alert. Do not ignore explanatory notes, and use your dictionary freely. Allow the similes and metaphors to resonate in your mind. Try tentative solutions and possibilities, and, if these do not help you with the sense, reject them. Keep trying, however, until you have a satisfactory understanding.

WRITING ABOUT METAPHOR AND SIMILE

When you undertake your study, you will need to note those places in your work where you find metaphors or similes. Similes are easier to recognize than metaphors, because of the *like* or *as* with which they usually begin. Metaphors are recognizable because of the transference of the subject or vehicle to the actual meaning or tenor. If the subject is memory, for example, but the poem speaks of law courts, you are looking at a metaphor.

Once you have identified the figures, try to answer questions such as these: What metaphors or similes does the work contain? How extensive are they? Are they contained by a single word, or are they more fully detailed? What ideas and values do the figures signify—what impressions of experience, what attitudes? How do the figures convey and underscore the work's thought and development? What relationships can you find among the metaphors and similes, if any (such as the judicial and financial relationships in Shakespeare's Sonnet 30)? How are the similes or metaphors related to the structure of the work?

Introduction

In determining your central idea you should relate the quality of the figures to the general nature of the work. Thus, metaphors and similes of suffering might be appropriate to a religious, redemptive work, while those of sunshine and cheer might be right for a romantic one. If there is any discrepancy between the metaphorical language and the topic material, think of using this contrast as your central idea. For example, suppose that love is the topic of the work but that the metaphorical language refers to darkness and cold: What would the writer be saying about the situation of the lovers? You should also justify any claims that you make about similes or metaphors. A simile in Coleridge's "Kubla Khan," for example, compares a "mighty fountain" with the sounds of "fast thick pants" of the earth itself. How is this simile to be taken? As a reference to the animality of the earth? As a suggestion that the fountain, and the earth, are dangerous? Or simply as a comparison suggesting immense, forceful noise? How do you explain the answer or answers you select? Your introduction is the place to establish ideas and justifications of this sort. Once you have determined your central idea, you should determine the major points of your thesis sentence.

Body

There are a number of approaches for discussing simile and metaphor. They are not mutually exclusive, and you may combine them as you wish. In fact, your essay will most likely touch on most of the following classifications.

1. THE MEANING AND EFFECT OF THE FIGURES. This approach is direct, requiring that you explain your interpretation of the various metaphors and similes, and also that you introduce necessary references and allusions to make your explanations fully meaningful. In stanza 2 of "A Valediction: Forbidding Mourning," for example, Donne introduces a metaphor equating the condition of love with the hierarchical structure of the church:

'Twere profanation of our joys
  To tell the laity our love.

Here Donne describes the private and mystical relationship of two lovers, drawing the metaphor from the religious tradition that explaining religious mysteries is a desecration. His idea is that love is rare, heaven-sent, private, privileged, and so fragile that telling the world about it would injure it.

2. THE FRAMES OF REFERENCE OF THE FIGURES AND THEIR APPROPRIATENESS TO THE SUBJECT MATTER. Here you locate and classify the sources and types of the figures, and you also determine the appropriateness of the references to the subject matter. The study topics are similar to those for considering imagery: Does the writer favor figures from nature, science, warfare, politics, business, reading, or from anywhere else? Why? Are these references right, given the subject? For example, Shakespeare in Sonnet 30, as we have seen, expands a metaphor equating personal reverie with courtroom proceedings. Because such proceedings are public and methodical, while personal self-evaluation is private and relatively unplanned, how appropriate is the metaphor? Does Shakespeare make it seem right as he develops it in the poem? How?

3. THE INTERESTS / SENSIBILITIES OF THE WRITER. This approach is like the one we just discussed, but the emphasis here is on what the writer's selectivity might show about his or her vision and interests. Begin by listing the figures and their sources, but then raise and try to answer questions like the following: Does the writer use figures derived from one sense rather than another (i.e., sight, hearing, taste, smell, touch)? Does he or she record color, brightness, shadow, shape, depth, height, number, size, slowness, speed, emptiness, fullness, richness, drabness? Has the writer relied on the associations of figures of sense? Do metaphors and similes referring to green plants and trees, to red roses, or to rich fabrics, for example, suggest that life is full and beautiful, or do references to touch suggest amorous warmth? This approach is designed to help you draw whatever conclusions you can about the author's—or the speaker's—taste or sensibility as a result of your study.

4. THE INTERACTIONS OF METAPHORS AND SIMILES. The presupposition of this approach is that each literary work is unified and organically whole so that each part is closely related to every other part. Usually it is best to pick a simile or metaphor from the beginning of the work and then determine how this figure influences your perception of the rest of the work. In this sort of analysis, you consider the relationship of part to parts, and part to whole. The beginning of Donne's "A Valediction: Forbidding Mourning," for example, contains a simile that compares the quiet dying of "virtuous men" to the speaker's taking a trip away from his woman friend. What is the effect of this comparison upon the rest of the poem? To help you in approaching such a question, you might suppose something quite different, say in this instance the violent death of a condemned criminal, or the slaughter of a domestic animal. Such suppositions, out of place and inappropriate as they would obviously be in Donne's poem, may help you in seeing and then explaining what is actually there in the work you are analyzing.

Conclusion

In your conclusion you might summarize your main points, describe your general impressions, try to describe the impact of the figures, indicate your personal responses, or show what might further be done along the lines you have been developing in the body. If you know of comparable or contrasting figures in other works by the same writer or by other writers, you might briefly consider these other sources and the light they shed on your present analysis.

Sample Theme

A Study of Shakespeare's Metaphors in Sonnet 30

When to the sessions of sweet silent thought,
I summon up remembrance of things past,
I sigh the lack of many a thing I sought,
And with old woes new wail my dear time's waste:
Then I can drown an eye (un-used to flow)   5
For precious friends hid in death's dateless night,
And weep afresh love's long since cancelled woe,
And moan th' expense of many a vanished sight.
Then can I grieve at grievances foregone,
And heavily from woe to woe tell o'er   10
The sad account of fore-bemoaned moan,
Which I new pay, as if not paid before.
　　　But if the while I think on thee (dear friend)
　　　All losses are restored, and sorrows end.

[1]　　In this sonnet Shakespeare's speaker describes the sadness and regret of remembered experience, but he states that such sadness may be overcome by the thought of a friend. Shakespeare gets his ideas across not by direct statement, however, but rather by metaphors, which enlarge private, personal concerns to areas of public activity. The metaphors are unusual and clever; in fact, a first response is that they seem too clever for the seriousness of the speaker's personal revelation. How, for example, can a person's memories be the same as stored financial accounts? But on consideration the metaphors are not just clever, but also correct, bold, and revealing. Through them, Shake-

[1] speare creates new and fresh ways of seeing personal life.° His metaphors are drawn from the worlds of law courts, investment, and accounting.▫

[2] The courtroom metaphor of the first four lines shows that memories of past experience are constantly present and influential. Like a judge commanding defendants to appear in court, the speaker "summon[s]" his memory of "things past" to appear on trial before him (line 2). This metaphor suggests that people are their own judges and that their ideals and morals are like laws by which they try themselves. The speaker finds himself guilty of wasting his past life. Removing himself from the strict punishment that a real judge might require, he does not condemn himself for his "dear time's waste," but instead laments it (line 4). The metaphor thus indicates that a person's consciousness is made up just as much of self-doubt and reproach as by more positive influences.

[3] With the closely related reference of investment in the next four lines, Shakespeare shows that living is also expenditure. According to the investment metaphor, life requires commitments to others, and also the spending of emotions. Love is one of life's major transactions, requiring a final payment penalty of weeping and "woe" when it is "cancelled" (line 7), and this fee must be repaid whenever that finished affair is remembered. One's friends also require emotional investment, and when they die, the speaker suggests that their loss is a contract with no terminating date ("dateless night"). Equally, the general passage of time, with all its experiences ("many a vanished sight"), causes the speaker to "moan" because he had gone to great "expense" for them (line 8).

Like the investment metaphor, the metaphor of accounting in the next four lines emphasizes that emotional reverses, or "grievances," are never over. Past grievances—sorrows, losses, regrets, disturbances, offenses, angers— are a part of memory, and calling them to mind is accompanied by a renewal of grief. The quatrain is quite effective:

> Then can I grieve at grievances foregone,
> And heavily from woe to woe tell o'er
[4]
> The sad account of fore-bemoaned moan,
> Which I new pay, as if not paid before.

Thus the speaker states that he counts out moans of anguish, and with them pays the bills for his past woes, just as an accountant counts, or _tells_, money. The tenor of the metaphor is that regret accompanies the memory of past mistakes forever, so that the speaker must pay again with "new" woe the accounts that he has already paid with past woe. In effect, this metaphor of payment indicates that memory puts human beings in lifelong double jeopardy.

[5] The legal and financial metaphors combine in the last two lines to show how present happiness overcomes past regrets. The "dear friend" of these lines has the resources (financial) to settle all the emotional judgments that the speaker as a self-judge has made against himself (legal). It is as though the friend is a rich patron who rescues him from emotional bankruptcy (legal and financial) and the possible doom resulting from the sentence (legal) of emotional misery and depression.

In these metaphors, therefore, Shakespeare's references are drawn from everyday legal and business actions, but his use of them is creative, unusual,

---

° Central idea
▫ Thesis sentence

and excellent. In particular, the idea of line 8 ("And moan th' expense of many a vanished sight") stresses that people spend much emotional energy on others. Without such personal commitment, one cannot have precious friends and [6] loved ones. In keeping with this metaphor of money and investment, one could measure life not in months or years, but in the spending of involvement and emotion with other people. Shakespeare, by inviting readers to explore the values brought out by his metaphors, gives new insights into the nature and value of life.

COMMENTARY ON THE THEME

This theme treats the three classes of metaphors that Shakespeare introduces in Sonnet 30. It thus illustrates the second approach, described on page 124. But the aim of the discussion is not to explore the extent and nature of the comparison between the metaphors and the personal situations in the sonnet. Instead the goal is to explain how the metaphors develop Shakespeare's meaning. This method therefore also illustrates the first approach (pp. 123–24).

Throughout, transitions from one topic to the next are brought about by linking words in the topic sentences. In paragraph 3, for example, the words "closely related" and "next four lines" move the reader from paragraph 2 to the new content. In paragraph 4, the words effecting the transition are "like the investment metaphor" and "the next four lines." The opening sentence of paragraph 5 refers collectively to the subjects of paragraphs 2, 3, and 4, thereby relating them to the new topic of paragraph 5.

(For a close look at the introductory paragraph, see below.) Paragraph 2 deals with the meaning of Shakespeare's courtroom metaphor. His investment metaphor is explained in paragraph 3. Paragraph 4 considers the accounting and money-handling figure. The fifth paragraph shows how Shakespeare's last two lines bring together the general strands of metaphor. The conclusion comments on the creativity of Shakespeare's metaphors, and it also further explains how the investment metaphor leads toward an increased understanding and valuation of life.

A Close Look at Paragraph 1

The primary objective of this paragraph, as in all introductions, is to include a brief general description of the work together with a brief specific description of the theme's topic, and also to express the central idea and the thesis sentence. Of particular note is that Shakespeare's metaphors are introduced in relation to the issue of their possibly being overly clever and farfetched, and, as a result, inappropriate. This issue is raised as a concession to be dealt with. From it, the assertion is presented that the metaphors, because they lead to new and fresh insights, serve the purpose of metaphors and thus are appropriate. Once this argument is established, the central idea and thesis sentence follow naturally. The introductory paragraph hence brings out all the necessary topics and issues to be considered in the body of the theme itself.

chapter 10

Writing About Symbolism and Allegory:
Keys to Extended Meaning

Like metaphors and smilies, symbolism and allegory are modes of expression designed to extend and expand meaning.

SYMBOLISM

Symbolism is derived from a Greek word meaning "to throw together" (*syn*, together, and *ballein*, to throw). In literature, a symbol pulls or draws together (1) a specific thing with (2) ideas, values, persons, or ways of life, into a direct relationship that normally would not be apparent. A symbol might also be regarded as a *substitute* for the elements being signified, much as the flag stands for the ideals of the nation.

In a literary work, whether story, drama, or poem, a symbol is usually a person, thing, place, action, group, art work, or situation. It has its own independent identity, and may function at an ordinary level of reality within a work. There is often a close relationship between the symbol and the things it stands for, but a symbol may also have no apparent connection. What is important, however, is that symbols point beyond their surface identity toward greater subtleties and complexities.

To test whether something is a symbol, you need to judge whether it consistently refers beyond itself to a significant idea, emotion, or quality. For example, the ancient mythological character *Sisyphus* is a symbol. According to Greek mythology, he is doomed in the underworld to roll a large boulder up a hill forever. Every time he gets it to the top, it rolls down, and then he is fated to roll it up again, and again, and again. His plight has been seen to symbolize the human condition: A person rarely if ever completes anything. Work must always be done over and over from day to day and from generation to generation, and the same problems confront humanity in each age. Because of such fruitless effort, life seems to have little or no meaning. Nevertheless, there is hope. People who meet frustration like that of Sisyphus stay involved and active, and even if they are only temporarily successful, their *work* makes their lives meaningful. A writer using Sisyphus as a symbol would want us to understand these ideas as a result of the reference. Symbolism, as you can see, is a shorthand form of communication.

Universal Symbols

Many symbols, like the myth of Sisyphus, are generally or universally recognized and are therefore termed **cultural** or **universal.** They embody ideas and emotions that writers and readers share as heirs of the same historical and cultural history. When using these symbols, a writer does not need to spend time investing people or objects with symbolic resonance within the work. The writer can assume that readers already know what the symbol represents. Thus ordinary water, the substance in the sacrament of baptism, is a recognized symbol of life. When clear water spouts up in a fountain, it symbolizes optimism (as upwelling, bubbling life). A stagnant pool symbolizes the pollution and diminution of life. In terms of psychology, water is also understood as a symbol of sexuality. Thus, lovers may meet by a quiet lake, a cascading waterfall, a murmuring stream, a wide river, or a stormy sea. The condition of the water in each instance may symbolize their romantic relationship. Another generally recognized symbol is the serpent, which represents the Devil, or Satan, or simply evil. This symbol is derived from the Book of Genesis (3:1–7), where Satan in the form of a serpent tempts Eve in the Garden of Eden. Drawing on this story, Hawthorne in "Young Goodman Brown" describes a walking staff that "bore the likeness of a great black snake," in this way instantly evoking the idea of Satanic evil. However, because the staff "might also be seen to twist and wriggle itself like a living serpent," it may also symbolize human tendencies to see evil where it does not exist.

Contextual Symbols

Objects and descriptions that are not universal symbols can be termed symbols only if they are made so within individual works. These types of symbols are **private, authorial,** or **contextual.** Unlike universal symbols, these are not derived from a common cultural, historical, or religious heritage, but rather gain their symbolic meaning within the context of a specific work. For example, the standing clock in the black and red room in Poe's "The Masque of the Red Death" (pp. 311–15) is used to symbolize not only the passage of time but the sinister forces of death. Another contextual symbol is the word *pattern* in Amy Lowell's poem "Patterns" (pp. 347–50). There it is made clear that patterns symbolize not only confining and stultifying cultural expectations, but the destructiveness of warfare. You should note again that symbolism of this sort applies *only within the context of an individual work*. If you were to encounter references to a standing clock or patterns in a context other than "The Masque of the Red Death" and "Patterns," they would not be symbolic unless they were invested with symbolic meaning by the authors of the other works.

Determining What Is Symbolic

In determining whether a particular object, action, or character is a symbol, you need to judge the importance the author gives to it. If the thing appears particularly prominent and also maintains a constancy of meaning, you may justify interpreting it as a symbol. For example, Miss Brill's furpiece in Mansfield's "Miss Brill" is shabby and moth-eaten. It has no value. But because Mansfield makes it specially important at both the beginning and ending of the story, it contextually symbolizes Miss Brill's poverty and isolation. At the end of Welty's "A Worn Path," Phoenix, the major character, plans to spend all her money for a toy windmill for her sick grandson. Readers may conclude that the windmill is small and will break soon, like her life and that of her grandson, but she wants to give the boy a little pleasure despite their poverty and general hopelessness. For these reasons it is a contextual or authorial symbol of her strong character, generous nature, and pathetic existence.

ALLEGORY

An **allegory** is like a symbol in that both use one thing to refer to something else. The term is derived from the Greek word *allegorein*, which means "to speak so as to imply other than what is said." Allegory, however, is more sustained than symbolism. An allegory is to a symbol as a motion picture is to a still picture. In form, an allegory is a complete and self-sufficient narrative, but it also signifies another series of events or conditions. While some works are allegories from beginning to end, many works that are not allegories may nevertheless contain brief sections or episodes that are allegorical.

Allegories and the allegorical method do not exist simply to enable authors to engage in literary exercises. Rather, thinkers and writers have concluded almost from the beginning of human existence that readers learn and memorize stories more easily than moral lessons. In addition, thought and expression have not always been free: The threat of censorship and reprisal has sometimes caused authors to express their views indirectly in the form of allegory rather than to write directly and risk being accused of libel or being subject to personal or political attack. The double meaning of many allegories is hence based in both need and reality.

Determining the Nature and Application of Allegory

As you study a work for allegory, you should determine how either an entire narrative or a brief episode may be construed as having an extended, allegorical meaning. The popularity of George Lucas's film *Star Wars* and its sequels, for example, is attributable at least partly to its being an allegory about the conflict between good and evil. Obi Wan Kenobi (intelligence) enlists the aid of Luke Skywalker (heroism, boldness) and instructs him in "the force" (moral or religious faith). Thus armed and guided, Skywalker opposes the powers of Darth Vader (evil) to rescue the Princess Leia (purity and goodness) with the aid of the latest spaceship and weaponry (technology). The story is accompanied by ingenious visual effects and almost tactile sound effects and music, and hence as an adventure film it stands by itself. With the obvious allegorical overtones, however, it stands for any person's quest for self-fulfillment.

To apply a part of the allegory more specifically, let us consider that the evil Vader is so strong that he imprisons Skywalker for a time, and Skywalker must exert all his skill and strength to get free and overcome Vader. In the allegorical application of the episode, this temporary imprisonment signifies those moments of doubt, discouragement, and depression that people experience while trying to better themselves through education, work, self-improvement, friendship, and marriage.

Almost from the beginning of recorded literature, similar heroic deeds have been represented in allegorical forms. From ancient Greece, the allegorical hero Jason sails the ship *Argo* to distant lands to gain the golden fleece (those who take risks are rewarded). Another such figure is Bellerophon, who rides the winged horse Pegasus to destroy the monster Chimera (both real and imagined fears can be overcome if they are confronted and attacked). From Anglo-Saxon England, the hero Beowulf saves the kingdom by killing Grendel and his monstrous mother (victory comes to those who rely on the forces of good). From seventeenth-century England, Bunyan's *Pilgrim's Progress* tells how the hero Christian overcomes difficulties and temptations to reach the Heavenly City (belief, perseverance, and resistance to temptation will save the faithful). As long as the parallel interconnections are close and consistent, like those mentioned here, an extended allegorical interpretation has validity.

FABLE, PARABLE, AND MYTH

Three additional forms that are close to allegory, but are special types, are **fable, parable,** and **myth.**

FABLE. The **fable** is an old and popular form. It is usually quite short and often features animals with human traits (these are called **beast fables**); writers and editors attach "morals" or explanations to these stories. Aesop (sixth century B.C.E.) was supposedly a slave who composed fables in ancient Greece. His fable of "The Fox and the Grapes," for example, signifies the trait of belittling things we cannot have. More recent contributions to the fable tradition are Walt Disney's "Mickey Mouse" and Walt Kelly's "Pogo."

PARABLE. The **parable** is a short, simple allegory with a moral or religious bent. Parables are often associated with Jesus, who used them to embody his own religious insights and truths. His parables of the Good Samaritan and the Prodigal Son, for example, are interpreted to show God's love, concern, understanding, and forgiveness.

MYTH. A **myth** is a story, like the myth of Sisyphus, that is associated with the religion, philosophy, and collective psychology of various societies or cultures. Myths embody truths for prescientific societies and codify the social and cultural values of the civilization in which they are composed. Sometimes, unfortunately, the words *myth* and *mythical* are used to mean "fanciful" or "untrue." This minimizing reflects a limited understanding of the psychological, philosophical, and scientific truths embedded in myths. In fact, the truths of mythology are not to be found literally in the stories themselves, but rather in their symbolic or allegorical interpretations.

ALLUSION IN SYMBOLISM AND ALLEGORY

Universal or cultural symbols and allegories often allude to other works from our cultural heritage, such as the Bible, ancient history and literature, and works of the British and American traditions. Sometimes understanding a work may require knowledge of politics and current events. For example, a major character in Hawthorne's "Young Goodman Brown" is Brown's wife, Faith, who stays at home when he leaves to go on his journey. Later, in the forest, when Brown is seeing his vision of sinful human beings, he exclaims, "My Faith is gone" (paragraph 50). On the realistic level, this statement makes sense, because Brown has concluded that his wife is lost. However, the symbol of his being married to Faith takes on additional meaning when one notes that it is also an allusion to the Biblical Book of Ephesians (2:8), and to the Pauline and Protestant-Calvinist tradition that faith is a key to salvation:

> For by grace you have been saved through faith; and this is not your own doing, it is the gift of God—

This Biblical passage might easily take a volume of explication, but in brief the allusion makes clear that the loss of faith also symbolizes the loss of God's grace. Here is an instance where a symbol gains meaning because of allusion.

This example brings up the issue of how to detect allusions. You can often rely on your own knowledge, but equally often you will need a dictionary or other reference work. The scope of your college dictionary will surprise you. If you cannot find an entry there, however, try one of the major encyclopedias, or ask your reference librarian, who can direct you to shelves loaded with helpful books. A few standard guides are *The Oxford Companion to English Literature, The Oxford Companion to Classical Literature,* and William Rose Benet's *The Reader's Encyclopedia.* A useful aid in finding Biblical references is *Cruden's Complete Concordance,* which in various editions has been used by readers since 1737. This work lists all the major words used in the King James Bible so that you may easily locate the chapter and verse of any Biblical quotation. If you still have trouble using sources like those, see your instructor.

WRITING ABOUT SYMBOLISM AND ALLEGORY

SYMBOLS. Take careful notes, and, in the light of whatever equivalent parallels you find, determine the use of symbols. A helpful aid is to make two-column, parallel lists to show how qualities of the symbol may be lined up with qualities of a character or action. Such a list can give you many details for your essay, and it can also help you in thinking more deeply about the effectiveness of the symbol. Here is such a list for the symbol of the toy windmill in Welty's "A Worn Path":

Qualities in the Windmill	Comparable Qualities in Phoenix and Her Life
1. Cheap	1. Poor, but she gives all she has for the windmill

2. Breakable   2. Old, and not far from death
3. A gift   3. Generous
4. Not practical   4. Needs relief from reality.
5. Colorful   5. Needs something new and cheerful

ALLEGORY.   An aid for figuring out an allegory or allegorical passage can work well with a diagram of parallel lines or boxes. You can place corresponding characters, actions, things, or ideas along these lines as following (using the film *Star Wars* as the specimen work):

STAR WARS

Luke Skywalker	Obi Wan Kenobi	Darth Vader	Princess Leia	Capture	Escape, and defeat of Vader

ALLEGORICAL APPLICATION TO MORALITY AND FAITH

Forces of good	Education and faith	Forces of evil	Object to be saved, ideals to be rescued and restored	Doubt, spiritual negligence	Restoration of faith

ALLEGORICAL APPLICATION TO PERSONAL AND GENERAL CONCERNS

Individual in pursuit of goals	The means by which goals may be reached	Obstacles to be overcome	Occupation, happiness, goals	Temporary failure, depression, discouragement, disappointment	Success

Once you have developed materials from your notes augmented by aids like these, develop your central idea and supporting details. A good way is to begin with a general idea about the work and then determine whether supporting details may be construed as symbols. A general idea about "Young Goodman Brown," for example, is that the acceptance of fanatic ideas darkens and limits the human soul. An early incident in the story may be used as a symbol of this idea. Specifically, when Goodman Brown enters the woods, he resolves "to stand firm against the devil," and he then looks up "to heaven above." As he looks, a "black mass of cloud" appears to hide the "brightening stars." Within the limits of our central idea, the cloud may be seen as a symbol, just like the widening path or the night walk itself. As long as you make solid connections in this way, your symbolic ascriptions will be acceptable.

Also, for your theme development you will need to prepare justifications for your symbols or allegorical parallels. In "The Masque of the Red Death," for example, Prince Prospero's seemingly impregnable "castelated abbey" is a line of defense against the plague raging the countryside. But the Red Death personified easily invades the castle and conquers Prospero and his misguided guests. In treating the abbey as a symbol, it would be important for you to demonstrate its possible applicability to measures that people take (medicine, escapist activity, etc.) to keep death distant and remote from concern. In the same way, in an allegorical treatment of "Young Goodman Brown," you would need to establish a connecting link like the following: that people lose their ideals and forsake their principles not because they are evil, but because they misperceive and misunderstand the events and people around them.

Introduction

The introduction should establish the grounds for your discussion. There may be a recurring symbol, for example, or a regular symbolic pattern. Or there may be actions with allegorical applications. Your discussion should determine such characteristics. The central idea will refer to the nature of the symbols or allegory, like Miss Brill's opening and closing of the box for her shabby furpiece, the darkness in "Young Goodman Brown," or the freezing cold in Glaspell's *Trifles*. The thesis sentence will determine the topics for the body. These topics may be presented as specific things, like the guide's walking staff or Minnie Wright's broken preserve jars, or to classes or groups of symbols, like "regenerative symbols" or symbols of death.

Body

There are a number of approaches for discussing symbolism and allegory. You might use one exclusively, or a combination. If you choose symbols and symbolism, you might consider the following:

1. THE MEANING OF A MAJOR SYMBOL. Here you interpret the symbol and what it stands for. Answer questions like these: Is the symbol contextual or universal? How do you decide? How do you derive your interpretation of the symbolic meaning? What is the extent of the meaning? Does the symbol undergo modification or new applications if it reappears? How does the symbol affect your understanding of the total work? Does the symbol bring out any ironies? How does the symbol add strength and depth to the work?

2. THE DEVELOPMENT AND RELATIONSHIP OF SYMBOLS. For two or more symbols: Do the symbols have a connection or common bond (like night and the cloud in "Young Goodman Brown")? What is this bond? Do they develop additional meanings? Do they suggest a unified reading or a contradictory one (like the windmill and the medicine in "A Worn Path," which suggest cheer and hopelessness)? Do the symbols control the form of the work? How? For example, the horse Toby in Chekhov's *The Bear* symbolizes Mrs. Popov's shifting attitudes that govern the shape of the play. The symbol of the snowy field in Frost's "Desert Places" becomes a dual symbol as the poem unfolds, referring to bleakness both of soul and of landscape. The star of Keats's "Bright Star" is a symbol governing the movement of ideas from personal integrity to love. Other questions are whether the symbols fit naturally or artificially into the context of the work, and whether and how the writer's symbols make for unique qualities or excellences.

If you write about allegory, you might use one of the following approaches:

1. THE APPLICATION AND MEANING OF THE ALLEGORY. Does the allegory (fable, parable, myth) refer to anyone or anything specific? How may it be more generally applied to ideas or qualities of human character, not only of its own time but of our own? Does it illustrate, either closely or loosely, particular philosophies or religious views? If so, what are these? How do you know? If the allegory seems outdated, how much can be salvaged for people today?

2. THE CONSISTENCY OF THE ALLEGORY. Is the allegory used consistently throughout the work, or is it intermittent? Explain and detail this use. Would it be correct to call your work *allegorical* rather than an *allegory*? Can you determine how parts of the work are introduced for their allegorical importance, such as the natural obstacles in the woods in Welty's "A Worn Path," which are allegorical equivalents of life's difficulties; or as the entertainment scene in "The Masque of the Red Death," which corresponds to the ways by which people try to avoid the realities of disease and death.

Conclusion

You might summarize main points, describe general impressions, explain the impact of the symbolic or allegorical methods, indicate personal responses, or suggest further lines of thought and application. You might also assess the quality and appropriateness of the symbolism or allegory (such as the opening of "Young Goodman Brown" being in darkness, with the closing in gloom).

Sample Theme

Allegory and Symbolism in Hawthorne's "Young Goodman Brown" *

[1]
It is hard to read beyond the third paragraph of Nathaniel Hawthorne's "Young Goodman Brown" without finding allegory and symbolism. The opening at first seems realistic—Goodman Brown, a young Puritan, leaves his home in colonial Salem to take an overnight trip. His wife's name, "Faith," however, suggests a symbolic reading, and as soon as Brown goes into the forest, his journey becomes an allegorical trip into evil. The idea that Hawthorne shows by this trip is that rigid belief destroys the best human qualities.° He develops this thought in the allegory and in many symbols, particularly the sunset, the walking-stick, and the path.▫

[2]
The allegory is about how people develop destructive ideas. Most of the story is dreamlike and unreal, and the ideas that Brown gains are also unreal. At the weird "witch meeting" in the dream forest, he becomes persuaded that everyone he knows is sinful, and he then permits mistrust and loathing to distort his previous love for his wife and neighbors. As a result, the rest of his life is harsh and gloomy. That Hawthorne locates the story in colonial Salem village indicates that his allegorical target is the overly zealous pursuit of religious principles which dwell on sinfulness rather than on love. However, modern readers may also apply the allegory to the ways in which people uncritically accept *any* ideal (most often political loyalties or racial or national prejudices), and thereby reject the individuality, rights, and integrity of others. If people like Brown apply a rigid standard, they can condemn anyone, particularly if they never try to understand those they condemn. In this way, Hawthorne's allegory applies to any narrow-minded acceptance of ideals or systems that exclude the importance of forgiveness and love.

[3]
Hawthorne's attack on such dehumanizing belief is found not just in the allegory, but also in his many symbols. For example, the seventh word in the story, "sunset," may be taken as a symbol. In reality, sunset merely indicates the end of day. Coming at the beginning of the story, however, it suggests that Goodman Brown is beginning his long night of hatred, his spiritual death. For him the night will never end, because his final days are shrouded in "gloom" (paragraph 72).

[4]
The next symbol, the guide's walking-stick or staff, suggests the arbitrariness of the standard by which Brown judges his neighbors. Hawthorne's description indicates the symbolic nature of this staff:

> . . . the only thing about him [the guide] that could be fixed upon as remarkable, was his staff, which bore the likeness of a great black snake, curiously wrought, that it might almost be seen to twist and

---

* For the text of this story, See Appendix C, pages 302–11.
° Central idea
▫ Thesis sentence

wriggle itself like a living serpent. This, of course, must have been an ocular deception, assisted by the uncertain light. (paragraph 13)

[4] The serpent symbolically suggests Satan, who in Genesis (3:1–7) is the originator of all evil, but the phrase "ocular deception" creates an interesting and realistic ambiguity about the symbol. Since the perception of the snake may depend on nothing more than the "uncertain" light, the staff may be less symbolic of evil than of the human tendency to find evil where it does not exist (and could the light itself symbolize the tentative, temporary condition of all human knowledge?).

[5] In the same vein, the path through the forest is a major symbol of the destructive mental confusion that overcomes Brown. As he walks, the path grows "wilder and drearier, and more faintly traced," and "at length" it vanishes (paragraph 50). This is like the Biblical description of the "broad" way that leads "to Destruction" (Matthew 7:13). As a symbol, the path shows that most human acts are bad, while a small number, like the "narrow" way to life (Matthew 7:14), are good. Goodman Brown's path is at first clear, as though sin is at first unique and unusual. Soon, however, it is so indistinct that he can see only sin wherever he turns. The symbol suggests that, as people follow evil, their moral vision becomes blurred and they cannot choose the right way even if it is in front of them, and they soon fall prey to "the instinct that guides mortal man to evil" (paragraph 50).

[6] Through Hawthorne's allegory and symbols, then, "Young Goodman Brown" presents the paradox of how outwardly noble beliefs can backfire destructively. Goodman Brown dies in gloom because he believes that his wrong vision is real. This form of evil is the hardest to stop, because wrongdoers who are convinced of their own goodness are beyond reach. In view of such self-righteous evil, whether cloaked in the apparent virtues of Puritanism or some other blindly rigorous doctrine (political as well as religious), Hawthorne writes that "the fiend in his own shape is less hideous than when he rages in the breast of man" (paragraph 53). Young Goodman Brown thus is the central symbol of the story. He is one of those who walk in darkness while thinking that they are bathed in the brightest of light.

COMMENTARY ON THE THEME

The introduction justifies the treatment of allegory and symbolism on the grounds that Hawthorne early in the story invites such a reading. The central idea relates Hawthorne's method to the idea that rigid belief destroys the best human qualities. The thesis sentence outlines two major areas of discussion: (1) allegory, and (2) symbolism.

Paragraph 2 considers the allegory as a criticism of rigid Puritan morality. Paragraphs 3, 4, and 5 deal with three major symbols: sunset, the staff, and the path. The aim of this discussion is to show the meaning and applicability of these symbols to Hawthorne's attack on unquestioning belief. Throughout these three paragraphs the central idea—the relationship of rigidity to destructiveness—is stressed. Hawthorne's allusions to both the Old and New Testaments are pointed out in paragraphs 4 and 5. The last paragraph raises questions leading to the conclusion that Brown himself symbolizes Hawthorne's idea that the primary cause of evil is the inability to separate reality from unreality.

A Close Look at Paragraph 2

This paragraph briefly treats the allegory of "Young Goodman Brown" in three major steps. The first is a three-sentence recapitulation designed not as a summary but rather as a reflection of the story's major thrust. The second step moves to Hawthorne's primary parallel topic (seventeenth-century religious rigorism as symbolized by the village of Salem, where, we might remember, young women were hanged for witchcraft), which is also his target. This second phase of the paragraphs fulfills two purposes: (a) the application of the allegory, and (b) an explanation of why Hawthorne chooses to make the story so clearly allegorical. With the primary allegorical meaning thus established, the paragraph concludes with a more general and current application (the uncritical and dehumanizing acceptance of any fanatic system). The major thread running through each of the major parts of the paragraph is the hurtful effect of monomaniacal views like those of Brown.

Should you be discussing any work as allegory, this paragraph's structure would be useful as a guide either for a single paragraph or, as expanded, for an entire theme. If "Young Goodman Brown" were to be considered further as an allegory, for example, additional topics might be Brown's gullibility, the meaning of Faith and the requirements for maintaining it, and the causes for preferring to think evil rather than good of other people. The point is that the more extensive the analysis of any allegory, the more separate points may be explored.

chapter 11

Writing About Tone:
The Writer's Control
over Attitudes and Feelings

Tone refers to the methods by which writers and speakers reveal attitudes or feelings. Tone may be perceived in everything spoken and written, such as earnest declarations of love, requests to pass a dish at dinner, or letters from government offices threatening penalties if certain fines are not paid. Often tone is confused with attitude, and it is therefore important to realize that tone refers not to attitudes themselves but rather those techniques and modes of presentation that *reveal* or *create* attitudes.

LITERARY TONE AND SPEAKING TONE OF VOICE

In literary study the word *tone* is borrowed from the phrase *tone of voice* in speech. Tone of voice reflects attitudes toward a particular thing or situation and also toward listeners. Let us suppose that Mary has a difficult assignment, on which she expects to work all day. Things go well, and she finishes quickly. She happily tells her friend Anne, "I'm so pleased. I needed only two hours for that." Then she decides to buy tickets for a popular play, and must wait through a long and slow line. After getting her tickets, she tells the people at the end of the line, "I'm so pleased. I needed only two hours for that." The sentences are exactly the same, but by changing her emphasis and vocal inflection, Mary indicates her disgust

141

and impatience with her long wait, and also shows her sympathy with the people still in line. By controlling the *tone* of her statements, in other words, Mary conveys pleasure at one time and indignation and also sympathy at another.

TONE IN LITERATURE

As this example of Mary indicates, an attitude itself may be summarized with a word or phrase (pleasure, indignation; love, contempt; deference, command; persistence, negligence; and so on), but the study of tone is concerned with examining those aspects of situation, language, action, and background that bring out the attitude. In Poe's "The Masque of the Red Death," for example, Prince Prospero declares his outrage at the intruder costumed as the Red Death. His words indicate anger, imperiousness, and intimidation:

> "Who dares"—he demanded hoarsely of the courtiers who stood near him—"who dares insult us with this blasphemous mockery? Seize him and unmask him—that we may know whom we have to hang, at sunrise, from the battlements!" (paragraph 11)

Prospero's words demonstrate his estimate of his own power to command. He is judge, jury, and executioner, and he leaves no opportunity for debate about his rights. In contrast, at the end of "A Worn Path," the attendant offers Phoenix "a few pennies," but Phoenix wants more. Being a recipient of charity, but also being an independent sort, Phoenix makes her request indirectly (paragraph 99):

> "Five pennies is a nickel," said Phoenix stiffly.

This deferential request is not the same as Prince Prospero would make, but it is nevertheless demanding. Though Phoenix is not a literary master, she is a master of tone in this situation.

The tone may be determined similarly in everything you read. Quite often authors wish to be helpfully informative and therefore present descriptions as simply and clearly as possible, as though the words are like clear windows overlooking scenes and situations. When authors decide to communicate special attitudes, they may use specially connotative words, as Keats does in "On First Looking into Chapman's Homer," with the line "Much have I travelled in the realms of gold." He is saying that he has read a good deal of literature, but the expression "realms of gold" indicates his profound admiration for his subject and his wonderment at the things he has read.

Tone Within Works

In pursuing the ways in which tone is embodied within works, you may study the following:

1. THE APPARENT AUTHORIAL ATTITUDE TOWARD THE MATERIAL. An author may indicate an attitude or a number of attitudes toward the material. In the short poem "Anthem for Doomed Youth," for example, Wilfred Owen shows detestation toward war, and sympathy for those whose loved ones have been killed. In the poem "Echo," Christina Rossetti's speaker addresses a lover who is long dead, and by this means Rossetti renders attitudes of yearning and sorrow. In a broader perspective, authors may view human nature with amused affection, as does Chekhov in *The Bear*, or with amused resignation, as does Hardy in "Channel Firing." An important authorial attitude is that of irony, to be considered later (pp. 146–47).

2. INTERNALLY EXPRESSED ATTITUDES. Beyond the general authorial tone, there are many internally expressed attitudes. In effect, a work may have as many tones as there are speakers and situations. The speaker of Lowell's "Patterns," for example, is a prim and proper upper-class young lady. Yet at the news of her fiancé's death, her sorrowful meditation brings out that she had made a promise to him to make love outside, on a "shady seat" in the garden (lines 86–89). This personal confession reveals the inner warmth that her external appearance would never suggest, and it also makes the poem pathetically poignant.

In addition, characters interact, and their tone reflects their judgments about other characters and situations. The brusque young woman in "Miss Brill" compares Miss Brill's fur muff to a "fried whiting," an insult which she makes no attempt to prevent Miss Brill herself from hearing (paragraph 14). Her speech indicates contempt, indifference, and cruelty. A complicated expression of tone occurs in Glaspell's *Trifles*, where the two major characters, Mrs. Hale and Mrs. Peters, decide to cover up the conclusive evidence that Minnie Wright has murdered her husband. Of the two characters, Mrs. Peters has been the slower one to support the cover-up, and to do so she must indicate understanding and support for Minnie. In the speech in which she indicates her support, she does not say any such thing, but rather speaks as she might be expected to speak—of the embarrassment she might feel if she and Mrs. Hale were to reveal the "trifles" to the nearby husbands (paragraph 137):

> My, it's a good thing the men couldn't hear us. Wouldn't they just laugh! Getting all stirred up over a little thing like a—dead canary. As if that could have anything to do with—with—wouldn't they *laugh*!

Notice that neither she nor Mrs. Hale makes any statement violating legal principles. Instead, she takes advantage of her knowledge that men scoff at feminine things, like Minnie's quilting knots, and therefore she openly anticipates the men's amusement. But we know that by these words she has joined Mrs. Hale in sympathizing with Minnie and in hiding the evidence. In addition, Mrs. Peters is also asserting her own independence from the interests of her sheriff-husband, if only to a limited degree. The tone of her speech, in other words, is quite complex.

   3. ATTITUDES TOWARD READERS.   Authors recognize that readers are participants in the creative act and that all elements of a work—word choice, characterization, allusiveness, levels of reality—must take audience response into account. When Hawthorne makes his woodland guide refer to King Philip's War, for example (paragraph 18), he is assuming that his readers will identify that war as having been savagely greedy and cruel. By not explaining this part of history, he indicates respect for the knowledge of his readers, and he also assumes identity with readers by relying on their agreement with his interpretation.

   Authors always make similar considerations about readers, by implicitly complimenting them on their knowledge and also by satisfying their curiosity and desire to be interested, stimulated, and pleased. Keats assumes that readers will concur with his speaker's excitement on discovering Homer's greatness. Coleridge assumes that his readers will savor the mouth-filling words which he uses in "Kubla Khan." Updike assumes that readers will understand that he does not normally speak like Sammy but that he uses Sammy's diction to reveal Sammy as a perceptive and independent but somewhat insecure young man. Hawthorne assumes that readers will understand that Young Goodman Brown's walk to the woods bordering Salem is allegorical and nightmarish, and not realistic. Such textual manifestations of authorial evaluations of readers are vital in the consideration of tone.

LAUGHTER, COMEDY, AND FARCE

A major aspect of tone is laughter and the methods of comedy and farce. Everyone likes to laugh, but not everyone can explain the reasons for laughing. It seems clear that smiles, shared laughter, and good human relationships go together, so that laughter is essential to a person's mental health. Laughter is unplanned, often unpredictable, and sometimes personal and idiosyncratic. It resists close analysis. Despite the difficulty of explaining all the causes of laughter, however, we may note a number of common elements:

   1. *An object to laugh at.* There must be something to laugh at, whether a person, a thing, situation, custom, a habit of speech or dialect, or arrangement of words.

2. *Incongruity*. Human beings normally know what to expect under given conditions, and anything contrary to these expectations is **incongruous** and may therefore generate laughter. When the temperature is 100 F., for example, you expect people to dress lightly. But if you see a person who is dressed in a heavy overcoat, a warm hat, a muffler, and large gloves, and who is waving his arms and stamping his feet to keep warm, this person violates your expectations. Because his garments and behavior are inappropriate or incongruous, you would likely laugh at him. If you hear a standup comedian say, "Yesterday afternoon I was walking down the street and turned into a drugstore," this remark is funny because "turned into" has two incompatible meanings. A student in a language class once wrote of the need for understanding the "congregation of verbs." This inadvertent verbal mistake is called a *malapropism*, after Mrs. Malaprop, a character in Sheridan's eighteenth-century play *The Rivals*. He meant, of course, the "conjugation" of verbs but wrote a word that is more appropriate to people in church than to a grammatical list. The mistake produces laughter, or at least a smile. Incongruity is common to all these laughter-producing examples. In the literary creation of such verbal slips, the tone is directed against the speaker, and both readers and author alike share the enjoyment.

3. *Safety and/or good will*. Seeing a person slipping on a banana peel and hurtling through the air may cause laughter as long as we ourselves are not that person, for laughter depends on insulation from danger and pain. In farce, where much physical abuse takes place (such as falling through trapdoors or being hit in the face by cream pies), the abuse never harms the participants. The incongruity of such situations causes laughter, and one's safety from personal consequences—together with the insulation from pain of the participants—prevents grave or even horrified responses. Good will enters into laughter in romantic comedy or in works where you are drawn into general sympathy with the major figures, such as Smirnov and Mrs. Popov in Chekhov's *The Bear*. Here the infectiousness of laughter and happiness governs your responses. As the author leads the characters toward recognizing their love, your involvement produces happiness, smiles, and even sympathetic laughter.

4. *Unfamiliarity, newness, uniqueness, spontaneity*. Laughter depends on seeing something new or unique, or on experiencing a known thing freshly. Because laughter is prompted by flashes of insight or sudden revelations, the circumstances promoting laughter are always spontaneous. Perhaps you have had someone explain a joke or funny situation, only to find that the explanation doused your chance to laugh. Although spontaneity is most often a quality of the unfamiliar, it is not lost just because a thing is well-known. Indeed, the task of the comic writer is to develop ordinary materials to a point where spontaneity frees readers to laugh. Thus it is possible to read and reread *The Bear* and laugh each time because, even though you know what will happen, the work shapes your responses to the emergence of love out of anger. The love between Mrs. Popov and

Smirnov is and always will be comic because it is so illogical, unexpected, incongruous, and spontaneous.

IRONY

One of the most human traits is the capacity to have two or more attitudes toward someone or something. We know that people are not perfect, but we love a number of them anyway. Therefore we speak to them not only with love and praise, but also with banter and criticism. (And they may choose to inform us, in turn, about our own imperfections.) On occasion, you may have given mildly insulting greeting cards. If you give such cards, you do so expecting to amuse rather than affront your loved ones, for as you share smiles and laughs, you also remind your loved ones of your affection.

The word **irony** describes such situations and expressions by which a writer conveys an idea or attitude by making an opposite or contradictory statement. Irony is natural to human beings who are aware of the ambiguities and complexities in life. It is a function of the realization that life does not always measure up to promise, that friends and loved ones are sometimes angry and bitter toward each other, that the universe contains incomprehensible mysteries, that doubt exists even in the certainty of knowledge and faith, and that human character is built through chagrin, regret, and pain as much as through emulation and praise. In expressing an idea ironically, writers pay the greatest compliment to their readers, for they assume that readers have sufficient skill and understanding to discover the real meaning of quizzical or ambiguous statements and situations.

The Major Types of Irony:
Verbal, Situational, and Dramatic

VERBAL IRONY. **Verbal irony** is a statement in which one thing is said and another is meant. For example, one of the American astronauts was asked how he would feel if all his safety equipment broke down during reentry. He answered, "A thing like that could ruin your whole day." His words would have been appropriate for day-to-day minor mishaps, but since failed safety equipment would cause his death, his answer was ironic (doubly so since the loss in 1986 of the space shuttle *Challenger*). This form of verbal irony is **understatement.** By contrast, **overstatement** or **hyperbole** is deliberate exaggeration for effect, as in "And I will love thee still, my Dear, / Till all the seas go dry" (from Burns's "A Red, Red Rose").

Often verbal irony is ambiguous, having double meaning or **double entendre.** Midway through "Young Goodman Brown," for example, the woodland guide leaves Brown alone while stating, "when you feel like moving again, there is my staff to help you along" (paragraph 41). The word "staff" is ambiguous, for it refers to the staff that has earlier been described to resemble a serpent (paragraph 13). The word therefore suggests that the devilish guide is leaving Brown not only with a real staff, but also with the spirit of evil (unlike the divine "staff" that gives comfort as described in Psalm 23). Ambiguity, of course, may be used in relation to any topic. Quite often double entendre is used in statements about sexuality and love, usually for the amusement of listeners or readers.

SITUATIONAL IRONY AND COSMIC IRONY. **Situational irony**, or **irony of situation**, refers to conditions emphasizing that human beings have little or no control over their lives or anything else. The situation is not temporary, one might add, but permanent and universal. People are enmeshed in circumstances in which their own actions are puny when compared with the forces arrayed against them, as in Hardy's "Channel Firing," which is built on the situation that warfare has been permanent from earliest times to the present. A happier example of situational irony is in Chekhov's *The Bear*, for the two characters shift from anger to love as they fall into the grips of emotions that are "bigger than both of them."

A special kind of situational irony, which emphasizes the pessimistic and fatalistic side of life, is **cosmic irony**, or **irony of fate**. By the standard of cosmic irony, the universe is indifferent to individuals, who are subject to blind chance, accident, uncontrollable emotions, perpetual misfortune, and misery. Even if things temporarily go well, people's lives inevitably end badly, and their best efforts will not rescue them or make them happy. A work illustrating cosmic irony is Glaspell's *Trifles*, which develops out of the stultifying conditions of farm life experienced by Minnie Wright. She has no profession, no other hope, no other life except the lonely, dreary farm—nothing. After 29 years of wretchedness, she buys a canary who warbles for her to make life a little pleasant. But after a year, her boorish and insensitive husband wrings the bird's neck, and she in turn, with her only meager pleasure destroyed, strangles him at night in his bed. She thus illustrates the irony of fate, for she is caught in a hopeless web of circumstance from which there is no constructive escape.

DRAMATIC IRONY. Like cosmic irony, **dramatic irony** is a special kind of situational irony; it applies when a character perceives a situation in a limited way while the audience, and other characters, may see it in greater perspective. The character therefore is able to understand things in only one way while the audience can perceive two ways. The classic example of dramatic irony is *Oedipus Rex* by the ancient Greek dramatist Sophocles. All his life Oedipus has been driven by fate, which he can never escape. As the play draws to its climax and Oedipus believes that he is about to discover the murderer of his father, the audience knows—as he does not—that he is approaching his own self-destruction: As he condemns the murder, he also condemns himself.

WRITING ABOUT TONE

In preparing to write about tone, you will, as always, need to begin with a careful reading. As you study, it is important to note those elements of the work that touch particularly on attitudes or authorial consideration. Thus, for example, you may be studying Hughes's "Theme for English B," where it is necessary to consider the force of the poet's claim for equality. How serious is the claim? Does the speaker's apparent matter-of-factness make him seem less than enthusiastic? Or does this tone indicate that equality is so fundamental a right that its realization should be an everyday part of life? Depending on the work, your devising and answering such questions can help you understand the degree to which authors show control of tone.

Similar questions apply when you study internal qualities such as style and characterization. Do all the speeches seem right for speaker and situation? Are all descriptions appropriate, all actions believable? If the work is comic, does the writer seem to be laughing too? In serious situations, is there evidence of understanding and sympathy? Does the writer ask you to lament the human condition? What kind of character is the speaker? Is he or she intelligent? Friendly? Idealistic? Realistic? Do any words seem unusual or especially noteworthy, such as dialect, polysyllabic words, foreign words or phrases that the author assumes you know, or especially connotative or emotive words?

Introduction

The introduction describes the general situation of the work and its dominant moods or impressions. The central idea should be about the aspect or aspects you will develop, such as that the work leads to cynicism, as in "Channel Firing," or to laughter and delight, as in *The Bear*. Or your central idea might be that the author's diction is designed to portray the life of ordinary people, or to show the pretentiousness of various speakers or characters, or to call on the reader's ability to visualize experience. Problems connected with interpreting the tone should also be mentioned here. The thesis sentence contains the major aspects for the body.

Body

In the body, you should examine all aspects bearing on tone. Some of the things to cover might be these:

1. THE AUDIENCE, SITUATION, AND CHARACTERS. Is any person or group directly addressed by the speaker? What attitude is expressed (love, respect, condescension, confidentiality, confidence, etc.)? What is the basic situation in the work? Do you find irony? If so, what kind is it? What does the irony show (optimism or pessimism, for example)? How is the situation controlled to shape your responses? That is, can actions, situations, or characters be seen as expressions of attitude, or as embodiments of certain favorable or unfavorable ideas or positions? What is the nature of the speaker or persona? Why does the speaker seem to speak exactly as he or she does? How is the speaker's character manipulated to show apparent authorial attitude and to elicit reader response? Does the work promote respect, admiration, dislike, or other feelings about character or situation? How?

2. DESCRIPTIONS, DICTION. Analysis of these is stylistic, but your concern here is to relate style to attitude. Are there any systematic references, such as to colors, sounds, noises, natural scenes, and so on, that collectively reflect an attitude? Do connotative meanings of words control response in any way? Is any special knowledge of references or hard words expected of readers? What is the extent of this knowledge? Do speech or dialect patterns indicate attitudes about speakers or their condition of life? Are speech patterns normal and standard, or slang or substandard? What is the effect of these patterns? Are there unusual or particularly noteworthy expressions? If so, what attitudes do these show? Does the author use verbal irony? To what effect?

3. HUMOR. Is the work funny? How funny, how intense? How is the humor achieved? Does the humor develop out of incongruous situations or language, or both? Is there an underlying basis of attack in the humor, or are the objects of laughter still respected or even loved despite having humor directed against them?

4. IDEAS. Ideas may be advocated, defended mildly, or attacked. What approach to ideas do you have in the work you have been studying? How does the author make his or her attitude clear—directly, by statement, or indirectly, through understatement, overstatement, or the language of a character? In what ways does the work assume a common ground of assent between author and reader? That is, are there apparently common assumptions about religious views, political ideas, moral and behavioral standards, and so on? Are these commonly assumed ideas readily acceptable, or is any concession needed by the reader to approach the work? (For example, a major subject of "Dover Beach" is that absolute belief in the truth of Christianity has been lost. This subject may not be important to everyone, but even an irreligious reader, or a follower of another faith, may find common ground in the poem's psychological situation, or in the desire to learn as much as possible about so important a phenomenon of modern western society.)

5. Unique characteristics.   Each work has unique properties that contribute to the tone. Rossetti's "Echo," for example, considers the speaker's general memory of her dead lover and presents details suggesting the poignancy and despair of her solitude. Hardy's "Channel Firing" develops from the comic idea that the firing of guns at sea is so loud it could awaken the dead. Glaspell's *Trifles* depends on the inquisitiveness and also the feminine understanding of the two women. Without them, we would not learn about Minnie, for their husbands understand nothing about her plight. Be alert for such special circumstances in any work, whether story, poem, or play, and as you plan and develop your theme, try to take these things into account.

Conclusion

The conclusion may summarize your main points and from there go on to any needed redefinitions, explanations, or afterthoughts, together with ideas reinforcing earlier points. If you have changed your mind, or have discovered awakening awareness, a brief account of these thoughts would also be appropriate. Finally, you might mention some other major aspect of the work's tone that you did not develop in the body.

Sample Theme

*The Tone of Confidence in "Theme for English B" by Langston Hughes**

---

[1] "Theme for English B" grows from the situational irony of racial differences. The situation is unequal opportunity, seen from the perspective of a college student from the oppressed race. This situation might easily produce bitterness, anger, outrage, or vengefulness. However, the poem contains none of these. It is not angry or indignant; it is not an appeal for revenge or revolution. It is rather a declaration of personal independence and individuality. The tone is one of objectivity, daring, occasional playfulness, but above all, confidence.° These attitudes are made plain in the speaker's situation, the ideas, the poetic form, the diction, and the expressions.▫

[2] Hughes's treatment of the situation is objective, factual, and personal, not emotional or political. The poem contains a number of factual details presented clearly, like these: The speaker is black in an otherwise all-white College English class. He has come from North Carolina and is now living alone at the

* For the text of this poem, see Appendix C, pages 352–53.
° Central idea
▫ Thesis sentence

[2] Harlem YMCA, away from family and roots. He is also, at 22, an older student. The class is for freshmen (English B), yet he is the age of many seniors. All this is evidence of disadvantage, yet the speaker does no more than present the facts objectively, without comment. He is in control, presenting the details straightforwardly, in a tone of total objectivity.

[3] Hughes's thoughts about equality—the idea underlying the poem—are presented in the same objective, cool manner. The speaker writes to his instructor as an equal, not as an inferior. In describing himself he does not deal in abstractions, but rather in reality. Thus he defines himself in language descriptive of everyday abilities, needs, activities, and likes. He is cool and direct here, for his presentation takes the form of a set of inclusive principles emphasizing the sameness and identity of everyone regardless of race or background. The idea is that everyone should put away prejudices and begin to treat people as people, not as representatives of any race. By causing the speaker to avoid emotionalism and controversy, Hughes makes counterarguments difficult if not impossible. He is so much in control that the facts themselves carry his argument for equality.

[4] The selection of a poetic form demonstrates bravery and confidence. The title here is the key, for it does not promise the most exciting of topics. Normally, in fact, one would expect nothing much more than a short prose theme in response to and English assignment, but a poem is unexpected and therefore daring and original, particularly one like this that touches on the topic of equality and identity. The wit, ability, and skill of the speaker's use of the form itself demonstrate the self-confidence and self-sufficiency that reinforce the theoretical basis for equality.

Hughes's diction is in keeping with the tone of confidence and daring. The words are simple, showing the speaker's confidence in the truth and power of his ideas. Almost all the words are short, of no more than one or two syllables. This high proportion of short words reflects a conscious attempt to keep the diction clear and direct. A result is that Hughes avoids any possible ambiguities, as the following section of the poem shows:

[5]
Well, I like to eat, sleep, drink, and be in love.
I like to work, read, learn, and understand life.
I like a pipe for a Christmas present,
or records—Bessie, bop, or Bach. (lines 21–24)

With the exception of what it means to "understand life," these words are descriptive and are free of emotional overtones. They reflect the speaker's confidence in his belief that equality should replace inequality and prejudice.

[6] A number of the speaker's phrases and expressions also show this same confidence. Although most of the material is expressed straightforwardly, one can perceive playfulness and irony. In lines 18–20 there seems to be a deliberate use of confusing language to bring about a verbal merging of the identities of the speaker, the instructor, Harlem, and the greater New York area:

Harlem, I hear you:
hear you, hear me—we two—you, me talk on this page.
(I hear New York, too.) Me—who? (18–20)

The speaker's confidence is so strong that he writes an expression that seems almost childish. This expression is in the second line of the following excerpt:

> I guess being colored doesn't make me not like
> the same things other folks like who are other races. (25–26)

There is also whimsicality in the way in which the speaker treats the irony of the black–white situation:

[6]   So will my page be colored that I write? (27)

Underlying this last expression is an awareness that, despite the claim that people are equal and are tied to each other by common humanity, there are also strong differences among individuals. The speaker is confidently asserting grounds for independence as well as equality.

Thus, an examination of "Theme for English B" reveals vitality and confidence. The poem is a statement of trust and an almost open challenge on the personal level to the unachieved ideal of equality. Hughes is saying that since it is American to have such ideals, there is nothing to do but to live up to them.

[7]   He makes this point through the deliberate simplicity of the speaker's words and descriptions. Yet the poem is not without irony, particularly at the end, where the speaker mentions that the instructor is "somewhat more free" than he is. "Theme for English B" is complex and engaging. It shows the speaker's confidence through objectivity, daring, and playfulness.

COMMENTARY ON THE THEME

Because this theme embodies a number of approaches by which tone may be studied in any work (situation, common ground, diction, special characteristics), it is typical of many essays that use a combined, eclectic approach. The central idea is that the dominant attitude in "Theme for English B" is the speaker's confidence, and that this confidence is shown in the similar but separable attitudes of objectivity, daring, and playfulness. The purpose of the theme is to discuss how Hughes makes plain these and other related attitudes in five separate aspects of the poem.

Paragraph 2 deals with situational irony in relation to the social and political circumstances of racial discrimination (see approach 1, pp. 148–49). Paragraph 3 considers the objectivity with which Hughes considers the idea of equality (approach 4). (For paragraph 4, see below.) Paragraphs 5 and 6 consider how Hughes's word choices exhibit his attempts at clarity, objectivity, playfulness, and confidence (approach 2). The attention given in these paragraphs to Hughes's monosyllabic words is justified by their importance in the poem's tone.

The concluding paragraph stresses again the attitude of confidence in the poem and also notes additional attitudes of trust, challenge, ingenuousness, irony, daring, and playfulness.

A Close Look at Paragraph 4

The fourth paragraph is particularly instructive, for it shows how a topic that might ordinarily be taken for granted, such as the basic form of expression, can be seen as a unique feature of tone (approach 5). The paragraph contrasts the expected student response (no more than a brief prose theme) with the actual response (the poem itself, with its interesting twists and turns). Since the primary tone of the poem is that of self-confidence, which is the unspoken basis for the speaker's assertion of independence and equality, the paragraph stresses that the form itself embodies this attitude. The concluding sentence stresses the important idea that the attitude of confidence buttressing the concept of self-sufficiency is an essential justification for equality. The paragraph thus combines the poem's dominant attitude with its underlying political argument.

chapter 12

Writing About a Problem:
Challenges to Overcome
in Reading

A **problem** is any question that you cannot answer easily and correctly about a body of material that you know. The question, "Who is the major character in *Hamlet?*" is not a problem, because the obvious answer is Hamlet.

Let us, however, ask another question: "Why is it *correct* to say that Hamlet is the major character?" This question is not as easy as the first, and for this reason it is a problem. It requires that we think about our answer, even though we do not need to search very far. Hamlet is the title character. He is involved in most of the actions of the play. He is so much the center of our liking and concern that his death causes sadness and regret. To "solve" this problem has required a set of responses, all of which provide answers to the question "why?" With variation, most readers of Shakespeare's play would likely be satisfied with the answers.

More complex, however, and more typical of most problems, are questions like these: "Why does Hamlet talk of suicide in his first soliloquy?" "Why does he treat Ophelia so coarsely in the 'nunnery' scene?" "Why does he delay in avenging his father's death?" It is with questions like these that themes on a problem are normally concerned. Simple factual responses do not answer such questions. A good deal of thought, together with a number of interpretations knitted together into a whole theme, is required.

THE USEFULNESS OF PROBLEM SOLVING

Problem solving is one of the most beneficial of skills. In an art course, for example, you will need to think about whether representationalism or realism is superior or inferior to impressionism or expressionism. To consider this problem requires much knowledge and thought about art. In philosophy you will encounter the problem of whether reality is to be found in particulars or universals. An answer will take you creatively into ways of understanding that you do not anticipate. In your classes in literature and writing, you will encounter many problems and questions in classroom discussions, but, beyond these, you should also make it your regular task to ask and answer your own questions. Whatever their origin, all questions will cause you to search the material deeply and pick out the best and most suitable answers. In short, wherever you go, you will find challenging problems, and in overcoming them you will develop your powers to read carefully, to think pointedly, and to argue effectively.

STRATEGIES FOR DEVELOPING
A THEME ABOUT A PROBLEM

The first purpose in a theme about a problem is to convince your reader that your solution is a good one. This you do by making sound conclusions from supporting evidence. In nonscientific subjects such as literature you rarely find absolute proofs, so your conclusions will not be *proved* in the way you prove triangles congruent. But your organization, your use of facts from the text, your interpretations, and your application of general or specific knowledge should all make your conclusions *convincing*. Your basic strategy is thus *persuasion*.

Because problems and solutions change with the works being studied, each theme on a problem is different from any other. Despite these differences, however, a number of common strategies may be adapted to whatever problem you face. You might use one or more of these, keeping in mind that your goal is to solve your problem in the most direct, convenient way.

1. THE DEMONSTRATION THAT CONDITIONS FOR A SOLUTION ARE FULFILLED. In effect, this development is the most basic in writing—namely, illustration. You first explain that certain conditions need to exist for your solution to be plausible. Your central idea—really a brief answer to the question—is that the conditions do indeed exist. Your development is to show how the conditions may be found in the work.

Suppose that you are writing on the problem of why Hamlet delays revenge against his uncle, Claudius (who before the play opens has murdered Hamlet's father, King Hamlet, and has become the new king of Denmark). Suppose that, in your introduction, you make the point that Hamlet delays because he is never sure that Claudius is guilty. This is your "solution" to the problem. In the body of your theme you support your answer by showing the flimsiness of the information Hamlet receives about the crime (i.e., the two visits from the Ghost and Claudius's distress at the play within the play). Once you have "attacked" these sources of data on the grounds that they are unreliable, you have succeeded because your solution is consistent with the details of the play.

2. THE ANALYSIS OF WORDS IN THE PHRASING OF THE PROBLEM. Another good approach is to explore the meaning and limits of important words or phrases in the question. Your object is to clarify the words and show how applicable they are. You may wish to define the words and to show whether they have any special meaning.

Such attention to words might give you enough material for all or part of your essay. The sample theme in this chapter, for example, briefly considers the meaning of the word *effective* when applied to Robert Frost's poem "Desert Places." Similarly, a theme on the problem of Hamlet's delay would benefit from a treatment of the word *delay*: What, really, does *delay* mean? For Hamlet, is there a difference between delay that is reasonable and delay that is unreasonable? Does Hamlet in fact delay unreasonably? Is his delay the result of a psychological fault? Would speedy revenge be more or less reasonable than the delay? By the time you have answered such pointed questions, you will also have written a goodly amount of material for your full theme.

3. THE REFERENCE TO LITERARY CONVENTIONS OR EXPECTATIONS. What appears to be a problem can often be treated as a normal characteristic, given the particular work you are studying. In this light, the best argument is to establish that the problem can be solved by reference to the literary mode or conventions of a work, or to the work's own self-limitations. For example, a question might be raised about why Mathilde in "The Necklace" does not tell her friend Jeanne about the loss of the necklace. A plausible answer is that, all motivation aside, the story builds up to a surprise, which could be spoiled by an early disclosure. To solve the problem, in other words, one has recourse to the structure of the story—to the literary convention which Maupassant was observing when he wrote "The Necklace."

Similarly, a problem about Shakespeare's "My Mistress' Eyes" (p. 340) might be that the speaker is insulting rather than complimenting the Mistress. The base for this assertion is that the woman's physical attributes are denigrated (i.e., her hair is like "wires," while her eyes are "nothing like the sun"). An answer to the problem may be found, however, in the conventions of the Elizabethan love sonnet, which often described qualities that could never exist in real life. Shakespeare is therefore doing two things: (1) He is criticizing the sonnet convention on the grounds that it is "false" and overly elaborate, and (2) he is also claiming that there is great beauty in reality and truth, even if living people are not ideally perfect.

Other problems that may be dealt with in this way might concern levels of reality. Hawthorne's "Young Goodman Brown," for example, is fanciful and dreamlike (or nightmarish), for in everyday life, things could not happen as they do in the forest near Hawthorne's Salem. Similarly, although Jackson's "The Lottery" presents ordinary village folk at a public event, the stoning at the end indicates something other than everyday reality. Thus, problems about the unreality of either the lottery or Goodman Brown's walk can be readily answered by reference to the dreamlike and symbolic qualities of both works. In the same way, a question about the sudden falling in love of Smirnov and Mrs. Popov in Chekhov's *The Bear* can be answered with reference to the play's being a farce: Because in farces unlikely things occur rapidly and without apparent logic, such a quick infatuation is not unusual at all. The principal strategy in dealing with questions like these is to resolve difficulties by establishing a context in which the difficulties vanish. Problems, in other words, may be seen as resulting from no more than normal occurrences, granted the generic qualities or levels of reality of particular works.

4. The argument against possible objections: procatalepsis. With this strategy, you raise your own objections and then argue against them. This strategy, called **procatalepsis** or **anticipation,** helps you sharpen your arguments, for *anticipating* and dealing with objections forces you to make analyses and use facts that you might otherwise overlook. Although procatalepsis may be used point by point throughout your theme, you may find it most useful at the end. (See the last paragraph of the sample theme, p. 161.)

Imagine that someone is raising objections to your solution to the problem. It is then your task to show that the objections (1) are not accurate or valid, (2) are not strong or convincing, or (3) are based on unusual rather than usual conditions (on an exception and not the rule). Here are some examples of these approaches. The objections raised are underlined, so that you can easily distinguish them from the answers.

a. *The objection is not accurate or valid.* Here you reject the objection by showing that either the interpretation or the conclusions are wrong and also by emphasizing that the evidence supports your solution.

Although Hamlet's delay is reasonable, the claim might be made that his duty is to kill Claudius in revenge immediately after the Ghost's accusations. This claim is not persuasive because it assumes that Hamlet knows everything the audience knows. The audience accepts the

Ghost's word that Claudius is guilty, but from Hamlet's position there is every reason to doubt the Ghost and not to act. Would it not seem foolish and insane for Hamlet to kill Claudius, who is king legally, and then to claim that he did it because the Ghost told him to do so? The argument for speedy revenge is not good, because it is based on an incorrect view of Hamlet's situation.

b. *The objection is not strong or convincing.* Here you concede that the objection has some truth or validity, but you then try to show that it is weak and that your own solution is stronger.

One might claim that Claudius's distress at the play within the play is evidence for his guilt and that therefore Hamlet should carry out his revenge right away. This argument has merit, and Hamlet's speech after Claudius has fled the scene ("I'll take the Ghost's word for a thousand pound") shows that the "conscience of the king" has been caught. But this behavior is not a strong case for killing him. Hamlet could justify a claim for an investigation of his father's death on these grounds, but he could not justify a revenge killing. Claudius could not be convicted in any court on the testimony that he was disturbed at seeing the Murder of Gonzago. Even after the play within the play, the reasons for delay are stronger than for action.

c. *The objection is based on unusual rather than usual conditions.* Here you reject the objection on the grounds that it could be valid only if normal conditions were suspended. The objection depends on an exception, not a rule.

The case for quick action is simple: Hamlet should kill Claudius right after seeing the Ghost (I.3), or else after seeing the King's reaction to the stage murder of Gonzago (III.2) or else after seeing the Ghost again (III.4). This argument wrongly assumes that due process does to exist in the Denmark of Hamlet and Claudius. Redress under these circumstances, goes the argument, must be both personal and extra-legal. However, the fact is that Hamlet's Denmark is a civilized place where legality and the rules of evidence are precious. Thus Hamlet cannot rush out to kill Claudius, because he knows that the King has not had anything close to due process. The argument for quick action is poor because it rests on an exception being made from civilized law.

WRITING ABOUT A PROBLEM

Writing a theme on a problem requires you to argue a position: Either there is a solution or there is not. To develop this position requires that you show the steps to your conclusion. Your general thematic form is thus (1) a description of the conditions that need to be met for the solution you propose, and then (2) a demonstration that these conditions exist. If you assert that there is no solution, then your form would be the same for the first part, but your second part—the development—would show that these conditions have *not* been met.

As with most themes, you may assume your reader's familiarity with the work, and you should therefore avoid retelling stories. Your job is to select only those materials that support your argument, so that you create an effective solution to your problem.

Introduction

Begin with a statement of the problem, and refer to the conditions that must be established for the problem to be solved. It is unnecessary to say anything about the author or the general nature of the work unless you plan to use this material as a part of your development. Your central idea is your answer to the question, and your thesis sentence indicates the main heads of your development.

Body

The body should convince your reader that your solution to the problem is sound. In each paragraph, the topic sentence is a major aspect of your answer, and this should be followed with supporting detail. Your goal should be to bring about your reader's agreement.

You might use one or more of the strategies described in this chapter. These are, again, (1) the demonstration that conditions for a solution are fulfilled, (2) the analysis of words in the phrasing of the problem, (3) the reference to literary expectations or limitations, and (4) the argument against possible objections. You might combine these. Thus, if we assume that your argument is that Hamlet's delay is reasonable, you might first consider the word *delay* (strategy 2). Then you might use strategy 1 to explain the reasons for which Hamlet does delay. Finally, to answer objections to your argument, you might show that he acts when he feels justified in acting (strategy 4). Whatever your topic, the important thing is to use the method or methods that best help you make a good argument for your solution.

Conclusion

Here you should affirm the validity of your solution in view of the supporting evidence. You might do this by reemphasizing your strongest points, or you might simply present a brief summary. Or you might think of your argument as still continuing and thus use the strategy of procatalepsis to raise and answer possible objections to your solution, as in the last paragraph of the sample theme.

Sample Theme

*The Problem of Frost's Use of the Term "Desert Places"
in the Poem "Desert Places"**

[1] In the last line of "Desert Places," the meaning suggested by the title undergoes a sudden shift. At the beginning it clearly refers to the snowy setting described in the first stanza, but in the last line it refers to a negative state of soul. The problem is this: Does the change happen too late to be effective? That is, does the new meaning come out of nowhere, or does it really work as a closing thought? To answer these questions, one must grant that the change cannot be effective if there is no preparation for it before the last line of the poem. But if there is preparation—that is, if Frost does provide hints that the speaker feels an emptiness like that of the bleak, snowy natural world—then the shift is both understandable and effective even though it comes at the very end. It is clear that Frost makes the preparation and therefore that the change is effective.° The preparation may be traced in Frost's references, word choices, and concluding sentences.□

[2] In the first two stanzas, Frost includes the speaker in his reference to living things being overcome. His opening scene is one of snow which covers "weeds and stubble" (line 4) and which almost literally smothers hibernating animals, "in their lairs" (6). The speaker then focuses on his own mental state, saying that he is "too absent-spirited to count," and that the "loneliness" of the scene "includes" him "unawares" (7, 8). This movement—from vegetable, to animal, to human—shows that everything alive is changed by the snow. Obviously the speaker will not die like the grass or hibernate like the animals, but he indicates that the "loneliness" overcomes him. These first eight lines thus connect the natural bleakness with the speaker.

[3] In addition, a number of words in the third stanza are preparatory because they may be applied to human beings. The words "lonely" and "loneliness" (9), "more lonely" (10), "blanker" and "benighted" (11), and "no expression, nothing to express" (12) may all refer equally to human or to natural conditions. The word "benighted" is most important, because it suggests not only the darkness of night, but also intellectual or moral ignorance. Because these words invite the reader to think of negative mental and emotional states, they provide a context in which the final shift of meaning is both logical and natural.

[4] The climax of Frost's preparation for the last two words is in the sentences of the fourth stanza. All along, the speaker claims to feel an inner void that is similar to the bleakness of the cold, snowy field. This idea emerges as the major focus in the last stanza, where in two sentences the speaker talks about his feelings of emptiness or insensitivity:

> They cannot scare me with their empty spaces
> Between stars—on stars where no human race is.

---

* For the text of this poem, see Appendix C, pages 350–51.
° Central idea
□ Thesis sentence

I have it in me so much nearer home
[4]   To scare myself with my own desert places.

[5]   In the context of the poem, therefore, the shift in these last two words does not seem sudden or illogical. The words rather pull together the two parts of the comparison that Frost has been building from the first line. Just as "desert places" refers to the snowy field, it also suggests human coldness, blankness, unconcern, insensitivity, and cruelty. The phrase does not spring out of nowhere, but is a strong climax of the poem.

[6]   Although Frost's conclusion is effective, a critic might still claim that it is weak because Frost does not develop the thought about the negative soul. He simply mentions "desert places" and stops. But the poem is not a long psychological study. To ask for more than Frost gives would be to expect more than sixteen lines can provide. A better claim against the effectiveness of the concluding shift of meaning is that the phrase "desert places" is both vague and perhaps boastfully humble. If the phrase were taken away from the poem, this criticism might be acceptable. But the fact is that the phrase is in the poem, and that it must be judged only in the poem. There, it takes on the associations of the previous fifteen lines, and does so with freshness and surprise. Thus the shift of meaning is a major reason for Frost's success in "Desert Places."

COMMENTARY ON THE THEME

The general development of this essay illustrates strategy 1 described in this chapter (pp. 155–56). The attention to the word "effective" in paragraph 1 briefly illustrates the second strategy (p. 156). The concluding paragraph shows two approaches to the fourth strategy (pp. 157–58), using the arguments that the objections are not good because they (4a) are not accurate or valid (here the inaccuracy is related to strategy 3), and (4c) are based on the need for an exception, namely that the phrase in question be removed from the context in the poem.

After introducing the problem, the first paragraph emphasizes that a solution is available only if the poem prepares the reader for the problematic shift of meaning. The central idea is that the poem satisfies this requirement and that the shift is effective. The thesis sentence indicates three subjects for development.

Paragraph 2 asserts that there is preparation even early in the poem. (For a discussion of paragraph 3, see below.) The fourth paragraph asserts that the concluding sentences build toward a climax of Frost's pattern of development.

Paragraphs 5 through 6 form a two-part conclusion to the theme. The fifth paragraph summarizes the arguments and offers an interpretation of the phrase. The last paragraph raises and answers two objections. The theme thus shows that a careful reading of the poem eliminates the grounds for claiming that there is any problem about the last line.

A Close Look at Paragraph 3

The argument of paragraph 3, like that of paragraph 2, is that the texture of the poem, right from the start, demonstrates the central idea (stated in the introductory paragraph) that the conditions for a solution to the problem are met. The method in this paragraph is to show how particular words and expressions, because they are applicable to both nature and human beings, connect the bleak opening scene with the speaker's professed spiritual numbness. The words are therefore not explained *outside the context* of "Desert Places," but rather *for the support they lend to the solution/central idea*. The specially emphasized word "benighted" (line 11) is the most illustrative, because it particularly refers to cultural and intellectual bleakness. The paragraph hence demonstrates how the careful selection and analysis of key words can be part of a total argument.

chapter 13

Writing the Themes of Comparison–Contrast and Extended Comparison–Contrast:

Learning by Seeing Things Together

A comparison–contrast theme is used to compare and contrast different authors, two or more works by the same author, different drafts of the same work, or characters, incidents, techniques, and ideas in the same work or in different works. The virtue of comparison–contrast is that it enables the study of works in perspective. No matter what works you consider together, the method helps you isolate and highlight individual characteristics, for the quickest way to get at the essence of one thing is to compare it with another. Similarities are brought out by comparison, and differences are shown by contrast. In other words, you can enhance your understanding of what a thing *is* by using comparison–contrast to determine what it *is not.*

For example, our understanding of Shakespeare's Sonnet 30, "When to the Sessions of Sweet Silent Thought" (p. 125), may be enhanced if we compare it with Christina Rossetti's poem "Echo" (p. 206). Both poems treat personal recollections of past experiences, told by a speaker to a listener who is not intended to be the reader. They also both refer to persons, now dead, with whom the speakers were closely involved.

There are important differences, however. Shakespeare's speaker numbers the dead persons as friends whom he laments generally, while Rossetti refers specifically to one person with whom the speaker was in love. Rossetti's topic is the sorrow of dead love, the irrevocability of the past, and the present loneliness of the speaker. Shakespeare includes the references to dead friends as a way of accounting for present sorrows, but then his speaker turns to the present and asserts that thinking about the "dear friend" being addressed enables him to restore past "losses" and end all "sorrows." In Rossetti's poem, there is no reconciliation of past and present; instead the speaker focuses entirely upon the sadness of the present moment. Though both poems are retrospective, then, Shakespeare's poem looks toward the present while Rossetti's looks to the past.

While more could be said, this example shows how the comparison–contrast method enables us to identify leading similarities and distinguishing differences in both works. It is usually the rule that you may overcome difficulty with one work by comparing and contrasting it with another work on a comparable subject.

CLARIFY YOUR INTENTION

When planning a comparison–contrast theme, you should first decide on your goal, for you may use the method in a number of ways. One objective may be *the equal and mutual illumination of both (or more) works.* For example, an essay comparing Welty's "A Worn Path" (pp. 322–28) with Hawthorne's "Young Goodman Brown" (pp. 302–11) might be designed (1) to compare ideas, characters, or methods in these stories equally, without stressing or favoring either. But you might also wish (2) to emphasize "Young Goodman Brown," and therefore you would use "A Worn Path" as material for highlighting Hawthorne's work. In addition, you might use the comparison–contrast method (3) to show your liking of one work at the expense of another, or (4) to emphasize a method or idea that you think is especially noteworthy or appropriate.

A first task therefore is to decide what to emphasize. The first sample theme (pp. 170–72) gives "equal time" to both works being considered, without any claims for the superiority of either. Unless you want to pursue a different rhetorical goal, this theme is a suitable model for most comparisons.

FIND COMMON GROUNDS FOR COMPARISON

The second stage in prewriting for this theme is to select a common ground for discussion. It is pointless to compare dissimilar things, for the resulting conclusions will not have much value. Instead, find a common ground. Compare like with like: idea with idea, characterization with characterization, imagery with imagery, point of view with point of view, tone with tone, problem with problem. Nothing much can be learned from a comparison of "Welty's view of courage and Chekhov's view of love," but a comparison of "The relationship of love to stability and courage in Chekhov and Welty" suggests common ground, with the promise of important things to be learned through the examination of similarities and differences.

In seeking common ground, you will need to be inventive and creative. For instance, Maupassant's "The Necklace" and Chekhov's *The Bear* at first seem dissimilar. Yet a common ground can be found, such as "The treatment of Self-Deceit," "The Effects of Chance on Human Affairs," "The View of Women," and so on. Although other works may seem even more dissimilar than these, it is usually possible to find a common ground for comparison and contrast. Much of your success with this theme depends on your finding a workable basis—a common denominator—for comparison.

METHODS OF COMPARISON

Let us assume that you have decided on your rhetorical purpose and on the basis of your comparison. You have done your reading, taken notes, and have a rough idea of what to say. The remaining problem is the treatment of your material. Here are two ways:

A common way is to make your points first about one work and then about the other. Unfortunately, this methods makes your paper seem like two big lumps. ("Work 1" takes up one half of your paper, and "work 2" takes up the other half.) Also, the method involves repetition because you must repeat many points when you treat the second subject.

A superior method therefore is to treat the major aspects of your main idea and to refer to the two (or more) works as they support your arguments. Thus you refer constantly to *both* works, sometimes within the same sentence, and remind your reader of the point of your discussion. There are reasons for the superiority of this method: (1) You do not repeat your points needlessly, for you document them as you ___ them. (2) By constantly referring to the two works, you make you ___ points without requiring sections.
a reader with a poor memory to reread pre___ral References as a Basis of

As a model, here is a paragraph on Shakespeare's Sonnet 73 ['That Comparison in Frost's 'Desert Place___']" (pp. 350 and 339). The virtue Time of Year Thou Mayest in M___ial from both poems simultaneously of the paragraph is that it us___ sentences allows) as the substance f___ (as nearly as the time se___

the development of th___ their ideas to events occurring in the natural
      ___ parallel with death is common to both poems, with
      [1] B___out it in his first line, and Shakespeare introducing i___
world. [2___
Fros___

his seventh. [3] Along with night, Frost emphasizes the onset of winter and snow as a time of death and desolation. [4] With this natural description, Frost also symbolically refers to empty, secret, dead places in the inner spirit—crannies of the soul where bleak winter snowfalls correspond to selfishness and indifference to others. [5] By contrast, Shakespeare uses the fall season, with the yellowing and dropping of leaves and also the flying away of birds, to stress the closeness of real death and therefore also the need to love fully during the time remaining. [6] Both poems therefore share a sense of gloom, because both present death as inevitable and final, just like the oncoming season of barrenness and waste. [7] Because Shakespeare's sonnet is addressed to a listener who is also a loved one, however, it is more outgoing than the more introspective poem of Frost. [8] Frost turns the snow, the night, and the emptiness of the universe inwardly in order to show the speaker's inner bleakness, and by extension, the bleakness of many human spirits. [9] Shakespeare instead uses the bleakness of seasons, night, and dying fires to state the need for loving "well." [10] The poems thus use common and similar references for different purposes and effects.

The paragraph links Shakespeare's references to nature with those of Frost. Five sentences speak of both authors together; three speak of Frost alone, and two of Shakespeare alone, but all the sentences are unified topically. This interweaving of references indicates that the writer has learned both poems well enough to think of them at the same time, and it also enables the writing to be more pointed and succinct than if the works were separately treated.

You can learn from this example: If you develop your theme by putting your two subjects constantly together, you will write economically and pointedly (not only for themes, but also for tests). Beyond that, if you digest the material as successfully as this method indicates, you demonstrate that you are fulfilling a major educational goal—the assimilation and use of material. Too often, because you learn things separately (in separate works and courses, at separate times), you tend also to compartmentalize them. Instead, should always try to relate them, to *synthesize* them. Comparison and contrast help in this process of putting together, of seeing things not as fragments but as parts of wholes.

AVOID THE "TENNIS-BALL" METHOD

As you make your comparison, do not confuse an interlocking method with a "tennis-ball" method, in which you bounce your subject back and forth constantly and repetitively, almost as though you were hitting observations back and forth over a net. The tennis-ball method is shown in the following example from a comparison of the characters Mathilde (Maupassant's "The Necklace") and Miss Brill (Mansfield's "Miss Brill"):

Mathilde is a young married woman, while Miss Brill is single and getting older. Mathilde has at least some kind of social life, even though she doesn't have more than one friend, while Miss Brill leads a life of solitude. Mathilde's daydreams about wealth are responsible for her misfortune, but the shattering of Miss Brill's daydreams about her self-importance is done by someone from the outside. Therefore, Mathilde is made unhappy because of her own shortcomings, but Miss Brill is a helpless victim. In Mathilde's case, the focus is on adversity not only causing trouble but also strengthening character. In Miss Brill's case the focus is on the weak getting hurt and being made weaker.

Imagine the effect an entire essay written in this boring "1,2—1,2—1,2" order. Aside from the repetition and unvaried patterning of subjects, the tennis-ball method does not permit much illustrative development. You should not feel so cramped that you cannot take two or more sentences to develop a point about one writer or subject before you include comparative references to another. If you remember to interlock the two subjects of comparison, however, as in the paragraph about Frost and Shakespeare, your method will give you the freedom to develop your topics fully.

THE EXTENDED
COMPARISON–CONTRAST THEME

For limited research papers and extended end-of-the-semester themes (and also comprehensive exam questions), you may be asked to treat a number of works from the standpoint of topics such as ideas, plot, structure, character, and setting. For extended assignments of this sort, the comparison–contrast method is applicable, although with more works you will need to adjust your treatment.

Let us assume that you have been assigned not just two works but five or six. You need first to find a common ground which you may use as your central, unifying idea, just as you do for a comparison of only two works. Once you establish your idea for comparison, you should classify or group your works on the basis of their similarities and differences with regard to the topic.

Let us assume that three or four works treat a topic in one way, while two or three do it in another (e.g., either criticism or praise of wealth and trade, or the joys or sorrows of love, or the enthusiasm or disillusionment of youth). In writing about these works, you might treat the topic itself in a straightforward comparison–contrast method but use details from the works within the groupings as the material that you use for illustration and argument. To make your theme as specific as possible, it is probably best to stress only two major works with each of your subpoints. Once you have established these points in detail, there is no need to go into similar detail with all the other works you are studying. Instead, you may refer to the other works briefly, with your purpose being to strengthen your points but not to create more and more examples. Once you go to another subpoint, you may use different works for illustration, so that by the end of your theme you will have given due attention to each work in your assignment. In this way—by treating many works in comparative groups of twos—you can keep your essay reasonably brief, for there is no need for unproductive detail.

For illustration, the second sample theme shows how this grouping may be done (pp. 174–79). There, six works are included in a general category of how love and service offer guidance and stability. This group is contrasted with another group of four works (including two characters from one of the works in the first group), in which love is shown as an escape or retreat.

DOCUMENTATION AND THE EXTENDED COMPARISON–CONTRAST THEME

For the longer comparison–contrast theme you may need to document your references. Generally you do not need to identify page numbers for references to major traits, ideas, and actions. For example, if you refer to the end of Poe's "The Masque of the Red Death," where Prince Prospero rushes through his suite of seven rooms and dies in the last, you may assume that your reader also knows about this action. You do not need to do any more than make the reference.

But if you quote lines or passages, or if you cite actions or characters in special ways, you may need to use parenthetical pages references, as described in Joseph Gibaldi and Walter S. Achtert, *MLA Handbook for Writers of Research Papers*, 3rd ed. (discussed in Appendix B, pp. 297–98). If you are using lines or parts of lines of poetry, use line numbers parenthetically, as in the second sample essay. Be guided by the following principle: If you make a specific reference that you think your reader might want to examine in more detail, supply the line or page number. If you refer to minor details that might easily be unnoticed or forgotten, also supply the line or page number. Otherwise, if you refer to major ideas, actions, or characterizations, be sure to make your internal reference clear enough so that your reader can easily recall it from his or her memory of the work.

WRITING COMPARISON–CONTRAST THEMES

First, narrow and simplify your subject so that you can handle it conveniently. For example, if you compare Amy Lowell and Wilfred Owen (as in the first sample theme), pick out one or two of each poet's poems on identical or similar topics, and write your theme about these. For the longer comparison–contrast theme, you will need no more than one work by each author. Be wary, however, of the limitations of your selection, because generalizations made from one or two works may not apply to all works of the same writer.

Once you have found an organizing principle along with the relevant works, begin to refine and focus the direction of your theme. As you study each work, note common or contrasting elements, and use these to form your central idea. At the same time, you can select the most illustrative works and classify them according to your topic, such as war (first sample theme) or love (second).

Introduction

State the works, authors, characters, or ideas which you are considering. Then show how you have narrowed the topic. Your central idea should briefly highlight the principal grounds of comparison and contrast, such as that both works treat a common topic, exhibit a similar idea, use a similar form, develop an identical attitude, and so on, and also that major or minor differences help to make the works unique. You may also assert that one work is superior to the other, if you wish to make this judgment and defend it. Your thesis sentence should list the topics to be developed in the body.

Body

The body depends on the works and your basis of comparison (ideas and themes, depictions of character, uses of setting, qualities of style, uses of point of view, and so on). For a comparison–contrast treatment on such a basis, your goal should be to shed light on both (or more) of the works you are treating. For example, you might examine a number of stories that are written in the first-person point of view (see Chapter 6, pp. 87–89). A theme on this topic might compare the ways each author uses this point of view to achieve similar or distinct effects. Or you might compare a group of poems that employ similar images, symbols, or ironic methods. Sometimes the process can be as simple as identifying female or male protagonists and comparing the ways in which their characters are developed. Another approach is to compare the *subjects,* as opposed to the *theme.* You might identify works dealing with general subjects like love, death, youth, race, or war. Such groupings provide a basis of excellent comparisons and contrasts.

As you develop the body, remember to keep comparison–contrast foremost. That is, your discussion of point of view, metaphorical language, or whatever should not so much explain these topics as topics, but rather explore similarities and differences about the works being compared. Let us say that your topic is an idea. You will of course need to explain the idea, but only enough to establish points of similarity or difference. As you develop such a theme, you might illustrate your arguments by referring to related uses of elements such as setting, characterization, rhythm or rhyme, symbolism, point of view, or metaphor. When you introduce these new subjects, you will be right on target as long as you use them comparatively.

Conclusion

Here you may reflect on other ideas or techniques in the works you have compared, make observations about similar qualities, or summarize briefly the grounds of your comparison. The conclusion of an extended comparison–contrast theme should represent a final bringing together of your materials. In the body of your theme, you may not have referred to all the works in each paragraph, but in your conclusion you should try to include them. If your writers belong to any "period" or "school" (information about such topics would require research and use of correct documentation), you might also show how they relate to these larger movements. References of this sort provide an obvious common ground for comparison and contrast.

First Sample Theme (Two Works)

The Treatment of Responses to War in Amy Lowell's "Patterns" and Wilfred Owen's "Anthem for Doomed Youth"*

---

[1] "Patterns" and "Anthem for Doomed Youth" are both powerful and unique condemnations of war.° Owen's short poem speaks broadly and generally about the ugliness of war and also about large groups of bereaved people, while Lowell's longer poem focuses upon the personal grief of just one person. In a real sense, Lowell's poem begins where Owen's ends, a fact which accounts for both the similarities and differences between the two works. The anti-war themes may be compared on the basis of their subjects, their lengths, their concreteness, and their use of a common major metaphor.□

* For the texts of these works, please see Appendex C, pages 347–50, 352.
° Central idea
□ Thesis sentence

"Anthem for Doomed Youth" attacks war more directly than "Patterns." Owen's opening line, "What passing bells for those who die as cattle," suggests that in war human beings are depersonalized before they are slaughtered, like so much meat, while his observations about the "monstrous" guns and the "shrill, demented" shells unambiguously condemn the horrors of war. By contrast, in "Patterns" warfare is far away, on another continent, intruding only [2] when the messenger delivers the letter stating that the speaker's fiancé has been killed (lines 63–64). Similar news governs the last six lines of Owen's poem, quietly describing how those at home respond to the news that their loved ones have died in war. Thus the anti-war focus in "Patterns" is the contrast between the calm, peaceful life of the speaker's garden and the anguish of her responses, while in Owen's poem the stress is more the external horrors of war which bring about the need for ceremonies honoring the dead.

Another difference, which is surprising, is that Owen's poem is less than 1/7 as long as Lowell's. "Patterns" is an interior monologue or meditation of 107 lines, but it could not be shorter and still be convincing. In the poem the speaker thinks about the present and past, and contemplates the future loneliness to which her intended husband's death has doomed her. Her final outburst, "Christ, what are patterns for?", can make no sense if she does not explain her situation as extensively as she does. On the other hand, "Anthem for Doomed Youth" is brief—a 14-line sonnet—because it is more general and less personal [3] than "Patterns." Although Owen's speaker shows great sympathy, he or she views the sorrows of others distantly, unlike Lowell, who goes right into the mind and spirit of the grieving woman. Owen's use, in his last six lines, of phrases like "tenderness of patient minds" and "drawing down of blinds" is a short but powerful representation of deep grief. He gives no further detail even though thousands of individual stories might be told. In contrast, Lowell tells one of these stories as she focuses on her solitary speaker's lost hopes and dreams. Thus the contrasting lengths of the poems are governed by each poet's treatment of the topic.

Despite these differences of approach and length, both poems are similarly concrete and real. Owen moves from the real scenes and sounds of far-off battlefields to the homes of the many soldiers who have been killed in battle, while Lowell's scene is a single place—the garden of the estate where the speaker has just received news of her lover's death. Her speaker walks on real gravel along garden paths which contain daffodils, squills, a fountain, and a lime [4] tree. She thinks of her clothing and her ribboned shoes, and also of her fiancé's boots, sword hilts, and buttons. The images in Owen's poem are equally real, but are not associated with individuals as in "Patterns." Thus his images refer to cattle, bells, rifle shots, shells, bugles, candles, and window blinds. While both poems thus reflect reality, Owen's details are more general and public, whereas Lowell's are more personal and intimate.

Along with this concreteness, the poems share a major metaphor: that cultural patterns both control and frustrate human wishes and hopes. In "Patterns" this metaphor is shown in warfare itself (line 106), which is the supremely destructive political structure, or pattern. Further examples of the metaphor are [5] found in details about clothing (particularly the speaker's stiff, confining gown in lines 5, 18, 21, 73, and 100, but also the lover's military boots in lines 46 and 49); the orderly, formal garden paths in which the speaker is walking (lines 1, 93); her restraint at hearing about her lover's death; and her courtesy, despite her grief, in ordering refreshment for the messenger (line 69). Within such rigid patterns, her hopes for happiness have vanished, along with the sensuous spontaneity symbolized by her lover's plans to make love with her on a "shady seat" in the garden (lines 85–89). The metaphor of the constricting pattern may also be seen in "Anthem for Doomed Youth," except that in this poem the pattern is the funeral, not love or marriage. Owen's speaker contrasts the calm, peaceful tolling of "passing bells" (line 1) with the frightening sounds of war [5]   represented by the "monstrous anger of the guns," "the rifles' rapid rattle," and "the demented choirs of wailing shells" (lines 2–8). Thus, while Lowell uses the metaphor to reveal the irony of hope and desire being destroyed by war, Owen uses it to reveal the irony of war's nullification and perversion of peaceful ceremonies.

Though the poems in these ways share topics and some aspects of treatment, they are distinct and individual. "Patterns" is visual and kinesthetic, whereas "Anthem for Doomed Youth" is strongly auditory. Both poems conclude on powerfully emotional although different notes. Owen's poem dwells on the pathos and sadness that war brings to many unnamed people, while Lowell's expresses the most intimate thoughts of a particular woman in the first [6]   agony of sorrow. Although neither poem directly attacks the usual platitudes and justifications for war (the needs to mobilize, to sacrifice, to achieve peace through fighting, and so on), the attack is there by implication, for both poems make their appeal by stressing how war destroys the relationships that make life worth living. For this reason, despite their differences, both "Patterns" and "Anthem for Doomed Youth" are parallel anti-war poems, and both are strong portrayals of human feeling.

COMMENTARY ON THE THEME

This example illustrates how approximately "equal time" may be given to the similarities and differences of each work being compared. Because the theme shifts constantly from one work to the next, particular phrases may be noticed. When the works are similar or even identical, terms are "common," "share," "and," "both," "similar," "also," and "both." For comparative situations, words like "longer," and "more" are useful. Marking differences are "by contrast," "while," "whereas," "different," "dissimilar," and "on the other hand." Transitions from paragraph to paragraph are not different in this type of theme from those in other themes. Thus, "despite," "along with concreteness," and "in these ways" are used here, but they could be used anywhere for the same transitional purpose.

The central idea of the theme is that the poems mutually condemn war. This idea is brought out in the introductory paragraph, together with the supporting idea that the poems blend into each other because both show responses to news of battle casualties. The thesis sentence concluding the first paragraph indicates four topics for detailed comparison and contrast.

Paragraph 2, the first in the body, discusses how each poem brings out its attack on warfare. Paragraph 3 explains the differing lengths of the poems as a function of differences in perspective. Because Owen's sonnet views war and its effects at a distance, it is brief, while Lowell's interior monologue views death intimately, needing more detail and greater length. (See the discussion of paragraph 4 below.) Paragraph 5, the last in the body, considers the similar and dissimilar ways in which the poems treat a common metaphor.

The final paragraph summarizes the central idea, and it also stresses the ways in which both poems, while being similar, are distinct and unique.

A Close Look at Paragraph 4

Paragraph 4, on the topic of concreteness and reality, shows how equal time may be given to two works without the bouncing back and forth of the tennis-ball method. To show the content of each sentence, let us use *O* for "Anthem for Doomed Youth" and *L* for "Patterns"; the paragraph may be schematized, sentence by sentence, as follows:

$$1 = O,L. \quad 2 = O,L. \quad 3 = L. \quad 4 = L. \quad 5 = O,L. \quad 6 = O. \quad 7 = O,L.$$

Thus there are five references to Owen in the paragraph, and six to Lowell, as close as one can get to "equal time." Three of the sentences (3, 4, and 6) are devoted exclusively to details in one or the other poem, while sentences 1, 2, 5, and 7 refer to both works, stressing points of broad or specific comparison. The scheme demonstrates that the two works are, in effect, interlocked within the paragraph.

Because the paragraph does not exist independently but is a part of the theme, it opens with a transitional emphasis on the "differences" in the preceding paragraph, with the intention of stressing the point of comparison to follow (concreteness and reality). The second sentence introduces a major difference, namely that Lowell's poem concerns individuals while Owen's broadly concerns many persons. Sentences 3 and 4 refer to Lowell's poem alone, and the topic shifts to Owen's poem in sentence 5. To make the transition less abrupt, the transition word *equally* keeps the reader's mind on "Patterns" while it also deals with "Anthem for Doomed Youth." The seventh sentence, referring to both works, offers a brief summary of the similarities and differences explored in the paragraph.

Second Sample Theme
(Extended Comparison–Contrast)

The Complexity of Love and Devoted Service

[1]   On the surface, sexual attraction, love, and devoted duty are simple, and their results should be good. When love works and is in balance, a person loves and devotes attention to someone, or serves a cause with respect and willingness. Such devotion leads to stability and a healthy sense of identity. It is a way of saying "yes." When love and devotion do not work, the effect is extreme unhappiness, a way of saying "no." Love, in short, is not simple. It is complex, and its results are not uniformly good.° This idea can be traced in a comparison of works: Shakespeare's Sonnet 116, Keats's "Bright Star," Rossetti's "Echo," Arnold's "Dover Beach," Hardy's "Channel Firing," Owen's "Anthem for Doomed Youth," Chekhov's The Bear, Glaspell's Trifles, Updike's "A & P," and Welty's "A Worn Path."* The complexity in these works is that love and devotion do not operate in a vacuum but rather in the context of personal, philosophical, economic, and national difficulties. The works show that love and devotion may be forces for stability and refuge, but also for harm.°

[2]   Love as an ideal and stabilizing force is a major principle asserted by Shakespeare in Sonnet 116, Keats in the sonnet "Bright Star," and Rossetti in "Echo." All three writers think of love as a constant, and associate it with guidance and illumination. Shakespeare states that love gives lovers strength and stability in a complex world of opposition and difficulty. Such love is like a "star" that guides wandering ships (line 7), and like a "fixed mark" that stands against the shaking of life's tempests (lines 5 and 6). Fixity is also the condition stressed by Keats in "Bright Star," where the speaker contrasts his own apparent instability with his desire to be as steadfast in his loving as the star is in the sky (line 1). Rossetti refers to love as a light in darkness (stanza 1), even though the light, to her speaker, has been snuffed out by the death of her beloved.

[3]   For these three writers, then, love grows out of the need for stability and guidance, just as it also supplies this need. To this degree, love is a simplifying force, but it simplifies primarily because the darkness and the "tempests" complicating life are so strong. Such love is one of the best things that happen to human beings, because it fulfills them and prepares them to face life. It is fair to say that all the writers being considered here, either directly or indirectly, are working with this same positive assumption about love.

[4]   The desire to seek identity in love is so strong that it can also cause people to do strange and funny things. The two major characters in Chekhov's short comedy-farce The Bear are examples, as is Sammy of Updike's story "A & P." Sammy watches the three girls in the store with great sexual curiosity, and within minutes after they leave, he quits his job in a gesture that combines

---

° Central idea
* For the texts of these poems, see Appendix C, pages 339, 345, 206, 345–46, 346–47, 352, 354–63, 363–73, 334–38, 322–28.
□ Thesis sentence

[4]

sexual adoration, chivalric respect, and a sense of individuality. A similar quick change is shown by Chekhov's Mrs. Popov and Smirnov, who as <u>The Bear</u> opens are enmeshed in their own confusions. She is devoted to the memory of her dead husband, while he is disillusioned and cynical about women because of mismanaged love affairs. But Chekhov makes them go through hoops for love. As the two argue, insult each other, and reach the point of dueling with real pistols, their need for love overcomes their anger. In their case, as in Sammy's, it is as though the impulse for love and admiration overcomes all the contrary influences, because the common need for a stabilizing base is so strong.

[5]

<u>Either seriously or comically, then, love and love interest are like a rudder, guiding people in powerful and conflicting currents.</u> The results may be sudden and passionate kisses, as with Chekhov's characters, or they may be the establishment of a new condition or ideal, as in Shakespeare, Keats, and Rossetti, and in the decision that Updike's Sammy makes. All these works, however, demonstrate that love shapes lives in ways that go beyond a person's immediate intentions.

[6]

<u>This thought is somewhat like the view presented by Eudora Welty in "A Worn Path."</u> Welty's story describes how love is manifested in loving service, in this respect being not only a guide, but a controlling force. A poor grandmother, Phoenix Jackson, has a hard life in caring for her incurably ill grandson. The walk she takes along the "worn path" to Natchez symbolizes the hardships she endures because of her single-minded love. Her care is the closest thing to pure simplicity that may be found in all the works examined, with the possible exception of the sudden falling in love in Chekhov's play.

[7]

<u>Even Phoenix's devoted service, however, does not solve problems, but rather brings them out.</u> She is not surrounded by the joyless, loveless, violent world described by Hardy, Owen, and Arnold, but her life is nevertheless quite grim. She is poor and ignorant, and her grandson has nowhere to go but down. If she would only think deeply about her condition, she might be as despairing as Arnold and Hardy. But her strength is her ability either to accept her difficult life or to ignore the grimness of it. With her service as her "star" and "ever-fixed mark," to recall Shakespeare's words in Sonnet 116, she stays cheerful and lives in friendship with the animals and the woods. Her life has meaning and dignity.

[8]

Arnold's view of love and devotion under such bad conditions marks a departure from the views of love's power as a guiding and governing force. For Arnold, the public world seems to be so far gone that there is nothing left but personal relationships. <u>Thus love is not so much a guide as a refuge, a condition accepted for sanity and safety.</u> After describing what he considers the worldwide shrinking of the "Sea of Faith" (i.e., the loss of absolute belief in the existence of a personal and caring God), he states:

Ah, love, let us be true
To one another! for the world, which seems
To lie before us like a land of dreams,
So various, so beautiful, so new,
Hath really neither joy, nor love, nor light,
Nor certitude, nor peace, nor help for pain;
And we are here as on a darkling plain
Swept with confused alarms of struggle and flight
Where ignorant armies clash by night.

—lines 29–37

Here the word <u>true</u> should be underlined, as Shakespeare emphasizes "<u>true</u> minds" and as Welty gives us in Phoenix a portrait of true service. "True" in Arnold's poem involves the creation of a small area of fidelity and certainty in

[8] the world of horrible naval gunnery and rattling rifles of "Channel Firing" and "Anthem for Doomed Youth," where there is only madness and death. Love is not so much a guide as a condition of hope, a retreat where truth can still have meaning.

In practice, perhaps, Arnold's idea of love as a refuge is not different from the view that love is a guide. Once the truthful pledge is made, it is a force for goodness, at least for the lovers making the pledge, just as love creates stability and purpose for Shakespeare, Chekhov, Welty, and Keats. <u>Yet Arnold's view is weaker.</u> It does not come from within, as with the longing of Rossetti's speaker,

[9] Sammy's final gesture of support for the rights of the young ladies to wear bathing suits in a public place, or the abrupt love of Chekhov's major characters. Rather Arnold's appeal for truth and fidelity results from a philosophical decision to ignore political and philosophical forces, which are beyond control, and to seek meaning and fidelity only in small and private relationships.

Thus far love and devotion have been considered more or less as ideals, but the ideal is always subject to the reality of human personality. <u>A major idea is hence that the character of a person may turn love sour and damage life.</u> Such destructiveness is brought out best in this set of works by Susan Glaspell

[10] in <u>Trifles.</u> Ideally, the love of John and Minnie Wright should have given them the strength and stability to live satisfactory if not happy lives on their isolated small farm. Instead, John has used his power to suppress Minnie's femininity and love of song. The result is her simmering anger for the thirty years of their life together, resulting in the outburst of her strangling John in his sleep.

Minnie's anger is not dissimilar to that of Mrs. Popov, whose dead husband Nicolai had been neglectful and unfaithful. John, however, is not unfaithful, but overbearing and cruel, thus justifying Minnie's rage. Mrs. Popov has some of the same rage, but submerges it at the start of <u>The Bear</u> by devoting her life to the role of a grieving (but angry) widow. She of course is more

[11] fortunate than Minnie, for fate takes her husband Nicolai while Minnie, in desperation and presumed rage, takes the burden of eliminating her husband herself. <u>Even though neither husband appears in</u> The Bear <u>and</u> Trifles, <u>they both demonstrate the worst possible result of love—its use for personal power rather than for mutual understanding, tenderness, and devoted caring.</u>

John Wright and Nicolai Popov are minor compared with those unseen, unnamed and distant persons firing the big guns during the "gunnery practice out at sea" of Hardy's "Channel Firing" (line 10) and also those who create "the monstrous anger of the guns" of Owen's "Anthem for Doomed Youth" (line 2). Neither poet treats the gunners as individuals but as an evil collective force made up of persons who, under the sheltering claim of devoted service to country, are "striving strong to make / Red war yet redder" (Hardy, lines 13, 14)

[12] and to create great hordes of "these who die as cattle" (Owen, line 1). <u>For them, love of country is a last refuge and not a guide, and it is therefore a misuse of devoted service.</u> In their blind obedience, as Hardy's God says, they are not much better than the dead because they do nothing "for Christés sake" (line 15). They operate the ships and fill the columns of Arnold's "ignorant armies," and, like Wright and Nicolai, they have forsaken the guidance that love should give while they pursue mindless and destructive ends.

In summary, love and devotion as seen in these various works may be
[13] compared with a continuous line formed out of the human need for love and for

the stability and guidance that love offers. At one end love is totally good and ideal; at the other it becomes totally bad. Shakespeare, Keats, Rossetti, Welty, Chekhov's Smirnov and Mrs. Popov, and Updike's Sammy are at the end that is good. Still at the good end, but moving toward the center, is Arnold's use of

[13]   love as a refuge. On the other side of the line are Chekhov's Nicolai Popov and Glaspell's John Wright, while all the way at the bad end are the insensible and invisible gunners in Hardy's "Channel Firing" and Owen's "Anthem for Doomed Youth."

The difficulty noted in all the works, and a major problem in life, is to keep oneself on the stabilizing, constructive part of the line. Although in his farce Chekhov causes love to win against almost impossible odds, he shows the problem most vividly of all the authors studied. Under normal conditions, people like Mrs. Popov and Smirnov would not find love. Instead, they would continue

[14]   following their destructive and false guides. They would be unhappy and disillusioned, and would continue to spread talk about their own confused ideas (as Smirnov actually does almost right up to his sudden conversion to loving Mrs. Popov). Like the military and naval forces of Arnold and Hardy, they would then wind up at the destructive end of the line.

Change, death, opposition, confusion, anger, resignation, economic difficulty, illness—these are only some forms of the forces that attack people as they try to find meaning and stability in love and service as in Sonnet 116, "Bright Star," "Echo," the major characters in The Bear, "A Worn Path," and, to smaller degrees, "A & P" and "Dover Beach." If confusion wins, they are

[15]   locked into harmful positions, like the gunners in "Channel Firing" and "Anthem for Doomed Youth" and like Nicolai Popov of The Bear and John Wright of Trifles. Thus love is complicated by circumstances, and it not by itself alone the simple force for good that it should ideally be. The works compared and contrasted here have shown these difficulties and complexities.

COMMENTARY ON THE THEME

This theme, combining for discussion all three of the genres, is visualized as an assignment at the end of a unit of study. The expectation prompting the assignment is that a fairly large number of literary works can be profitably compared on the basis of a unifying subject, idea, or technique. For this sample, the works—six poems, two stories, and two plays—are compared and contrasted on the common ground or central idea of the complexity of love and service. The theme develops this central idea in three major sections: (1) love as an ideal and guide, in paragraphs 2 to 7, (2) love as a refuge or escape, in paragraphs 8 and 9, and (3) love as an excuse for doing harm, as in paragraphs 10 to 12.

The various works are grouped generally according to these sections. Thus Sonnet 116, "Bright Star," "Echo," The Bear, "A & P," and "A Worn Path" are together in the first group—love as an ideal and guide. "Dover Beach" and "Channel Firing" are considered in the second section but are also introduced for comparison in paragraph 7 as part of a point about the nature of Phoenix's condition in "A Worn Path." Similarly, some of the works in the first group are included as subjects of comparison and contrast in all the sections.

It is obviously impossible for all works being considered to be discussed in detail in every paragraph of a comparison–contrast theme. Thus, in paragraph 2 of this theme, only three of the works are introduced on the common topic, and paragraph 3 consists of a reflection on these three works. Paragraph 4 introduces two works on a slightly different point ("strange and funny things") than that of paragraphs 2 and 3. Paragraph 5 is like the third paragraph because it, too, serves as a point of reflection—this time about all the works considered to that point. The form of comparison and contrast throughout the theme might hence be thought of as one of expansion (when a number of works are introduced) and contraction (when there are just a few).

Paragraph 6 introduces references to just one work, Welty's "A Worn Path," with a brief comparison of only one other work at the end. The seventh paragraph continues the subject of the sixth and introduces two additional works for comparison. (For paragraph 8, see below.) Like paragraph 8, paragraph 9 uses Arnold's "Dover Beach" as the key work, with reference to a number of other works for comparison.

The third major section of the theme, consisting of paragraphs 10 to 12, is devoted primarily to four works, although the general idea of love, as established early in the theme, provides the subject of an implicit contrast.

The technique of comparison–contrast used in this way shows how the various works may be defined and distinguished in relation to the common idea. Paragraph 13, the first in the conclusion, summarizes these distinctions by suggesting a continuous line along which each of the works may be placed. Paragraphs 14 and 15 continue the summary by showing the prominence of complicating difficulties, and, by implication, the importance of love and devoted duty.

One may readily grant that an extended comparison–contrast theme does not present a "full treatment" of each of the works. Indeed, the works are unique, and there are many elements that would not yield to the comparison–contrast method. In "Channel Firing," for example, there are ideas that human beings need eternal rest and not eternal life, that God is amused by—or indifferent to—human affairs, that religious service may be futile, and that war itself is the supreme form of cruelty. To introduce the poem into this comparison–contrast structure requires questioning the motives for patriotic duty of the distant gunners. While this consideration forms a link with the other works, it is by no means the major idea in Hardy's poem. So it is with the other works, each of which could be the subject of analysis from a number of separate standpoints. The effect of the comparison of all the works collectively, however, is the enhanced understanding of each of the works separately. To achieve such an understanding and explain it is the major goal of the extended comparison–contrast method.

A Close Look at Paragraph 8

The use of a great number of works may be seen in paragraph 8, which constitutes the beginning of a brief new section of the theme. The principal topic is the use of love as a refuge or retreat, and the central work of the paragraph is "Dover Beach." However, the first sentence contrasts Arnold's view with the common idea in the six works in the first group—that love is a guide. The fifth sentence shows how Arnold is similar in one respect to Shakespeare and Welty, and the sixth sentence shows a similarity of Arnold with Owen and Hardy. The paragraph alone thus brings together most of the works being studied in the theme, with a few receiving specific attention but more receiving general attention, without being specifically named, for comparison and contrast.

chapter 14

Writing About Prosody:

Rhythm, Sound,
and Rhyme in Poetry

Prosody (*the pronunciation of a song or poem*) refers to the study of sounds and rhythms in poetry. Poets, being especially attuned to language, select words not just for content but also for sound, and they arrange words so that important ideas coincide with climaxes of sound. Sensitive readers, when reading poetry aloud, interpret the lines and develop an appropriate speed and expressiveness of delivery—a proper rhythm. Indeed, some people think of rhythm and sound as the **music** of poetry, since it refers to measured sounds much like rhythms and tempos in music. Like music, poetry requires regularity of beat, but the tempo and loudness may be freer and less regular, and also a reader may linger over certain sounds and words, depending on their position in a line. **Prosody** is the word most often used in reference to sound and rhythm, but other descriptive words are **metrics, versification,** and **mechanics of verse.**

It is important to realize that *prosody is never to be separated from the content of a poem.* It is significant only as it supports and underscores content. Alexander Pope wrote that "the sound [of poetry] must seem an echo to the sense." In short, words count, and not only for their meanings, but also for their sounds and their contributions to a poem's rhythmical flow. Thus, the study of prosody is an attempt to determine how poets have arranged the words of their poems to make sound complement content.

To consider prosody you need to command a few basic linguistic facts. Words are made up of individually meaningful sounds (*segmental phonemes*), or **segments.** Thus, in the word *top* there are three segments: t, ŏ, and *p.* When you hear these three sounds in order, you recognize the word *top.* It takes three alphabetical letters—*t, o,* and *p*—to spell (**graph**) *top,* because each letter is identical with a segment. Sometimes it takes more than one letter to spell a segment. In the word *enough,* for example, there are four segments (*ē, n, ŭ, f*) but six letters: *e, n, ou,* and *gh.* The last two segments (*u* and *f*) require two letters each (two letters forming one segment are called a **digraph**). In the word *through* there are three segments but *seven* letters. To be correctly spelled in this word, the ōō segment must have four letters (*ough*). Note, however, that in the word *flute* the ōō segment requires only one letter, *u.*

Segments in combination make up words, and in combination make up lines of poetry. When we study the combined flow of words, we are concerned with **rhythm,** and when we study the effects of various segments in relationship to the rhythms and the content, we are concerned with **sound,** more specifically **alliteration, assonance,** and **rhyme.**

It is also essential to distinguish between spelling, or **graphics,** and pronunciation, or **phonetics.** Not all English sounds are spelled and pronounced in the same way, as with *top.* Thus the letter *s* has three very different sounds in the words *sweet, sugar,* and *flows: s, sh* (as in "sharp") and *z.* On the other hand, the words *shape, ocean, nation, sure,* and *machine* use different letters or combinations of letters (as digraphs) to spell the same *sh* sound.

Vowel sounds may also be spelled in different ways. The *ē* sound, for example, can be spelled *i* in *machine, ee* in *speed, ea* in *eat, e* in *even,* and *y* in *funny,* yet the vowel sounds in *eat, break,* and *bear* are not the same even though they are spelled the same. Remember this: With both consonants and vowel sounds, *do not confuse spellings with sounds.*

I. RHYTHM

Rhythm in speech is a combination of vocal speeds, rises and falls, starts and stops, vigor and slackness, and relaxation and tension. Every spoken utterance is rhythmical, but in ordinary speech and in prose, rhythm is less important than the flow of ideas. Rhythm is more significant in poetry, however, because poetry is so emotionally charged, compact, and intense. This is not to say that writers of prose ignore sound and rhythm, but rather that poets devote greater attention and skill to these qualities of language. Poets invite readers to stop at words, to linger over sounds, to slow down at times and speed up at others. As language becomes more dramatic and intense, it also becomes more rhythmical. When you read poetry, therefore, you give great attention to individual words; your units of expression are shorter than in prose; your voice will go through a wider range of pitch; and you can rely on greater ranges of dramatic intensity.

SYLLABLES

The unit of rhythm in poetry and prose is the **syllable,** which consists of a single strand of sound such as in the article *a* in "*a* table," *fine* in "fine linen," *sleds* in "new sleds," and *flounce* in "the little girls flounce into the room." (While "a" is a syllable of only one segment, "flounce" consists of six segments: *f, l, ow, n, t,* and *s*). In pronouncing words, you give some syllables more force and intensity than others (note the comparative intensities of the syllables as you say "the bucket," for example, or "the old oaken bucket"). The more intense syllables (created by a combination of loudness, length, and energy) are **heavily stressed,** while the less intense syllables are **lightly stressed.** For metrical discussion, the term in common use is the **foot,** which consists of measured combinations of heavy and light stresses.

There are various types of **feet,** each with a definite pattern. Poets of traditional forms usually fill their lines with a specific number of the same feet, and that number determines the **meter,** or measure of that line. Thus five feet in a line are **pentameter,** four are **tetrameter,** three are **trimeter,** and two are **dimeter.** (To these may be added the less common line lengths **hexameter,** a six-foot line; **heptameter** or **septenary,** seven feet; and **octameter,** eight feet.) Normally, **accent** or **beat** falls on each stressed syllable, although *beat* is often loosely equated with *foot.*

Frequently, rhetorical needs cause poets to **substitute** other feet for the regular foot established in the poem. Whether there is **substitution** or not, however, the number and kind of feet in each line constitute the metrical description of that line. To discover the prevailing metrical system in any poem, you **scan** the poem. The act of scanning is called **scansion.**

A Notational System to Indicate Rhythms

In scansion, it is important to use an agreed-upon notational system to record stress or accent. A heavy or primary accent is commonly indicated by a prime mark or acute accent (´). A light accent may be indicated by a bowl-like half-circle called a **breve** (˘), or by a raised circle or degree sign (°). To separate one foot from another, a **virgule** (/) or slash is used. The following line, from Coleridge's "The Rime of the Ancient Mariner," may be schematized formally in this way:

Wá - tĕr, / wá - tĕr / éve - r̆y whére,

Here the virgules show that the line may be divided into two two-syllable feet and one three-syllable foot.

METRICAL FEET

Equipped with this knowledge, you are ready to scan poems to determine the rhythmical patterns of feet. The most important ones, the specific names of which are derived from Greek poetry, are the two-syllable foot, the three syllable foot, and the imperfect (or one-syllable) foot.

The Two-syllable Foot

1. IAMB. This is a light stress followed by a heavy stress:

t h̆e wínds

The iamb is the most common foot in English poetry because it most nearly reflects natural speech while also elevating speech to poetry. It is the most versatile and adaptable of all the poetic feet. Even within the same line, iambic feet may vary in intensity, so that they may support or undergird the shades of meaning designed by the poet. For example, in this line from Wordsworth, each foot is unique:

T h̆e wínds / thăt wíll / b̆e hówl- / ĭng át / ăll hóurs.

Even though *will* and *at* are stressed syllables, they are not as heavily stressed as *winds, howl-,* and *hours* (indeed, they are also less strong than *all,* which is in an unstressed position in the concluding iamb). Such variability, approximating the stresses and rhythms of actual speech, makes the iamb suitable for both serious and light verse, and it therefore helps poets focus attention on ideas and emotions. If they use it with skill, it never becomes monotonous, for it does not distract readers by drawing attention to its own rhythm.

2. TROCHEE. This is a heavy accent followed by a light:

flów - ĕr

Rhythmically, most English words are trochaic (examples: *wátĕr, snówfăll, aúthŏr, wíllŏw, mórnĭng, eárlў, fóllŏw, síngĭng, présĕnce, sómethĭng*) unless they have prefixes (e.g., *sŭblíme, bĕcáuse, ĭmpél*) or are borrowed from another language and are still pronounced as in that language (e.g., *măchíne, tĕchníque, găráge, chĕmíse*). Because trochaic rhythm has often been called *falling, dying, light,* or *anticlimactic,* while iambic rhythm is *rising, elevating, serious,* and *climactic,* poets have preferred the iambic foot. They therefore have arranged various placements of two syllable words, using single-syllable words and a variety of other means, so that the stressed syllable is at the end of the foot, as in Shakespeare's *hĭs bénd - / ĭng síck - / lĕ's cóm - / păss cóme /,* in which three successive trochaic words are arranged to match the iambic meter.

3. Spondee. The **spondee**—also called a **hovering accent**—consists of two successive, equally heavy accents, as in *men's eyes* in Shakespeare's line:

When, ín / dĭs - gráce / wĭth fór - / tŭne ańd / men's ⌢ eyes.

The spondee is mainly a substitute foot in English verse because successive spondees usually become iambs or trochees. For this reason it is virtually impossible within traditional metrical patterns for an entire poem to be written in spondees (unless a poet uses only one-syllable stressed words while leaving out functional words like prepositions and articles, which are unstressed). As a substitute, however, the spondee creates emphasis. The usual way to indicate the **spondaic foot** is to link the two syllables together with chevronlike marks (⌢).

4. Pyrrhic. The **pyrrhic** consists of two unstressed syllables (even though one of them may be in a normally stressed position), as in *on their* in Pope's line:

Nŏw sleép - / ĭng flocks / ŏn theĭr / soft fleec - / ĕs líe.

The pyrrhic is made up with weakly accented words such as prepositions (e.g., *on*), articles (e.g., *the, a*), inflections (sleep*ing,* fleec*es*), and the concluding syllables of many words (e.g., read*er*). Like the spondee, it is usually substituted for an iamb or trochee, and therefore a complete poem cannot be in pyrrhics. As a substitute foot, however, the pyrrhic acts as a rhythmic catapult to move the reader swiftly to the next strongly accented syllable, and therefore it undergirds the ideas conveyed by more important words.

The Three-Syllable Foot

1. Anapest. This consists of two light stresses followed by a heavy:

bў thĕ dáwn's / eăr - lў líght (Key)

2. Dactyl. This is a heavy stress followed by two lights:

gréen ăs oŭr / hópe ĭn ĭt, / whíte ăs oŭr / faíth ĭn ĭt (Swinburne)

The Imperfect Foot

The **imperfect foot** consists of a single syllable (´) or (˘) by itself. This foot is a variant or substitute occurring in a poem in which one of the major feet forms the metrical pattern. The second line of "The Star-Spangled Banner," for example, is anapestic, but it contains an imperfect foot at the end:

What so proud - / ly we hailed / at the twi - / light's last gleam - / ing.

Uncommon Meters

Many poems contain variants other than those described above. Poets such as Browning, Tennyson, Poe, and Swinburne experimented with uncommon meters. Other poets manipulate pauses or **caesurae** (discussed below) to create the effects of uncommon meters. For these reasons, you might need to refer to metrical feet such as the following:

1. AMPHIBRACH. This is a light, heavy, and light:

Ah feed me / and fill me / with pleas - sure (Swinburne).

2. AMPHIMACER OR CRETIC. This is a heavy, light, and heavy:

Love is best (Browning).

3. BACCHIUS OR BACCHIC This is a light stress followed by two heavy stresses:

Some late lark / sing - ing (Henley).

4. DIPODIC or SYZYGY. Dipodic measure (literally, "two feet" combining to make one) develops in longer lines when a poet submerges two regular feet under a stronger beat, so that a "galloping" or "rollicking" rhythm results. The following line from Masefield's "Cargoes," for example (p. 351), may be scanned as five trochees followed by an iamb:

Quin-que / reme of / Nin- e- / veh from / dis-tant / O-phir.

In reading, however, a stronger beat is superimposed on groups of four syllables, making one foot out of two—dipodic measure or syzygy:

Quinquereme of / Nineveh from / distant Ophir

OTHER RHYTHMIC DEVICES

Accentual, Strong-Stress, and "Sprung" Rhythms

Accentual or strong-stress lines are historically derived from the poetry of Old English (A.D. 700–1100). At that time, each line was divided in two, with two major stresses occurring in each half. In the nineteenth century, Gerard Manley Hopkins (1844–1889) developed what he called "sprung" rhythm, a rhythm in which the major stresses would be released or "sprung" from the line. The method is complex, but one characteristic is the juxtaposing of one-syllable stressed words, as in this line from "Pied Beauty":

With swift, slow; sweet, sour; adazle, dim;

Here a number of elements combine to create six major stresses in the line, which contains only nine syllables. Many of Hopkins's lines combine alliteration (see p. 189) and strong stresses in this way to create the same effect of heavy emphasis.

The Caesura, or Pause

Whenever we speak, we utter a number of syllables without pause of any sort and stop only after a definite group of meaningful words is finished. These groups of words, rhythmically, are **cadence groups.** In poetry, the short or heavy pause separating cadence groups is called a **caesura** (plural **caesurae**). For scansion, the caesura may be noted by two diagonal lines or **virgules** (//) to distinguish it from the single **virgule** separating feet. Sometimes the caesura coincides with the end of a foot, as in this line by William Blake ("To Mrs. Anna Flaxman"):

With hands / di - vine / / he mov'd / the gen - / tle Sod./

The caesura, however, may fall within a foot, and there may be more than one in a line, as in this line by Ben Jonson:

Thou art / not, / / Pens - / hurst, / / built / to en - / vious show./

When a caesura ends a line, usually marked by a comma, semicolon, or period, that line is **end-stopped,** like this line which opens Keats's "Endymion" (1818):

A thing / of beau - / ty / / is / a joy / for - ev - er. / /

If a line has no punctuation at the end and runs over to the next line, it is called **run-on.** A term also used to indicate run-on lines is **enjambement.** The following passage, a continuation of the line from Keats, contains three run-on lines:

> Its loveliness increases; / / it will never
> Pass into nothingness; / / but still will keep
> A bower quiet for us, / / and a sleep
> Full of sweet dreams, / / . . .

Emphasis by Formal Substitution

Most closed form poems follow a regular pattern that may be formally analyzed according to the regular feet we have been describing here. For interest and emphasis, however (and also because of the natural rhythms of English speech), poets **substitute** other feet for the regular feet of the poem. For example, the following line is from the "January" Eclogue of Edmund Spenser's *Shepherd's Calendar.* Although the pattern of the poem is iambic pentameter (i.e., five iambs per line), Spenser includes two substitute feet in the line:

All in / a sun - / shine day, / as did / be - fall./

In the first foot, *All in* is a trochee, and *shine day* is a spondee. These are formal substitutions; that is, Spenser uses separate, formally structured feet in place of the normal iambic feet. The effect is to move from "All" to "sunshine day" in a rapid, climactic sweep, in keeping with the idea that a springlike day in winter brings indescribable pleasure.

Emphasis by Rhetorical Substitution

The effects provided by formal substitution may also be achieved by the manipulation of the caesura. If the pauses are arranged within feet, they may create the actual *hearing* of trochees, amphibrachs, and other variant feet even though the line may scan regularly in the dominant meter. This variation is **rhetorical substitution.** A noteworthy example in an iambic pentameter line is this one from Pope's *Essay on Man:*

His ac - / tion's, / / pas - / sion's, / / be - / ing's, / / use / and end.

Ordinarily there is one caesura in a line of this type (after the fourth syllable), but in this one Pope has made three, each producing a strong pause. The line is regularly iambic, but speaking it aloud creates a different effect. Because of the caesurae after the third, fifth, and seventh syllables, the rhythm produces an amphibrach, a trochee, another trochee, and an amphimacer, thus:

His ăc - tĭon's, / / păs - sion's, / / bĕ - ĭng's, / / ŭse / ănd end.

Thus the spoken substitutions produced by the caesurae in this regular line produce the tension and interest of substitution.

When studying rhythm, then, your main concern in noting substitutions is to determine the formal metrical pattern and then to analyze the formal and rhetorical variations on this pattern and their principal techniques and effects. Always try to show how these variations have enabled the poet to get points across and to achieve emphasis.

II. SEGMENTAL POETIC DEVICES

Once you have completed your analysis of rhythms, you may go on to consider the segmental poetic devices in the poem. Usually these devices are used to create emphasis, but somethimes in context they may echo or imitate some of the things being described. The segmental devices most common in poetry are **assonance, alliteration,** and **onomatopoeia.**

ASSONANCE

Assonance is the repetition of identical *vowel* sounds in different words— for example, the short ĭ in "swĭft Camĭlla skĭms." It is a strong means of emphasis, as in the following line, where the ŭ sound connects the two words *lull* and *slumber,* and short ĭ connects *him, in,* and *his:*

And more, to lull him in his slumber soft.

In some cases, poets may use assonance elaborately, as in the first line of Pope's *An Essay on Criticism:*

'Tis hard to say, if greater want of skill.

Here the line is framed and balanced with the short ĭ in *'Tis, if,* and *skill.* The ä in *hard* and *want* forms another, internal frame, and the ā in *say* and *greater* creates still another frame. Such a balanced use of vowels is unusual, however, for in most lines assonance occurs primarily as a means of highlighting important words, without such elaborate patterning.

ALLITERATION

Alliteration is a means of highlighting ideas by the selection of words containing the same *consonant* sound—for example, the repeated *m* in Spenser's "Mixed with a *m*ur*m*uring wind," or the *s* sound in Waller's "Your never-failing *s*word made war to *c*ease," which emphasizes the connection between the words *sword* and *cease*."

There are two kinds of alliteration. (1) Most commonly, alliteration is regarded as the repetition of identical consonant sounds that begin syllables in close patterns—for example, in Pope's line "*L*aborious, heavy, *b*usy, *b*old, and *b*lind," and "While *p*ensive *p*oets *p*ainful vigils keep." Used judiciously, alliteration gives strength to ideas by emphasizing key words, but too much can cause comic and catastrophic consequences. (2) Another form of alliteration occurs when a poet repeats identical or similar consonant sounds that do not begin syllables but nevertheless create a pattern—for example, the *z* segment in the line "In these places freezing breezes easily cause sneezes," or the *b, m,* and *p* segments (all of which are made *bilabially,* that is, with both lips) in "The *m*u*mb*ling and *m*ur*m*uring *b*eggar throws *p*egs and *p*e*bb*les in the *b*u*bb*ling *p*ool." Such patterns, apparently deliberately organized, are hard to overlook.

ONOMATOPOEIA

Onomatopoeia is a blending of consonant and vowel sounds designed to imitate or suggest a situation or action. It is made possible in poetry because many words in English are **echoic** in origin; that is, they are verbal echoes of the actions they describe, such as *buzz, bump, slap, spirit,* and so on. Tennyson utilizes onomatopoeia effectively in the fragment from "The Passing of Arthur" analyzed in the first sample theme (below, pp. 199–205). There, in describing the panting of the man exerting himself heavily while carrying King Arthur from the height of a cliff to the level of a lake, he uses many words beginning with the aspirate *h* sound. Since panting creates a breathy, aspirated sound, speaking Tennyson's lines duplicates the sounds he describes.

EUPHONY AND CACOPHONY

Words describing smooth or jarring sounds, particularly those resulting from consonants, are **euphony** and **cacophony,** respectively. Euphony ("good sound") refers to words containing consonants that permit an easy and smooth flow of spoken sound. Although there is no rule that some consonants are inherently more pleasant than others, students of poetry often cite the sounds *m, n, ng, l, v,* and *z,* together with *w,* and *y,* as being especially easy on the ears. The opposite of euphony is cacophony ("bad sound"), in which percussive and choppy sounds make for particularly vigorous and noisy pronunciation. It is the combination of words and sounds that creates harshness, as in tongue-twisters like "black bug's blood" and "selfish shellfish in a sushi." Obviously, unintentional cacophony is a mark of imperfect control. When a poet deliberately creates it for effect, however, as in Tennyson's line "The bare black cliff clang'd round him," Pope's "The hoarse, rough verse should like the torrent roar," and Coleridge's "Huge fragments vaulted like rebounding hail, / Or chaffy grain beneath the thresher's flail," cacophony is a mark of poetic skill. Although poets generally aim at easily flowing, euphonious lines, cacophony does have a place, always depending on the poet's intention and subject matter.

III. RHYME AND ITS FUNCTIONS

Rhyme is the repetition of identical or similar concluding syllables in different words, most often at the ends of lines. Words with the same concluding vowel sounds rhyme; such rhymes are a special kind of assonance. Thus *day* rhymes with *weigh, grey, bouquet,* and *matinee.* Rhyme may also combine assonance and idential consonant sounds, as in *ache, bake, break,* and *opaque,* or *turn, yearn, fern,* and *adjourn.* As these examples illustrate, rhyme is a function of *sound* rather than spelling; the words do not have to be spelled the same way or look alike to rhyme.

When rhyme is employed to good effect in poetry, it becomes much more than a simple ornament. Rhyme adds to the sensory impact of poetry by providing a pleasing network of related sounds that echo in the mind. Through rhyme, sound may join with sense in a coherent whole. Rhyme can also contribute significantly to the impression that a given poem makes on our memories. In its simplest form, it jingles in the mind, with rhymes like *bells* and *tells,* but rhyme also provides emphasis and reinforces ideas. It is a powerful way of clinching a thought by the physical link of related sound.

Wherever rhyme is employed with skill and originality, it leads the mind into fresh, unusual, and even surprising turns of thought. Poets may thus be judged, at least to some extent, on their rhymes. Some rhymers are satisfied with easy rhymes, or *cliché rhymes,* like *trees* and *breeze* (a rhyme criticized by Pope). But good rhymes and good poets go together, in creative cooperation. For example, the seventeenth-century poet John Dryden, who wrote volumes of rhyming couplets, acknowledged that the need to find rhymes inspired ideas that he had not anticipated. In this sense, rhyme has been—and still is—a vital element of poetic creativity.

RULES AND VARIANTS IN RHYME

While languages like Italian or French contain large numbers of rhyming words, making rhyme comparatively easy to achieve, the English language is short on rhyming words. Therefore there are not many "rules" for poets using rhymes. About the only restriction is that the same forms are not to be used, even if they appear in different words. *Turn* should not be matched with *taciturn, verse* with *universe,* or *stable* with *unstable.* Aside from this, the major guide is taste and propriety.

Also, because of the difficulty of finding rhyming words in English, a wide latitude in rhyming forms has been accepted. There is **eye rhyme** or **sight rhyme,** the pairing of words that look alike but do not sound alike. Thus according to sight rhyme "I *wind* [a clock]" may be joined to "the North *wind.*" In **slant rhyme,** the rhyming vowel segments are different while the consonants are the same; for example *bleak* and *broke; could* and *solitude.*

RHYME AND RHYTHM

The effects of rhyme are closely connected with rhythm. In general, rhymes falling on accented syllables lend themselves to serious effects. These rhymes have traditionally been called **masculine,** although terms like **heavy-stress rhyme** or **accented rhyme** are now more appropriate. The accenting of heavy-stress rhyme may be seen in the opening lines of Robert Frost's "Stopping by Woods on a Snowy Evening":

> Whose woods / these are / I think / I know.
> His house / is in / the vil- / lage though.

Rhymes concluding with either one or two light stresses have been called **feminine,** but this term may now be distasteful. Preferable terms are the accurate **trochaic** or **double rhyme** for rhymes of two syllables, and **dactylic** or **triple rhyme** for rhymes of three syllables. Abstractly, such rhymes are called **falling** or **dying.** Falling rhymes are most appropriate in comic and lighter subject matter, as in the second and fourth lines of the first stanza of "Miniver Cheevy" by Edwin Arlington Robinson:

> Miniver Cheevy, child of scorn
> Grew lean while he assailed the *seasons.*
> He wept that he was ever born,
> And he had *reasons.*

Dactylic or triple rhyme is unusual. It may be seen in these lines from Browning's "The Pied Piper of Hamelin," which also illustrate **internal rhyme,** that is, a rhyming word within a line:

Small feet were ***pattering,*** wooden shoes ***clattering,***
Little hands clapping and little tongues ***chattering.***
And, like fowls in a farm-yard where barley was ***scattering***. . . .

DESCRIBING RHYMES

In the description of rhymes, alphabetical letters are used. Each repeated letter indicates a rhyme (a, a). Each new letter indicates a new rhyme (b, b; c, c; d, d; etc.). An *x* indicates no rhyme. To formulate a rhyme pattern, you should include (1) the meter and number of feet of each line, and (2) the letters indicating rhymes. Here is such a formulation:

Iambic pentameter: a, b, b, a, c, c, a.

This scheme shows that all the lines are iambic; with five feet in each line. The rhyming lines are 1, 4, and 7; 2 and 3; and 5 and 6.

Should the number of feet in lines vary, show this fact with a number in front of each letter:

Iambic: 5a, 5b, 4a, 3a, 2b, 6a.

Always make a note of any deviations from the predominant pattern. If there is a variation in the meter of any of the rhymes, note that variation the first time you use the letter, as follows:

Iambic: 5a, 4b (trochee), 5a, 4b, 5a, 5b.

Here lines 2, 4, and 6 are rhyming trochees; there is no need to indicate this fact on any but the first use of the letter, because the subsequent appearances of the letter automatically indicate the variation.

RHYME SCHEMES

Along with the line length, rhyme is a determinant in the classification of poetic forms. Here are the major ones:

1. The Couplet.

a, a; b, b; c, c; d, d; etc.

Couplets of iambic pentameter are called **heroic** or **neoclassic.** Also common, especially for light and satiric purposes, are couplets in iambic tetrameter (four iambic feet).

2. The Italian or Petrarchan Sonnet.

Iambic pentameter: a, b, b, a, a, b, b, a, c, d, c, d, c, d.

The first eight lines form the **octave,** the last six the **sestet.** There is usually a shift in thought from the octave to the sestet.

3. The Shakespearean Sonnet.

Iambic pentameter: a, b, a, b, c, d, c, d, e, f, e, f, g, g.

Note that the Shakespearean sonnet has seven rhyming sounds, contrasted with the four in the Italian sonnet. Each rhyming group of four lines, like any four-line group, is called a **quatrain.** Each quatrain usually contains a separate development of the thought, with the couplet providing a conclusion or climax.

4. Ballad Measure, or Common Measure.

Iambic: 4x, 3a, 4x, 3a; 4x, 3b, 4x, 3b; etc.

Each quatrain forms a separate unit, analogous to the paragraph, called a **stanza.** A typical ballad consists of many stanzas. Ballads are often narrative in development, like the anonymous "Sir Patrick Spens." Coleridge uses ballad measure for "The Rime of the Ancient Mariner" and adds variations with extra lines for some of his stanzas.

5. The Song.

The song is a free stanzaic form designed to be sung to a repeated melody. The scheme for one stanza therefore describes all the stanzas. There is no limit to the number of stanzas, although there are usually no more than five or six. Here are some rhyme schemes of song stanzas:

Donne's "The Canonization":
    Iambic: 5a, 4b, 5b, 5a, 4c, 4c, 4a, 3a.

Browing's "Two in the Campagna":
    Iambic tetrameter: a, b, a, b, (3)x.

(Note that line 5 is not paired in rhyme with any of the other lines and that this line has three rather than four feet.)

Burns's "To a Mouse":
    Iambic tetrameter: a, a, b, (2)c, b, (2)c.
In stanzas 1, 2, 4, and 6 the rhyming feet are in amphibrachs.
In stanzas 3, 5, 7, and 8 the rhyming feet are iambic.

A regular variant of the song is the **hymn,** a song used in religious services. Hymns usually contain from three to six stanzas. Common measure is most frequently used, but there are many schemes. To enable hymns to be sung to a number of separate tunes, most hymnals contain an analytical table of the hymns based on the number of syllables in each line of the stanza.

6. Terza Rima.

Terza rima is a rhyming pattern of three lines in iambic pentameter: a, b, a; b, c, b; c, d, c; etc. Dante invented this form for *The Divine Comedy*. Shelley uses it in the first stanzas of "Ode to the West Wind." Roethke uses it in "The Waking."

7. The Ode.

The ode is a stanzaic form more complex than the song, with varying line lengths and sometimes intricate rhyme schemes. Some odes have repeating stanzaic patterns, whereas others are totally free. Although some odes have been used as a setting for music, they usually do not fit repeating melodies. There is no set form for the ode; poets have developed their own types according to their needs. Keats's great odes were particularly congenial to his ideas, like the "Ode to a Nightingale," which consists of ten stanzas in iambic pentameter with the repeating form a, b, a, b, c, d, e, (3)c, d, e. By constrast, Wordsworth's "Ode: Intimations of Immortality" consists of ten stanzas but each of the stanzaic patterns is unique.

WRITING ABOUT PROSODY

Because studying prosody requires a good deal of specific detail and also much specific description, it is best to limit your choice of poem to a short passage or a complete short poem. A sonnet, a stanza of a lyric poem, or a fragment from a long poem will usually be sufficient for your study. If you choose a fragment, it should be self-contained, such as an entire speech or short episode or scene (like the example from Tennyson chosen for the first sample theme, pp. 199–205).

The analysis of even a short poem, however, can grow long because of the need to describe word positions and stresses and also to determine the various effects. For this reason, you do not have to exhaust all aspects of your topic. Try to make your discussion representative of the prosody of the poem or passage you have chosen.

Your first reading in preparation for your theme should be for comprehension. On second and third readings, make notes of sounds, accents, and rhymes by reading the poem aloud. To perceive sounds, one student helped herself by reading aloud in an exaggerated way in front of a mirror. If you have privacy, or are not self-conscious, you might do the same. Let yourself go a bit. As you dramatize your reading (maybe even before fellow students), you will find that heightened levels of reading also accompany the poet's expression of important ideas. Mark these spots for later analysis, so that you will be able to make good points about the relationship of the poem's prosody to its content.

In planning your theme, it is vitally important to prepare study sheets so that your observations will be correct, for if your factual analysis is wrong, some of your writing will also be wrong. Furthermore, your writing task will be made easy by careful preparation. Experience has shown that it is best to make four triple-spaced copies of the poem or passage (with carbon paper or duplicating machine). These will be for the separate analysis of (1) rhythm, (2) assonance, (3) alliteration, and (4) rhyme. If you have been assigned just one of these, of course only one copy will be necessary. Leave spaces between syllables and words for marking out the various feet of the poem. Ultimately, this duplication of the passage, with your markings, should be included as a first page, as in the sample themes.

Carry out your study of the passage in the following way:

1. Number each line of the passage, regardless of length, beginning with *1*, so that you may use these numbers as location references in your theme.

2. Determine the formal pattern of feet, using the short acute accent for heavily stressed syllables (´), and the breve for lightly stressed syllables (˘). Use chevrons to mark spondees (⌢).

3. Indicate the separate feet by a diagonal line or virgule (/). Indicate caesurae and end-of-line pauses by double virgules (//).

4. Use colored pencils to underline, circle, make boxes, or otherwise mark the formal and rhetorical substitutions that you discover. Because such substitutions may occur throughout the poem, develop a numbering system for each type (e.g., 1 = anapest, 3 = spondee, etc., as in the sample worksheet, pp. 200-202). Provide a key to your numbers at the bottom of the page.

5. Do the same for alliteration, assonance, onomatopoeia, and rhyme. It has proved particularly effective to draw lines to connect the repeating

sounds, for these effects will be close together in the poem, and your connections will dramatize this closeness. The use of a separate color for each effect with each separate sound is particularly useful, for the distinctions made by different colors make possible the exact observation needed for this theme.

6. Use your worksheets as a reference for your reader. In writing your theme, however, you need to make your examples specific by making brief quotations, as in the examples (i.e., words, phrases, and entire lines, with proper marks and accents). Do not rely on line numbers alone.

Once you have analyzed the various effects in the poem under consideration and have recorded these on your worksheets and in your notes, you will be ready to formulate a central idea and organization for your theme. The focus of the theme should reflect what you have found to be the most significant features of prosody in relationship to some other element of the poem, such as speaker, tone, or ideas. Thus, in planning a theme about Masefield's "Cargoes" you might argue that the dipodic rhythms undergird the poem's alternating notes of admiration and irony. In studying Coleridge's "Kubla Khan" you might take the view that the segmental effects, through onomatopoeia, graphically complement the poem's descriptions.

After forming a tentative idea, you can gather examples of supporting prosodic evidence. These examples can be grouped into units of related or similar effects that will eventually become paragraphs. Make sure that all examples are relevant to your central idea. If you find the prosodic evidence leading you in new directions, revise your central idea accordingly.

Depending on your assignment, you might show the operation of all the component elements of prosody, or you may wish to focus on just one aspect. It would be possible, for example, to devote an entire theme to the discussion of (1) regular meter, (2) one particular variation in meter, such as the anapest or spondee, (3) the caesurae, (4) assonance, (5) alliteration, (6) onomatopoeia, or (7) rhyme. For brevity of illustration, we here treat rhythm and segments together as one theme, and rhyme as a separate theme.

Introduction

The introduction should lead as quickly as possible to the central idea. After a brief description of the poem (such as that it is a sonnet, a two-stanza lyric, an iambic pentameter description of a character or action, a dipodic burlesque poem, and so on), establish the scope of your theme. Your central idea will outline the thought you wish to carry out through your prosodic analysis, such as that regularity of meter is consistent with a happy, firm vision of love or life, or that the use of the spondee emphasizes the solidity of the speaker's wish to love, or that particular sounds emphasize some of the poem's actions. Your thesis sentence should outline the aspects to be treated in the body.

Body

A. RHYTHM. First, establish the formal metrical pattern. What is the dominant metrical foot and line length? Are some lines shorter than the pattern? What relationship do the variable lengths have to the subject matter? If the poem is a lyric or a sonnet, is the poet successful in placing important words and syllables in stressed positions to achieve emphasis? Try to relate line lengths to whatever exposition and development of ideas and whatever rising and falling emotions you find. It is also important to look for either repeating or varying metrical patterns as the subject matter reaches peaks or climaxes. Generally, deal with the relationship between the formal rhythmical pattern and the poet's ideas and attitudes.

When noting substitutions, you might analyze the formal variations and the principal effects of these, as nearly as you can determine what the effects are. If you concentrate on only one substitution, describe any apparent pattern in its use—that is, its locations, recurrences, and effects on meaning.

For caesurae, treat the effectiveness of the poet's control. Can you see any pattern of use? Are the pauses regular, or do they seem randomly placed? Describe any noticeable principles of placement, such as (1) the creation of rhythmical similarities in various parts of the poem, (2) the development of particular rhetorical effects, or (3) the creation of interest through rhythmical variety. Do the caesurae lead to important ideas and attitudes? Are the lines all end-stopped, or do you discover enjambement? How do these rhythmical characteristics aid in the poet's expression of subject matter?

B. SEGMENTAL EFFECTS. Here you might be discussing, collectively or separately, the use and effects of assonance, alliteration, onomatopoeia, and cacophony and euphony. Be sure to establish that the instances you choose have really occurred systematically enough within the poem to be grouped as a pattern. You should illustrate sounds by including relevant words within parentheses. You might wish to make separate paragraphs on alliteration, assonance, and any other seemingly important pattern. Also, because space in a theme is always at a premium, you might concentrate on one noteworthy effect, like a certain pattern of assonance, rather than on everything. Throughout your discussion, always keep foremost the relationship between content and sound.

Note: To make illustrations clear, underline all sounds to which you are calling attention. If you use an entire word to illustrate sound, underline only the sound and not the entire word, but put the word within quotation marks (for example, The poet uses a t ["tip," "top," and "terrific"]). When you refer to entire words containing particular segments, however, underline these words (for example, "The poet uses a t in tip, top, and terrific).

C. **RHYME.** This discussion should include a description of the major features of rhyme, including the scheme and variants, the lengths and rhythms of the rhyming words, and noteworthy segmental characteristics. In discussing the grammatical features of the rhymes, you might note the kinds of words (i.e., verbs, nouns, etc.) used for rhymes: Are they all the same? Does one form predominate? Is there variety? Can you determine the grammatical positions of the rhyming words? How may these characteristics be related to the idea or theme of the poem?

You might also discuss the qualities of the rhyming words. Are the words specific? Concrete? Abstract? Are there any striking rhymes? Any surprises? Any rhymes that are clever and witty? Do any rhymes give unique comparisons or contrasts? How?

Generally, you might also be able to note striking or unique rhyming effects. Without becoming overly subtle or farfetched, you can make valid and interesting conclusions. Do any sounds in the rhyming words appear in patterns of assonance or alliteration elsewhere in the poem to an appreciable degree? Do the rhymes produce onomatopoeia? Broadly, can you detect any aspects of rhyme that are uniquely effective because they are at one with the thought and mood of your poem?

Conclusion

Beyond summarizing your main idea, you might try to develop a short evaluation of the poet's prosodic performance. If we accept the premise that poetry is designed not only to inform but also to transfer attitudes and to stimulate, to what degree did the prosodic techniques of the poem you have studied contribute to these goals? Without going into excessive detail (and in effect writing another body), what more can you say here? What has been the value of your study to your understanding and appreciation of the poem? If you think your analysis has helped you to develop new awareness of the poet's craft, it would be appropriate to state what you have learned.

First Sample Theme

A Study of Tennyson's Rhythm and Segments in "The Passing of Arthur," lines 349–360

1. *RHYTHMICAL ANALYSIS*

But the o- / ther swift- / ly strode / / from ridge / to ridge, / /   1

Clothed with / his breath, / / and look- / ing, / / as / he walk'd, / /   2

Lar-ger / than hu- / man / / on / the fro- / zen hills. / /   3

He heard / the deep / be-hind / him, / / and / a cry   4

Be-fore. / / His own / thought drove / him / / like / a goad. / /   5

Dry clash'd / his har- / ness / / in / the i / cy caves   6

And bar- ren / chasms, / / and all / to left / and right   7

The bare / black cliff / clang'd round / him, / / as / he based   8

His feet / on juts / of slip- / pe-ry crag / / that rang   9

Sharp- smit- / ten / / with / the / dint / of ar- / med heels— / /   10

And on / a sud- / den, / / lo! / / the lev- / el lake, / /   11

And the / long glor- / ies / / of / the win- / ter moon. / /   12

1 = Anapaest, or effect of anapaest.
2 = Amphibrach, or the effect of amphibrach.
3 = Spondee.

4 = Effect of imperfect foot.
5 = Pyrrhic.
6 = Trochee, or the effect of trochee.

2. ALLITERATION

But the other (s) wiftly (s) trode from ridge to ridge,   1

Clothed with his breath, and looking, as (h) e walked,   2

Larger than (h) uman on the frozen (h) ills.   3

(H) e (h) eard the deep be (h) ind (h) im, and a cry   4

Before. (H) is own thought drove him like a goad.   5

Dry (c) lashed (h) is (h) arness in the icy (c) aves   6

And (b) arren (ch) asms, and all to left and right   7

The (b) are (b) (l) ack (c) (l) iff (c) (l) anged round him, as he (b) ased 8

His feet on juts of s (l) ippery (c) rag that rang   9

Sharp-smitten with the dint of armed heels—   10

And on a sudden, (l) o! the (l) evel (l) ake,   11

And the (l) ong g (l) ories of the winter moon.   12

〰〰〰 = s   ———— = b

‒‒‒‒‒‒ = h   〰〰〰 = l as second consonant
                                                            sound in words

•••••••• = k   —·—·—· = l

3. ASSONANCE

But the other sw (i) ftly str (o) de from r (i) dge to r (i) dge,   1

Cl (o) thed w (i) th h (i) s breath, and looking, as he walked,   2

Larger than human on the fr (o) zen hills.   3

He heard the deep beh (i) nd him, and a cr (y)   4

Before. His (ow) n thought dr (o) ve him l (i) ke a g oa d.   5

Dr (y) clashed his harness in the (i) cy caves   6

And barren ch (a) sms, and all to left and r (i) ght   7

The bare bl (a) ck cliff cl (a) nged round him, as he based   8

H (i) s feet on juts of sl (i) ppery cr (a) g that r (a) ng   9

Sh (ar) p-sm (i) tten w (i) th the d (i) nt of (ar) med heels—   10

And on a sudden, lo, the level lake,   11

And the long glories of the winter moon!   12

———————— = ō *   •—•—•—• = ä

- - - - - - - - = ī   ᴧᴧᴧᴧᴧ = ĭ

• • • • • • • • • = a

* Pronunciation symbols as in *Webster's New World Dictionary*, 2nd ed.

Note: *For illustrative purposes, this theme analyzes a passage from Tennyson's "The Passing of Arthur," which is part of* Idylls of the King. *Containing 469 lines, "The Passing of Arthur" describes the last battle and death of Arthur, legendary king of early Britain. After the fight, in which Arthur has been mortally wounded by the traitor Mordred, only Arthur and his follower Sir Bedivere remain alive. Arthur commands Bedivere to throw the royal sword "Excalibur" into the lake from which Arthur had originally received it. After great hesitation and some false claims, Bedivere does throw the sword into the lake, and a hand rises out of the water to catch it. Bedivere then carries Arthur to the lake shore, where the dying king is taken aboard a magical funeral barge. The passage selected for discussion here is Tennyson's description of Bedivere's carrying Arthur down the hills and cliffs from the battlefield to the lake below.*

[1]
This passage describes the ordeal of Sir Bedivere as he carries the dying Arthur from the mountainous heights, where he was wounded, down to the lake, where the king will be sent to his final rest. Tennyson devotes great attention to the ghostly, deserted landscape, emphasizing the bleakness and hostility of the scenes. The passage is in unrhymed iambic pentameter—blank verse. But Tennyson's verse is alive; it constantly augments his descriptions and conveys an impression of Bedivere's mood, whether of anguish or relaxation.° The control over prosody enables a true blending of sound and sense, as may be seen in Tennyson's use of rhythm and in his manipulation of segmental devices, including onomatopoeia.□

[2]
Tennyson controls his meter to emphasize Bedivere's exertions and moods. In line 1 the meter is regular, except for an anapaest in the first foot. This regularity may be interpreted as emphasizing the swiftness and surefootedness of Bedivere. But he is about to undergo a severe test, and the rhythm quickly becomes irregular, as though to strain the pentameter verse in illustration of Bedivere's exertions. Tennyson therefore uses variations to highlight key words. For example, he uses the effect of anapaests in a number of lines. In line 2 he emphasizes the chill air and Bedivere's vitality in the following way:

Clothéd with / his bréath, / /

The image is one of being surrounded by one's own breath that vaporizes on hitting the cold air, and the rhythmical variation—a trochaic substitution in the first foot—enables the voice to build up to the word breath, a most effective internal climax.

[3]
Tennyson uses a similar rhythmical effect in line 3. He emphasizes the frozen hills by creating a caesura in the middle of the third foot and then by making the heavy stress of the third foot fall on the preposition on, which with the creates in effect the two unstressed syllables of an anapaest including the first, stressed, syllable of frozen. The effect is that the voice builds up to the word and thus emphasizes the extreme conditions in which Bedivere is walking:

/ / on / the fro - / zen hills. / /

Tennyson uses this effect twelve times in the passage. It is his major means of rhetorical emphasis.

° Central idea
□ Thesis sentence

[4]   Perhaps the most effective metrical variation is the spondee, which appears in lines 5, 6, 8, (twice), 10, and 12. These substituitions, occurring mainly in the section in which Sir Bedivere is forcing his way down the frozen hills, permit the lines to ring out, as in:

     The băre / bláck cliff / cláng'd róund /

and

     Drý clásh'd / hĭs hár - / nĕss.

The best use of the spondee is in line 5, where the stresses reach a climax on the word <u>drove</u>, which suggests the torment Bedivere is feeling:

     Hĭs ówn / thóught dróve / hĭm / / lĭke / ă góad

To put a case, let us suppose that Tennyson had been an inferior poet and had written instead, "He was goaded by his thought," or "His thought was like a goad to him." When one realizes how rhythmically inferior such choices are, Tennyson's achievement stands out even more.

[5]   There is other substitution, too, both formal and rhetorical, and the tension these variations create keeps the responsive reader aware of Bedivere's tasks. One type of variation is the appearance of amphibrachic rhythm, which is produced in lines 2, 3, 4, 6, 7, and 11. The effect is achieved by a pattern which complements the rhetorical anapaests. A caesura in the middle of a foot leaves the three preceding syllables as a light, heavy, and light, the rhythmical form of the amphibrach. In line 2, for example, it appears thus:

     / / ănd lóok - / ĭng / /

In line 6 it takes this form:

     / hĭs hár - / nĕss / /

       Still another related variation is that of the apparently imperfect feet in lines 5, 8, 11, and 12. These imperfect feet are produced by a caesura, which isolates the syllable, as *him* is in line 8:

[6]

     The băre / bláck cliff / cláng'd róund / hĭm, / /

In line 11 the syllable (on the word <u>lo</u>!) is surrounded by two caesurae and is therefore thrust into a position of great stress:

     Ănd ón / ă súd - / dĕn / / ló! / / thĕ lével - / ĕl láke

Other, less significant substitutions are the trochees in lines 3 and 7, and the pyrrhic in line 12. All the described variations support the heroic action described in the passage.

Many of the variations described are produced by Tennyson's handling of his sentence structure, which results in a free placement of the caesurae and in a free use of end-stopping and enjambement. It is interesting that four of the first five lines are end-stopped (two by commas, two by periods). Bedivere is exerting himself during these lines and apparently he is making short tests to gather strength for his ordeal. The ordeal comes during the next four lines, when he makes his precarious descent; none of the lines containing this de-

[7]   scription is end-stopped. Bedivere is disturbed (being goaded by "his own thought"), but he must keep going, and we may presume that the free sentence structure and the free metrical variation enforce his difficulty and mental disturbance. But in the last two lines, when he has reached the lake, the lines "relax" with falling caesurae exactly at the fifth syllables. In other words, the sentence structure of the last two lines is regular, an effect designed to indicate the return to order and beauty after the previous, rugged chaos.

This rhythmical virtuosity is accompanied by a similarly brilliant control over segmental devices. Alliteration is the most obvious, permitting Tennyson to tie key words and their signifying actions together, as in the s's in "swiftly strode" in line 1, or the b's in "barren," "bare," "black," and "based" in lines 7 and 8. Other notable examples are the aspirated h's in lines 2–6 (he, human,

[8]   hill, heard, behind, him, his, harness); the k's in lines 6–9 (clash'd, caves, chasms, cliff, clang'd, crag); and the l's in lines 11 and 12 (lo, level, lake, long, glories). One might compare these l's with l's in the more anguished context of lines 8 and 9, where the sounds appear as the second segment in the heavy, ringing words there (black, cliff, clang'd, slippery). The sounds are the same, and the emphasis is similar, but the effects are different.

Assonance is also present throughout the passage. In the first five lines, for example, the ō appears in six words. The first three ō's are in descriptive or metaphoric words (strode, clothed, frozen), while the last three are in words describing the pain and anguish that Bedivere experiences as a result of his efforts in the barren landscape (own, drove, goad). The o therefore ties the physical to the psychological. Other patterns of assonance are the ă in lines 7,

[9]   8, and 9 (chasms, clang'd, black, crag, rang), the ä of line 10 (sharp, armed), the ī of lines 4–7 behind, cry, like, dry, icy, right), and the short ĭ of lines 1 and 2, and 9 and 10 (swiftly, ridge, with, his, slippery, smitten, with, dint). One might remark also that in the last two lines, which describe the level lake and the moon, Tennyson introduces a number of relaxed ō and ōō and similar vowel sounds (ô, ŭ, ō, ô, ô, ŭ, ōō).

The last two lines are, in fact, onomatopoeic, since the liquid l sounds suggest the gentle lapping of waves on a lake shore. There are other examples of onomatopoeia, too. In line 2 Tennyson brings out the detail of Sir Bedivere's walking in the presumably cold air "Clothed with his breath," and in the follow-

[10]   ing five lines Tennyson employs many words with the aspirate h (e.g., his harness); in this context, these sounds suggest Sir Bedivere's labored breath as he carries his royal burden. Similarly, the explosive stops b, k, d, and t in lines 6–10 seem to be imitative of the sounds of Sir Bedivere's feet on the "juts of slippery crag."

This short passage is filled with many examples of poetic excellence. The sounds and the rhythms of the words and lines, put into this context by Ten-

[11]   nyson, actually speak along with the meaning; they emphasize the grandeur of Arthur and his faithful follower, and for one brief moment bring out the magic that Tennyson associated with the fading past.

COMMENTARY ON THE THEME

This theme presents a full discussion of the prosody of the passage from Tennyson. Paragraphs 2 through 7 discuss the relationship of the rhythms to the content. Note that prosody is not discussed in isolation, but as it serves Tennyson's description of the actions and scenes. Paragraphs 8 and 9 present a discussion of the alliteration and assonance of the passage, and paragraph 10 considers onomatopoeia. The concluding paragraph, 11, is not so much a summary of the prosodic technique as a tribute to Tennyson's poetic skill.

A Close Look at Paragraph 4

Paragraph 4 refers to the use of the spondee as a substitute foot to reinforce ideas. Since it is difficult to visualize the effects without actually hearing the relevant lines, three lines are quoted, with the chevron marks included to assist the reader in listening to the effects. For comprehensiveness, the first sentence numbers all the lines in which the substitution occurs. In this paragraph there is also a short comparison of alternative ways of saying what Tennyson says so well. While such a speculative comparison should not be attempted often, it is effective here in bringing out the quality of Tennyson's use of the spondee as a means of emphasis.

Second Sample Theme

The Rhymes in Christina Rossetti's "Echo"

1	Come to me in the silence of the *n* night;	5a
2	Come in the speaking silence of a *n* dream;	5b
3	Come with soft rounded cheeks and eyes as *adj* bright	5a
4	As sunlight on a *n* stream;	3b
5	Come back in *n* tears,	2c
6	O memory, hope, love of finished *n* years.	5c

7	O dream how sweet, too sweet, too bitter sweet, *(adj)*	5d
8	Whose wakening should have been in Paradise, *(n)*	5e
9	Where souls brimful of love abide and meet; *(v)*	5d
10	Where thirsty longing eyes *(n)*	3e
11	Watch the slow door *(n)*	2f
12	That opening, letting in, lets out no more. *(adv)*	5f
13	Yet come to me in dreams, that I may live *(v)*	5g
14	My very life again though cold in death: *(n)*	5h
15	Come back to me in dreams, that I may give *(v)*	5g
16	Pulse for pulse, breath for breath: *(n)*	3h
17	Speak low, lean low, *(adj)*	2i
18	As long ago, my love, how long ago! *(adj)*	5i

Repeated words:		n = noun
～～～	dream, dreams	v = verb
——————	sweet	adj = adjective
–.–.–.	breath	adv = adverb
......	low	
- - - -	long ago	
～～～	come	

In the three-stanza lyric poem "Echo," Christina Rossetti uses rhyme as a way of saying that one might regain in dreams a love that is lost in reality.° As the dream of love is to the real love, so is an echo to an original sound. From
[1] this comparison comes the title of the poem and also Rossetti's unique use of rhyme. Aspects of her rhyme are the lyric pattern, the forms and qualities of the rhyming words, and the special use of repetition.□

The rhyme pattern is simple, and, like rhyme generally, it may be thought
[2] of as a pattern of echoes. Each stanza contains four lines of alternating rhymes concluded by a couplet, as follows:

Iambic: 5a, 5b, 5a, 3b, 2c, 5c.

° Central idea.
□ Thesis sentence.

There are nine separate rhymes throughout the poem, three in each stanza. Only two words are used for each rhyme; no rhyme is used twice. Of the eighteen rhyming words, sixteen—almost all—are of one syllable. The remain

[2] ing two words consist of two and three syllables. With such a great number of single-syllable words, the rhymes are all rising ones, on the accented halves of iambic feet, and the end-of-line emphasis is on simple words.

The grammatical forms and positions of the rhyming words lend support to the inward, introspective subject matter. Although there is variety, more than half the rhyming words are nouns. There are ten in all, and eight are placed as the objects of prepositions. Such enclosure helps the speaker emphasize her yearning to relive her love within dreams. Also, the repeated verb "come" in stanzas 1 and 3 is in the form of commands to the absent lover. A careful study shows that most of the verbal energy in the stanzas is in the first parts of the

[3] lines, leaving the rhymes to occur in elements modifying the verbs, as in these lines:

> Come to me in the silence of the <u>night</u> (1)
>
> Yet come to me in dreams, that I may <u>live</u> (13)
> My very life again though cold in <u>death</u>; (14)

Most of the other rhymes are also in such internalized positions. The free rhyming verbs occur in subordinate clauses, and the nouns that are not the objects of prepositions are the subject (10) and object (11) of the same subordinate clause.

The qualities of the rhyming words are also consistent with the poem's emphasis on the speaker's internal life. Most of the words are impressionistic. Even the concrete words—<u>stream, tears, eyes, door,</u> and <u>breath</u>—reflect the speaker's mental condition rather than describe reality. In this regard, the rhyming words of 1 and 3 are effective. These are <u>night</u> and <u>bright,</u> which contrast

[4] the bleakness of the speaker's condition, on the one hand, with the vitality of her inner life, on the other. Another effective contrast is in 14 and 16, where <u>death</u> and <u>breath</u> are rhymed. This rhyme may be taken to illustrate the sad fact that even though the speaker's love is past, it can yet live in present memory just as an echo continues to sound.

It is in emphasizing how memory echoes experience that Rossetti creates the special use of rhyming words. There is an ingenious but not obtrusive repetition of a number of words—echoes. The major echoing word is of course the verb <u>come,</u> which appears six times at the beginnings of lines in stanzas 1 and 3. But rhyming words, stressing as they do the ends of lines, are also repeated systematically. The most notable is <u>dream,</u> the rhyming word in 2.

[5] Rossetti repeats the word in 7 and uses the plural in 13 and 15. In 7 the rhyming word <u>sweet</u> is the third use of the word, a climax of "how <u>sweet,</u> too <u>sweet,</u> too bitter <u>sweet.</u>" Concluding the poem, Rossetti repeats <u>breath</u> (16), <u>low</u> (17), and the phrase <u>long ago</u> (18). This special use of repetition justifies the title "Echo," and it also stresses the major idea that it is only in one's memory that past experience has reality, even if dreams are no more than echoes.

Thus rhyme is not just ornamental in "Echo," but integral. The skill of Rossetti here is the same as in her half-serious, half-mocking poem "Eve,"

[6] even though the two poems are totally different. In "Eve," she uses very plain rhyming words thogether with comically intended double rhymes. In "Echo," her subject might be called fanciful and maybe even morbid, but the easiness of the rhyming words, like the diction of the poem generally, keeps the focus on regret

[6] and yearning rather than self-indulgence. As in all rhyming poems, Rossetti's rhymes emphasize the conclusions of her lines. The rhymes go beyond this effect, however, because of the internal repetition—echoes—of the rhyming words. "Echo" is a poem in which rhyme is inseparable from meaning.

COMMENTARY ON THE THEME

Throughout, illustrative words are italicized, and numbers are used to indicate the lines from which the illustrations are drawn. The introductory paragraph asserts that rhyme is important in Rossetti's poem. It also attempts to explain the title "Echo." The thesis sentence indicates the four topics to be developed in the body.

Paragraph 2 deals with the mechanical, mathematical aspects of the rhyme. As the means of explaining the rising, heavy-stress rhyme, the paragraph cites the high number of monosyllabic rhyming words. (For paragraph 3, see below.) Paragraph 4 emphasizes the impressionistic nature of the rhyming words and also points out two instances in which rhymes stress the contrast between real life and the speaker's introspective life. Paragraph 5 deals with repetition of five rhyming words within the poem. This repetition is quite important in the total meaning and effect of the poem, for it may be seen as a pattern of echoes, in keeping with the title.

In the concluding paragraph, the rhymes in "Echo" are compared briefly with those in "Eve," another of Rossetti's poems. The conclusion is that Rossetti is a skilled rhymer because she uses rhyme appropriately in both poems. At the end of the theme, the central idea is reiterated.

A Close Look at Paragraph 3

This paragraph illustrates the way in which the discussion of rhyme may be heightened by emphasis on the grammatical structure of the studied poem. With "Echo," for example, an analysis and count reveal that there are ten rhyming nouns and three rhyming verbs. The verb of command, *come*, is mentioned to show that most of the rhyming words exist within groups modifying this word, and three lines of the poem are quoted as illustration. Because this meditative poem is internalized and introspective, the rhymes thus embody and complement the speaker's thoughts. It is difficult to predict what the effects of grammatical study would be on the rhymes of other poems, but this example shows that such study, whatever its results, can render unexpected insights into the poet's technique (whether intentional or unintentional).

chapter 15

Writing Two Themes Based on a Close Reading:
I. General content and
II. Style

A theme on a close reading is a detailed study of a passage of prose or poetry. The passage may be a fragment of a longer work, such as an entire speech from a play, story, or novel, or it may be a paragraph of descriptive or analytic prose. It may also be an entire short poem, such as a sonnet or short lyric.

The close-reading theme is at once specific and general. It is specific because it requires you to concentrate on the selected passage. It is general because you do not need to study a single topic (such as character, setting, or point of view) but need to deal with any or all of those things that may be found in the passage. Should your passage describe a specific person, of course, you would need to discuss character, but your emphasis would be on what the passage itself brings out about the character. You would also stress action, setting, and ideas, or even make comparisons, if you find that these matters are important. In other words, the content of a close-reading theme is variable; your passage dictates your content.

STUDYING YOUR PASSAGE

Whenever you are to write a close-reading theme, you should first read the *entire* work, so that you can understand the relationship of all the parts. Read carefully. Then study the passage you are to write about. First, be sure to use a dictionary to help you understand all words that are even slightly obscure. Sometimes you may not get the sense of a passage on the first or second reading, perhaps because some of the words are not clear to you, even though they may appear so at first. Therefore, look up *all* the words, even the simple ones, in the obscure sentence or sentences. In Shakespeare's Sonnet 73, for example, this famous line occurs:

Bare ruined choirs, where late the sweet birds sang.

If you think *choirs* means organized groups of singers (as you might at first), you will be puzzled by the line. The dictionary will tell you that *choirs* is also an architectural term for that part of a church in which singers are often placed. Thus Shakespeare's word takes in the range of both empty branches and destroyed churches, and the phrase *sweet birds* refers to vanished human singers as well as birds that have flown away because of winter's cold. Let us take another line, this time from John Donne's first *Holy Sonnet:*

And thou like Adamant draw mine iron heart.

Unless you look up *Adamant* and realize that Donne uses it to mean a magnet, you will not understand the sense of *draw*. You will thus miss Donne's image and his idea of God's immense power over human beings.

Once you have mastered the words to the best of your ability, look at the sentence structures, particularly in poetry, where you will often find variations in the ordinary English subject-verb-object word order. If you read the line "Thy merit hath my duty strongly knit," be sure that you get the subject and object straight (i.e., "Thy merit hath strongly knit my duty"). Or, look at lines 15 and 16 from Pope's *Essay on Criticism:*

Let such teach others who themselves excell,
And censure freely who have written well.

On first reading, these lines are difficult. A person might conclude that Pope is asking the critic to condemn those writers who have written well (but as an exercise, look up *censure* in the *Oxford English Dictionary*), until the lines are unraveled:

Let such who themselves excell teach others,
And [let such] who have written well censure freely.

There is a great difference here between the misreading and the correct reading. What you must keep in mind is that an initial failure to understand a sentence structure that is no longer common can prevent your full understanding of a passage. Therefore, you must be sure to untie all the syntactic knots.

TYPES OF CLOSE-READING THEMES

These are two types of close-reading themes. The first deals with the general content of the passage and its relationship to the entire work. The second type is also concerned with the general content but goes on to deal with the style of the passage.

I. THE GENERAL CONTENT OF A PASSAGE

This kind of close-reading theme emphasizes the content of the passage and the relationship of the passage to the rest of the work. The theme is designed as a first approach to close reading and does not require detailed knowledge about diction, grammar, and style. Thus, although you may wish to discuss special words and phrases, it should be your aim primarily to consider the content of your passage.

Once you have clarified the passage to your satisfaction, you should develop materials for your theme. Try to make some general statements about your passage: Does the passage (1) describe a natural or artificial scene, (2) develop a character or characters, (3) describe an action, (4) describe or analyze a character's thoughts, or (5) develop an argument? Is the passage a speech by one character or a dialogue or discussion by two or more? What is the content of the passage? That is, are there themes and ideas that are brought up elsewhere in the work? In this respect, how does the passage connect to what has gone on before and to what comes after? (To deal with this question, you may assume that your reader is familiar with the entire work.) Following are some obvious points to think about:

For an Early Passage

For an early passage, you may expect that the author is setting things in motion (exposition, complication). Thus, you should try to determine how ideas, themes, characterizations, and arguments that you find in the passage are related to these matters as they appear later in the work. You may assume that everything in the passage is there for a purpose. Try to find that purpose.

For a Later, Midpoint Passage

For a later passage, which might be characterized as a "turning point" (crisis) a character's fortunes take either an expected or unexpected turn. If the change is expected, you should explain how the passage focuses the various themes or ideas and then propels them toward the climax. If the change is unexpected, it is necessary to show how the contrast is made in the passage. It may be that the work is one that features surprises, and the passage thus is read one way at first but on second reading may be seen to have a double meaning. Or it may be that the speaker has had one set of assumptions while the readers have had others, and that the passage marks a point of increasing self-awareness on the part of the speaker. Many parts of works are not what they seem at first reading, and it is your task here to determine how the passage is affected by events at or near the end of the work.

For a Concluding Passage

You may assume that a passage at or near the end of the work is designed to solve problems or to be a focal point or climax for all the situations and ideas that have been building up. You will need to show how the passage brings together all themes, ideas, and details. What is happening? Is any action described in the passage a major action, or a step leading to the major action? Has everything in the passage been prepared for earlier?

GENERAL PURPOSES
OF THE CLOSE-READING THEME

In light of what we have seen, the general purposes of a close-reading theme should be clear. If you can read a paragraph, you can read the entire book; if you can read a speech, you can read the entire play or story; if you can read one poem by a poet, you can read other poems by the same poet. This is not to say that the writing of a close-reading theme automatically means that at first reading you will understand every work by the same author. Few people would insist that reading passages from Joyce's *Dubliners* makes it possible to understand *Finnegans Wake*. What a close-reading theme gives you is a skill upon which you can build, an approach to any other text you will encounter.

You will find use for the general technique of close reading in other courses also. In political science, for example, parts of political speeches can and should be scrutinized carefully, not just for what is said but for what is half-said or left out entirely. A close study of a philosophical work or biblical passage will yield much that might not be found in a casual first reading. No matter what course you are taking or what your personal interests may be, you can use close-reading techniques to improve your understanding.

WRITING ABOUT GENERAL CONTENT
IN A PASSAGE

Introduction

Because the close-reading theme is concerned with details in the passage, you may find a problem in creating a thematic structure. This difficulty is surmountable if you work either with a generalization about the passage itself or else with a central idea based on the relationship of the passage to the work. Suppose, for example, that the passage is factually descriptive, or intensely emotional, or that it introduces a major character or idea, or that it sets in motion forces that will create a climax later in the work. Any one of these observations may serve as your central idea.

Body

You may develop the body according to what you find in the passage. Suppose you have a passage of character description; you might wish to analyze what is said about the character, together with a comparison of how these qualities are modified later. In addition, you might consider how these qualities are to affect other characters and/or later events in the work. Suppose your passage is particularly witty, and you decide to discuss the quality of the wit and then show how this wittiness bears upon earlier and later situations. The idea here is to focus on details in the passage and also on the relationship of these details to the entire work.

Conclusion

As you make your major points for the body of the theme, you may also notice subpoints that are worth mentioning but do not merit full consideration. You might bring these points into your conclusion. For example, there may be a particular word or type of word, or there may be an underlying assumption that you found in the passage, or there may be some quality that you find hard to describe. The conclusion is the place for you to mention these things. If you haven't discussed anything about the way some of the things are said but want to say that the diction is plain and monosyllabic, or difficult and polysyllabic, and if you do not believe that you can go into great detail about these matters, then you can bring them up in your conclusion. You may also, of course, summarize your main points from the body of your theme.

NUMBERS FOR EASY REFERENCE

Include a copy of your passage at the beginning of your theme, as in the samples in this chapter. For your reader's convenience, number lines in poetry and sentences in prose.

Sample Theme

A Study of Paragraph 31 of Updike's "A & P"*

> [1] Lengel sighs and begins to look very patient and old and gray. [2] He's been a friend of my parents for years. [3] "Sammy, you don't want to do this to your Mom and Dad," he tells me. [4] It's true, I don't. [5] But it seems to me that once you begin a gesture it's fatal not to go through with it. [6] I fold the apron, "Sammy" stitched in red on the pocket, and put it on the counter, and drop the bow tie on top of it. [7] The bow tie is theirs, if you've ever wondered. [8] "You'll feel this for the rest of your life," Lengel says, and I know that's true, too, but remembering how he made that pretty girl blush makes me so scrunchy inside I punch the No Sale tab and the machine whirs "pee-pul" and the drawer splats out. [9] One advantage to this scene taking place in summer, I can follow this up with a clean exit, there's no fumbling around getting your coat and galoshes, I just saunter into the electric eye in my white shirt that my mother ironed the night before, and the door heaves itself open, and outside the sunshine is skating around on the asphalt.

[1]   This is the next to last paragraph of "A & P," and it is part of Sammy's gesture supporting the right of the three girls to wear bathing suits in the store. The action is simple: Sammy takes off his apron and tie, and walks outside. But the issues in the paragraph are not simple. Even though Sammy's decision to quit his job is abrupt, a number of reasons are evident, such as that Sammy supports the girls' rights, that he feels sympathy for their embarrassment, that he objects to Lengel's grayness of spirit as well as of hair, and that he perceives (if dimly) the contrast between restrictiveness and freedom. In all these reasons there is a common denominator of growth brought about by his sudden decision and action.° These qualities are shown in his diction, his self-awareness, and also in the greater issue of independence.▫

[2]   A major aspect of Sammy's diction indicates the limited world which he is growing away from. He uses the present tense rather than the past, for example

---

* For the text of this story, see Appendix C, pages 334–38.

° Central idea

▫ Thesis sentence

[2] (see verbs like <u>sighs,</u> <u>begins,</u> <u>fold,</u> and so on), a characteristic of his place in the ordinary life of his home town, where this use of present-for-past tense is probably common. His use of the slang words <u>scrunchy</u> and <u>splats</u> (8), also reflecting this background, demonstrates his lack of sophistication and polish.

[3] <u>The diction also suggests an aspect in which Sammy is limited.</u> He is aware of the meaning of his gesture, but does not—or cannot—express its significance. He is a young man of nineteen, with two alternatives ahead of him for his future. One is the routine represented by the store and by the various respectable zombies who walk through it. The other is the freedom, independence, and unconventionality represented by the girls wearing bathing suits in the store. But he goes no farther in considering his situation except to note his embarrassment at the way in which Lengel admonishes the "Queen" (8). His limited explanation hence shows that his feelings and perceptions are far ahead of his ability for expression.

[4] <u>Though the language in the paragraph reveals Sammy's shortcomings, there are also words of perceptiveness and skill that show his growth.</u> His memory of Lengel's checkout-counter advice suggests objectivity and accuracy. Also, his observations about Lengel show greater understanding than his abrupt decision to resign would indicate (1, 3, 6). Some of the paragraph is devoted to description, and Sammy's words here are economical and to the point, ably appropriate for the subject matter. Sammy's most skillful and imaginative language is contained in the last sentence, in which he observes that the sun is "skating around on the asphalt" (9).

[5] <u>Also demonstrative of Sammy's strength is his strong sense of self-awareness.</u> His self-awareness is so great, in fact, that the paragraph resembles a scene which he himself stages and directs. His sauntering out to make his "clean exit" at the end suggests that he is adopting an outward appearance of defiance to correspond with his gesture. Interestingly, he theorizes not about the implications of his actions, but rather about the proper pose to go along with his new independence. His idea is that he recognizes his obligations to his parents and his future (respectability?) to continue working, but that he has a larger duty to be consistent with himself. In this context, his surprising observation that "it is fatal not to go through with" a gesture once it has begun is mildly comic (5). Thus the paragraph brings out Sammy's bravery and daring, even if he expends these virtues on nothing more than suddenly quitting his job.

[6] <u>Because of this daring and insouciance, the paragraph also suggests the major idea that turmoil and sacrifice go along with growth and independence.</u> Even though the circumstances are minor, Sammy's need for independence is great. The paragraph of course is not argumentative but rather narrative, and the difficulties of making choices are therefore made no more prominent than Lengel's statement that Sammy will "feel this for the rest of . . . [his] life." (8). While Lengel means that Sammy will likely suffer because of the action, and therefore regret it, Sammy probably means that he will be proud for having asserted himself. His going through with his gesture thus points toward the final words of the story, about how hard life will be for him "hereafter" (paragraph 32). The suggestion is that choosing independence creates turmoil and difficulty, of which quitting the A & P is only a small symbol. It is this aspect of the paragraph that makes it so vital in the story. Sammy has been a part of his town, with its slang and substandard speech habits; its banks, church, and real-estate offices; and its resistance to unconventional or inappropriate dress. But in cutting himself free he leaves a great deal behind, and in recognizing the possibly difficult consequences, he accepts the burden of growth.

The paragraph is therefore a major one. As an action, it moves Sammy out of the store in completion of his gesture, and in this respect it climaxes the comedy of a nineteen-year-old losing his job in protest against a prudish boss. As a symbol, it brings out the movement from restrictiveness to freedom, thereby touching on the difficulty and turmoil that go along with growth and independence. There are other potential issues in the paragraph as well, like [7] those of young against old, or of sexual admiration and appreciation against conventional respectability, but though these are major in the story, they are not as prominent in the paragraph. This close study shows the paragraph to be a packed one, vital in the narrative itself, and also touching on the important issues underlying Sammy's chivalric protest against the store's dress code. In all these respects, it is a rough sketch of Sammy's subsequent life while it also moves the story quickly toward its end.

COMMENTARY ON THE THEME

The sample theme shows that a close study depends on the substance of the text paragraph. Because the topic is Sammy's leaving the store, together with the words immediately preceding this action, the theme is devoted to the effect of this action on the process of Sammy's growth (the central idea). If a text paragraph had been selected from earlier in the story, by contrast, the close reading could deal with the growth only incidentally, because the earlier passage would be part of the exposition of the story and would not yet be treating the effects of Sammy's decision.

In paragraph 1, the introduction, the central idea is presented as the link connecting possible topics that might be considered in the text paragraph. Three subjects are listed for development in the body.

The body contains three major sections. The first consists of three separate paragraphs and is concerned with what the diction shows about the narrator, Sammy. Paragraphs 3 and 4 emphasize the limitations of Sammy's background and analytical ability. Paragraph 5 takes a new direction, emphasizing that the diction also demonstrates Sammy's power and perceptiveness. Cumulatively, therefore, the three paragraphs bring out the central idea that the text paragraph concentrates on Sammy's capacities for growth.

Paragraph 5 continues the emphasis on Sammy's growth, being concerned with a more abstract topic, that of self-awareness and self-control. (For paragraph 6, see below.)

The concluding paragraph, 7, contains a summary in the form of a contrast between the paragraph as action and symbol. Because an important goal of a close-reading theme is to stress the function of the text paragraph within the story, the final note is that the text paragraph points both toward the story's end and also toward the general condition of young people moving out on their own.

A Close Look at Paragraph 6

This paragraph demonstrates how the discussion of a general issue may be approached in a close reading for general content. The topic—that growth produces disturbance and turmoil—is a major one in the story. Even though the idea has broad applications, however, it is not discussed abstractly or generally but is connected closely with the paragraph. Lengel's speech (as Sammy reports it) is the subject of the discussion, with the paragraph placing stress on how the idea is applied specifically to Sammy as a young man quitting his job. In addition, the structural relationship of the issue to the very conclusion of the story is emphasized. The paragraph hence shows how important it is to anchor all discussions in both text and central idea.

II. THE STYLE OF A PASSAGE

The second type of close-reading theme is like the first in that both deal with a passage in the context of the entire work. The second goes beyond the first, however, because it concentrates on the *style* of the passage rather than the content.

To carry out a discussion of style, you will need to apply many of the things you previously learned or are learning about the mechanics of language. You might feel hesitant at first, but you will unquestionably find that you know much more than you think you know. In addition, many of the approaches you might try are not especially difficult. As an instance, the sample theme shows what might be done with the application of no more than a moderate knowledge of language.

The word *style* is not easy to define to everyone's satisfaction, but for the present theme you may deal with it as an analysis of word choice and sentence development resulting from an author's judgment about the following matters:

1. The speaker, or narrator, of the work
2. The character being analyzed or described
3. The circumstances of the passage
4. The type or purpose of the work
5. The audience

Any close reading for style should take these and related elements into account as they become relevant to the details of the passage.

And they do become relevant. Authors do not always write in their own persons, but take on the voice of a particular narrator, or they present the speech of a character just as they think that character would likely say it. (For further development of this fact, see Chapter 6, *Writing About Point of View*.) Also, the writer's perception of his or her audience governs the amount of detail and kinds of diction that you will find in your passage. It is not possible to write a close-reading theme for style without also considering the entire context of the passage.

EXAMPLES OF STYLE
AND ITS RELATION TO CHARACTER

To look at a specific example, let us consider the character of Portia from Shakespeare's *The Merchant of Venice*. Late in the play Portia masquerades brilliantly as a lawyer, and because of her ingenuity in argument she brings Antonio out of danger. It would seem natural that Shakespeare, in giving her speeches elsewhere in the play, would emphasize and demonstrate her intelligence. In I.ii, for example, Portia says the following:

> If to do were as easy as to know what were good to do, chapels had been churches and poor men's cottages princes' palaces. It is a good divine that follows his own instructions: I can easier teach twenty what were good to be done, than to be one of the twenty to follow mine own teaching.

From the style of this passage, one may conclude that Shakespeare is indeed showing that Portia has a rapid mind. Her first sentence uses simple diction but a complex structure. Of her first fourteen words, six are infinitives and two are verbs; that is, more than half of the words (about 57 percent) are verbs or verbals. One may conclude that such a proportion suggests great mental power. Also, the first fourteen words form an *if-*clause, dependent on the verb in the following main clause. The ability to control subordination in sentences is regarded as the mark of a good mind and a good style. Portia shows an ability to use rhetoric—in this sentence ellipsis in a parallel structure: the main clause of the first sentence equals two clauses, but the verb is used only once: "chapels had been churches and poor men's cottages [had been] princes' palaces." Portia's language is concrete and vivid, and she has control over her balanced sentence.

To be contrasted with Portia's speech is this one by Ophelia in *Hamlet*, IV. v:

> Well, God 'ild you. They say, the owl was a baker's daughter. Lord, we know what we are, but not what we may be. God be at your table.

Ophelia makes this speech after she has gone mad. Her words are simple, and her sentences are disconnected. Just when she seems to become coherent (in sentence 3) her thought is broken, and her last sentence seems as random as her first. Had Shakespeare introduced the mental toughness of Portia's speech here, he would not have shown a broken mind but an alert one in all its powers. Thus, he gives Ophelia these disconnected sentences, so unlike her coherent speeches earlier in the play.

The point about both passages is that the differences in style are appropriate to the two characterizations and also to the differing dramatic situations. Please note that our analyses of style are related to the contexts of the plays. It would not be fruitful to discuss style independently of the context, particularly in a dramatic passage, for the language is likely to be indicative of the immediate situation and is also likely to involve comparisons with other sections of the work.

TWO MAJOR APPROACHES TO STYLE

There are two major topics, or approaches, to close reading for style: (1) diction, and (2) rhetoric. Technically, rhetoric includes diction, but here they are separated for ease of analysis. Naturally, either approach can become complex and subtle, so much so that any aspect, such as connotation or parallelism, can furnish materials for an entire theme.

DICTION: CHOICE OF WORDS

The study of style begins with words, and **diction** refers to a writer's selection of specific words. The selection should be accurate and explicit, so that all actions and ideas are clear. It is perhaps difficult to judge accuracy and completeness, inasmuch as often we do not have any basis of comparison. Nevertheless, if a passage comes across as effective, if it conveys an idea well or gets at the essence of an action vividly and powerfully, we may confidently say that the words have been the right ones. In a passage describing action, for example, there should be active verbs, whereas in a description of a place there should be nouns and adjectives that provide locations, relationships, colors, and shapes. An explanatory or reflective passage should include a number of words that convey thoughts, states of mind and emotion, and various conditions of human relationships.

Formal, Neutral, and Informal Diction

Words fall naturally into three basic groups, or classes, that may be called **formal** or *high*, **neutral** or *middle*, and **informal** or *low*. Formal or high diction consists of standard and often elegant words (frequently polysyllabic), the retention of correct word order, and the absence of contractions.

The sentence "It is I," for example, is formal. The following sentences from Poe's "The Masque of the Red Death" use formal language:

> They resolved to leave means neither of ingress nor egress to the sudden impulses of despair or of frenzy from within. The abbey was amply provisioned. With such precautions the courtiers might bid defiance to contagion. (Paragraph 2)

Note here words like *ingress, egress, provisioned, bid defiance,* and *contagion.* These words are not in ordinary, everyday vocabulary; they have what we may call *elegance.* Though they are used accurately and aptly, and though the sentences are brief and simple, the diction is high.

Neutral or middle diction is ordinary, everyday, but still standard vocabulary, with a shunning of longer words but with the use of contractions when necessary. The sentence "It's me," for example, is neutral, the sort of thing many people say in preference to "It is I" when identifying themselves on the phone. The following passage from Langston Hughes's poem "Theme for English B" illustrates middle, neutral diction:

> I am twenty-two, colored, born in Winston-Salem.
> I went to school there, then Durham, then here
> to this college on the hill above Harlem.
> I am the only colored student in my class. (lines 7–10)

In this passage the words are easy and ordinary, words that are in common use in everyday conversation. They do not draw attention to themselves but are centered directly on the topic. In a sense, such words in the neutral style are chosen because they are like clear windows, while words of the high style are more like stained glass.

Informal or low diction may range from colloquial—the language used by people in relaxed, common activities—to the level of substandard or slang expressions. A person speaking to a close friend uses diction and idiom that would not be appropriate in public and formal situations, and even in some social situations. Low language is thus appropriate for dialogue in stories and plays, depending on the characters speaking, and for stories told in the first-person point of view as though the speaker is talking directly to a group of sympathetic and relaxed close friends. An amusing example of low diction may be seen in the first sentence of the following speech from Chekhov's *The Bear.* Smirnov, the speaker, talks angrily and insultingly to a servant, using low words. The humor develops when he shifts to a formal style speaking to the aristocratic lady, Mrs. Popov:

> SMIRNOV (to LUKA). You idiot, you talk too much. . . . Ass! (*Sees* MRS. POPOV *and changes to dignified speech.*) Madam, may I introduce myself:

retired lieutenant of the artillery and landowner, Grigory Stepanovich Smirnov! I feel the necessity of troubling you about a highly important matter. . . . (Speech 19)

By graphically juxtaposing low and high diction, the passage marks Chekhov's skill over comic dramatic style.

Specific–General and Concrete–Abstract Language

Specific refers to a real thing or things that may be readily perceived or imagined. "My pet dog Woofie is barking" is specific. **General** statements refer to broad classes of persons or things. Assertions like "All people like pets" and "Dogs make good pets" are generalizations. There is an ascending order from (1) very specific, to (2) less specific, to (3) general, as though the words themselves mount a stairway. Thus *peach* is a specific fruit. *Fruit* is specific but more general because it may also include apples, oranges, and all other fruits. *Dessert* is a still more general word, which can include all sweets, including fruits and peaches, and also some cheeses. *Food* is more general yet, for the word includes everything that human beings may eat under any circumstances. If you report that you are having "food" for dinner, you are being vague and overly general, but if you say that the main course is a London broil with peaches for dessert, you are quite specific.

While *specific–general* refers to numbers, *concrete–abstract* refers to qualities or conditions. **Concrete** words describe qualities of immediate perception. If you say "Ice cream is cold," the word *cold* is concrete because it describes a condition that you may perceive or feel. **Abstract** words refer to broader, less palpable qualities; they may therefore apply to many separate things. Thus, ice cream may also be *sweet, creamy,* and *peachy.* If we describe it as *good,* however, we are becoming abstract because the word *good* is far removed from ice cream itself and conveys no descriptive information about it. A wide number of things may be good, just as they may be *bad, fine, "cool," excellent,* and so on.

Usually, narrative and descriptive writing features specific and concrete words in preference to general and abstract ones. It stands to reason: When we confront many general and abstract words that may mean a number of things at once, we become uncertain and confused. Usually, therefore, such words are out of place in stories and novels. On the other hand, we can visualize and understand passages containing words about specific things and actions, for with more specificity and concreteness there is less ambiguity. Because vividness is a goal of most fiction, specific and concrete words are the fiction writer's basic tool.

The point, however, is not that abstract and general words do not belong, but rather that words should be *appropriate in the context.* Good writers manipulate style to match their narrative and descriptive purposes. As an example, we may consider Eudora Welty's description of the forest near Natchez where her heroine Phoenix Jackson walks. Although Welty states that the woods are "deep and still," which is the extent of her use of abstraction, she emphasizes specific things in the forest such as the "frozen earth," the bright "pine needles," the dropping pine cones, a thorn bush, and "a tree in a pearly cloud of mistletoe" (paragraphs 1–15).

Welty's descriptive words might be contrasted with Hawthorne's rendering of the forest in "Young Goodman Brown." In an early paragraph (8), Brown begins what seems like an ordinary walk into the neighboring woods. But this walk is not ordinary, for it is in the woods where his perceptions are to be distorted permanently by his witnessing a demonic ritual. To develop the impression of uncertainty and unreality of Brown's experience, Hawthorne uses a number of abstract words, such as *dreary, gloomiest, narrow, lonely, peculiarity, solitude, innumerable, thick,* and *unseen.* Thus Welty uses specific words to match Phoenix's age and difficulty, while Hawthorne's abstract words augment the unreality and illogicality of Brown's distrust of others. In both cases, the words make a perfect fit.

Denotation and Connotation

Another way of understanding style is to study the author's management of **denotation** and **connotation,** that famous pair. *Denotation* refers to what a word means, and *connotation* to what the word suggests. It is one thing to call a person *skinny,* for example, another to use the words *thin* or *gaunt,* and still something else to say *svelte* or *shapely.* Similarly, both *cat* and *kitten* are close to each other denotatively, but *kitten* connotes more playfulness and cuteness than *cat.* If a person in a social situation behaves in ways that are *friendly, warm, polite,* or *correct,* these words all suggest slight differences in behavior, not because the words are not close in meaning, but because they have different connotations.

It is through the careful choice of words not only for denotation but also for connotation that authors create unique effects even though they might be describing similar or even identical situations. Let us look briefly at Eudora Welty's description of Phoenix Jackson in "A Worn Path," as Phoenix walks through the woods:

> Her eyes were blue with age. Her skin had a pattern all its own of numberless branching wrinkles and as though a whole little tree stood in the middle of her forehead, but a golden color ran underneath, and the two knobs of her cheeks were illumined by a yellow burning under the dark. Under the rag her hair came down on her neck in the frailest of ringlets, still black, and with an odor like copper. (paragraph 2)

Though the description skillfully portrays an aging woman, it also contains a compelling note of admiration. Specifically, the words *golden color* and *illumined* would be appropriate in the description of delicate and lovely medieval book paintings, while *frailest of ringlets, still black* suggests girlishness and personal care, despite Phoenix's advancing age and weakness. With this description you might compare Sammy's words depicting the "queen" in "A & P" (paragraphs 2–4), which suggest his admiration not only of her sexual beauty but also of her grace. Shirley Jackson's less full description of Tessie Hutchinson in "The Lottery" (paragraph 8) is designed to minimize her as no more than an average woman of the village. (The meager details are that she has a "sweater thrown over her shoulders" and that she "dried her hands on her apron.") All these descriptive examples demonstrate the ways in which connotation may complement an author's descriptive intentions.

RHETORIC

Broadly, **rhetoric** refers to the art of persuasive writing and, even more broadly, to the general art of writing. Any passage can be studied for its rhetorical qualities. For this reason it is necessary to develop both the methods and the descriptive vocabulary with which to carry out an analysis. Some things that may easily be done involve counting various elements in a passage and analyzing the types of sentences the author uses.

Counting

Doing a count of the number of words in a sentence; or the number of verbs, adjectives, prepositions, and adverbs; or the number of syllables in relation to the total number of words, can often lead to valuable conclusions about style, especially if the count is related to other aspects of the passage. The virtue of counting is that it is easy to do and therefore it provides a "quick opening" into at least one aspect of style. Always remember that conclusions based on a count will provide *tendencies* of a particular author rather than absolutes. For illustration, let us say that Author *A* uses words mainly of 1 or 2 syllables while Author *B* includes many words of 3, 4, and 5 syllables. Going further, let us say that *A* uses an average of 12 words per sentence while *B* uses 35. It would be fair to conclude that Author *A* is brief while Author *B* is more expansive. This is not to say that Author *A*'s passage would be superior, however, for a long string of short sentences with short words might become choppy and tiresome and might cause your mind to wander.

Sentence Types

You can learn much about a passage by determining the types of sentences it contains. Though you have probably learned the basic sentence types at one time or another, let's review them here:

1. **Simple sentences** contain one subject and one verb, together with modifiers and complements. They are often short and are most appropriate for actions and declarations. Often they are idiomatic, particularly in dialogue.

2. **Compound sentences** contain two simple sentences joined by a conjunction (*and, but, for, or, nor* and so on) and a comma, or by a semicolon without a conjunction. Frequently, compound sentences are strung together as a series of three or four or more simple sentences.

3. **Complex sentences** contain a main clause and a subordinate clause. Because of the subordinate clause, the complex sentence is often suitable for describing cause-and-effect relationships in narrative, and also for analysis and reflection.

4. **Compound-complex sentences** contain two main clauses and a dependent clause. In practice, many authors produce sentences that may contain a number of subordinate clauses together with many more than two main clauses. Usually, the more clauses, the more difficult the sentence.

Loose and Periodic Sentences

A major way to describe sentences in terms of the development of their content is to use the terms *loose* and *periodic*. A **loose sentence** unfolds easily, with no surprises. Because it is fairly predictable, it is the most commonly used sentence in stories. Here is an example:

In America, the idea of equality was first applied only to white males.

Periodic sentences are arranged as much as possible in an order of climax, with the concluding information or thought being withheld to make the sentence especially interesting or surprising. Usually the periodic sentence begins with a dependent clause so that the content may be built up to the final detail, as in this sentence:

Although in America the idea of equality was first applied only to males of European ancestry, in this century, despite the reluctance and even the opposition of many men who have regarded equality as a mark of their own status and not as a right for everyone, it has been extended to women and to persons of all races.

In narrative prose, sentences of this type are usually carefully placed in spots of crucial importance. Often the sentence alone might be said to contain the crisis and resolution at the same moment, as in this example from Edgar Allan Poe's "The Fall of the House of Usher":

> For a moment she remained trembling and reeling to and fro upon the threshold, then, with a low moaning cry, fell heavily inward upon the person of her brother, and in her violent and now final death-agonies, bore him to the floor a corpse, and a victim to the terrors he had anticipated.

Parallelism

To create interest, authors often rely on the rhetorical device called **parallelism**, which is common and easily recognized. Parallelism is the repetition of the same grammatical form (nouns, verbs, phrases, clauses) to balance expressions, conserve words, and build up to climaxes. Here, for example, is another sentence from Poe, which occurs in the story "The Black Cat":

> I grew, day by day, more moody, more irritable, more regardless of the feelings of others.

Arrangements like this are called *parallel* because they may actually be laid out graphically, according to parts of speech, in parallel lines, as in the following (with the phrase "day by day" left out):

```
                more moody
    I grew       more irritable
                more regardless of the feelings of others
```

Poe's sentence achieves an order of increasing severity of psychological depression developing from the personal to the social.

The same parallel arrangements may be seen in individual sentences within a paragraph or longer unit. In "The Necklace," for example, Maupassant uses parallel sentences to describe Mathilde's ten years of household drudgery. The effect of the repeated patterns—"she" followed by active past-tense verbs—is to suggest the sameness and also the boredom of her life:

> She learned to do the heavy housework, dirty kitchen jobs. She washed the dishes, wearing away her manicured fingernails on greasy pots and encrusted baking dishes. She handwashed dirty linen, shirts, and dish towels that she hung out on the line to dry. Each morning, she took the garbage down to the street, and she carried up water, stopping at each floor to catch her breath. And, dressed in cheap house dresses, she went to the fruit dealer, the grocer, the butcher, with her basket under her arms,

haggling, insulting, defending her measly cash penny by penny. (paragraph 99)

CUMULATIO OR ACCUMULATION. The paragraph from "The Necklace" also illustrates another rhetorical device much used by writers, namely **cumulatio** or **accumulation.** While *parallelism* refers to grammatical constructions, *cumulatio* refers to the building up of details, such as the materials in the "she" sentences in Maupassant's paragraph. The device is therefore a brief way of introducing much information, for once the parallel rhythm of the buildup begins, readers readily accept new material. The device thus acts as a series of quick glimpses or vignettes, and vividness is established through the parallel repetition.

CHIASMUS OR ANTIMETABOLE. Also fitting into the pattern of parallelism is a favorite device called **chiasmus** or **antimetabole.** This pattern is designed to create vividness though memorable repetition. The pattern is *A B B A,* which can be arranged graphically at the ends of an *X* (which is the same as the Greek letter *chi*):

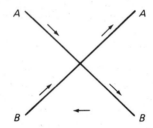

Mark Twain, in the story "Luck," creates a sentence that shows the pattern:

| *A* | *B* | *B* | *A* |
| I drilled him and crammed him, and crammed him and drilled him.(Paragraph 8) |

You may not always encounter such easily observed patterns, but you should always be alert to positions and arrangements that you think are particularly noticeable or effective. Even though you may not be able to use a technically correct name, your analysis should go well as long as you focus your attention on noticeable aspects of effective writing.

WRITING ABOUT THE STYLE OF A PASSAGE

In prewriting, you should consider the selected passage in the context of the entire story. What sort of passage is it? Narrative? Descriptive? Does it contain any dialogue? Is there a speaker with clearly established characteristics? How does the passage reflect his or her personality? Try to determine the level of the diction: Did you need to use a dictionary to discover the meaning of any of the words? Are there any unusual words? Any especially difficult or uncommon words? Do any of the words distract you as you read? Is there any slang? Are any words used only in particular occupations or ways of life (such as words used about drink, or automobiles, or horses, words from other languages, and so on)? Are there any contractions? Do they indicate a conversational, intimate level of speech? Are the words the most common ones that might be used? Can you think of more difficult ones? Easier ones? More accurate ones? Are there many short words? Long words?

Can you easily imagine the situations described by the words? If you have difficulty, can you find any reasons that stem out of the level of diction?

Are the sentences long or short? Is there any variation in length? Can you observe any relationship between length and topic material? Are the sentences simple, compound, or complex? Does one type predominate? Why? Can you describe noteworthy rhetorical devices? Are there any sentences that are periodic rather than loose? What effect is gained by such sentences? Are there any other noticeable devices? What are they? How are they used? What is their effect?

Introduction

In your introduction you should establish the particulars about the passage you are studying and should present a central idea that relates the style to these particulars. You should mention the place of the passage in the work, the general subject matter, any special ideas, the speaker, the apparent audience (if any except the general reader), and the basic method of presentation (that is, monologue, dialogue, or narration, all of which might be interspersed with argument, description, or comparison).

Body

In the body you should describe and evaluate the style of the passage. Always remember to consider style in relationship to circumstances. For example, suppose the speaker is in a plane crashing to the ground, or in a racing car approaching the finish line, or hurrying to meet a sweetheart; or suppose the speaker is recalling the past or considering the future. Keep such conditions foremost throughout your analysis.

To focus your theme, you might single out one aspect of style, or might discuss everything, depending on the length of the assignment. Be sure to treat things like levels of diction, categories like specific-general and concrete-abstract, the degree of simplicity or complexity, length, numbers of words (an approach that is easy for a beginning), and denotation-connotation. In discussing rhetorical aspects, go as far as you can. Consider things like sentence types and any rhetorical devices you notice and can describe. If you can draw attention to the elements in a parallel structure by using grammatical terms, do so. If you are able to detect the ways in which the sentences are kept simple or made complex, describe these ways. Be sure to use examples from the passage to illustrate your point; indent them and leave spaces between them and your own material.

The sort of theme envisaged here is designed to sharpen your levels of awareness at your own stage of development as a reader. Later, to the degree that you will have gained sharper perceptions and a wider descriptive vocabulary, you will be able to enhance the sophistication of your analyses.

Conclusion

Whereas the body is the place for detailed descriptions and examples, your conclusion is the place where you can make evaluations of the author's style. To what extent have your discoveries in your analysis increased or reinforced your appreciation of the author's technique? Does the passage take on any added importance as a result of your study? Is there anything elsewhere in the work comparable to the content, words, or ideas that you have discussed in the passage?

First Sample Theme (Style in a Passage from a Play)

Hamlet's Self-Revelation: A Reading of Hamlet, I. v. 92–109

Oh all you host of Heaven! Oh Earth; what else?	92
And shall I couple Hell? Oh fie; hold my heart;	93
And you my sinews, grow not instant old;	94
But bear me stiffly up: Remember thee?	95
Aye, thou poor Ghost, while memory holds a seat	96
In this distracted globe: Remember thee?	97
Yea, from the table of my memory,	98
I'll wipe away all trivial fond records,	99
All saws of books, all forms, all pressures past,	100
That youth and observation copied there;	101
And thy commandment all alone shall live	102
Within the book and volume of my brain,	103
Unmixed with baser matter; yes, yes, by Heaven:	104
Oh most pernicious woman!	105
Oh villain, villain, smiling damned villain!	106
My tables, my tables; meet it is I set it down,	107
That one may smile, and smile and be a villain;	108
At least I'm sure it may be so in Denmark;	109

[1]   In this passage from Act I of <u>Hamlet,</u> Hamlet is alone after the Ghost of his father has left the stage. His speech builds upon the Ghost's command to be remembered, and he begins by addressing that departed figure. After the first thirteen lines, however, he really is addressing himself, in soliloquy. <u>A close reading of the speech reveals Hamlet as an imaginative, reflective person undergoing great stress.°</u> These qualities are apparent in the scholarly diction, the development of the "book and volume" comparison, the blending of grammatical structure and line, the poetic rhythms, and the contradiction within the speech.□

[2]   <u>The diction indicates Hamlet's background as a student,</u> for many of his words might be expected from someone who has been immersed in arguments and ideas. <u>Table, records, saws</u> (sayings) of books, copied, book and volume, <u>set it down</u>—all these smack of the classroom. They show that Hamlet, who before the play's opening has returned from the university for his father's funeral (and his mother's marriage), turns naturally to the language of a student even under stress, or perhaps especially under stress.

[3]   <u>A turn of mind characteristic of a student is shown in lines 97–103.</u> This is the knack of seizing a thought and developing it fully. Hamlet is promising to remember the Ghost, but he goes beyond that. He deals at great length with the thought that his memory is like a "book and volume" on which all his previous life's experiences have been written. He states that he will "wipe away" this entire record, which is "trivial" compared to the "commandment" for vengeance that the Ghost has just made. In short, Hamlet is the sort of person who pursues an idea to its logical extension, using the exactly right vocabulary.

[4]   <u>The grammatical control in the passage seems also designed to suggest Hamlet's mental strength.</u> Everything is correct. The adverbial clause <u>while-. . .globe</u> modifies the opening verb <u>Remember</u> (95), which itself echoes the Ghost's departing words. The long sentence extending from 98 to 104 shows a perfect blending of grammar and poetic lines. Thus, 98 contains an adverb (prepositional) phrase modifying the main clause of 99. Line 100 contains three noun units which are in apposition to the noun in 99 (<u>records</u>). Lines 102 and 104 contain the second element in the compound sentence, and the major parts of this, too, are coextensive with their respective lines. In 103 the phrase <u>With-in. . .brain</u> modifies the verb <u>shall live</u> in 102, and the phrase in 104 (<u>Unmixed . . . matter</u>) complements the same verb. The reader must here assume that Shakespeare is exerting this control over the lines to show that Hamlet's mind is powerful, and under the right circumstances capable of great control. Fortinbras says, after Hamlet's death, that the young Prince was potentially a great leader. Surely the control over language shown in this passage is evidence of the capacity for analysis and discernment that should characterize leadership.

[5]   <u>Despite this mental power, however, there are many rhythmic indications that Hamlet is going through stress.</u> The large number of interjections throughout the speech creates heavy interruptions in the thought, most likely to suggest a mind that is being upset and overwhelmed. These are: <u>Aye</u> (96) <u>Yea</u> (98); <u>yes, yes, by heaven</u> (104); the exclamations against Gertrude and Claudius which take up lines 105 and 106; and the repetition of <u>smile</u> (108). In addition, the major rhythm of the speech from 104 to the end is complementary to the morbidity that characterizes Hamlet in the rest of the play. This section contains many trochaic rhythms, which would have been described in Shakespeare's day as having a "dying fall." There are falling rhythms on

° Central idea
□ Thesis sentence

yés, bý héaven

and

[5]   Ŏ villaĭn, villaĭn, smiliĭng dámneĕd villaĭn.

The last two lines end with trochees (villaĭn; Dénmaĕrk). These rhythms anticipate the interjections in the "To be or not to be" soliloquy, where Hamlet is so
depressed that he thinks of suicide.

        Along with these rhythmic indications, a close reading of the content of
the speech reveals great agitation. Hamlet is a person of normal sensibility, and
a normal person would be upset by much less than he has just been through.
A natural result, however brief, would be a loss of composure, with wrong
words, hesitations, or even contradictions in thought. While Shakespeare sees
[6]   to it that Hamlet's diction is perfect, he leads Hamlet into an apparent contradiction. Thus, after he exclaims that his mother is "pernicious" and his uncle is
a "villain," he frantically writes in his "tables" that one "may smile, and smile,
and be a villain." Here the contradiction between his promise to forget trivialities
and his writing this platitude indicates his confused state after seeing the Ghost.

        Because this passage reveals the disturbance in Hamlet's character so
fully, it is important to the rest of the play. From this point on, Hamlet is goaded
by his promise to the Ghost that he will think of nothing but revenge. He will feel
guilty and will be overwhelmed with self-doubt and self-destructiveness, be-
[7]   cause he delays acting on this promise. His attitude toward Claudius, which
previously was scorn, will now be hatred and the obsession for vengeance. His
love for Ophelia will be wrecked by this obsession, and as a result Ophelia, a
tender plant, will die. Truly, this passage may be regarded as the climax of the
first act, and it points the way to the grim but inevitable outcome of the play.

COMMENTARY ON THE THEME

This theme is based on details of style that reflect a careful but not exhaustive close reading. Thus, the discussion of diction in paragraph 2 deals only
with those words that reflect Hamlet's concerns as a student. In paragraph
3 the "book and volume" analogy is related to this same studiousness.
While the details of this analogy are mentioned, they are not examined
extensively because fuller treatment would go beyond the length of a normal theme.

        (For paragraph 4, see below.) The discussion of rhythm in paragraph
5 is focused on two prominent aspects of Hamlet's speech: the interjections
to indicate mental turbulence, and the trochees to complement the growth
of Hamlet's morbid frame of mind. Paragraph 6 is based on the interpretation (which the concentration of a close reading permits) that Hamlet's
contradictory behavior is a normal response to his just having seen the

Ghost. Throughout the theme there is an effort to fit the passage into the context of the play, and the concluding paragraph relates Hamlet's mental state, as revealed in the speech, to important aspects of the later acts.

A Close Look at Paragraph 4

The most detailed paragraph in the theme is the fourth, where the connection is made between grammar and Hamlet's mental power. An operative use of grammatical terms is illustrated here to describe parts of sentences. Although the paragraph contains technical detail, the nomenclature is neither obscure nor difficult, for the descriptive terms are in common use in most literature and composition classes. To write a comparable paragraph, you would need to lay out the sentences of a passage grammatically, relying on whatever methods you have developed about parsing or structural analysis.

Second Sample Theme (Style in a Prose Passage)

Mark Twain's Blending of Style and Purpose in "Luck" *

---

[1] The battle was awfully hot; the allies were steadily giving way all over the field. [2] Our regiment occupied a position that was vital; a blunder now must be destruction. [3] At this crucial moment, what does this immortal fool do but detach the regiment from its place and order a charge over a neighboring hill where there wasn't a suggestion of an enemy! [4] "There you go!" I said to myself; "this *is* the end at last."

[5] And away we did go, and were over the shoulder of the hill before the insane movement could be discovered and stopped. [6] And what did we find? [7] An entire and unsuspected Russian army in reserve! [8] And what happened? [9] We were eaten up? [10] That is necessarily what would have happened in ninety-nine cases out of a hundred. [11] But no; those Russians argued that no single regiment would come browsing around there at such a time. [12] It must be the entire English army, and that the sly Russian game was detected and blocked; so they turned tail, and away they went, pell-mell, over the hill and down into the field, in wild confusion, and we after them; they themselves broke the solid Russian center in the field, and tore through, and in no time there was the most tremendous rout you ever saw, and the defeat of the allies was turned into a sweeping and splendid victory! [13] Marshall Canrobert looked on, dizzy with astonishment, admiration, and delight; and sent right off for Scoresby, and hugged him, and decorated him on the field in presence of all the armies!

*For the text of this story, see Appendix C, pages 316–18.

[1] Appearing close to the end of "Luck," these two paragraphs are important in Twain's satiric design to puncture the bubble of Scoresby, a widely recognized and decorated British hero who is nothing more than a lucky boob. In the story, the paragraphs come as a climax. By presenting a brief account of a decisive battle in the Crimean War, in which Scoresby's regiment figures prominently, they bring out his stupidity and luck to the highest degree. Though the passages are narrative, the mark of Twain's style is to underscore how the hero's blundering foolishness is always saved by luck.° In every respect—description, word level, use of general and abstract diction, grammatical patterns, and the narrator's involvement—the passage embodies Twain's satiric and comic goal.□

[2] The descriptions in the paragraphs are directed toward the idiocy of the main character. In fact, the descriptions are not about the battle at all. The military matter presented in the thirteen sentences is that the allies are giving way, that Scoresby orders a charge, and that the Russians turn tail and dash away. There is no report of clashing soldiers and dying men and horses beyond the claim that the Russians themselves "tore through" their own ranks, and there are no vivid words, beyond these, describing the circumstances of victory. Indeed, the descriptions are minimal, containing just enough to exemplify Scoresby's lucky blunder, but no more. The paragraphs would be unsuccessful as an account of a battle, but as part of this story they superbly serve Twain's purposes.

[3] In keeping with the exposé, Twain uses a middle, or neutral level of diction. The words are not unusual or difficult. What could be more ordinary, for example, than words like battle, awfully, steadily, occupied, discovered, stopped, argued, and victory? One may grant that splendid, astonishment, pell-mell, immortal, and crucial are not common in everyday speech, but in this context they are appropriate, for they fall within the vocabulary of responses to battle. Because of their aptness, they enable the reader to focus on the subject and on the narrator's expressions of humor, and in this respect they fit the middle level of diction.

[4] Not only is the level neutral, but many words are general and abstract, in accord with the intention of the story to debunk Scoresby. The "allies were steadily giving way," for example, and the "movement" of many individuals is described as "insane." These broad words are fitting for groups and mass actions, but not for specific individuals. When the Russians conclude from Scoresby's senseless charge that their "game" is "detected," they turn "tail" and run "pell-mell," dashing in such "wild confusion" that there is "the most tremendous rout you ever saw," resulting in "sweeping and splendid victory"—all general and abstract words. Even the "hero," Scoresby, is not detailed anywhere as a specific leader and fighter; it is as though he is less significant than the gigantic forces of blind stupidity he unleashes. The last sentence of the paragraphs, the thirteenth, continues in this mode with the abstract but worshipful responses of the commander, Marshall Canrobert; he is "dizzy with astonishment, admiration, and delight." These abstract words reflect the public renown of Scoresby, which we, as the narrator's listeners, know to be untrue. Both general and abstract words thus jell perfectly with Twain's debunking humor.

Grammatically, as well, there is great emphasis on the contrast between Scoresby's stupidity and his success. Twain's first two sentences are neatly

° Central idea
□ Thesis sentence

balanced with contrasting ideas: Sentence 1 tells us that the battle is "hot" (part 1) and that the allies are losing (part 2). Sentence 2 tells us that the regiment is important (part 1) and that a mistake would be disastrous (part 2). But as the battle descends into the sweeping chaos caused by the charge of Scoresby's regiment, the grammar takes on the same chaotic pattern. Sentence 12, con-

[5] taining all the battle details, is eighty-one words long. It is broken up by semi-colons and commas into a variety of separate statements and structures describing the pell-mell retreat and victory. In other words, the sentence has the same wildness, sweep, and madness of the events being described–a blending of grammar and subject.

The major quality of Twain's style in the passage, however, is the amused, debunking language contributed directly by the narrator. The narra-tor's ideas keep the passage short, and his words frame the suspense and anticlimax of the battle, as is shown in the first paragraph (sentences 1–4). He tells us (sentence 3) that the "immortal fool" orders a mistaken charge. His lamenting prediction, "this *is* the end at last" (sentence 4), is designed for full dramatic and suspenseful effect. The narrator's involvement is also shown by

[6] his simply phrased questions just before he tells about the results of the charge: "And what did we find?" "And what happened?" "We were eaten up?" His continual effect on the language is apparent in his reconstruction of the military logic of the Russians, and his attitude is most amusingly shown by the word browsing (sentence 11), which suggests grazing animals, not charging armies. This word emphasizes the dimwittedness of Scoresby's command to attack. Throughout the paragraphs, the speaker thus lends his own wry insights to the language. The skill, naturally, belongs to Twain.

In all respects, the passage is a model of the right use of words in the right places. If the writing were about an actual military combat, it would be poor. But because it is part of a comic exposé of a fortunate fool, it is hard to imagine a better way to put things. Twain's speaker gives us what we need to know:

[7] namely that Scoresby has a Midas touch in everything he does, no matter how potentially disastrous. The sentences are clear and direct, and convey the facts about Scoresby that show his imbecility. Even the longest and most confused sentence, the twelfth, is appropriate to the confusion that Scoresby converts to triumph. For these reasons, the paragraphs are examples of accurate, pur-poseful narrative prose.

COMMENTARY ON THE THEME

This theme shows how separate stylistic topics may be unified. Important in this objective are the transitions from paragraph to paragraph, such as "not only . . . but," "in keeping with the exposé," "as well," and "in all respects." These transition phrases enable reader concentration to move smoothly from one topic to the next.

The introduction demonstrates the importance of relating the passage being studied to the work as a whole. Because the central idea is connected to Twain's debunking objective, the point is made that style and satiric intention are merged and integrated. The thesis sentence indicates five aspects of style to be considered in the essay. Any one of these, if it were necessary, could be separately developed.

In the body, paragraph 2 treats the absence of specifically descriptive words, explaining this lack by reference to the satiric subject. Paragraph 3 treats the neutral diction, making the point that this language is appropriate because it permits a direct focus on the asinine blunders of the major character. Twain's use of general and abstract language is treated in paragraph 4, the point being that this language is appropriate because the story exposes the emptyheadedness of Scoresby. In paragraph 5, the subject is the grammar of the passage, indicating that the movement from balance to chaos complements the chaos of the battle. (For paragraph 6, see below.) The concluding paragraph, 7, is a tribute to Twain's style, emphasizing again how his satiric objective governs word choices.

A Close Look at Paragraph 6

Paragraph 6, the last of the body, is designed as the high point of the discussion of style, asserting that the most important aspect of the writing is the narrative speaker. It is this speaker whose ideas and words permit Twain to keep the narrative brief while emphasizing his hero's blundering stupidity. Theoretically, details about a battle description might be exhaustive and exhausting, particularly if the goal is descriptive reality. Since the topic is style, however, the paragraph demonstrates that the effect of the narrator is to provide only enough details to be consistent with the story's thesis. Thus the layout of the battle, the questions, and the characterization of the Russian army as "browsing" are all stylistically the most significant aspect of Twain's style.

chapter 16
_____

Writing an Evaluation:
Deciding on Literary Quality

Evaluation is the act of deciding what is good, bad, or mediocre. It requires a steady pursuit of the best—to be satisfied with less is to deny the best efforts of our greatest writers. Evaluation implies that there are ideal standards of excellence by which decisions about quality can be made, but it must be remembered that these standards are flexible and may be applicable to works of literature written in all places and ages.

An evaluation is different from an essay on what you might like or dislike in a work (see Chapter 2, pp. 41–50). While your preferences are important in your evaluation, they are not as important as your judgment, and your judgment may lead you into positions that seem contrary to your preferences. In other words, it is possible to grant the excellence of a work or writer that you personally may not like.

STANDARDS FOR EVALUATION

There is no precise answer to the problem of how to justify an evaluation. Evaluation is the most abstract, philosophical, and difficult writing about literature you will do. Standards of taste, social mores, and even morals differ from society to society and from age to age; nonetheless, some works of art have been judged as great by generation after generation in many cultures. There are many standards to help you evaluate a literary work.

Some of the major ones are described below, and many have been suggested in earlier chapters.

Truth

Although *truth* or *truthful* is often used in speaking of literature to
mean *realism* or *realistic*, its meaning here is carefully restricted. To speak of
the truth is to imply generality and universality. Let us take a concrete
illustration. Sophocles' *Oedipus the King* has survived the turbulence of
almost 2,500 years. It was written within social contexts that no longer
exist, and it concerns circumstances that are difficult to imagine in the
twentieth century. Nevertheless, it remains as true (and relevant) for our
time as it was when it was first performed before the Athenian public. This
is so because it embodies situations that human beings have always and
will always face; it reflects patterns of human error, guilt, and punishment
that are as valid today as they were in Sophocles' day.

While many works have not withstood such an extended test of time,
those that survive and prosper beyond their initial publication do so because they, too, embody some essential truth about the human condition.
Such works measure up to basic standards we use in deciding whether a
work of art is good or bad, great or mediocre.

Affirmativeness

Affirmativeness means here that human beings are worth caring about
and writing about, no matter how debased their condition of living or how
totally they abuse their state. If a character like Mathilde Loisel experiences
loss and difficulties, the author must demonstrate that this loss has value
and meaning. Human worth is here affirmed (through Mathilde herself)
even as a major character is hurt. If a character is happy at the end of the
work, the author must show that this character's qualities have justified
such good fortune. Life is again affirmed. If an unworthy character is
fortunate at the end, the author still affirms human worth by suggesting a
world in which such worth may become triumphant. In short, authors may
portray the use and abuse of life, the love and the hate, the heights and the
depths, but their vision is always that life is valuable and worthy of respect
and dignity. The best works are those that make this affirmation forcefully,
without platitudes.

"The Joint Force and Full Result of All"

In his *Essay on Criticism* (1711), Alexander Pope insists that a critic
should not judge a work simply by its parts but should judge the *whole*—
"the joint force and full result of all." You can profit from Pope's wisdom.

Consider the total effect of the work, both as an artistic form and as a cause of impressions and emotions in yourself. Bear in mind that a great work may contain imperfections, but if the sum total of the work is impressive, the flaws assume minor importance.

By the same token, excellent technique in itself does not justify a claim for excellence. An interesting plot, a balanced and carefully handled structure, a touching love story, a valid or important moral—none of these attributes alone can support a total judgment of "good" unless everything in the work is balanced.

Another important phase of the "joint force and full result of all" is the way in which you become involved as you read. Most of what you read, if it has merit, will cause you to become emotionally involved with the characters and actions. You have perhaps observed that characters in some works seem real to you or that incidents are described so vividly that you feel as though you have witnessed them. The problem here is whether the involvement you experienced was fleeting and momentary or whether it has assumed more permanence.

Vitality

A good work of literature has a life of its own and can be compared to a human being. A work can grow in the sense that your repeated experience with it will produce insights that you did not have in your previous readings. Examples of such works are poems like Shakespeare's sonnets and Lowell's "Patterns," stories like Jackson's "The Lottery" and Poe's "The Masque of the Red Death," and plays like Chekhov's *The Bear* and Glaspell's *Trifles*. Readers and critics alike constantly find new insights and understanding in such works.

Beauty

Beauty is closely allied with unity, symmetry, harmony, and proportion. To discover the relationship of parts to whole—their logical, chronological, and associational functions within the work—is to perceive beauty. In the eighteenth century people believed that "variety within order" constituted beauty. The Romantic and post-Romantic periods held that beauty could be found only through greater freedom. This belief has produced such characteristics as originality for its own sake, experimentation in form, freedom of syntax, stream-of-consciousness narration, and personal diction. Despite the change of emphasis, however, the concepts of unity and proportion are still valid and applicable. Therefore, studies of style, structure, point of view, tone, and imagery are all ways of determining whether works are beautiful.

WRITING AN EVALUATION

In your theme you will attempt to answer the question of whether the work you have studied is good. If so, why? If not, why not? The grounds for your evaluation must be artistic. Although some works may be good pieces of political argument, or may be successfully controversial, your goal is to judge them as works of art.

Introduction

In the introduction you can briefly summarize your evaluation, which will be your central idea, and list the points by which you expect to demonstrate the validity of your assessment. To assist your reader's comprehension of your ideas, you should note any unique facts or background about the work you are evaluating.

Body

In the body, demonstrate the grounds for your judgment; your principal points will be the positive or negative features of the work you are evaluating. Positive features include qualities of style, idea, structure, character, logic, point of view, and so on. Your discussion will analyze the probability, truth, force, or power with which the work embodies these positive aspects.

Avoid analysis for its own sake, and do not retell stories. If you are showing the excellence or deficiency of a character portrayal, you can include a description of the character, but remember that your discussion is to be pointed toward *evaluation*, not *description*. Therefore you must select details for discussion that will illustrate whether the work is good or bad. Similarly, if you are evaluating a sonnet of Shakespeare, you might argue that the superb imagery contributes to the general excellence. At this point you might introduce some of the imagery, but your purpose is not to analyze imagery as such; it should be used only for illustration. If you remember to keep your thematic purpose foremost, you should have little difficulty in making your discussion relate to your central idea.

Conclusion

The conclusion should be a statement on the total result of the work you are evaluating. Your concern here is with total impressions. This part of evaluation should reemphasize your central idea.

Sample Theme

An Evaluation of Shirley Jackson's "The Lottery"*

[1] To evaluate Jackson's "The Lottery" one needs to overcome possible objections that might be made to it. One is that the story is impossible; we don't murder ritual scapegoats any more to pacify angry gods who might destroy the earth's fertility if their lust for human blood is not satisfied. Another is that the story is improbable and untrue because the specific cruelty it reveals is less likely than individual concern, kindness, respect, and legal due process. It is possible to defend "The Lottery" against these objections, and, in addition, to point out the story's power and artistic vitality.° Its worth may be found in its symbolism, truth, satire, and artistic excellence.□

[2] A major reason for considering "The Lottery" negatively is the mistaken judgment that it is about an abandoned ritual practice, and that to put it into the present time is a falsification. While such practices are admittedly a thing of the past in more civilized societies, the argument itself is invalid if the story is taken not realistically but symbolically. As symbolism, the story represents the many institutional and quasi-legal means through which people justify cruelty, such as marital violence, child abuse, and various forms of discrimination. (Examples can be multiplied each day from newspapers and TV news reports.) In such a symbolic reading, Jackson's 300 villagers collectively represent cruelty which is inflicted without thought or knowledge. Because Jackson draws attention to the forgotten meaning of the ritual, she emphasizes that the lottery is no more than an official sanction for mob barbarity. She is careful to emphasize this mean-inglessness when the townfolk begin to descend on Tessie Hutchinson:

> Although the villagers had forgotten the ritual and lost the original black box, they still remembered to use stones. The pile of stones the boys had made earlier was ready; there were stones on the ground with the blowing scraps of paper that had come out of the box. (paragraph 74)

The symbolic value here is that cruelty is constant in human nature, and it persists from age to age as the real reason for action, as opposed to the justifications, which are forgotten.

Also, because of the symbolic value, the negative judgment that the story is improbable and untrue cannot be maintained. Rather, the story is solidly grounded in truth about human beings. One may concede that the individuals carrying the stones would each, individually, be kind and helpful. But in a vast group they give in to violence against a member of their own group. Of partic-ular note, for example, is that it is Mrs. Delacroix who selects "a stone so large she. . . [has] to pick it up with both hands," and who urges Mrs. Dunbar to hurry

---

* For the text of this story, see Appendix C, pages 328–34.
° Central idea
□ Thesis sentence

up to the stoning (paragraph 74). Ironically, this is the same Mrs. Delacroix who has just been chatting with Mrs. Hutchinson in as friendly a way as possible (paragraphs 8, 9). One might like to insist that people never hurt their friends, but Mrs. Delacroix is a symbol denying the validity of this ideal claim about friendship and commnunity.

[3]

In this vein, "The Lottery" may be taken as a satire against complacency and self-congratulation. To those who would like to believe that the dominating virtue of human beings is their kindness, Jackson satirically offers the brutality of the lottery's ultimate "prize." There can be no exceptions, because the people joining in the stoning are all good, plain, everyday, hardworking folks, including the playful children who pile stones together for the final sacrifice. This fact makes kind and sensitive readers uncomfortable; in fact, it makes them squirm. But as a satire the entire story shocks us into the truth that horror is a part of everyday life. A cutting illustration of the satire is the last part of the opening paragraph, which explains the time needed for the lottery to take place:

[4]

> . . . in this village, where there were only about three hundred people, the whole lottery took less than two hours, so it could begin at ten o'clock in the morning and still be through in time to allow the villagers to get home for noon dinner. (paragraph 1)

The concluding clause of this paragraph is brilliant, for it implies that the insensitivity of the villagers is so great that they could go calmly home and eat lunch after stoning one of their neighbors to death! The real bite of this observation is not clear until the story's end, but, in retrospect, the clause is an incisive satirization of indifference and cruelty.

This opening excellence is also typical of the story's general artistic quality. The ending is designed as a wrenching surprise, and it succeeds in this aim, even though throughout the story Jackson drops hints that prepare for the brutal stoning. At the beginning, Jackson makes the gathering of the villagers in the square seen usual and ordinary. Although readers are therefore unsuspecting, and notice nothing unusual, a second look reveals that the people are uneasy. When the men gather, for example, we learn that "their jokes were quiet and they smiled rather than laughed" (paragraph 3). When one of the fathers speaks "sharply" to his son, there is nothing to indicate anything beyond fatherly annoyance, but in the context of the conclusion, the sharpness suggests great mental tension.

[5]

In fact, Jackson has constructed so fine a story that readers are kept constantly in suspense. She withholds the ominousness of the events until paragraph 45, when she writes that Bill Hutchinson is "standing quiet" after his family has drawn the prize. This is the first major clue that something is going wrong, and that the seeming festiveness is not producing the expected result of happiness. This realization is confirmed when Tessie Hutchinson claims that the drawing is unfair (paragraph 45). Even so, Jackson keeps readers guessing about the true horror of the prize until almost the very end, and the concluding sentence is an abrupt and jarring cry of pain:

[6]

> "It isn't fair, it isn't right," Mrs. Hutchinson screamed, and then they were upon her. (paragraph 79)

This overwhelmingly powerful ending, a climax as well as a conclusion, is the justification for valuing "The Lottery" so highly. Once readers have experienced (not just read) the story, they can never forget its "joint force and full result," just as they can never forget its uncomfortable truths about human beings. In negation, one might claim that "The Lottery" is too disturbing, too dark, and too bleak, for the common, everyday folks of Jackson's village become literally revenging monsters in their concluding attack. But because the ritual execution forces consideration of those extremes of brutality that most of us would prefer not to confront, Jackson succeeds in stimulating awareness. For this reason the story is affirmative, despite its satirical presentation of human beings. "The Lottery," in all respects, is a great and unforgettable masterpiece.

[7]

COMMENTARY ON THE THEME

The theme illustrates that evaluation, because it emphasizes judgment, requires the development of some kind of argument. It is not enough, in other words, to claim that a work is either good or bad, but this claim must be argued convincingly, with materials from the work being used as support.

In this specific theme, the claim is that "The Lottery" is an excellent story, and this position is argued throughout, with reference to the story's truth, vitality, artistic quality, and "joint force and full result." The introductory paragraph makes plain the theme's major strategy of anticipating objections to "The Lottery" and then answering them—and building upon the answers—so as to create a favorable judgment about the story. There are thus two parts of the theme: (1) a refutation of the arguments that the story is outdated and untrue, and (2) an argument in favor of the story's artistic excellence.

(For paragraph 2, see below.) Paragraph 3 deals with the issue of truth and gives evidence to support the reality of Jackson's revelations about the villagers. In paragraph 4, the argument for truth is shifted to the artistic evidence that the story is a satire, with its truth becoming evident in the validity of its attack on smugness and complacency about human nature.

The fifth and sixth paragraphs continue to treat the story artistically. Paragraph 5 considers the way in which Jackson masterfully withholds and masks the gruesome intentions of the villagers, while paragraph 6 considers the powerful impact of the conclusion. The arguments in favor of evaluating "The Lottery" favorably are brought together in paragraph 7, where an additional assertion is made that the story is to be valued not only because of its satiric views of human cruelty, but also because of its affirmative effect of increasing awareness.

A Close Look At Paragraph 2

This paragraph illustrates the argumentative method of **anticipation,** or **procatalepsis** (see also pp. 157–58). The method is to develop a point by arguing against a possible objection. In this case, the objection is both conceded on one level and nullified on another, for the answer is based on the assertion that "The Lottery" is to be read not realistically (which would make the objection valid) but symbolically (which makes the objection meaningless). It is not enough just to assert that the story is symbolic, however, and hence the paragraph moves to demonstrate how the symbolism may be applied. The first application is to the outside evidence of a number of examples of human cruelty. As long as such evidence is general in nature, as in this paragraph, and not political or sectarian, it is acceptable. The second application of the symbol is made to the mindlessness of cruelty. In support, the paragraph asserts that the villagers have forgotten the reasons for their lottery but have retained only its brutal enactment. The quoted passage from the story supports the claim that Jackson is exposing the reflexive, unthinking nature of the villagers' evil. The paragraph thus supports the theme's positive evaluation of "The Lottery," it raises valid arguments, and it is based solidly in the story.

chapter 17

Writing About Film:
Visual and Auditory Literature

Film is the word most often used for motion pictures, although you may often hear "picture," or simply "movie." It is a highly specialized kind of drama, and like drama, it utilizes the techniques of dialogue, monologue, and action. Like drama also, it employs movement and spectacle. Unlike drama, it embodies the technology of photography and lighting, film chemistry, sound, and editing. In writing about film, you may make purely literary considerations, such as character, structure, tone, ideas, or symbolism. In addition, however, since the techniques of film are so specialized, you will also need to take at least some of these into account.

FILM AND STAGE PLAYS

Film may be compared with the stage production of a play. A play may be produced many times, in many different places, with many different people. In bringing a play to life, the producer and director not only employ actors, but also artists, scene designers, carpenters, painters, lighting technicians, costume makers, choreographers, and music directors and musicians. Each production is therefore different from every other, because not only the actors, but also the accessories of the staging, are unique. A film, however, because of high production costs and because it reaches a mass audience through movie theaters, television, and videocassettes, usually exists in only one version ("remakes" being excepted). Thus Shakespeare's play *Hamlet* has been staged innumerable times since Shakespeare's Globe Theatre company first produced it at the beginning of the seventeenth century, while Orson Welles's *Citizen Kane* (1941) is in only one form and cannot ever change.

As might be expected, then, stage and movie productions are radically different. In a play, actors enter, speak to each other, and remain in front of the audience until they exit. The stage itself limits what can be done. The makers of the film, however, have few such limitations, and the absence of restrictions permits the inclusion of any detail whatever, from a car chase to a scene in the Napoleonic wars. If there is to be a scene on a desert island, the film-maker goes to such an island and presents it in all its reality, complete with beach, palm trees, huts, and authentic natives-turned-actors. Nothing is left to your imagination. If the scene is a distant planet, obviously the film-maker cannot go on location there, but instead creates a working location in the studio, with lighting, props, costumes, and special effects. Film, in short, enables a dramatic production to approach almost complete freedom.

THE PAINTER, THE PHOTOGRAPHER, AND THE FILM-MAKER

To the degree that film is confined to a screen, it may visually be compared to the art of the painter and the still photographer. There is a whole language of visual art. One object in a painting may take on special relationships to others as the artist directs the eyes of the observer. A color used in one part may be balanced with same color, or with its complement, in another part. Painters and photographers may introduce certain details as symbols and may suggest allegorical interpretations through the inclusion of mythical figures or universally recognized objects. Particular effects may be achieved with the use of the textures of the paint and control over shutter speed, focus, and various techniques of development. The techniques and effects are extensive.

The film-maker is able to utilize most of the resources of the still photographer and many of those of the painter, and may augment these with special effects. Artistically, the most confining aspect of film is the rectangular screen, but aside from that, film is unrestricted. With a basis in a dramatic text called a "script" or "film-script," film uses words and their effects but it also employs the language of visual art, and especially the particular vividness and power of moving pictures. When considering film, then, you should realize that it communicates not just by words, but also by various techniques. You can treat the ideas, the problems, and the symbolism in a film, but you should also recognize that the visual presentation is inseparable from the medium of film itself.

TECHNIQUES OF FILM

There are many techniques of film, and a full description and documentation of them can, and has, become extensive.[1] In preparing to write a theme about film, however, you need to familiarize yourself only with those aspects of technique that have an immediate bearing on your responses and interpretations.

Editing or *Montage:* The Heart of the Film-Maker's Craft

A finished film is not a continuous work, filmed from start to end, but is instead a composite. The putting together of the film is the process of **editing**, or **montage** (assemblage, mounting, construction), which is a cutting and gluing. Depending on the flexibility of the film-script, the various scenes of the film are planned before shooting begins, but the major task of montage is done in a studio, by special film editors.

If we again compare film with a stage play, we may note that a theatrical production moves continuously, with pauses only for intermissions and scene changes. Your perception of the action is caused by your distance from the stage (perhaps aided by opera glasses or binoculars). Also, even as you move your eyes from one character to another, you still perceive the entire stage. In a film, however, the directors and editors *create* these continuous perceptions for you by piecing together different parts. The editors begin with many "takes" (separately filmed scenes, including many versions of the same scenes). What they select, or mount, will be the film, and we never see the discarded scenes. Thus, it is editing or montage, that puts everything together.

The Uses of Montage

NARRATIVE CONTINUITY. The first use of montage, already suggested, is narrative continuity. For example, a journey may be illustrated by selected shots of a person buying a plane ticket, boarding the plane, taking a seat, drinking a complimentary soda, and walking in a terminal. A climb up a steep cliff may be shown at the bottom, middle, and top (with backward slips and falls to show the danger of the climb and to make viewers catch their breaths). All such narrative sequences result from the assembling of individual pieces, each one representing phases of the activity. A classic example of a large number of separate parts forming a narrative unit is the well-known shower murder in Alfred Hitchcock's

---

[1] See, for example, Ephraim Katz, *The Film Encyclopedia* (New York: Crowell, 1979); Daniel Talbot, ed., *Film: An Anthology* (Berkeley: University of California Press, 1969); Louis D. Gianetti, *Understanding Movies*, 5th ed. (Englewood Cliffs, NJ: Prentice Hall, 1990); and James Monaco, *How to Read a Film*, rev. ed. (New York: Oxford University Press, 1981).

Psycho (1959), where a 45-second sequence is made up of more than seventy different shots (e.g., the woman in the shower, the murderer behind the curtain, the attack, the slumping figure, the running water, the dead woman's eye, the bathtub drain, etc.).

EXPLANATION OF CHARACTER AND MOTIVATION. Montage is used in "flashbacks" to explain present, ongoing actions or characteristics, or in illustration of a character's thoughts and memories, or in brief examples from the unremembered past of a character suffering from amnesia. It also supplies direct visual explanation of a character. A famous example occurs in Welles's *Citizen Kane* (the subject of the sample theme, pp. 251–54). The concluding scene shows overhead views of Kane's vast collection of statues and mementos. At the very end, the camera focuses on a raging incinerator, into which workmen have thrown his boyhood sled, which bears the brand name "Rosebud" (and which we have fleetingly seen him playing with as a boy). Because "Rosebud" is Kane's dying word, which everyone in the film is trying to learn about, this final scene shows that Kane's dying thoughts are about his lost boyhood, before he was taken away from his parents, and that his unhappy life has resulted from feelings of rejection and personal pain.

DIRECTORIAL COMMENTARY. In addition, montage is used symbolically as commentary, as is an early sequence in Charlie Chaplin's *Modern Times* (1936), which shows a large group of workers rushing to their factory jobs. Immediately following this scene is a view of a large, milling herd of sheep. By this symbolic montage, Chaplin suggests that the men are being herded and dehumanized by modern industry. Thus, montage and editorial statement go hand in hand.

OTHER USES. Montage may also produce other characteristics through camera work, development, and special effects. For example, filmmakers may reverse an action to emphasize its illogicality or ridiculousness. Editing may also speed up action (which makes even the most serious things funny), or slow things down. It may also blend one scene with another, or juxtapose two or more actions in quick succession to show what people may be doing while they are separated. The possibilities for creativity and uniqueness are extensive.

Visual Techniques

THE CAMERA. Whereas editing or montage is a finishing technique, the work of film *begins* with the camera, which permits great freedom in the presentation of characters and actions. In a film, the visual viewpoint may shift. Thus, a film may begin with a distant shot of the actors—a **long shot**—much like the views of actors on stage. Then the camera may zoom in to give a **closeup,** or may zoom out to present a wide and complete panorama. Usually a speaking actor will be the subject of a closeup, but the camera may also show closeups of other actors who are reacting. You must decide on the effects of closeups and long shots yourself, but it should be plain that the use of either—or of middle-distance photographs—is a means by which film directors control perceptions of their characters and situations.

The camera may also move from character to character, or from character to a natural or manufactured object. In this way a film may show a series of reactions to an event. It may also concentrate the viewer's attention on a character's attitude, or it may be a visual commentary on his or her actions. If a man and woman are in love, for example, the camera may shift, either directly or through montage, from the couple to flowers and trees, thus associating their love visually with objects of beauty and growth. Should the flowers be wilted and the trees leafless, however, the visual commentary might be that the love is doomed and hopeless.

The camera may also create unique effects. For example, slow motion can focus on a certain aspect of a person's character. The concentrated focus on a child running happily in a meadow (as in *The Color Purple* [1985] by Steven Spielberg) suggests the joy inherent in such a movement. Surprisingly, speed is sometimes indicated by slow motion, which emphasizes strong muscular effort (as in the running scenes in Hugh Hudson's *Chariots of Fire* [1981]).

Many other camera techniques bear on action and character. The focus may be sharp at one point, indistinct at another. Moving a speaking character out of focus may suggest that listeners are bored. Sharp or blurred focus may also show that a character has seen things exactly or inexactly. In action sequences, the camera may be mounted in a moving vehicle to "track" or follow running human beings or horses, speeding bicycles and cars, or moving sailboats, canoes, speedboats, or rowboats. A camera operator on foot may also be the tracker, or the camera may track ground movement from an aircraft. Movement may also be captured by a rotating camera that follows a moving object or character. Then, too, the camera may be fixed while the moving object goes from one side to the other.

LIGHT SHADOW, AND COLOR.   As in the theater, the film-maker uses light, shadow, and color to reinforce ideas and to create realistic and symbolic effects. A scene in sunshine, which brings out colors, and the same scene in rain and clouds or in twilight, all of which mute colors, create different moods. Characters in bright light are presumably open and frank, whereas characters in shadow may be hiding something, particularly in black and white films. Flashing or strobe lights might show a changeable or sinister character or situation.

Colors, of course, have much the same meaning that they have in any other artistic medium. Blue sky and clear light suggest happiness, while greenish light may indicate something ghoulish. A memorable control of colors occurs midway through David O. Selznick's *Gone with the Wind* (1939), when Scarlet O'Hara reflects upon the devastation of her plantation home, Tara. She resolves never to be hungry again, and as she speaks she is silhouetted against a flaming orange sky—an angry background which suggests how totally the way of life she knew as a young woman has been destroyed. As in this example, you may expect colors to underscore the story of the film. Thus, lovers may wear clothing with the same or complementary colors, while people who are not "right" for each other may wear clashing colors.

Action and the Human Body

ACTION.   The strength of film is direct action. Actions of all sorts—running, swimming, driving a car, fighting, embracing and kissing, or even just sitting; chases, trick effects, ambushes—all these and more create a sense of immediate reality, and all are tied (or should be) to narrative development. Scenes of action may run on for several minutes with little or no accompanying dialogue, to carry on the story or to convey ideas about the interests and abilities of the characters.

THE BODY.   Closely related to the portrayal of action is the way in which film shows the human body (and animal bodies), together with bodily motion and gesture (or body language). The view or perspective that the film-maker presents is particularly important. A torso shot of a character may stress no more than the content of that character's speech. A closeup shot, however, with the character's head filling the screen, may put emphasis on motives as well as content. The camera may also distort ordinary expectations of reality. With wide-angle lenses and closeups, for example, human subjects may be made to seem bizarre or grotesque, as with the faces in the crowd in Woody Allen's *Stardust Memories* (1980). Sometimes the camera creates other bodily distortions, enlarging certain limbs, for example, as with the forest dweller in Ingmar Bergman's *Virgin Spring* (1959), or throwing into unnatural prominence a scolding mouth or a suspicious eye. If distortion is used, it invites interpretation: The film-maker may be asserting that certain human beings, even supposedly normal ones, are odd, sinister, intimidating, or psychotic.

Sound

DIALOGUE AND MUSIC.   The first business of the sound track is the spoken dialogue, which is "mixed" in editing to be synchronized with the action. There are also many other elements in the sound track. Music, the most important element, creates and augments moods. A melody in a major or minor key, or in a slow or fast tempo, may affect our perception of actions. If a character is thinking deeply, muted strings may create a complementary sound. But if the character is going insane, the music may become discordant and percussive. Sometimes music gives a film a special identity. In Hudson's *Chariots of Fire*, for example, Vangelis Papathanassiou wrote music that has become popular in itself but which is always identified with the film. In addition, musical accompaniments may directly render dramatic statement, without dialogue. An example occurs in Welles's *Citizen Kane*. Beginning that portion of the narrative derived from the autobiography of a character who is now dead (the scene first focuses on his statue), the musical sound track by Bernard Herrmann quotes the *Dies Irae* theme from the traditional Mass for the Dead. The instrumentation, however, makes the music funny, and we do not grieve but rather smile. Herrmann, incidentally, varies this theme elsewhere in the film, usually for comic effect.

SPECIAL SOUND EFFECTS. Special sound effects may also augment a film's action. The sound of a blow, for example, may be enhanced electronically to cause an impact similar to the force of the blow itself (as in the boxing scenes from the many *Rocky* films). At times sounds, such as the noises of wailing people, squeaking or slamming doors, marching feet, or moving vehicles, may be filtered through an electronic apparatus to create weird or ghostly effects. Often a character's words may echo rapidly and sickeningly to show dismay or anguish. In a word, sound is a vital part of film.

WRITING ABOUT FILM

Obviously the first requirement is to see the film, either in a theater or on videocassette. No matter how you see it, you should do so at least twice, making notes as you go, because your discussion takes on value the more thoroughly you know the material. Write down the names of the script writer, director, composer, special effects editor, chief photographer, and major actresses and actors. If particular speeches are worth quoting, remember the general circumstances of the quotation, and also, if possible, key words. Take notes on costume and color, or (if the film is in black and white) light and shade. You will need to rely on memory, but if you have videotape, you may easily check important details.

Introduction

Here, state your central idea and thesis sentence. You should also include the background necessary to support points to be made in the body. It is also appropriate to name the major creative and performing persons of the film.

Body

If you have no other instructions, you might decide on usual literary subjects such as plot, structure, character, ideas, or setting. Remember, however, to consider not only dialogue and action, but also film techniques.

In discussing the film's action, answer questions like these: What is the relationship of action to theme and character? Is the action realistic? Does the camera stay at a distance, showing the persons as relatively small in a vast natural or artificial world? Do closeups show smiles, frowns, eagerness, or anxiety? Is any attempt made to render temperature by action, say cold by a character's stamping of feet, or warmth by the character's removing a coat or shirt? Does the action show any changing of mood, from sadness to happiness, or from indecision to decision?

Then, too, you may stress cinematographic techniques, showing their relationship to the theme, their appropriateness, and their quality. If you discuss technique, be sure to have good notes, so that your supporting details are accurate. A good method is to concentrate on technique in only a few scenes. If you analyze the effects of montage, for example, you may use your stop-action control (for a videocassette recorder) and rewind button to go over the scene a number of times.

You might emphasize the quality of the acting. You do not need to be a drama critic to answer questions like these: How well do the actors adapt to the medium of film? How convincing are their performances? Do they control their facial expressions? Does their appearance lend anything to your understanding of their characters? How well do they control bodily motion? Are they graceful? Awkward? Does it seem that the actors are genuinely creating their roles, or just reading through the parts?

Conclusion

You might conclude by evaluating the effectiveness of the cinematic form to story and idea. Are all the devices of film used in the best possible way? Is anything overdone? Is anything underplayed? Is the film good, bad, or indifferent up to a point, and then does it change? How? Why?

Sample Theme

Orson Welles's Citizen Kane: *Whittling a Giant Down to Size*

[1] Citizen Kane (1941) is a well-crafted film in black and white. The script is by Herman Mankiewicz and Orson Welles, with photography by Gregg Toland, music by Bernard Herrmann, direction by Welles, and the leading role by Welles. It is the story of a wealthy and powerful man, Charles Foster Kane, who exemplifies the American Dream of economic self-sufficiency, self-determination, and self, period. The film does not explore the "greatness" of the hero, however, but rather exposes him as a misguided, unhappy person who tries to buy love and remake reality.° All aspects of the picture—characterization, structure, and technique—are directed to this goal.□

[2] At the film's heart is the character and deterioration of Kane, the newly deceased newspaper magnate and millionaire. He is not all bad, for he begins well and then goes downward, in a tragic sequence. For example, the view we see of him as a child, being taken away from home, invites sympathy. When we next see him as a young man, he idealistically takes over a daily newspaper, the Inquirer. This idealism makes him admirable but also makes his deterioration tragic. As he says to his associate, Thatcher, in a moment of insight, he could have been a great person if he had not been so wealthy. His corruption begins when he tries to alter the world to suit himself, such as his insane attempt to make an opera star out of his second wife, Susan, and his related attempt to shape critical praise for her despite her terrible singing. Even though he builds an opera house for her, and also sponsors many performances, he cannot change reality. This tampering with truth indicates how completely he loses his youthful integrity.

[3] The structure is progressively arranged to bring out such weaknesses. The film flows out of the opening obituary newsreel, from which we learn that Kane's dying word was the name Rosebud (the brand name of his boyhood sled, which is spoken at the beginning by a person whose mouth is shown in closeup). The newsreel director, wanting to get an inside story, assigns a reporter named Thompson to learn about "Rosebud." Thompson's search unifies the rest of the film; he goes from place to place and person to person to collect materials and conduct interviews which disclose Kane's increasing strangeness and alienation. At the end, although the camera leaves Thompson to focus on the burning sled, he has been successful in uncovering the story of Kane's deterioration (even though he himself never learns what "Rosebud" means). Both the sled and the reporter therefore tie together the many aspects of the film.

[4] It is through Thompson's searches that the film presents the flashback accounts of Kane's deterioration. The separate persons being interviewed (including Thatcher's handwritten account) each contribute something different to the narrative because their experiences with Kane have all been unique. As a

° Central idea
□ Thesis sentence

result of these individual points of view, the story is quite intricate. We learn in the Bernstein section, for example, that Jedediah proudly saves a copy of Kane's declaration about truth in reporting. We do not learn in Jedediah's interview, however, that he, Jedediah, sends the copy back to Kane as an indictment of Kane's betrayal of principle. Rather, it is in <u>Susan's</u> account that [4] we learn about the return, even though she herself understands nothing about it. This subtlety, so typical of the film, marks the ways in which the biography of Kane is perceptively revealed.

<u>Thus, the major importance of these narrating characters is to reveal and reflect Kane's disintegration.</u> Jedediah (Joseph Cotten) is a person of principle who works closely with Kane, but after the lost election he rebels when he understands the falseness of Kane's personal life. He is totally alienated after Kane completes the unfinished attack on Susan's performance. Jedediah's change, or perhaps his assertion of principle, thus reveals Kane's increasing [5] corruption. Susan, Kane's second wife (Dorothy Comingore), is naive, sincere, and warm, but her drinking, her attempted suicide, and her final separation show the harm of Kane's warped visions. Bernstein (Everett Sloane), the first person Thompson interviews, is a solitary figure who is uncritical of Kane, but it is he who first touches on the theme about the mystery of Kane's motivations. Bernstein also takes on life when he speaks poignantly of his forty-five year memory of the girl in white. Even though this revelation is brief, it suggests layers of feeling and longing.

<u>In addition to these perceptive structural characterizations,</u> Citizen Kane <u>is a masterpiece of film technique.</u> The camera images are sharp, with clear depths of field. In keeping with Kane's disintegration and mysteriousness, the screen is rarely bright. Instead, the film makes strong use of darkness and contrasts, almost to the point at times of blurring distinctions between people. [6] Unique in Gregg Toland's camera work are the many shots taken from waist high or below, which distort the bodies of the characters by distancing their heads—suggesting that the characters are preoccupied by their own concerns and oblivious to normal perspectives. Nowhere is this distortion better exemplified than in the scene between Kane and Jedediah in the empty rooms after the lost election.

<u>As might be expected in a film so dominated by its central figure, the many symbols create strong statements about character.</u> The most obvious is the sled "Rosebud," the dominating symbol of the need for love and acceptance in childhood. Another notable symbol is glass and, in one scene, ice. In the party scene, two ice statues are in the foreground of the employees of the Inquirer. In another scene, a bottle looms large in front of Jedediah, who is drunk. In another, a pill bottle and drinking glass are in front of Susan, who has [7] just used them in her suicide attempt. The suggestion of these carefully photographed symbols is that life is brittle and temporary. Particularly symbolic is the bizarre entertainment in the party scene. Because Kane joins the dancing and singing, the action suggests that he is doing no more than taking a role in life, never being himself or knowing himself. Symbols that frame the film are the wire fence and the "No Trespassing" signs at both beginning and end. These symbols suggest that even if we understand a little about Kane, or anyone, there are boundaries we cannot pass, depths we can never reach.

<u>There are also amusing symbols which suggest not only the diminution of Kane, but also of the other characters.</u> An example is Bernstein's high-backed [8] chair, which makes him look like a small child. Similarly, the gigantic fireplace at Xanadu makes both Kane and Susan seem like pigmies—a symbol that

great wealth dwarfs and dehumanizes people. Especially comic is Kane's picnic at Xanadu. In going into the country, Kane and his friends do not walk, but ride in a long line of cars—more like a funeral procession than a picnic—and they stay overnight in a massive tent. Quite funny is the increasing distance between Kane and Emily, his first wife, in the rapid-fire shots that portray their developing [8] separation. Even more comic is the vast distance at Xanadu between Kane and Susan when they discuss their life together. They are so far apart that they must shout to be heard. Amusing as these symbols of diminution and alienation are, however, they are also pathetic, because at first Kane finds closeness with both his wives.

In all respects, <u>Citizen Kane</u> is a masterly film. This is not to say that the characters are likable, or that the amusing parts make it a comedy. Instead, the film pursues truth, suggesting that greatness and wealth cannot give happiness. <u>It is relentless in whittling away at its major figure.</u> Kane is likable at times, and he is enormously generous (as shown when he sends Jedediah $25,000 in [9] severance pay). But these high moments show the contrasting depths to which Kane falls, with the general point being that people who are powerful and great may deteriorate even at their height. The goal of the newsreel director at the beginning is to get at the "real story" behind the public man. There is more to any person than a two-hour film can reveal, but within its limits, <u>Citizen Kane</u> gets at the real story, and the real story is both sad and disturbing.

COMMENTARY ON THE THEME

The major point is that the film diminishes the major figure, Kane. In this respect the theme illustrates the analysis of character (Chapter 4, pp. 64–74), and it therefore emphasizes how film may be considered as a form of literature. Also shown in the theme are other methods of literary analysis: structure (pp. 57–63) and symbolism (pp. 129–40). Of these topics, only the use of symbols, because they are visually presented in the film, is unique to the medium of film as opposed to the medium of words.

Any one of the topics might be developed as a separate essay. There is more than enough about the character of Susan, for example, to sustain a complete theme, and the film's structure could be extensively explored. *Citizen Kane* itself as a repository of film techniques is rich enough for an exhaustive, book-length account.

(For paragraph 1, see below.) Paragraph 2 begins the body and carries out a brief analysis of the major character. Paragraphs 3–5 discuss various aspects of the film's structure (the second topic announced in the thesis sentence) as they bear on Kane. In paragraph 3 the unifying importance of the sled and the reporter, Thompson, is explained. Paragraph 4 focuses on the film's use of flashback as a structural technique, while paragraph 5 discusses three of the flashback characters as they either intentionally or unintentionally reveal Kane's flaws.

In paragraphs 6–8 the topic is film technique, the third and last topic of the thesis sentence. Paragraph 6 focuses on light, camera angles, and distortion; paragraph 7 treats visual symbols; paragraph 8 continues the topic of symbols but extends it to amusing ones.

The final paragraph, 9, restates the central idea and also relates the theme of deterioration to the larger issue of how great wealth and power affect character. Thus, as a conclusion, this paragraph not only presents a summary but also gives a tribute to the film's general implications.

A Close Look at Paragraph 1

Like all first paragraphs, this one fulfills the goal of getting the theme under way. To this end, it includes a central idea that is not unlike central ideas of most themes, and its principal topics—characterization, structure, and technique—are not unexpected. Because the theme is about a film, however, the unique aspect of the paragraph is the opening brief description and the credits to the script writers, principal photographer, composer, and director. Unlike works written by a single author, film is a collaborative medium, and therefore it is appropriate to recognize the separate creative contributions of the principal persons. If you look at the scrolling credits at the end of most films, you will note that huge numbers of people have been involved, but for your theme, recognition of the major individuals is sufficient.

chapter 18

Writing the Research Theme:
Extra Resources for Understanding

Research, as distinguished from pure criticism, refers to using both primary and secondary sources for assistance in treating a literary subject. That is, in merely *discussing* a work you consult only the work itself (the primary source), whereas in doing *research*, you consult not only the work but many other works that were written about it or that may shed light on it (secondary sources). Typical research tasks are to find out more about the historical period in which a story was written or about prevailing opinions of the times or about what modern (or earlier) critics have said. It is obvious that a certain amount of research is always necessary in any critical job, or in any theme. Looking up words in a dictionary, for example, is only minimal research; more vigorous research, and the type we are considering here, involves the use of introductions, critical articles, encyclopedias, biographies, critical studies, histories, and the like.

It is necessary to put research in perspective. In general, students and scholars do research to uncover some of the accumulated "lore" of our civilization. This lore—the knowledge that currently exists—may be compared to a large cone that is constantly being filled. At the beginnings of human existence there was little knowledge, and the cone was at its narrowest point. As civilization progressed, people learned more and more, and the cone began to fill. Each time a new piece of information or a new conclusion was recorded, a little more knowledge or lore was in effect poured into the cone, which became slightly fuller. Though at present our cone of knowledge is quite full, it seems capable of infinite growth. Knowledge keeps piling up and new disciplines keep developing. It becomes more and more difficult for one person to accumulate more than a small portion of the entirety. Indeed, historians generally agree that the last person to know virtually everything about every existing discipline was Aristotle—2,400 years ago.

If you grant that you cannot learn everything, you can make a positive start by recognizing that research can provide two things: (1) a systematic understanding of a portion of the knowledge filling the cone, and (2) an understanding of, and ability to handle, the methods by which you might someday be able to make your own contributions.

Thus far we have been speaking broadly about the relevance of research to any discipline. The chemist, the anthropologist, the ecologist, the marine biologist—all employ research. Our problem here, however, is literary research, the systematic study of library sources in order to illuminate a topic connected with a work of fiction.

SELECTING A TOPIC

Frequently your instructor will ask for a research essay on a specific topic. However, if you have only a general research assignment, your first problem is to make your own selection. It may be helpful to have a general notion of the kind of research essay you would find most congenial. Here are some possibilities.

1. A PARTICULAR WORK. You might treat character (for example, "The Character of Smirnov in *The Bear*," or "The Question of Whether Young Goodman Brown is a Hero or a Dupe"), or tone, point of view, setting, structure, and the like. A research paper on a single work is similar to a theme on the same work, except that the research paper takes into account more views and facts than those you are likely to have without the research. See the sample research theme, on Katherine Mansfield's "Miss Brill," to see how materials may be handled for such an assignment (pp. 271–79).

2. A PARTICULAR AUTHOR. This theme is about an idea or some facet of style, imagery, setting, or tone of the author, tracing the origins and development of the topic through a number of different stories, poems, or plays. An example might be "The Idea of Sin and Guilt as Developed by Hawthorne." This paper is suitable for a number of shorter works, though it is also applicable for a single major work, such as a longer story, novel, or play.

3. A PAPER BASED ON COMPARISON AND CONTRAST. There are two types:

a. *A theme about an idea or artistic quality common to two or more authors.* Your intention might be to show points of similarity or contrast, or else to show that one author's work may be read as a criticism of another's. Typical subjects are "The Use of the Third-Person Limited Point of View by Hawthorne and Mansfield," or "The Theme of Love and Sexuality in Shakespeare, Chekhov, and Donne."

b. *Contrasting or opposing critical views of a particular work of body of works.* Sometimes much is to be gained from an examination of differing critical opinions on topics like "The Meaning of Shirley Jackson's 'The Lottery,' " "The Interpretations of Hawthorne's 'Young Goodman Brown,' " or "The Question of Chekhov's Attitude Toward Women as Seen in *The Bear.*" Such a study would attempt to determine the critical opinion and taste to which a work does or does not appeal, and it might also aim at conclusions about whether the work was or is in the advance or rear guard of its time.

4. A PAPER SHOWING THE INFLUENCE OF AN IDEA, AUTHOR, PHILOSOPHY, POLITICAL SITUATION, OR ARTISTIC MOVEMENT ON SPECIFIC WORKS OF AN AUTHOR OR AUTHORS.   A paper on influences can be fairly direct, such as "Details of Black American Life as Reflected in Hughes's 'Theme for English B,' " or else more abstract and critical, such as "The Influence of Racial Oppression and the Goal of Racial Equality on the Speaker of 'Theme for English B.' "

5. A PAPER ON THE ORIGINS OF A PARTICULAR WORK OR TYPE OF WORK.   One avenue of research for such a theme might be to examine an author's biography to discover the germination and development of a work—for example, " 'Kubla Khan' as an Outgrowth of Coleridge's Reading." Another way of discovering origins might be to relate a work to a particular type or tradition: " 'Theme for English B' and the Harlem Renaissance," or " 'Patterns' and Its Relationship to the Anti-War Literature of World War I."

If you consider these types of topics, an idea of what to write may come to you. Perhaps you have particularly liked one author, or several authors. If so, you might start to think along the lines of types 1, 2 and 3. If you are interested in influences or in origins, then types 4 or 5 may suit you better.

If you still cannot decide on a topic after rereading the works you have liked, then you should carry your search for a topic into your school library. Look up your author or authors in the card or computer catalogue. Your first goal should be to find a relatively recent book-length critical study published by a university press. Use your judgment: Look for a title indicating that the book is a general one dealing with the author's major works rather than just one work. Study those chapters relevant to the work or works you have chosen. Most writers of critical studies describe their purpose and plan in their introduction or first chapter, so begin with the first part of the book. If there is no separate chapter on the primary text, use the index and go to the relevant pages. Reading in this way should soon suggest a topic for further study. Once you have made your decision, you are ready to develop a working bibliography.

SETTING UP A BIBLIOGRAPHY

The best way to begin to develop a working bibliography of books and articles is to refer to major critical studies of the writer or writers. Again, go to the catalogue and pick out books that have been published by university presses. These books usually contain selective bibliographies. Be particularly careful to read the chapters on your primary work or works, and look for the footnotes or endnotes, for you can save time if you record the names of books and articles listed in these notes. Then look at the bibliographies at the ends of the books and select likely looking titles. Now look at the dates of publication of the critical books. Let us suppose that you have been looking at three, published in 1963, 1975, and 1987. The chances are that the bibliography in a book published in 1987 will be complete up through about 1985, for the writer will usually have completed the manuscript two (but sometimes more) years before the book was published. What you should do then is to gather a bibliography of works published since 1985; you may assume that writers of critical works will have done the selecting for you of the most relevant works published before that time.

Bibliographical Guides

Fortunately for students doing literary research, the Modern Language Association of America (MLA) has been providing a virtually complete bibliography of literary studies for years, not just in English and American literatures, but in the literatures of most modern foreign languages. The MLA started achieving completeness in the late 1950s, and by 1969 had reached such an advanced state that it divided the bibliography into four parts. Most university and college libraries have these bibliographies readily available on open shelves or tables. There are, of course, many other bibliographies useful for students doing literary research, such as the *Essay and General Literature Index,* the *International Index* and various specific indexes. There are many more than can be mentioned here meaningfully. For most purposes, however, the *MLA International Bibliography* is more than adequate. Remember that as you progress, the notes and bibliographies in the works you consult will also constitute an unfolding bibliography. For the sample research essay in this chapter, for example, a number of entries were discovered not from the bibliographies, but from the reference lists in critical works.

The *MLA International Bibliography* is conveniently organized by period and author. If your author is Katherine Mansfield, for example, look her up under "English Literature X. Twentieth Century," the relevant listing for all twentieth-century English writers. If your author is Hawthorne, refer to "American Literature III. Nineteenth Century, 1800–1870." You will find most books and articles listed under the author's last name. For special help for students and researchers, the MLA has recently developed an exhaustive topics list that is keyed to the bibliographical entries. Using these topics, you may locate important works that you might miss with only the authors list. In the MLA bibliographies, journal references are abbreviated, but a lengthy list explaining abbreviations appears at the beginning of the volume. You should begin with the most recent MLA bibliography and then go backward to your stopping point. Be sure to get the complete information, especially volume numbers and years of publication, for each article and book. You are now ready to find your sources and to take notes.

TAKING NOTES AND PARAPHRASING MATERIAL

There are many ways of taking notes, but the consensus is that the best method is to use notecards. If you have never used cards before, you might profit from consulting any one of a number of handbooks and special workbooks on research. A lucid and methodical explanation of using cards and taking notes can be found in Lynn Troyka, *Simon & Schuster Handbook for Writers,* 2nd ed. (Englewood Cliffs, N.J.: Prentice Hall, 1990), Chapter 32. The principal virtue of cards, aside from the fact that they stack neatly and do not tear easily, is that they may be classified, numbered, renumbered, shuffled, tried out in one place, rejected, and then used in another (or thrown away), and arranged in order when you start to write.

Taking Notes

WRITE THE SOURCE ON EACH CARD.   As you take notes, write down the source of your information on each card. This may sound like a lot of bother, but it is easier than going back to the library to find the correct source after you have begun your theme. You can save time if you take the complete data on one card—a master card for that source—and then make up an abbreviation for your notes. Here is an example, which also, you will observe, includes the location where the reference was originally found (e.g., card catalogue, bibliography in a book, the *MLA International Bibliography,* etc.).

> *Donovan, Josephine, ed. Feminist*   PN
> *Literary Criticism: Explorations*   98
> *in Theory.*   .W64
> *Lexington: The University Press*   F4
> *of Kentucky, 1975.*
>
> DONOVAN
>
> *Card Catalogue, "Women"*

If you plan to write many notes from this book, then the name "Donovan"
will serve as a shorthand identification on each card. Be sure not to lose
your complete master card, because you will need it in preparing your list
of works cited.

    RECORD THE PAGE NUMBER FOR EACH NOTE.   It would be hard to guess
how much exasperation has been caused by the failure to record page
numbers of notes. Be sure to get the page number down first, *before* you
begin your note. If the detail you are noting goes from one page to the next
in your source, record the exact spot where the page changes, as in this
example:

> *Heilbrun and Stimson,* in DONOVAN, pp. 63–64
>
> ^63 *After the raising of the feminist*
> *consciousness it is necessary to*
> *develop/^64 "the growth of moral*
> *perception" through anger and the*
> *correction of social inequity.*

The reason for such care is that you may wish to use only a part of a note you have taken, and when there are two pages you will need to be accurate in locating what goes where.

RECORD ONLY ONE FACT OR OPINION PER CARD.   Record only one thing on each card—one quotation, one paraphrase, one observation—never two or more. You might be tempted to fill up the entire card, but such a try at economy often gets you in trouble because you might want to use different details recorded on the same card in other spots, which may mean copying the material again or else using a scissors to chop up your original card. If you have only one entry per card, you will avoid such hassles and also retain the freedom you need.

ENTITLE YOUR CARDS.   To help plan and develop the various parts of your essay, write a title for each of your notes as in the examples in this chapter. This practice is a form of outlining. Let us continue discussing the structure of Mansfield's "Miss Brill," the subject of the sample research essay (pp. 271–79). As you do your research, you discover that there is a divergence of critical thought about how the ending of the story should be understood. Here is a note about one of the diverging interpretations:

> Daly 90   last sentence
>
> "Miss Brill's "complete" "identification" with the shabby fur piece at the very end may cause readers to conclude that she is the one in tears but bravely does not recognize this fact, and also to conclude that she may never use the fur in public again because of her "complete" defeat. Everything may be for "perhaps" the very last time." 90

Notice that the title classifies the topic of the note. If you use such classifications, a number of like-titled cards could underlie a section in your theme about how to understand the concluding sentence of "Miss Brill." In addition, once you decide to explore the last sentence, the topic itself will guide you in further study and note taking. (See paragraphs 19–24 of the sample theme, which concern this topic.)

Use quotation marks for all quoted material. Of major importance in taking notes is distinguishing copied material from your own words. Here you must be extremely cautious. Always put quotation marks around *every direct quotation you copy verbatim from a source*. Make the quotation marks immediately, before you forget, so that you will always know that the words of your notes within quotation marks are the words of another writer.

Often, as you take a note, you may use some of your own words and some of the words from your source. In cases like this it is even more important to be cautious. Put quotation marks around *every word* that you take directly from the source, even if you find yourself literally with a note that resembles a picket fence. Later, when you begin writing, your memory of what is yours and not yours will become dim, and if you use another's words in your own paper but do not grant recognition, you lay yourself open to the charge of plagiarism—using someone else's writing without giving them credit, thus representing that writing as your own. Statistics are not available, but it is clear that a great deal of outright plagiarism has been caused not by deliberate deception but rather by sloppy note-taking habits.

Paraphrasing

When you take notes, it is best to *paraphrase* the sources. A paraphrase is a restatement in your own words, and therefore actually a first step in writing. The challenge in paraphrasing is to capture the idea in the source without duplicating the words. The best way to do this is to read and reread the passage you are noting, then turn over the book or journal and write out the idea *in your own words* as accurately as you can. Once you have this note, compare it with the original and make corrections to improve your thought and emphasis. Add a short quotation if you believe it is needed, but be sure to use quotation marks. If your paraphrase is too close to the original, throw out the note and try again. All this is worth the effort, because often you can use *part or all of your note directly at an appropriate place in your theme.*

To see the problems of paraphrase, let us look at a paragraph of criticism and then see how a student doing research might take notes on it. The paragraph is by Richard F. Peterson, from an essay entitled "The Circle of Truth: The Stories of Katherine Mansfield and Mary Lavin," which was published in *Modern Fiction Studies* 24 (1978): 383–394. In the passage to be quoted, Peterson is considering the structures of two Mansfield stories, "Bliss" and "Miss Brill":

Peterson 385

    "Bliss" and "Miss Brill" are flawed stories, but not because the truth they reveal about their protagonists is too brutal or painful for the tastes of the common reader. In each story, the climax of the narrative suggests an arranged reality that leaves a lasting impression, not of life, but of the author's cleverness. This strategy of arrangement for dramatic effect or revelation, unfortunately, is common in Katherine Mansfield's fiction. Too often in her stories a dropped remark at the right or wrong moment, a chance meeting or discovery, an intrusive figure in the shape of a fat man at a ball or in the Café de Madrid, a convenient death of a hired man or a stranger dying about a ship, or a *deus ex machina* in the form of two doves, a dill pickle, or a fly plays too much of a role in/[386] creating a character's dilemma or deciding the outcome of the narrative.

Because taking notes necessarily forces a shortening of this or any criticism, it also requires you to discriminate, judge, interpret, and select; good note taking is no easy task. There are some things that can guide you, however, when you go through the many sources you uncover.

THINK OF THE PURPOSE OF YOUR RESEARCH THEME. You may not know exactly what you are "fishing for" when you start to take notes, for you cannot predict what your theme will contain. Research is a form of discovery. But soon you will notice patterns or large topics that your sources constantly explore. If you can accept one of these as your major topic, or focus of interest, you should use that as your guide in all your note taking.

For example, suppose you start to take notes on criticism about Katherine Mansfield's "Miss Brill," and after a certain amount of reading you decide to focus on the story's structure. This decision guides your further research and note taking. Thus, for example, Richard Peterson (above) criticizes Mansfield's technique of arranging climaxes in her stories. With your topic being structure, it would therefore be appropriate to take a note on Peterson's judgment. The following note is adequate as a brief reminder of the content in the passage:

Peterson 385   structure: negative.

Peterson claims that Mansfield creates climaxes that are too artificial, too unlifelike, giving the impression not of reality but of Mansfield's own "Cleverness." 385

Let us now suppose that you want a fuller note in the expectation that you will need not just Peterson's general idea but also some of his supporting detail. Such a note might look like this:

Peterson 385   *structure: negative*

Peterson thinks that "Bliss" and "Miss Brill" are "flawed" because they have contrived endings that give the impression "not of life but of "Mansfield's "cleverness". She arranges things artificially, according to Peterson, to cause the endings in many other stories. Some of these things are chance remarks, discoveries, or meetings, together with other unexpected or chance incidents and objects. These contrivances make their stories imperfect. 385

When you actually write your theme, you would find any part of this note useful. The words are almost all the note taker's own, and the few quotations are within quotation marks. Note that Peterson, the critic, is properly recognized as the source of the criticism, so that the note could be adapted readily to the theme almost as it is. The key here is that your taking of notes should be guided by your developing plan for your essay.

WRITE YOUR OWN THOUGHTS AS THEY OCCUR TO YOU. As you take your notes, you will develop many thoughts of your own. Do not let these go, to be remembered later (maybe), but write them down immediately. Often you may notice a detail that your source does not mention, or you may get a hint for an idea that the critic does not develop. Often, too, you may get thoughts which can serve as "bridges" between details in your notes or as introductions or concluding observations. Be sure to title your comment and also to mark it as your own thought. Here is such a note, which is on the emphasis on character as opposed to action in "Miss Brill":

My Own   Last Sentence

Mansfield's letter of Jan. 17, 1921,
indicates that action as such
was less significant in her scheme
for the story than the sympathetic
evocation of "Miss Brill's observations,
impressions, and moods. She
wanted to reveal character.

Observe that in paragraph 5 of the sample research theme, the substance of this note, and a good deal of the language, is used to introduce new material once the passage from the Mansfield letter has been quoted.

SORT YOUR CARDS. If you have taken your notes well, your essay will have been taking shape in your mind already. The titles of your cards will suggest areas to be developed as you do your planning and prewriting. Once you have assembled a stack of notecards derived from a reasonable number of sources (your instructor may have assigned a minimum number), you can sort them into groups according to the topics and titles. For the sample essay, after some shuffling and retitling, the following groups of cards were distributed:

1. Writing and publication
2. The title: amusement and seriousness
3. General structure
4. Specific structures: season, time of day, levels of cruelty, Miss Brill's own "hierarchies" of unreality
5. The concluding paragraphs, especially the last sentence
6. Concluding remarks

If you look at the major sections of the sample essay, you will see that the topics are adapted with only slight changes from these groups of cards. In other words, the arrangement of the cards is an effective means of outlining and organizing a research essay.

ARRANGE THE CARDS IN EACH GROUP. There is still much to be done with these individual groups. You cannot use the details as they fall ran-

CHAPTER 18

domly; you need to decide which notes are important. You might also retitle some cards and use them elsewhere. Of those that remain in the group, you will need to lay them out in an order to be used in the theme.

Once you have your cards in order, you can write whatever comments or transitions that are needed to move from detail to detail. Write this material directly on the cards, but be sure to separate it in some way from the original note (by using a different color of ink, or by blocking it off) so that you can distinguish it later when you put your theme together. Here is an example of such a "developed" notecard:

By adding such commentary to your notecards, you are also simplifying the writing of your first draft. In many instances, the note and the comment may be moved directly into the paper with minor adjustments (some of the content of this note appears in paragraph 6 of the sample essay, and almost all the topics introduced here are developed in paragraphs 9–14).

Be Creative and Original in Your Research Theme

This is not to say you can always settle for the direct movement of the cards into your essay. The major trap to avoid in a research paper is that your use of sources can become an end itself and therefore a shortcut for your own thinking and writing. Quite often students introduce details in a research paper the way a master of ceremonies introduces performers in a variety show. This is unfortunate because it is the *student* whose theme will be judged, even though the sources, like the performers, do all the work. Thus it is important to be creative and original and to do your own thinking and writing, even though you are relying heavily on sources. Here are four ways in which research essays may offer chances for originality:

1. *Selection.* In each section of your theme you include many details from many separate sources. Though you rely on the sources for conclusions and supporting details, you can be original to the extent that you are bringing *these* materials together for the first time and that you are choosing to emphasize some details and minimize others. Inevitably, your assemblage of details from your sources will be unique and therefore original.

2. *Development.* A way to be original is closely related to selection on the development of various points. Your arrangement is an obvious area of originality: One detail seems to precede another, and certain conclusions stem out of certain details. As you present details, conclusions, and arguments, you also add your own original stamp by using supporting details that are different from those in your sources. You may also add your own emphasis to particular points—an emphasis that you do not find in your sources.

Naturally, the words that you use will be original with you. Your topic sentences, for example, are all your own. As you introduce details and conclusions, you need to write "bridges" to get from point to point. These may be introductory remarks or transitions. In other words, as you write, you are not just stringing things out but are actively tying thoughts together in a variety of creative ways. Your success in these efforts constitutes your greatest originality.

3. *Explanation of controversial views.* Also closely related to your selection is the fact that in your research you may have found conflicting or differing views. It is original for you, as you describe and distinguish these views, to explain the differences. In other words, as you explain a conflict or difference, you are writing an original analysis. To see how differing views may be handled, see paragraphs 19–21 of the sample theme.

4. *Creation of your own insights and positions.* There are three possibilities here, all related to how well you have learned the primary texts on which your research in secondary sources is based.

   a. *Your own interpretations and ideas.* Remember that an important part of taking notes is to make your own points precisely when they occur to you. Often you can expand these as truly original parts of your theme. Your originality does not need to be extensive; it may consist of no more than a single insight. Here is such a card, which was written during the research on the structure of "Miss Brill":

> *My Own*   *Miss Brill's unreality*
>
> It is ironic that the boy and girl sit down on the bench next to Miss Brill just when she is at the height of her fancies. By allowing her to overhear their insults, they introduce objective reality to her. The result is that she is plunged instantly from the height of rapture to the depth of pain.

The originality here is built around the contrast between Miss Brill's exhilaration and her rapid and cruel deflation. The observation is not unusual or startling, but it nevertheless represents an attempt at original thought. When modified and adapted, the material of the note supplies much of paragraph 18 of the sample theme. You can see that here the development of a "my own" notecard is an important part of the prewriting stage for your research essay.

b. *Gaps in the sources.* As you read your secondary sources you may realize that an obvious conclusion is not being made, or that an important detail is not being stressed. Here is an area that you can develop on your own. You conclusions may involve a particular interpretation or major point of comparison, or they may rest on a particularly important but understressed word or fact. For example, paragraphs 21–24 in the sample theme form an argument based on the observations that critics have overlooked, or neglected to mention, about the conclusion of "Miss Brill." In your research, whenever you find such a critical "vacuum" (assuming that you cannot read all the articles about some of your topics, where your discovery may already have been made a number of times), it is right to move in with whatever is necessary to fill it.

c. *Disputes with the sources.* You may also find that your sources present arguments that you wish to dispute. As you develop your disagreement, you will be arguing originally, for you will be using details in a different way from that of the critic or critics whom you are disputing, and your conclusions are yours alone. This area of originality is similar to the laying out of controversial critical views, except that you furnish one of the opposing views yourself. The approach is limited, however, because it is difficult to find many substantive points of interpretation on which there are not already clearly delineated opposing views. Paragraph 13 of the sample research theme shows how a disagreement can lead to a different if not original interpretation.

WRITING THE RESEARCH THEME

Introduction

In planning, keep in mind that for a research theme, the introduction may be expanded beyond the length of an ordinary essay because of the need to relate the research to your topic. You may bring in relevant historical or biographical information (see, for example, the introduction of the sample theme). You might also summarize critical opinion or describe any relevant problems. The idea is to introduce interesting and significant materials that you have found during your research. Obviously, you should plan to include your usual guides—your central idea and your thesis sentence.

Because of the greater length of most research essays, some instructors require a topic outline, which is in effect a brief table of contents. This pattern is observed in the sample essay. *Inasmuch as the inclusion of any outline is a matter of choice with various instructors, be sure that you understand whether your instructor requires it.*

Body and Conclusion

Your development for both the body and the conclusion will be governed by your choice of subject. Consult the relevant chapters in this book about what to include for whatever approach or approaches you select (setting, point of view, character, tone, or any other).

The research theme may be from five to fifteen or more pages long. Clearly, a theme on only one work may be shorter than one on two or more. If you narrow your topic as suggested in the approaches described above, you can readily keep your paper within the assigned length. The sample research theme, for example, illustrates the first approach by being limited to the structural aspects of one story. Were you to write on characteristic structures in a number of other stories by Mansfield or any other writer (the second approach), you could limit the number of pages by stressing comparative treatments and by avoiding excessive detail about problems pertaining to each and every story. In short, you will decide to include or exclude materials by compromising between the importance of the materials and the limits of your assignment.

Although you limit your topic yourself in consultation with your instructor, you may encounter problems because you will be dealing not with one text alone but with many. Naturally the sources will provide you with details and also with many of your ideas. The problem is to handle the many strands without piling on too many details, and also without being led into digressions. It is important therefore to keep your central idea foremost, for the constant stressing of your central idea will help you both in selecting relevant materials and rejecting irrelevant ones.

Documenting Your Sources

Your reader will automatically assume that everything you write is your own unless you indicate otherwise. As we noted earlier, you leave yourself open to a charge of plagiarism if you give no recognition to details, interpretations, or specific language that you clearly derive from a source. To handle this problem, you must be especially careful in the use of quotation marks and in the granting of recognition. Most commonly, if you are simply presenting details and facts, you can write straightforwardly and let parenthetical references suffice as your authority, as the following sentence from the sample essay will show:

> Because Katherine Mansfield's "Miss Brill"—one of the eighty-eight short stories and fragments she wrote in her brief life (Magalaner 5)—succeeds so well as a portrait of the protagonist's inner life, it has become well known and frequently anthologized (Gargano).

Here the parenthetical references to secondary texts adequately recognize the authority beyond your own (the Gargano reference, incidentally, contains no page number because it is an unpaginated one-page article).

If you are using an interpretation that is unique to a particular writer or writers, however, or if you are relying on a significant quotation from your source, you should grant recognition and use quotation marks as an essential part of your discussion, as in this sentence:

> While Cheryl Hankin suggests that the structuring is perhaps more "instinctive" than deliberate (474), Marvin Magalaner, using "Miss Brill" as an example, speaks of Mansfield's power to weave "a myriad of threads into a rigidly patterned whole" (39).

Here there can be no question about plagiarism, for the names of the authorities are acknowledged in full, the page numbers are specific, and the quotation marks clearly show the important word and phrase that are introduced from the sources. If you grant recognition as recommended here, no confusion can possibly result about the authority underlying your essay. Refer to Appendix B, "A Note on Documentation" for more detailed information on acknowledging your sources.

Sample Research Theme

*The Structure of Mansfield's "Miss Brill"**

I. INTRODUCTION
  A. THE WRITING OF "MISS BRILL"
  B. THE CHOICE OF THE NAME "BRILL"
  C. THE NATURE OF THE STORY'S STRUCTURE
II. SEASON AND TIME AS STRUCTURE
III. INSENSITIVE OR CRUEL ACTIONS AS STRUCTURE
IV. MISS BRILL'S "HIERARCHY OF UNREALITIES" AS STRUCTURE
V. THE STORY'S CONCLUSION
VI. CONCLUSION

1. Introduction

A. The Writing of "Miss Brill"

    Because Katherine Mansfield's "Miss Brill"—one of the eighty-eight short stories and fragments she wrote in her brief life (Magalaner 5)—succeeds so well as a portrait of the protagonist's inner life, it has become well known and frequently anthologized (Gargano). She apparently wrote it on the evening of November 11, 1920, when she was staying at Isola Bella, an island retreat in north Italy where she had gone in her desperate search to overcome tuberculosis. In her own words, she describes the night of composition:

> Last night I walked about and saw the new moon with the old moon in her arms and the lights in the water and the hollow pools filled with stars—and lamented there was no God. But I came in and wrote Miss Brill instead; which is my insect Magnificat now and always (Letters 594).

[1] Her husband, J. Middleton Murry, who had remained in London, published the story in the November 26, 1920 issue of the journal Athenaeum, which he was then editing. In 1922, Mansfield included "Miss Brill" in her collection entitled The Garden Party and Other Stories (Daly 134)

[2]   She was particularly productive at the time of "Miss Brill" despite her illness, for she wrote a number of superb stories then. The others, as reported by her biographer Antony Alpers, were "The Lady's Maid," "The Young Girl," "The Daughters of the Late Colonel," and "The Life of Ma Parker" (304–305).

---

* For the text of this story, see Appendix C, pages 319–22. The type of documentation used here is that recommended in the *MLA Handbook for Writers of Research Papers* 3rd ed. See Appendix B, pages 292–301.

[2]   All these stories share the common bond of "love and pity" rather than the "harshness or satire" that typifies many of her earlier stories (Alpers 305).

B. The Choice of the Name "Brill"

"Miss Brill," however, does contain at least a minor element of humor. James W. Gargano notes that the title character, Miss Brill, is named after a lowly flatfish, the brill. This fish, with notoriously poor vision, is related to the
[3]   turbot and the whiting (it is the whiting that the rude girl compares to Miss Brill's fur piece). The Oxford English Dictionary records that the brill is "inferior in flavour" to the turbot. One may conclude that Mansfield, in choosing the name, wanted to minimize her heroine.

While Mansfield's use of the name suggests a small trick on poor Miss Brill, the story is not amusing, but is rather poignant and powerful. Miss Brill is portrayed as one who has been excluded from "public history" (Gubar 31) because she lives exclusively in the "feminine world" (Maurois 337). Her main concerns, in other words, are not power and greatness but the privacy of personal moments which may be upset by no more than a contemptuous giggle (Gubar 38). The poignancy of the story stems from Miss Brill's eagerness to be "part of a scene that ruthlessly excludes her" and thus which makes her "the
[4]   loneliest of all . . . [characters in] Katherine Mansfield's stories about lonely women" (Fullbrook 103), while the story's power results from the feeling with which Mansfield renders the "inarticulate longings and tumultuous feelings that lie beneath the surface of daily life" (McLaughlin 381). A mark of her skill is the way in which she enters the soul of her heroine and turns it "outward, for her reader to see and understand" (Magill 710), so much so that Claire Tomalin declares that the story is "conceived virtually as [a] dramatic" monologue (213). Mansfield's own description in writing "Miss Brill" bears out these claims, for it shows how deeply she feels the pathetic inner life of her character:

> In Miss Brill I choose not only the length of every sentence, but even the sound of every sentence. I choose the rise and fall of every paragraph to fit her, and to fit her on that day at that very moment. After I'd written it I read it aloud—numbers of times—just as one would play over a musical composition—trying to get it nearer to the expression of Miss Brill—until it fitted her. (Letter to Richard Murry of January 17, 1921, qtd. in Sewell, 5–6).

C. The Nature of the Story's Structure

Mansfield's description strongly indicates that action in the story was less significant in her scheme than the sympathetic evocation of Miss Brill's mood and impressions—in other words, the depths of her character. Such a design might lead readers to conclude that the story is not so much formed as forming, a free rather than planned development. In reference to Mansfield's talent generally, Edward Wagenknecht reflects that the stories, including "Miss Brill,"
[5]   are "hardly even episodes or anecdotes. They offer reflections [instead] of some aspect of experience or express a mood" (163). In many ways, Wagenknecht's observation is true of "Miss Brill." The story seems to be built up from within the character, and it leaves the impression of an individual who experiences a "crisis in miniature," a "deep cut into time" in which life changes and all hopes and expectations are reversed (Hankin 465).
[6]   It therefore follows that Mansfield's achievement in "Miss Brill" is to fash-

credible character in a pathetic and shattering moment of life, <u>and the story</u> <u>embodies an intricate set of structures that simultaneously complement the</u> <u>movement downward.</u>° Mansfield's control over form is strong. While Cheryl Hankin suggests that the structuring is perhaps more "instinctive" than deliberate (474), Marvin Magalaner, using "Miss Brill" as an example, speaks of

[6] Mansfield's power to weave "a myriad of threads into a rigidly patterned whole" (39). <u>These complementary threads, stages, or "levels" of "unequal length"</u> (Harmat uses the terms "niveaux" and "longueur inégale," 49, 51) <u>are the fall</u> <u>season, the time of day, insensitive or cruel actions, Miss Brill's own unreal</u> <u>perceptions, and the final section or denouement.</u>□

II. Season and Time as Structure

<u>A significant aspect of structure is Mansfield's use of the season and the times</u> <u>of day.</u> The autumnal season is integral to the deteriorating circumstances of the heroine. In the very first paragraph, for example, we learn that there is a "faint chill" in the air (is the word "chill" chosen to rhyme with "Brill"?), and this phrase is repeated in paragraph 10. Thus the author establishes autumn and the approaching end of the year as the beginning of the movement toward dashed hopes. This seasonal reference is also carried out when we read that

[7] "yellow leaves" are "down drooping" in the local <u>Jardins Publiques</u> (paragraph 6) and that leaves are drifting "now and again" from almost "nowhere, from the sky" (paragraph 1). It is of course the autumn cold that has caused Miss Brill to take out her bedraggled fur piece at which the young girl later is so amused. Thus the chill, together with the fur, forms a structural setting integrated both with the action and mood of the story. In a real way, the story begins and ends with the fur (Sewell 25), which is almost literally the direct cause of Miss Brill's deep hurt at the end.

 <u>Like this seasonal structuring, the times of day parallel the darkening</u> <u>existence of Miss Brill.</u> At the beginning, the day is "brilliantly fine—the blue sky powdered with gold," and the light is "like white wine." This metaphorical language suggests the brightness and crispness of full sunlight. In paragraph 6,

[8] where we also learn of the yellow leaves, "the blue sky with gold-veined clouds" indicates that time has been passing as clouds drift in during late afternoon. By the end of the story, Miss Brill has returned to her "little dark room" (paragraph 18). In other words, the time moves from day to evening, from light to darkness, as an accompaniment to the psychological pain of Miss Brill.

III. Insensitive or Cruel Actions as Structure

 <u>What seems to be Mansfield's most significant structural device, which is</u> <u>nevertheless not emphasized by critics, is the introduction of insensitive or cruel</u> <u>actions.</u> It is as though the hurt experienced by Miss Brill on the bright Sunday afternoon in the Public Gardens is also being experienced by many others.

[9] Because she is the spectator who is closely related to Mansfield's narrative voice, Miss Brill is the filter through whom these negative examples reach the reader. Considering the patterns that emerge, one may conclude that Mansfield intends the beauty of the day and the joyousness of the band as an ironic contrast to the pettiness and insensitivity of people in the park.

 The first characters are the silent couple on Miss Brill's bench (paragraph
[10] 3), and the incompatible couple of the week before (paragraph 4). Because

---

° Central idea
□ Thesis sentence

[10] these seem no more than ordinary, they are not at first perceived as a part of the story's pattern of cruelty and rejection. But the incompatibility suggested by their silence and one-way complaining establishes a structural parallel with the young and insensitive couple who insult Miss Brill. Thus the first two couples prepare the way for the third, and all exhibit behavior of increasing insensitivity.

[11] Almost unnoticed as a second level of negative life is the vast group of "odd, silent, nearly all old" people filling "the benches and green chairs" (paragraph 5). These people are nevertheless significant structurally because the "dark little rooms—or even cupboards" that Miss Brill associates with them describe her circumstances at the story's end (paragraph 18). The reader may conclude from Miss Brill's silent, eavesdropping behavior that she herself is one of these nameless and faceless ones.

[12] Once Mansfield has set these levels for her heroine, she introduces examples of more active rejection and cruelty. The beautiful woman of paragraph 8, who throws down the bunch of violets, is the first of these. The causes of her scorn are not made clear, and Miss Brill does not know what to make of the incident, but the woman's actions indicate that she has been involved in a relationship that has ended bitterly.

[13] The major figure involved in rejection, who is important enough to be considered a structural double of Miss Brill, is the woman wearing the ermine toque (paragraph 8). She tries to please the "gentleman in grey," but this man insults her by blowing smoke in her face. It could be, as Peter Thorpe observes, that the woman is "obviously a prostitute" (661). More likely, from the conversation overheard by Miss Brill, is that the "ermine toque" has had a broken relationship with the gentleman. Being familiar with his Sunday habits, she deliberately comes to the park to meet him, as though by accident, to attempt a reconciliation. After her rejection, her hurrying off to meet someone "much nicer" (there is no such person, for Mansfield uses the phrase "as though" to introduce the ermine toque's departure) is her way of masking her hurt. Regardless of the precise situation, however, Mansfield makes plain that the encounter is characterized by vulnerability, unkindness, and pathos.

[14] Once Mansfield has established this major incident, she introduces two additional examples of insensitivity. At the end of paragraph 8, the hobbling old man "with long whiskers" is nearly knocked over by the troupe of four girls—arrogance if not contempt. The final examples involve Miss Brill herself. These are the apparent indifference of her students, together with the old invalid gentleman "who habitually sleeps" when Miss Brill reads to him.

[15] Although "Miss Brill" is a brief story, Mansfield creates a large number of structural parallels to the sudden climax brought about by the insulting young couple. The boy and girl do not appear until the very end, in other words (paragraphs 11–14), but actions like theirs have been anticipated structurally throughout the entire narrative. The story does not take us to the homes of the other victims as we follow Miss Brill, but readers may conclude that the silent couple, the complaining wife and long-suffering husband, the unseen man rejected by the beautiful young woman, the ermine toque, and the funny gentleman, not to mention the many silent and withdrawn people sitting in the park, all return to similar loneliness and personal pain.

IV. Miss Brill's "Hierarchy of Unrealities" as Structure

[16] The intricacy of the structure of "Miss Brill" does not end here. Of great importance is the structural development of the heroine herself. Peter Thorpe notes a "hierarchy of unrealities" which govern the reader's increasing awareness of her plight (661). By this measure, the story's actions progressively bring

[16] out Miss Brill's failures of perception and understanding—failures which in this respect make her like her namesake fish, the brill (Gargano).

These unrealities begin with Miss Brill's fanciful but harmless imaginings about her shabby fur piece. This beginning sets up the pattern of her pathetic inner life. When she imagines that the park band is a "single, responsive, and very sensitive creature" (Thorpe 661), we are to realize that she is simply making a great deal out of nothing more than an ordinary band. Though she cannot interpret the actions of the beautiful young woman with the violets, she does see the encounter between the ermine toque and the gentleman in grey

[17] as an instance of rejection. Her response is certainly correct, but then her belief that the band's drumbeats are sounding out "The Brute! The Brute!" indicates her vivid overdramatization of the incident. The "top of the hierarchy of unrealities" (Thorpe 661) is her fancy that she is an actor with a vital part in a gigantic drama played by all the people in the park. The most poignant aspect of this daydream is her imagining that someone would miss her if she were absent, for this fancy shows how far she is from reality.

With regard to this structure or hierarchy of unrealities, it is ironic that the boy and girl sit down next to her just when she is at the height of her fancy about her own importance in life. By allowing her to overhear their insults, the couple introduces objective reality to her with a vengeance, and she is plunged from

[18] rapture to pain. The following, and final, two paragraphs hence form a rapid dénouement which reflects her loneliness and despair.

V. The Story's Conclusion

Of unique importance in the structure of the story are the final two paragraphs—the conclusion or dénouement—in which Miss Brill returns to her miserable little room. This conclusion may easily be understood as a total, final defeat. For example, Saralyn Daly, referring to Miss Brill as one of Mansfield's "isolatoes"—that is, solitary persons cut off from normal human contacts (88)— fears that the couple's callous insults have caused Miss Brill to face the outside world with her fur piece "perhaps for the very last time" (90). Eudora Welty

[19] points out that Miss Brill is "defenseless and on the losing side" and that her defeat may be for "always" (87). Miss Brill has experienced a pattern described by Zinman as common in Mansfield stories, in which the old are destroyed "by loneliness and sickness, by fear of death, by the thoughtless energy of the younger world around them" (457). With this disaster for the major character, the story may be fitted to the structuring of Mansfield stories observed by André Maurois: "moments of beauty suddenly broken by contact with ugliness, cruelty, or death" (342–343).

Because some critics have stated that Miss Brill's downfall is illogically sudden, they have criticized the conclusion. Peterson, for example, complains that the ending is artificial and contrived because of the improbability that the

[20] young couple would appear at just that moment to make their insults (385). On much the same ground, Berkman declares that the ending is excessive, mechanical, and obvious (162, 175).

Cheryl Hankin, however, suggests another way in which the conclusion may be taken, a way which makes the story seem both ironic and grimly humorous. In describing patterns to be found in Mansfield's stories, Hankin

[21] notes the following situation that may account for the ending of "Miss Brill":

. . . an impending disillusionment or change in expectations may be deflected by the central character's transmutation of the experience into something positive (466).

[21] There is no question that the ending indicates that Miss Brill has been totally shattered. Her deflation is shown by her quietness and dejection on returning to her small "cupboard" room.

Mansfield's last sentence, however, may be interpreted as a way of indicating that Miss Brill is going back to her earlier habit of making reality over to fit her own needs:

> But when she put the lid on she thought she heard something crying. (paragraph 18)

[22] It is hard to read this last sentence without finding irony and pathos. By hearing "something crying," Miss Brill may likely be imagining that the fur piece, and not she, has been hurt. One might remember that the thoughtless young girl has laughed at the fur because it resembles a "fried whiting" (paragraph 14). The irony here is that Miss Brill, like the Boss in another Mansfield story, "The Fly," is forgetting about the pain of remembrance and slipping back into customary defensive behavior.

This pattern of evasion is totally in keeping with Miss Brill's character. Despite her poverty and loneliness, she has been holding a job (as a teacher of English, presumably to French pupils), and has also been regularly performing her voluntary task of reading to the infirm old man. She has clearly not had a life filled with pleasure, but her Sunday afternoons of eavesdropping have enabled her, through "the power of her imagination," to share the lives of many [23] others (Hanson and Gurr 81). Mansfield establishes this vicarious sociability as Miss Brill's major strength, which Hanson and Gurr call "the saving grace of her life" (81). Her method makes her both strange and pathetic, but nevertheless she has been functioning if not excelling. Within such a framework, the deflating insults of paragraphs 13 and 14 may be seen as another incentive for her to adjust by strengthening her fancy, not abandoning it.

This is not to interpret the story's conclusion as an indication that Miss Brill has shaken off the couple's insults. She is first and foremost a "victim" (Zinman 457), if not of others, then of her own reality-modifying imagination. But she is presented as a character who has positive qualities. Indeed, Mansfield herself expressed her own personal liking of Miss Brill (despite the name "brill"). Her husband, J. Middleton Murry, shortly after receiving the story from her for publication, sent her a letter in which he expressed his fondness for the heroine. In a return letter to him of November 21, 1920, Mansfield wrote that [24] she shared this fondness. She went on in the same letter to say:

> One writes (one reason why is) because one does care so passionately that one must show it—one must declare one's love (qtd. in Magalaner 17).

Surely the author could love her creation out of pity alone, but if she had added an element of strength, such as the brave but sad ability to adjust to "impossible and intolerable conditions" in life (Zinman 457), then her love would have an additional cause. Therefore it is plausible that the last sentence of "Miss Brill" shows the resumption of the heroine's way of surviving.

VI. Conclusion

[25] "Miss Brill" is a compact story intricately built up from a number of coexisting structures. It is alive, so much so that it justifies the tribute of Antony Alpers that it is a "minor masterpiece" (305). The structural contrast between

the heroine and the world around her is derived from a deeply felt dichotomy about life attributed to Mansfield herself, a sense that the human soul is beau-
[25] tiful, on the one hand, but that people are often vile, on the other (Moore 245). It is the vileness from which Miss Brill seems to be escaping at the end.

The greater structure of "Miss Brill" is therefore a hard, disillusioned view of life itself, in which the lonely, closed out, and hurt are wounded even more. This pattern of exclusion affects not only the restricted lives of the lonely, but it also reaches directly into their minds and souls. Miss Brill's response is to
[26] retreat further and further into an inner world of unreality, but also to continue life, even at an almost totally subdued level, within these confines. It is Mansfield's "almost uncanny psychological insight" (Hankin 467) into the operation of this characteristic response that gives "Miss Brill" its structure and also accounts for its excellence as a story.

Works Cited

Alpers, Antony. Katherine Mansfield, A Biography. New York: Knopf, 1953.

Berkman, Sylvia. Katherine Mansfield, A Critical Study. New Haven: Yale U. P. (for Wellesley College), 1951.

"Brill." Oxford English Dictionary. 1933 ed.

Daly, Saralyn R. Katherine Mansfield. New York: Twayne, 1965.

Fullbrook, Kate. Katherine Mansfield. Bloomington and Indianapolis: Indiana U.P., 1986.

Gargano, James W. "Mansfield's MISS BRILL." Explicator 19, No. 2 (Nov., 1960): item 10 (one page, unpaginated).

Gubar, Susan. "The Birth of the Artist as Heroine: (Re)production, the Kunstlerroman Tradition, and the Fiction of Katherine Mansfield," The Representation of Women in Fiction. Eds. Carolyn Heilbrun and Margaret R. Higonnet, Selected Papers from the English Institute, 1981 (Baltimore: Johns Hopkins U.P., 1983) 19–58.

Hankin, Cheryl. "Fantasy and the Sense of an Ending in the Work of Katherine Mansfield." Modern Fiction Studies 24 (1978): 465–74.

Hanson, Clare, and Andrew Gurr. Katherine Mansfield. New York: St. Martin's, 1981.

Harmat, Andrée-Marie. "Essai D'Analyse Structurale D'Une Nouvelle Lyrique Anglaise: 'Miss Brill' de Katherine Mansfield." Les Cahiers de la Nouvelle 1 (1983):49–74.

Heiney, Donald W. Essentials of Contemporary Literature. Great Neck: Barron's, 1954.

Magalaner, Marvin. The Fiction of Katherine Mansfield. Carbondale: Southern Illinois U.P., 1971.

Magill, Frank N., Ed. English Literature: Romanticism to 1945. Pasadena: Salem Softbacks, 1981.

Mansfield, Katherine. Katherine Mansfield's Letters to John Middleton Murry, 1913–1922. Ed. John Middleton Murry. New York: Knopf, 1951. Cited as "Letters."

———. The Short Stories of Katherine Mansfield. New York: Knopf, 1967.

Maurois, André. Points of View from Kipling to Graham Greene. New York: Ungar, 1935, rpt. 1968.

McLaughlin, Ann L. "The Same Job: The Shared Writing Aims of Katherine Mansfield and Virginia Woolf." Modern Fiction Studies 24 (1978): 369–82.

Moore, Virginia. Distinguished Women Writers. Port Washington: Kennikat, 1934, rpt. 1962.

Peterson, Richard F. "The Circle of Truth: The Stories of Katherine Mansfield and Mary Lavin." Modern Fiction Studies 24 (1978): 383–94.

Sewell, Arthur. Katherine Mansfield: A Critical Essay. Auckland: Unicorn, 1936.

Thorpe, Peter. "Teaching "Miss Brill.' " College English 23 (1962): 661–63.

Tomalin, Claire. Katherine Mansfield: A Secret Life. New York: Knopf, 1988.

Wagenknecht, Edward. A Preface to Literature. New York: Holt, 1954.

Welty, Eudora. The Eye of the Story: Selected Essays and Reviews. New York: Random House, 1977. 85–106.

Zinman, Toby Silverman. "The Snail under the Leaf: Katherine Mansfield's Imagery." Modern Fiction Studies 24 (1978): 457–64.

COMMENTARY ON THE THEME

This theme fulfills an assignment of 2,500–3,000 words, with 15–25 sources. The bibliography was developed from a college library card catalogue, together with lists of references in some of the critical books (Magalaner, Daly, Berkman), the *MLA International Bibliography,* and the *Essay and General Literature Index.* The sources were contained in a college library with selective, not exhaustive, holdings, supplemented by the use of a local public library. There is only one rare source, an article (Harmat) which was obtained in Xerox through Interlibrary Loan from one of only two United States libraries holding the journal in which it appears. For most quarterly or semester-long classes, you will likely not have the time to extend your sources by this method, but the article in question refers specifically to "Miss Brill" and it was therefore desirable to examine it.

The sources for the sample theme consist of a mixture of books, articles, and chapters or portions of books. One article (Sewell) is published as a separate short monograph. Also a part of the sources is the story "Miss Brill" itself, from Appendix C (with locations made by paragraph number) together with editions of Mansfield's letters and stories. The sources are used in the theme for facts, interpretations, reinforcement of conclusions, and general guidance and authority. The theme also contains passages taking issue with some specific matters in certain of the sources.

All necessary thematic devices, including overall organization and transitions, are unique to the sample theme. Additional particulars about the handling of sources and developing a research theme are included in the discussion of note taking and related matters in this chapter.

The introduction to the sample theme contains essential details about the writing of the story and the title, and it also contains a pointed summary of critical appraisals of the story itself. The idea explored here is that the story dramatizes the heroine's emotional responses first to exhilarating and then to deflating experiences. The central idea (paragraph 6) is built out of this idea, explaining that the movement of emotions is accompanied by an intricate and complementary set of structures. The thesis sentence at the end of paragraph 6, presents the topics to be developed in the body.

Sections II–V examine various elements of the story for their structural relationship to Miss Brill's emotions. Section II details the structural uses of the settings of autumn and times of day, pointing out how they parallel Miss Brill's experiences. The longest section is part III (paragraphs 9–15), which is based on an idea not found in the sources. The aspect of the central idea stressed here is that the story describes a number of characters experiencing difficulties and cruelties like those of Miss Brill. Paragraph 10 cites the three couples of the story, paragraph 11 the silent old people, and paragraph 12 the woman with violets. (For paragraph 13, see below.) Paragraph 14 contains brief descriptions of additional examples of insensitivity, two of them involving Miss Brill herself. Paragraph 15 both concludes and summarizes the instances of insensitivity and cruelty, emphasizing again the "structural parallels" to the situation of the heroine.

Section IV (paragraphs 16–18) is based on ideas of the story's structure found in one of the sources (Thorpe). It hence is more derivative than the previous section. Section V (paragraphs 19–24) is devoted to the dénouement of the story. Paragraphs 19 and 20 consider critical disparagements and interpretations of the ending. In paragraph 21, however, a hint found in a source (Hankin) is used to interpret the story's final sentence. An argument in support of this reading is developed in paragraphs 22–24, concluding with a reference to the author's own personal approval of the main character.

Section VI, the conclusion of the sample theme (paragraphs 25,26), relates the central idea to further biographical information and also to Mansfield's achievement in the story. Of the three sources used here, two are used earlier in the essay, and one (Moore) is new.

The list of works cited is the basis of all references in the text of the essay, in accord with the *MLA Handbook for Writers of Research Papers*, 3rd ed. By locating the parenthetical references, a reader might readily examine, verify, and further study any of the ideas and details drawn from the sources and developed in the theme.

A Close Look at Paragraph 13

This paragraph demonstrates Mansfield's technique of using characters parallel to Miss Brill as a focal point of insensitive or cruel actions (one
of the theme's major topics as listed in the thesis sentence in paragraph 6).
The topic sentence of paragraph 13 comes at the end, thereby serving not
only as the topic idea but also the climax. The connection of the woman in
the ermine toque to Miss Brill is made in sentences 1 and 4, while the bulk
of the paragraph establishes how the "ermine toque" figures into the story's pattern of insensitivity. The paragraph development also depends on
the positive assertion (about the "ermine toque") which is made in disagreement with one of the sources. In this way, the paragraph illustrates
one of the means by which a research theme may make an original point,
even though sources form the basis for its assertions and development (see
also pp. 266–69)

appendix a

Taking Examinations
on Literature

Taking an examination on literature is not difficult if you prepare correctly. Preparing means (1) studying the material assigned in conjunction with the comments made in class by your instructor and by fellow students in discussion, (2) developing and reinforcing your own thoughts, (3) anticipating the questions by writing your own practice answers to these questions, and (4) understanding the precise function of the test in your education.

You should realize that the test is not designed to plague you or to hold down your grade. The grade you receive is a reflection of your achievement at a given point in the course. If your grades are low, you can improve them by studying coherently and systematically. Those students who can easily do satisfactory work might do superior work if they improve their method of preparation. From whatever level you begin, you can increase your achievement by improving your method of study.

Your instructor has three major concerns in evaluating your tests (assuming literate English): (1) to see the extent of your command over the subject material of the course ("How good is your retention?"), (2) to see how well you are able to think about the material ("How well are you educating yourself?"), and (3) to see how well you can actually respond to a question or address yourself to an issue.

There are many elements that go into writing good answers on tests, but this last point, about responsiveness, is the most important. A major cause of low exam grades is that students really do not *answer* the questions asked. Does that seem surprising? The problem is that some students do no more than retell a story or restate an argument, never confronting the issues in the question. This is the common problem that has been treated throughout this book. Therefore, if you are asked, "Why does . . . ," be sure to emphasize the *why*, and use the *does* only to exemplify the *why*. If the question is about organization, focus on that. If a problem has been raised, deal with the problem. In short, always *respond* directly to the question or instruction. Let us compare two answers to the same question:

Q. How does the setting of Jackson's "The Lottery" figure in the development of the story?

A

The setting of Jackson's "The Lottery" is a major element in the development of the story. The scene is laid in the village square, between the bank and the post office. There are many flowers blooming, and the grass is green. A pile of stones is set up in the square. Into this place, just before ten o'clock in the morning, come the villagers to hold their annual lottery. There are 300 of them—children, men, and housewives. In the center of the square the black lottery box is set up on a three-legged stool. This box has been around for years, and looks broken and shabby. The setting requires that the villagers gather around the box and that the male head representing each village family draw a slip of paper for that family. Once they have all drawn, it is discovered that Bill Hutchinson is the "winner." He is not a lucky winner, however, because his family of five has to draw again individually. Bill's wife Tessie draws the black spot that Bill had drawn for the family. Then all the villagers in the square fall upon her to stone her to death, because that is the fate of the "winner." The setting here is therefore all important in the development of the story.

B

The setting of Jackson's "The Lottery" is a major element in the development of the story. As a setting for all the action, the town square of the unnamed village is large enough to contain all 300 villagers, piles of stones which they can pick up and hurl, and the black box on a three-legged stool. As a setting in time, the entire action takes place within a two-hour period between ten in the morning and noon. As a seasonal setting, the date of June 27, specifically mentioned as the day of the action, suggests an anachronistic and mindless but nevertheless cruel early summer ritual. As a setting in character and society, the homey, simple lifestyle of the people indicates inertia and fallibility, not sophistication and innovativeness. It is *likely* that such people would preserve cruel and meaningless customs without thinking about their horrible effects. In all respects, then, the setting in place, time, season, and culture is all important in the development of the story.

While column A introduces the important elements of the story's setting, it does not stress the importance of these elements in the story itself. It is also cluttered with details that have no bearing on the question. On the other hand, column B, focusing directly on the connection, stresses how four aspects of setting relate to the story. Because of this emphasis, B is shorter than A. That is, with the focus directly on the issue, there is no need for irrelevant narrative details. Thus, A is unresponsive and unnecessarily long, while B is responsive and includes only enough detail to exemplify the major points.

PREPARATION

Your problem is how best to prepare yourself to have a knowledgeable and ready mind at examination time. If you simply cram facts into your head for the examination in hopes that you will be able to adjust to whatever questions are asked, you will likely flounder.

Read and Reread

Above all, keep in mind that your preparation should begin not on the night before the exam, but as soon as the course begins. When each assignment is given, you should complete it by the date due, for you will understand your instructor's lecture and the classroom discussion only if you know the material being discussed (see also the guides for study in Chapter 1, pp. 13–17). Then, about a week before the exam, you should review each assignment, preferably rereading everything completely. With this preparation, your study on the night before the exam will be fruitful, for it might be viewed as a climax of preparation, not the entire preparation itself.

Make Your Own Questions: Go on the Attack

Just to read or reread is too passive to give you the masterly preparation you want for an exam. You should instead go on the attack by trying to anticipate the specific conditions of the test. The best way to reach this goal is to compose and answer your own practice questions. Do not waste your time trying to guess the question you think your instructor might ask. That might happen—and wouldn't you be happy if it did?—but do not turn your study into a game of chance. What is of greatest importance is to arrange the subject matter by asking yourself questions that help you get things straight.

How can you make your own questions? It is not as hard as you might think. Your instructor may have announced certain topics or ideas to be tested on the exam, and you might develop questions from these. Or you might apply general questions to the specifics of your assignments, as in the following examples:

1. *About a character and the interactions of characters* (see also Chapter 4, pp. 64–74): What sort of character is A? How does A grow or change in the work? What does A learn, or not learn, that brings about the conclusion? To what degree is A representative of any particular type? How does B influence A? Does a change in C bring about any corresponding change in A?

2. *About technical and structural questions:* These may be quite broad, covering everything from point of view (Chapter 6) to prosody (Chapter 14). The best guide here is to study those technical aspects that have been discussed in class, for it is unlikely that you will be asked to go beyond the levels reached in classroom discussion.

3. *About events or situations* (see also Chapter 3, pp. 51–63): What relationship does episode A have to situation B? Does C's thinking about situation D have any influence on the outcome of event E?

4. *About a problem* (see also Chapter 12, pp. 154–62): Why is character A or situation X this way and not that way? Is the conclusion justified by the ideas and events leading up to it?

Adapt Your Notes to Make Questions

Perhaps the best way to construct questions is to adapt your classroom notes, for notes are the fullest record you have about your instructor's views of the subject material. As you work with your notes, you should refer to passages from the text that were studied by the class or stressed by your instructor. If there is time, memorize as many important phrases or lines as you can; plan to incorporate these into your answers as evidence to support the points you make. Remember that it is good to work not only with main ideas from your notes, but also with matters such as style, imagery, and organization.

Obviously, you cannot make questions from all your notes, and you will therefore need to select from those that seem most important. As an example, here is a short but significant note from a classroom lecture about John Dryden's poem *Absalom and Achitophel* (1681): "A political poem— unintelligible unless one learns about the politics of the time." It is not difficult to use this note to make two practice questions:

1. Why is *Absalom and Achitophel* unintelligible unless one learns about the politics of the time?

2. What knowledge of the politics of the time is needed to make *Absalom and Achitophel* intelligible?

The first question consists of the adaptation of the word *why* to the phrasing of the note. For the second, the word *what* has been adapted. Either question would force pointed study. The first would require an explanation of how various parts of Dryden's poem become clear only when they are related to aspects of the politics of 1681. The second would emphasize the politics, with less reference to the poem. If you spent fifteen or twenty minutes writing practice answers to each of these questions, you could be confident in taking an examination on the material. It is likely that you could adapt your preparation to any question related to the politics of the poem.

Work with Questions Even When Time Is Short

Whatever your subject, it is important that you spend as much study time as possible making and answering your own questions. You will have limited time and will not be able to write extensive answers indefinitely. Even so, do not give up on the question method. If time is too short for full practice answers, write out the main heads, or topics, of an answer. When the press of time (or the need for sleep) no longer permits you to make even such a brief outline answer, keep thinking of questions, and think about the answers on the way to the exam. Try never to read passively or unresponsively, but always with a creative, question-and-answer goal. Think of studying as a prewriting experience.

The time you spend in this way will be valuable, for as you practice, you will develop control and therefore confidence. If you have ever known anyone who has had difficulty with tests, or who has claimed a phobia about them, you may find that a major cause has been passive rather than active preparation. A passively prepared student finds that test questions compel thought, arrangement, and responsiveness, but the student is not ready for this challenge and therefore writes answers that are both unresponsive and filled with summary. The grade, needless to say, is low, and the student's fear of tests is reinforced. It seems clear that active, creative study is the best way to break such long-standing patterns of fear and uncertainty, because it is the best form of preparation. There is no moral case to make against practice question-and-answer study, either, for everyone has the right and obligation to prepare—and all of this is preparation—in the best way possible.

Study with a Fellow Student

Often the thoughts of another person can help you understand the material to be tested. Try to find a fellow student with whom you can work, for both of you can help each other. In view of the need for steady preparation throughout a course, regular conversations are a good idea. You might also make your joint study systematic by setting aside a specific evening or afternoon for work sessions. Make the effort; working with someone else can be stimulating and rewarding.

TWO BASIC TYPES OF QUESTIONS
ABOUT LITERATURE

There are two types of questions you will find on any examination about literature. Keep them in mind as you prepare. The first type is *factual*, or *mainly objective*, and the second is *general, comprehensive, broad*, or *mainly subjective*. In a literature course very few questions are purely objective, except multiple-choice questions.

Factual Questions

MULTIPLE-CHOICE QUESTIONS.   These are the most factual questions. In a literature course, your instructor will most likely reserve them for short quizzes, usually on days when an assignment is due, to make sure that you are keeping up with the reading. Multiple choice tests your knowledge of facts, and it also tests your ingenuity in perceiving subtleties of phrasing, but on a literature exam this type of question is rare.

IDENTIFICATION QUESTIONS.   These questions are more interesting and challenging. They test not only your factual knowlege but also your ability to relate this knowledge to your understanding. This type of question will frequently be used as a check on the depth and scope of your reading. In fact, an entire exam could be composed of only identification questions, each demanding perhaps five minutes to write. Typical examples of what you might be asked to identify are:

1. *A character.* It is necessary to describe briefly the character's position, main activity, and significance. Let us assume that "Prince Prospero" is the character to be identified. Our answer should mention that he is the prince (position) who invites a thousand followers to his castle to enjoy themselves while keeping out the plague of the red death in Poe's "The Masque of the Red Death" (main activity). He is the major cause of the action, and he embodies the story's theme that pride is vain and that death is inescapable (significance). Under the category of "significance," of course, you might develop as many ideas as you have time for, but the short example here is a general model for most examinations.

2. *Incidents or situations.* These may be illustrated as follows: "A woman mourns the death of her husband." After giving the location of the situation or incident (Mrs. Popov in Chekhov's play *The Bear*), try to demonstrate its significance in the work. (That is, Mrs. Popov is mourning the death of her husband when the play opens, and in the course of the play Chekhov uses her feelings to show amusingly that life with real emotion is stronger than duty to the dead.)

3. *Things, places, and dates.* Your instructor may ask you to identify a cavalry charge (Twain's "Luck"), a village square (Jackson's "The

Lottery"), or the dates of Mansfield's "Miss Brill" (1920) or Amy Low-ell's "Patterns" (1916). For dates, you may be given a leeway of five or ten years if you must guess. What is important about a date is not so much exactness as historical and intellectual perspective. The date of "Patterns," for example, was the third year of Word War I, and the poem consequently reflects a reaction against the protracted and senseless loss of life that war was producing. Thus, to claim "World War I" as the date of the poem would likely be acceptable as an answer, if it happens that you cannot remember the exact date.

4. *Quotations.* You should remember enough of the text to identify a passage taken from it, or at least to make an informed guess. Generally, you should (1) locate the quotation—if you remember it—or else describe the probable location, (2) show the ways in which the quotation is typical of the content and style of the work you have read, and (3) describe the importance of the passage. You can often salvage much from a momentary lapse of memory by writing a reasoned and careful explanation of your guess, even if the guess is wrong.

TECHNICAL AND ANALYTICAL QUESTIONS AND PROBLEMS. On a scale of ascending importance, the third and most difficult type of factual question is on those matters with which this book has been concerned: technique, analysis, and problems. You might be asked to discuss the *setting, images, point of view,* or *principal idea* of a work; you might be asked about a *specific problem;* you might be asked to analyze a poem that may or may not be duplicated for your benefit (if it is not duplicated, woe to students who have not studied their assignments). Questions like these assume that you have technical knowledge, while they also ask you to examine the text within the limitations imposed by the terms.

Obviously, technical questions occur more frequently in advanced courses than in elementary ones, and the questions become more subtle as the courses become more advanced. Instructors of elementary courses may use main-idea or special-problem questions but will probably not use many of the others unless they state their intentions to do so in advance, or unless technical terms have been studied in class.

Questions of this type are fairly long, with perhaps from fifteen to twenty-five minutes allowed for each. If you have two or more of these questions, try to space your time sensibly; do not devote 80 percent of your time to one question and leave only 20 percent for the rest.

Basis of Judging Factual Questions

IDENTIFICATION QUESTIONS. In all factual questions, your instructor is testing (1) your factual command, and (2) your quickness in relating a part of the whole. Thus, suppose you are identifying the incident "A man kills a canary." It is correct to say that Susan Glaspell's *Trifles* is the location of the incident, that the dead farmer John Wright was the killer, and that the canary belonged to his wife. Knowledge of these details clearly establishes that you know the facts. But a strong answer must go further. Even in the brief time you have for short answers, you should always aim to connect the facts to (1) major causation in the work, (2) an important idea or ideas, (3) the development of the work, and (4) for a quotation, the style. Time is short and you must be selective, but if you can make your answer move from facts to significance, you will always fashion superior responses. Along these lines, let us look at an answer identifying the action from *Trifles:*

> The action is from Glaspell's *Trifles.* The man who kills the bird is Mr. Wright, and the owner is Mrs. Wright. The killing is important because it is shown as the final indignity in Mrs. Wright's long-developing rage, which prompts her to strangle Wright in his sleep. It is thus the cause not only of the murder but also of the investigation bringing the officers and their wives on stage. In fact, the wringing of the bird's neck makes the play possible because it is the wives who discover the dead bird, and it is the means by which Glaspell highlights them as the major characters in the play. Because the husband's brutal act shows how bleak the life of Mrs. Wright actually was, it dramatizes the lonely plight of women in a male-dominated way of life like that on the Wright farm. The discovery also raises the issue of legality and morality, because the two wives decide to conceal the evidence, therefore protecting Mrs. Wright from conviction and punishment.

Any of the points in this answer could be developed as a separate theme, but the paragraph is successful as a short answer because it goes beyond fact to deal with significance. Clearly, such answers are possible at the time of an exam only if you have devoted considerable thought to the various exam works beforehand. The more thinking and practicing you do before an exam, the better your answers will be. You may remember this advice as a virtual axiom: *A really superior answer cannot be written if your thinking originates entirely at the time you first see the question.* By studying well, you will be able to reduce surprise on an exam to an absolute minimum.

LONGER FACTUAL QUESTIONS. More extended factual questions also require more thoroughly developed organization. Remember that here your knowledge of essay writing is important, for the quality of your composition will determine a major share of your instructor's evaluation of your answers. It is therefore best to take several minutes to gather your thoughts together before you begin to write, because a ten-minute planned answer is preferable to a twenty-five–minute unplanned answer. You do not need to write every possible fact on each particular question. Of greater significance is the use to which you put the facts you know and the organization of your answer. When the questions are before you, use a sheet of scratch paper to jot down the facts you remember and your ideas about them in relation to the question. Then put them together, phrase a thesis sentence, and use your facts to illustrate or prove your thesis.

It is always necessary to begin your answer pointedly, using key words or phrases from the question or direction if possible, so that your answer will have thematic shape. You should never begin an answer with "Because" and then go on from there without referring again to the question. To be most responsive during the short time available for an exam, you should use the questions as your guide for your answer. Let us suppose that you have the following question on your test: "How does Glaspell use details in *Trifles* to reveal the character of Mrs. Wright?" The most common way to go astray on such a question, and the easiest thing to do also, is to concentrate on Mrs. Wright's character rather than on how Glaspell uses detail to bring out her character. The word *how* makes a vast difference in the nature of the final answer, and hence a good method on the exam is to duplicate key phrases in the question to ensure that you make your major points clear. Here is an opening sentence that uses the key words and phrases (underlined here) from the question to direct thought and provide focus.

> Glaspell <u>uses details</u> of setting, marital relationships, and personal habits <u>to reveal the character of Mrs. Wright,</u> as a person of great but unfulfilled potential whom anger has finally overcome.

Because this sentence repeats the key phrases from the question, and also because it promises to show *how* the details are to be focused on the character, it suggests that the answer to follow will be totally responsive.

General or Comprehensive Questions

General or comprehensive questions are particularly important on final examinations, when your instructor is interested in testing your total comprehension of the course material. Considerable time is usually allowed for answering this type of question, which may be phrased in a number of ways:

1. A direct question asking about philosophy, underlying attitudes, main ideas, characteristics of style, backgrounds, and so on. Here are some possible questions in this category:

   "What use do _____ , _____, and _____ make of the topic of _____ ?"

   "Define and characterize the short story as a genre of literature."

   "Explain the use of dialogue by Hawthorne, Welty, and Maupassant."

"Contrast the technique of point of view as used by
_____ , _____ , and _____ ."

2. A "comment" question, often based on an extensive quotation borrowed from a critic or written by your instructor for the occasion, about
a broad class of writers, or about a literary movement, or the like. Your
instructor may ask you to treat this question broadly (taking in many
writers) or else to apply the quotation to a specific writer.

3. A "suppose" question, such as "What advice might Mrs. Wright of
Trifles give the speakers of Lowell's 'Patterns' and Keats's 'Bright
Star'?" or "What might the speaker of Rossetti's poem 'Echo' say if
she learned that her dead lover was Goodman Brown of Hawthorne's
'Young Goodman Brown'?" Although "suppose" questions might
seem whimsical at first sight, they have a serious design and should
prompt original and radical thinking. The first question, for example,
should cause a test writer to bring out, from Mrs. Wright's perspective,
that the love of both speakers was/is potential, not actual. She would
likely sympathize with the speaker's loss in "Patterns," but might also
say the lost married life might not have been as totally happy as the
speaker assumes. For the speaker of "Bright Star," a male, Mrs.
Wright might say that the steadfast love sought by him should also be
linked to kindness and toleration as well as passion. Although such
questions, and answers, are speculative, the need to respond to them
causes a detailed consideration of the works involved, and in this
respect the "suppose" question is a salutary means of learning. Needless to say, it is difficult to prepare for a "suppose" question, which you
may therefore regard as a test not only of your knowledge, but also of
your inventiveness and ingenuity.

Basis of Judging General Questions

When answering broad, general questions, you are in fact dealing
with an unstructured situation, and you not only must supply an *answer*
but—equally important—must also create a *structure* within which your
answer can have meaning. You might say that you make up your own
specific question out of the original general question. If you were asked to
"Consider the role of women as seen in Lowell, Mansfield, and Glaspell,"
for example, you would do well to structure the question by focusing a
number of clearly defined topics. A possible way to begin answering such
a question might be this:

Lowell, Mansfield, and Glaspell present a view of female resilience by
demonstrating inner control, power of adaptation, and endurance.

With this sort of focus you would be able to proceed point by point,
introducing supporting data as you form your answer.

As a general rule, the best method for answering a comprehensive question is comparison–contrast (see also Chapter 13, pp. 163–79). The reason is that in dealing with, say, a general question on Rossetti, Chekhov, and Keats, it is too easy to write *three* separate essays rather than *one*. Thus, you should try to create a topic like "The treatment of real or idealized love," or "The difficulties in male–female relationships," and then develop your answer point by point rather than writer by writer. By creating your answer in this way, you can bring in references to each or all of the writers as they become relevant to your main idea. If you were to treat each writer separately, your comprehensive answer would lose focus and effectiveness, and it would be needlessly repetitive.

Remember these things, then: In judging your response to a general question, your instructor is interested in seeing: (1) how effectively you perceive and explain the significant issues in the question, (2) how intelligently and clearly you organize your answer, (3) how relevantly and persuasively you use materials from the work as supporting evidence.

Bear in mind that in answering comprehensive questions, though you are ostensibly free, the freedom you have been extended has been that of creating your own structure. The underlying idea of the comprehensive, general question is that you possess special knowledge and insights that cannot be discovered by more factual questions. You must therefore formulate your own responses to the material and introduce evidence that reflects your own particular insights and command of information.

A final word, always: Good luck.

A Note
on Documentation

In any writing not derived purely from your own mind, you must document your facts. In writing about literature, you must base your conclusions on material in particular literary works and must document this material. If you refer to secondary sources, you must be especially careful to document your facts. To document properly, you must use illustrative material in your discussion and mention your sources either in your discussion or in footnotes to it.

INTEGRATION AND MECHANICS
OF QUOTATIONS

DISTINGUISH YOUR THOUGHTS FROM THOSE OF YOUR AUTHOR. Ideally, your themes should reflect your own thought as it is prompted and illustrated by an author's work. Sometimes a problem arises, however, because it is hard for your reader to know when *your* ideas have stopped and your *author's* have begun. You must therefore arrange things to make the distinction clear, but you must also blend your materials so that your reader may follow you easily. You will be moving from paraphrase, to general interpretation, to observation, to independent application of everything you choose to discuss. It is not always easy to keep these various elements integrated. Let us see an example in which the writer moves from reference to an author's ideas—really paraphrase—to an independent application of the idea:

[1] In the "Preface to the Lyrical Ballads," Wordsworth states that the language of poetry should be the same as that of prose. [2] That is, poetic diction should not be artificial or contrived in any sense, but should consist of the words normally used by people in their everyday lives (791–793). [3] If one follows this principle in poetry, then it would be improper to refer to the sun as anything but *the sun*. [4] To call it a *heavenly orb* or the *source of golden gleams* would be inadmissible because these phrases are not used in common speech.

Here the first two sentences paraphrase Wordsworth's ideas about poetic diction, the second going so far as to locate a passage where Wordsworth develops the idea. The third and fourth sentences apply Wordsworth's idea to examples chosen by the writer. Here the blending is provided by the transitional clause, "If one follows this principle," and the reader is thus not confused about who is saying what.

INTEGRATE MATERIAL BY USING QUOTATION MARKS. Sometimes you will use short quotations from your author to illustrate your ideas and interpretations. Here the problem of distinguishing your thoughts from the author's is solved by quotation marks. In this sort of internal quotation you may treat prose and poetry in the same way. If a poetic quotation extends from the end of one line to the beginning of another, however, indicate the line break with a virgule (/) and use a capital letter to begin the next line, as in the following:

Wordsworth states that in his boyhood all of nature seemed like his own personal property. Rocks, mountains, and woods were almost like food to him, and he claimed that "the sounding cataract / Haunted . . . [him] like a passion" (lines 76–80).

BLEND QUOTATIONS INTO YOUR OWN SENTENCES. Making internal quotations still creates the problem of blending materials, however, for quotations should never be brought in unless you prepare your reader for them in some way. Do not, for example, bring in quotations in the following manner:

Alexander Pope's pastoral sky is darkened by thick clouds, bringing a feeling of gloom that is associated with the same feeling that can be sensed at a funeral. "See gloomy clouds obscure the cheerful day."

This abrupt quotation throws the reader off balance. It is better to prepare the reader to move from the discourse to the quotation, as in the following revision:

Alexander Pope's pastoral scene is marked by sorrow and depression, as though the spectator, who is asked to "see gloomy clouds obscure the cheerful day," is present at a funeral.

Here the quotation is made an actual part of the sentence. This sort of blending is satisfactory, provided that the quotation is brief.

INDENT AND BLOCK LONG QUOTATIONS. The standard for how to place quotations should be not to quote within a sentence any passage longer than 20 or 25 words (but consult your instructor, for the exact number of words allowable may vary [*MLA Handbook*, pp. 56–58]). Quotations of greater length demand so much separate attention that they interfere with your own sentence. It is possible but not desirable to have one of your sentences conclude with a quotation, but you should never make an *extensive* quotation in the middle of a sentence. By the time you finish such an unwieldy sentence, your reader will have lost sight of how it began. When your quotation is long, you should make a point of introducing it and setting it off separately as a block.

The physical layout of block quotations should be as follows: Double-space between your own discourse and the quotation. Double-space the quotation (like the rest of your theme) and indent it ten spaces from the left margin to distinguish it from your own writing. You might use fewer spaces for longer lines of poetry, but the standard should always be to create a balanced, neat page. After the quotation double-space again and resume your own discourse. Here is a specimen, from a theme about John Gay's "Trivia," an early eighteenth-century poem:

In keeping with this general examination of the anti-

heroic side of life, Gay takes his description into

the street, where constant disturbance and even ter-

ror were normal conditions after dark. A person try-

ing to sleep was awakened by midnight drunkards, and

the person walking late at night could be attacked by

gangs of thieves and cutthroats who waited in dark

corners. The reality must have been worse than Gay

implies in his description of these sinister inhab-

itants of the darkened streets:

```
Now is the time that rakes their revels keep;

Kindlers of riot, enemies of sleep.

His scattered pence the flying Nicker flings,

And with the copper shower the casement rings.

Who has not heard the Scourer's midnight fame?

Who has not trembled at the Mohock's name? (lines

321-326)


Gay mentions only those who have "trembled" at the

Mohocks, not those who have experienced their bru-

tality.
```

When quoting lines of poetry, always remember to quote them *as lines*. Do not run them together. When you create such block quotations, as in the example above, you do *not* need quotation marks.

USE THREE SPACED PERIODS (AN ELLIPSIS) TO SHOW OMISSIONS. Whether your quotation is long or short, you will often need to change some of the material in it to conform to your own sentence requirements. You might wish to omit something from the quotation that is not essential to your point. Indicate such omissions with three spaced periods (. . .). If your quotation is very brief, however, do not use spaced periods, since they might be more of a hindrance than a help. See, for example, the absurdity of an ellipsis in the following:

Keats asserts that ". . . a thing of beauty . . ." always gives joy.

USE SQUARE BRACKETS FOR YOUR OWN WORDS WITHIN QUOTATIONS. If you add words of your own to integrate the quotation into your own train of discourse or to explain words that may seem obscure, put square brackets around these words, as in the following passage:

In the "Tinturn Abbey Lines," Wordsworth refers to a trance-like state of illumination, in which the "affections gently lead . . . [him] on." He is unquestionably describing a state of extreme relaxation, for he mentions that the "motion of . . . human blood [was] / Almost suspended [his pulse slowed]" and that in these states he became virtually "a living soul" (lines 42–49).

DO NOT CHANGE YOUR SOURCE. Always reproduce your source exactly. Although most anthologies modernize the spelling of older writers, the works of British authors may include words like *tyre* and *labour*. Also, you may encounter "old-spelling" editions in which all words are spelled exactly as they were centuries ago. Your principle should be *to duplicate everything exactly as you find it,* even if this means spelling words like *achieve* as *atchieve* or *joke* as *joak.* A student once took the liberty of amending the word *an* to "and" in the construction "an I were" in an Elizabethan text. The result was inaccurate, because *an* really meant *if* (or *and if*) and not *and* in introductory clauses. Difficulties like this one are rare, but you will avoid them if you reproduce the text as you find it. Should you think that something is either misspelled or confusing as it stands, you may do one of two things:

1. Within brackets, clarify or correct the confusing word or phrase, as in the following:

   In 1714, fencing was considered a "Gentlemany [i.e., gentlemanly] subject."

2. Use the word *sic* [Latin for *thus*, meaning "It is this way in the text"] immediately after the problematic word or obvious mistake:

   He was just "finning [sic] his way back to health" when the next disaster struck.

DO NOT OVERQUOTE. A word of caution: *Do not use too many quotations.* You will be judged on your own thought and on the continuity and development of your own theme. It is tempting to include many quotations on the theory that you need to use examples from the text to illustrate and support your ideas. Naturally, it is important to introduce examples, but please realize that too many quotations can disturb the flow of *your own* thought. If your theme consists of many illustrations linked together by no more than your introductory sentences, how much thinking have you actually shown? Try, therefore, to create your own discussion, using examples to connect your thought appropriately to the text or texts you are analyzing.

DOCUMENTATION: NOTES AND PARENTHETICAL REFERENCES

It is essential to acknowledge—to document—all sources from which you have quoted *or* paraphrased factual and interpretive information. If you do not grant recognition, you run the risk of being challenged for representing as your own the results of others' work; this is *plagiarism*. As the means of documentation, there are many reference systems, some using parenthetical references and others using footnotes or endnotes. Whatever the system, they have in common a carefully prepared bibliography or list of works cited.

The first system, which uses parenthetical references within the theme itself, is described in detail in Joseph Gibaldi and Walter S. Achtert, *MLA Handbook for Writers of Research Papers*, 3rd ed., 1989, which should be in the hands of all students. The second system, which features footnotes or endnotes, is still widely used. Because this system is still widely recommended, it is appropriate to review it here also.

LIST OF WORKS CITED (MLA FORMAT)

The key to any reference system is a carefully prepared list of *Works Cited* at the end of the essay. "Works Cited" means exactly that; the list should contain just those books and articles which you have actually *used* within your theme. If, on the other hand, your instructor has required that you use footnotes or endnotes, you may extend your concluding list to be a complete bibliography of works both cited and also consulted but not actually used. Always, always, check your instructor's preferences.

For the *Works Cited* list, you should include all the following information in each entry:

For a Book

1. The author's name, last name first, period.
2. Title, underlined, period.
3. City of publication (not state), colon; publisher (easily recognized abbreviations may be used; see the *MLA Handbook*, pp. 213–16), comma; date, period.

For an Article

1. The author's name, last name first, period.
2. Title of article in quotation marks, period.
3. Name of journal or periodical, underlined, followed by volume number in Arabic (*not* Roman) numbers with no punctuation, followed by the years of publication within parentheses (including month and day of weekly or daily issues), colon. Inclusive page numbers, period (without any preceding "p." or "pp.").

   The list of works cited should be arranged alphabetically by author, with unsigned articles being listed by title. Bibliographical lists are begun at the left margin, with subsequent lines being indented, so that the key locating work—usually the author's last name—may be easily seen. The many unpredictable and complex combinations, including ways to describe works of art, musical or other performances, and films, are detailed extensively in the *MLA Handbook* (pp. 86–154). Here are two model entries:

BOOK: Alpers, Antony. Katherine Mansfield, A Biog-

           raphy. New York: Knopf, 1953.

ARTICLE: Hankin, Cheryl. "Fantasy and the Sense of

           an Ending in the Work of Katherine Mans-

           field." Modern Fiction Studies   24

           (1978): 465–474.

PARENTHETICAL REFERENCES
TO THE LIST OF WORKS CITED

Within the text of the essay, you may refer parenthetically to the list of works cited. The parenthetical reference system recommended in the *MLA Handbook* (pp. 155–77) is that the author's last name and the relevant page number or numbers be included in the body of the essay. If the author's name is mentioned in the discussion, only the page number or numbers are given in parentheses. Here are two examples:

> Mansfield shapes the story "Miss Brill" as a development from pleasant daydreams to wakefulness, accompanied by the downfall of hope and imagination (Hankin 472).
>
> Cheryl Hankin points out that Mansfield shapes the story "Miss Brill" as a development from daydreams to wakefulness, accompanied by the downfall of hope and imagination (472).

For a full discussion of the types of in-text references and the format to use, see the *MLA Handbook*.

FOOTNOTES AND ENDNOTES

The most formal system of documentation still widely used is that of footnotes (references at the bottom of each page) or endnotes (references listed numerically at the end of the essay). If your instructor wants you to use one of these formats, do the following: The first time you quote or refer to the source, make a note with the details in this order:

For a Book

1. The author's name, first name or initials first, comma.
2. The title: underlined for a book, no punctuation. If you are referring to a story found in a collection, use quotation marks for that, but underline the title of the book. (Use a comma after the title if an editor, translator, or edition follows.)
3. The name of the editor or translator, if relevant. Abbreviate "editor" or "edited by" as *ed.*, "editors" as *eds.* Use *trans.* for "translator" or "translated by."
4. The edition (if indicated), abbreviated thus: *2nd ed., 3rd ed.,* and so on.
5. The publication facts should be given in parentheses, without any preceding or following punctuation, in the following order:
   a. City (but *not* the state) of publication, colon.
   b. Publisher (clear abbreviations are acceptable), comma.
   c. Year of publication.
6. The page number(s), for example, 65, 65f., 6–10. If you are referring to longer works, such as novels or longer stories that may have division or chapter numbers, include these numbers for readers who may be using an edition different from yours.

For an Article

1. The author, first name or initials first, comma.
2. The title of the article, in quotation marks, comma.
3. The name of the journal, underlined, no punctuation.
4. The volume number, in Arabic letters, no punctuation.
5. The year of publication in parentheses, colon.
6. The page number(s); for example, 65, 65f., 6–10.

For later notes to the same work, use the last name of the author as the reference unless you are referring to two or more works by the same author. Thus, if you refer to only one work by, say, Joseph Conrad, the name "Conrad" will be enough for all later references. Should you be referring to other works by Conrad, however, you will also need to make a short reference to the specific works to distinguish them, such as "Conrad, 'Youth,' " and "Conrad, 'The Secret Sharer.' "

Footnotes are placed at the bottom of each page, and endnotes are included in separate page(s) at the end of the theme. The first lines of both footnotes and endnotes should be paragraph-indented, and continuing lines should be flush with the left margin. Both endnote and footnote numbers are positioned slightly above the line (as superior numbers) like this ([12]). Generally, you may single-space footnotes and endnotes, and leave a single space between them, but be sure to ask your instructor about what is acceptable. For more detailed coverage of footnoting practices, see the *MLA Handbook,* pp. 185–200.

Sample Footnotes

In the examples below, book titles and periodicals, which are usually *italicized* in print, are shown underlined, as they would be in your typewritten or carefully handwritten essay.

[1] André Maurois, Points of View from Kipling to Graham Greene (New York: Ungar, 1968) 342.

[2] Susan Gubar, "The Birth of the Artist as Heroine: (Re)production, the Kunstlerroman Tradition, and the Fiction of Katherine Mansfield," in The Representation of Women in Fiction, eds. Carolyn G. Heilbrun and Margaret R. Higonnet, Selected Papers from the English Institute, 1981 (Baltimore: Johns Hopkins UP, 1982), 25.

[3] Ann L. McLaughlin, "The Same Job: The Shared Writing Aims of Katherine Mansfield and Virginia Woolf," Modern Fiction Studies 24 (1978): 375.

[4] Gubar 55.

[5] Maurois 344.

[6] McLaughlin 381.

As a principle, you do not need to repeat in a note any material you have already mentioned in your own discourse. For example, if you recognize the author and title of your source, then the note should merely give no more than the data about publication. Here is an example:

In <u>The Fiction of Katherine Mansfield</u>, Marvin Magalaner points out that Mansfield was as skillful in the development of epiphanies (that is, the use of highly significant though perhaps unobtrusive actions or statements to reveal the depths of a particular character) as Joyce himself, the "inventor" of the technique.[9]

---

[9] (Carbondale: Southern Illinois UP, 1971) 130.

OTHER REFERENCE SYSTEMS

There are many other reference systems and style manuals, which have been adopted by various disciplines (e.g., mathematics, medicine, psychology) to serve their own particular needs. If you receive no instructions from your instructors in other courses, you may adapt the current MLA system described here. If you need to use the documentation methods of other fields, however, use the *MLA Handbook,* pp. 201–2, for guidance about what style manual to select.

FINAL WORDS

As long as all you want from a reference is the page number of a quotation or a paraphrase, the parenthetical system described briefly here—and detailed fully in the *MLA Handbook*—is the most suitable and convenient one you can use. It saves your reader the trouble of searching the bottom of the page or thumbing through pages at the end to find a reference in a long list of notes. However, you may wish to use footnotes or endnotes if you need to add more details or refer your readers to other materials that you are not using.

Whatever method you follow, *there is an unchanging need to grant recognition to sources.* Remember that whenever you begin to write and make references, you might forget a number of specific details about documentation, and you will certainly discover that you have many questions. Be sure then to ask your instructor, who is your final authority.

appendix c

Works Used for Sample Themes and References

STORIES

Nathaniel Hawthorne (1804–1864)

Young Goodman Brown 1835

Young Goodman Brown came forth at sunset, into the street of Salem village,° but put his head back, after crossing the threshold, to exchange a parting kiss with his young wife. And Faith, as the wife was aptly named, thrust her own pretty head into the street, letting the wind play with the pink ribbons of her cap, while she called to Goodman Brown.

"Dearest heart," whispered she, softly and rather sadly, when her lips were close to his ear, "prithee, put off your journey until sunrise, and sleep in your own bed to-night. A lone woman is troubled with such dreams and such thoughts, that she's afeard of herself, sometimes. Pray, tarry with me this night, dear husband, of all nights in the year!"

"My love and my Faith," replied young Goodman Brown, "of all nights in the year, this one night must I tarry away from thee. My journey, as thou callest it, forth and back again, must needs be done 'twixt now and sunrise. What, my sweet, pretty wife, dost thou doubt me already, and we but three months married!"

"Then God bless you!" said Faith with the pink ribbons, "and may you find all well, when you come back."

5   "Amen!" cried Goodman Brown. "Say thy prayers, dear Faith, and go to bed at dusk, and no harm will come to thee."

So they parted; and the young man pursued his way, until, being about to turn the corner by the meeting-house, he looked back and saw the head of Faith still peeping after him, with a melancholy air, in spite of her pink ribbons.

° *Salem village:* in Massachusetts, about 15 miles north of Boston. The time of the story is the late seventeenth century.

"Poor little Faith!" thought he, for his heart smote him. "What a wretch am I, to leave her on such an errand! She talks of dreams, too. Methought, as she spoke, there was trouble in her face, as if a dream had warned her what work is to be done to-night. But no, no! 't would kill her to think it. Well; she's a blessed angel on earth; and after this one night, I'll cling to her skirts and follow her to Heaven."

With this excellent resolve for the future, Goodman Brown felt himself justified in making more haste on his present evil purpose. He had taken a dreary road, darkened by all the gloomiest trees of the forest, which barely stood aside to let the narrow path creep through, and closed immediately behind. It was all as lonely as could be; and there is this peculiarity in such a solitude, that the traveller knows not who may be concealed by the innumerable trunks and the thick boughs overhead; so that, with lonely footsteps, he may yet be passing through an unseen multitude.

"There may be a devilish Indian behind every tree," said Goodman Brown to himself; and he glanced fearfully behind him, as he added, "What if the devil himself should be at my very elbow!"

His head being turned back, he passed a crook of the road, and looking forward again, beheld the figure of a man, in grave and decent attire, seated at the foot of an old tree. He arose at Goodman Brown's approach, and walked onward, side by side with him.

10

"You are late, Goodman Brown," said he. "The clock of the Old South° was striking, as I came through Boston; and that is full fifteen minutes agone."

"Faith kept me back awhile," replied the young man, with a tremor in his voice, caused by the sudden appearance of his companion, though not wholly unexpected.

It was now deep dusk in the forest, and deepest in that part of it where these two were journeying. As nearly as could be discerned, the second traveller was about fifty years old, apparently in the same rank of life as Goodman Brown, and bearing a considerable resemblance to him, though perhaps more in expression than features. Still, they might have been taken for father and son. And yet, though the elder person was as simply clad as the younger, and as simple in manner too, he had an indescribable air of one who knew the world, and would not have felt abashed at the governor's dinner-table, or in King William's° court, were it possible that his affairs should call him thither. But the only thing about him that could be fixed upon as remarkable, was his staff, which bore the likeness of a great black snake, so curiously wrought, that it might almost be seen to twist and wriggle itself like a living serpent. This, of course, must have been an ocular deception, assisted by the uncertain light.

"Come, Goodman Brown!" cried his fellow-traveller, "this is a dull pace for the beginning of a journey. Take my staff, if you are so soon weary."

"Friend," said the other, exchanging his slow pace for a full stop, "having kept covenant by meeting thee here, it is my purpose now to return whence I came. I have scruples, touching the matter thou wot'st° of."

15

Old South: The Old South Church, in Boston, is still there.
King William: William IV was King of England from 1830 to 1837; William III was King from 1688 to 1701. Readers may choose the William that Hawthorne intends.
Thou wot'st: you know

"Sayest thou so?" replied he of the serpent, smiling apart. "Let us walk on, nevertheless, reasoning as we go, and if I convince thee not, thou shalt turn back. We are but a little way in the forest, yet."

"Too far, too far!" exclaimed the goodman, unconsciously resuming his walk. "My father never went into the woods on such an errand, nor his father before him. We have been a race of honest men and good Christians, since the days of the martyrs.° And shall I be the first of the name of Brown that ever took this path and kept—"

"Such company, thou wouldst say," observed the elder person, interrupting his pause. "Well said, Goodman Brown! I have been as well acquainted with your family as with ever a one among the Puritans; and that's no trifle to say. I helped your grandfather, the constable, when he lashed the Quaker woman so smartly through the streets of Salem. And it was I that brought your father a pitch-pine knot, kindled at my own hearth, to set fire to an Indian village, in King Philip's war.° They were my good friends, both; and many a pleasant walk have we had along this path, and returned merrily after midnight. I would fain be friends with you, for their sake."

"If it be as thou sayest," replied Goodman Brown, "I marvel they never spoke of these matters. Or, verily, I marvel not, seeing that the least rumor of the sort would have driven them from New England. We are a people of prayer, and good works to boot, and abide no such wickedness."

20   "Wickedness or not," said the traveller with twisted staff, "I have a very general acquaintance here in New England. The deacons of many a church have drunk the communion wine with me; the selectmen, of divers towns, make me their chairman; and a majority of the Great and General Court are firm supporters of my interest. The governor and I, too—but these are state secrets."

"Can this be so!" cried Goodman Brown, with a stare of amazement at his undisturbed companion. "Howbeit, I have nothing to do with the governor and council; they have their own ways, and are no rule for a simple husbandman like me. But, were I to go on with thee, how should I meet the eye of that good old man, our minister, at Salem village? Oh, his voice would make me tremble, both Sabbath-day and lecture-day!"

Thus far, the elder traveller had listened with due gravity, but now burst into a fit of irrepressible mirth, shaking himself so violently, that his snakelike staff actually seemed to wriggle in sympathy.

"Ha! ha! ha!" shouted he, again and again; then composing himself, "Well, go on, Goodman Brown, go on; but, prithee, don't kill me with laughing!"

"Well, then, to end the matter at once," said Goodman Brown, considerably nettled, "there is my wife, Faith. It would break her dear little heart; and I'd rather break my own!"

25   "Nay, if that be the case," answered the other, "e'en go thy ways, Goodman

---

days of the martyrs: The martyrdoms of Protestants in England during the reign of Queen Mary (1553–1558).
King Philip's War (1675–1676): Infamous for its cruelties, this war resulted in the suppression of Indian tribal life in New England and prepared the way for unlimited settlement of the area by European immigrants. "Philip" was the English name of Chief Metacomet of the Wampanoag Indian Tribe.

Brown. I would not, for twenty old women like the one hobbling before us, that Faith should come to any harm."

As he spoke, he pointed his staff at a female figure on the path, in whom Goodman Brown recognized a very pious and exemplary dame, who had taught him his catechism in youth, and was still his moral and spiritual adviser, jointly with the minister and Deacon Gookin.

"A marvel, truly, that Goody° Cloyse should be so far in the wilderness, at nightfall!" said he. "But, with your leave, friend, I shall take a cut through the woods, until we have left this Christian woman behind. Being a stranger to you, she might ask whom I was consorting with, and whither I was going."

"Be it so," said his fellow-traveller. "Betake you to the woods, and let me keep the path."

Accordingly, the young man turned aside, but took care to watch his companion, who advanced softly along the road, until he had come within a staff's length of the old dame. She, meanwhile, was making the best of her way, with singular speed for so aged a woman, and mumbling some indistinct words, a prayer, doubtless, as she went. The traveller put forth his staff, and touched her withered neck with what seemed the serpent's tail.

"The devil!" screamed the pious old lady. 30

"Then Goody Cloyse knows her old friend?" observed the traveller, confronting her, and leaning on his writhing stick.

"Ah, forsooth, and is it your worship, indeed?" cried the good dame. "Yea, truly is it, and in the very image of my old gossip,° Goodman Brown, the grandfather of the silly fellow that now is. But, would your worship believe it? My broomstick hath strangely disappeared, stolen, as I suspect, by that unhanged witch, Goody Cory,° and that, too, when I was all anointed with the juice of smallage and cinquefoil and wolf's-bane°—"

"Mingled with fine wheat and the fat of a new-born babe," said the shape of old Goodman Brown.

"Ah, your worship knows the recipe," cried the old lady, cackling aloud. "So, as I was saying, being all ready for the meeting, and no horse to ride on, I made up my mind to foot it; for they tell me there is a nice young man to be taken into communion to-night. But now your good worship will lend me your arm, and we shall be there in a twinkling."

"That can hardly be," answered her friend. "I will not spare you my arm, 35 Goody Cloyse, but here is my staff, if you will."

So saying, he threw it down at her feet, where, perhaps, it assumed life, being one of the rods which its owner had formerly lent to the Egyptian Magi.° Of this fact, however, Goodman Brown could not take cognizance. He had cast up his eyes in astonishment, and looking down again, beheld neither Goody Cloyse nor

---

Goody: a shortened form of "goodwife," a respectful name for a married woman of low rank. A "Goody Cloyse" was one of the women sentenced to execution by Hawthorne's great grandfather, Judge John Hathorne.
gossip: from "good sib" or "good relative."
Goody Cory: the name of a woman who was also sent to execution by Judge Hathorne.
smallage and cinquefoil and wolf's bane: plants especially associated with ointments made by witches.
lent to the Egyptian Magi: See Exodus 7:10–12.

the serpentine staff, but his fellow-traveller alone, who waited for him as calmly as if nothing had happened.

"That old woman taught me my catechism!" said the young man; and there was a world of meaning in this simple comment.

They continued to walk onward, while the elder traveller exhorted his companion to make good speed and persevere in the path, discoursing so aptly, that his arguments seemed rather to spring up in the bosom of his auditor, than to be suggested by himself. As they went he plucked a branch of maple, to serve for a walking stick, and began to strip it of the twigs and little boughs, which were wet with evening dew. The moment his fingers touched them, they became strangely withered and dried up, as with a week's sunshine. Thus the pair proceeded, at a good free pace, until suddenly, in a gloomy hollow of the road, Goodman Brown sat himself down on the stump of a tree, and refused to go any farther.

"Friend," said he, stubbornly, "my mind is made up. Not another step will I budge on this errand. What if a wretched old woman do choose to go to the devil, when I thought she was going to Heaven! Is that any reason why I should quit my dear Faith, and go after her?"

40   "You will think better of this by and by," said his acquaintance, composedly. "Sit here and rest yourself a while; and when you feel like moving again, there is my staff to help you along."

Without more words, he threw his companion the maple stick, and was as speedily out of sight as if he had vanished into the deepening gloom. The young man sat a few moments by the roadside, applauding himself greatly, and thinking with how clear a conscience he should meet the minister, in his morning walk, nor shrink from the eye of good old Deacon Gookin. And what calm sleep would be his, that very night, which was to have been spent so wickedly, but purely and sweetly now, in the arms of Faith! Amidst these pleasant and praiseworthy meditations, Goodman Brown heard the tramp of horses along the road, and deemed it advisable to conceal himself within the verge of the forest, conscious of the guilty purpose that had brought him thither, though now so happily turned from it.

On came the hoof-tramps and the voices of the riders, two grave old voices, conversing soberly as they drew near. These mingled sounds appeared to pass along the road, within a few yards of the young man's hiding-place; but owing, doubtless, to the depth of the gloom, at that particular spot, neither the travellers nor their steeds were visible. Though their figures brushed the small boughs by the wayside, it could not be seen that they intercepted, even for a moment, the faint gleam from the strip of bright sky, athwart which they must have passed. Goodman Brown alternately crouched and stood on tiptoe, pulling aside the branches, and thrusting forth his head as far as he durst, without discerning so much as a shadow. It vexed him the more, because he could have sworn, were such a thing possible, that he recognized the voices of the minister and Deacon Gookin, jogging° along quietly, as they were wont to do, when bound to some ordination or ecclesiastical council. While yet within hearing, one of the riders stopped to pluck a switch.

"Of the two, reverend Sir," said the voice like the deacon's, "I had rather miss an ordination dinner than to-night's meeting. They tell me that some of our

jogging: riding a horse at a slow trot.

community are to be here from Falmouth and beyond, and others from Connecticut and Rhode Island; besides several of the Indian powwows,° who, after their fashion, know almost as much deviltry as the best of us. Moreover, there is a goodly young woman to be taken into communion."

"Mighty well, Deacon Gookin!" replied the solemn old tones of the minister. "Spur up, or we shall be late. Nothing can be done, you know, until I get on the ground."

The hoofs clattered again, and the voices, talking so strangely in the empty   45
air, passed on through the forest, where no church had ever been gathered, nor solitary Christian prayed. Whither, then, could these holy men be journeying, so deep into the heathen wilderness? Young Goodman Brown caught hold of a tree, for support, being ready to sink down on the ground, faint and over-burthened with the heavy sickness of his heart. He looked up to the sky, doubting whether there really was a Heaven above him. Yet, there was the blue arch, and the stars brightening in it.

"With Heaven above, and Faith below, I will yet stand firm against the devil!" cried Goodman Brown.

While he still gazed upward, into the deep arch of the firmament, and had lifted his hands to pray, a cloud, though no wind was stirring, hurried across the zenith, and hid the brightening stars. The blue sky was still visible, except directly overhead, where this black mass of cloud was sweeping swiftly northward. Aloft in the air, as if from the depths of the cloud, came a confused and doubtful sound of voices. Once, the listener fancied that he could distinguish the accents of town's-people of his own, men and women, both pious and ungodly, many of whom he had met at the communion-table, and had seen others rioting at the tavern. The next moment, so indistinct were the sounds, he doubted whether he had heard aught but the murmur of the old forest, whispering without a wind. Then came a stronger swell of those familiar tones, heard daily in the sunshine, at Salem village, but never, until now, from a cloud at night. There was one voice, of a young woman, uttering lamentations, yet with an uncertain sorrow, and entreating for some favor, which, perhaps, it would grieve her to obtain. And all the unseen multitude, both saints and sinners, seemed to encourage her onward.

"Faith!" shouted Goodman Brown, in a voice of agony and desperation; and the echoes of the forest mocked him, crying—"Faith! Faith!" as if bewildered wretches were seeking her, all through the wilderness.

The cry of grief, rage, and terror was yet piercing the night, when the unhappy husband held his breath for a response. There was a scream, drowned immediately in a louder murmur of voices fading into far-off laughter, as the dark cloud swept away, leaving the clear and silent sky above Goodman Brown. But something fluttered lightly down through the air, and caught on the branch of a tree. The young man seized it and beheld a pink ribbon.

"My Faith is gone!" cried he, after one stupefied moment. "There is no good   50
on earth, and sin is but a name. Come, devil! for to thee is this world given."

And maddened with despair, so that he laughed loud and long, did Goodman Brown grasp his staff and set forth again, at such a rate, that he seemed to fly

powwow: a Narragansett Indian word describing a ritual ceremony of dancing, incantation, and magic.

along the forest path, rather than to walk or run. The road grew wilder and drearier, and more faintly traced, and vanished at length, leaving him in the heart of the dark wilderness, still rushing onward, with the instinct that guides mortal man to evil. The whole forest was peopled with frightful sounds; the creaking of the trees, the howling of wild beasts, and the yell of Indians; while, sometimes, the wind tolled like a distant church bell, and sometimes gave a broad roar around the traveller, as if all Nature were laughing him to scorn. But he was himself the chief horror of the scene, and shrank not from its other horrors.

"Ha! ha! ha!" roared Goodman Brown, when the wind laughed at him. "Let us hear which will laugh loudest! Think not to frighten me with your deviltry! Come witch, come wizard, come Indian powwow, come devil himself! and here comes Goodman Brown. You may as well fear him as he fear you!"

In truth, all through the haunted forest, there could be nothing more frightful than the figure of Goodman Brown. On he flew, among the black pines, brandishing his staff with frenzied gestures, now giving vent to an inspiration of horrid blasphemy, and now shouting forth such laughter, as set all the echoes of the forest laughing like demons around him. The fiend in his own shape is less hideous, than when he rages in the breast of man. Thus sped the demoniac on his course, until, quivering among the trees, he saw a red light before him, as when the felled trunks and branches of a clearing have been set on fire, and throw up their lurid blaze against the sky, at the hour of midnight. He paused, in a lull of the tempest that had driven him onward, and heard the swell of what seemed a hymn, rolling solemnly from a distance, with the weight of many voices. He knew the tune. It was a familiar one in the choir of the village meeting-house. The verse died heavily away, and was lengthened by a chorus, not of human voices, but of all the sounds of the benighted wilderness, pealing in awful harmony together. Goodman Brown cried out; and his cry was lost to his own ear, by its unison with the cry of the desert.

In the interval of silence, he stole forward, until the light glared full upon his eyes. At one extremity of an open space, hemmed in by the dark wall of the forest, arose a rock, bearing some rude, natural resemblance either to an altar or a pulpit, and surrounded by four blazing pines, their tops aflame, their stems untouched, like candles at an evening meeting. The mass of foliage, that had overgrown the summit of the rock, was all on fire, blazing high into the night, and fitfully illuminating the whole field. Each pendent twig and leafy festoon was in a blaze. As the red light arose and fell, a numerous congregation alternately shone forth, then disappeared in shadow, and again grew, as it were, out of the darkness, peopling the heart of the solitary woods at once.

55   "A grave and dark-clad company!" quoth Goodman Brown.

In truth they were such. Among them, quivering to-and-fro, between gloom and splendor, appeared faces that would be seen, next day, at the council-board of the province, and others which, Sabbath after Sabbath, looked devoutly heavenward, and benignantly over the crowded pews, from the holiest pulpits in the land. Some affirm that the lady of the governor was there. At least, there were high dames well known to her, and wives of honored husbands, and widows a great multitude, and ancient maidens, all of excellent repute, and fair young girls, who trembled lest their mothers should espy them. Either the sudden gleams of light, flashing over the obscure field, bedazzled Goodman Brown, or he recognized a score of the church members of Salem village, famous for their especial sanctity. Good old Deacon Gookin had arrived, and waited at the skirts of that venerable saint, his reverend pastor. But, irreverently consorting with these grave, reputable, and pious people, these elders of the church, these chaste dames and dewy virgins, there were men of dissolute lives and women of spotted fame, wretches given over to all mean and filthy vice, and suspected even of horrid crimes. It was strange to see, that the good shrank not from the wicked, nor were the sinners abashed by the saints. Scattered, also, among their pale-faced enemies, were the Indian priests, or powwows, who had often scared their native forest with more hideous incantations than any known to English witchcraft.

"But, where is Faith?" thought Goodman Brown; and, as hope came into his heart, he trembled.

Another verse of the hymn arose, a slow and mournful strain, such as the pious love, but joined to words which expressed all that our nature can conceive of sin, and darkly hinted at far more. Unfathomable to mere mortals is the lore of fiends. Verse after verse was sung, and still the chorus of the desert swelled between, like the deepest tone of a mighty organ. And, with the final peal of that dreadful anthem, there came a sound, as if the roaring wind, the rushing streams, the howling beasts, and every other voice of the unconverted wilderness were mingling and according with the voice of guilty man, in homage to the prince of all. The four blazing pines threw up a loftier flame, and obscurely discovered shapes and visages of horror on the smoke-wreaths, above the impious assembly. At the same moment, the fire on the rock shot redly forth, and formed a glowing arch above its base, where now appeared a figure. With reverence be it spoken, the apparition bore no slight similitude, both in garb and manner, to some grave divine of the New England churches.

"Bring forth the converts!" cried a voice, that echoed through the field and rolled into the forest.

At the word, Goodman Brown stepped forth from the shadow of the trees, and approached the congregation, with whom he felt a loathful brotherhood, by the sympathy of all that was wicked in his heart. He could have well-nigh sworn, that the shape of his own dead father beckoned him to advance, looking downward from a smoke-wreath, while a woman, with dim features of despair, threw out her hand to warn him back. Was it his mother? But he had no power to retreat one step, nor to resist, even in thought, when the minister and good old Deacon Gookin seized his arms, and led him to the blazing rock. Thither came also the slender form of a veiled female, led between Goody Cloyse, that pious teacher of the catechism, and Martha Carrier, who had received the devil's promise to be queen of hell. A rampant hag was she! And there stood the proselytes, beneath the canopy of fire.

"Welcome, my children," said the dark figure, "to the communion of your race! Ye have found, thus young, your nature and your destiny. My children, look behind you!"

They turned; and flashing forth, as it were, in a sheet of flame, the fiend-worshippers were seen; the smile of welcome gleamed darkly on every visage.

"There," resumed the sable form, "are all whom ye have reverenced from youth. Ye deemed them holier than yourselves, and shrank from your own sin, contrasting it with their lives of righteousness and prayerful aspirations heavenward. Yet, here are they all, in my worshipping assembly! This night it shall be granted you to know their secret deeds; how hoary-bearded elders of the church have whispered wanton words to the young maids of their households; how many a woman, eager for widow's weeds, has given her husband a drink at bedtime, and let him sleep his last sleep in her bosom; how beardless youths have made haste to inherit their father's wealth; and how fair damsels—blush not, sweet ones!—have dug little graves in the garden, and bidden me, the sole guest, to an infant's funeral. By the sympathy of your human hearts for sin, ye shall scent out all the places—whether in church, bed-chamber, street, field, or forest—where crime has been committed, and shall exult to behold the whole earth one stain of guilt, one mighty blood-spot. Far more than this! It shall be yours to penetrate, in every bosom, the deep mystery of sin, the fountain of all wicked arts, and which inexhaustibly supplies more evil impulses than human power—than my power, at its utmost!—can make manifest in deeds. And now, my children, look upon each other."

They did so; and, by the blaze of the hell-kindled torches, the wretched man beheld his Faith, and the wife her husband, trembling before that unhallowed altar.

65   "Lo! there ye stand, my children," said the figure, in a deep and solemn tone, almost sad, with its despairing awfulness, as if his once angelic nature° could yet mourn for our miserable race. "Depending upon one another's hearts, ye had still hoped that virtue were not all a dream! Now are ye undeceived!—Evil is the nature of mankind. Evil must be your only happiness. Welcome, again, my children, to the communion of your race!"

"Welcome!" repeated the fiend-worshippers, in one cry of despair and triumph.

And there they stood, the only pair, as it seemed, who were yet hesitating on the verge of wickedness, in this dark world. A basin was hollowed, naturally, in the rock. Did it contain water, reddened by the lurid light? or was it blood? or, perchance, a liquid flame? Herein did the Shape of Evil dip his hand, and prepare to lay the mark of baptism upon their foreheads, that they might be partakers of the mystery of sin, more conscious of the secret guilt of others, both in deed and thought, than they could now be of their own. The husband cast one look at his pale wife, and Faith at him. What polluted wretches would the next glance show them to each other, shuddering alike at what they disclosed and what they saw!

"Faith! Faith!" cried the husband. "Look up to Heaven, and resist the Wicked One!"

Whether Faith obeyed, he knew not. Hardly had he spoken, when he found himself amid calm night and solitude, listening to a roar of the wind, which died heavily away through the forest. He staggered against the rock, and felt it chill and damp, while a hanging twig, that had been all on fire, besprinkled his cheek with the coldest dew.

70   The next morning, young Goodman Brown came slowly into the street of Salem village staring around him like a bewildered man. The good old minister was taking a walk along the grave-yard, to get an appetite for breakfast and meditate his sermon, and bestowed a blessing, as he passed, on Goodman Brown. He shrank from the venerable saint, as if to avoid an anathema. Old Deacon Gookin was at

---

once angelic nature: Lucifer, or the devil, had led the traditional revolt of the angels, and was thrown into hell as his punishment. See Isaiah 14:12—15.

domestic worship, and the holy words of his prayer were heard through the open window. "What God doth the wizard pray to?" quoth Goodman Brown. Goody Cloyse, that excellent old Christian, stood in the early sunshine, at her own lattice, catechising a little girl, who had brought her a pint of morning's milk. Goodman Brown snatched away the child, as from the grasp of the fiend himself. Turning the corner by the meetinghouse, he spied the head of Faith, with the pink ribbons, gazing anxiously forth, and bursting into such joy at sight of him that she skipt along the street, and almost kissed her husband before the whole village. But Goodman Brown looked sternly and sadly into her face, and passed on without a greeting.

Had Goodman Brown fallen asleep in the forest, and only dreamed a wild dream of a witch-meeting?

Be it so, if you will. But, alas! it was a dream of evil omen for young Goodman Brown. A stern, a sad, a darkly meditative, a distrustful, if not a desperate man did he become, from the night of that fearful dream. On the Sabbath day, when the congregation were singing a holy psalm, he could not listen, because an anthem of sin rushed loudly upon his ear, and drowned all the blessed strain. When the minister spoke from the pulpit, with power and fervid eloquence, and with his hand on the open Bible, of the sacred truths of our religion, and of saint-like lives and triumphant deaths, and of future bliss or misery unutterable, then did Goodman Brown turn pale, dreading lest the roof should thunder down upon the gray blasphemer and his hearers. Often, awaking suddenly at midnight, he shrank from the bosom of Faith, and at morning or eventide, when the family knelt down at prayer, he scowled, and muttered to himself, and gazed sternly at his wife, and turned away. And when he had lived long, and was borne to his grave, a hoary corpse, followed by Faith, an aged woman, and children and grandchildren, a goodly procession, besides neighbors not a few, they carved no hopeful verse upon his tombstone; for his dying hour was gloom.

Edgar Allan Poe (1809–1849)

The Masque of the Red Death 1842

The "Red Death" had long devastated the country. No pestilence had ever been so fatal, or so hideous. Blood was its Avatar° and its seal—the redness and the horror of blood. There were sharp pains, and sudden dizziness, and then profuse bleeding at the pores, with dissolution. The scarlet stains upon the body and especially upon the face of the victim, were the pest ban which shut him out from the aid and from the sympathy of his fellow-men. And the whole seizure, progress, and termination of the disease, were the incidents of half an hour.

Avatar: model, incarnation, manifestation.

But the Prince Prospero° was happy and dauntless and sagacious. When his dominions were half depopulated, he summoned to his presence a thousand hale and light-hearted friends from among the knights and dames of his court, and with these retired to the deep seclusion of one of his castellated abbeys. This was an extensive and magnificent structure, the creation of the prince's own eccentric yet august taste. A strong and lofty wall girdled it in. This wall had gates of iron. The courtiers, having entered, brought furnaces and massy hammers and welded the bolts. They resolved to leave means neither of ingress nor egress to the sudden impulses of despair or of frenzy from within. The abbey was amply provisioned. With such precautions the courtiers might bid defiance to contagion. The external world could take care of itself. In the meantime it was folly to grieve, or to think. The prince had provided all the appliances of pleasure. There were buffoons, there were improvisatori, there were ballet-dancers, there were musicians, there was Beauty, there was wine. All these and security were within. Without° was the "Red Death."

It was toward the close of the fifth or sixth month of his seclusion, and while the pestilence raged most furiously abroad, that the Prince Prospero entertained his thousand friends at a masked ball of the most unusual magnificence.

It was a voluptuous scene, that masquerade. But first let me tell of the rooms in which it was held. There were seven—an imperial suite. In many palaces, however, such suites form a long and straight vista, while the folding doors slide back nearly to the walls on either hand, so that the view of the whole extent is scarcely impeded. Here the case was very different; as might have been been expected from the duke's love of the *bizarre.* The apartments were so irregularly disposed that the vision embraced but little more than one at a time. There was a sharp turn at every twenty or thirty yards, and at each turn a novel effect. To the right and left, in the middle of each wall, a tall and narrow Gothic window looked out upon a closed corridor which pursued the windings of the suite. These windows were of stained glass whose color varied in accordance with the prevailing hue of the decorations of the chamber into which it opened. That at the eastern extremity was hung, for example, in blue—and vividly blue were its windows. The second chamber was purple in its ornaments and tapestries, and here the panes were purple. The third was green throughout, and so were the casements. The fourth was furnished and lighted with orange—the fifth with white—the sixth with violet. The seventh apartment was closely shrouded in black velvet tapestries that hung all over the ceiling and down the walls, falling in heavy folds upon a carpet of the same material and hue. But in this chamber only, the color of the windows failed to correspond with the decorations. The panes here were scarlet—a deep blood color. Now in no one of the seven apartment was there any lamp or candelabrum, amid the profusion of golden ornaments that lay scattered to and fro or depended from the roof. There was no light of any kind emanating from lamp or candle within the suite of chambers. But in the corridors that followed the suite, there stood, opposite to each window, a heavy tripod, bearing a brazier of fire, that projected its rays through the tinted glass and so glaringly illumined the room. And thus were produced a mul-

Prospero: that is, "prosperous." In Shakespeare's play *The Tempest,* the principal character is Prospero.
without: outside, beyond the abbey walls.

titude of gaudy and fantastic appearances. But in the western or black chamber the effect of the fire-light that streamed upon the dark hangings through the blood-tinted panes was ghastly in the extreme, and produced so wild a look upon the countenances of those who entered, that there were few of the company bold enough to set foot within its precincts at all.

It was in this apartment, also, that there stood against the western wall, a 5 gigantic clock of ebony. Its pendulum swung to and fro with a dull, heavy, monotonous clang; and when the minute-hand made the circuit of the face, and the hour was to be stricken, there came from the brazen lungs of the clock a sound which was clear and loud and deep and exceedingly musical, but of so peculiar a note and emphasis that, at each lapse of an hour, the musicians of the orchestra were constrained to pause, momentarily, in their performance, to hearken to the sound; and thus the waltzers perforce ceased their evolutions; and there was a brief disconcert of the whole gay company; and, while the chimes of the clock yet rang, it was observed that the giddiest grew pale, and the more aged and sedate passed their hands over their brows as if in confused revery or meditation. But when the echoes had fully ceased, a light laughter at once pervaded the assembly; the musicians looked at each other and smiled as if at their own nervousness and folly, and made whispering vows, each to the other, that the next chiming of the clock should produce in them no similar emotion; and then, after the lapse of sixty minutes (which embrace three thousand and six hundred seconds of the Time that flies), there came yet another chiming of the clock, and then were the same disconcert and tremulousness and meditation as before.

But, in spite of these things, it was a gay and magnificent revel. The tastes of the duke were peculiar. He had a fine eye for colors and effects. He disregarded the *decora*° of mere fashion. His plans were bold and fiery, and his conceptions glowed with barbaric lustre. There are some who would have thought him mad. His followers felt that he was not. It was necessary to hear and see and touch him to be *sure* that he was not.

He had directed, in great part, the movable embellishments of the seven chambers, upon occasion of this great fête,° and it was his own guiding taste which had given character to the masqueraders. Be sure they were grotesque. There were much glare and glitter and piquancy and phantasm—much of what has been since seen in "Hernani."° There were arabesque figures with unsuited limbs and appointments. There were delirious fancies such as the madman fashions. There were much of the beautiful, much of the wanton, much of the *bizarre*, something of the terrible, and not a little of that which might have excited disgust. To and fro in the seven chambers there stalked, in fact, a multitude of dreams. And these—the dreams—writhed in and about, taking hue from the rooms, and causing the wild music of the orchestra to seem as the echo of their steps. And, anon, there strikes the ebony clock which stands in the hall of the velvet. And then, for a moment, all is still, and all is silent save the voice of the clock. The dreams are stiff-frozen as they stand. But the echoes of the chime die away—they have endured but an instant—and a light, half-subdued laughter floats after them as they depart. And

decora: schemes, patterns.
fête: party, revel.
Hernani: a tragedy (1830) by Victor Hugo (1802–1885), featuring elaborate scenes and costumes.

now again the music swells, and the dreams live, and writhe to and fro more merrily than ever, taking hue from the many-tinted windows through which stream the rays from the tripods. But to the chamber which lies most westwardly of the seven there are now none of the maskers who venture; for the night is waning away; and there flows a ruddier light through the blood-colored panes; and the blackness of the sable drapery appalls; and to him whose foot falls upon the sable carpet, there comes from the near clock of ebony a muffled peal more solemnly emphatic than any which reaches *their* ears who indulge in the more remote gaieties of the other apartments.

But these other apartments were densely crowded, and in them beat feverishly the heart of life. And the revel went whirlingly on, until at length there commenced the sounding of midnight upon the clock. And then the music ceased, as I have told; and the evolutions of the waltzers were quieted; and there was an uneasy cessation of all things as before. But now there were twelve strokes to be sounded by the bell of the clock; and thus it happened, perhaps that more of thought crept, with more of time, into the meditations of the thoughtful among those who revelled. And thus too, it happened, perhaps, that before the last echoes of the last chime had utterly sunk into silence, there were many individuals in the crowd who had found leisure to become aware of the presence of a masked figure which had arrested the attention of no single individual before. And the rumor of this new presence having spread itself whisperingly around, there arose at length from the whole company a buzz, or murmur, expressive of disapprobation and surprise—then, finally, of terror, of horror, and disgust.

In an assembly of phantasms such as I have painted, it may well be supposed that no ordinary appearance could have excited such sensation. In truth the masquerade license of the night was nearly unlimited; but the figure in question had out-Heroded Herod,° and gone beyond the bounds of even the prince's indefinite decorum. There are chords in the hearts of the most reckless which cannot be touched without emotion. Even with the utterly lost, to whom life and death are equally jests, there are matters of which no jest can be made. The whole company, indeed, seemed now deeply to feel that in the costume and bearing of the stranger neither wit nor propriety existed. The figure was tall and gaunt, and shrouded from head to foot in the habiliments of the grave. The mask which concealed the visage was made so nearly to resemble the countenance of a stiffened corpse that the closest scrutiny must have had difficulty in detecting the cheat. And yet all this might have been endured, if not approved, by the mad revellers around. But the mummer had gone so far as to assume the type of the Red Death. His vesture was dabbed in *blood*—and his broad brow, with all the features of the face, was besprinkled with the scarlet horror.

10   When the eyes of Prince Prospero fell upon this spectral image (which, with a slow and solemn movement, as if more fully to sustain its *role*, stalked to and fro among the waltzers) he was seen to be convulsed, in the first movement with a strong shudder either of terror or distaste; but, in the next, his brow reddened with rage.

"Who dares"—he demanded hoarsely of the courtiers who stood near him—

---

out-Heroded Herod: quoted from Shakespeare's *Hamlet,* act 3, scene 2, line 13, in reference to extreme overacting.

"who dares insult us with this blasphemous mockery? Seize him and unmask him—that we may know whom we have to hang, at sunrise, from the battlements!"

It was in the eastern or blue chamber in which stood the Prince Prospero as he uttered these words. They rang throughout the seven rooms loudly and clearly, for the prince was a bold and robust man, and the music had become hushed at the waving of his hand.

It was in the blue room where stood the prince, with a group of pale courtiers by his side. At first, as he spoke, there was a slight rushing movement of this group in the direction of the intruder, who, at the moment was also near at hand, and now, with deliberate and stately step, made closer approach to the speaker. But from a certain nameless awe with which the mad assumptions of the mummer had inspired the whole party, there were found none who put forth hand to seize him; so that, unimpeded, he passed within a yard of the prince's person; and while the vast assembly, as if with one impulse, shrank from the centres of the rooms to the walls, he made his way uninterruptedly, but with the same solemn and measured step which had distinguished him from the first, through the blue chamber to the purple—through the purple to the green—through the green to the orange— through this again to the white—amd even thence to the violet, ere a decided movement had been made to arrest him. It was then, however, that the Prince Prospero, maddening with rage and the shame of his own momentary cowardice, rushed hurriedly through the six chambers, while none followed him on account of a deadly terror that had seized upon all. He bore aloft a drawn dagger, and had approached, in rapid impetuosity, to within three or four feet of the retreating figure, when the latter, having attained the extremity of the velvet apartment, turned suddenly and confronted his pursuer. There was a sharp cry—and the dagger dropped gleaming upon the sable carpet, upon which, instantly afterward, fell prostrate in death the Prince Prospero. Then, summoning the wild courage of despair, a throng of the revellers at once threw themselves into the black apartment, and seizing the mummer, whose tall figure stood erect and motionless within the shadow of the ebony clock, gasped in unutterable horror at finding the grave cerements and corpse-like mask, which they handled with so violent a rudeness, untenanted by any tangible form.

And now was acknowledged the presence of the Red Death. He had come like a thief in the night.° And one by one dropped the revellers in the blood-bedewed halls of their revel, and died each in the despairing posture of his fall. And the life of the ebony clock went out with that of the last of the gay. And the flames of the tripods expired. And Darkness and Decay and the Red Death held illimitable dominion over all.

thief in the night: 2 Peter 3:10.

Mark Twain (1885–1910)

Luck[1]   1891

It was at a banquet in London in honor of one of the two or three conspicuously
illustrious English military names of this generation. For reasons which will presently appear, I will withhold his real name and titles and call him Lieutenant-
General Lord Arthur Scoresby, Y.C., K.C.B., etc., etc. What a fascination there is
in a renowned name! There sat the man, in actual flesh, whom I had heard of so
many thousands of times since that day, thirty years before, when his name shot
suddenly to the zenith from a Crimean battlefield,° to remain forever celebrated. It
was food and drink to me to look, and look, and look at that demi-god; scanning,
searching, noting: the quietness, the reserve, the noble gravity of his countenance;
the simple honesty that expressed itself all over him; the sweet unconsciousness of
his greatness—unconsciousness of the hundreds of admiring eyes fastened upon
him, unconsciousness of the deep, loving, sincere worship welling out of the
breasts of those people and flowing toward him.

The clergyman at my left was an old acquaintance of mine—clergyman now,
but had spent the first half of his life in the camp and field and as an instructor in
the military school at Woolwich. Just at the moment I have been talking about a
veiled and singular light glimmered in his eyes and he leaned down and muttered
confidentially to me—indicating the hero of the banquet with a gesture:

"Privately—he's an absolute fool."

This verdict was a great surprise to me. If its subject had been Napoleon, or
Socrates, or Solomon, my astonishment could not have been greater. Two things I
was well aware of: that the Reverend was a man of strict veracity and that his
judgment of men was good. Therefore I knew, beyond doubt or question, that the
world was mistaken about this hero: he *was* a fool. So I meant to find out, at a
convenient moment, how the Reverend, all solitary and alone, had discovered the
secret.

5   Some days later the opportunity came, and this is what the Reverend told me:

About forty years ago I was an instructor in the military academy at Woolwich. I was present in one of the sections when young Scoresby underwent his
preliminary examination. I was touched to the quick with pity, for the rest of the
class answered up brightly and handsomely, while he—why, dear me, he didn't
know *anything*, so to speak. He was evidently good, and sweet, and lovable, and
guileless; and so it was exceedingly painful to see him stand there, as serene as a
graven image, and deliver himself of answers which were veritably miraculous for
stupidity and ignorance. All the compassion in me was aroused in his behalf. I said

---

[1] This is not a fancy sketch. I got it from a clergyman who was an instructor at Woolwich forty
years ago, and who vouched for its truth. [Twain's note.]
Crimean battlefield: In the Crimean War (1853–1856), England was one of the allies that fought
against Russia.

to myself, when he comes to be examined again he will be flung over, of course; so it will be simply a harmless act of charity to ease his fall as much as I can. I took him aside and found that he knew a little of Caesar's history; and as he didn't know anything else, I went to work and drilled him like a galley-slave on a certain line of stock questions concerning Caesar which I knew would be used. If you'll believe me, he went through with flying colors on examination day! He went through on that purely superficial "cram," and got compliments too, while others, who knew a thousand times more than he, got plucked. By some strangely lucky accident—an accident not likely to happen twice in a century—he was asked no question outside of the narrow limits of his drill.

It was stupefying. Well, all through his course I stood by him, with something of the sentiment which a mother feels for a crippled child; and he always saved himself—just by miracle, apparently.

Now, of course, the thing that would expose him and kill him at last was mathematics. I resolved to make his death as easy as I could; so I drilled him and crammed him, and crammed him and drilled him, just on the line of questions which the examiners would be most likely to use, and then launched him on his fate. Well, sir, try to conceive of the result: to my consternation, he took the first prize! And with it he got a perfect ovation in the way of compliments.

Sleep? There was no more sleep for me for a week. My conscience tortured me day and night. What I had done I had done purely through charity, and only to ease the poor youth's fall. I never had dreamed of any such preposterous results as the thing that had happened. I felt as guilty and miserable as Frankenstein. Here was a wooden-head whom I had put in the way of glittering promotions and prodigious responsibilities, and but one thing could happen: he and his responsibilities would all go to ruin together at the first opportunity.

The Crimean War had just broken out. Of course there had to be a war, I said   10
to myself. We couldn't have peace and give this donkey a chance to die before he is found out. I waited for the earthquake. It came. And it made me reel when it did come. He was actually gazetted to a captaincy in a marching regiment! Better men grow old and gray in the service before they climb to a sublimity like that. And who could ever have foreseen that they would go and put such a load of responsibility on such green and inadequate shoulders? I could just barely have stood it if they had made him a cornet°; but a captain—think of it! I thought my hair would turn white.

Consider what I did—I who so loved repose and inaction. I said to myself, I am responsible to the country for this, and I must go along with him and protect the country against him as far as I can. So I took my poor little capital that I had saved up through years of work and grinding economy, and went with a sigh and bought a cornetcy in his regiment, and away we went to the field.

And there—oh, dear, it was awful. Blunders?—why he never did anything *but* blunder. But, you see, nobody was in the fellow's secret. Everybody had him focused wrong, and necessarily misinterpreted his performance every time. Consequently they took his idiotic blunders for inspirations of genius. They did, honestly! His mildest blunders were enough to make a man in his right mind cry; and they did make me cry—and rage and rave, too, privately. And the thing that kept

---

cornet: the fifth ranking officer in a British cavalry troop.

me always in a sweat of apprehension was the fact that every fresh blunder he made increased the luster of his reputation! I kept saying to myself, he'll get so high that when discovery does finally come it will be like the sun falling out of the sky.

He went right along, up from grade to grade, over the dead bodies of his superiors, until at last, in the hottest moment of the battle of————down went our colonel, and my heart jumped into my mouth, for Scoresby was next in rank! Now for it, said I; we'll all land in Sheol° in ten minutes, sure.

The battle was awfully hot; the allies were steadily giving way all over the field. Our regiment occupied a position that was vital; a blunder now must be destruction. At this crucial moment, what does this immortal fool do but detach the regiment from its place and order a charge over a neighboring hill where there wasn't a suggestion of an enemy! "There you go!" I said to myself; "this *is* the end at last."

15   And away we did go, and were over the shoulder of the hill before the insane movement could be discovered and stopped. And what did we find? An entire and unsuspected Russian army in reserve! And what happened? We were eaten up? That is necessarily what would have happened in ninety-nine cases out of a hundred. But no; those Russians argued that no single regiment would come browsing around there at such a time. It must be the entire English army, and that the sly Russian game was detected and blocked; so they turned tail, and away they went, pell-mell, over the hill and down into the field, in wild confusion, and we after them; they themselves broke the solid Russian center in the field, and tore through, and in no time there was the most tremendous rout you ever saw, and the defeat of the allies was turned into a sweeping and splendid victory! Marshal Canrobert looked on, dizzy with astonishment, admiration, and delight; and sent right off for Scoresby, and hugged him, and decorated him on the field in presence of all the armies!

And what was Scoresby's blunder that time? Merely the mistaking his right hand for his left—that was all. An order had come to him to fall back and support our right; and, instead, he fell *forward* and went over the hill to the left. But the name he won that day as a marvelous military genius filled the world with his glory, and that glory will never fade while history books last.

He is just as good and sweet and lovable and unpretending as a man can be, but he doesn't know enough to come in when it rains. Now that is absolutely true. He is the supremest ass in the universe; and until half an hour ago nobody knew it but himself and me. He has been pursued, day by day and year by year, by a most phenomenal astonishing luckiness. He has been a shining soldier in all our wars for a generation; he has littered his whole military life with blunders, and yet has never committed one that didn't make him a knight or a baronet or a lord or something. Look at his breast; why, he is just clothed in domestic and foreign decorations. Well, sir, every one of them is the record of some shouting stupidity or other; and, taken together, they are proof that the very best thing in all this world that can befall a man is to be born lucky. I say again, as I said at the banquet, Scoresby's an absolute fool.

Sheol: In the Hebrew Scriptures, Sheol is the region of the dead (Psalm 6:5) where worms destroy the body and the dead are alienated from God (Isaiah 14:11–19). Here, *Sheol* loosely means *Hell.*

Katherine Mansfield (1888–1923)

Miss Brill

1920

Although it was so brilliantly fine—the blue sky powdered with gold and great spots of light like white wine splashed over the Jardins Publiques°—Miss Brill was glad that she had decided on her fur. The air was motionless, but when you opened your mouth there was just a faint chill, like a chill from a glass of iced water before you sip, and now and again a leaf came drifting—from nowhere, from the sky. Miss Brill put up her hand and touched her fur. Dear little thing! It was nice to feel it again. She had taken it out of its box that afternoon, shaken out the moth-powder, given it a good brush, and rubbed the life back into the dim little eyes. "What has been happening to me?" said the sad little eyes. Oh, how sweet it was to see them snap at her again from the red eiderdown! . . . But the nose, which was of some black composition, wasn't at all firm. It must have had a knock, somehow. Never mind—a little dab of black sealing-wax when the time came—when it was absolutely necessary. . . . Little rogue! Yes, she really felt like that about it. Little rogue biting its tail just by her left ear. She could have taken it off and laid it on her lap and stroked it. She felt a tingling in her hands and arms, but that came from walking, she supposed. And when she breathed, something light and sad—no, not sad, exactly—something gentle seemed to move in her bosom.

There were a number of people out this afternoon, far more than last Sunday. And the band sounded louder and gayer. That was because the Season had begun. For although the band played all the year round on Sundays, out of season it was never the same. It was like some one playing with only the family to listen; it didn't care how it played if there weren't any strangers present. Wasn't the conductor wearing a new coat, too? She was sure it was new. He scraped with his foot and flapped his arms like a rooster about to crow, and the bandsmen sitting in the green rotunda blew out their cheeks and glared at the music. Now there came a little "flutey" bit—very pretty!—a little chain of bright drops. She was sure it would be repeated. It was; she lifted her head and smiled.

Only two people shared her "special" seat: a fine old man in a velvet coat, his hands clasped over a huge carved walking-stick, and a big old woman, sitting upright, with a roll of knitting on her embroidered apron. They did not speak. This was disappointing, for Miss Brill always looked forward to the conversation. She had become really quite expert, she thought, at listening as though she didn't listen, at sitting in other people's lives just for a minute while they talked round her.

She glanced, sideways, at the old couple. Perhaps they would go soon. Last Sunday, too, hadn't been as interesting as usual. An Englishman and his wife, he

Jardins Publiques: public gardens, or public park. The setting of the story is a seaside town in France.

wearing a dreadful Panama hat and she button boots. And she'd gone on the whole time about how she ought to wear spectacles; she knew she needed them; but that it was no good getting any; they'd be sure to break and they'd never keep on. And he'd been so patient. He'd suggested everything—gold rims, the kind that curved round your ears, little pads inside the bridge. No, nothing would please her. "They'll always be sliding down my nose!" Miss Brill had wanted to shake her.

5   The old people sat on the bench, still as statues. Never mind, there was always the crowd to watch. To and fro, in front of the flower-beds and the band rotunda, the couples and groups paraded, stopped to talk, to greet, to buy a handful of flowers from the old beggar who had his tray fixed to the railings. Little children ran among them, swooping and laughing; little boys with big white silk bows under their chins, little girls, little French dolls, dressed up in velvet and lace. And sometimes a tiny staggerer came suddenly rocking into the open from under the trees, stopped, stared, as suddenly sat down "flop," until its small high-stepping mother, like a young hen, rushed scolding to its rescue. Other people sat on the benches and green chairs, but they were nearly always the same, Sunday after Sunday, and—Miss Brill had often noticed—there was something funny about nearly all of them. They were odd, silent, nearly all old, and from the way they stared they looked as though they'd just come from dark little rooms or even—even cupboards!°

Behind the rotunda the slender trees with yellow leaves down drooping, and through them just a line of sea, and beyond the blue sky with gold-veined clouds.

Tum-tum-tum tiddle-um! tiddle-um! tum tiddley-um tum ta! blew the band.

Two young girls in red came by and two young soldiers in blue met them, and they laughed and paired and went off arm-in-arm. Two peasant women with funny straw hats passed, gravely, leading beautiful smoke-coloured donkeys. A cold, pale nun hurried by. A beautiful woman came along and dropped her bunch of violets, and a little boy ran after to hand them to her, and she took them and threw them away as if they'd been poisoned. Dear me! Miss Brill didn't know whether to admire that or not! And now an ermine toque° and a gentleman in grey met just in front of her. He was tall, stiff, dignified, and she was wearing the ermine toque she'd bought when her hair was yellow. Now everything, her hair, her face, even her eyes, was the same colour as the shabby ermine, and her hand, in its cleaned glove, lifted to dab her lips, was a tiny yellowish paw. Oh, she was so pleased to see him—delighted! She rather thought they were going to meet that afternoon. She described where she'd been—everywhere, here, there, along by the sea. The day was so charming—didn't he agree? And wouldn't he, perhaps? . . . But he shook his head, lighted a cigarette, slowly breathed a great deep puff into her face, and, even while she was still talking and laughing, flicked the match away and walked on. The ermine toque was alone; she smiled more brightly than ever. But even the band seemed to know what she was feeling and played more softly, played tenderly, and the drum beat, "The Brute! The Brute!" over and over. What would she do? What was going to happen now? But as Miss Brill wondered, the ermine toque turned, raised her hand as though she'd seen some one else, much

---

cupboards: rooms designed for china but remodeled for a lodger; the tiniest of rooms.
toque: a hat. The phrase "ermine toque" refers to a woman wearing a hat made of the fur of a weasel.

nicer, just over there, and pattered away. And the band changed again and played more quickly, more gaily than ever, and the old couple on Miss Brill's seat got up and marched away, and such a funny old man with long whiskers hobbled along in time to the music and was nearly knocked over by four girls walking abreast.

Oh, how fascinating it was! How she enjoyed it! How she loved sitting here, watching it all! It was like a play. It was exactly like a play. Who could believe the sky at the back wasn't painted? But it wasn't till a little brown dog trotted on solemn and then slowly trotted off, like a little "theatre" dog, a little dog that had been drugged, that Miss Brill discovered what it was that made it so exciting. They were all on the stage. They weren't only the audience, not only looking on; they were acting. Even she had a part and came every Sunday. No doubt somebody would have noticed if she hadn't been there; she was part of the performance after all. How strange she'd never thought of it like that before! And yet it explained why she made such a point of starting from home at just the same time each week—so as not to be late for the performance—and it also explained why she had quite a queer, shy feeling at telling her English pupils how she spent her Sunday afternoons. No wonder! Miss Brill nearly laughed out loud. She was on the stage. She thought of the old invalid gentleman to whom she read the newspaper four afternoons a week while he slept in the garden. She had got quite used to the frail head on the cotton pillow, the hollowed eyes, the open mouth and the high pinched nose. If he'd been dead she mightn't have noticed for weeks; she wouldn't have minded. But suddenly he knew he was having the paper read to him by an actress! "An actress!" The old head lifted; two points of light quivered in the old eyes. "An actress—are ye?" And Miss Brill smoothed the newspaper as though it were the manuscript of her part and said gently: "Yes, I have been an actress for a long time."

The band had been having a rest. Now they started again. And what they played was warm, sunny, yet there was just a faint chill—a something, what was it?—not sadness—no, not sadness—a something that made you want to sing. The tune lifted, lifted, the light shone; and it seemed to Miss Brill that in another moment all of them, all the whole company, would begin singing. The young ones, the laughing ones who were moving together, they would begin, and the men's voices, very resolute and brave, would join them. And then she too, she too, and the others on the benches—they would come in with a kind of accompaniment—something low, that scarcely rose or fell, something so beautiful—moving. . . . And Miss Brill's eyes filled with tears and she looked smiling at all the other members of the company. Yes, we understand, we understand, she thought—though what they understood she didn't know.   10

Just at that moment a boy and a girl came and sat down where the old couple had been. They were beautifully dressed; they were in love. The hero and heroine, of course, just arrived from his father's yacht. And still soundlessly singing, still with that trembling smile, Miss Brill prepared to listen.

"No, not now," said the girl. "Not here, I can't."

"But why? Because of that stupid old thing at the end there?" asked the boy. "Why does she come here at all—who wants her? Why doesn't she keep her silly old mug at home?"

"It's her fu-fur which is so funny," giggled the girl. "It's exactly like a fried whiting."

15   "Ah, be off with you!" said the boy in an angry whisper. Then: "Tell me, ma petite chérie—"

"No, not here," said the girl. "Not *yet*."

On her way home she usually bought a slice of honeycake at the baker's. It was her Sunday treat. Sometimes there was an almond in her slice, sometimes not. It made a great difference. If there was an almond it was like carrying home a tiny present—a surprise—something that might very well not have been there. She hurried on the almond Sundays and struck the match for the kettle in quite a dashing way.

But to-day she passed the baker's by, climbed the stairs, went into the little dark room—her room like a cupboard—and sat down on the red eiderdown. She sat there for a long time. The box that the fur came out of was on the bed. She unclasped the necklet quickly; quickly, without looking, laid it inside. But when she put the lid on she thought she heard something crying.

Eudora Welty (b. 1909)

A Worn Path   1941

It was December—a bright frozen day in the early morning. Far out in the country there was an old Negro woman with her head tied in a red rag, coming along a path through the pinewoods. Her name was Phoenix Jackson. She was very old and small and she walked slowly in the dark pine shadows, moving a little from side to side in her steps, with the balanced heaviness and lightness of a pendulum in a grandfather clock. She carried a thin, small cane made from an umbrella, and with this she kept tapping the frozen earth in front of her. This made a grave and persistent noise in the still air, that seemed meditative like the chirping of a solitary little bird.

She wore a dark striped dress reaching down to her shoe tops, and an equally long apron of bleached sugar sacks, with a full pocket: all neat and tidy, but every time she took a step she might have fallen over her shoelaces, which dragged from her unlaced shoes. She looked straight ahead. Her eyes were blue with age. Her skin had a pattern all its own of numberless branching wrinkles and as though a whole little tree stood in the middle of her forehead, but a golden color ran underneath, and the two knobs of her cheeks were illumined by a yellow burning under the dark. Under the rag her hair came down on her neck in the frailest of ringlets, still black, and with an odor like copper.

Now and then there was a quivering in the thicket. Old Phoenix said, "Out of my way, all you foxes, owls, beetles, jack rabbits, coons and wild animals! . . .

Keep out from under these feet, little bob-whites. . . . Keep the big wild hogs out of my path. Don't let none of those come running my direction. I got a long way." Under her small black-freckled hand her cane, limber as a buggy whip, would switch at the brush as if to rouse up any hiding things.

On she went. The woods were deep and still. The sun made the pine needles almost too bright to look at, up where the wind rocked. The cones dropped as light as feathers. Down in the hollow was the mourning dove—it was not too late for him.

The path ran up a hill. "Seem like there is chains about my feet, time I get this far," she said, in the voice of argument old people keep to use with themselves. "Something always take a hold of me on this hill—pleads I should stay." 5

After she got to the top she turned and gave a full, severe look behind her where she had come. "Up through pines," she said at length. "Now down through oaks."

Her eyes opened their widest, and she started down gently. But before she got to the bottom of the hill a bush caught her dress.

Her fingers were busy and intent, but her skirts were full and long, so that before she could pull them free in one place they were caught in another. It was not possible to allow the dress to tear. "I in the thorny bush," she said. "Thorns, you doing your appointed work. Never want to let folks pass, no sir. Old eyes thought you was a pretty little *green* bush."

Finally, trembling all over, she stood free, and after a moment dared to stoop for her cane.

"Sun so high!" she cried, leaning back and looking, while the thick tears went over her eyes. "The time getting all gone here." 10

At the foot of this hill was a place where a log was laid across the creek. "Now comes the trial," said Phoenix.

Putting her right foot out, she mounted the log and shut her eyes. Lifting her skirt, leveling her cane fiercely before her, like a festival figure in some parade, she began to march across. Then she opened her eyes and she was safe on the other side.

"I wasn't as old as I thought," she said.

But she sat down to rest. She spread her skirts on the bank around her and folded her hands over her knees. Up above her was a tree in a pearly cloud of mistletoe. She did not dare to close her eyes, and when a little boy brought her a plate with a slice of marble-cake on it she spoke to him. "That would be acceptable," she said. But when she went to take it there was just her own hand in the air. 15

So she left that tree, and had to go through a barbed-wire fence. There she had to creep and crawl, spreading her knees and stretching her fingers like a baby trying to climb the steps. But she talked loudly to herself: she could not let her dress be torn now, so late in the day, and she could not pay for having her arm or her leg sawed off if she got caught fast where she was.

At last she was safe through the fence and risen up out in the clearing. Big dead trees, like black men with one arm, were standing in the purple stalks of the withered cotton field. There sat a buzzard.

"Who you watching?"

In the furrow she made her way along.

20   "Glad this not the season for bulls," she said, looking sideways, "and the good Lord made his snakes to curl up and sleep in the winter. A pleasure I don't see no two-headed snake coming around that tree, where it come once. It took a while to get by him, back in the summer."

She passed through the old cotton and went into a field of dead corn. It whispered and shook and was taller than her head. "Through the maze now," she said, for there was no path.

Then there was something tall, black, and skinny there, moving before her.

At first she took it for a man. It could have been a man dancing in the field. But she stood still and listened, and it did not make a sound. It was as silent as a ghost.

"Ghosts," she said sharply, "who be you the ghost of? For I have heard of nary death close by."

25   But there was no answer—only the ragged dancing in the wind.

She shut her eyes, reached out her hand, and touched a sleeve. She found a coat and inside that an emptiness, cold as ice.

"You scarecrow," she said. Her face lighted. "I ought to be shut up for good," she said with laughter. "My senses is gone. I too old. I the oldest people I ever know. Dance, old scarcrow," she said, "while I dancing with you."

She kicked her foot over the furrow, and with mouth drawn down, shook her head once or twice in a little strutting way. Some husks blew down and whirled in streamers about her skirts.

Then she went on, parting her way from side to side with the cane, through the whispering field. At last she came to the end, to a wagon track where the silver grass blew between the red ruts. The quail were walking around like pullets, seeming all dainty and unseen.

30   "Walk pretty," she said. "This is the easy place. This the easy going."

She followed the track, swaying through the quiet bare fields, through the little strings of trees silver in their dead leaves, past cabins silver from weather, with the doors and windows boarded shut, all like old women under a spell sitting there. "I walking in their sleep," she said, nodding her head vigorously.

In a ravine she went where a spring was silently flowing through a hollow log. Old Phoenix bent and drank. "Sweet-gum makes the water sweet," she said, and drank more. "Nobody know who made this well, for it was here when I was born."

The track crossed a swampy part where the moss hung as white as lace from every limb. "Sleep on, alligators, and blow your bubbles." Then the track went into the road.

Deep, deep the road went down between the high green-colored banks. Overhead the live-oaks met, and it was as dark as a cave.

35   A black dog with a lolling tongue came up out of the weeds by the ditch. She was meditating, and not ready, and when he came at her she only hit him a little with her cane. Over she went in the ditch, like a little puff of milkweed.

Down there, her senses drifted away. A dream visited her, and she reached her hand up, but nothing reached down and gave her a pull. So she lay there and presently went to talking. "Old woman," she said to herself, "that black dog come up out of the weeds to stall you off, and now there he sitting on his fine tail smiling at you."

A white man finally came along and found her—a hunter, a young man; with his dog on a chain.

"Well, Granny!" he laughed. "What are you doing there?"

"Lying on my back like a June-bug waiting to be turned over, mister," she said, reaching up her hand.

He lifted her up, gave her a swing in the air, and set her down. "Anything   40
broken, Granny?"

"No sir, them old dead weeds is springy enough," said Phoenix, when she had got her breath. "I thank you for your trouble."

"Where do you live, Granny?" he asked, while the two dogs were growling at each other.

"Away back yonder, sir, behind the ridge. You can't even see it from here."

"On your way home?"

"No sir, I going to town."   45

"Why, that's too far! That's as far as I walk when I come out myself, and I get something for my trouble." He patted the stuffed bag he carried, and there hung down a little closed claw. It was one of the bob-whites, with its beak hooked bitterly to show it was dead. "Now you go on home, Granny!"

"I bound to go to town, mister," said Phoenix. "The time come around."

He gave another laugh, filling the whole landscape. "I know you old colored people! Wouldn't miss going to town to see Santa Claus!"

But something held old Phoenix very still. The deep lines in her face went into a fierce and different radiation. Without warning, she had seen with her own eyes a flashing nickel fall out of the man's pocket onto the ground.

"How old are you, Granny?" he was saying.   50

"There is no telling, mister," she said, "no telling."

Then she gave a little cry and clapped her hands and said, "Git on away from here, dog! Look! Look at that dog!" She laughed as if in admiration. "He ain't scared of nobody. He a big black dog." She whispered, "Sic him!"

"Watch me get rid of that cur," said the man. "Sic him, Pete! Sic him!"

Phoenix heard the dogs fighting, and heard the man running and throwing sticks. She even heard a gunshot. But she was slowly bending forward by that time, further and further forward, the lids stretched down over her eyes, as if she were doing this in her sleep. Her chin was lowered almost to her knees. The yellow palm of her hand came out from the fold of her apron. Her fingers slid down and along the ground under the piece of money with the grace and care they would have in lifting an egg from under a setting hen. Then she slowly straighened up, she stood erect, and the nickel was in her apron pocket. A bird flew by. Her lips moved. "God watching me the whole time. I come to stealing."

The man came back, and his own dog panted about them. "Well, I scared him   55
off that time," he said, and then he laughed and lifted his gun and pointed it at Phoenix.

She stood straight and faced him.

"Doesn't the gun scare you?" he said, still pointing it.

"No, sir, I seen plenty go off closer by, in my day, and for less than what I done," she said, holding utterly still.

He smiled, and shouldered the gun. "Well, Granny," he said, "you must be a hundred years old, and scared of nothing. I'd give you a dime if I had any money with me. But you take my advice and stay home, and nothing will happen to you."

60   "I bound to go on my way, mister," said Phoenix. She inclined her head in the red rag. Then they went in different directions, but she could hear the gun shooting again and again over the hill.

She walked on. The shadows hung from the oak trees to the road like curtains. Then she smelled wood-smoke, and smelled the river, and she saw a steeple and the cabins on their steep steps. Dozens of little black children whirled around her. There ahead was Natchez shining. Bells were ringing. She walked on.

In the paved city it was Christmas time. There were red and green electric lights strung and crisscrossed everywhere, and all turned on in the daytime. Old Phoenix would have been lost if she had not distrusted her eyesight and depended on her feet to know where to take her.

She paused quietly on the sidewalk where people were passing by. A lady came along in the crowd, carrying an armful of red-, green- and silver-wrapped presents; she gave off perfume like the red roses in hot summer, and Phoenix stopped her.

"Please, missy, will you lace up my shoe?" She held up her foot.

65   "What do you want, Grandma?"

"See my shoe," said Phoenix. "Do all right for out in the country, but wouldn't look right to go in a big building."

"Stand still then, Grandma," said the lady. She put her packages down on the sidewalk beside her and laced and tied both shoes tightly.

"Can't lace 'em with a cane," said Phoenix. "Thank you, missy. I doesn't mind asking a nice lady to tie up my shoe, when I gets out on the street."

Moving slowly and from side to side, she went into the big building, and into a tower of steps, where she walked up and around and around until her feet knew to stop.

70   She entered a door, and there she saw nailed up on the wall the document that had been stamped with the gold seal and framed in the gold frame, which matched the dream that was hung up in her head.

"Here I be," she said. There was a fixed and ceremonial stiffness over her body.

"A charity case, I suppose," said an attendant who sat at the desk before her.

But Pheonix only looked above her head. There was sweat on her face, the wrinkles in her skin shone like a bright net.

"Speak up, Grandma," the woman said. "What's your name? We must have your history, you know. Have you been here before? What seems to be the trouble with you?"

75   Old Phoenix only gave a twitch to her face as if a fly were bothering her.

"Are you deaf?" cried the attendant.

But then the nurse came in.

"Oh, that's just old Aunt Phoenix," she said. "She doesn't come for herself— she has a little grandson. She makes trips just as regular as clockwork. She lives away back off the Old Natchez Trace." She bent down. "Well, Aunt Phoenix, why don't you just take a seat? We won't keep you standing after your long trip." She pointed.

The old woman sat down, bolt upright in the chair.

80   "Now, how is the boy?" asked the nurse.

Old Phoenix did not speak.

"I said, how is the boy?"

But Phoenix only waited and stared straight ahead, her face very solemn and withdrawn into rigidity.

"Is his throat any better?" asked the nurse. "Aunt Phoenix, don't you hear me? Is your grandson's throat any better since the last time you came for the medicine?"

With her hands on her knees, the old woman waited, silent, erect and mo-   85
tionless, just as if she were in armor.

"You mustn't take up our time this way, Aunt Phoenix," the nurse said. "Tell us quickly about your grandson, and get it over. He isn't dead, is he?"

At last there came a flicker and then a flame of comprehension across her face, and she spoke.

"My grandson. It was my memory had left me. There I sat and forgot why I made my long trip."

"Forgot?" the nurse frowned. "After you came so far?"

Then Phoenix was like an old woman begging a dignified forgiveness for   90
waking up frightened in the night. "I never did go to school, I was too old at the Surrender," she said in a soft voice. "I'm an old woman without an education. It was my memory fail me. My little grandson, he is just the same, and I forgot it in the coming."

"Throat never heals, does it?" said the nurse, speaking in a loud, sure voice to old Phoenix. By now she had a card with something written on it, a little list. "Yes. Swallowed lye. When was it—January—two, three years ago—"

Phoenix spoke unasked now. "No, missy, he not dead, he just the same. Every little while his throat begin to close up again, and he not able to swallow. He not get his breath. He not able to help himself. So the time come around, and I go on another trip for the soothing medicine."

"All right. The doctor said as long as you came to get it, you could have it," said the nurse. "But it's an obstinate case."

"My little grandson, he sit up there in the house all wrapped up, waiting by himself," Phoenix went on. "We is the only two left in the world. He suffer and it don't seem to put him back at all. He got a sweet look. He going to last. He wear a little patch quilt and peep out holding his mouth open like a little bird. I remembers so plain now. I not going to forget him again, no, the whole enduring time. I could tell him from all the others in creation."

"All right." The nurse was trying to hush her now. She brought her a bottle   95
of medicine. "Charity," she said, making a check mark in a book.

Old Phoenix held the bottle close to her eyes, and then carefully put it into her pocket.

"I thank you," she said.

"It's Christmas time, Grandma," said the attendant. "Could I give you a few pennies out of my purse?"

"Five pennies is a nickel," said Phoenix stiffly.

"Here's a nickel," said the attendant.   100

Phoenix rose carefully and held out her hand. She received the nickel and then fished the other nickel out of her pocket and laid it beside the new one. She stared at her palm closely, with her head on one side.

Then she gave a tap with her cane on the floor.

"This is what come to me to do," she said. "I going to the store and buy my child a little windmill they sells, made out of paper. He going to find it hard to believe there such a thing in the world. I'll march myself back where he waiting, holding it straight up in this hand."

She lifted her free hand, gave a little nod, turned around, and walked out of the doctor's office. Then her slow step began on the stairs, going down.

Shirley Jackson (1919–1965)

The Lottery   1948

The morning of June 27th was clear and sunny, with the fresh warmth of a full-summer day; the flowers were blossoming profusely and the grass was richly green. The people of the village began to gather in the square, between the post office and the bank, around ten o'clock; in some towns there were so many people that the lottery took two days and had to be started on June 26th, but in this village, where there were only about three hundred people, the whole lottery took less than two hours, so it could begin at ten o'clock in the morning and still be through in time to allow the villagers to get home for noon dinner.

The children assembled first, of course. School was recently over for the summer, and the feeling of liberty sat uneasily on most of them; they tended to gather together quietly for a while before they broke into boisterous play, and their talk was still of the classroom and the teacher, of books and reprimands. Bobby Martin had already stuffed his pockets full of stones, and the other boys soon followed his example, selecting the smoothest and roundest stones; Bobby and Harry Jones and Dickie Delacroix—the villagers pronounced this name "Dellacroy"—eventually made a great pile of stones in one corner of the square and guarded it against the raids of the other boys. The girls stood aside, talking among themselves, looking over their shoulders at the boys, and the very small children rolled in the dust or clung to the hands of their older brothers or sisters.

Soon the men began to gather, surveying their own children, speaking of planting and rain, tractors and taxes. They stood together, away from the pile of stones in the corner, and their jokes were quiet and they smiled rather than laughed. The women, wearing faded house dresses and sweaters, came shortly after their menfolk. They greeted one another and exchanged bits of gossip as they went to join their husbands. Soon the women, standing by their husbands, began to call to their children, and the children came reluctantly, having to be called four or five times. Bobby Martin ducked under his mother's grasping hand and ran, laughing, back to the pile of stones. His father spoke up sharply, and Bobby came quickly and took his place between his father and his oldest brother.

The lottery was conducted—as were the square dances, the teen-age club, the Halloween program—by Mr. Summers, who had time and energy to devote to civic activities. He was a round-faced, jovial man and he ran the coal business, and people were sorry for him, because he had no children and his wife was a scold. When he arrived in the square, carrying the black wooden box, there was a murmur of conversation among the villagers, and he waved and called, "Little late today, folks." The postmaster, Mr. Graves, followed him, carrying a three-legged stool, and the stool was put in the center of the square and Mr. Summers set the black box down on it. The villagers kept their distance, leaving a space between themselves and the stool, and when Mr. Summers said, "Some of you fellows want to give me a hand?" there was a hesitation before two men, Mr. Martin and his oldest son, Baxter, came forward to hold the box steady on the stool while Mr. Summers stirred up the papers inside it.

The original paraphernalia for the lottery had been lost long ago, and the black box now resting on the stool had been put into use even before Old Man Warner, the oldest man in town, was born. Mr. Summers spoke frequently to the villagers about making a new box, but no one liked to upset even as much tradition as was represented by the black box. There was a story that the present box had been made with some pieces of the box that had preceded it, the one that had been constructed when the first people settled down to make a village here. Every year, after the lottery, Mr. Summers began talking again about a new box, but every year the subject was allowed to fade off without anything's being done. The black box grew shabbier each year; by now it was no longer completely black but splintered badly along one side to show the original wood color, and in some places faded or stained.

Mr. Martin and his oldest son, Baxter, held the black box securely on the stool until Mr. Summers had stirred the papers thoroughly with his hand. Because so much of the ritual had been forgotten or discarded, Mr. Summers had been successful in having slips of paper substituted for the chips of wood that had been used for generations. Chips of wood, Mr. Summers had argued, had been all very well when the village was tiny, but now that the population was more than three hundred and likely to keep on growing, it was necessary to use something that would fit more easily into the black box. The night before the lottery, Mr. Summers and Mr. Graves made up the slips of paper and put them in the box, and it was then taken to the safe of Mr. Summers' coal company and locked up until Mr. Summers was ready to take it to the square next morning. The rest of the year, the box was put away, sometimes one place, sometimes another; it had spent one year in Mr. Graves' barn and another year underfoot in the post office, and sometimes it was set on a shelf in the Martin grocery and left there.

There was a great deal of fussing to be done before Mr. Summers declared the lottery open. There were the lists to make up—of heads of families, heads of households in each family, members of each household in each family. There was the proper swearing-in of Mr. Summers by the postmaster, as the official of the lottery; at one time, some people remembered, there had been a recital of some sort, performed by the official of the lottery, a perfunctory, tuneless chant that had been rattled off duly each year; some people believed that the official of the lottery used to stand just so when he said or sang it, others believed that he was supposed to walk among the people, but years and years ago this part of the ritual had been allowed to lapse. There had been, also, a ritual salute, which the official of the lottery had had to use in addressing each person who came up to draw from the box, but this also had changed with time, until now it was felt necessary only for the official to speak to each person approaching. Mr. Summers was very good at all this; in his clean white shirt and blue jeans, with one hand resting carelessly on the black box, he seemed very proper and important as he talked interminably to Mr. Graves and the Martins.

Just as Mr. Summers finally left off talking and turned to the assembled villagers, Mrs. Hutchinson came hurriedly along the path to the square, her sweater thrown over her shoulders, and slid into place in the back of the crowd. "Clean forgot what day it was," she said to Mrs. Delacroix, who stood next to her, and they both laughed softly. "Thought my old man was out back stacking wood," Mrs. Hutchinson went on, "and then I looked out the window and the kids was gone, and then I remembered it was the twenty-seventh and came a-running." She dried her hands on her apron, and Mrs. Delacroix said, "You're in time, though. They're still talking away up there."

Mrs. Hutchinson craned her neck to see through the crowd and found her husband and children standing near the front. She tapped Mrs. Delacroix on the arm as a farewell and began to make her way through the crowd. The people separated good-humoredly to let her through; two or three people said, in voices just loud enough to be heard across the crowd, "Here comes your Missus, Hutchinson," and "Bill, she made it after all." Mrs. Hutchinson reached her husband, and Mr. Summers, who had been waiting, said cheerfully, "Thought we were going to have to get on without you, Tessie." Mrs. Hutchinson said, grinning, "Wouldn't have me leave m'dishes in the sink, now, would you, Joe?," and soft laughter ran through the crowd as the people stirred back into position after Mrs. Hutchinson's arrival.

10   "Well, now," Mr. Summers said soberly, "guess we better get started, get this over with, so's we can go back to work. Anybody ain't here?"

"Dunbar," several people said. "Dunbar, Dunbar."

Mr. Summers consulted his list. "Clyde Dunbar," he said. "That's right. He's broke his leg, hasn't he? Who's drawing for him?"

"Me, I guess," a woman said, and Mr. Summers turned to look at her. "Wife draws for her husband," Mr. Summers said. "Don't you have a grown boy to do it for you, Janey?" Although Mr. Summers and everyone else in the village knew the answer perfectly well, it was the business of the official of the lottery to ask such questions formally. Mr. Summers waited with an expression of polite interest while Mrs. Dunbar answered.

"Horace's not but sixteen yet," Mrs. Dunbar said regretfully. "Guess I gotta fill in for the old man this year."

15   "Right," Mr. Summers said. He made a note on the list he was holding. Then he asked, "Watson boy drawing this year?"

A tall boy in the crowd raised his hand. "Here," he said. "I'm drawing for m'mother and me." He blinked his eyes nervously and ducked his head as several voices in the crowd said things like "Good fellow, Jack," and "Glad to see your mother's got a man to do it."

"Well," Mr. Summers said, "guess that's everyone. Old Man Warner make it?"

"Here," a voice said, and Mr. Summers nodded.

A sudden hush fell on the crowd as Mr. Summers cleared his throat and looked at the list. "All ready?" he called. "Now, I'll read the names—heads of families first—and the men come up and take a paper out of the box. Keep the paper folded in your hand without looking at it until everyone has had a turn. Everything clear?"

The people had done it so many times that they only half listened to the directions; most of them were quiet, wetting their lips, not looking around. Then Mr. Summers raised one hand high and said, "Adams." A man disengaged himself from the crowd and came forward. "Hi, Steve," Mr. Summers said, and Mr. Adams said, "Hi, Joe." They grinned at one another humorlessly and nervously. Then Mr. Adams reached into the black box and took out a folded paper. He held it firmly by one corner as he turned and went hastily back to his place in the crowd, where he stood a little apart from his family, not looking down at his hand.

"Allen," Mr. Summers said. "Anderson. . . . Bentham."

"Seems like there's no time at all between lotteries any more," Mrs. Delacroix said to Mrs. Graves in the back row. "Seems like we got through with the last one only last week."

"Time sure goes fast," Mrs. Graves said.

"Clark. . . . Delacroix."

"There goes my old man," Mrs. Delacroix said. She held her breath while her husband went forward.

"Dunbar," Mr. Summers said, and Mrs. Dunbar went steadily to the box while one of the women said, "Go on, Janey," and another said, "There she goes."

"We're next," Mrs. Graves said. She watched while Mr. Graves came around from the side of the box, greeted Mr. Summers gravely, and selected a slip of paper from the box. By now, all through the crowd there were men holding the small folded papers in their large hands, turning them over and over nervously. Mrs. Dunbar and her two sons stood together, Mrs. Dunbar holding the slip of paper.

"Harburt. . . . Hutchinson."

"Get up there, Bill," Mrs. Hutchinson said, and the people near her laughed.

"Jones."

"They do say," Mr. Adams said to Old Man Warner, who stood next to him, "that over in the north village they're talking of giving up the lottery."

Old Man Warner snorted. "Pack of crazy fools," he said. "Listening to the young folks, nothing's good enough for *them*. Next thing you know, they'll be wanting to go back to living in caves, nobody work any more, live *that* way for a while. Used to be a saying about 'Lottery in June, corn be heavy soon.' First thing you know, we'd all be eating stewed chickweed and acorns. There's *always* been a lottery," he added petulantly. "Bad enough to see young Joe Summers up there joking with everybody."

"Some places have already quit lotteries," Mrs. Adams said.

"Nothing but trouble in *that*,'" Old Man Warner said stoutly. "Pack of young fools."

"Martin." And Bobby Martin watched his father go forward. "Overdyke. . . . Percy."

"I wish they'd hurry," Mrs. Dunbar said to her older son. "I wish they'd hurry."

"They're almost through," her son said.

"You get ready to run tell Dad," Mrs. Dunbar said.

Mr. Summers called his own name and then stepped forward precisely and selected a slip from the box. Then he called, "Warner."

40   "Seventy-seventh year I been in the lottery," Old Man Warner said as he went through the crowd. "Seventy-seventh time."

"Watson." The tall boy came awkwardly through the crowd. Someone said, "Don't be nervous, Jack," and Mr. Summers said, "Take your time, son."

"Zanini."

After that, there was a long pause, a breathless pause, until Mr. Summers, holding his slip of paper in the air, said, "All right, fellows." For a minute, no one moved, and then all the slips of paper were opened. Suddenly, all the women began to speak at once, saying, "Who is it?" "Who's got it?" "Is it the Dunbars?" "Is it the Watsons?" Then the voices began to say, "It's Huchinson. It's Bill," "Bill Hutchinson's got it."

"Go tell your father," Mrs. Dunbar said to her older son.

45   People began to look around to see the Hutchinsons. Bill Hutchinson was standing quiet, staring down at the paper in his hand. Suddenly, Tessie Hutchinson shouted to Mr. Summers. "You didn't give him time enough to take any paper he wanted. I saw you. It wasn't fair!"

"Be a good sport, Tessie," Mrs. Delacroix called, and Mrs. Graves said, "All of us took the same chance."

"Shut up, Tessie," Bill Hutchinson said.

"Well, everyone," Mr. Summers said, "that was done pretty fast, and now we've got to be hurrying a little more to get done in time." He consulted his next list. "Bill," he said, "you draw for the Hutchinson family. You got any other households in the Hutchinsons?"

"There's Don and Eva," Mrs. Hutchinson yelled. "Make *them* take their chance!"

50   "Daughters draw with their husbands' families, Tessie," Mr. Summers said gently. "You know that as well as anyone else."

"It wasn't *fair*," Tessie said.

"I guess not, Joe," Bill Hutchinson said regretfully. "My daughter draws with her husband's family, that's only fair. And I've got no other family except the kids."

"Then, as far as drawing for families is concerned, it's you," Mr. Summers said in explanation, "and as far as drawing for households it concerned, that's you, too. Right?"

"Right," Bill Hutchinson said.

55   "How many kids, Bill?" Mr. Summers asked formally.

"Three," Bill Hutchinson said. "There's Bill, Jr., and Nancy, and little Dave. And Tessie and me."

"All right, then," Mr. Summers said. "Harry, you got their tickets back?"

Mr. Graves nodded and held up the slips of paper. "Put them in the box, then," Mr. Summers directed. "Take Bill's and put it in."

"I think we ought to start over," Mrs. Hutchinson said, as quietly as she could. "I tell you it wasn't *fair.* You didn't give him time enough to choose. *Every-body* saw that."

Mr. Graves had selected the five slips and put them in the box, and he 60 dropped all the papers but those onto the ground, where the breeze caught them and lifted them off.

"Listen, everybody," Mrs. Huchinson was saying to the people around her.

"Ready, Bill?" Mr. Summers asked, and Bill Hutchinson, with one quick glance around at his wife and children, nodded.

"Remember," Mr. Summers said, "take the slips and keep them folded until each person has taken one. Harry, you help little Dave." Mr. Graves took the hand of the little boy, who came willingly with him up to the box. "Take a paper out of the box, Davy," Mr. Summers said. Davy put his hand into the box and laughed. "Take just *one* paper," Mr. Summers said. "Harry, you hold it for him." Mr. Graves took the child's hand and removed the folded paper from the tight fist and held it while little Dave stood next to him and looked up at him wonderingly.

"Nancy next," Mr. Summers said. Nancy was twelve, and her school friends breathed heavily as she went forward, switching her skirt, and took a slip daintily from the box. "Bill, Jr.," Mr. Summers said, and Billy, his face red and his feet over-large, nearly knocked the box over as he got a paper out. "Tessie," Mr. Summers said. She hesitated for a minute, looking around defiantly, and then set her lips and went up to the box. She snatched a paper out and held it behind her.

"Bill," Mr. Summers said, and Bill Hutchinson reached into the box and felt 65 around, bringing his hand out at last with the slip of paper in it.

The crowd was quiet. A girl whispered, "I hope it's not Nancy," and the sound of the whisper reached the edges of the crowd.

"It's not the way it used to be," Old Man Warner said clearly. "People ain't the way they used to be."

"All right," Mr. Summers said. "Open the papers. Harry, you open little Dave's."

Mr. Graves opened the slip of paper and there was a general sigh through the crowd as he held it up and everyone could see that it was blank. Nancy and Bill, Jr., opened theirs at the same time, and both beamed and laughed, turning around to the crowd and holding their slips of paper above their heads.

"Tessie," Mr. Summers said. There was a pause, and then Mr. Summers 70 looked at Bill Hutchinson, and Bill unfolded his paper and showed it. It was blank.

"It's Tessie," Mr. Summers said, and his voice was hushed. "Show us her paper, Bill."

Bill Hutchinson went over to his wife and forced the slip of paper out of her hand. It had a black spot on it, the black spot Mr. Summers had made the night before with the heavy pencil in the coal-company office. Bill Hutchinson held it up, and there was a stir in the crowd.

"All right, folks," Mr. Summers said. "Let's finish quickly."

Although the villagers had forgotten the ritual and lost the original black box, they still remembered to use stones. The pile of stones the boys had made earlier was ready; there were stones on the ground with the blowing scraps of paper that had come out of the box. Mrs. Delacroix selected a stone so large she had to pick it up with both hands and turned to Mrs. Dunbar. "Come on," she said. "Hurry up."

75   Mrs. Dunbar had small stones in both hands, and she said, gasping for breath, "I can't run at all. You'll have to go ahead and I'll catch up with you."

The children had stones already, and someone gave little Davy Hutchinson a few pebbles.

Tessie Hutchinson was in the center of a cleared space by now, and she held her hands out desperately as the villagers moved in on her. "It isn't fair," she said. A stone hit her on the side of the head.

Old Man Warner was saying, "Come on, come on, everyone." Steve Adams was in the front of the crowd of villagers with Mrs. Graves beside him.

"It isn't fair, it isn't right," Mrs. Hutchinson screamed, and then they were upon her.

John Updike (b. 1932)

A & P°   1961

In walks these three girls in nothing but bathing suits. I'm in the third checkout slot, with my back to the door, so I don't see them until they're over by the bread. The one that caught my eye first was the one in the plaid green two-piece. She was a chunky kid, with a good tan and a sweet broad soft-looking can with those two crescents of white just under it, where the sun never seems to hit, at the top of the backs of her legs. I stood there with my hand on a box of HiHo crackers trying to remember if I rang it up or not. I ring it up again and the customer starts giving me hell. She's one of these cash-register-watchers, a witch about fifty with rouge on her cheekbones and no eyebrows, and I know it made her day to trip me up. She'd been watching cash registers for fifty years and probably never seen a mistake before.

By the time I got her feathers smoothed and her goodies into a bag—she gives me a little snort in passing, if she'd been born at the right time they would have burned her over in Salem—by the time I get her on her way the girls had circled around the bread and were coming back, without a pushcart, back my way along the counters, in the aisle between the checkouts and the Special bins. They didn't even have shoes on. There was this chunky one, with the two-piece—it was bright green and the seams on the bra were still sharp and her belly was still pretty pale so I guessed she just got it (the suit)—there was this one, with one of those chubby berry-faces, the lips all bunched together under her nose, this one, and a tall one, with black hair that hadn't quite frizzed right, and one of these sunburns right

A & P: "The Great Atlantic and Pacific Tea Company." This large grocery chain flourishes today in twenty-six states.

across under the eyes, and a chin that was too long—you know, the kind of girl other girls think is very "striking" and "attractive" but never quite makes it, as they very well know, which is why they like her so much—and then the third one, that wasn't quite so tall. She was the queen. She kind of led them, the other two peeking around and making their shoulders round. She didn't look around, not this queen, she just walked straight on slowly, on these long white prima-donna legs. She came down a little hard on her heels, as if she didn't walk in her bare feet that much, putting down her heels and then letting the weight move along to her toes as if she was testing the floor with every step, putting a little deliberate extra action into it. You never know for sure how girls' minds work (do you really think it's a mind in there or just a little buzz like a bee in a glass jar?) but you got the idea she had talked the other two into coming in here with her, and now she was showing them how to do it, walk slow and hold yourself straight.

She had on a kind of dirty-pink—beige, maybe. I don't know—bathing suit with a little nubble all over it and, what got me, the straps were down. They were off her shoulders looped loose around the cool tops of her arms, and I guess as a result the suit had slipped a little on her, so all around the top of the cloth there was this shining rim. If it hadn't been there you wouldn't have known there could have been anything whiter than those shoulders. With the straps pushed off, there was nothing between the top of the suit and the top of her head except just *her*, this clean bare plane of the top of her chest down from the shoulder bones like a dented sheet of metal tilted in the light. I mean, it was more than pretty.

She had sort of oaky hair that the sun and salt had bleached, done up in a bun that was unraveling, and a kind of prim face. Walking into the A & P with your straps down, I suppose it's the only kind of face you *can* have. She held her head so high her neck, coming up out of those white shoulders, looked kind of stretched, but I didn't mind. The longer her neck was, the more of her there was.

She must have felt in the corner of her eye me and over my shoulder Stokesie   5
in the second slot watching, but she didn't tip. Not this queen. She kept her eyes moving across the racks, and stopped, and turned so slow it made my stomach rub the inside of my apron, and buzzed to the other two, who kind of huddled against her for relief, and then they all three of them went up the cat-and-dog-food-breakfast-cereal-macaroni-rice-raisins-seasonings-spreads-spaghetti-soft-drinks-crackers-and-cookies aisle. From the third slot I look straight up this aisle to the meat counter, and I watched them all the way. The fat one with the tan sort of fumbled with the cookies, but on second thought she put the package back. The sheep push-ing their carts down the aisle—the girls were walking against the usual traffic (not that we have one-way signs or anything)—were pretty hilarious. You could see them, when Queenie's white shoulders dawned on them, kind of jerk, or hop, or hiccup, but their eyes snapped back to their own baskets and on they pushed. I bet you could set off dynamite in an A & P and the people would by and large keep reaching and checking oatmeal off their lists and muttering "Let me see, there was a third thing, began with A, asparagus, no ah, yes, applesauce!" or whatever it is they do mutter. But there was no doubt, this jiggled them. A few houseslaves in pin curlers even looked around after pushing their carts past to make sure what they had seen was correct.

You know, it's one thing to have a girl in a bathing suit down on the beach, where what with the glare nobody can look at each other much anyway, and another thing in the cool of the A & P, under the fluorescent lights, against all those stacked packages, with her feet paddling along naked over our checkerboard green-and-cream rubber-tile floor.

"Oh Daddy," Stokesie said beside me. "I feel so faint."

"Darling," I said. "Hold me tight." Stokesie's married, with two babies chalked up on his fuselage already, but as far as I can tell that's the only difference. He's twenty-two, and I was nineteen this April.

"Is it done?" he asks, the responsible married man finding his voice. I forgot to say he thinks he's going to be manager some sunny day, maybe in 1990 when it's called the Great Alexandrov and Petrooshki° Tea Company or something.

10   What he meant was, our town is five miles from the beach, with a big summer colony out on the Point, but we're right in the middle of town, and the women generally put on a shirt or shorts or something before they get out of the car into the street. And anyway these are usually women with six children and varicose veins mapping their legs and nobody, including them, could care less. As I say, we're right in the middle of town, and if you stand at our front doors you can see two banks and the Congregational church and the newspaper store and three real-estate offices and about twenty-seven old freeloaders tearing up Central Street because the sewer broke again. It's not as if we're on the Cape;° we're north of Boston and there's people in this town haven't seen the ocean for twenty years.

The girls had reached the meat counter and were asking McMahon something. He pointed, they pointed, and they shuffled out of sight behind a pyramid of Diet Delight peaches. All that was left for us to see was old McMahon patting his mouth and looking after them sizing up their joints. Poor kids, I began to feel sorry for them, they couldn't help it.

Now here comes the sad part of the story, at least my family says it's sad, but I don't think it's so sad myself. The store's pretty empty, it being Thursday afternoon, so there was nothing much to do except lean on the register and wait for the girls to show up again. The whole store was like a pinball machine and I didn't know which tunnel they'd come out of. After a while they come around out of the far aisle, around the light bulbs, records at discount of the Caribbean Six or Tony Martin Sings or some such gunk you wonder they waste the wax on, sixpacks of candy bars, and plastic toys done up in cellophane that fall apart when a kid looks at them anyway. Around they come, Queenie still leading the way, and holding a little gray jar in her hand. Slots Three through Seven are unmanned and I could see her wondering between Stokes and me, but Stokesie with his usual luck draws an old party in baggy gray pants who stumbles up with four giant cans of pineapple juice (what do these bums *do* with all that pineapple juice? I've often asked myself) so the girls come to me. Queenie puts down the jar and I take it into my fingers icy cold. Kingfish Fancy Herring Snacks in Pure Sour Cream: 49¢. Now her hands are empty, not a ring or a bracelet, bare as God made them, and I wonder where the money's coming from. Still with that prim look she lifts a folded dollar bill out of the

---

    Great Alexandrov and Petrooshki: Apparently a reference to the possibility that someday Russia might rule the United States, and might then change the names of American businesses and institutions.

    the Cape: Cape Cod, the southeastern area of Massachusetts, a place of many resorts and beaches.

hollow at the center of her nubbed pink top. The jar went heavy in my hand. Really, I thought that was so cute.

Then everybody's luck begins to run out. Lengel comes in from haggling with a truck full of cabbages on the lot and is about to scuttle into that door marked MANAGER behind which he hides all day when the girls touch his eye. Lengel's pretty dreary, teaches Sunday school and the rest, but he doesn't miss that much. He comes over and says, "Girls, this isn't the beach."

Queenie blushes, though maybe it's just a brush of sunburn I was noticing for the first time, now that she was so close. "My mother asked me to pick up a jar of herring snacks." Her voice kind of startled me, the way voices do when you see the people first, coming out so flat and dumb yet kind of tony, too, the way it ticked over "pick up" and "snacks." All of a sudden I slid right down her voice into her living room. Her father and the other men were standing around in ice-cream coats and bow ties and the women were in sandals picking up herring snacks on toothpicks off a big glass plate and they were all holding drinks the color of water with olives and sprigs of mint in them. When my parents have somebody over they get lemonade and if it's a real racy affair Schlitz in tall glasses with "They'll Do It Every Time"° cartoons stenciled on.

"That's all right," Lengel said. "But this isn't the beach." His repeating this   15
struck me as funny, as if it had just occurred to him, and he had been thinking all these years the A & P was a great big dune and he was the head lifeguard. He didn't like my smiling—as I say he doesn't miss much—but he concentrates on giving the girls that sad Sunday-school-superintendent stare.

Queenie's blush is no sunburn now, and the plump one in plaid, that I liked better from the back—a really sweet can—pipes up, "We weren't doing any shopping. We just came in for the one thing."

"That makes no difference," Lengel tells her, and I could see from the way his eyes went that he hadn't noticed she was wearing a two-piece before. "We want you decently dressed when you come in here."

"We *are* decent," Queenie says suddenly, her lower lip pushing, getting sore now that she remembers her place, a place from which the crowd that runs the A & P must look pretty crummy. Fancy Herring Snacks flashed in her very blue eyes.

"Girls, I don't want to argue with you. After this come in here with your shoulders covered. It's our policy." He turns his back. That's policy for you. Policy is what the kingpins want. What the others want is juvenile delinquency.

All this while, the customers had been showing up with their carts but, you   20
know, sheep, seeing a scene, they had all bunched up on Stokesie, who shook open a paper bag as gently as peeling a peach, not wanting to miss a word. I could feel in the silence everybody getting nervous, most of all Lengel, who asks me, "Sammy, have you rung up their purchase?"

I thought and said "No" but it wasn't about that I was thinking. I go through the punches, 4, 9, GROC, TOT—it's more complicated than you think, and after you do it often enough, it begins to make a little song, that you hear words to, in my case "Hello (*bing*) there, you (*gung*) hap-py *pee*-pul (*splat*)!—the *splat* being the

---

"They'll Do It Every Time": A syndicated daily and Sunday cartoon created by Jimmy Hatlo.

drawer flying out. I uncrease the bill, tenderly as you may imagine, it just having come from between the two smoothest scoops of vanilla I had ever known were there, and pass a half and a penny into her narrow pink palm, and nestle the herrings in a bag and twist its neck and hand it over, all the time thinking.

The girls, and who'd blame them, are in a hurry to get out, so I say "I quit" to Lengel quick enough for them to hear, hoping they'll stop and watch me, their unsuspected hero. They keep right on going, into the electric eye; the door flies open and they flicker across the lot to their car, Queenie and Plaid and Big Tall Goony-Goony (not that as raw material she was so bad), leaving me with Lengel and a kink in his eyebrow.

"Did you say something, Sammy?"

"I said I quit."

25   "I though you did."

"You didn't have to embarrass them."

"It was they who were embarrassing us."

I started to say something that came out "Fiddle-de-doo." It's a saying of my grandmother's, and I know she would have been pleased.

"I don't think you know what you're saying," Lengel said.

30   "I know you don't," I said. "But I do." I pull the bow at the back of my apron and start shrugging it off my shoulders. A couple customers that had been heading for my slot begin to knock against each other, like scared pigs in a chute.

Lengel sighs and begins to look very patient and old and gray. He'd been a friend of my parents for years. "Sammy, you don't want to do this to your Mom and Dad," he tells me. It's true. I don't. But it seems to me that once you begin a gesture it's fatal not to go through with it. I fold the apron, "Sammy" stitched in red on the pocket, and put it on the counter, and drop the bow tie on top of it. The bow tie is theirs, if you've ever wondered. "You'll feel this for the rest of your life," Lengel says, and I know that's true, too, but remembering how he made that pretty girl blush makes me so scrunchy inside I punch the No Sale tab and the machine whirs "pee-pul" and the drawer splats out. One advantage to this scene taking place in summer, I can follow this up with a clean exit, there's no fumbling around getting your coat and galoshes, I just saunter into the electric eye in my white shirt that my mother ironed the night before, and the door heaves itself open, and outside the sunshine is skating around on the asphalt.

I look around for my girls, but they're gone, of course. There wasn't anybody but some young married screaming with her children about some candy they didn't get by the door of a powder-blue Falcon° station wagon. Looking back in the big windows, over the bags of peat moss and aluminum lawn furniture stacked on the pavement, I could see Lengel in my place in the slot, checking the sheep through. His face was dark gray and his back stiff, as if he'd just had an injection of iron, and my stomach kind of fell as I felt how hard the world was going to be to me hereafter.

Falcon: A small car that had recently been introduced by the Ford Motor Company.

POEMS

William Shakespeare (1564–1616)

Sonnet 73: That Time of Year Thou Mayest in Me Behold

1609

That time of year thou mayest in me behold,
When yellow leaves, or none, or few do hang
Upon those boughs which shake against the cold,
Bare ruined choirs, where late the sweet birds sang.
In me thou seest the twilight of such day,   5
As after Sunset fadeth in the West,
Which by and by black night doth take away,
Death's second self that seals up all in rest.
In me thou seest the glowing of such fire,
That on the ashes of his youth doth lie,   10
As the death bed, whereon it must expire,
Consumed with that which it was nourished by.
    This thou perceiv'st, which makes thy love more strong.
    To love that well, which thou must leave ere long.

Sonnet 116: Let Me Not to the Marriage of True Minds

1609

Let me not to the marriage of true minds
Admit impediments; love is not love
Which alters when it alteration finds
Or bends with the remover to remove.
O no, it is an ever fixed mark   5
That looks on tempests and is never shaken;
It is the star to every wandering bark
Whose worth's unknown, although his height be taken.
Love's not Time's fool, though rosy lips and cheeks

10   Within his bending sickle's compass come;
       Love alters not with his brief hours and weeks.
       But bears it out even to the edge of doom:
           If this be error and upon me proved,
           I never writ, nor no man ever loved.

Sonnet 130: My Mistress' Eyes Are Nothing Like the Sun   1609

       My Mistress' eyes are nothing like the Sun,
       Coral is far more red, than her lips' red,
       If snow be white, why then her breasts are dun:
       If hairs be wires, black wires grow on her head:
5   I have seen Roses damasked, red and white,
       But no such Roses see I in her cheeks,
       And in some perfumes is there more delight,
       Than in the breath that from my Mistress reeks.
       I love to hear her speak, yet well I know,
10   That Music hath a far more pleasing sound:
       I grant I never saw a goddess go,
       My Mistress when she walks treads on the ground.
           And yet by heaven I think my love as rare,
           As any she belied with false compare.

John Donne (1572–1631)

A Valediction: Forbidding Mourning   1633

       As virtuous men pass mildly away,
           And whisper to their souls to go,
       Whilst some of their sad friends do say
           The breath goes now, and some say, No;

5   So let us melt, and make no noise,
           No tear-floods, nor sigh-tempests move,

'Twere profanation° of our joys
  To tell the laity° our love.

Moving of th'earth brings harms and fears,
  Men reckon what it did and meant;
But trepidation° of the spheres,
  Though greater far, is innocent.°   10

Dull sublunary lovers' love
  (Whose soul is sense°) cannot admit
Absence, because it doth remove
  Those things which elemented it.   15

But we by a love so much refined
  That our selves know not what it is,
Inter-assured of the mind,
  Care less, eyes, lips, and hands to miss.   20

Our two souls therefore, which are one,
  Though I must go, endure not yet
A breach, but an expansion,
  Like gold to airy thinness beat.°

If they be two, they are two so   25
  As stiff twin compasses° are two;
Thy soul, the fixt foot, makes no show
  To move, but doth, if th'other do.

And though it in the center sit,
  Yet when the other far doth roam,   30
It leans and harkens after it,
  And grows erect, as that comes home.

Such wilt thou be to me, who must
  Like th'other foot, obliquely run;
Thy firmness draws my circle just,°   35
  And makes me end where I begun.

---

profanation, laity: as though the two lovers are priests of love, while ordinary people are ignorant of their relationship.
trepidation: Before Sir Issac Newton explained the precession of the equinoxes, it was assumed that the positions of heavenly bodies should be constant and perfectly circular. The clearly observable irregularities (caused by the slow wobbling of the earth's axis) were explained by the concept of *trepidation,* or a trembling or oscillation that occurred in the outermost of the spheres that were believed to surround the earth.
innocent: harmless.
soul is sense: lovers whose attraction is totally physical.
gold to airy thinness beat: a reference to the malleability of gold.
compasses: a compass used for drawing circles.
just: perfectly round.

Edmund Waller (1606–1687)

Go, Lovely Rose

1645

Go, lovely rose,
Tell her that wastes her time and me
That now she knows,
When I resemble° her to thee,
How sweet and fair she seems to be.

Tell her that's young,
And shuns to have her graces spied,
That hadst thou sprung
In deserts, where no men abide,
Thou must have uncommended died.

Small is the worth
Of beauty from the light retired;
Bid her come forth,
Suffer herself to be desired,
And not blush so to be admired.

Then die, that she
The common fate of all things rare
May read in thee:
How small a part of time they share
That are so wondrous sweet and fair.

resemble: compare.

Robert Burns (1759–1796)

O My Luve's Like a Red, Red Rose

1796

O my Luve's like a red, red, rose,
That's newly sprung in June:
O my Luve's like the melodie
That's sweetly play'd in tune.

As fair art thou, my bonnie lass,
So deep in luve am I;

And I will luve thee still, my Dear,
  Till a'° the seas gang° dry.

Till a' the seas gang dry, my Dear,
  And the rocks melt wi'° the sun: 10
And I will luve thee still, my Dear,
  While the sands o'° life shall
run.

And fare thee weel, my only Luve!
  And fare thee weel, awhile!
And I will come again, my Luve,   15
  Tho' it were ten thousand mile!

a': all. *gang*: go. *wi'*: with. *o'*: of.

Samuel Taylor Coleridge (1772–1834)

Kubla Khan   1816

In Xanadu did Kubla Kahn
A stately pleasure dome decree:
Where Alph, the sacred river, ran
Through cavern measureless to man
  Down to a sunless sea.   5
So twice five miles of fertile ground
With walls and towers were girdled round:
And there were gardens bright with sinuous rills,
Where blossomed many an incense-bearing tree;
And here were forests ancient as the hills,   10
Enfolding sunny spots of greenery.

But oh! that deep romantic chasm which slanted
Down the green hill athwart a cedarn cover!
A savage place! as holy and enchanted
As e'er beneath a waning moon was haunted   15
By woman wailing for her demon lover!
And from this chasm, with ceaseless turmoil seething,
As if this earth in fast thick pants were breathing,
A mighty fountain momently was forced:
Amid whose swift half-intermitted burst   20
Huge fragments vaulted like rebounding hail,
Or chaffy grain beneath the thresher's flail;
And 'mid these dancing rocks at once and ever

It flung up momently the sacred river.
25   Five miles meandering with a mazy motion
Through wood and dale the sacred river ran,
Then reached the caverns measureless to man,
And sank in tumult to a lifeless ocean:
And 'mid this tumult Kubla heard from far
30   Ancestral voices prophesying war!
    The shadow of the dome of pleasure
    Floated midway on the waves;
    Where was heard the mingled measure
    From the fountain and the caves.
35   It was a miracle of rare device,
A sunny pleasure dome with caves of ice!

    A damsel with a dulcimer
    In a vision once I saw:
    It was an Abyssinian maid,
40   And on her dulcimer she played,
    Singing of Mount Abora.
Could I revive within me
    Her symphony and song,
To such a deep delight 'twould win me,
45   That with music loud and long,
I would build that dome in air,
That sunny dome! those caves of ice!
And all who heard should see them there,
And all should cry. Beware! Beware!
50   His flashing eyes, his floating hair!
Weave a circle round him thrice,
And close your eyes with holy dread,
For he on honeydew hath fed,
And drunk the milk of Paradise.

John Keats (1795–1821)

On First Looking into Chapman's Homer   1816

Much have I travell'd in the realms of gold,
    And many goodly states and kingdoms seen;
    Round many western islands have I been
Which bards in fealty to Apollo hold.

Oft of one wide expanse had I been told   5
   That deep-brow'd Homer ruled as his demesne;
   Yet did I never breathe its pure serene
Till I heard Chapman speak out loud and bold:
Then felt I like some watcher of the skies
   When a new planet swims into his ken: 10
Or like stout Cortez when with eagle eyes
   He star'd at the Pacific—and all his men
Look'd at each other with a wild surmise—
   Silent, upon a peak in Darien.

Bright Star   1819

Bright star! would I were steadfast as thou art—
   Not in lone splendor hung aloft the night,
And watching, with eternal lids apart,
   Like Nature's patient, sleepless eremite,°
The moving waters at their priestlike task   5
   Of pure ablution round earth's human shores,
Or gazing on the new soft-fallen mask
   Of snow upon the mountains and the moors;
No—yet still steadfast, still unchangeable,
   Pillowed upon my fair love's ripening breast,   10
To feel forever its soft fall and swell,
   Awake forever in a sweet unrest,
Still, still to hear her tender-taken breath,
And so live ever—or else swoon to death.

eremite: hermit.

Matthew Arnold (1822–1888)

Dover Beach   1849

The sea is calm to-night.
The tide is full, the moon lies fair
Upon the straits:—on the French coast the light

Gleams and is gone; the cliffs of England stand,
Glimmering and vast, out in the tranquil bay.
Come to the window, sweet is the night air!
Only, from the long line of spray
Where the sea meets the moon-blanched land,
Listen! You can hear the grating roar
Of pebbles which the waves draw back, and fling,
At their return, up the high strand,
Begin, and cease, and then again begin,
With tremulous cadence slow, and bring
The eternal note of sadness in.

Sophocles long ago
Heard it on the Ægean, and it brought
Into his mind the turbid ebb and flow
Of human misery; we
Find also in the sound a thought,
Hearing it by this distant northern sea.
The Sea of Faith
Was once, too, at the full, and round earth's shore
Lay like the folds of a bright girdle furled.
But now I only hear
Its melancholy, long, withdrawing roar,
Retreating, to the breath
Of the night wind, down the vast edges drear
And naked shingles of the world.

Ah, love, let us be true
To one another! for the world, which seems
To lie before us like a land of dreams,
So various, so beautiful, so new,
Hath really neither joy, nor love, nor light,
Nor certitude, nor peace, nor help for pain;
And we are here as on a darkling plain
Swept with confused alarms of struggle and flight
Where ignorant armies clash by night.

Thomas Hardy (1840–1928)

Channel Firing   1914

That night your great guns unawares,
Shook all our coffins as we lay,
And broke the chancel window squares.
We thought it was the Judgment-day

And sat upright. While drearisome   5
Arose the howl of wakened hounds:
The mouse let fall the altar-crumb,
The worms drew back into the mounds,

The glebe cow drooled. Till God called, "No;
It's gunnery practice out at sea   10
Just as before you went below;
The world is as it used to be:

"All nations striving strong to make
Red war yet redder. Mad as hatters
They do no more for Christés sake   15
Than you who are helpless in such matters.

"That this is not the judgment-hour
For some of them's a blessed thing,
For if it were they'd have to scour
Hell's floor for so much threatening . . .   20

"Ha, ha. It will be warmer when
I blow the trumpet (if indeed
I ever do; for you are men,
And rest eternal sorely need)."

So down we lay again. "I wonder,   25
Will the world ever saner be,"
Said one, "than when He sent us under
In our indifferent century!"

And many a skeleton shook his head.
"Instead of preaching forty year,"   30
My neighbor Parson Thirdly said,
"I wish I had stuck to pipes and beer."

Again the guns disturbed the hour,
Roaring their readiness to avenge,
As far inland as Stourton Tower,   35
And Camelot, and starlit Stonehenge.

Amy Lowell (1874–1925)

Patterns   1916

I walk down garden paths,
And all the daffodils

Are blowing, and the bright blue squills.
I walk down the patterned garden-paths
5   In my stiff, brocaded gown.
With my powdered hair and jewelled fan,
I too am a rare
Pattern. As I wander down
The garden paths.

10 My dress is richly figured,
And the train
Makes a pink and silver stain
On the gravel, and the thrift
Of the borders.
15 Just a plate of current fashion
Tripping by in high-heeled, ribboned shoes.
Not a softness anywhere about me,
Only whalebone° and brocade.
And I sink on a seat in the shade

20 Of a lime tree. For my passion
Wars against the stiff brocade.
The daffodils and squills
Flutter in the breeze
As they please.
25 And I weep;
For the lime-tree is in blossom
And one small flower has dropped upon my bosom.

And the plashing of waterdrops
In the marble fountain
30 Comes down the garden-paths.
The dripping never stops.
Underneath my stiffened gown
Is the softness of a woman bathing in a marble basin,
A basin in the midst of hedges grown
35 So thick, she cannot see her lover hiding.
But she guesses he is near,
And the sliding of the water
Seems the stroking of a dear
Hand upon her.
40 What is Summer in a fine brocaded gown!
I should like to see it lying in a heap upon the ground.
All the pink and silver crumpled up on the ground.

whalebone: Used as a stiffener in tightly laced corsets.

I would be the pink and silver as I ran along the paths,
And he would stumble after,
Bewildered by my laughter.
I should see the sun flashing from his sword-hilt and buckles on his shoes. 45
I would choose
To lead him in a maze along the patterned paths,
A bright and laughing maze for my heavy-booted lover.
Till he caught me in the shade, 50
And the buttons of his waistcoat bruised my body as he clasped me,
Aching, melting, unafraid.
With the shadows of the leaves and the sundrops,
And the plopping of the waterdrops,
All about us in the open afternoon— 55
I am very like to swoon
With the weight of this brocade,
For the sun sifts through the shade.

Underneath the fallen blossom
In my bosom,
Is a letter I have hid. 60
It was brought to me this morning by a rider from the Duke.
Madam, we regret to inform you that Lord Hartwell
Died in action Thursday se'nnight°
As I read it in the white, morning sunlight, 65
The letters squirmed like snakes.
"Any answer, Madam," said my footman.
"No," I told him.
"See that the messenger takes some refreshment.

No, no answer."
And I walked into the garden. 70
Up and down the patterned paths,
In my stiff, correct brocade.
The blue and yellow flowers stood up proudly in the sun,
Each one. 75
I stood upright too,
Held rigid to the pattern
By the stiffness of my gown.
Up and down I walked.
Up and down. 80

In a month he would have been my husband.
In a month, here, underneath this lime,
We would have broken the pattern;
He for me, and I for him,
He as Colonel, I as Lady, 85
On this shady seat.

se'nnight: i.e. a week ago (seven nights) last Thursday

He had a whim
That sunlight carried blessing.
And I answered, "It shall be as you have said."
90 Now he is dead.

In Summer and in Winter I shall walk
Up and down
The patterned garden-paths
In my stiff, brocaded gown.
95 The squills and daffodils
Will give place to pillared roses, and to asters, and to snow.
I shall go
Up and down,
In my gown.
100 Gorgeously arrayed,
Boned and stayed.
And the softness of my body will be guarded from embrace
By each button, hook, and lace.
For the man who should loose me is dead,
105 Fighting with the Duke in Flanders,°
In a pattern called a war.
Christ! What are patterns for?

Flanders: A place of frequent warfare in Belgium. The speaker's clothing (lines 5,6) suggests
the time of the Duke of Marlborough's Flanders campaigns of 1702–10. The Battle of Waterloo
(1815) was also fought nearby under the Duke of Wellington. During World War I, fierce
fighting against the Germans occurred in Flanders in 1914 and 1915, with great loss of life.

Robert Frost (1875–1963)

Desert Places   1936

Snow falling and night falling fast, oh, fast
In a field I looked into going past,
And the ground almost covered smooth in snow,
But a few weeds and stubble showing last.

5 The woods around it have it—it is theirs.
All animals are smothered in their lairs.
I am too absent-spirited to count;
The loneliness includes me unawares.

And lonely as it is that loneliness
10 Will be more lonely ere it will be less—

A blanker whiteness of benighted snow
With no expression, nothing to express.

They cannot scare me with their empty spaces
Between stars—on stars where no human race is.
I have it in me so much nearer home   *15*
To scare myself with my own desert places.

John Masefield (1878–1967)

Cargoes   1902

Quinquereme° of Nineveh° from distant Ophir,°
Rowing home to haven in sunny Palestine,
With a cargo of ivory,
And apes and peacocks,°
Sandalwood, cedarwood,° and sweet white wine.   *5*

Stately Spanish galleon coming from the Isthmus,°
Dipping through the Tropics by the palm-green shores,
With a cargo of diamonds,
Emeralds, amethysts,
Topazes, and cinnamon, and gold moidores.°   *10*

Dirty British coaster with a salt-caked smoke-stack,
Butting through the Channel in the mad March days,
With a cargo of Tyne coal,°
Road-rails, pig-lead,
Firewood, iron-ware, and cheap tin trays.   *15*

Quinquereme: the largest of the ancient ships. It was powered by three tiers of oars, and was named "quinquereme" because five men operated each vertical oar station. Two oars were each taken by two men, while the third was taken by one man alone.
Nineveh: "an exceeding great city," Jonah 3:3.
Ophir: Ophir probably was in Africa, and was known for its gold, I Kings 10:11; 1 Chron.29:4.
apes and peacocks: I Kings 10:22, and 2 Chron. 9:21. These goods were brought to King Solomon.
cedarwood: I Kings 9:11.
Isthmus: the Isthmus of Panama.
moidores: Coin in use in Portugal and Brazil during the early times of new world exploration.
Tyne coal: Newcastle upon Tyne, a coal-producing area in north England.

Wilfred Owen (1893–1918)

Anthem for Doomed Youth   1920

What passing-bells for these who die as cattle?
Only the monstrous anger of the guns.
Only the stuttering rifles' rapid rattle
Can patter out their hasty orisons.
5 No mockeries for them from prayers or bells,
Nor any voice of mourning save the choirs—
The shrill, demented choirs of wailing shells;
And bugles calling for them from sad shires.

What candles may be held to speed them all?
10 Not in the hands of boys, but in their eyes
Shall shine the holy glimmers of good-byes.
The pallor of girls' brows shall be their pall;
Their flowers the tenderness of patient minds,
And each slow dusk a drawing-down of blinds.

Langston Hughes (1902–1967)

Theme for English B   1951

The instructor said,

   Go home and write
   a page tonight.
   And let that page come out of you—
5 Then, it will be true.

I wonder if it's that simple?

I am twenty-two, colored, born in Winston-Salem.
I went to school there, then Durham, then here
to this college on the hill above Harlem.
I am the only colored student in my class.
The steps from the hill lead down to Harlem,   10
through a park, then I cross St. Nicholas,
Eighth Avenue, Seventh, and I come to the Y°,
the Harlem Branch Y, where I take the elevator
up to my room, sit down, and write this page: 15

It's not easy to know what is true for you or me
at twenty-two, my age. But I guess I'm what
I feel and see and hear. Harlem, I hear you:
hear you, hear me—we two—you, me talk on this page.
(I hear New York, too.) Me—who?   20

Well, I like to eat, sleep, drink, and be in love.
I like to work, read, learn, and understand life.
I like a pipe for a Christmas present,
or records—Bessie, bop, or Bach.°

I guess being colored doesn't make me not like   25
the same things other folks like who are other races.
So will my page be colored when I write?
Being me, it will not be white.
But it will be
a part of you, instructor.   30
You are white—
yet a part of me, as I am a part of you.
That's American.
Sometimes perhaps you don't want to be a part of me.
Nor do I often want to be part of you.   35
But we are, that's true!
As I learn from you,
I guess you learn from me—
although you're older—and white—
and somewhat more free.   40

This is my page for English B.

Harlem . . . Y: Places near Columbia University, in New York City.
Bessie: Bessie Smith (c. 1898–1937), American jazz singer, famed as "Empress of the Blues."
bop: A type of popular music in vogue from the 1930s through the 1960s; also called *bebop* and
rebop.   *Bach:* Johann Sebastian Bach (1685–1750), German composer, considered the master of
the Baroque style of music.

PLAYS

Anton Chekhov (1860–1904)

The Bear:
A Joke in One Act   1888

CAST OF CHARACTERS

> **Mrs. Popov.** *A widow of seven months,* Mrs. Popov *is small and pretty, with dimples. She is a landowner. At the start of the play, she is pining away in memory of her dead husband.*
> **Grigory Stepanovich Smirnov.** *Easily angered and loud,* Smirnov *is older. He is a landowner, too, and a gentleman farmer of substance.*
> **Luka.** *Luka is* Mrs. Popov's *footman (a servant whose main tasks were to wait table and attend the carriages, in addition to general duties.) He is old enough to feel secure in telling* Mrs. Popov *what he thinks.*
> **Gardener, Coachman, Workmen,** *who enter at the end.*

The drawing room of Mrs. Popov's *country home.*

(Mrs. Popov, *in deep mourning, does not remove her eyes from a photograph.*)

LUKA. It isn't right madam . . . you're only destroying yourself. . . . The chambermaid and the cook have gone off berry picking; every living being is rejoicing; even the cat knows how to be content, walking around the yard catching birds, and you sit in your room all day as if it were a convent, and you don't take pleasure in anything. Yes, really! Almost a year has passed since you've gone out of the house!

MRS. POPOV. And I shall never go out. . . . What for? My life is already ended. *He* lies in his grave; I have buried myself in these four walls . . . we are both dead.

LUKA. There you go again! Your husband is dead, that's as it was meant to be, it's the will of God, may he rest in peace. . . . You've done your mourning and that will do. You can't go on weeping and mourning forever. My wife died when her time came, too. . . . Well? I grieved, I wept for a month, and that was enough for her; the old lady wasn't worth a second more. (*Sighs.*) You've forgotten all your neighbors. You don't go anywhere or accept any calls. We live, so to speak, like spiders. We never see the light. The mice have eaten my uniform. It isn't as if there weren't any nice neighbors—the district is full of them . . . there's a regiment stationed at Riblov, such officers—they're like candy—you'll never get your fill of them! And in the barracks, never a Friday goes by without a dance; and, if you

Slightly altered from the Bantam Press edition of *Ten Great One-Act Plays,* Morris Sweetkind, ed. (1968).

please, the military band plays music every day. . . . Yes, madam, my dear lady: you're young, beautiful, in the full bloom of youth—if only you took a little pleasure in life . . . beauty doesn't last forever, you know! In ten years' time, you'll be wanting to wave your fanny in front of the officers—and it will be too late.

Mrs. Popov (*determined.*) I must ask you never to talk to me like that! You know that when Mr. Popov died, life lost all its salt for me. It may seem to you that I am alive, but that's only conjecture! I vowed to wear mourning to my grave and not to see the light of day. . . . Do you hear me? May his departed spirit see how much I love him. . . . Yes, I know, it's no mystery to you that he was often mean to me, cruel . . . and even unfaithful, but I shall remain true to the grave and show him I know how to love. There, beyond the grave, he will see me as I was before his death. . . .

Luka. Instead of talking like that, you should be taking a walk in the garden   5
or have Toby or Giant harnessed and go visit some of the neighbors . . .

Mrs. Popov. Ai! (*She weeps.*)

Luka. Madam! Dear lady! What's the matter with you! Christ be with you!

Mrs. Popov. Oh, how he loved Toby! He always used to ride on him to visit the Korchagins or the Vlasovs. How wonderfully he rode! How graceful he was when he pulled at the reins with all his strength! Do you remember? Toby, Toby! Tell them to give him an extra bag of oats today.

Luka. Yes, madam.

(*Sound of loud ringing.*)

Mrs. Popov (*shudders*). Who's that? Tell them I'm not at home!   10

Luka. Of course, madam. (*He exits.*)

Mrs. Popov (*alone. Looks at the photograph.*) You will see, Nicholas, how much I can love and forgive . . . my love will die only when I do, when my poor heart stops beating. (*Laughing through her tears.*) Have you no shame? I'm a good girl, a virtuous little wife. I've locked myself in and I'll be true to you to the grave, and you . . . aren't you ashamed, you chubby cheeks? You deceived me, you made scenes, for weeks on end you left me alone . . .

Luka (*enters, alarmed*). Madam, somebody is asking for you. He wants to see you. . . .

Mrs. Popov. But didn't you tell them that since the death of my husband, I don't see anybody?

Luka. I did, but he didn't want to listen; he spoke about some very impor-   15
tant business.

Mrs. Popov. I am *not at home!*

Luka. That's what I told him . . . but . . . the devil . . . he cursed and pushed past me right into the room . . . he's in the dining room right now.

Mrs. Popov (*losing her temper*). Very well, let him come in . . . such manners! (Luka *goes out.*) How difficult these people are! What does he want from me? Why should he disturb my peace? (*Sighs.*) But it's obvious I'll have to go live in a convent. . . . (*Thoughtfully.*) Yes, a convent. . . .

Smirnov (*to* Luka). You idiot, you talk too much. . . . Ass! (*Sees* Mrs. Popov *and changes to dignified speech.*) Madam, may I introduce myself: retired lieutenant of the artillery and landowner, Grigory Stepanovich Smirnov! I feel the necessity of troubling you about a highly important matter. . . .

Mrs. Popov (*refusing her hand*). What do you want?   20

SMIRNOV.   Your late husband, whom I had the pleasure of knowing, has remained in my debt for two twelve-hundred-ruble notes. Since I must pay the interest at the agricultural bank tomorrow, I have come to ask you, madam, to pay me the money today.

MRS. POPOV.   One thousand two hundred. . . .And why was my husband in debt to you?

SMIRNOV.   He used to buy oats from me.

MRS. POPOV. (*sighing, to* LUKA).   So, Luka, don't you forget to tell them to give Toby an extra bag of oats.

(LUKA *goes out*.)

(*To* SMIRNOV).   If Nikolai, my husband, was in debt to you, then it goes without saying that I'll pay; but please excuse me today. I haven't any spare cash. The day after tomorrow, my steward will be back from town and I will give him instructions to pay you what is owed; until then I cannot comply with your wishes. . . . Besides, today is the anniversary—exactly seven months ago my husband died, and I'm in such a mood that I'm not quite disposed to occupy myself with money matters.

25   SMIRNOV.   And I'm in such a mood that if I don't pay the interest tomorrow, I'll be owing so much that my troubles will drown me. They'll take away my estate!

MRS. POPOV.   You'll receive your money the day after tomorrow.

SMIRNOV.   I don't want the money the day after tomorrow. I want it today.

MRS. POPOV.   You must excuse me. I can't pay you today.

SMIRNOV.   And I can't wait until after tomorrow.

30   SMIRNOV.   What can I do, if I don't have it now?

SMIRNOV.   You mean to say you can't pay?

MRS. POPOV.   I can't pay. . . .

SMIRNOV.   Hm! Is that your last word?

MRS. POPOV.   That is my last word.

35   SMIRNOV.   Positively the last?

MRS. POPOV.   Positively.

SMIRNOV.   Thank you very much. We'll make a note of that. (*Shrugs his shoulders.*) And people want me to be calm and collected! Just now, on the way here, I met a tax officer and he asked me: why are you always so angry, Grigory Stepanovich? Goodness' sake, how can I be anything but angry? I need money desperately . . . I rode out yesterday early in the morning, at daybreak, and went to see all my debtors; and if only one of them had paid his debt . . . I was dog-tired, spent the night God knows where—a Jewish tavern beside a barrel of vodka. . . . Finally I got here, fifty miles from home, hoping to be paid, and you treat me to a "mood." How can I help being angry?

MRS. POPOV.   It seems to me that I clearly said: My steward will return from the country and then you will be paid.

SMIRNOV.   I didn't come to your steward, but to you! What the hell, if you'll pardon the expression, would I do with your steward?

40   MRS. POPOV.   Excuse me, my dear sir, I am not accustomed to such unusual expressions nor such a tone. I'm not listening to you any more. (*Goes out quickly.*)

SMIRNOV (*alone*).   Well, how do you like that? "A mood." . . . "Husband died seven months ago"! Must I pay the interest or mustn't I? I ask you: Must I pay, or must I not? So, your husband's dead, and you're in a mood and all that finicky stuff

. . . and your steward's away somewhere; may he drop dead. What do you want me to do? Do you think I can fly away from my creditors in a balloon or something? Or should I run and bash my head against the wall? I go to Gruzdev—and he's not at home; Yaroshevich is hiding, with Kuritsin it's a quarrel to the death and I almost throw him out the window; Mazutov has diarrhea, and this one is in a "mood." Not one of these swine wants to pay me! And all because I'm too nice to them. I'm a sniveling idiot, I'm spineless, I'm an old lady! I'm too delicate with them! So, just you wait! You'll find out what I'm like! I won't let you play around with me, you devils! I'll stay and stick it out until she pays. Rrr! . . . How furious I am today, how furious! I'm shaking inside from rage and I can hardly catch my breath. . . .Damn it! My God, I even feel sick! (*He shouts.*) Hey, you!

LUKA (*enters*).   What do you want?

SMIRNOV.   Give me some beer or some water! (LUKA *exits.*)   What logic is there in this! A man needs money desperately, it's like a noose around his neck—and she won't pay because, you see, she's not disposed to occupy herself with money matters! . . . That's the logic of a woman! That's why I never did like and do not like to talk to women. I'd rather sit on a keg of gunpowder than talk to a woman. Brr! . . . I even have goose pimples, this broad has put me in such a rage! All I have to do is see one of those spoiled bitches from a distance, and I get so angry it gives me a cramp in the leg. I just want to shout for help.

LUKA (*entering with water.*)   Madam is sick and won't see anyone.

SMIRNOV.   Get out! (LUKA *goes.*)   Sick and won't see anyone! No need to see   45
me . . . I'll stay and sit here until you give me the money. You can stay sick for a week, and I'll stay for a week . . . if you're sick for a year, I'll stay a year . . . I'll get my own back, dear lady! You can't impress me with your widow's weeds and your dimpled cheeks . . . we know all about those dimples! (*Shouts through the window.*) Semyon, unharness the horses! We're not going away quite yet! I'm staying here! Tell them in the stable to give the horses some oats! You brute, you let the horse on the left side get all tangled up in the reins again! (*Teasing.*) "Never mind". . . I'll give you a never mind! (*Goes away from the window.*) Shit! The heat is unbearable and nobody pays up. I slept badly last night and on top of everything else this broad in mourning is "in a mood". . . my head aches . . . (*Drinks, and grimaces.*) Shit! This is water! What I need is a drink! (*Shouts.*) Hey, you!

LUKA (*enters*).   What is it?

SMIRNOV.   Give me a glass of vodka. (LUKA *goes out.*) Oof! (*Sits down and examines himself.*) Nobody would say I was looking well! Dusty all over, boots dirty, unwashed, unkempt, straw on my waistcoat. . . .The dear lady probably took me for a robber. (*Yawns.*) It's not very polite to present myself in a drawing room looking like this; oh well, who cares? . . . I'm not here as a visitor but as a creditor, and there's no official costume for creditors. . . .

LUKA (*enters with vodka*).   You're taking liberties, my good man. . . .

SMIRNOV (*angrily*).   What?

LUKA.   I . . . nothing . . . I only . . .

SMIRNOV.   Who are you talking to? Shut up!   50

LUKA (*aside*).   The devil sent this leech. An ill wind brought him. . . . (LUKA *goes out.*)

SMIRNOV.   Oh how furious I am! I'm so mad I could crush the whole world into a powder! I even feel faint! (*Shouts.*) Hey, you!

MRS. POPOV (*enters, eyes downcast*).   My dear sir, in my solitude, I have long ago grown unaccustomed to the masculine voice and I cannot bear shouting. I must request you not to disturb my peace and quiet!

55   SMIRNOV.   Pay me my money and I'll go.

    MRS. POPOV.   I told you in plain language: I haven't any spare cash now; wait until the day after tomorrow.

    SMIRNOV.   And I also told you respectfully, in plain language: I don't need the money the day after tomorrow, but today. If you don't pay me today, then tomorrow I'll have to hang myself.

    MRS. POPOV.   But what can I do if I don't have the money? You're so strange!

    SMIRNOV.   Then you won't pay me now? No?

60   MRS. POPOV.   I can't. . . .

    SMIRNOV.   In that case, I can stay here and wait until you pay. . . . (*Sits down.*) You'll pay the day after tomorrow? Excellent! In that case I'll stay here until the day after tomorrow. I'll sit here all that time . . . (*Jumps up.*) I ask you: Have I got to pay the interest tomorrow, or not? Or do you think I'm joking?

    MRS. POPOV.   My dear sir, I ask you not to shout! This isn't a stable!

    SMIRNOV.   I wasn't asking you about a stable but about this: Do I have to pay the interest tomorrow or not?

    MRS. POPOV.   You don't know how to behave in the company of a lady!

65   SMIRNOV.   No, I don't know how to behave in the company of a lady!

    MRS. POPOV.   No, you don't! You are an ill-bred, rude man! Respectable people don't talk to a woman like that!

    SMIRNOV.   Ach, it's astonishing! How would you like me to talk to you? In French, perhaps? (*Lisps in anger.*) Madam, je vous prie° . . . how happy I am that you're not paying me the money. . . . Ah, pardon, I've made you uneasy! Such lovely weather we're having today! And you look so becoming in your mourning dress. (*Bows and scrapes.*)

    MRS. POPOV.   That's rude and not very clever!

    SMIRNOV (*teasing*).   Rude and not very clever! I don't know how to behave in the company of ladies. Madam, in my time I've seen far more women than you've seen sparrows. Three times I've fought duels over women; I've jilted twelve women, nine have jilted me! Yes! There was a time when I played the fool; I became sentimental over women, used honeyed words, fawned on them, bowed and scraped. . . . I loved, suffered, sighed at the moon; I became limp, melted, shivered . . . I loved passionately, madly, every which way, devil take me, I chattered away like a magpie about the emancipation of women, ran through half my fortune as a result of my tender feelings; but now, if you will excuse me, I'm on to your ways! I've had enough! Dark eyes, passionate eyes, ruby lips, dimpled cheeks; the moon, whispers, bated breath—for all that I wouldn't give a good goddamn. Present company excepted, of course, but all women, young and old alike, are affected clowns, gossips, hateful, consummate liars to the marrow of their bones, vain, trivial, ruthless, outrageously illogical, and as far as this is concerned (*taps on his forehead*), well, excuse my frankness, any sparrow could give pointers to a philosopher in petticoats! Look at one of those romantic creatures: muslin, ethereal demigoddess, a thousand raptures, and you look into her soul—a common crocodile! (*Grips the back of a chair; the chair cracks and breaks.*) But the most revolting part of it

Madam, je vous prie: Madam, I beg you.

all is that this crocodile imagines that she has, above everything, her own privilege, a monopoly on tender feelings. The hell with it—you can hang me upside down by that nail if a woman is capable of loving anything besides a lapdog. All she can do when she's in love is slobber! While the man suffers and sacrifices, all her love is expressed in playing with her skirt and trying to lead him around firmly by the nose. You have the misfortune of being a woman, you know yourself what the nature of a woman is like. Tell me honestly; Have you ever in your life seen a woman who is sincere, faithful, and constant? You never have! Only old and ugly ladies are faithful and constant! You're more liable to meet a horned cat or a white woodcock than a faithful woman!

MRS. POPOV.   Pardon me, but in your opinion, who is faithful and constant in   70
love? The man?

SMIRNOV.   Yes, the man!

MRS. POPOV.   The man! (*Malicious laugh.*) Men are faithful and constant in love! That's news! (*Heatedly*) What right have you to say that? Men are faithful and constant! For that matter, as far as I know, of all the men I have known and now know, my late husband was the best. . . . I loved him passionately, with all my being, as only a young intellectual woman can love; I gave him my youth, my happiness, my life, my fortune; he was my life's breath; I worshipped him as if I were a heathen, and . . . and, what good did it do—this best of men himself deceived me shamelessly at every step of the way. After his death, I found his desk full of love letters; and when he was alive—it's terrible to remember—he used to leave me alone for weeks at a time, and before my very eyes he flirted with other women and deceived me. He squandered my money, made a mockery of my feelings . . . and, in spite of all that, I loved him and was true to him . . . and besides, now that he is dead, I am still faithful and constant. I have shut myself up in these four walls forever and I won't remove these widow's weeds until my dying day. . . .

SMIRNOV.   (*laughs contemptuously*).   Widow's weeds! . . . I don't know what you take me for! As if I didn't know why you wear that black outfit and bury yourself in these four walls! Well, well! It's no secret, so romantic! When some fool of a poet passes by this country house, he'll look up at your window and think: "Here lives the mysterious Tamara, who, for the love of her husband, buried herself in these four walls." We know these tricks!

MRS. POPOV.(*flaring*).   What? How dare you say that to me?

SMIRNOV.   You may have buried yourself alive, but you haven't forgotten to   75
powder yourself!

MRS. POPOV.   How dare you use such expressions with me?

SMIRNOV.   Please don't shout. I'm not your steward! You must allow me to call a spade a spade. I'm not a woman and I'm used to saying what's on my mind! Don't you shout at me!

MRS. POPOV.   I'm not shouting, you are! Please leave me in peace!

SMIRNOV.   Pay me my money and I'll go.

MRS. POPOV.   I won't give you any money!   80

SMIRNOV.   Yes, you will.

MRS. POPOV.   To spite you, I won't pay you anything. You can leave me in peace!

SMIRNOV.   I don't have the pleasure of being either your husband or your fiancé, so please don't make scenes! (*Sits down*). I don't like it.

Mrs. Popov (*choking with rage*).   You're sitting down?
85 Smirnov.   Yes, I am.
Mrs. Popov.   I ask you to get out!
Smirnov.   Give me my money . . . (*Aside.*) Oh, I'm so furious! Furious!
Mrs. Popov.   I don't want to talk to impudent people! Get out of here! (*Pause.*)
You're not going? No?
Smirnov.   No.
90 Mrs. Popov.   No?
Smirnov.   No!
Mrs. Popov.   We'll see about that. (*Rings.*)

(Luka *enters.*)

Luka, show the gentleman out!
Luka (*goes up to* Smirnov).   Sir, will you please leave, as you have been asked.
You mustn't . . .
Smirnov (*jumping up*).   Shut up! Who do you think you're talking to? I'll
make mincemeat out of you!
95 Luka (*his hand to his heart*).   Oh, my God! Saints above! (*Falls into chair.*) Oh,
I feel ill! I feel ill! I can't catch my breath!
Mrs. Popov.   Where's Dasha? Dasha! (*She shouts.*) Dasha! Pelagea! Dasha!
(*She rings.*)
Luka.   Oh! They've all gone berry picking . . . there's nobody at home . . .
I'm ill! Water!
Mrs. Popov.   Will you please get out!
Smirnov.   Will you please be more polite?
100 Mrs. Popov (*clenches her fist and stamps her feet*).   You're nothing but a crude
bear! A brute! A monster!
Smirnov.   What? What did you say?
Mrs. Popov.   I said that you were a bear, a monster!
Smirnov (*advancing toward her*).   Excuse me, but what right do you have to
insult me?
Mrs. Popov.   Yes, I am insulting you . . . so what? Do you think I'm afraid
of you?
105 Smirnov.   And do you think just because you're one of those romantic cre-
ations, that you have the right to insult me with impunity? Yes? I challenge you!
Luka.   Lord in Heaven! Saints above! . . . Water!
Smirnov.   Pistols!
Mrs. Popov.   Do you think just because you have big fists and you can bellow
like a bull, that I'm afraid of you? You're such a bully!
Smirnov.   I challenge you! I'm not going to let anybody insult me, and I don't
care if you are a woman, a delicate creature!
110 Mrs. Popov (*trying to get a word in edgewise*).   Bear! Bear! Bear!
Smirnov.   It's about time we got rid of the prejudice that only men must pay
for their insults! Devil take it, if women want to be equal, they should behave as
equals! Let's fight!
Mrs. Popov.   You want to fight! By all means!
Smirnov.   This minute!
Mrs. Popov.   This minute! My husband had some pistols . . . I'll go and get

them right away. (*Goes hurriedly and then returns.*) What pleasure I'll have putting a bullet through that thick head of yours! The hell with you! (*she goes out.*)

SMIRNOV.   I'll shoot her down like a chicken! I'm not a little boy or a senti-   115
mental puppy. I don't care if she is delicate and fragile.

LUKA.   Kind sir! Holy father! (*Kneels.*) Have pity on a poor old man and go away from here! You've frightened her to death and now you're going to shoot her?

SMIRNOV (*not listening to him*).   If she fights, then it means she believes in equality of rights and emancipation of women. Here the sexes are equal! I'll shoot her like a chicken! But what a woman! (*Imitates her.*) "The hell with you! . . . I'll put a bullet through that thick head of yours! . . ." What a woman! How she blushed, her eyes shone . . . she accepted the challenge! To tell the truth, it was the first time in my life I've seen a woman like that. . . .

LUKA   Dear sir, please go away! I'll pray to God on your behalf as long as I live!

SMIRNOV.   That's a woman for you! A woman like that I can understand! A real woman! Not a sour-faced nincompoop but fiery, gunpowder! Fireworks! I'm even sorry to have to kill her!

LUKA (*weeps.*)   Dear sir . . . go away!   120

SMIRNOV.   I positively like her! Positively! Even though she has dimpled cheeks, I like her! I'm almost ready to forget about the debt. . . . My fury has diminished. Wonderful woman!

MRS. POPOV (*enters with pistols*).   Here they are, the pistols. Before we fight, you must show me how to fire. . . . I've never had a pistol in my hands before . . .

LUKA.   Oh dear Lord, for pity's sake. . . . I'll go and find the gardener and the coachman. . . . What did we do to deserve such trouble? (*Exit.*)

SMIRNOV (*examining the pistols*)   You see, there are several sorts of pistols . . . there are special dueling pistols, the Mortimer with primers. Then there are Smith and Wesson revolvers, triple action with extractors . . . excellent pistols! . . . they cost a minimum of ninety rubles a pair. . . . You must hold the revolver like this . . . (*Aside.*) What eyes, what eyes! A woman to set you on fire!

MRS. POPOV.   Like this?   125

SMIRNOV.   Yes, like this . . . then you cock the pistol . . . take air . . . put your head back a little . . . stretch your arm out all the way . . . that's right . . . then with this finger press on this little piece of goods . . . and that's all there is to do . . . but the most important thing is not to get excited and aim without hurrying . . . try to keep your arm from shaking.

MRS. POPOV.   Good . . . it's not comfortable to shoot indoors. Let's go into the garden.

SMIRNOV.   Let's go. But I'm giving you advance notice that I'm going to fire into the air.

MRS. POPOV.   That's the last straw! Why?

SMIRNOV.   Why? . . . Why . . . because it's my business, that's why.   130

MRS. POPOV.   Are you afraid? Yes? Aahhh! No, sir. You're not going to get out of it that easily! Be so good as to follow me! I will not rest until I've put a hole through your forehead . . . that forehead I hate so much! Are you afraid?

SMIRNOV.   Yes, I'm afraid.

MRS. POPOV.   You're lying! Why don't you want to fight?

SMIRNOV.   Because . . . because you . . . because I like you.

135   MRS. POPOV. (*laughs angrily*).   He likes me! He dares say that he likes me! (*Points to the door.*) Out!

SMIRNOV (*loads the revolver in silence, takes cap and goes; at the door, stops for half a minute while they look at each other in silence; then he approaches* MRS. POPOV *hesitantly*). Listen. . . . Are you still angry? I'm extremely irritated, but, do you understand me, how can I express it . . . the fact is, that, you see, strictly speaking . . . (*He shouts.*) Is it my fault, really, for liking you? (*Grabs the back of a chair, which cracks and breaks.*) Why the hell do you have such fragile furniture! I like you! Do you understand? I . . . I'm almost in love with you!

MRS. POPOV.   Get away from me—I hate you!

SMIRNOV.   God, what a woman! I've never in my life seen anything like her! I'm lost! I'm done for! I'm caught like a mouse in a trap!

MRS. POPOV.   Stand back or I'll shoot!

140   SMIRNOV.   Shoot! You could never understand what happiness it would be to die under the gaze of those wonderful eyes, to be shot by a revolver which was held by those little velvet hands. . . . I've gone out of my mind! Think about it and decide right away, because if I leave here, then we'll never see each other again! Decide . . . I'm a nobleman, a respectable gentleman, of good family. I have an income of ten thousand a year. . . .I can put a bullet through a coin tossed in the air . . . I have some fine horses. . . .Will you be my wife?

MRS. POPOV (*indignantly brandishes her revolver*).   Let's fight! I challenge you!

SMIRNOV.   I'm out of my mind . . . I don't understand anything . . . (*Shouts.*) Hey, you, water!

MRS. POPOV (*shouts*).   Let's fight!

SMIRNOV.   I've gone out of my mind. I'm in love like a boy, like an idiot! (*He grabs her hand, she screams with pain.*) I love you! (*Kneels.*) I love you as I've never loved before! I've jilted twelve women, nine women have jilted me, but I've never loved one of them as I love you. . . . I'm weak, I'm a limp rag. . . . I'm on my knees like a fool, offering you my hand. . . . Shame, shame! I haven't been in love for five years, I vowed I wouldn't; and suddenly I'm in love, like a fish out of water. I'm offering my hand in marriage. Yes or no? You don't want to? You don't need to! (*Gets up and quickly goes to the door.*)

145   MRS. POPOV.   Wait!

SMIRNOV (*stops*).   Well?

MRS. POPOV.   Nothing . . . you can go . . . go away . . . wait . . . No, get out, get out! I hate you! But—don't go! Oh, if you only knew how furious I am, how angry! (*Throws revolver on table.*) My fingers are swollen from that nasty thing. . . . (*Tears her handkerchief furiously.*) What are you waiting for? Get out!

SMIRNOV.   Farewell!

MRS. POPOV.   Yes, yes, go away! (*Shouts.*) Where are you going? Stop. . . . Oh, go away! Oh, how furious I am! Don't come near me! Don't come near me!

150   SMIRNOV (*approaching her*).   How angry I am with myself! I'm in love like a student. I've been on my knees. . . . It gives me the shivers. (*Rudely.*) I love you! A lot of good it will do me to fall in love with you! Tomorrow I've got to pay the interest, begin the mowing of the hay. (*Puts his arm around her waist.*) I'll never forgive myself for this. . . .

MRS. POPOV.   Get away from me! Get your hands away! I . . . hate you! I . . . challenge you!

(*Prolonged kiss.* LUKA *enters with an ax, the* GARDENER *with a rake, the* COACHMAN *with a pitchfork, and* WORKMAN *with cudgels.*)

LUKA (*catches sight of the pair kissing*).   Lord in heaven! (*Pause.*)   *155*

MRS. POPOV (*lowering her eyes*).   Luka, tell them in the stable not to give Toby any oats today.

CURTAIN

Susan Glaspell (1882–1948)

Trifles   1916

CAST OF CHARACTERS

George Henderson, *county attorney*
Henry Peters, *sheriff*
Lewis Hale, *a neighboring farmer*
Mrs. Peters
Mrs. Hale

Scene.*The kitchen in the now abandoned farmhouse of John Wright, a gloomy kitchen, and left without having been put in order—unwashed pans under the sink, a loaf of bread outside the breadbox, a dish towel on the table—other signs of incompleted work. At the rear the outer door opens and the Sheriff comes in followed by the County Attorney and Hale. The Sheriff and Hale are men in middle life, the County Attorney is a young man; all are much bundled up and go at once to the stove. They are followed by two women—the Sheriff's wife first; she is a slight wiry woman, a thin nervous face. Mrs. Hale is larger and would ordinarily be called more comfortable looking, but she is disturbed now and looks fearfully about as she enters. The women have come in slowly, and stand close together near the door.*

COUNTY ATTORNEY. (*Rubbing his hands.*)   This feels good. Come up to the fire, ladies.

MRS. PETERS. (*After taking a step forward.*)   I'm not—cold.

SHERIFF. (*Unbuttoning his overcoat and stepping away from the stove as if to mark the beginning of official business.*)   Now, Mr. Hale, before we move things about, you explain to Mr. Henderson just what you saw when you came here yesterday morning.

COUNTY ATTORNEY.   By the way, has anything been moved? Are things just as you left them yesterday?

5   SHERIFF. (*Looking about.*)   It's just the same. When it dropped below zero last night I thought I'd better send Frank out this morning to make a fire for us—no use getting pneumonia with a big case on, but I told him not to touch anything except the stove—and you know Frank.

COUNTY ATTORNEY.   Somebody should have been left here yesterday.

SHERIFF.   Oh—yesterday. When I had to send Frank to Morris Center for that man who went crazy—I want you to know I had my hands full yesterday, I knew you could get back from Omaha by today and as long as I went over everything here myself—

COUNTY ATTORNEY.   Well, Mr. Hale, tell just what happened when you came here yesterday morning.

HALE.   Harry and I had started to town with a load of potatoes. We came along the road from my place and as I got here I said, "I'm going to see if I can't get John Wright to go in with me on a party telephone." I spoke to Wright about it once before and he put me off, saying folks talked too much anyway, and all he asked was peace and quiet—I guess you know about how much he talked himself; but I thought maybe if I went to the house and talked about it before his wife, though I said to Harry that I didn't know as what his wife wanted made much difference to John—

10   COUNTY ATTORNEY.   Let's talk about that later, Mr. Hale. I do want to talk about that, but tell now just what happened when you got to the house.

HALE.   I didn't hear or see anything; I knocked at the door, and still it was all quiet inside. I knew they must be up, it was past eight o'clock. So I knocked again, and I thought I heard somebody say, "Come in." I wasn't sure, I'm not sure yet, but I opened the door—this door (*Indicating the door by which the two women are still standing*) and there in that rocker— (*Pointing to it*) sat Mrs. Wright.

(*They all look at the rocker.*)

COUNTY ATTORNEY.   What—was she doing?

HALE.   She was rockin' back and forth. She had her apron in her hand and was kind of—pleating it.

COUNTY ATTORNEY.   And how did she—look?

15   HALE.   Well, she looked queer.

COUNTY ATTORNEY.   How do you mean—queer?

HALE.   Well, as if she didn't know what she was going to do next. And kind of done up.

COUNTY ATTORNEY.   How did she seem to feel about your coming?

HALE.   Why, I don't think she minded—one way or other. She didn't pay much attention. I said, "How do, Mrs. Wright, it's cold, ain't it?" She said, "Is it?"—and went on kind of pleating at her apron. Well, I was surprised; she didn't ask me to come up to the stove, or to set down, but just sat there, not even looking at me, so I said, "I want to see John." And then she—laughed. I guess you would call it a laugh. I thought of Harry and the team outside, so I said a little sharp: "Can't I see John?" "No," she says, kind o' dull like. "Ain't he home?" says I. "Yes," says she, "he's home." "Then why can't I see him?" I asked her, out of patience. " 'Cause he's dead," says she. "*Dead?*" says I. She just nodded her head, not getting a bit excited, but rockin' back and forth. "Why—where is he?" says I, not knowing what to say. She just pointed upstairs—like that (*Himself pointing to the room above*). I got up, with the idea of going up there. I walked from there to here—then I says, "Why, what did he die of?" "He died of a rope round his neck," says she, and just went on pleatin' at her apron. Well, I went out and called Harry. I thought I might—need help. We went upstairs and there he was lyin'—

COUNTY ATTORNEY. I think I'd rather have you go into that upstairs, where   20
you can point it all out. Just go on now with the rest of the story.

HALE. Well, my first thought was to get that rope off. It looked . . . (*Stops, his face twitches*) . . . but Harry, he went up to him, and he said, "No, he's dead all right, and we'd better not touch anything." So we went back down stairs. She was still sitting that same way. "Has anybody been notified?" I asked. "No," says she, unconcerned. "Who did this, Mrs. Wright?" said Harry. He said it businesslike—and she stopped pleatin' of her apron. "I don't know," she says. "You don't *know*?" says Harry. "No," says she. "Weren't you sleepin' in the bed with him?" says Harry. "Yes," says she, "but I was on the inside." "Somebody slipped a rope round his neck and strangled him and you didn't wake up?" says Harry. "I didn't wake up," she said after him. We must 'a looked as if we didn't see how that could be, for after a minute she said, "I sleep sound." Harry was going to ask her more questions but I said maybe we ought to let her tell her story first to the coroner, or the sheriff, so Harry went fast as he could to Rivers' place, where there's a telephone.

COUNTY ATTORNEY. And what did Mrs. Wright do when she knew that you had gone for the coroner?

HALE. She moved from that chair to this one over here (*Pointing to a small chair in the corner*) and just sat there with her hands held together and looking down. I got a feeling that I ought to make some conversation, so I said I had come in to see if John wanted to put in a telephone, and at that she started to laugh, and then she stopped and looked at me—scared. (*The County Attorney, who has had his notebook out, makes a note.*) I dunno, maybe it wasn't scared. I wouldn't like to say it was. Soon Harry got back, and then Dr. Lloyd came, and you, Mr. Peters, and so I guess that's all I know that you don't.

COUNTY ATTORNEY. (*Looking around.*) I guess we'll go upstairs first—and then out to the barn and around there. (*To the Sheriff*) You're convinced that there was nothing important here—nothing that would point to any motive.

SHERIFF. Nothing here but kitchen things.   25

(*The County Attorney, after again looking around the kitchen, opens the door of a cupboard closet. He gets up on a chair and looks on a shelf. Pulls his hand away, sticky.*)

COUNTY ATTORNEY. Here's a nice mess.

(*The women draw nearer.*)

MRS. PETERS. (*To the other woman.*) Oh, her fruit; it did freeze. (*To the County Attorney*) She worried about that when it turned so cold. She said the fire'd go out and her jars would break.

SHERIFF. Well, can you beat the women! Held for murder and worryin' about her preserves.

COUNTY ATTORNEY. I guess before we're through she may have something more serious than preserves to worry about.

HALE. Well, women are used to worrying over trifles.   30
(*The two women move a little closer together.*)

COUNTY ATTORNEY. (*With the gallantry of a young politician.*) And yet, for all their worries, what would we do without the ladies? (*The women do not unbend. He goes to the sink, takes a dipperful of water from the pail and pouring it into a basin, washes his hands. Starts to wipe them on the roller towel, turns it for a cleaner place.*) Dirty towels! (*Kicks his foot against the pans under the sink.*) Not much of a housekeeper, would you say, ladies?

MRS. HALE. (*Stiffly.*) There's a great deal of work to be done on a farm.

COUNTY ATTORNEY. To be sure. And yet (*With a little bow to her*) I know there are some Dickson county farmhouses which do not have such roller towels.

(*He gives it a pull to expose its full length again.*)

MRS. HALE. Those towels get dirty awful quick. Men's hands aren't always as clean as they might be.

35   COUNTY ATTORNEY. Ah, loyal to your sex, I see. But you and Mrs. Wright were neighbors. I suppose you were friends, too.

MRS. HALE. (*Shaking her head.*) I've not seen much of her of late years. I've not been in this house—it's more than a year.

COUNTY ATTORNEY. And why was that? You didn't like her?

MRS. HALE. I liked her all well enough. Farmers' wives have their hands full, Mr. Henderson. And then—

COUNTY ATTORNEY. Yes—?

40   MRS. HALE. (*Looking about.*) It never seemed a very cheerful place.

COUNTY ATTORNEY. No—it's not cheerful. I shouldn't say she had the home-making instinct.

MRS. HALE. Well, I don't know as Wright had, either.

COUNTY ATTORNEY. You mean that they didn't get on very well?

MRS. HALE. No, I don't mean anything. But I don't think a place'd be any cheerfuller for John Wright's being in it.

45   COUNTY ATTORNEY. I'd like to talk more of that a little later. I want to get the lay of things upstairs now.

(*He goes to the left, where three steps lead to a stair door.*)

SHERIFF. I suppose anything Mrs. Peter does'll be all right. She was to take in some clothes for her, you know, and a few little things. We left in such a hurry yesterday.

COUNTY ATTORNEY. Yes, but I would like to see what you take, Mrs. Peters, and keep an eye out for anything that might be of use to us.

MRS. PETERS. Yes, Mr. Henderson.

(*The women listen to the men's steps on the stairs, then look about the kitchen.*)

MRS. HALE. I'd hate to have men coming into my kitchen, snooping around and criticising.

(*She arranges the pans under the sink which the County Attorney had shoved out of place.*)

50   MRS. PETERS. Of course it's no more than their duty.

MRS. HALE. Duty's all right, but I guess that deputy sheriff that came out to make the fire might have got a little of this on. (*Gives the roller towel a pull.*) Wish I'd thought of that sooner. Seems mean to talk about her for not having things slicked up when she had to come away in such a hurry.

MRS. PETERS. (*Who has gone to a small table in the left rear corner of the room, and lifted one end of a towel that covers a pan.*) She had bread set.

(*Stands still.*)

MRS. HALE. (*Eyes fixed on a loaf of bread beside the breadbox, which is on a low shelf at the other side of the room. Moves slowly toward it.*) She was going to put this in there. (*Picks up loaf, then abruptly drops it. In a manner of returning to familiar things.*) It's a shame about her fruit. I wonder if it's all gone. (*Gets up on the chair and looks.*) I think there's some here that's all right, Mrs. Peters. Yes—here; (*Holding it toward the window*) this is cherries, too. (*Looking again.*) I declare I believe that's the only one. (*Gets down, bottle in her hand. Goes to the sink and wipes it off on the outside.*) She'll feel awful bad after all her hard work in the hot weather. I remember the afternoon I put up my cherries last summer.

(*She puts the bottle on the big kitchen table, center of the room. With a sigh, is about to sit down in the rocking-chair. Before she is seated realizes what chair it is; with a slow look at it, steps back. The chair which she has touched rocks back and forth.*)

MRS. PETERS. Well, I must get those things from the front room closet. (*She goes to the door at the right, but after looking into the other room, steps back.*) You coming with me, Mrs. Hale? You could help me carry them.

(*They go in the other room; reappear, Mrs. Peters carrying a dress and skirt, Mrs. Hale following with a pair of shoes.*)

MRS. PETERS. My, it's cold in there.   55

(*She puts the clothes on the big table, and hurries to the stove.*)

MRS. HALE. (*Examining her skirt*). Wright was close. I think maybe that's why she kept so much to herself. She didn't even belong to the Ladies Aid. I suppose she felt she couldn't do her part, and then you don't enjoy things when you feel shabby. She used to wear pretty clothes and be lively, when she was Minnie Foster, one of the town girls singing in the choir. But that—oh, that was thirty years ago. This all you was to take in?

MRS. PETERS. She said she wanted an apron. Funny thing to want, for there isn't much to get you dirty in jail, goodness knows. But I suppose just to make her feel more natural. She said they was in the top drawer in this cupboard. Yes, here. And then her little shawl that always hung behind the door. (*Opens stair door and looks.*) Yes, here it is.

(*Quickly shuts door leading upstairs.*)

MRS. HALE. (*Abruptly moving toward her.*) Mrs. Peters?
MRS. PETERS. Yes, Mrs. Hale?
MRS. HALE. Do you think she did it?   60
MRS. PETERS. (*In a frightened voice.*) Oh, I don't know.
MRS. HALE. Well, I don't think she did. Asking for an apron and her little shawl. Worrying about her fruit.

MRS. PETERS. (*Starts to speak, glances up, where footsteps are heard in the room above. In a low voice.*) Mr. Peters says it looks bad for her. Mr. Henderson is awful sarcastic in a speech and he'll make fun of her sayin' she didn't wake up.

MRS. HALE. Well, I guess John Wright didn't wake when they was slipping that rope under his neck.

65 MRS. PETERS. No, it's strange. It must have been done awful crafty and still. They say it was such a—funny way to kill a man, rigging it all up like that.

MRS. HALE. That's just what Mr. Hale said. There was a gun in the house. He says that's what he can't understand.

MRS. PETERS. Mr. Henderson said coming out that what was needed for the case was a motive; something to show anger, or—sudden feeling.

MRS. HALE. (*Who is standing by the table.*) Well, I don't see any signs of anger around here. (*She puts her hand on the dish towel which lies on the table, stands looking down at table, one half of which is clean, the other half messy.*) It's wiped to here. (*Makes a move as if to finish work, then turns and looks at loaf of bread outside the breadbox. Drops towel. In that voice of coming back to familiar things.*) Wonder how they are finding things upstairs. I hope she had it a little more red-up° up there. You know, it seems kind of *sneaking*. Locking her up in town and then coming out here and trying to get her own house to turn against her!

MRS. PETERS. But Mrs. Hale, the law is the law.

70 MRS. HALE. I s'pose 'tis. (*Unbuttoning her coat.*) Better loosen up your things, Mrs. Peters. You won't feel them when you go out.

(*Mrs. Peters takes off her fur tippet, goes to hang it on hook at back of room, stands looking at the under part of the small corner table.*)

MRS. PETERS. She was piecing a quilt.

(*She brings the large sewing basket and they look at the pieces.*)

MRS. HALE. It's a log cabin pattern. Pretty, isn't it? I wonder if she was goin' to quilt it or just knot it?

(*Footsteps have been heard coming down the stairs. The Sheriff enters followed by Hale and the County Attorney.*)

SHERIFF. They wonder if she was going to quilt it or just knot it!

(*The men laugh; the women look abashed.*)

COUNTY ATTORNEY. (*Rubbing his hands over the stove.*) Frank's fire didn't do much up there, did it? Well, let's go out to the barn and get that cleared up.

(*The men go outside.*)

75 MRS. HALE. (*Resentfully.*) I don't know as there's anything so strange, our takin' up our time with little things while we're waiting for them to get the evidence. (*She sits down at the big table smoothing out a block with decision.*) I don't see as it's anything to laugh about.

MRS. PETERS. (*Apologetically.*) Of course they've got awful important things on their minds.

red-up: neat, arranged in order

(*Pulls up a chair and joins Mrs. Hale at the table.*)

MRS. HALE. (*Examining another block.*) Mrs. Peters, look at this one. Here, this is the one she was working on, and look at the sewing! All the rest of it has been so nice and even. And look at this! It's all over the place! Why, it looks as if she didn't know what she was about!

(*After she has said this they look at each other, then start to glance back at the door. After an instant Mrs. Hale has pulled at a knot and ripped the sewing.*)

MRS. PETERS. Oh, what are you doing, Mrs. Hale?
MRS. HALE. (*Mildly.*) Just pulling out a stitch or two that's not sewed very good. (*Threading a needle.*) Bad sewing always made me fidgety.
MRS. PETERS. (*Nervously.*) I don't think we ought to touch things.   *80*
MRS. HALE. I'll just finish up this end. (*Suddenly stopping and leaning forward.*) Mrs. Peters?
MRS. PETERS. Yes, Mrs. Hale?
MRS. HALE. What do you suppose she was so nervous about?
MRS. PETERS. Oh—I don't know. I don't know as she was nervous. I sometimes sew awful queer when I'm just tired. (*Mrs. Hale starts to say something, looks at Mrs. Peters, then goes on sewing.*) Well, I must get these things wrapped up. They may be through sooner than we think. (*Putting apron and other things together.*) I wonder where I can find a piece of paper, and string.
MRS. HALE. In that cupboard, maybe.   *85*
MRS. PETERS. (*Looking in cupboard.*) Why, here's a birdcage. (*Holds it up.*) Did she have a bird, Mrs. Hale?
MRS. HALE. Why, I don't know whether she did or not—I've not been here for so long. There was a man around last year selling canaries cheap, but I don't know as she took one; maybe she did. She used to sing real pretty herself.
MRS. PETERS. (*Glancing around.*) Seems funny to think of a bird here. But she must have had one, or why would she have a cage? I wonder what happened to it.
MRS. HALE. I s'pose maybe the cat got it.
MRS. PETERS. No, she didn't have a cat. She's got that feeling some people   *90*
have about cats—being afraid of them. My cat got in her room and she was real upset and asked me to take it out.
MRS. HALE. My sister Bessie was like that. Queer, ain't it?
MRS. PETERS. (*Examining the cage.*) Why, look at this door, It's broke. One hinge is pulled apart.
MRS. HALE. (*Looking too.*) Looks as if someone must have been rough with it.
MRS. PETERS. Why, yes.

(*She brings the cage forward and puts it on the table.*)

MRS. HALE. I wish if they're going to find any evidence they'd be about it. I   *95*
don't like this place.
MRS. PETERS. But I'm awful glad you came with me, Mrs. Hale. It would be lonesome for me sitting here alone.
MRS. HALE. It would, wouldn't it? (*Dropping her sewing.*) But I tell you what I do wish, Mrs. Peters. I wish I had come over sometimes when *she* was here. I—(*Looking around the room*)—wish I had.

MRS. PETERS. But of course you were awful busy, Mrs. Hale—your house and your children.

MRS. HALE. I could've come. I stayed away because it weren't cheerful—and maybe that's why I ought to have come. I—I've never liked this place. Maybe because it's down in a hollow and you don't see the road. I dunno what it is but it's a lonesome place and always was. I wish I had come over to see Minnie Foster sometimes. I can see now—

(*Shakes her head.*)

100   MRS. PETERS. Well, you mustn't reproach yourself, Mrs. Hale. Somehow we just don't see how it is with other folks until—something comes up.

MRS. HALE. Not having children makes less work—but it makes a quiet house, and Wright out to work all day, and no company when he did come in. Did you know John Wright, Mrs. Peters?

MRS. PETERS. Not to know him; I've seen him in town. They say he was a good man.

MRS. HALE. Yes—good; he didn't drink and kept his word as well as most, I guess, and paid his debts. But he was a hard man, Mrs. Peters. Just to pass the time of day with him—(*Shivers.*) Like a raw wind that gets to the bone. (*Pauses, her eye falling on the cage.*) I should think she would 'a wanted a bird. But what do you suppose went with it?

MRS. PETERS. I don't know, unless it got sick and died.

(*She reaches over and swings the broken door, swings it again. Both women watch it.*)

105   MRS. HALE. You weren't raised round here, were you? (*Mrs. Peters shakes her head.*) You didn't know—her?

MRS. PETERS. Not till they brought her yesterday.

MRS. HALE. She—come to think of it, she was kind of like a bird herself—real sweet and pretty, but kind of timid and—fluttery. How—she—did—change. (*Silence; then as if struck by a happy thought and relieved to get back to everyday things.*) Tell you what, Mrs. Peters, why don't you take the quilt in with you? It might take up her mind.

MRS. PETERS. Why, I think that's a real nice idea, Mrs. Hale. There couldn't possibly be any objection to it, could there? Now, just what would I take? I wonder if her patches are in here—and her things.

(*They look in the sewing basket.*)

MRS. HALE. Here's some red. I expect this has got sewing things in it. (*Brings out a fancy box.*) What a pretty box. Looks like something somebody would give you. Maybe her scissors are in here. (*Opens box. Suddenly puts her hand to her nose.*) Why—(*Mrs. Peters bends nearer, then turns her face away.*) There's something wrapped up in this piece of silk.

110   MRS. PETERS. Why, this isn't her scissors.

MRS. HALE. (*Lifting the silk.*) Oh, Mrs. Peters—it's—

(*Mrs. Peters bends closer.*)

MRS. PETERS. It's the bird.

MRS. HALE. (*Jumping up.*)   But, Mrs. Peters—look at it! Its neck! Look at its neck! It's all—other side *to.*

MRS. PETERS.   Somebody—wrung—its—neck.

(*Their eyes meet. A look of growing comprehension, of horror. Steps are heard outside. Mrs. Hale slips box under quilt pieces, and sinks into her chair. Enter Sheriff and County Attorney. Mrs. Peters rises.*)

COUNTY ATTORNEY. (*As one turning from serious things to little pleasantries.*)   Well,   115
ladies, have you decided whether she was going to quilt it or knot it?

MRS. PETERS.   We think she was going to—knot it.

COUNTY ATTORNEY.   Well, that's interesting, I'm sure. (*Seeing the birdcage.*) Has the bird flown?

MRS. HALE. (*Putting more quilt pieces over the box.*)   We think the—cat got it.

COUNTY ATTORNEY. (*Preoccupied.*)   Is there a cat?

(*Mrs. Hale glances in a quick covert way at Mrs. Peters.*)

MRS. PETERS.   Well, not *now.* They're superstitious, you know. They leave.   120

COUNTY ATTORNEY. (*To Sheriff Peters, continuing an interrupted conversation.*) No sign at all of anyone having come from the outside. Their own rope. Now let's go up again and go over it piece by piece. (*They start upstairs.*) It would have to have been someone who knew just the—

(*Mrs. Peters sits down. The two women sit there not looking at one another, but as if peering into something and at the same time holding back. When they talk now it is in the manner of feeling their way over strange ground, as if afraid of what they are saying, but as if they can not help saying it.*)

MRS. HALE.   She liked the bird. She was going to bury it in that pretty box.

MRS. PETERS. (*In a whisper.*)   When I was a girl—my kitten—there was a boy took a hatchet, and before my eyes—and before I could get there—(*Covers her face an instant*) If they hadn't held me back I would have—(*Catches herself, looks upstairs where steps are heard, falters weakly*)—hurt him.

MRS. HALE. (*With a slow look around her.*)   I wonder how it would seem never to have had any children around. (*Pause.*) No, Wright wouldn't like the bird—a thing that sang. She used to sing. He killed that, too.

MRS. PETERS. (*Moving uneasily.*)   We don't know who killed the bird.   125

MRS. HALE.   I knew John Wright.

MRS. PETERS.   It was an awful thing was done in this house that night, Mrs. Hale. Killing a man while he slept, slipping a rope around his neck that choked the life out of him.

MRS. HALE.   His neck. Choked the life out of him.

(*Her hand goes out and rests on the birdcage.*)

MRS. PETERS. (*With rising voice.*)   We don't know who killed him. We don't know.

MRS. HALE. (*Her own feeling not interrupted.*)   If there'd been years and years   130
of nothing, then a bird to sing to you, it would be awful—still, after the bird was still.

MRS. PETERS. (*Something within her speaking.*)   I know what stillness is. When we homesteaded in Dakota, and my first baby died—after he was two years old, and me with no other than—

MRS. HALE. (*Moving.*)   How soon do you suppose they'll be through, looking for the evidence?

MRS. PETERS.   I know what stillness is. (*Pulling herself back.*) The law has got to punish crime, Mrs. Hale.

MRS. HALE. (*Not as if answering that.*)   I wish you'd seen Minnie Foster when she wore a white dress with blue ribbons and stood up there in the choir and sang. (*A look around the room.*) Oh, I *wish* I'd come over here once in a while! That was a crime! That was a crime! Who's going to punish that?

135 MRS. PETERS. (*Looking upstairs.*)   We mustn't—take on.

MRS. HALE.   I might have known she needed help! I know how things can be—for women. I tell you, it's queer, Mrs. Peters. We live close together and we live far apart. We all go through the same things—it's all just a different kind of the same thing. (*Brushes her eyes; noticing the bottle of fruit, reaches out for it.*) If I was you I wouldn't tell her her fruit was gone. Tell her it *ain't*. Tell her it's all right. Take this in to prove it to her. She—she may never know whether it was broke or not.

MRS. PETERS. (*Takes the bottle, looks about for something to wrap it in; takes petticoat from the clothes brought from the other room, very nervously begins winding this around the bottle. In a false voice.*)   My, it's a good thing the men couldn't hear us. Wouldn't they just laugh! Getting all stirred up over a little thing like a—dead canary. As if that could have anything to do with—with—wouldn't they *laugh*!

(*The men are heard coming down stairs.*)

MRS. HALE. (*Under her breath.*)   Maybe they would—maybe they wouldn't.

COUNTY ATTORNEY.   No, Peters, it's all perfectly clear except a reason for doing it. But you know juries when it comes to women. If there was some definite thing. Something to show—something to make a story about—a thing that would connect up with this strange way of doing it—

(*The women's eyes meet for an instant. Enter Hale from outer door.*)

140 HALE.   Well, I've got the team° around. Pretty cold out there.

COUNTY ATTORNEY.   I'm going to stay here a while by myself. (*To the Sheriff.*) You can send Frank out for me, can't you? I want to go over everything. I'm not satisfied that we can't do better.

SHERIFF.   Do you want to see what Mrs. Peters is going to take in?

(*The County Attorney goes to the table, picks up the apron, laughs.*)

COUNTY ATTORNEY.   Oh, I guess they're not very dangerous things the ladies have picked out. (*Moves a few things about, disturbing the quilt pieces which cover the box. Steps back.*) No, Mrs. Peters doesn't need supervising. For that matter, a sheriff's wife is married to the law. Ever think of it that way, Mrs. Peters?

MRS. PETERS.   Not—just that way.

145 SHERIFF. (*Chuckling*)   Married to the law. (*Moves toward the other room.*) I just

---

team: that is, a team of horses drawing a wagon, or, more probably, a sleigh.

want you to come in here a minute, George. We ought to take a look at these windows.

COUNTY ATTORNEY (*Scoffingly.*)   Oh, windows!

SHERIFF.   We'll be right out, Mr. Hale.

(*Hale goes outside. The Sheriff follows the County Attorney into the other room. Then Mrs. Hale rises, hands tight together, looking intensely at Mrs. Peters, whose eyes make a slow turn, finally meeting Mrs. Hale's. A moment Mrs. Hale holds her, then her own eyes point the way to where the box is concealed. Suddenly Mrs. Peters throws back quilt pieces and tries to put the box in the bag she is wearing. It is too big. She opens box, starts to take bird out, cannot touch it, goes to pieces, stands there helpless. Sound of a knob turning in the other room. Mrs. Hale snatches the box and puts it in the pocket of her big coat. Enter County Attorney and Sheriff.*)

COUNTY ATTORNEY. (*Facetiously.*)   Well, Henry, at least we found out that she was not going to quilt it. She was going to—what is it you call it, ladies?

MRS. HALE. (*Her hand against her pocket.*)   We call it—knot it, Mr. Henderson.

CURTAIN

A Glossary of Key Literary
Terms and Concepts

This glossary presents brief definitions of terms boldfaced in the text. Page references indicate where readers may find additional detail and illustration, together with discussions about how the concepts may be utilized in the writing of themes about literature.

Abstract diction, Language describing qualities that pertain broadly to many things (e.g., "good," "interesting," "neat," and so on), and therefore applicable to many things rather than to one or a few; distinguished from *concrete diction, 221*

Accent or **beat** (*See* Beat)

Accented rhyme (prosody), The type of *foot* on which a *rhyme* falls, such as an *iamb*, a *trochee*, and so on, *186, 191*

Accentual, strong stress, or **"sprung" rhythm (prosody),** Lines relying not on traditional meters but rather on strong stresses, *191*

Accumulation (*See* Cumulatio)

Actions, or **incidents,** The events or occurrences in a work, *51*

Acute accent (prosody), A superior diacritical mark (') used in scansion to illustrate a heavy stress, *182*

Allegory, A complete *narrative* that may also be applied to a parallel set of situations, *129–30*

Alliteration, The repetition of identical consonant sounds (most often the sounds beginning words) in close proximity (e.g., "pensive poets," "grown grey"), *181, 189*

Amphibrach (prosody), A three-syllable *foot* consisting of a light, heavy, and light stress, *185*

Amphimacer, or **cretic (prosody),** A three-syllable *foot* consisting of a heavy, light, and heavy stress, *185*

Anapest (prosody), A three-syllable *foot* consisting of two light stresses followed by a heavy stress, *184*

Antagonist, The person, idea, force, or general set of circumstances opposing the *protagonist*, an essential element of *plot, 57*

Anticipation (*See* Procatalepsis)

Antimetabole (*See* Chiasmus)

Assertion, A sentence putting an *idea* (the subject) into operation (the predicate); necessary for both expressing and understanding the idea, *98–99*

Assonance (prosody), The repetition of identical vowel sounds in different words in close proximity, *181, 188*

Atmosphere, or **mood,** The emotional aura evoked by a work, *78*

Audience, or **mythical reader,** The intended group of readers for whom a writer writes, *32*

Authorial symbols, *Symbols* that are not derived from a common cultural heritage, but that gain their symbolic meaning within the context of a particular work, *130–31*

Authorial voice (*See also* Speaker, Point of View, and Third-Person Point of View), The *voice* or *speaker* used by authors when seemingly speaking for themselves, *68, 85–86*

Bacchius, or **bacchic (prosody),** A three-syllable *foot* consisting of a light stress followed by two heavy stresses, *185*

Ballad, or **common measure (prosody),** Quatrains in which lines of iambic tetrameter alternate with iambic trimeter, rhyming X–A–X–A, X–B–X–B, etc., *193*

Beat or **accent (prosody),** The heavy stresses or accents in lines of poetry. The number of beats in a line usually dictates the meter of the line (five beats in a pentameter line, etc.), *182*

Brainstorming, The exploration and discovery of details to be used in composition, *31–32*

Breve (prosody), A superior diacritical mark, in the form of a bowl-like half circle, which indicates light stresses, *182*

Cacophony (prosody), Meaning "bad sound," *cacophony* refers to words combining sharp or harsh sounds, *189–90*

Cadence group (prosody and style), A coherent word group spoken as a single rhythmical unit, such as a noun phrase ("our sacred honor") or prepositional phrase ("of parting day"), *186*

Caesura, caesurae (prosody), The pause(s) separating phrases within lines of poetry, an important aspect of poetic *rhythm, 186*

Central idea, (1) The thesis or main idea of an *essay* or *theme, 20–24;* (2) The theme of a literary work, *99*

Character, An extended verbal representation of a human being, the inner self that determines thought, speech, and behavior, *64–74*

Chiasmus, or **antimetabole,** A rhetorical pattern in which words and also ideas are repeated in the sequence A–B–B–A, *226*

Climax (Greek for *ladder*), The high point of *conflict* and tension preceding the resolution of a drama or story; the point of decision, of inevitability and no return. The climax is sometimes merged with the *crisis* in the consideration of dramatic and narrative structure, *57, 212*

Closeup (film), A detailed camera view, such as a character's head, or even mouth or eyes, etc.; distinguished from a *longshot,* or distant view, *246*

Common measure (*See* Ballad measure)

Comparison-Contrast, A means of studying two or more works based on a common element, such as *subject, point of view,* use of *setting,* etc.; the goal of the Comparison-Contrast technique is to illuminate characteristics and qualities of each work by showing similarities (*comparison*) and differences (*contrast*), *163–79*

Complex sentence (style), A main clause together with a subordinate or dependent clause, *224*

Complication, A stage of narrative and dramatic structure in which the major *conflicts* are brought out; the *rising action* of a drama, *57, 211*

Compound-complex sentence (style), Two or more independent clauses integrating one or more dependent clauses, *224*

Compound sentence (style), Two simple sentences joined by a conjunction, *224*

Conclusion, The final section of a work. In a *theme,* the conclusion is used for matters such as a summary of major points, a brief evaluation, the suggestion of new directions, etc., *26*

Concrete diction (style), Words that describe specific qualities or properties; distinguished from *abstract diction, 221*

Conflict, The opposition between two characters, between large groups of people, or between *protagonists* and larger forces such as natural objects, ideas, modes of behavior, public opinion, and the like. Conflict may also be internal and psychological, involving choices facing a *protagonist.* Conflict is the essence of *plot, 52*

Connotation, The meanings that words suggest beyond their bare dictionary definitions, *222*

Contextual symbols (*See* Authorial symbols)

Convention, An accepted feature of a *genre,* such as the *point of view* of a *story,* the form of a *poem* (e.g., sonnet, ode), the competence or brilliance of the detective in detective fiction, or the impenetrability of disguise and concealment in a Shakespearean play, *14*

Cosmic irony, or **irony of fate,** *Situational irony* that is connected to a pessimistic or fatalistic view of life, *147*

Counting (style), The action of counting numbers of words in sentences, numbers of syllables in words, and so on, as one of the means of describing a writer's *style, 223*

Couplet (prosody), Two successive rhyming lines, *192–93*

Cretic (*See* Amphimacer)

Crisis, The point of uncertainty and tension—the *turning point*—that results from the *conflicts* and difficulties brought about through the complications of the *plot.* The crisis leads to the *climax*—that is, to the decision made by the protagonist to resolve the conflict. Sometimes the *crisis* and *climax* are considered as two elements of the same stage of plot development, *57, 211–12*

Cultural or **universal symbols,** *Symbols* recognized and shared as a result of a common social and cultural heritage, *130*

Cumulatio, The parallel building up of much detail; a short way of introducing a considerable amount of material, *226*

Dactyl (prosody), A three-syllable *foot* consisting of a heavy stress followed by two lights, *184*

Dactyllic or **triple rhyme (prosody),** Rhyming *dactyls, 191–92*

Denotation (style), The standard dictionary meaning of a word, *222–23*

Dénouement (untying), or **resolution,** The final stage of *plot* development, in which mysteries are explained, characters find their destinies, and the work is completed. Usually the dénouement is done as speedily as possible, for it occurs after all conflicts are ended, *58, 212*

Device, A *rhetorical figure* or strategy, *14, 117*

Diction, Word choice, types of words, and the level of language:

Formal diction, Proper, elevated, elaborate, and often polysyllabic language, *219–20*

Informal or **low diction,** Relaxed, conversational, and familiar language, utilizing contractions and elisions, and sometimes employing slang and grammatical mistakes, *220–21*

Middle or **neutral diction,** Correct language characterized by directness and simplicity, *220*

Digraph (prosody), Two alphabetical letters spelling one sound, as in *digraph*, where ⟨ph⟩ spells the / f / sound, *181*

Dilemma, Two choices facing a *protagonist*, usually in a tragic situation, with either choice being unacceptable or damaging; a cause of both internal and external *conflict*, *52*

Dimeter (prosody), A line consisting of two metrical feet, *182*

Dipody or **syzygy (prosody),** The submergence of two normal *feet*, usually iambs or trochees, under a stronger beat, so that a "galloping" or "rollicking" rhythm results, *185–86*

Double entendre ("double meaning"), Deliberate ambiguity, often sexual, *146–47*

Double or **trochaic rhyme (prosody),** Two-syllable trochaic *rhymes*, *191*

Drama, An individual play; also plays considered as a group; one of the three major *genres* of literature, *3*

Dramatic irony, A special kind of *situational irony* in which a character perceives his or her plight in a limited way while the audience and one or more of the other characters understand it entirely, *147*

Dramatic, or **third-person objective point of view,** A third-person *narration* reporting speech and action, but rigorously excluding commentary on the actions and thoughts of the characters, *90*

Dying or **falling rhyme** (*See* Double or trochaic rhyme)

Dynamic character, A character who undergoes adaptation, change, or growth, unlike the *static character*, who remains constant. In a *short story*, there is usually only one dynamic character, whereas in a *novel* there may be many, *66*

Echoic words (prosody), Words echoing the actions they describe, such as *buzz, bump,* and *slap;* important in the device of *onomatopoeia*, *189*

Editing (*See* Montage)

Enclosing use of setting, (*See* Framing setting)

End-stopped line (prosody), A line ending in a full pause, usually indicated with a period or semi-colon, *186–87*

Enjambement, or **run-on (prosody),** A line having no end punctuation but running over to the next line, *187*

Epic, A long narrative poem elevating character, speech, and action, *3*

Essay (*See* Theme)

Euphony (prosody), Meaning "good sound," *euphony* refers to word groups containing consonants that permit an easy and pleasant flow of spoken sound; opposite of *cacophony*, *189–90*

Evaluation, The act of deciding what is good, bad, or mediocre, *235–42*

Exposition, That structural stage which introduces all things necessary for the development of the *plot*, *57, 211*

Eye rhyme (prosody), Words that seem to rhyme because they are spelled similarly (e.g., *bear, fear*), but which in fact do not sound alike, *191*

Fable, A brief *story* illustrating a moral truth, most often associated with the ancient Greek writer Aesop, *133*

Falling rhyme (*See* Double rhyme)

Farce, A work, most often a short play, featuring exaggerated and boisterous action and speech, *354–63*

Feminine rhyme (*See* Double rhyme)

Fiction, *Narratives* based in the imagination of the author, not in literal, reportorial facts; one of the three major *genres* of literature, *3*

Figurative language, Words and expressions that conform to a particular pattern or form, such as *metaphor, simile,* and *parallelism*, *3, 117–18, 225*

Figures, rhetorical (*See* Figurative language)

Film script, The written text of a film, including descriptions of actions and effects, *244*

First-person point of view, The use of an "I," or first-person, *speaker* or *narrator* who tells about things that he/she has seen, done, spoken, heard, thought, and also learned about in other ways. Sometimes the first-person speaker is a major participant in the action, sometimes not, but such a speaker is integral to the story and therefore is worthy of independent study in her or his own right, *87–89, 91–92*

Flashback, A method of *narration* in which past events are introduced into a present action, *58–59*

Flat character, A character, usually minor, who is not individual, but rather useful and structural, static and unchanging; distinguished from *round character*, *66–67*

Foot (prosody), Measured combinations of heavy and light *stresses*, such as the iamb, which contains a light and a heavy stress, *182, 183–85*

Framing setting, The same features of *setting* used at both the beginning and ending of a work so as to "frame" or "enclose" the work, *78*

General language (style), Words referring to broad classes of persons or things; distinguished from *specific language*, *221*

Genre, A type of literature, such as *fiction* and *poetry;* also a type of work, such as detective fiction, epic poetry, tragedy, etc., *3*

Graph (prosody, style), Writing or spelling; the appearance of words on a page, as opposed to their actual sounds, *181*

Heavy-stress rhyme (prosody), A *rhyme*, such as rhyming iambs or anapests, ending with a strong stress, *191*

Heptameter (prosody), A line consisting of seven metrical *feet, 182*

Hero, heroine, The major male or female *protagonist* in a *narrative* or *drama;* the terms are often used to describe leading characters in adventures and romances, *66*

Hexameter (prosody), A line consisting of six metrical *feet, 182*

Hovering accent, (*See* Spondee)

Hymn (prosody), A religious song, consisting of one and usually many more replicating rhythmical stanzas, *194*

Hyperbole (style), A figure in which emphasis is achieved through exaggeration, *146–47*

Iamb (prosody), A two-syllable *foot* consisting of a light stress followed by a heavy stress (e.g., *the winds*), *183*

Iambic pentameter (prosody), A line consisting of five iambic *feet, 192*

Idea, A concept, thought, opinion, or belief; in literature, a unifying, centralizing conception or *theme, 98–107*

Image, imagery, Language, making for vividness, that triggers the mind to fuse together memories of sights (*visual*), sounds (*auditory*), tastes (*gustatory*), smells (*olfactory*), and sensations of touch (*tactile*). The word "image" refers to a single mental picture, such as Coleridge's image of a damsel playing a dulcimer (in "Kubla Khan"). "Imagery" refers to images throughout a work or throughout the works of a writer or groups of writers, *3, 108–116, 118*

Imperfect foot (prosody), A metrical *foot* consisting of a single syllable, either heavily or lightly stressed, *185*

Incidents (*See* Actions)

Invention, The process of discovering and determining materials to be included in a composition, whether a theme or an imaginative work; a vital phase of *prewriting, 18–27*

Irony, Broadly, a means of indirection. Language that states the opposite of what is intended is *verbal irony.* The placement of characters in a state of ignorance is *dramatic irony*, while an emphasis on powerlessness is *situational irony, 79, 146–47*

Italian or **Petrarchan sonnet**, An iambic pentameter poem of fourteen lines, divided between the first eight lines (the *octet*) and the last six (the *sestet*), *193*

Kinesthetic images, Words describing human or animal motion and activity, *111*

Kinetic images, Words describing general motion, *111*

Limited, or **Limited-omniscient point of view**, A third-person *narration* in which the actions, and often the thoughts, of the *protagonist* are the focus of attention, *90–91*

Literature, Written compositions (but also, in preliterate societies, oral compositions) designed to engage readers emotionally as well as intellectually, with the major genres being *fiction, poetry, drama*, and *nonfiction prose*, and with many separate subforms, *2–3*

Longshot (film), A distant camera view, including not only characters but also their surroundings; distinguished from a *closeup, 246*

Loose sentence (style), A straightforward sentence, usually in subject-verb-object order, with no climax and no surprises, *224*

Lyric, A short poem written in a repeating stanzaic form, often designed to be set to music; a *song, 194*

Major mover, A major participant in a work's action, who either causes things to happen or who is the subject of major events. If the first-person narrator is also a major mover, such as the *protagonist*, that fact gives first-hand authenticity to the narration, *185–86*

Masculine rhyme (prosody), *Rhymes* falling on a stressed syllable such as iambic or anapestic *rhyme, 191*

Meaning, That which is to be understood in a work; the total combination of ideas, actions, descriptions, and effects, *99*

Mechanics of verse (*See* Prosody)

Metaphor, *Figurative language* which makes the direct verbal equation of two or more things that may at first seem unlike each other, *14, 117–28*

Metaphorical language (*See* Figurative language)

Meter (prosody), The number of *feet* within a line of traditional verse, such as *iambic pentameter* referring to a line containing five *iambs, 182*

Metrical foot (*See* Foot)

Montage (film), The editing or assembling of the various camera "takes," or separate filmed scenes, to make a continuous film, *245–46*

Mood (*See* Atmosphere)

Music of poetry (prosody), Broadly, the rhythms, sounds, and rhymes of poetry; *prosody, 180–208*

Myth, A story that embodies truths about human experience and that codifies social and cultural values; also, myths considered collectively, *3, 133*

mythical reader *See* Audience

Narration, narrative fiction, The relating or recounting of a sequence of events or actions. While a *narration* may be reportorial and historical, *narrative fiction* is primarily creative and imaginative, 3

Nonfiction prose, A *genre* consisting of essays, articles, and books that are concerned with real as opposed to fictional things; one of the major *genres* of literature, 3

Novel, A long work of fictional prose, 3

Octave (prosody), The first eight lines of an Italian sonnet, 193

Ode (prosody), A stanzaic poetic form (usually long, to contrast it with the *song*) with varying line lengths and sometimes intricate *rhyme* schemes, 194

Omniscient point of view, A *third-person narrative* in which the *speaker* or *narrator*, with no apparent limitations, may describe intentions, actions, reactions, locations, and speeches of any or all of the characters, and may also describe their innermost thoughts (when necessary), 90

Onomatopoeia, A blending of consonant and vowel sounds designed to imitate or suggest the activity being described, 189

Outline, A formal pattern for a written composition, 25–27

Overstatement (*See* Hyperbole)

Parable, A short *allegory* designed to illustrate a religious truth, most often associated with Jesus as recorded in the Gospels, 3, 133

Parallelism (style), A rhetorical structure in which the same grammatical forms are repeated, 225–26

Pentameter (prosody), A line consisting of five metrical *feet*, 182

Periodic sentence (style), A sentence arranged in an order of climax, building toward a climactic and sometimes surprising idea, 224

Persona (The Greek word for **mask.** *See also* Speaker), The narrator or speaker of a *story* or *poem*, 87–92

Phonetics (prosody), The *actual pronunciation* of sounds, as distinguished from spelling or *graphics*, 181

Plausibility (*See* Verisimilitude)

Plot, The plan or groundwork for a story, with the actions resulting from believable and authentic human responses to a *conflict*. It is causation, conflict, response, opposition, and interaction that make a *plot* out of a series of *actions*, 51–63

Poem, poet, poetry: *Poetry* is a variable literary genre which is, foremost, characterized by the rhythmical qualities of language. While poems may be short (including *epigrams* and *haiku* of just a few lines) or long (*epics* of thousands of lines), the essence of poetry is compression, economy, and force, in contrast with the expansiveness of prose. There is no bar to the topics that poets may consider, and poems may range from the personal and lyric to the public and discursive. A *poem* is one poetic work. A *poet* is a person who writes poems. *Poetry* may refer to the poems of one writer, to poems of a number of writers, to all poems generally, or to the aesthetics of poetry considered as an art, 3, 180–208

Point of view, The *speaker, voice, narrator,* or *persona* of a work; the position from which details are perceived and related; a centralizing mind or intelligence; not to be confused with *opinion* or *belief*, 85–97

Point-of-view character, The central figure or *protagonist* in a *limited-point-of-view narration*, the character about whom events turn, the focus of attention in the narration, 91

Private symbols (*See* Authorial symbols)

Probability (*See* Verisimilitude)

Procatalepsis, or anticipation, A rhetorical strategy whereby the writer raises an objection and then answers it; the idea is to strengthen an argument by dealing with possible objections before someone else can raise them, 157–58

Prose fiction, Imaginative prose *narratives (short stories* and *novels)* that focus on one or a few characters who undergo a *change* or *development* and they interact with other characters and deal with their problems, 3

Prosody, The sounds and rhythms of poetry, 180–208

Protagonist, The central character and focus of interest in a *narrative* or *drama*, 66

Pyrrhic (prosody), A metrical *foot* consisting of two unaccented syllables, 184

Quatrain, (1) A four-line stanza or poetic unit. (2) In an *English* or *Shakespearean* sonnet, a group of four lines united by rhyme, 193

Representative character, A *flat character* with the qualities of all other members of a group (i.e., clerks, cowboys, detectives, etc.); a *stereotype*, 67

Research, literary, The use of both primary and secondary sources for assistance in treating a literary subject, 255–80

Resolution (*See* Dénouement)

Response, A reader's intellectual and emotional reactions to a literary work, 42–44

Rhetoric, The art of persuasive writing; broadly, the art of all effective writing, 223–26

Rhetorical figure (*See* Figurative language)

Rhyme (prosody), The repetition of identical concluding syllables in different words, most often at the ends of lines, 181, 190–94

Rhyme scheme (prosody), The pattern of *rhyme*, usually indicated by assigning a letter of the alphabet to each rhyming sound, 192–94

Rhythm (prosody, style), The varying speed, intensity, elevation, pitch, loudness, and expressiveness of speech, especially poetry, 181–88

Romance (1) Lengthy Spanish and French stories of the sixteenth and seventeenth centuries; (2) modern formulaic stories describing the growth of an enthusiastic love relationship, 3

Round character, A character who profits from experience and undergoes a change or development; usually but not necessarily the *protagonist*, 66–67

Run-on line (*See* Enjambement)

Scansion (prosody), The act of determining the prevailing *rhythm* of a poem, 182

Second-person point of view, A *narration* in which a second-person listener ("you") is the *protagonist* and the speaker is someone with knowledge the protagonist does not possess or understand about his or her own actions (e.g., doctor, parent, rejected lover, etc.), 89, 92

Segment (prosody), The smallest meaningful unit of sound, such as the /l/,/u/ and /v/ sounds in "love." Segments are to be distinguished from spellings, 181

Septenary (*See* Heptameter)

Sestet, (1) A six-line stanza or unit of poetry. (2) The last six lines of an *Italian* sonnet, 193

Setting, The natural, manufactured, and cultural environment in which characters live and move, including all the artifacts they use in their lives, 26–30, 75–84

Shakespearean (English) sonnet, A sonnet form developed by Shakespeare, with three quatrains concluded by a couplet, and with a total of seven rhymes, 193

Short story, A compact, concentrated work of *narrative fiction* that may also contain description, dialogue, and commentary. Poe used the term "brief prose tale" for the short story, and emphasized that it should create a major, unified impact, 3

Sight rhyme (*See* Eye rhyme)

Simile, A figure of comparison, using "like" with nouns and "as" with clauses, as in "the trees were bent by the wind *like actors bowing after a performance*," 14, 117–28

Simple sentence (style), A complete sentence containing one subject and one verb, together with modifiers and complements, 224

Situational irony, A type of *irony* emphasizing that human beings are enmeshed in forces beyond their comprehension and control, 147

Slant rhyme (prosody), A *near rhyme*, in which the consonant sounds are identical, but not the vowels, such as "should" and "food," "slum" and "slam," 191

Song (prosody), A lyric poem with a number of repeating stanzas, written to be set to music, 193

Sonnet, A poem of fourteen lines in *iambic pentameter*, 193

Speaker, The *narrator* of a story or poem, the *point of view*, often an independent character who is completely imagined and consistently maintained by the author. In addition to narrating the essential events of the work (justifying status as the *narrator*), the speaker may also introduce other aspects of his or her knowledge, and may interject judgments and opinions. Often the character of the speaker is of as much interest as the *actions* or *incidents*, 85

Specific language (style), Words referring to a real thing or things that may be readily perceived or imagined; distinguished from *general language*, 221

Spondee (prosody), A two-syllable *foot* consisting of successive, equally heavy accents (e.g., *men's eyes*), 184

Spring rhythm (prosody), A method of accenting, developed by Gerard Manley Hopkins, in which major stresses are "sprung" from the poetic line, 186

Stanza (prosody), A group of poetic lines corresponding to paragraphs in prose; the meters and rhymes are usually repeating or systematic, 193

Static character, A character who undergoes no change; contrasted with a *dynamic character*, 66

Stereotype, A character who is so ordinary and unoriginal that he/she seems to have been cast in a mold; a *representative* character, 67

Stock character, A *flat character* in a standard role with standard *traits*, such as the irate police captain, the bored hotel clerk, etc.; a *stereotype*, 67

Stress (prosody), The emphasis given to a syllable, either strong or light, 182

Strong-stress rhythm (*See* Heavy-stress rhythm)

Structure The arrangement and placement of materials in a work, 57–63

Style, The manipulation of language, the placement of words in the service of content, 209–34

Substitution, *Formal substitution* is the use of a variant foot within a line. *Rhetorical substitution* is the manipulation of the *caesura* to create the effect of a differing *rhythm* from the prevailing one, 182, 187–88

Syllable (prosody), A separately pronounced part of a word (e.g., the *eat* and *ing* parts of "eating"), or, in some cases, a complete word (e.g., *flounced*), 182

Symbol, symbolism, A specific word, idea, or object that may stand for ideas, values, persons, or ways of life, 129–40

Syzygy (*See* Dipodic)

Tenor, The sense, or meaning, of a *metaphor*, *symbol* or other *rhetorical figure*, 119–20

Terza rima (prosody), A three-line stanza form with the pattern A–B–A, B–C–B, etc., 194

Tetrameter (prosody), A line consisting of four metrical *feet*, 182

Theme, (1) The major or central idea of a work, 99. (2) A short composition developing an interpretation or advancing an argument, *passim.* (3) The main point or idea that a writer of a *theme* asserts and illustrates, *17–18,* and *passim*

Thesis statement, or thesis sentence, An introductory sentence that names the topics to be developed in the body of a theme, *24–25* and *passim*

Third-person point of view, A third-person method of *narration* (i.e., *she, he, it, they, them,* etc.), in which the *speaker* or *narrator* is not a part of the story, as with the *first-person point of view.* Because the third-person speaker may exhibit great knowledge and understanding, together with other qualities of character, he or she is often virtually identified with the author, but this identification is not easily decided, *89–92. See also* Authorial voice, Omniscient point of view

Tone, The methods used by writers to control attitudes, *141–53*

Topic sentence, The sentence determining the subject matter of a paragraph, *25* and *passim*

Trait, A typical mode of behavior; the study of major traits provides a guide to the description of *character, 64–65*

Trimeter (prosody), A line consisting of three metrical *feet, 182*

Trochee, trochaic (prosody), A two-syllable *foot* consisting of a heavy followed by a light stress, *183–84*

Understatement, The deliberate underplaying or undervaluing of a thing to create emphasis, *146*

Universal symbols (*See* Cultural symbols)

Value, values, The expression of an idea or ideas that concurrently asserts their importance and desirability as goals, standards, and ideals, *99*

Vehicle, The image or reference of a *rhetorical figure,* such as a *metaphor* or *simile;* it is the vehicle that carries or embodies the *tenor, 119*

Verbal irony, Language stating the opposite of what is meant, *146*

Verisimilitude (i.e., **"like truth"**), A characteristic whereby the setting, circumstances, characters, dialogue, actions, and outcomes in a work are designed to seem true, lifelike, real, plausible, and probable, *69–70*

Versification (*See* Prosody)

Virgule (prosody), A diacritical mark (/) separating feet in a metrical scansion, *182.* A double virgule (//) is used to indicate a *caesura,* or pause, *186*

Voice (*See* Speaker)

Index of Authors, Directors, Topics, and Chapter Titles

Works are included alphabetically under the name of the author or director. Anonymous works and collectively-authored works are indexed under the titles. For brief definitions of important words and terms, please consult the *Glossary*.

Patterson, Freeman,
1937-
                    87617
Photography of
 natural things

DATE		
JUL 3 1 1985		

MAY 2 0 1986

© THE BAKER & TAYLOR CO.

PHOTOGRAPHY OF NATURAL THINGS

Books by Freeman Patterson

Photography for the Joy of It
Photography and the Art of Seeing
Photography of Natural Things
Namaqualand: A Garden of the Gods

PHOTOGRAPHY
OF NATURAL THINGS

FREEMAN PATTERSON

VNR VAN NOSTRAND REINHOLD · TORONTO · NEW YORK

Published by Van Nostrand Reinhold Publishers
A Division of International Thomson Limited
1410 Birchmount Road, Scarborough, Ontario, Canada M1P 2E7

Published in the United States of America
by Van Nostrand Reinhold Company Inc.
135 West 50th Street, New York, NY 10020

Library of Congress Catalogue Number 82-060051

Canadian Cataloguing in Publication Data

Patterson, Freeman, 1937-
Photography of natural things
ISBN 0-7706-0020-4 (bound)   ISBN 0-7706-0022-0 (pbk)
1. Nature photography   I. Title.
TR721.P38   778.9′3   C82-094680-X

Design by Keith Scott   Editing by Susan Kiil
Typesetting by Compeer Typographic Services Limited
Colour separations and printing by Herzig Somerville Limited
Bound by The Bryant Press Limited
All photographs are by the author

Printed and bound in Canada
82 83 84 85 86 87 88 10 9 8 7 6 5 4 3 2 1

Preface

In nature, nothing exists in isolation. Whether photographing the striking patterns of light and shade in the drifting snow, documenting the nesting habits of a cedar waxwing, or capturing the soft movement of grasses tossing in the breeze, we can sense the interactions between all natural things. When we learn to focus not only on individual organisms, but also on whole communities and how they are linked together in ecological systems, we begin to develop a better understanding of natural things and how to photograph them.

The photography of natural things includes all forms of plants and animals and the air, water, and soil habitats where they live and interact. The possibilities for making nature pictures are almost endless. We can photograph natural things almost anywhere – even in the cracks of a city sidewalk. We can start at home with, say, a pot of African violets, or a freshly sliced tomato, an insect on a leaf of lettuce, frost patterns on the windowpane, the cat, or a bowl of goldfish. As we observe and photograph what is near at hand, our experience will prepare us to take better advantage of other photographic opportunities that may arise farther afield.

When we photograph nature we want to observe our subject matter carefully and sometimes to record exactly what we see – a cluster of red mushrooms, a colourful sunset, or a frog catching a fly. In trying to document plant and animal life like this, we must first look for and try to understand the functions and behaviour of our subjects. We should try to show not only what certain plants and animals look like, but also the natural relationships between them.

At other times, we may want to express the impact nature has on us by conveying a mood or a feeling through photography, or by singling out a natural design. The finest images – the images that stir our souls – combine documentation of natural things with a sense of what they mean to us. They use both documentary and interpretive approaches. Sometimes we should forget a strictly realistic approach, and use our cameras to portray intangible qualities – the freedom of a bird in flight, the gentleness of an early morning mist, the struggle for survival of a lone seedling. We should try to clarify our personal response, then use natural designs and colours, and selected photographic techniques, to express these feelings through our pictures. Through the photography of natural things, we can explore freely our interests in, and our relationship to, the natural world, the vast system in which each of us is a tiny part.

I am grateful for the contributions of several persons to this book – to Mary Ferguson, Bill Haney, Mary Majka, Mark Majka, and Michael Clugston for valuable information and specific suggestions; to my editor, Susan Kiil, whose professional expertise and commitment I appreciate more than I can ever express; and to Liz and Keith Scott for providing me a home-away-from-home for many weeks of writing and editing.

Freeman Patterson
Shampers' Bluff
New Brunswick
May 1982

Contents

Relationships between natural things

July 23   05:30   Alarm clock rings. Jump out of bed and look out of several windows. Nearly daylight – sunrise at six o'clock. Sky clear, mist rising off Kingston Creek and Gorham's pasture. No wind. Have a quick bite of toast and tea.

05:45   In my car going down the driveway. (Cameras loaded with film and packed in trunk last night; extra film and one camera on tripod beside me.) Quickly check two favourite spots, but mist conditions not quite right. May be sorry, but will gamble on Gorham's pasture.

06:00   Arrive at hill overlooking Gorham's farm and Belleisle Bay. Sun rising through golden fog bank at far end of bay. Stunning! Within 30 seconds of arrival, shooting directly toward sun and mist, using 85-200mm zoom lens (and tripod, naturally). Ten minutes of spectacular sunrise.

06:10   Leave tripod in position, but swing lens almost 180 degrees. Gravel road (soft brown in early light) cuts through field between meadow and pasture, hay forming triangular patterns; bit of mist rising near trees at top. Eliminate sky – too bright.

06:15   Swing lens back 90 degrees toward small valley, cattle lying in grass, lines of soft sunlight starting to stream across pasture. Make pictures with various focal lengths; eliminate sky and scrub bushes.

06:20   Aim camera in direction of sun again to photograph section of dew-covered hay field. Move tripod for first time, and find spiders' webs here and there. Concentrate exclusively on webs hanging with dew, long shots to close-ups using a variety of lenses (100mm macro for close-ups); use lots of back lighting. Deliberately overexpose one-half f/stop to retain delicate hues. All of a sudden two strands of a web (one out of focus) turn into prisms – all the rainbow colours. What's causing it? Get same effect on another web when shooting at same angle. This has never happened before. No wonder! Always concentrated on dew-covered webs – the prismatic lines are strands of web that have lost their water drops. Zero in on dry parts of web or combinations of wet and dry strands, shooting at widest aperture. Incredible colour! Gone are "webs" and "dew." Have entered an ever-changing world of form, colour, and light; beyond definitions and assumptions. Must just look, look, look.

07:30   Slowly drive back along gravel road. Banks of summer wildflowers too good to pass up – vetch, swamp candles, daisies, fireweed. A few overall shots, then several compositions of swamp candles close up.

08:15   More than two hours gone; must get home. Put cameras away and head off. Successful for two kilometres, then can't stand it any longer. Ditch with sparse clumps of back-lighted timothy grass in peak condition, heads saturated with dew. More close-ups, carefully designed.

08:30   Tall, narrow cat-tail leaves translucent in the back lighting – incredible colours and lines. Move in on groups of leaves, contrasted against dark background. Stay with shallow depth of field, so edges of leaves go in and out of focus. Very strong designs. Becoming more and more abstract as I work.

09:15   Move on a few metres to new clump of cat-tails. Nope, doesn't work. Try again, and again. Can't match what I've just done. Make only two shots.

09:35   Finally head home, determined not to stop. Stop at mailbox. Long line of fireweed soars across a distant bank. Passed it up last year, can't bear to pass it by again. Dig out 300mm lens to flatten perspective and emphasize the line of reddish-purple cutting through the green – must shoot from a distance. Looks good – keep going. Move to the left, now away over to the right. Try a few shots with a streak of red at the bottom, wall of green above, and line of sky at top. That's good and that's enough.

09:55   Pack cameras in car trunk once more. Gather up exposed film from back seat. Nine rolls! I remember reloading the camera only twice.

10:15   Bacon and eggs.

I viewed the slides from my morning trip several days later. First, I evaluated them for technical quality – especially exposure. Next, on a large light box I laid out all the photographs that either surpassed my expectations or disappointed me. By identifying the reasons for the successes and failures, I was able to develop guidelines to help me come closer to the results I want in making future images. Then, I sat back and recollected the events of that morning. Questions began to come to my mind. Questions about nature, about relationships between natural things, such as "Why were there no insects on the flowers of the timothy grass? Was it the temperature, or are they always free of insects?" and "Why did the fireweed grow in a long narrow line instead of in a broad clump or expanse as it usually does?" I decided to examine the timothy grass each time I passed by it during the day, and to return to the fireweed to examine the soil and the general habitat to see if I could find answers to my questions.

10

To learn about nature and to convey useful information about it through the photographs you make, you must consider the relationships that exist between natural things and processes. For example, if you see a snake sunning itself on a rock on a hot morning, you will convey more about nature if your photograph includes the snake, the rock, and a bit of shadow to indicate the sun is shining, rather than just making a close-up of the snake. There is a relationship between these things. The sun has heated up the rock and the snake is lying on it to raise its body temperature. A warm snake is able to do things that a cold snake can't. So, a picture that includes some of the snake's habitat may tell more about the snake than a portrait of it alone would.

A habitat, or environment, together with the interactions between all of the living and non-living things within it, is called an ecological system, or *ecosystem*. The plants and animals depend on each other, directly or indirectly, for their existence. They make up a *biotic* (or living) community. This biotic community could not survive, however, without an *abiotic* (or non-living) support system – soil, mineral elements, sunlight, moisture, heat, and so on.

Within this structure there are two fundamental processes at work. In one process, the sun's energy manufactures food from inorganic substances. In the other, this food is consumed, digested and re-arranged, and the remains returned to the earth. Where there is light and green plants, food is manufactured through photosynthesis and used for the growth and propagation of the plants. The plant material, in turn, becomes food for a host of living things – from an insect feeding on leaves, to a bird catching that insect and, finally, to the bird being food for a fox. In turn, bacteria and fungi utilize plant and animal matter. These small consumers are also vital links in the food chain. They break down complex materials, use some of them, and release the rest into the system as simple compounds.

What each organism does (not merely where it lives) is called its *niche*. Think of a baseball diamond as a habitat, and the diamond plus the game being played there as an ecosystem. In this ecosystem every player has a different location and function. The pitcher has a niche, so does the catcher, the fielder, and so on. As each carries out his or her responsibility, the entire team functions successfully. Every ecosystem is like that. The players change, but the game remains the same.

Ecosystems are everywhere: a tiny pond overgrown with bulrushes, a dense clump of bushes surrounded by an expanse of grass, or a desert that stretches over hundreds of kilometres. Ecosystems are also located in urban areas – in parks, waterfronts, golf courses, cemeteries, perhaps your own backyard.

The bog in the woods behind my house is an ecosystem that I photograph frequently. I have learned a great deal about the relationships that exist in nature by developing a knowledge of this one ecosystem. Each year, usually in the spring, the bog becomes a very shallow pond teeming with insect larvae and other life. More of the time it is like a deep, damp, spongy, forest pasture with hummocks of sphagnum moss and plants that like the wet, heavily acid soil (such as cinnamon ferns and bog beans), frogs, birds, and a happy moose who finds the menu very much to her taste. In the spring, green plants at the water's surface are the major food producers, but as the water evaporates and the bog becomes drier, ferns, mosses, Labrador tea, and other vegetation take over the responsibilities for basic food production. As the food supply alters during the summer and fall, so do the consumers. By midsummer, insect larvae and the number of birds have dwindled, but fungi appear on fallen branches or dying leaves, aiding decomposition. In winter, when the bog is frozen, hares make paths through the hummocks, ruffed grouse sit in the alders and surrounding birches feeding on the leaf buds, and now and then an owl or hawk drops in to hunt for a supply of fresh meat. All year long, the processes of the ecosystem carry on, and I photograph them whenever I can.

However, an ecosystem does not merely repeat the same cycle – it changes. Like any other organism it has a past, a present, and a future. As the years go by in the bog, the moss grows thicker and alder bushes invade a little farther. Each year their leaves, in increasing numbers, are added to the collection of organic material on the ground. Gradually, the soil builds up and the bog becomes drier. The changing conditions favour the germination of seeds from trees that currently do not grow there, and so the tree cover changes. Birds that favoured the old habitat are seen less frequently, but new species have appeared. This change in the ecosystem is called *succession*, and it will continue until the ecosystem reaches maturity. At that time the habitat will be neither very wet nor very dry, and will contain a community of species of a fairly constant population. The ecosystem will probably remain stable until it is subjected to outside influences, such as fire, flood, or exploitation by people.

The relationships between living and non-living things within ecosystems, and between ecosystems themselves, are vital to the existence of everything else. Just as a bee cannot survive apart from the social life of its hive, nor a fielder play ball without the rest of the team, neither can any other creature, including a human being, exist for long apart from its ecosystem.

By making pictures in a small ecosystem near your home, you will learn a great deal about nature and be better prepared to understand and photograph the activities of a larger or wilder ecosystem when you have the opportunity to visit one. In addition to documenting nature subjects, look for ways to convey your personal response through images that evoke the struggle for survival or inspire viewers with their beauty. By making both kinds of photographs you will express more fully your respect and caring for natural things.

All natural things are linked in relationships with other natural things. While a bilberry tree in blossom is the central element of this photograph, the details of the forest ecosystem in the background help to give the tree a sense of place and indicate the season. Since both the tree and its surroundings appear to have a random sort of pattern, I decided on a loosely organized composition. In both documentary and interpretive nature photography, the physical characteristics of the subject matter should guide your composition and choice of techniques.

A wide-angle lens is a useful tool for photographing wildflowers close up while showing something of their habitat. For these California poppies I used a 28mm lens, moved in very close to the foreground flowers, focused on blossoms about one-third of the way up from the bottom edge of the picture frame, and used the smallest lens opening (f/16) for maximum depth of field. The result is a clear description of both the flowers and their hilly, meadow habitat. If I had positioned my camera vertically, I would have reduced the feeling of broad expanse, but increased the sense of flowers stretching from my feet to the horizon.

Invisible natural forces have to be portrayed indirectly. By using a shutter speed slower than the movement of the daisies and grasses, I was able to capture the blur and document the presence of wind. The shutter speed you might choose in a similar situation will depend on the strength of the wind, your distance from the plants, and the pictorial effect you want. In a stiff breeze, a shutter speed of 1/60 second will permit blurring of the moving flowers or branches, but slower shutter speeds (1/30, 1/15, 1/8, and 1/4 second) are more often necessary.

Many flowers, especially annuals, close at night or in chilly weather and open only when flying insects that pollinate them are active. This picture was taken on a cool, cloudy day when the flowers were closed, and brilliant highlights and dark shadows were absent. Because temperature affects natural relationships, and because indirect lighting often improves the richness of colours in flowers and other natural things, a nature photographer should take advantage of overcast days.

I visited this clump of flowers on several days, hoping for the wind to abate and for special lighting conditions. At sunset on this day, the wind suddenly dropped and warm light gently illuminated the plants, the rock, and the mountain. Since the lighting was changing rapidly, I quickly waded into the water to set up my tripod on the rocky bottom, and then stood perfectly still to avoid making ripples. I captured the image I wanted seconds before the sun dipped below the horizon.

The action of water, wind, and temperature helps to convert rock into soil. Lichens are the first plants to colonize a rock face. As the processes of weathering and erosion continue, organic material and moisture accumulate in crevices that develop in the rock, and other plants establish themselves. These higher forms of plant life speed up the disintegration of the rock, as their roots penetrate more deeply into cracks and their dead leaves add to the collection of organic material. This natural process can be documented anywhere in the world – here, in southern Africa, or, on the facing page, in Alberta.

Both this picture and the one opposite were made on the shady side of a rock on a bright sunny day – continents apart. Light from a blue sky is reflected off the rocks giving them a bluish tint. It would have been easy to eliminate this tint by using a warming filter; but since the blue cast occurs naturally, I decided to include it in both photographs. I selected a film sensitive to blue (the same film in each case) to make sure that the tint would be recorded accurately. Also, I devoted the largest part of each picture to the rock, as it dominates the plants growing in the crevices.

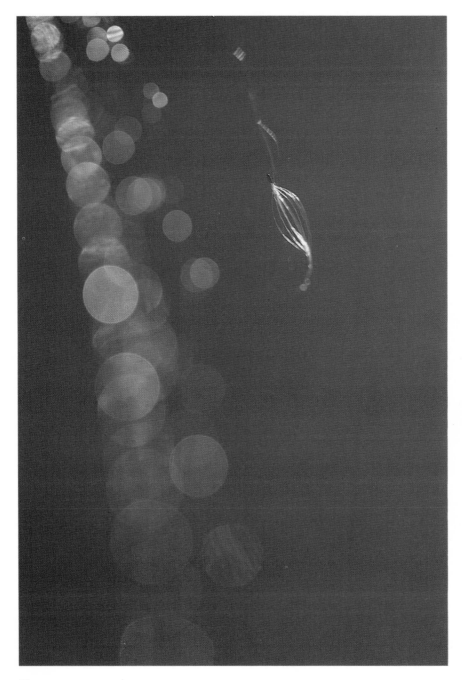

Part of the story of plant life is how a species disperses its seeds. This seed was travelling on the wind when it was caught and held by a spider's web. When the web is destroyed, the sagging strands will carry the seed to the ground. Heavy rain may transport the seed farther and help to bury it with soil and organic material, assuring its eventual germination. By focusing on the seed and using minimum depth of field (f/2.8), I was able to document the process of seed dispersal as well as to convey the delicate beauty of the web.

Grasses and wildflowers grow just about anywhere there is soil and moisture. I found this grouping in a meadow near my home, and photographed it with a 135mm lens. This lens and a standard 50mm lens are useful for moderate close-up pictures when you set the lens at or near its minimum focusing distance. To avoid formality, I normally would not place the rose as close to the centre of the picture as I did in this image. But because of the informal arrangement of blue hare bells, I decided on this composition, which for me conveyed the natural design of the subject matter.

I photographed these frosted leaves just before rays from the rising sun reached into their shaded corner of a field. Because the darker tones in the picture are about equal in area to the lighter tones, I used the exposure indicated by the camera's light meter. If there had been more frost on the leaves, I would have given more exposure than the meter suggested in order to render the whites correctly. Had there been less frost, I would have under-exposed slightly. In order to determine appropriate exposure in situations like this, it's important to examine the tones in all areas of the composition, including the spaces between the leaves.

This image was made in the same place, at the same time, and with the same equipment as the photograph on the facing page. However, by moving farther away from the subject matter and deliberately avoiding a design with a strong centre of interest, I was able to show more of the tapestry of frosted autumn leaves. The cue for my composition was simply the natural arrangement of the material. Before you settle on a composition, wander around the area and try to detect the visible natural relationships within your subject matter. After photographing, linger a little while to see if you can find other camera positions that will be as effective.

Cloudy damp days in November provide an opportunity to see and photograph some of nature's most subtle, beautiful hues, and to notice that beyond affecting our emotions, colour also helps us tell the time of year. The brown weeds and grasses immediately indicate the season. Soon these plants will be beaten down by wind and snow, and will eventually decompose into humus, adding important nutrients to the soil for succeeding plant generations. Thus, in both life and death, plants contribute to the successful functioning of the natural system.

Nature in the city

The growth of cities has increased interest in nature photography, as an antidote to the pressures of urban living, a readily available therapy, and a stimulating creative outlet. Many of the world's finest nature photographers live in cities or towns, and many of these make most of their pictures close to home. In fact, if you're interested in photographing nature, you can begin practically anywhere – even in the downtown area of a large city, or in parks and ravines. Both of these environments are good places to start, by the way, because nature carries on here as surely as it does anywhere else. If you can see and take advantage of what is near at hand, you'll be much better prepared for special opportunities when they do arise. Let me give you some examples.

It's a fact of nature that wet places tend to become dry, and dry places wet. That's why small lakes become marshes and why barren fields become forests. Nature constantly seeks to create "middle" environments, to balance the extremes. Even in urban deserts of concrete and asphalt, nature constantly seeks to alter this condition. Water seeps into an imperfection in a concrete sidewalk, washing dirt in with it. If the water freezes, it may enlarge the crack, allowing more dirt in. Seeds can germinate and grow in a surprisingly small amount of soil, even if the habitat at first may be very marginal. But, if a plant or two can establish themselves, their roots will gradually put pressure on the crack, opening it wider. As plants mature and die, their remains will fertilize the fissure, and the following year there will be more, healthier plants. Unless people intervene to "correct" the situation, the process will accelerate relentlessly until, perhaps centuries later, what was once a sidewalk will have become a habitat "balanced" for its particular climate – with typical vegetation and animal life.

Since people do intervene, and are forever "repairing" sidewalks, most city dwellers will rarely have the chance to photograph the natural process asserting itself fully. However, there is no end of opportunities to show the change beginning, and in some instances to show the entire process, perhaps a vacant lot becoming a wild place again, full of weeds and nesting birds. On a summer evening's stroll, even the most casual observer is apt to notice the little clump of goldenrod blooming in the crack between the sidewalk and the office tower. The more interested observer, or the nature photographer, may take a second look and be delighted to find that a spider has spun a few threads and is waiting for the vibrations that will tell it a fly has become entangled. If you're lucky, you may even see the spider move in for the kill.

Quite a few nature photographers would pass this situation by because they fear theft of either their cameras or their pride. It *is* embarrassing to be stretched out on a sidewalk with your camera lens pointed up at a spider and a crowd staring down at you. However, two photographers, or one photographer with a friend or two, are much less likely to lose either pride or equipment. Embarrassment, if it bothers you, will be greatly reduced if somebody else is involved or simply looks interested.

Parks, ravines, river valleys, and backyards offer the city dweller almost the same opportunities to learn about nature and nature photography as many country settings do. When I lived in Toronto, every February or March a piece of news would spread among city photographers like a wind-driven grass fire sweeping across the prairie: "The skunk cabbage are blooming in Edwards Gardens!" Once the word was out, the skunk cabbage didn't have another moment to call their own. The city nature photographer's year began, it seemed, with skunk cabbage. Their early bloom marked the emotional resurrection of thousands of photographers who were beginning to tire a little from a surfeit of icicles and snow drifts. After that, it was not uncommon to see a photographer with tripod in hand riding the subway to some favourite haunt in search of spring flowers.

A Montreal photographer I know takes her dog for a walk every evening in Mont Royal park, but she also takes her camera. You'll often find her crouched over a scattering of autumn leaves or a moth floating in a puddle. She keeps her photographic skills well sharpened through her nightly walks, so that when she is able to spend a rare weekend in the country or goes on holidays, she is familiar with her equipment and its operation.

One night I walked by a private school in Toronto when a concert was in progress. Bentleys, Rolls Royces, and Mercedes lined the driveway. Playing around them and on top of them was a family of raccoons. Six weeks later, at an exhibition of nature photographs in a local library, I saw a shot of three raccoons peering through some leaves. The photographer was a teacher at that private school.

Of course, in most large cities there are good opportunities to photograph animals at zoos and game farms. While there is a temptation to think of captive animals as being tame, and their physical surroundings as unnatural, many zoos are run by highly professional biologists with an excellent understanding of animal needs and behaviour, and these people try to reproduce the main features of the wild habitat. So, a photographer should not dismiss zoos lightly, because there is much to observe and learn there. Also, zoos offer excellent chances to make animal portraits that are very difficult to obtain in the wild, and to photograph many facets of behaviour at close range.

Any city dweller who has a clear view of even a little sky can photograph clouds, approaching storms, sunrises, sunsets, and rainbows. Weather changes provide endless challenges for the nature photographer – back-lighted streaks of rain against dark evergreens, icicles hanging from rose hips, sunlight streaming through spring leaves, lightning ricochetting off skyscrapers at night, snow-flakes settling gently on bare branches, trees in a pink twilight after a snowfall.

When it comes to equipment and film, nature photography in the city makes few demands you won't encounter elsewhere. It often helps to have a telephoto lens in order to isolate particular natural objects or to make more visually accessible any objects that are difficult to approach. If you don't have a telephoto lens, you may wish to purchase one. I'd suggest you consider a zoom lens, possibly in the 80-200mm range, as it will be useful in a wide variety of situations.

Although many photographers are unaware of it, the city provides some good lighting conditions less often available in the country. The smog or haze so prevalent in urban areas, while undesirable from a health standpoint, often acts as a kind of filter, softening the contrast of harsh sunlight and thereby helping the photographer. Tall buildings and expanses of concrete act as large reflectors, bouncing light in various directions and thus reducing contrast as well. Warm light early or late in the day may be reflected by a street or building into shadowy areas, casting a pleasant glow on objects in the shade. This soft, warm light is often used by photographers who make portraits of people on the street, and may be just as useful to nature photographers making pictures of plants, fallen leaves, insects, birds, and so on.

A city nature photographer should not always avoid showing the human influence. It's well to remember that a city is a habitat created and dominated by one species. It is a marginal environment for most other species of animals and plants. Although many live there successfully, they do so only because they have found a way to co-exist with the dominant species. It's worthwhile to consider a city as an ecosystem, indeed to photograph it from that point of view, and to include very deliberately the behaviour of the human species as it endeavours to obtain food, escape predation (crime), seek shelter, and propagate. Anthills, deer trails, and peacocks displaying their tail feathers – that's what supermarkets, expressways, houses, and beauty parlours are all about.

Nature in your home

Many people confined to a house or apartment think nature photography is beyond their reach. Some are caught up with important family responsibilities, others are restricted by physical handicaps. Some are experienced nature photographers cut off from their favourite outdoor activity; others are complete beginners longing for opportunities to learn. If you are among this number, or if you put away your camera for long periods every year, why not take advantage of the opportunities available to you every day in your own home?

In Edmonton, I met a handicapped photographer who was very fond of birds. Confined to his home and wheelchair, and with only partial use of his hands, he managed for many years to make remarkably good pictures of blue jays, waxwings, sparrows, and a whole host of other species. He had nests and feeders arranged in the yard outside his window, so he could observe the birds even when he wasn't photographing them. He also had a special tripod holder attached to his wheelchair. His wife would set up his camera, load it with film, and attach the lens he wanted. Then, Bill would watch and wait for hours, squeezing the cable release to capture birds in striking poses or at characteristic tasks. The birds became so fond of him they sometimes came into the open window for a visit. On one occasion he was able to make pictures of a blue jay walking over the keys of his typewriter. His photographs of birds were so good that they occasionally appeared in the local newspaper, and were frequently accepted for showing in international nature exhibitions.

Even if you don't photograph birds from your window or ask them inside for visits, the possibilities for making nature pictures in your home are almost endless. If you are interested in plants, begin with those growing in your home. The fact that they are domesticated is unimportant. Like all plants, they respond to light, heat, moisture, and nutrients; they grow and blossom; they provide food for insects (much to your annoyance) and add oxygen to the air; and their old leaves wither and turn brown. Furthermore, many species of house plants occur naturally in the wild. I've photographed one species of geranium both in my greenhouse and in semi-arid regions of southern Africa. Hybrids and new varieties of house plants all originate as wild plants. Most plant societies (and they are numerous) can provide literature on the origins and domestication of house plants, which is very useful to a nature photographer.

Photographically, you can do anything with a house plant that you can with a wild one – except show it in natural surroundings. You can make pictures of stems, leaves, and blossoms; you can move in very close to show nodes on stems, the veins of a leaf, and the many parts of a flower. You can pollinate many species of house plants artificially with a small camel's hair brush; they will set seeds and you can photograph the seed heads. Seeds of the geranium family are especially striking. Ask friends to bring in seed stalks of wildflowers, branches of evergreens, and the dry fertile fronds of ferns. You need never be short of material. You can use both natural light and flash to achieve front lighting, side lighting, back lighting, and even lighting. You can try the full range of close-up equipment, experiment with selective focus, and choose various backgrounds.

If plants interest you, don't stop with ornamental varieties. Bisect a cabbage and look at the incredible internal structure of its leaves. Save that rotting apple or orange, and photograph the molds as they develop. Study the shape of a pear or green pepper. Make abstracts of the skin of a squash. Abandon yourself to the colour and form of natural designs. Do visual leaps and dances!

However, plants are only one sort of subject matter. What about aphids and other "pests" that attack house plants? Or water in its various forms? There are rain drops on your windowpane in summer, frost patterns in winter, and snow on windowsills and on the trees outside your window. Photograph snow falling; if the background is a building, that doesn't mean the snow is less natural. You can even use a camera and macro lens in the bathtub – to photograph along the water surface.

If you have an aquarium, why not try photographing fish? Perhaps a friend can bring a few frogs' eggs or insect larvae for you to raise and photograph. But, don't overlook the spider in the kitchen – and let the web hang there for a while. You may find yourself photographing the predator and its prey, or making a very close-up picture of a single strand of the web to show how it acts as a prism.

If you can make excursions into the country or nearby parks and ravines, you'll realize that working at home has done wonders for your technical skills and your ability to see. In short, you can become a very skilled nature photographer by working in your home, where you can explore your individual interests, your personal responses to natural material, and develop your abilities to document nature.

29

Photographic approaches

Imagine an early morning in June. You are standing at the edge of a meadow, looking across it toward the spot where the sun will soon be rising. Your tripod stands beside you, supporting a camera with a 50mm lens. The camera and lens are tilted down slightly, so that when you look through the viewfinder you see several clumps of daisies and a few dew-laden spiders' webs among the grasses. Everything is in focus. When the first ray of sunlight spotlights the web in the foreground, you quickly determine your exposure and press the shutter release. Your photograph documents a web in a meadow habitat, the coming of morning to the meadow, and conveys something of your joy in being there.

Next, you lower your tripod and replace the 50mm lens with a 200mm lens. You carefully compose a picture in which the foreground web and flowers are entirely out of focus – a soft blur of light tones and delicate hues. Grasses in the distance are obscured, appearing as a mere tracery of lines. When every-thing is just right, you press the shutter release again. Through the expressive power of delicate tones and colour, the photograph records your mood as effectively as your first image and, in an abstract way, says just as much about a summer morning. But is it a photograph of nature?

For both pictures you selected the same subject matter – daisies, webs, grasses, and morning light. Both images record your response to this subject matter. Yet, the two photographs are very different in appearance. One includes a great deal of information about nature; the other does not. By changing a lens, camera position, and depth of field, you have raised a basic question: when is the photograhy of natural things "nature photography?"

Perhaps you'll be tempted to reply that a picture has to contain recognizable natural objects in order to be called a nature photograph. But, would you necessarily recognize the underbelly of a centipede, if it were photographed very close up? There are many things in nature that we don't recognize or understand unless we are very well informed about the particular subject matter.

Now consider another example. Imagine a cluster of spring violets blooming from a carpet of last year's beech leaves and fern stalks on the forest floor. The dead leaves and stalks are very bright and distracting, overwhelming the delicate beauty of the blossoms. So, in order to capture the image you want of the flowers, you sweep away all the old beech leaves and pull out the dead fern stalks, until only the violets and the rich brown soil remain. Finally, you set up your camera, focus on the flowers, set the lens at f/22 for maximum depth of field, and determine your exposure. When you press the shutter release, you will make a sharp, clear image in which every natural object is fully recognizable. But, will you be making a photograph of *nature*? When is the photography of natural things nature photography? Your answer to this important question will reveal a good deal about how you see nature and will determine the kinds of images you will want to make.

DOCUMENTARY PHOTOGRAPHS

In documenting natural objects, situations, and processes, your paramount concern is accuracy. For example, pay careful attention to where and how a plant grows or a bird nests, and try to present this information faithfully in your photographs. In documentary nature photography it's important to put aside human value judgements and preconceptions, and to try to view the natural system from nature's standpoint. Once you try this, you'll quickly see how essential such careful observation is. In fact, it's the basis of documentary photography.

The best place for observing natural things – though not always the easiest – is in their own habitat, where they are part of their normal processes and surroundings. A good way to begin learning how to observe is to choose one subject, let's say an anthill, and to visit it often. Watch for as long as you can, and try to get answers to basic questions. Ask yourself how, in this case, an ant determines its location, how it perceives time and change, and how it responds to basic drives, such as the need for food, the need to propagate, and the need to avoid predators. You won't get complete answers to these questions, even if you visit an anthill over a period of years, but you will learn a great deal and, even more important, you will learn *how* to observe. You can then apply your methods to the observation of other creatures and their habitats.

By combining observation with reading, you will be able to understand and to document nature more accurately. For example, you may observe that ants have an excellent sense of direction, but you may not know why. Reading will provide the answer. You could learn why some daisies have longer stems than others of the same species, which might help you decide whether or not to include the stems in your photograph. Also, when you are alert to the meaning of an animal's behaviour or know the reasons for a plant's structure, you will be able to select your photographic tools and techniques more wisely.

Try to make and collect photographs that reflect nature's balance. Balance is a basic principle of the universe, and nature's fundamental law. Nature will tolerate individual aberrations, such as a population explosion among foxes or people, but only for a while. It never allows an aberration to affect the functioning of the system permanently. As foxes multiply, they outstrip their food supply, which dwindles; as the food supply diminishes, the weaker foxes starve to death. Eventually, the number of foxes is just right for the amount of food available to support them, and the smaller population is healthier than the larger one had been. The same process works just as effectively with pitcher plants, and with people – sometimes more swiftly, often more slowly, but always surely. So, make pictures of lively young fox pups as well as images of foxes weak from starvation, because as a naturalist you should know that both illness and health are essential to the long-term survival of a species or population, and you will not value one sort of photograph above the other.

It is tempting to document only beautiful things – the perfect rose, the tranquil lake, the magnificent sunset – and to avoid the rotting fungus, the worm-eaten leaf, or the injured sparrow. If you repair cars or teach children all week, you may turn to photography as a way of forgetting your problems and frustrations, and not be at all inclined to go around looking for damaged plants or wounded rabbits, even if it was an insect that ate holes in the orchid or a hawk that mauled the rabbit in an attempt to get food for its young. If you, or others, regard your photographic efforts as being one-sided, it's well to remember that your seeking out of beautiful things is itself an example of nature at work. Your system demands not only physical stability, but also psychological balance; after a rough week at work you are feeding yourself the food you need to make your system healthy again.

In nature, physical beauty always has a function or reason. Beauty without function, or pure decoration does not occur. Some of the most striking displays of colour in the plant and animal kingdoms are warnings to predators or sexual lures. So are some of the loveliest fragrances. The purpose of beauty in these cases is to ensure that male meets female, and that a new generation is born.

Many nature stories are too complex to be recorded in a single image, so a series of pictures, or a photo essay, may provide more complete information and be a better document – although no photographs, however numerous, can ever be a complete document. But remember that in trying for accuracy, you needn't be bound to a literal or realistic style. For example, you may render a flower sharp and in focus, but throw the background out of focus. Or, you may use a slow shutter speed to photograph a flock of birds flying. The birds will be blurred, but that may document the concept of flight and the direction of movement more accurately than if you had used a fast shutter speed to "freeze" the birds in midair. (A fast shutter speed would provide a better physical description of the birds themselves.) When you do choose a realistic approach, it should be balanced. As a documentary nature photographer, you should strive – in the body of your work, if not in every individual image – to show that both beauty and imperfection have roles to play in the successful working of natural systems. If you can do this, your nature photography will be both honest and informative.

INTERPRETIVE PHOTOGRAPHS

Many good photographs of nature subjects may be more impressionistic than documentary. For instance, a picture of a tree barely glimpsed through morning mists may provide little factual information about either the tree or the mists, yet give an accurate sense of atmospheric and weather conditions, and an overall feeling of the scene. A photograph of a waterfall made with either a very slow or fast shutter speed is an interpretation of flowing water, not a record of what the eye actually sees. However, while these photographs are also documents of what is in front of your lens, their main purpose is to convey a mood or a feeling that nature has evoked, or to single out a natural design, rather than to provide specific, factual information. By emphasizing a mood, feeling, or natural design, you incorporate your own interpretation in the image.

When interpreting nature, you can use the same techniques you employ for documentary images – maximum depth of field, for example. That is what I chose for the photograph of an expanse of snow and ice on page 135, which is not recognizable as snow and ice. In this image I wanted to convey a sense of great space and of being above the clouds, which the subject matter stimulated. As you look at this picture, ask why the subject matter gives this impression and what techniques I used to express it photographically.

The photograph of sumach leaves on page 126 is also an interpretation. In this case I focused on part of one leaf and used minimum depth of field, so everything else would be soft and blurred. You can see the structure of the in-focus leaf, which is the only real information the picture provides. Apart from that, you receive a visual impression of how I saw autumn at a particular place and time. I deliberately blended tones and hues to soften the rich colour saturation and impart a sense of gentleness. I blurred the sharply defined shapes and lines of the leaves to add a dream-like quality to the image. These were very personal decisions, but they arose from the impact the subject matter made on me.

As with documentary pictures, of course, interpretive images depend on what you include in the picture space or on the point of view you select. For example, if I had used the same lens, but moved father away from the sumach leaves, I would not have been able to throw them out of focus to the same degree, and I would have had to include more leaves, thus providing more specific information. On the other hand, if I had moved closer to the expanse of snow and ice you would be able to recognize its texture, and the impression of space would have been greatly reduced. By focusing on a small section of a zebra's back, I would be making an abstract composition of black and white lines. The picture might be called a close-up document because of the way I placed the lines in the picture space. But if its main appeal is aesthetic then it really is more interpretive than documentary.

Interpretive images are an important aspect of the photography of nature, because they arouse our interest without overloading our minds with detail. They allow us to feel or savour the experience of being with nature, thus affecting us on an emotional level. Also, they can influence the attitudes of people who have little appreciation of the natural world and help to stimulate a sensitivity to it.

There is no absolute distinction between a documentary nature photograph and an interpretive one. Some images are more documentary because they provide a great deal of specific information or explain a process clearly. Some pictures are more interpretive because, above all else, they convey a mood, generate an attitude, or stimulate a feeling about nature which the subject matter evoked in the photographer. Many nature photographs are both documentary and interpretive, communicating both information and mood. Accept the two styles as valuable directions in the photography of nature, and don't be too concerned about classifying images in one category or the other. Allow yourself the freedom to move in either direction.

As you focus your lens on the natural world, remember that people are part of nature. Whether you are photographing waves or dunes, grasshoppers, whales, or falling leaves, you are capturing images of your community. What happens to all living things happens to you. The more you think about how people make use of the environment to satisfy the basic needs of life – food, shelter, and reproduction – the more you may want to document and interpret the activities of one particular mammal, *Homo sapiens,* in order to understand other creatures and photograph them better.

The sun and the atmosphere

Every living thing depends on air, water, and soil to provide its habitat and sustain its needs. These three mediums exist and support life because of an essential ingredient – energy. The source of energy is the sun, which radiates tremendous quantities of light and heat. While only a tiny fraction of the sun's energy ever reaches Earth, this amount is sufficient to create and maintain life. It's easy to understand why earlier civilizations regarded the sun as a god, and why sun and sunlight are our major symbols for life and hope. People have always been fascinated with sunrises and sunsets, with the varying colour of light, and the ways that light shapes and defines the visual world. The energy source that makes life possible also makes things visible, so let's think about photographing the sun and its influence on the atmosphere, the first medium of life the sun's rays encounter on their journey to our planet.

Earth is wrapped in an envelope of gases, water vapour, and fine particles that is hundreds of kilometres thick. This envelope, the atmosphere, is held against the planet's surface by gravity and exerts tremendous pressure on the earth. The sun's rays do not warm the atmosphere as they pass through it, but the earth absorbs heat and radiates it back into the air. Since the radiation is uneven, this stirs up the air and produces wind. Most weather occurs in the lower atmosphere, where heat and air pressure are greatest and where the air contains enough water vapour and fine particles of dust to form clouds.

Unlike water and soil, air is not a permanent home for living things, except micro-organisms, though many insects, birds, and some mammals spend large portions of their lives in aerial habitats – hunting food, escaping predators, mating, and resting. An albatross spends most of its long life (more than half a century) riding the west winds around the globe. Plants also travel in the atmosphere, particularly as pollen or seeds. The spores of various mushrooms are transported around the world in the jet stream.

While the sun is far beyond the earth's atmosphere, we see it through the atmosphere and associate it with air more than with water or soil – the sun appears to be part of the sky. So, when we photograph atmospheric conditions, we often have to consider the location of the sun in the sky and the visual effects of sunlight on clouds, mists, and rain.

PHOTOGRAPHING THE SUN AND THE DAYTIME SKY

Photographing the sun at different times of day and in varying atmospheric conditions requires learning some basic exposure information. Once you know the basics, you can alter, adapt, and experiment in order to obtain the particular results you want.

Whenever you include the sun in a photograph, your choice of exposure will be influenced to some extent by the lens you use. With a wide-angle or standard focal length lens, by far the largest part of the picture area will be sky or landscape. Since the sun is so small in the total area, it will affect your meter reading less than if you were using a longer lens. Regardless of the atmospheric conditions when you point your camera at the sun, your meter will indicate a need for less exposure the longer the lens you use, because the sun occupies more of the picture space. For instance, if you decide to photograph the sun with an exposure of 1/60 second at f/16 when using a wide-angle lens, you'll probably find that you need to reduce that to 1/125 second at f/16 for a 100mm or 135mm lens, and more still for a 300mm lens or longer. If you have lenses of different focal lengths, establish the basic adjustments you'll have to make for each lens by making your own comparison tests.

Bright sun

When you point your camera at the bright sun in a clear blue sky, your meter reading may be inaccurate, because the meter isn't designed to read such a high level of light intensity. So keep these exposure recommendations in mind as a guide. With ISO 25 film, try 1/125 second at f/22; with ISO 64 film use 1/250 second at f/22. (You'll find that these are also useful exposure guides for photographing sun dogs and brilliant light reflected off water.) With films of higher speeds, increase the shutter speed accordingly, though this is clearly a good time to use slow- or medium-speed film.

Sunrises and sunsets

As the sun's rays travel through the atmosphere, they encounter dust particles and air molecules, which bend the light rays. At sunrise and sunset, the sun is farther away from us than it is at other times of day, so the rays have to travel farther through the atmosphere to reach us; they encounter more particles and molecules, and are bent more, than when the sun is overhead. The short wave-lengths of light (blue, violet) are bent the most, and are deflected away from us. The long wave-lengths (red) are bent the least, and reach us more or less unadulterated by the other colours. This is why sunrises and sunsets are reddish. The more particles and air molecules encountered by the sun's rays at sunrise or sunset, the more pronounced the red hue will be.

Unlike the exposure for a bright sun in a clear sky, which remains the same sunny day after sunny day, exposures for sunrises and sunsets can vary tremendously. The light level increases constantly from well before sunrise to well after; it decreases in the same way, as the sun sets and darkness falls. There is no standard exposure guide for these situations, except that with all lenses one f/stop underexposure produces strong, well-saturated colour. However, there are metering practices that will ensure you get well-exposed sunrises and sunsets every time. With wide-angle and normal lenses, compose the picture and take a meter reading *with the sun in the picture*. Then, to obtain the colour saturation usually apparent to the eye, underexpose by one f/stop or one shutter speed. However, you must be careful not to include a lot of dark, foreground landscape, as this will affect the meter reading and result in an overexposed sky. If you want to include a large amount of land beneath the horizon, meter off the sun and sky areas *before* you compose the picture. With 100mm lenses or longer, it's better to meter off the sky *adjacent to the sun*, compose your picture, and then underexpose by one f/stop. The same metering procedures apply to sunrises, except that many sunrises are more delicate in hue and, if you want to retain that delicacy, you should only underexpose by half an f/stop or not at all. In both morning and evening situations, you should feel free to vary your exposures in order to intensify or reduce the colour density.

Rainbows

When sunlight passes through rain drops, the drops bend the light waves much as prisms do. This effect is easy to observe in wet grass after the clouds have blown away. When it's raining in part of the sky, but the sun is shining from the opposite direction, the same thing happens – a whole shower of rain drops bends the light rays, and a rainbow occurs. Because the long wave-lengths of light are bent the least and the short wave-lengths are bent the most, the outside rim of a rainbow is always red and the inside rim always violet.

In order to saturate the hues of a rainbow in your photographs, expose as you would for a sunset. If you obey your meter, the colour saturation will be diminished and you'll be disappointed. Try underexposing by one f/stop or shutter speed. If the sky behind the rainbow is very dark, as it sometimes is, try underexposing by one and a half f/stops. A polarizing filter will also improve the colour rendition. On rare occasions you may see a "fogbow" or a "mistbow" – a white arc against a bank of fog or mist. These are not easy to record on film, but you will succeed if you overexpose slightly.

Try photographing rainbows with lenses of various focal lengths, and experiment with the compositions. For example, you can show an entire rainbow (and much more) with a 16mm or 17mm lens. With a 200mm lens you can make a very striking vertical of one end of a rainbow meeting the earth. Any zoom lens will allow you to vary your compositions easily.

Sea fog and morning mists

When warm air blows across large bodies of cold water, you may have the opportunity to photograph fog. If cold air moves across warm water, such as lakes and marshes, you may have a chance to make pictures of morning mists – until the sun heats the air to the same temperature as the water, dissolving the mists.

In metering for fog and mist, simply follow the guidelines that apply to any light-toned subject matter. If the sun is behind you and falling on the mist, take your reading off the mist and open your lens by about one f/stop to lighten the mist. (If you follow the meter precisely, you'll get a middle grey mist.) If the sun is shining toward you through the mist, the same principle applies – to keep the lightness and mistiness, open the lens a little after reading your meter. If the mist appears quite pink or golden, you may want to adhere to the meter reading in order to keep the colour more saturated. With lenses of 100mm or longer, meter to either side of the sun's orb, and then come back to your original composition.

Rays of sunlight and shadow streaming through trees on a misty morning are often difficult to meter properly, and virtually impossible when you are facing the sun. However, appropriate exposure is easy to determine if you follow two simple steps. *1/* Check the sheet that comes with each roll of film to find the recommended exposure for front-lighted subjects on a sunny day. If you are using ISO 64 film, that will be 1/250 second at f/8. *2/* Think of the exposure for shooting a bright sun in a clear sky. For ISO 64 film, that will be 1/250 second at f/22. You'll notice immediately that there are only two f/stops between f/8 and f/22 – these are f/11 and f/16. Now, as you face the sun, judge the brightness of its rays streaming toward you through the trees. They are probably brighter than most front-lighted subjects on a sunny day, but not as bright as the sun in a clear sky, so your lens opening will be either f/11 or f/16, or in between. Any of these exposures will likely produce excellent results.

If you are not facing the sun, but are standing at an angle to the light rays, the intensity of the light will be reduced. Now you can use your meter effectively. Take a reading from your subject and use the indicated setting, if the composition is divided more-or-less equally between light rays and darker material. If two-thirds or more of the space is *brighter* than middle grey, overexpose by half an f/stop or more to record the brightness accurately. If two-thirds or more of the area is darker than middle grey, underexpose by half an f/stop or more to make sure the darks are not washed out. You'll find that the few rays in the darker picture are properly exposed. Deciding on the exposure for rays of light streaming through a misty woods is a splendid exercise for developing your own judgement.

Clouds

Clouds, with their ever-changing patterns and colours, can be fascinating subjects for photographers. While there are several quite different kinds of them, all clouds are formed when water vapour in the air is cooled to the point that it condenses. Clouds are composed of billions of water droplets or ice particles. The drops of water form around particles like dust, smoke, or salt in the air; so if the air is very clean, condensation can't occur and the sky will remain cloudless.

When you photograph clouds, the exposure to choose will depend on the effect you want. For example, if the sky is dark and ominous, use your meter to obtain a reading, and then underexpose anywhere from one to three f/stops to retain the dark foreboding sense of the sky. If you decide on maximum underexposure (two or three f/stops or shutter speeds), it helps to have a brilliant highlighted area, such as back-lighted water, in the composition. This will contrast sufficiently with the dark sky to prevent your image from appearing merely underexposed. The photograph on page 130 illustrates this point. Very often skyscapes that include clouds (and most skyscapes do, because it's clouds that make them attractive or interesting) will benefit from a little underexposure. This is especially true if there is a clear contrast between the clouds and the sky, as in the photograph on page 128. Also, a polarizing screen can be used to darken the sky and make white clouds stand out dramatically, particularly if you are shooting at a right angle to the sun. Familiarize yourself with other filters as well, since they can produce dramatic differences in the way clouds and the sky are recorded on film. (See "Filters" on page 165.)

After sunset, but before the sky is dark, try making time exposures of clouds to indicate wind movement. The results may be both good documents and striking impressions of a windy evening.

There are some natural phenomena and objects in the sky that can be photographed only at night, such as northern lights and stars. There are others that are visible during the day, but which can be photographed more easily and effectively when the sky is dark, for example the moon or lightning.

Lightning

The next time you watch an electrical storm or photograph lightning, contemplate some "electrifying" facts. Lightning strikes the earth somewhere one hundred times every second, more than eight and a half million times a year. As destructive as lightning is, its absence would mean the speedy and total destruction of life on this planet. In less than an hour Earth would lose to the upper atmosphere the negative electrical charge that enables it to convert atmospheric nitrogen into other forms of nitrogen, which almost all plants require. Without plants, there would be no animal life.

If you should capture lightning on film during the daytime, it would be an accident of timing rather than a matter of good planning. The best way to go about photographing lightning at night is to: *1/* load a slow-speed film in your camera;   *2/* put your camera on a tripod;   *3/* choose a wide-angle or normal lens;   *4/* compose your picture with a bit of foreground and a lot of black sky, and focus at infinity;   *5/* set the lens at its smallest aperture, say f/16, set the shutter-speed dial for a time exposure, and press the shutter release. Since the sky is so dark, the film is not being exposed (or is being exposed very, very slowly) even though the shutter gate is open. It will only be exposed when lightning flashes, and then only the narrow path of the bolt itself will be exposed. You can wait for more bolts, if you want, without advancing the film. Obviously, in cities, where street and building lights reflect off clouds, nights are not nearly as dark as they are in the country. This means film kept on time exposure may be fully exposed after a few seconds, and whether lightning has occurred or not, you'll need to advance the film to the next frame. If you live in a city and want to photograph lightning, it will help to use the film with the slowest speed available and to make sure your lens is set at minimum aperture.

The moon

For most people the moon is a haunting symbol and an object of pictorial beauty. Once you have tried any night photography, you'll be ready to photograph moonlit landscapes and the moon itself.

Pictures of the moon in the night sky without any scene below are very easy to make. For a rich, yellow, full moon with detail in its surface use a long telephoto lens (300mm to 1000mm) and expose as you would for any other front-lighted object in sunlight – 1/250 second at f/8 on ISO 64 film. If there is a light cloud cover or haze, you may want to open the lens one f/stop. You can also give the impression of haze by breathing lightly on your lens.

If you want to photograph a *landscape illuminated by moonlight, but without the moon* in your picture, here are some suggestions.

1/ The easiest time of the year to make good landscape pictures by moonlight is in the winter, when snow covers the ground and substantially reduces the contrast between the sky and the earth.

2/ Twilight is usually the best time for night pictures of the land, with the sky a deep, glowing blue, and the horizon line visible. If you are facing east, try shooting approximately 20 to 40 minutes after sunset; facing west, you can photograph about 40 to 60 minutes after sunset. If the sky is overcast and you can't see the moon, you'll still get the same rich colour; but you can start shooting a little earlier and you won't need to worry about differences in brightness between the eastern and western sky.

3/ In order to convey the sense of moonlight on the landscape, you should underexpose; but the longer your exposure time the less you will have to underexpose. Let me explain. If your light meter suggests a setting of 1/2 second at f/2.8, underexpose by one full f/stop. (You can underexpose even more if there is a contrasting light source in the picture.) However, if you want maximum depth of field (f/22) for the same scene, you will require a time exposure of 32 seconds. In this case you should not underexpose. While a setting of f/2.8 at 1/2 second is theoretically the exposure equivalent of f/22 at 32 seconds, the shorter time will actually produce a lighter exposure than the longer one. The reason is that, on long exposures in dark situations, film reacts more slowly than it would in normal light, so the film speed or ISO rating is effectively reduced. For photographing a light-coloured or snowy landscape illuminated by a full moon long after twilight, the basic exposure guideline is f/2 for 30 seconds with ISO 64 film.

4/ You can heighten the blue in your scene by using tungsten film or a blue filter. Also, you can simulate moonlight by shooting during the day with tungsten film or a blue filter and underexposing two or three f/stops. Your picture will appear more authentic if you include an area of reflected light, such as a patch of bright back-lighted water. If you are intent on documenting the colour of the moonlight you may reject this method, but it is well to remember that all pictures of moonlight are impressions. It is virtually impossible to show a night landscape the way our eyes actually see it.

If you want to photograph a *night landscape with the moon* in the sky, plan to be in the right place as the moon rises or goes down. However, you may find that to expose the land properly, you must overexpose the moon, or conversely, to expose the moon correctly, you must underexpose the land. Here's an alternative. It may require a little practice, but it's not difficult and will ensure success. The trick is to shoot the moon and landscape at different times – and to add the one to the other. Let's say you start with the landscape. Here's how you do it.

Start with an empty camera. *1/* Cock the shutter, so it will be impossible for the film advance lever to move. *2/* Insert a roll of film in your camera and put the tip of the film leader in the take-up spool. *3/* Advance the film, turning the spool with your fingers, until the sprocket holes on both sides of the film just reach the take-up spool or some other identification point in the back of your camera – which you must remember. *4/* Close the camera, and press the shutter release. *5/* Advance the film two more times, which means shooting off two more frames – something you should do with every roll of film anyway. Now you are ready to make your evening landscape pictures.

Proceed in the way I described earlier, only this time make sure you leave some empty sky space in each frame, where you can add the moon later. Also, keep an accurate record of what you have done, or will need to do when you add the moon. Your notes should look like this. Photo 1 – vertical, place 135mm moon upper left; Photo 2 – horizontal, place 300mm moon far upper right; and so on. Continue shooting until you have finished the film, then rewind it carefully, so you don't roll the leader inside the cassette. Put the film in its canister and use an elastic band to attach your notes. Then, store the film in your refrigerator until the night you add the moons.

When you put that roll of film into your camera again, you must load it exactly as before, if you want the moons to be positioned properly in the land-scapes. Remember to align the film with the same identification point in the camera, as you did the first time through. If you are photographing the moon with lenses shorter than 300mm, you should probably use different exposure settings from the ones I suggested earlier (page 41); otherwise the moon may seem rather insignificant. If the moon is full and bright, try 1/250 second at f/3.5 on ISO 64 film. For a half moon, try 1/60 second at the same f/stop, and for a crescent moon, 1/15 second. You may want to shorten exposure times after you've seen your first roll, if you prefer more surface detail in the moon.

Treat my suggestions as guidelines, and vary them if adaptations will produce photographs that seem more authentic or are more to your liking. Experiments with composition, exposure, and other techniques may produce unusual or striking images.

Stars

There are other features of the night sky to challenge the nature photographer – the pattern of stars and planets, the dance of northern lights. Unless you have access to a telescope, it may not occur to you to photograph stars, but if so think again – you can make star pictures with your basic equipment. All you need is a tripod, a camera and lens, film, and a black sky in which stars appear clear and bright.

A picture of stars made with a short exposure may look no more interesting than pin pricks in unexposed film. However, if you leave your camera for a period of time on a tripod, lens pointed heavenward, with the shutter locked open, the rotation of the earth will trace out delicate star trails across your photograph. It helps to include some land or trees at the bottom of the picture to give scale and a sense of vastness. Using a medium-speed film (ISO 64 or ISO 100) and a lens opening of f/2.8, try exposures of 15 seconds to one hour. For longer exposures, use a smaller aperture. The longer the exposure, the longer the star trails will be.

Use a wide-angle lens to show a large expanse of sky. A 16mm or 17mm wide-angle lens pointed at the North Star or the Southern Cross will produce a marvelous, circular pattern of whirling star trails, if you leave the lens open for several hours. Any bright constellation will produce more striking trails than a random section of sky. Of course, while your camera is at work, you could be in your tent or your house studying about stars.

Aurora borealis or aurora australis

The polar auroras are magnificent displays of light in the night-time sky. In northern latitudes they are called northern lights, and in southern latitudes, southern lights. The auroras are caused by electrified particles shot out by the sun during periods of sunspot activity, generally in the equinoctial periods. These particles contact thin gases very high in the atmosphere, making them glow. When the particles encounter nitrogen, the auroral display may be reddish; when they encounter oxygen, the "lights" may look quite green, as in the photograph on page 138. These displays may appear at any time of night, all year around. The greater the sunspot activity, the more frequent and intense the displays are likely to be.

Good photographs of the northern or southern lights are not common. Again, sky conditions have to be right and you have to be on location when they occur. Even though I live in the country and see northern lights more often than city dwellers, I still miss many excellent displays because they frequently occur very late at night, or simply because I haven't looked outside. However, if you want to capture the spectacle on film and are willing to wait for that special night, here's what to do. Set up your tripod and camera, and attach either a wide-angle or normal lens, preferably one that has a large maximum lens opening (f/1.4 to f/2.8). With the lens fully open, make exposures of 15 to 40 seconds with ISO 64 film. Check carefully for overhead wires in the picture space. It's easy for you to miss them at night, but your camera won't. Also avoid including nearby house or street lights in the frame, because they are much brighter than the aurora and will appear as "burned out" hot spots in the final image. More distant artificial lights may not present this problem. Try to photograph the aurora on different occasions. You'll be amazed at how varied your images will be.

PHOTOGRAPHING INVISIBLE THINGS

Although air is invisible, we document its presence every time we photograph a blue sky, a sunset, or a morning mist. None of these things would be visible without the atmosphere for light to pass through. The atmosphere also transmits the sun's energy in the form of heat. This and other natural forces such as wind and air pressure are vital to our existence, and yet they are the most difficult to capture on film. We must be content to record the changes they work in the world.

Heat

Unless you have the special equipment that can actually photograph heat itself, you can only portray it through its visible effects, such as dried mud, scorched plants, and desert mirages. Since temperature is the measurement of heat intensity, you're photographing a relative kind of heat when you show the low end of the scale – cold – through winter pictures, for example. Differences in the amounts of heat present, that is differences in temperature, produce fog, mist, and clouds. Temperature affects the whole spectrum of plant functions and animal behaviour. For example, you can indicate the presence of heat through a picture of a bee pollinating a flower, or a snake lying on a rock. When you think about it, it's practically impossible to make pictures without, at the same time, documenting the presence and effects of heat.

Wind

Differences in temperature help set up differences in air pressure, which in turn make the air move, producing everything from zephyrs to cyclones. Since wind, like heat, is impossible to photograph directly, a photographer must show it indirectly or by implication, through its patterns and effects. A time exposure of clouds after sunset on a blustery evening will capture the wind's force and direction; and so will the blurred motion of plants or branches tossing in the wind, as in the photograph on page 15. Even in a high wind, you will need a fairly slow shutter speed (1/60 second or slower) to convey the impression of movement of something that is fixed in one place, such as a delicate plant. Also, by photographing snow blowing into drifts, or sand dunes after the wind has abated, you can record very clear stories of air movement.

Because the sun provides heat and light that make the atmosphere a place for life, nature photographers should look up as often as they look down. However, the sun also makes life possible in water and soil, and air interacts with these two mediums to ensure the development and growth of living things. So, let's consider water and soil in turn and how to photograph the natural things and processes that are part of them.

Water and natural processes

Water assumes many forms, appears in many places, and does many things. As a liquid, water is part of all living things and has a powerful influence on their functions and behaviour. It collects in ponds, lakes, rivers, and oceans, providing major habitats for plants and animals; it aids in the processes of erosion and decomposition. As a solid – snow, ice, and frost – water blankets both terrestrial and aquatic habitats, insulating them against heat loss and the harshest effects of cold air. As vapour, water helps make weather possible; but because water vapour is invisible, it can only be photographed when it condenses into mist, clouds, and precipitation, in other words, when it changes into its liquid or solid states. However, these two states of water offer the photographer continual opportunities to learn about nature and to make exciting images.

PHOTOGRAPHING WATER

Since the colour appearance of water is so changeable, you should examine it very carefully if you want to avoid surprises in your pictures. This is particularly true for large surfaces on days when there are clouds in the sky, because neither the colour nor the tone of water is uniform. In fact, one of the best exercises for a nature photographer is to sit beside a lake or stream and immerse your attention in the play of tones and colours on the surface. If you learn to really "see" water, your overall visual awareness will be heightened.

Water is often in motion. Waves, ripples, and falling rain are not as easy to study as calm water, simply because the patterns of colour and tone move more swiftly than your eyes can grasp. However, it's still possible to perceive overall hue and tone, and to select the film and techniques that will record them the way you want.

Rain

Falling rain can be difficult to capture on film. If you open a window and point your lens at a downpour, you'll probably record only a greyish blur, no matter what shutter speed you choose. However, special opportunities may arise that make it possible to get very good pictures of rain falling, but you must have your camera ready and be prepared to act quickly. If it rains heavily during the late afternoon or early evening, watch carefully. In zones of westerly winds most storms and showers move from west to east, so that while it's still raining where you are the sun may break through clouds to the west, back-lighting the rain. In other wind zones, morning showers often provide the same opportunities. If you have pre-selected a composition, preferably with a background of dark tones (evergreen trees or buildings, for example), the brilliant back-lighted streaks of rain will stand out clearly, especially if you underexpose about one f/stop to keep the background fairly dark. You'll record longer streaks of rain and show the downpour more clearly if you use speeds of 1/8 to 1/30 second.

Water drops

Much of the earth's surface is shielded from the direct impact of falling rain by a covering of plants. Drops of water collect on branches and twigs and combine to form larger drops which fall to the ground at widely-spaced intervals. Hence a tree protects the soil beneath it from a heavy overall impact, but also subjects particular spots to bigger single splashes than they would get if the trees were not there. Certain species of fungi have adapted to this situation magnificently. You'll find them growing under trees because there they are protected from the force of heavy rainfall; however, when they reach maturity, they need the impact of a large water drop to shatter their spore cases and release the spores. So, if you are photographing drops of water, you may want to show their function in a larger process of life. Like everything else in nature, water drops are not merely things-in-themselves, but are part of the endless chain of life and death.

   Rain drops and dew drops are beautiful natural objects, and rare is the nature photographer who has not tried to capture their delicate structures and shimmering reflections. Water drops are not always spherical. If you watch water dripping slowly from a blade of grass, you will notice that even though each drop wants to escape from the grass, it resists leaving until the last instant. The drop stretches to its limit before it falls. The surface tension of water creates a dilemma for the molecules in a droplet – they want to escape, but at the same time they want to stick together because they are more attracted to their own kind than to air molecules. Using a macro lens or other close-up equipment, try to capture images of water droplets at various stages of departure from their source.

Water drops frequently act as prisms, breaking up rays of sunlight into the full colour spectrum. While you may want to document this phenomenon, you should also regard it as an opportunity for uninhibited visual exploration and interpretive photography. The best way to begin is to crawl around in the grass with some close-up equipment on your camera – practically any close-up equipment will do. (If you don't want to get wet, pull on a pair of light plastic rain pants. Protect your lens with an ultraviolet or skylight filter.) To capture the prismatic effect, you will usually have to face the sun, so that the drops are back-lighted. Look at drops in the grass with, or without, your lens. If you don't see any drops showing the colour spectrum, tilt your lens down at about a right angle to the sun's rays, and look again. It helps to have the lens set at its widest aperture and focused at a fixed distance (10 to 30 centimetres, depending on the close-up equipment you are using), since it's easier to move the camera slightly forward or backward than to refocus continually. You will often find that out-of-focus drops show the prismatic effect most clearly. Using that effect, you can make pure abstractions of colour, or you can focus on the tip of a blade of grass and use the colour patterns as a dramatic background.

When you calculate the exposures for close-ups of water drops, remember that, unless the drop is very large in the picture space, it will have no effect on the meter reading. Instead, the meter will measure the background. So, you must note the difference in brightness between the drop and the background. If the background is dark, you will need to underexpose in order to keep it that way and to prevent the water drop from looking washed out in appearance. More often than not, you will find it necessary to underexpose by at least one f/stop or shutter speed, and if there is strong back lighting, two f/stops or shutter speeds. Only on rare occasions (usually on cloudy days) should you follow your meter exactly when photographing water drops close up. In these cases, the tone (brightness) of the drop and the background will be about the same, but a contrasting colour in the image may provide visual separation and make the drop stand out clearly. When there is no colour contrast, you can achieve separation by focusing on the drop and using the shallowest possible depth of field, putting the background out of focus.

No other subject offers a nature photographer such a range of possibilities for documentary and interpretive images, and few subjects are as easy to find. Even if you are confined to your home, you have access to this enchanting miniature world.

Bodies of water

Just as water drops may be photographed in motion (rain falling) or in a more static configuration as single drops, so large bodies of water may be recorded in either a more active or a more passive state. What constitutes a large body of water depends entirely on the size of the creature viewing it. To me a puddle is small, but to an insect it may be gigantic. However, since insects have yet to take up nature photography, let's look at bodies of water that seem large to human beings – such as lakes, rivers, and oceans. From a purely visual point of view they constitute a major pictorial feature in any composition where they appear. A photographer should think of them in terms of colour and form (shape, line, texture, and perspective) – and look for their emotional or symbolic qualities. Vast bodies of water are often "felt" as much as seen – an emotional response that sometimes seems stronger than the purely biological one.

Most of us see and photograph only the surfaces of lakes, rivers, and oceans. Therefore, the texture of the surface has to be considered for both the information it provides and the mood it evokes. A very rough texture, marked by peaks and troughs, indicates a strong disturbance, a turbulence that will threaten us if we venture into the water. Medium-rough texture evokes caution. Ripples have a calming effect, as they suggest gentleness. A smooth surface stimulates feelings of safety and peace. While it's relatively easy to photograph the calmness of water, showing *turbulence and roughness* requires more judgement. Choosing a shutter speed that will show the power of the waves racing toward the shore and breaking on the rocks is part of it, but there's more. Embedded in the idea of turbulence is the sense of darkness. Even when the ocean is studded with white caps, we may describe it as a dark and stormy sea. What we feel can be as important as what we see. A photographer recording the scene must decide which truth to tell – the physical fact or the emotional impact. Will you take a documentary or an interpretive approach? Your decision will determine the technical adjustments you make (exposure, for example) and thus the appearance of the final image.

Large waves suggest raw power. If you want to express that impression you may select a fast shutter speed, wait for a moment when waves are smashing against rocks, and freeze the shattered water in midair. Or, you may trip the shutter a fraction of a second earlier to suspend the waves above the rocks – the uncompleted action suggesting the impact that is about to occur. However, a shutter speed slow enough to allow waves to move across the picture space during the exposure will produce a greater sense of motion, although it may not be as effective in expressing sheer power. If you underexpose any of these images, you can also evoke dark turbulence and rage. On the other hand, your intentions may be more documentary. You may want to show wave action or wave patterns. If description is your goal, a high vantage point will allow you to show many waves and, at the same time, the distances between them. Use a shutter speed fast enough to arrest the motion. Such a picture could also document the effect of wind on water.

Calmer water provides an opportunity to photograph the pattern of *ripples*, which can be especially striking at sunrise or sunset. Experiment with various shutter speeds. Fast speeds will arrest the pattern, but if the light is low you may have to open the aperture fairly wide – sacrificing depth of field in order to expose the ripples properly. Slower shutter speeds will produce some blurring, but you may be surprised at how attractive the results are. Time exposures of ripples made before sunrise or after sunset can be very beautiful. Use a slow-speed film (perhaps ISO 25) and maximum depth of field (f/16 or f/22), so that you can easily make a long exposure (30 seconds) while the water still reflects the warm hues. Although many ripples will flow across the picture space during the time exposure, they will all crest more or less in the same places. So, a lengthy time exposure may look quite a lot like an image made with a much faster shutter speed.

Clear, still water surfaces produce perfect *reflections*, which you may want to record. However, you'll find even greater challenges and exciting opportunities for natural abstracts, if you photograph reflections in gently swelling or rippled water. Observe the water surface carefully until you begin to see the possibilities. Then, after you have composed a picture, try shooting it at various shutter speeds. You won't be able to predict the results exactly, but you'll have some good images and lots of ideas for your next attempt.

When shooting a large water surface, notice that the water often appears lighter in the distance and darker near you, especially if it's clear and shallow near you. The bottom of a pond or river absorbs light (especially if it's dark in pigment), and since the bottom is close to the surface in shallow water, the absorption there is greater. If your meter is of the "bottom-weighted" type (is influenced more by the level of light intensity in the lower half of the view-finder), you will have to compensate by underexposing slightly in order to keep the nearer water dark and to avoid washing out colour and texture in the distance. However, you may be able to overcome the problem entirely by changing the camera's position and its angle to the water.

Because of its infinite changeability, few subjects are worthy of more careful observation than the surface of a large lake or river. You can study it for the information it provides about nature, or lose yourself in the changing patterns of its hues and tones.

Waterfalls

All photographs of flowing water are impressions, so the techniques you choose for photographing a waterfall should be determined by the effect you want to convey. You may want to make an overall shot of the waterfall to show its general appearance. If the waterfall is neither large nor steep, you could try a slow shutter speed (1/2, 1/4, or 1/8 second, for example) so the water will appear to flow gently, as I did in the photograph on page 129. If it's a huge, churning torrent that tumbles down from a great height, a fast shutter speed (perhaps 1/500 second) would likely express the power of the cataract more fully. You may also want to zero in more closely on the gentle flow or the raging torrent and try to capture images of abstract designs in the water. Experiment with close-ups of the falling water, trying various shutter speeds and exposures to see what you can capture. A slow shutter speed may produce a delicate tracery of lines or a misty blur; but if you arrest the movement with a very fast shutter speed, you may show patterns of water surging and ebbing as it falls, since the flow over a waterfall is seldom truly constant. A close-up of a gentle waterfall from a low angle may capture reflected colours in the water, and your shutter speed will influence the way the colours are recorded. A slow shutter speed may produce the effect of flowing colour. A fast shutter speed could freeze the colours in a more static pattern and reduce their visual importance, but also intensify certain shapes. Any waterfall is worth a lot of exploring, and each image you make can reveal something of its character and mood.

PHOTOGRAPHING SNOW AND ICE

After a blizzard, the land is covered by a shallow body of "water," though we rarely think of a blanket of snow as a vast lake, because the visual differences are too great. So are physical and biological differences. Nature adapts to snow cover in both the short and the long term. Where snow is present for only a few months, some animals, such as the varying hare, develop white colouration for winter protection against predators. Where snow is present for much of the year, as it is in the Arctic, some animals are white all year long. Because snow traps enormous quantities of air and possesses high specific and latent heat, it is a natural insulator against the effects of extreme cold. Many animals and some birds make use of this insulating quality by burrowing into snow, and less hardy plants will be more successful in surviving the winter if the snow covering prevents the soil from freezing deeply. Snow is one of nature's devices for protecting living things against the effects of cold – except for nature photographers, who should protect themselves by dressing warmly.

Snow plays an important role in the natural selection of plant life. For example, if the branches of a tree become overburdened by the weight of snow and ice until they cannot support the load any longer, they may break off or cause the tree to topple. Thus, the stronger trees nearby will have more space and food to grow and propagate. This natural process can be recorded in a series of images taken in various places during the winter, or in the same place over several winter and summer seasons.

Snow

Snow provides more opportunities to learn about photography than virtually any other subject. That's because the appearance of snow is so readily altered by changes in the quality, direction, colour, and intensity of light. When you study light you are dealing with the basis of photography, indeed with vision itself.

The *quality* of light is its harshness or softness. Harsh light emanates from a direct, unshaded source, like the sun in a clear sky. Soft light is what we experience on a cloudy day, or in a shaded area. Both the physical appearance of snow and the evocative power of that appearance change radically when the quality of the light changes. Harsh light, for example, brings out texture. Soft light diminishes it. A photographer has to adapt immediately to the change and to what it suggests.

The *direction* of light has a powerful effect on the appearance of texture in snow, as well as on image design. Both back lighting and side lighting emphasize the roughness of the snow's surface. A direction between the two (light and shadow streaming in from an upper corner of the picture space) is equally emphatic. Only front lighting tends to reduce the appearance of texture, but even then snow seems rougher than it does under soft or indirect light.

The colour of snow is the *colour* of the light source. Whether we perceive that or not, the film usually will. The colour of shadows is the opposite to the colour of the light source. That's why, late on a sunny winter afternoon, when the snow appears very warm (gold or pink), the shadows are very blue. If you want red shadows, shine a strong blue-green light on a snowy object some night. Only when the sun is high in the sky is snow truly white and shadows reversed in grey or black. If you don't want to be surprised by the colour of snow in your photographs, be sure you look carefully at the colour of shadows. Even so, your eyes may play tricks on you, or film may not record exactly what you thought you saw.

The *intensity* of light is the measure of its brightness. The more brilliant the light source, the brighter the snow and the darker the shadows in relation to the open areas. Just as light causes colour contrasts between shaded and unshaded areas, it also produces tonal contrasts. In weak illumination (fading sun, for example) all contrasts are reduced. A few minutes after sunset or on a cloudy day there are virtually no contrasts in snow – it is both monochromatic and monotonal.

Regardless of the intensity of the light source, we normally perceive snow to be lighter in tone than "middle grey," which is what all reflected-light exposure meters are designed to indicate. (All meters in cameras are of this type.) So, if you set your camera on "automatic" or follow your meter exactly, you will get middle grey snow (or middle blue, middle gold, and so on). Since most of the time you won't want your pictures looking as if the snow is covered with soot or a dull haze, you must "open up" or overexpose to "put the white back in." This is particularly important for front lighting and for even lighting (cloudy days) because then there are no shadows. So, in order to get white snow in a photograph, you must regard your meter only as a guide, and overexpose approximately one full f/stop with colour film – "approximately" because conditions vary. For example, if you overexpose bright front-lighted snow by much more than one stop, you'll wipe out all appearance of texture, which is normally not desirable. If you overexpose the deep pink snow of sunset too much, you'll wash out the colour. Generally speaking, the more white snow in the picture, the more you should overexpose. The less white snow or the richer the colour of the snow, the less you should overexpose. If there's only a little snow (a patch here or there, or branches rimmed with snow against a blue sky), you won't need to overexpose at all.

While many snow pictures show texture, there is no rule saying that they must do so. If you want to wipe out all detail in snow, in order, say, to make dark tree trunks stand out starkly, go ahead and overexpose more than one f/stop. Don't forget, though, that the trees will also start to get lighter, so there's a point when the benefit of extreme overexposure may be lost. If you want all kinds of texture and sparkles in back-lighted snow, and don't care about whiteness, follow your meter.

Learn to evaluate the extent of bright areas in your compositions, so you can make reasonable judgements about how they will affect your exposures. Nobody can provide you with hard and fast rules that will work every time; besides, you'll learn far more through a bit of trial and error. Select a situation you can work on easily, perhaps a snow drift beside your home. Start off with long shots and medium close-ups; then try making back-lighted macro photographs of edges and bumps in the drift. It might help to do this over a period of days. Such exercises will help you learn how to expose for snow in various lighting conditions, and will provide chances for exploring your subject in great depth.

Falling snow

Snow, of course, is not a static phenomenon. It moves and changes. Flakes fall from the sky. Snow melts and refreezes as ice. Sometimes its consistency is like cornmeal; sometimes it's fluffy and feather-like. Wind hurls it into the air, and drives it into huge drifts. The variations are endless, and each has a way of reaching into our psyche and affecting us in profound ways. Each of these winter moods is worth photographing, but few will give you as much of a challenge as a good, old-fashioned snowstorm or blizzard.

You can photograph falling snow with or without a flash unit. If you use flash, especially at dusk when the background will be black, the individual flakes will stand out clearly. They will give the impression of arrested motion, of a world and a storm frozen in time. However, you may prefer to show the movement, because a blizzard is a howling, raging event. A lot is going on. For this you probably won't use flash, but will choose a slow shutter speed (1/15 to 1/60 second, depending on how fast the wind is moving the flakes) so the flakes will be blurred. If you've included areas of dark tones in your composition (evergreen trees or dark red brick buildings, for instance), the blurred flakes will stand out clearly and you'll "feel" the blizzard.

Another technique for making snowy winter pictures is double exposure. First, focus through the falling snow, on a background such as the edge of a forest with trees covered by snow. After you make that exposure, refocus at minimum distance using a shallow depth of field and a fast shutter speed. Shoot again on the same frame, after rewinding one frame or using the double-exposure lever. Your photograph will show large soft blobs of white all over the scene, and will capture the sensation of being out in the storm.

Frost

Frost can be treated rather like snow when you are shooting a field covered with it. As with snow you should keep the exposure slightly on the light side. However, if you are making close-ups of leaves or berries rimmed with frost, you'll have to note carefully the overall distribution of tones and adjust the exposures accordingly. Meter the major tonal area carefully and base your exposure calculations on how light or dark you think it should appear in your photograph. For example, the exposure for a composition of tufts of frost on stems, leaves, or berries will probably be a little darker than middle grey and will require slight underexposure. (See the photograph on page 22.) Highly back-lighted frost on the edge of a leaf may lose its detail and crystalline appearance, unless you underexpose by a full f/stop. If you think that the side of the leaf nearest you (in the shade) will lose colour and detail through under-exposure, use a piece of silver foil to reflect light onto its dark side. While back lighting often heightens the dramatic effect, you can also make excellent frost pictures in shaded locations, where exposures are usually easier to calculate.

Frost often accumulates on windowpanes, as well. Water vapour condensing on glass, and then freezing, can create remarkable patterns which lend themselves to both documentary and interpretive treatment. Even if the pane of glass is very large, you'll want to use a macro lens or some other close-up equipment to select the details that will produce the most exciting images. Since glass is a flat surface, you may be able to render all parts of a design in sharp focus even with a narrow depth of field – lens openings of f/5.6, f/8, or f/11. However, if you are positioned at a slight angle to the pane, don't hesitate to use f/16 or f/22, as out-of-focus areas may be very distracting. It's tempting to make your windowpane pictures only at sunrise or sunset when warm light colours the frost or the sun appears as a fiery orb behind the crystal patterns. However, any time of day can produce attractive tones and hues – soft, indirect light, in particular, lends itself to very subtle renditions of the frost. The photograph on page 83 was made when tonal transitions were gradual and hues delicate and restrained.

Ice

Ice is usually easier to photograph than water, simply because it's less likely to change as rapidly. Normally you will have plenty of time to consider ice compositions with care. The opportunities for photographing ice are numerous – sheets of ice full of cracks and bubbles (see the photograph on page 155), puddles in which leaves and grasses show through the ice, ice on trees after a period of freezing rain, ice in rock crevices, frozen waterfalls (especially early in winter when ice columns aren't buried in snow), and icicles. As with most subjects, you can be as factual or as imaginative in your treatment as you want – documenting the effects of freezing in various ecosystems, or abandoning yourself to the delight of finding pure visual abstractions.

Ice ranges in tone from almost white to almost black. If it's on the light side, overexpose a little in order to achieve realistic tone; if it's grey, follow your meter; and, if it's dark, underexpose, provided the ice contains some highlights. Dark ice often has lines or bumps that capture light and provide unusual patterns. These lines are much brighter than the main sheet of ice, but they are so narrow that you can safely ignore them in calculating your exposures. If you determine the exposure that will make ice appear as dark in your image as it is to your eye, then the lines of light should also turn out satisfactorily.

When winter comes, set out with your camera and lenses to photograph the cold, hard truths of snow and ice, but allow yourself time for fantasy too.

Soil and the natural landscape

Soil covers the continents like patchwork quilts and just as quilts are composed of many different colours, so our globe displays a great array of different soils. Although vegetation hides much of the soil, remember that what is beneath is an important component of a landscape. Soil types and climatic conditions determine to a great degree the kind of ecosystem that develops in an area. For example, a loose granular soil in an extremely dry area might become a desert, although the same sort of soil in a region of high rainfall could be forested. Conversely, a very dry area might include both desert and grassland, because of differences in soil type. Naturally, as a plant cover develops and organic material accumulates, the composition of the soil is altered. All soil has a history. In fact, in any area where a vegetative cover has been established for a long time, the soil will show the history of the whole ecosystem.

PHOTOGRAPHING SOIL

Every kind of habitat – from deserts to rainforests – provides a natural laboratory for the study and photography of soil and soil processes.

In most major desert ecosystems, the struggle among those plants that manage to grow is not for light and space, but for moisture. You can record the way these plants compete and adapt even if you have very limited photographic equipment. For instance, if you have only a 50mm lens, you could photograph desert shrubs, showing that they are spaced fairly evenly apart. These spaces reveal how much soil each plant requires in order to get enough moisture to live. Also the stunted growth of most desert shrubs reflects the scarcity of moisture.

Desert-like conditions can exist where dry land has been misused – cultivated improperly, overgrazed, scarred by the tracks of trail bikes – and the vegetative cover destroyed. Search out a hillside or some other area that has both desert-like conditions and a healthier, thicker plant covering. Visit the area from time to time, and make photographs contrasting the healthy plants and sod in one section with the lines and ditches of exposed soil in the other. When it rains or the wind blows strongly, document how each section is affected. The grass mat in one part will protect the earth from the driving wind and rain, which you can show through pictures of blowing grasses made with a slow shutter speed, and through photographs of water lying on and around grasses. On the other part of the hillside, show dust blowing or soil being washed away. Record how the lines of exposed soil have deepened – the more porous the soil, the more obvious the impact will be. If you pick an area near your home, you can easily document the changes over a period of months or years, and show not only the differences in vegetation between the two sections, but also the differences in animal life. For example, grasses and sod support an insect and bird life that exposed soil does not. In areas that manage to regenerate after some serious destruction of plant and animal communities, a similar project can be extremely instructive for both photographers and viewers, and give you a feeling of closeness to a natural landscape.

In forests a constant supply of moisture allows a dense and diverse growth of plant and animal life. Soil is often very rich: minerals and humus combine, and are often buried under layers of decaying organic matter. A documentary shot of soil in the forest, with the vegetative cover cleared away, may tell us about its richness, drainage, and other matters; but more can be told about the soil with images showing the relationships between the forest creatures, the plants, and the non-living things. You could document the competition for light and space among plants, perhaps by showing a thick stand of young firs that contains both living and dead trees. Illustrate decomposition with a row of fungi growing on a fallen branch, or through a scattering of dead, brown leaves scarred by ants or caterpillars. Make comparison shots of the forest floor under a cedar tree and under a birch. Show new life, perhaps a maple seedling emerging from the humus. Consider why the maple is growing under a birch, but not under a cedar or in an open glen; then, try to document the reasons.

In nature, nothing exists in isolation. Everything has its place in the natural scheme of things. When we learn to focus not only on individual organisms, but also on communities and how they are linked together in ecosystems, we have a better understanding of the landscape and how to photograph it.

SEEING THE NATURAL LANDSCAPE

A landscape is a surface configuration of the earth, a countenance. It changes constantly, expressing the effects of both underlying forces and external pressures. We read landscapes the same way we read faces. A landscape photograph is a portrait of the earth's face. It is also a visual record of one or more ecosystems, or parts of the same ecosystem – revealing the topographical mosaic of the land and various habitats in which plant and animal communities live and interact. However, like the features of a face, the surface patterns of the land and the natural communities on it often seem to be more than the sum of the parts. Just as we study a face in order to know a person, so we examine a landscape in order to understand the land itself. While we may notice a person's eyes, ears, nose, mouth, and other facial features, it is the whole face – the way the features are put together – that we see first. So it is with the features of the landscape; in looking at rocks, trees, rivers, and hills, we grasp first the total natural configuration, the character of the whole.

The major challenge of landscape photography is to isolate the key pictorial elements. You must keep your senses engaged and ask *why* a certain landscape is so compelling, if you hope to show this effectively on film. If you feel that a canyon is the dominant natural and visual feature, you may wait for side lighting to emphasize the erosion pattern in the rocks and de-emphasize other pictorial elements. If that lighting does not occur, you may have to return many times in the hope that it will, or you may have to use other visual devices, points of view, or photographic techniques to achieve the same effect. Photographing the land well is often a challenge to your photographic skills – and your patience.

An important part of analysing a landscape is recognizing the symbols it bears. Great images of the land are usually both documentary and interpretive. They are visual records of natural objects, situations, and ecosystems that allow a person to experience the immensity and complexity of the external world in a manner that is simple enough to grasp; but at the same time they surpass physical description, moving a person powerfully through subjective associations awakened by symbolism. Natural symbols are everywhere: people who live in arid regions look at rain, but see *life*; ancient people listened to thunder, but heard the *wrath of God*. Rocks may suggest certainty and dependability, vital emotional requirements of the human psyche. The more closely the physical characteristics of a natural object parallel important aspects of human life the more likely we are to regard the object symbolically. In addition to objects, nature's designs may be both visually and symbolically arresting. The play of sunlight may establish strong contrasts, accenting certain parts of a landscape or creating powerful lines and shapes. Colours, shapes, lines, textures, and perspective can affect our emotions directly because of their graphic impact, but they too can serve as symbols. Reds may suggest one thing, greens another. A circle will indicate completeness; a square, stability; an oblique line, tension, instability, and movement. Because design and function are so closely linked in nature, the symbolic properties of natural objects are often very easy to identify.

Great photographs of the land, images that stir our souls, are almost always pictures in which some natural object or design is intensified or heightened to the point where it ceases to be only a physical representation and becomes an emotional force as well. Images of this sort do not merely describe nature, they evoke a sense of wonder and a feeling of awe.

Seeing analytically is one of the two major challenges of photographing the natural landscape. Photographers must learn to isolate the key visual and emotional elements; you must identify the most significant parts if you want to photograph the whole landscape effectively. Only then can you hope to meet the second challenge – making sure that these key elements are emphasized in the pictorial image through photographic techniques.

MAKING LANDSCAPE PHOTOGRAPHS

Making a picture of a landscape may take only moments, or it may be a very prolonged activity. Sometimes you have to work quickly before conditions change – especially the light. Sometimes you have to wait hours or return to a spot repeatedly before you find conditions just right – again, especially the light. More than anything else, it is light (its intensity, quality, direction, and colour) that establishes the landscape you want. It illuminates the scene and shapes it visually. It affects your emotional response. Photographing the land is, above all, an exercise in managing light.

The tools available to do this are few – cameras, lenses, films, and filters. The basic technical considerations are only slightly more numerous – camera position, choice of focal length, depth of field, and exposure. Despite that apparent simplicity, you can find an infinite variety of ways to manage light merely by varying lenses and camera positions, while keeping everything else constant.

Most of the time you should proceed in this order when you make a landscape photograph. *1/* Visualize the image you want, along with its key pictorial elements; *2/* compose the scene (choose the lens and the exact camera position); *3/* select the point of focus and depth of field, which will give you a specific aperture or lens opening; *4/* determine the exposure you want. Since you already know what the lens opening will be as a result of determining the depth of field, this means choosing the shutter speed. As a general rule, decide on exposure last, since lighting conditions may change in all or part of the landscape while you are making your composition, and render any previous calculations inaccurate. Let's consider these four steps in order.

1/ The image and pictorial elements. In most landscapes, it is the lighting that draws your attention to the subject matter. You will ignore a scene one day, but be arrested by it the next – because of the lighting. Analyse why the lighting affects you so strongly. On a sunny day, pay special attention to the play of light and shadow, especially to parts highlighted by the sun. On an overcast day, observe carefully the gradual transitions from one area of brightness to another. Tonal contrasts are always significant – both in landscapes and in photographs of them. They establish the *form* of the landscape, and stimulate your emotional response to it. Form is one of the two primary visual elements (the other is *colour*), both of which are products of light. You see the four components of form – *shape, line, texture, and perspective* – because of tonal contrasts. You should also analyse a landscape for the configurations and emotional impact of colours.

2/ Choosing a lens and camera position. You must think of a lens as a design tool, because the lens you choose will help determine how the form of the land is rendered on film. Three of the four components of form – shape, line, and perspective – are tremendously affected by the lens you choose. Texture is also affected, but less obviously. For example, a short-focal-length (or wide-angle) lens, if properly used, will dramatically increase perspective by distorting shapes and lines especially at the edges of the picture. Vertical lines at the edges become curved or oblique, thus giving the illusion of depth. Conversely, a long-focal-length (or telephoto) lens compresses distance, making objects in the picture seem closer together than they actually are.

Once you have selected your lens, which means once you have chosen the components of form you will emphasize in the picture, you should have a good idea of where to position your tripod and camera. Once your camera is in place, the major decision about design has been made.

Most landscapes can be broken down into three areas or "grounds" – foreground, middle ground, and background, even if there are no clear demarcation lines, which there seldom are. When you analysed the scene in order to select a lens and camera position, you should have noted the content of each "ground" and assigned each a relative importance. Now, with your camera in position, study the three areas again. Let's say that you've selected a wide-angle lens – which likely means that you've decided to emphasize the foreground. By moving in close with this lens you will enlarge objects in the foreground, but not in the middle ground or background. The result will be increased perspective, since big things normally seem closer and small things seem farther away. Keeping your objective firmly in mind, move your camera slightly forward or backward, to one side or the other, up a little or down a little, until you find exactly the location you want. Then, lock your camera in position on the tripod.

Now come the refinements. Examine the edges and corners of the viewfinder carefully to make certain you aren't wasting or overcrowding the space.

For example, is the rock in the foreground touching the frame of the picture? Do you want it touching, or do you want a thin line of grass (a darker tone) between the rock and the edge? Look at the very top of the picture. Does the amount of sky balance with the small line of grass beneath the rock, or do you have far more sky than you need, a large blue or grey area which draws attention away from the foreground rock? If there is too much sky, then you can reduce it by moving your tripod forward slightly and tilting your camera down a little more at the same time. You'll end up with the same amount of grass, a slightly larger rock, and a reduced sky area. Chances are that once the foreground and background are in balance, the middle ground will be all right, too. However, you should always be alert to spots or lines of distracting tone or colour anywhere in the picture space, especially when you think that the composition is completed. Make a final check. Is the blade of grass in the extreme lower left much brighter than other grasses and, hence, annoying? If so, you should either remove it or adjust the camera very slightly. You can never be too careful about looking at the corners and edges of your composition. When you are satisfied that everything is the way you want it, you can go on to the next step.

3/ *Point of focus and depth of field.* What will you focus on and how much depth of field does your composition require? Usually, you'll find it quite easy to answer these questions, and you won't need very much time to complete this step. However, let's go slowly in order to understand just what's involved.

Point of focus and depth of field are related. No matter what lens and aperture you are using, *a/* the closer the point of focus is to the lens, the less depth of field you'll have, and *b/* there is always twice as much depth of field behind the point of focus as there is in front of it. Most landscapes seem to require considerable depth of field. Out-of-focus areas can be visually annoying. Assuming that you want all the depth of field you can get, here are a couple of ways you can decide where to focus in order to get maximum depth of field. Before you begin, set your lens at its smallest opening (let's say f/16), since depth of field increases as you "close down" the lens opening.

The first way is to use the depth-of-field scale on your lens. (It may help to get out a lens and follow along.) There are two f/16 settings on the depth-of-field scale. Set the infinity mark on the focusing ring beside whichever f/16 setting on the depth-of-field scale your lens permits. Now look at the other f/16 setting and note what distance on the focusing ring is beside it on the depth-of-field scale – let's say three metres. This means that everything between the two f/16 settings will be in focus – that is, everything between infinity and three metres. If you want things closer than three metres to be in focus, set the nearest distance you want in focus (say one metre) opposite the f/16 mark on the depth-of-field scale where you previously had three metres.

Then see what distance is now beside the other f/16 mark. You'll have a much smaller depth of field. If you want less depth of field in general, choose a wider lens opening (f/8, for example), follow the above procedure using f/8 instead of f/16, and read how much the depth of field has been reduced.

The second method for deciding where to focus in order to get maximum depth of field is by inspection. Press the depth-of-field preview button or lever on your camera (sometimes there's one on the lens too; use either one) and focus on whatever point gives you the depth of field that appears most suitable. If you are using a small lens opening (f/16) to ensure a lot of depth, you'll find the viewfinder becomes quite dark while the preview button is engaged. This may make determining the best point of focus difficult for some people. If you are one of them, either stay with the first method, or open the lens a little for previewing only. However, make sure to reset the lens at f/16 after previewing. Once you have decided on the point of focus and depth of field, disengage the preview button, so the viewfinder is bright again and easy to see through. Releasing the preview lever will *not* change the depth of field in your final picture, only in the viewfinder.

4/ Exposure. Since you already have selected a lens opening, the only remaining technical step is to choose a shutter speed that, in combination with the lens opening, will give you the appropriate exposure. How do you decide which shutter speed to use, that is, what exposure is most appropriate for the photograph you are making?

Your first consideration must be what you want the image to convey. Is it to be a descriptive picture of a geographical area that provides a good deal of information about the topography and the plant communities growing on it? If so, you will want to show detail throughout the picture and will probably decide on an average exposure. This should produce some detail in both light and dark areas, and excellent detail everywhere else. If you have been attracted to the scene by the interplay of light and shadow, and especially by the graphic quality of the hills, which become almost black when clouds pass over them, you will want to render the hills black in the final image. Or, if there is a band of snow occupying a large part of the foreground, you may want to make certain that it is rendered clean and white. Are you concerned about the exposure of every part of the scene, or especially about specific areas or objects? Ask yourself basic questions.

No matter what exposure you finally choose, begin by measuring the light intensity with a light meter. Most 35mm cameras have a light meter built in, designed for a very specific purpose – to determine the average brightness in the picture space and to indicate which combinations of lens and shutter settings will produce "middle grey." If you want an overall average exposure, follow it. If you don't, then switch your camera from the automatic to the manual mode (or use the manual over-ride), treat the meter as a general guide, and prepare to use your own good judgement.

If you want your final photograph to have a light, "airy" feeling about it, or if you are photographing snow, find the average (middle grey) exposure from the meter, and then *overexpose*. If you want a dark, moody image, find the middle grey setting and then *underexpose*. These principles apply to all subjects, not just landscapes. How much you deviate from the meter reading in any situation will depend on the effect you want to create. If you want to emphasize dramatically the darkness of an approaching storm, you can underexpose by two, even three, f/stops, provided there is a highlight somewhere in the scene. The underexposure will convert all tones below middle grey into black or near-black, but will not reduce a bright highlight to a tone below middle grey, so effective contrast will be retained in your image. If you want to soften the mood of a landscape by desaturating colours slightly, try half an f/stop overexposure.

An independent reflected-light meter operates in the same way as a built-in meter, and you will have to exercise personal judgement with it as well. However, a separate meter can be very useful if you want to measure the light reflected from a particular area of the picture. You can move to that area, measure the light, and return to your camera without having to alter the composition. A spot meter, a reflected-light meter that measures a very narrow angle of view (usually about one degree), is the most useful of all, because you can stay at your camera position and measure light intensity in as many parts of the scene as you want. However, a spot meter is a very expensive piece of equipment for the average photographer, and you should learn to work without one unless you are regularly making compositions in which precise exposures of distant objects is vital.

There are some situations that are difficult to meter no matter what equipment you use, and you should engage in some trial-and-error in order to gain experience and confidence. If you take 10 minutes to practise now and then near your home, you'll soon gain that confidence. You can aim your lens at anything for these exercises in learning to calculate appropriate exposures; you don't have to make any pictures, but if you make two or three each time, you'll have something to evaluate. Except for very special circumstances, don't get into the habit of writing down lens openings and shutter speeds for future reference, because you'll soon need a filing system. Besides, you won't want to carry all this data with you when you set out on a photographic jaunt. On those rare occasions when you may wish to note how much you deviated from the meter reading, indicate only that you overexposed or underexposed by one f/stop, or whatever the specific amount. This is sufficient information, because when you find yourself in the same circumstances again, although you may decide to overexpose or underexpose by the same amount, your lens opening/shutter speed combination could be very different.

CAPTURING THE COLOUR OF THE LANDSCAPE

Most landscape photographs are made with colour film because the colours determine much of our response to nature, colour is nature's clearest method of indicating time, and patterns of colour help to organize space visually.

In an image that contains only one hue, such as a golden scene at sunset, the emotional impact and symbolic power of the colour are strengthened since there are no competing hues; but, in those circumstances, visual organization will depend entirely on patterns of tone that form shapes, lines, texture, and perspective.

However, colour plays an important role in design when two or more hues are present, making colour contrasts or colour harmonies possible. By manipulating the placement, size, and intensity of the different colour areas, a photographer can emphasize particular features of a landscape, while de-emphasizing others. Nature photographers should be especially sensitive to the role of colour in landscape compositions, because in nature all colours are there for a reason. The gentle yellow-greens of aspen leaves in spring may appeal to your eyes, but they also inform you that the process of photosynthesis is just beginning. To show seasonal transition, therefore, you should give prominence in your composition to those colours that signal the processes under way in the landscape at that time of year. Colour is one of nature's clocks, and will tell you the time of day, the time of year, and the age of things.

Whether your photographic approach to the land is subjective or documentary, effective control of colour rendition will be one of your main technical concerns. Colours in the landscape come from both incident and reflected light, that is the light that emanates from the sun and the light reflected back from objects. The colour of reflected light is a blend of the colour of incident light and the pigments in the reflecting objects. These pigments act as natural filters, absorbing some wave lengths of light while reflecting others. At certain times of day, just before sunset for example, the colour of incident light tends to overwhelm the visual effect of the pigments, and an entire landscape will take on the colour of the light falling on it.

In any case, it's well to remember that there is no such thing as "true colour." When you photograph the landscape or other natural things you must endeavour to determine what is "appropriate colour" – suitable for the mood or information you want your photograph to convey.

Every type of colour film renders hues differently. Some produce warm images; others seem cool. One film may have a marked tendency toward magenta; another may show a vague hint of yellow. A photographer should learn to identify the colour tendencies of films. Here is an easy way to compare the colour rendition of two films. When you are at the end of a roll of film, leave the camera on your tripod as you load with another brand. With the new film, duplicate the last shot you made on the previous roll. If you do this regularly when you change from one brand of film to another, you'll soon know which film to choose for particular situations.

Experiments with different films under a variety of weather and lighting circumstances should not wait for trips to faraway places where mistakes could cost you once-in-a-lifetime pictures, but should be tried near your home. There is no photographic asset more valuable than a *sense* of which film (or which other tools and techniques) will give you what you want. Such intuition is acquired; a "hunch" is not a wild guess.

Because each person's colour sense is at least a little different from everybody else's, we respond emotionally to the hues of a landscape in very personal ways. You'll find that various tools and techniques (film, filters, composition) enhance some colours and reduce the impact of others. Some photographers will agree with your choices, others won't. However, if you are documenting the land, you should avoid "decorating" it with colourful objects (such as people in red coats) that don't normally belong, especially in the wilderness. Wilderness images call for special care. It's very easy to alter wilderness photographically, not only by stressing inappropriate colour, but also by eliminating evidence of disorder, competition, and hardship, and by imposing harmonious pictorial design that is not characteristic of the land itself. Just as human beings have radically altered, in fact domesticated, much of the natural landscape, so as photographers we can "tame" the land by the artistic and technical choices we make – even when we don't want to. All of our aesthetic and technical decisions should be based on the expressive qualities of the landscape, even when we are clearly enhancing or emphasizing certain qualities for personal reasons.

Plants

Every season is a time for plants. In the spring, deciduous and mixed forests are carpeted with hepaticas, goldthreads, trilliums, and a host of other flowers. These woodland plants grow and bloom while the light is plentiful. By the time the forests have developed heavy canopies of leaves, meadows are awash with the colours of grasses, dandelions, daisies, clovers, and vetch, which give way as summer passes to sorrels, goldenrods, and asters. In ditches, bogs, ponds, and other open places, fireweed, orchids, pitcher plants, and lilies abound.

Although flowering plants bloom mainly in the spring and summer, fall and winter also provide superb opportunities for studying and photographing plants. With the first frosts comes the spectacle of autumn colours; after the leaves have fallen the structures of plants are clearly revealed, and the seed heads of many plants remain for weeks or months. The red fruit of the high-bush cranberry never looks better than when it is hanging against a snowy landscape, and conifers, such as cedar, pine, and hemlock, become striking shapes against expanses of white. The long shadows of trees and smaller plants make patterns and designs as they fall across the snow. On wet days in late fall and early spring, grasses appear as rich, glowing, brown blankets on fields and meadows, no less beautiful than the white covering of winter or the green of spring. The opportunities for making both documentary and interpretive images of plants continue year round.

MAKING PICTURES OF PLANTS

Before you begin your photography of plants, decide what interests you most about them. Is it the variety of shapes and lines, or the colour of leaves and flowers? Is it the way plants adapt to different habitats, or the way they lure insects with flowers? Whatever it is, begin with what interests you – perhaps flowers. Make a picture of a wood lily or a clump of Indian paint brush. In order to do it well, ask yourself two simple, but important questions, then proceed step by step.

You should ask the two questions *after* you have found a flower you want to photograph, but *before* you set to work. These are: *1/* "what approach do I want to take – documentary or interpretive?"; and *2/* "what equipment will I require?"

Determining your approach in advance establishes in your mind an initial point of view, or theme, but does not prevent you from exploring that point of view or trying new ones. It helps you to pick your tools, saving you time and sparing you frustration; but you can always make changes if you don't achieve the results you expected.

Documenting plants

You may be documenting plants because you have an interest in botany, or simply because you have come across a forest, a meadow, or an individual plant that you find striking or beautiful. If you are photographing communities of plants, you should be aware of both natural relationships and visual organization. The two are related.

Let's say you decide to document a stand of maple trees to illustrate relationships within a plant population. An important natural relationship would be the competition for light and space among the trees. The soil and climate can support only a limited number of trees in any given area. This results in an observable pattern – the maples will be spaced at more or less regular intervals. In any area, the younger the maples, the more there will be; the older the trees, the fewer there will be, and the greater the distance between them. As you compose your picture, consider which format (vertical or horizontal) portrays the competition more effectively. Do you need to show many trees, or will just a few illustrate the struggle better? Should you include some blue sky for pictorial reasons, or will it detract from good documentation of the maple population – its density, average age, general health, and other facts vital for comprehending the stand as an ecological unit?

If you are documenting a single plant, perhaps a bluebell in the crevice of a huge boulder, see if you can describe more than just the plant itself. Think of the bluebell's habitat. Can you compose a picture that not only shows the plant clearly, but also tells something about its tenacity and how it aids in the weathering and conversion of rock to soil. If you can do this, you will be recording a natural relationship between living and non-living things. Also, your choice of photographic tools and techniques will be made easier. You will choose a lens and camera position that will enable you to show the plant, the crevice, and as much of the boulder as you feel is necessary to the story. You might try a 135mm lens in order to zero in on the important picture elements, but then step back a bit, to give a little more feeling of space.

If you want to record part of a plant, let's say an oak leaf chewed by an insect, you'll show the leaf's physical appearance (its colour, shape, vein structure) and the fact that it's used as food. So, use your close-up equipment near enough to the leaf to reveal its appearance clearly, and be careful to include the damaged part of the leaf as evidence of the insect's feeding. By examining the leaf, can you tell the sort of insect that chewed the hole? Can you make a picture that would help somebody else identify the insect?

Try as well to document plants interacting with other aspects of their ecosystem. Use a slow shutter speed to show trees and grasses tossing in the wind. Make a picture of burrs in your dog's coat to illustrate how some seeds are dispersed. Photograph the effect of permanent flooding on plants by focusing on a stand of dead trees in a beaver pond, and also show the trees the beaver used to build its dam.

When you document plants, many questions will come to mind as you encounter different natural situations and relationships. Some of these questions may concern nature itself, while others may involve pictorial considerations. It's very important to remember that the answer you find to a pictorial question may affect the accuracy and clarity of your documentation, or conversely, that to achieve the documentation you want, you may have to rethink a picture's design.

Interpretive pictures of plants

When you are photographing plants purely for the love of it, you may be unconcerned about how insects pollinate flowers, or why a jewel weed grows in damp places. Your interest is in the designs or moods of nature for their own sake, or in conveying your own feelings. Perhaps you'll want to show patterns of line in leaves or grasses, as in the photograph on page 78, or to portray a meadow as a wash of brilliant colour, or to convey a feeling of euphoria by overexposing and blurring a branch of cherry blossoms.

To make pictures like these, you can use the same equipment and techniques that you employ for documentary images. What differs is when and how you use them. Take camera position, for instance. For a documentary picture, you might compose three tiny bluets from ground level to show their basal leaves, thin stems, and size compared with surrounding grasses. For an interpretive image, you might compose from ground level in order to have grasses masking the lens as you focus through them on the bluets beyond, thus creating an impression of mistiness and flowers barely glimpsed. Or, consider maximum depth of field (f/16 or f/22). In a documentary image of trees, you might employ maximum depth of field to show every detail clearly. In an interpretive picture you might use the same technique, but position your camera extremely close to the nearest tree, so that each succeeding tree is farther away and slightly more out of focus, thus giving the impression of a long line of marchers receding gradually into the distance. In an interpretive image, how you choose to apply a technique may depend as much on how you see and respond to nature as on what is actually happening. For example, if you silhouette an orchid against the setting sun, you may provide little documentary information, but create a lasting impression of the flower, the mood, and your feeling, which others can relate to easily.

Keeping these distinctions in mind, let's explore a special area – the woods behind my house. Because natural things and processes are subject to all forms of weather, I often venture out when weather forecasters are warning me to stay at home. In fact, rainy days are my favourite time for photographing plants.

PHOTOGRAPHING ON A DAMP DAY IN THE WOODS

Cloudy or wet weather eliminates a host of lighting and exposure problems in the forest. Gone are the harsh highlights and black shadows of a sunny day, and the abrupt divisions between them that make composition and good exposure so difficult. In their place are gradual tonal changes, perceptible but gentle transitions from darks to lights. All forms of plant life seem robust, and there is a chance of finding many species of mushrooms in good condition. Colours seem to glow. Wind is seldom a worry, because the forest is its own wind shield, and damp days are often calm.

My equipment

Before leaving home, I don a light-weight rain suit and use two clear plastic bags to protect my cameras and lenses. One has a hole in it, so I can pull it over a camera and still have an open window for the lens to peer out. This bag goes over the camera and 100mm macro lens on my tripod. I carry the other camera (with a 35-70mm zoom lens attached) on a strap around my neck, sometimes buttoning it inside my rain jacket, but I put a plastic bag around it only when I have to lay it on very damp ground. In my pockets, I take along extra films, a folded piece of kitchen foil, a right-angle viewfinder for easy viewing of close-ups near the ground, a cable release which I use mostly for time exposures, a small chamois for wiping moisture off a lens or my glasses, and a package of raisins (which I sometimes share with a chipmunk). I do not take an umbrella, a ground sheet, or flash equipment, because I find them cumbersome. However, some photographers will consider a small flash unit essential, and others may find that an orange garbage bag makes a good kneeling pad – one that is difficult to forget when you leave a site.

First impressions

In the spring, the woods near my home are full of things to see and photo-graph. Adolescent ferns guard mossy rocks, carpets of bunchberry blossoms stretch across the brighter areas, white sentinel trunks of birch trees recede into mists, both pink lady's slippers and their white form may bloom where I have never found them before. A rain-drenched clump of clintonia growing beside a fallen log seems to be carefully tended by an unknown woodland gardener, and masses of *Marasmius* fungi are scattered across expanses of rotting cedar twigs that lie dark, brown, and mildewy beneath the trees to which they once belonged.

The first thing I want to do is to capture an overall view and impression of the woods, as I did one rainy day in the photograph on page 74. On that day I decided to record an expanse of bunchberries stretching across an old clearing among the trees. I set up my tripod and camera with the 35-70mm zoom lens. After previewing the scene, I moved closer to the foreground flowers, lowered the camera a little, and pointed the lens down at a slight angle. After focusing carefully about one-third of the way into the scene, I set the aperture at f/22, because I wanted everything from front to back to be in focus. Finally, I took a meter reading. The meter indicated a shutter speed of 1/2 second at f/22. Examining the different tones within the picture space, I noticed that the white flowers and birch trees provided good highlights and that there were tiny areas of pure black, but overall the tones were near to or slightly darker than middle grey. So, I decided to underexpose by half an f/stop. I set my lens at 1/4 second, halfway between f/16 and f/22, and pressed the shutter release.

Making close-ups

After trying some variations on this composition, I moved in for close-ups. I switched to my 100mm macro lens and began working with three or four bunchberry blossoms among the carpet of leaves. The water drops were glistening with reflected light and the wet leaves seemed to glow. (By then, I had completely forgotten about telephone calls and tax bills.) My next pictures were interpretive images. I put my camera and lens on a plastic bag on the damp ground while I attached a right-angle viewfinder, and I began to crawl around and see the plants from a worm's-eye view. As I moved my camera through the wet leaves, the lens element was protected by an ultraviolet filter, which was soon covered with water. The water on the filter did not interfere with the images, as there was no sunlight shining on it. I continued to alter camera positions until I found exactly the composition I wanted – a blend of rain drops and leaves in an abstract pattern of silver and green.

I depressed the depth-of-field preview button and slowly decreased the lens opening from f/2.8 (wide open) to f/11. The more depth of field I used, the shaper the edges of leaves appeared and the less attractive the design became; so I went back to maximum aperture. Then I selected a shutter speed that would give the slight overexposure I wanted, and pressed the shutter release. But that was only the first composition. I spent at least another half-hour exploring and photographing the spot in this way.

When I take the time to explore a small area carefully, I may discover things a casual observer would miss, such as the red *Hygrophorus* mushrooms on page 73. These were growing on a mossy hummock under some fern fronds – an extraordinary find! As I contemplated my good fortune that day, I decided on my approach. Because the fungi were so rich in colour and texture, I wanted all their detail to stand out clearly – my approach would be purely documentary.

It was very dark under the ferns, and the mushrooms required a two-minute exposure at f/22 (for maximum depth of field) on Kodachrome 25 film. Before making the picture, I attached a cable release to my camera. I also studied the tones in the picture area very carefully, and concluded that the underside of the larger mushroom would be too dark to show the gill structure unless I reflected light up into it. So, I pulled a piece of kitchen foil from my hip pocket and unfolded it below the mushroom just outside the picture space. It did the trick! When I pressed the cable release to begin the long exposure, I also began to jiggle the foil slightly in order to bounce the reflected light evenly on the underside of the mushroom.

Even though the light meter in the camera I was using only permitted me to calculate exposures as long as one second, *determining the two-minute exposure* for the mushrooms was not difficult. Here is how I did it. My aperture was already set at f/22. I set my shutter speed at one second and started opening the aperture from f/22 to f/16, then to f/11, f/8, f/5.6, f/4, f/2.8 – six full f/stops. At that point, my meter indicated proper exposure. (If it hadn't, I would have started doubling my ISO rating and calculated each double as one shutter speed.) By then, I had doubled my light six times. Next I put my aperture back to f/22 and set the shutter speed dial at the "B" setting for a time exposure. Then I doubled six times my shutter speed of one second – that is 2 seconds, 4 seconds, 8, 16, 32, and 64 seconds, or about one minute. However, at that exposure time, I knew there would be *reciprocity failure*, which would make the mushrooms underexposed. To overcome this problem, I simply had to double my one-minute exposure time to two minutes. (If my exposure time had been less than one minute, I would have added only about half the calculated time.) I could also have opened my lens one f/stop to f/11 to get the correct exposure, but I would have lost some of the depth of field. So, I exposed the image for two minutes at f/22.

Sometimes with long exposures, the normal colour rendition of a film changes. This *colour shift* did not happen with the mushrooms. Part of the reason for the accuracy of hue was the atmospheric condition – heavy overcast and light drizzle, which are essentially grey (lacking colour). If I had photographed the same mushrooms in deep shade on a sunny day, blue light reflecting from the sky would have altered the colours of the fungi and mosses, especially over a long exposure. Had I used a different brand of film, it would have produced a purplish cast, which becomes more pronounced during long exposures. Generally speaking, very slow shutter speeds and time exposures seem to overemphasize the normal colour "bias" of any particular brand of film.

Colour shift is neither good nor bad, merely desirable or undesirable from the individual photographer's point of view. With each picture I make, I have to decide whether I want the predicted colour change, or want to eliminate it,   *1/* by using filters (this requires quite a storehouse of filters to match up with light conditions and films), or   *2/* by using flash (even flash may be too cool or too warm, and may require filtration), or   *3/* by choosing another brand of film. Of course, I could make a shorter exposure by using a film that is very sensitive to light (that is, film with a high ISO rating, say ISO 200 or 400). But even with a high-speed film, exposure will be considerably longer on a dark day than it will be in bright light, and colour saturation seems to deteriorate more rapidly on high-speed films used for long exposures than on slow-speed films used for even longer ones. Given a choice, I'd rather make a two-minute exposure on ISO 25 film than a six- or seven-second exposure on ISO 400 film, unless I am deliberately trying to produce less saturated hues. Since I prefer to carry as little as possible, I leave behind filters and flash and use familiar films with low ISO ratings. And most of the time this produces the results I want.

After I had photographed the bunchberry blossoms, the water drops, and the red mushrooms, I made pictures of ferns, coral root, British soldier lichens, and a small waterfall. With only three exposures left on my last roll of film, I started to wander home – only 200 metres away. Just as I was emerging from the woods, a ruffed grouse flew up from the ferns in front of me, nearly striking me in the face. Without taking another step, I bent down and photographed her nest – my last three pictures.

Mushrooms and other fungi are consumer plants. Their mycelia (root-like structures) feed on plant material, usually dead plants, breaking it down into simple substances and hastening its conversion to humus. The part of a mushroom you see is the fruiting body, a structure that forms billions of tiny reproductive spores. The visible part of a mushroom, like the ones in this photograph, are an important food source for insects, birds, and mammals. My approach to photographing these red mushrooms was purely documentary (see pages 71 and 72), since I wanted to record their colour and their natural habitat.

There's no better time for photographing in the forest than a wet day in spring. Plant and animal activity is at a peak during this season, and the moisture seems to make colours glow. While you will have the opportunity to make many close-up pictures, take time to look at whole sections of the woods and to photograph plant communities. Many natural processes can be understood best this way. For example, you might notice that the bunchberries are blooming abundantly because the canopy of leaves is not yet thick enough to cut off the full light they require. A 35-70mm zoom lens is useful for habitat pictures like this one.

While bright sunlight produces very harsh tonal contrasts that make forest photography difficult, sunshine diffused by clouds or mist offers restrained contrast and gentle highlights. Usually such weather conditions last for only a short time, so it's wise to be in the woods before the sun begins to break through the mist. For this photograph I placed my camera and 85-200mm zoom lens on a tripod, composed carefully, and hoped that the sun's rays would highlight the ferns before they burned off the softening effect of the mist.

These tiny "bird's nests" are really mushrooms. The "eggs" in the nests are cases containing spores. When a large drop of water falls from a tree and hits a mushroom, the cases splash out and shatter, releasing the spores. In this way a very large plant helps a very small one to reproduce – by accumulating many small drops into one drop large enough to open the cases. At the same time, the small plant aids in the decomposition of dead plant material helping to create new soil for the tree. The sprigs of moss in the picture provide scale, revealing how tiny these bird's nest fungi are.

Exposure was the critical technical factor in making this image of timothy grass blossoms. The illuminated flower at the bottom was much brighter than the rest of the picture, and impossible to meter because it was so small. However, determining the correct exposure was easy; I simply exposed the film for normal sunny-day conditions. This kept the shaded blossoms properly subdued and retained detail in the bright flower. An alternative approach would be to take a meter reading of the entire picture space (to determine a setting for middle grey), and then to underexpose one f/stop or more to make sure the dark areas stayed dark.

The main purpose of interpretive photographs of natural things is to convey a mood or feeling or to single out a natural design, rather than to provide specific factual information. By choosing certain equipment and techniques, the photographer clarifies or intensifies the design or experience that nature provides. While the photographer's personal way of seeing may strongly affect the appearance of the final image, nature is the source for the interpretation. Interpretive photographs of natural things, like documentary images, should express the maker's interest in and respect for the subject matter.

While I used the same lens (100mm macro) and techniques (minimum focusing distance and depth of field) for both this picture and the one on the facing page, this image is more documentary than the other. The reason is the difference in specific information provided by the two photographs. Here you can see very clearly the shape and detail of the spore case of a moss. The out-of-focus spore cases add information about the reproductive abundance of the moss, and provide pictorial support for the in-focus spore case.

Fire is an important natural force in many forest ecosystems. While it destroys both animal and plant communities, its long-term effect is often beneficial. For example, it opens up heavily shaded areas to light, assuring rapid regeneration and growth. Some seeds require the intense heat of a fire in order to germinate. In this image, I devoted most of the space to the charred tree trunk, because the fire had occurred recently and death seemed to dominate life. However, here and there new plants were beginning to grow, so I included the tiny leaves to suggest rebirth.

80

White is difficult to expose for correctly, especially when it is surrounded by a mixture of hues and darker tones. Often, the problem is to retain detail in the white areas. Side lighting, which brings out texture, can help; so can back lighting, if the subject matter is translucent. For the Indian pipes, I made use of gentle natural back lighting and underexposed slightly, but to keep the plants bright, I used a piece of silver kitchen foil to reflect extra light onto the near side of the plants.

Photographing wild mammals in their natural environment requires knowledge of animal behaviour and consideration for the mammal. Think of your own reactions – sometimes you are willing to let strangers enter your private space; other times you want to be left alone. Because the rutting season was over, this bull elk accepted my slow, careful approach. A telephoto lens allowed me to photograph the elk close up, but a standard 50mm lens was necessary in this case for including the animal's snowy surroundings as well.

Frost patterns on windowpanes are natural designs which result from water vapour in the air condensing and freezing when it contacts the cold glass surface. These patterns assume the hues of both direct and reflected light, so their appearance will vary tremendously during the course of a day. It's a good idea to leave your camera and a close-up lens (I use a 100mm macro) in position on a tripod, so you will be ready to make pictures on repeated occasions. If your lens is aimed at a slight angle to the glass, you will need to use maximum depth of field in order to have all the crystals in focus.

Mist or fog can form a dramatic backdrop for large natural objects, just as out-of-focus leaves or grasses are a useful background for close-ups of flowers or seeds. Unobtrusive backgrounds enable a photographer to concentrate attention on the structure, colour, or activity of the main subject. However, because the tone and colour of the background may contribute substantially to the mood, it's important to choose a camera position or control other variables in a way that captures visual harmony between the two picture areas. For example, here the curving lines of the branches are in keeping with the softness of the mist.

Hawks and owls feed on insects, small mammals, amphibians, reptiles, and other birds. Normally, neither will attack a bird as large as a ruffed grouse. But, when food is scarce, they must attempt the difficult. The wing patterns in the snow and the tuft of grouse feathers tell the story in this image. I positioned the pattern on an oblique in order to make the composition dynamic, in keeping with the struggle that took place here, and overexposed by nearly one f/stop to keep the snow bright.

By using a 300mm lens and an 80-200mm zoom from the same position, I was able to make both close-up and habitat photographs of lions eating their kill. This image shows the animals on a typical east African plain. Outside the picture area several young lions waited their turn to feed. The feeding order – adults first, children second – is important in maintaining the population, because it means that animals of breeding age are more likely to survive periods when food is scarce.

Most lions don't climb trees, but if they live in areas where trees are abundant, they will adapt to the habitat. This female was sated from a full meal and showed no interest whatever in me. The main technical problem was the bright sky, which I could not avoid. However, by careful manoeuvring, I was able to break it up with branches and leaves, and then select an exposure suitable for recording the lion's face.

It's often easier to photograph large mammals than small ones, particularly mice, which may scurry away at the first hint of danger. The white-footed mouse you see here was also exhibiting a characteristic animal response to a threat – "freezing." When I popped up suddenly from behind a rock, I unwittingly shocked it into immobility. Notice the colour pattern in its fur. The upper part of its body is grey, which blends in with the rock, camouflaging the mouse from aerial predators as long as it remains still.

If you think this is an abstract pattern of light-coloured grasses, look again. It's really a very literal document of a small section of meadow. The brownish, cropped areas indicate where field mice bit off grasses to use for nest building and food (they eat the seeds). This happened under a blanket of deep snow. The whitish grasses were beaten down and bleached by the weather to complete the pattern. Many animals leave evidence of their activities that an observant nature photographer may want to include in a photo essay.

While it's often easy to photograph a frog close up, it's also a good idea to stand back and show the amphibian as we usually see it – peering through grasses or reeds as it rests in shallow water, waiting for a passing insect. For this picture, I used a 135mm lens about one and a half to two metres from the frog. I ignored my meter reading, which was strongly influenced by the dark water, and exposed for bright sunlight in order to record the colour of the frog and the plants accurately.

Because it takes a garter snake a few minutes to swallow a toad, I was able, after spotting this event, to run for a camera and return in time to make several pictures. I hand-held my camera so I could follow easily the movement of the snake. At 1/250 second, I was able to arrest the action, though I was restricted to an aperture of f/5.6 and a fairly shallow depth of field, as the sun was slightly obscured by a cloud. While ingesting, the snake itself is quite vulnerable to predation, as its ability to move easily and quickly is reduced. Nevertheless, it will try to escape, so it helps to have a friend with you who will keep steering the snake toward the lens.

While the placement of the main subject and the surroundings is important in a photograph, choosing the right moment to press the shutter release is often what makes a composition successful. This gull and its chick were constantly moving their necks and heads, so I had to watch carefully and make several exposures before I captured a moment that conveyed the relationship between the birds. Soft light from an overcast sky reduced the contrast between the lightest and darkest tones, and helped to show detail in all parts of the picture space.

Another image in which timing was critical. From a small boat, I had been observing the mother hippopotamus and her calf lying in water near the shore. Suddenly they started to move away. To indicate their relative size and relationship, I had to release the shutter at a moment when the mother was far enough out of the water to dominate her baby visually. Being aware of the elements and principles of visual design helps you to tell any nature story more clearly, because you will recognize expressive configurations more readily.

This giraffe belongs to a small wild group that has been separated for several generations from other giraffes, so no interbreeding has occurred. Because the group lives in a heavily forested area, the process of natural selection has favoured those individuals with darker coats, and now the entire population is darker than giraffes living in more open areas. The colouration of most wild creatures evolves in relation to their habitat. In many cases, it's a method for escaping detection by predators.

These towering cliffs on the south coast of Newfoundland are an ideal nesting site for gulls, gannets, and other birds. The grandeur of the location and the sound of the sea and the birds provide a memorable wilderness experience. A visitor becomes deeply aware of the value of leaving large areas of land undisturbed for the protection of natural things. The size of the birds in relation to the cliffs helps to produce the sense of height, and side lighting defines the shapes of the landscape.

To see and hear a small bird singing at sunrise is a common event, but one that touches the human spirit nonetheless. I decided against using a long telephoto lens to enlarge the bird, and to allow the sky and the rock to occupy almost the entire picture. The tiny bird seems alone in a big world, but undaunted by circumstances. It represents how we often feel about our own insignificance in the world and how we would like to respond.

Mammals

Before I ever started photographing wild animals, I lived on a farm for years, and if there is one thing I learned it's that cows, horses, and pigs are insatiably curious. Animals have to be curious – their survival may depend on it. So, later, when I went looking for creatures in the wild, I applied my knowledge of animal psychology and found that it worked. However, you don't need a farm background in order to understand animals – observing people will do just fine. Remember that human behaviour, like the behaviour of all other animals, is related to survival. Analyse your own actions in terms of how you seek food, obtain shelter, avoid predators and other dangers, and engage in courtship, reproduction, and child rearing. It will help you make better pictures of other animals.

If you aren't too keen about analysing yourself and your neighbours, you can learn a lot about animal behaviour and animal photography by watching your pets – canaries, goldfish, turtles, gerbils, cats, and dogs. That's what I'm doing these days – observing my two German shepherds, Tanja and her daughter, Genesis. Because my dogs' behaviour is similar to that of many wild animals, I'll be better prepared to understand and photograph similar behaviour in the wild.

When Genny was three, she gave birth to 12 pups. Watching the birth was a moving experience, and one I could easily photograph. As each pup emerged, Genny immediately bit the umbilical cord and started to lick the pup dry – instinctive actions. She had to stimulate breathing and begin the process of "bonding" her offspring to her. The behaviour of the pups was equally instinctive – responding to the source of warmth, each one in turn found a nipple and began to nurse. After eight pups had been born, Genny wanted to go outdoors. She seemed very frisky, and I thought her delivery was completed. What she needed was exercise, so she brought me sticks to toss for her. Then, suddenly, she sat down and eased slightly on her side. Within a minute, another pup was born. Again Genny nipped the umbilical cord and licked the pup thoroughly, then she gently took the pup in her mouth and carried it back to the litter. Within the hour she had three more pups. This experience has sensitized me to the meaning and importance of small acts of animal behaviour, and helped me to anticipate sequential actions when I photograph animals. As a result, I pay more attention to timing.

Not all animal behaviour is instinctive. Animals learn. The speed and accuracy with which they adapt to sudden changes in their environment may determine whether or not they will survive. Tanja was now a grandmother, but the moment she appeared at the door to see the kids, Genny bared her fangs and snarled. Genny had never done this before. Tanja is the dominant dog; in the relationship between the two dogs, only she has the right to snarl at the other. Clearly, roles had suddenly reversed. Tanja stopped. Genny continued to snarl. Slowly, Tanja backed away and did not return, despite the fact that the pups were in her favourite bed. She soon learned that any approach closer than 10 metres was risking a fight. She literally tiptoed, if she had to pass near this invisible boundary, and she developed other defensive behaviour as well. The most striking was to show total disinterest in the pups. If I carried a pup to her and held it to her nose, she acted as if the pup did not exist. She showed no reaction whatsoever. Later on, when the pups were weaned and started to run about the yard, Tanja would snarl very sharply if one came near her. It was her way of telling Genny that she knew she should have nothing to do with the pups. The pups were at least eight weeks old before Tanja began to associate with them, her signal being that Genny no longer snarled. But only after all the pups had been given homes of their own did Genny and Tanja assume their old roles and relationships. The birth and rearing of Genny's pups taught me a lot about animal behaviour and how to document it more effectively.

MAKING PICTURES OF MAMMALS

Some species of mammals are very difficult to photograph in their natural environment. Others can be photographed only in a zoo or by people who have special equipment and skills. Nevertheless, many species can be approached in their normal habitat, provided you know where to look and what behaviour to expect. Try to make pictures that can be combined in an informative photo essay – habitat shots, examples of both group and individual behaviour, portraits, and so on.

The territory of many mammals is directly related to their size. A female field mouse, under ordinary circumstances, never travels more than 10 metres from her birthplace. A moose, on the other hand, will range over many kilometres. This doesn't mean that the mouse is easier to photograph than a moose. In fact, the opposite is likely to be true. Usually, a mouse remains better hidden within its territory and, when it moves, it moves more quickly than a moose – in relation to its distance from a camera. Also, its movements may be more erratic. These and other differences in behaviour will affect how a photographer approaches each species.

Photographing small mammals in habitat

A mouse is a small mammal which frequently adapts itself to the habitat of people, scavenging both food and shelter. Because of this, people often forget that many species of mice also live in other surroundings. The problem with mice is that they are very active during the night. This can be annoying if you are trying to fall asleep, but it's no less a problem if you want to photograph mice (except for field mice, which are also active during the day). Indoors, it means trying to lure mice with food to a spot where you have set up your camera and flash – and having a device the mouse will activate unwittingly when it is in the right position for a picture. Such a procedure is much too tedious and time-consuming for most photographers. So, let's give mice another try – in the wild.

First, a couple of pointers. *1/* Don't be too fussy about species; chances are you'll have more than one kind of mouse living in the nearest meadow or woodlot, so to begin with, take whatever you can get. Along the edge of a meadow near trees, you'll probably meet the very busy field mouse, the meadow jumping mouse, and the white-footed mouse. *2/* Any season is mouse season. If you find your interest in other photographic projects is flagging, why not turn to mice? They are always around.

Perhaps you'll want to start in March, when you may be biding your time, waiting for spring flowers. As you cross a meadow, watch for patches where the brown grass has been chewed short. The field mouse (or meadow vole) has gathered food here or built a winter nest under the snow. This species clips stalks of grass in order to get at the seed heads or to gather material for its home. They are natural lawn mowers. You should make your first pictures here, not only because they show how mice gather food, but also because the designs in the grass can be quite striking, as in the photograph on page 89. You may also be able to photograph impressions on the grass, of tunnels made under the snow in winter. Some of these vestigial trails may lead to snow banks still lying at the edge of the woods. Dig down into the snow around young deciduous trees, for example maple and wild cherries, to see if mice have been nibbling at the bark. (Mice often girdle young trees, killing them, and causing major damage to young orchards. In the wild, pruning and killing of young shrubs and trees is nature's way of thinning out and keeping open spaces for other things to grow.) Make some pictures of trees nibbled by mice; move in close enough to show clearly the extent of the damage and teeth marks on stems and branches. Next, check any piles of brush at the edge of the woods or accumulations of grasses, and don't be surprised if mice start fleeing as you lift the roof off their homes. If somebody else does the lifting while you wait with camera raised at the ready, you may even capture a mouse on film as it scampers away. If you do, it will probably appear only as a small dark spot in the beaten, brown grass, but that's fine. Can you imagine how it looks to a hawk hovering 50 metres above you? Before you leave the spot, take another look; perhaps you'll find mouse tracks on the lingering snow, although they would be easier to spot in fluffy, fresh snow.

Every season will give you opportunities to photograph evidence of this common little mammal interacting with its environment. By reading about mice, you'll learn more about where and what to look for in your area. By continuing to prowl about with your camera, you'll be ready for one of those special opportunities that come to photographers who are patient and persistent. It happened to me one day without warning. As I rose from behind a small lichen-covered boulder I'd been photographing, I came face to face with a white-footed mouse, who was sitting on top. Normally this is no place for a mouse to be – in clear view of the sharp eyes of a hawk – so it must have been bothered by my crawling about. When it saw me, it "froze," a protective reaction to fear not uncommon in the animal kingdom. By remaining perfectly still, it blended with the rock, so it was making use of its colouration as well. As for me, I had only a 50mm lens; there was no chance of getting a close-up. But the mouse didn't move, so after making a few quick shots from half a metre, I decided to run to my house – 100 metres away – for my macro lens. I made it there, and back, in time! The little white-foot had not moved. You'll see its picture on page 88.

Many small mammals are fairly easy to observe, especially those that have homes which they leave and return to regularly. For example, I've been successful in photographing marmots and badgers by positioning myself outside their dens, setting up a camera and telephoto lens on a tripod, focusing on the entrance, and being patient. After a while, an animal will poke its nose out to investigate, and gradually become bolder and bolder as it realizes I am not a threat. Some small mammals move slowly or are relatively unafraid of people and can be photographed while they are engaged in daytime activities.

A porcupine nibbling the bark of a tree is a good example; and so is a rabbit, because it's likely to be curious. Others are easier to photograph at night, because they are basically nocturnal. Raccoons are very common in cities, partly because of food left out by humans. You can lure raccoons into the range of your lens with food, and photograph them with flash. Some raccoons will become so accustomed to the arrangement that they will resent your terminating it. Deer, coyotes, and foxes will also come for food in winter, but other small mammals such as mink, otters, and fishers may always present a problem, because they are rare, elusive, or swift. If you start by working with a mammal common to your area, you will gain experience in anticipating how other mammals may behave and be better prepared to capture them on film when the opportunity arises.

Photographing large mammals in habitat

The moose is the world's largest and most powerful deer. It ranges across the northlands of Europe, Asia, and North America. If you want to photograph one, a good place to look is in a marsh or pond early or late in the day. Moose feed on lily pads and other aquatic plants, pulling some up by the roots, but willow shrubs are their favourite diet.

Coming face to face with a moose is not the same thing as coming eye to eye with a mouse. If you get that close, you may be in trouble. Much of the year a bull moose is an elusive creature. When you arrive, he will leave. But, during the autumn rutting season he may charge, especially if his current mate is nearby. In the spring, after the cow has given birth (sometimes to twins), she is the one that displays aggressive behaviour, and she will not hesitate to attack an intruder. In other words, if a moose is showing a lot of interest in you, just stay where you are or make sure you can easily escape into a tall, sturdy tree. Moose can run very quickly, and the front feet of a cow or the antlers of a bull can do a great deal of damage.

If you know where and when moose feed, are aware of their characteristic defence behaviour (elusiveness, aggression), and exercise caution, you'll find stalking and observing moose an exhilarating and informative experience. To photograph them, it helps to have a long telephoto lens (300mm or more) for close-ups, and a medium-length zoom lens (80-200mm) for more general shots. There's always a tendency to try to fill the picture space with a wild mammal, but close-ups and portraits may tell less about them than more distant shots which show them in their natural context, as in the photograph of a bull elk on page 82. You should try for both kinds, as well as for typical mammal signs – tracks, droppings, rubbings, winter browsing scars on young trees, and so on. When you look for good pictures of mammals in groups, remember that many mammals will gather in areas that offer wind protection; in deer or elk country, go slowly as you near the brow of a hill, so you won't startle a herd by appearing suddenly. Then you can shoot down on them to show the extent and pattern of the herd.

Tracking mammals by using your knowledge of their habits is only one way to find them. The other way is to bring them to you. If you think a mammal is curious, test it. Many large North American mammals have white tails or patches ("signal" markings) on their rumps, so try waving a white handkerchief to see if the mammal takes more than a casual look at you. Crawl on your hands and knees, or do something it partly understands (but senses you are doing in a rather odd fashion), because then it will feel compelled to make an appropriate response. Be careful not to make abrupt movements or loud noises that may scare it off. Communicate that while you are odd, you are not a threat. In other cases, you may try familiar sounds or calls and, even better, match these with specific actions the mammals recognize. If you come across a herd of deer, for example, who are uneasy about your presence, don't stop dead in your tracks. The deer already know you are there. What they are worried about is your next move, so do something they will understand, like starting to graze. Blueberries are excellent for this purpose, if you are lucky enough to find any, but chances are you'll have to pretend with grass. Keep on grazing slowly and show no interest in the deer – until they have ceased to be concerned about you and have resumed grazing themselves. Then, using slow and gentle movements, start to make your pictures.

Other techniques and equipment

The quality, colour, and direction of light will affect the appearance of mammals, especially when photographed close up. Soft, indirect lighting produces natural colour and eliminates harsh contrast. Side lighting brings out the texture of hair or fur; it adds a vitality to portraits, and makes it easier to get a "catch light" in your subject's eye, so it seems more alert. However, sunny days in winter can cause severe contrasts between the snow and the tones in a dark mammal's coat, so you may have to sacrifice some detail in either the coat or the light areas, depending on which tone you expose for. The simplest solution to excessive contrast in close-ups and moderate close-ups of dark mammals is to keep light areas within the picture as small as possible, letting snow outside the composition (or light sand, if you are in a desert) reflect light onto the mammal's coat to reveal details. A cloudy bright day, or a low sun that gives warm side lighting, seems to produce the most desirable pictorial results and best colour. At high altitudes on a sunny day, light may be bluish, so a warming filter is needed to produce more natural hues in a mammal's coat.

You may or may not want to use a tripod when you make pictures of large mammals. I use one whenever possible because it frees me from the weight of a long lens, and I can relax. This helps to prolong my patience, if my subjects are slow to put in an appearance. (I normally hand-hold a second camera with a shorter lens.) A tripod is particularly useful when you station yourself at a spot where you expect mammals to come for food or water, because you can compose your image to a certain extent before they arrive. A tripod also makes possible the use of slow- and medium-speed films, which may be desirable for a variety of reasons, such as colour rendition, resolution, and easy access to shallow depth of field. However, there are times when a tripod is too cumbersome, especially on long, arduous hikes. You'll have to decide what is best for each particular situation.

You'll also have to make decisions about other equipment. If you are keenly interested in photographing animal behaviour, you should consider a motor drive for your camera. Some actions are so quick and so brief that you'll miss the best part if you have to advance the film yourself. That happened to me once when a lion charged the vehicle I was riding in. Before I could cock the shutter, I was covered with shattered window glass. Other animal actions, such as courting rituals, are often performed in a rapid sequential pattern, and you'll want to record each consecutive movement. A motor drive is fairly expensive, so invest in one only if you intend to use it fairly often. Also, a gun stock for your camera will help you follow animal movement, makes panning easy, and is not too expensive.

If you are shooting from a vehicle, which is mandatory in most African game parks and wise anywhere if mammals are near a highway during their rutting season, a large beanbag tossed over a lowered window can serve as an effective cushion for a long lens. Flash is useless unless you are photographing mammals fairly close up, except that you can use it to add a "catch light" to the eye of a distant subject photographed with a long telephoto lens. Flash may startle your subjects and make them flee; but it may be useful when you are working from a blind at a site to which mammals will return regularly – perhaps a water hole. They will become accustomed to the bursts of light. Also, large, home-made reflectors can be useful; you can prop one outside a den, for example, to bounce light onto the shady side of an emerging creature. If you can leave it in place for a few hours or days, your subject will ignore it.

These suggestions for techniques and equipment should help you to photograph many mammals anywhere in the world. However, the most important preparation for success is learning about animal behaviour. Observe and photograph the behaviour of domestic animals, and people; practise with pets and people the photographic techniques you may need in the field. Read about animals that interest you, and learn about their individual and group behaviour, both instinctive and learned. When you go into the wild you won't always succeed, but if you communicate that your intentions are harmless, you will succeed often enough to be rewarded with many fine photographs.

Birds

The colours, movements, and songs of birds arouse the human spirit. We gaze at an eagle soaring in a blue sky, and we sense freedom. We watch robins feeding their young, and we feel happiness. We listen to the song of a thrush, and hear music. The finest photographers of birds, those who combine documentation with a sense of what birds mean to the human psyche, employ both the documentary and the interpretive approaches. As you photograph birds, try also to capture their intangible qualities. Will a flock of birds photographed with a slow shutter speed give the impression of grace? How do you *feel* when you see a goldfinch swaying on a wind-blown thistle, or watch birds cavorting in a puddle? Try to identify your personal response, and then use shapes, colours, shutter speed, and depth of field to express your feelings in pictures.

PHOTOGRAPHING THE ACTIVITIES OF BIRDS

Although you may sometimes want to have a bird filling the entire picture, there are many occasions when you will not. Birds move about, they fly; and they don't do these things in cramped quarters. No other kind of nature photography requires a better understanding of how to use open space. A bird sitting on a rock, branch, or a waving bulrush may be occupying a characteristic perch. The perch and surroundings can add to your photograph in two ways – they will identify the bird's habitat, and they can be used as part of the pictorial design. The bird itself may be small in the picture space, as in the photograph on page 96, but that will seem appropriate if you compose the overall space well. At other times, you will want to make close-ups of birds engaged in characteristic activities, such as preening and nesting, or portraits to show structures and markings. You can also describe the activities of birds by photographing physical evidence of bird behaviour – holes drilled in trees by woodpeckers, abandoned nests, and wing patterns on the snow.

Social behaviour

Sight is the chief sense of birds, just as it is of people. In this respect we are more like birds than like our mammalian cousins, most of whom have large, elongated noses and live in a world of smells. Because birds depend on their vision for so much information, they communicate in large part by visual language, especially by markings, displays, and performances. If you learn to read the visual language of birds, you will be able to anticipate their actions better. This will help you not only to select the right lenses and other equipment, but also to document social behaviour more accurately. Nobody can learn the visual language of every bird species, but you can learn the fundamentals common to most, such as signals and displays related to recognizing one's own species and to breeding, and those related to daily contact, such as pecking order and flocking. These will guide you when you are photographing unfamiliar birds.

The visual signals associated with breeding and reproduction are myriad, and any photographer interested in birds will want to document some of them. To get a good overview, you should photograph several species of birds, using each species to illustrate different signals. Let's proceed step by step.

1/ Territory. Most activities related to breeding occur within a defended area, which varies in size according to the aggression of the males. They seem to be hostile in direct proportion to the amount of territory needed around their nests to supply enough food for their young, although many species (such as swallows or gannets) have only a small nesting territory and range considerable distances to obtain food. To show territoriality, use a medium-length telephoto lens on a section of a gannet colony to document the even spacing between nests. Also use the same lens or a longer one to film a couple of male robins displaying red breasts to each other, or having a tussle on your lawn.

2/ Courtship. Each species has its own visual language for courtship. Try to learn and document the stages or displays of several languages. For example, if you position yourself near a gannet colony, you can photograph five signals – *bowing* (aggressive male head-shaking and bowing to intimidate other males), *advertising* (gentle head-shaking without bowing, to attract females), *facing away* (a female hiding her bill as she enters a male's territory, indicating lack of aggression), *mutual fencing* (a complex display of bowing by the male, and mutual scissoring of bills to reduce fear), and *skypointing* (indicating a departure, and telling the mate not to leave the nest site unguarded).

In large sea-bird colonies, you can often approach closely enough to use a 50mm lens for habitat shots, but you'll need a longer lens to document courtship rituals clearly. In these situations, as with herds of wild animals, you'll find the birds pay less attention to you the longer you stay and the more gently you move. But, try for courtship rituals among other species too – a cormorant flapping its wings to expose its white thigh patch, African crowned cranes leaping and dancing, various species presenting nest-building material, or peacocks and other pheasants displaying colourful feathers.

3/ Nesting. With many birds, the nesting period can be divided into three stages – nest building, incubation, and child rearing. With some species all three stages are easy to observe and photograph. What you learn about nesting activities from these birds will guide you in photographing other nesting situations. For example, every year a pair of barn swallows builds a nest under the roof of my house, just over the front deck. Since I make no attempt to alter my usual behaviour, the swallows soon become accustomed to my walking or sitting within a metre or two of their nest. From this vantage point I can observe all three phases of nesting, starting with the swallows bringing mud and grass to the roof eaves. Also, I can photograph the adults when they perch near me on the railing of the deck, so I always keep a camera loaded with medium-speed film nearby.

After the rather quiet incubation period comes the rearing of the young. This provides many chances for pictures of the young birds peering out of the nest and the parents arriving with insects. But the culmination of nesting comes with the young swallows learning to fly. A few hours before they are ready, several adults (parents and others) swoop past the nest repeatedly, encouraging the young to try their wings. If this happens during the afternoon, chances are good that the young birds will make their first flights the following morning. When they leave for the first few times, they will probably go only a few metres to the railing of the deck. Last year I was able to approach very closely with my 100mm macro lens, and photographed three fledglings sitting together with their heads all turned in the same direction. If you have swallows nesting under the roof of your house or barn, but no railing near by, string up a clothesline closer to the nest than any other resting point, and at an easy height to photograph. The young swallows will probably light upon it when they leave the nest the first few times, and you'll be able to photograph them easily.

Part of the value of photographing easily-observable species is that you can apply the knowledge you acquire to the photography of other birds. While nesting activities of all species differ, you will be prepared for similar behaviour. For example, you may want to compare the building activities and nest sanitation of various species. The latter has a critical bearing on whether the young survive, and should be included in a photo essay on nesting. Also, ask how the fledglings signal for food, why baby ducks leave the nest so soon, and why most young birds are coloured much differently from their parents. Then, try to photograph the answers to these questions.

106

The social behaviour of birds is an endlessly fascinating subject, perhaps because the more we learn about it, the more we understand our own actions. Treat yourself to a good book on the subject, and read about pecking orders, contact and social distance, hostile behaviour, appeasement, species recognition, courtship, and nest building. Besides providing hours of enjoyment, it will be a stimulus to your photography of birds.

Maintenance behaviour

While social activity forms a large part of most birds' lives, personal activity, or maintenance behaviour, is extremely important too. You should look for three basic aspects – locomotion (flying, walking), keeping clean (bathing, preening and oiling, scratching, and anting), and feeding (shape and size of bill, use of feet, and food storage). Try to document important daily activities like these, not just periodic behaviour like nest building.

Flocking is an example of dual behaviour (maintenance activity in a social situation) that is very easy to photograph. Birds of many species increase the odds of personal survival by gathering in social units, especially for migration. As flocks, they seem to have a group mind, thousands of individuals soaring, turning, diving, and evading predators together in precise formation. Few sights in the animal kingdom evoke such a sense of wonder. You can observe huge flocks at feeding and resting points along the major flyways, for example at Point Pelee, Ontario, during the month of May, or on the tidal flats of the Bay of Fundy in late July and early August. Make sure you take along a 50mm lens for overall pictures of the flocks on the land or water, or rising against the sky. Use longer lenses to record swirling masses of birds close up. Try a range of shutter speeds – from fast speeds (to arrest a flock in midflight) to slow (panning to record a line of birds in fairly sharp detail while blurring the background, thus giving the impression of movement). Or, put your camera on a tripod and use a slow shutter speed in dim light or with a very slow film, so the birds are blurred while the background remains sharp. This may give a better sense of flight than a picture in which everything is sharp. (See the photograph on page 115.) Make use of warm side lighting for dramatic emphasis; but don't be deterred if the day is overcast – you can still get excellent colour and tone in flocks on the ground.

You may also want to document how birds that do not flock protect themselves against predators – for example, a bittern with its neck and head "frozen" in a position that simulates surrounding grasses. Camouflage is developed mostly among solitary birds. Try to document examples of camouflage created by a bird's actions and camouflage due to protective colouration.

From a human perspective, the difference between maintenance behaviour and social behaviour may often be difficult to distinguish. Birds, like humans, may carry on both kinds of activity at the same time – take care of personal business while in a group. For example, while you can photograph individuals of many species *bathing* in water or dust by themselves, the more gregarious species have pool parties with everybody jumping in together. If the pool is too small, there's often a line-up with much jostling, reminiscent of a summer afternoon at any community pool. At times like these, I've found it easy to approach a puddle closely enough to make overall shots of the activity with a 200mm lens. If the birds become wary and fly away, they soon return when I back off a little. Then I inch forward again.

One of the most fascinating methods many perching birds use for keeping clean is *anting*. For example, starlings apply masses of ants to their wing feathers for janitorial purposes. Jays are passive anters, perching where the insects will come aboard of their own accord. Birds that use ants for grooming seem to prefer those that squirt formic acid, which acts as an insecticide (killing parasites) and as a body lotion (making feathers glisten). Anting is similar to a cleaning crew – with brooms and cans of spray – boarding an airplane at a stop on a long overseas flight. To record a bird anting, you'll have to hunt carefully to find a site where anting takes place, and then position yourself closely enough (possibly in a blind) to record the activity.

Feeding is a basic maintenance activity, and you'll find some species fairly easy to photograph as they feed. When they are relatively unafraid of people, it's easy to lure birds into camera range with food. For example, chickadees and Clark's nutcrackers become very bold; Canada jays will even sit in your beard (if you have one) and take food from your mouth. If you are travelling abroad, you'll encounter species that are equally at ease with you and your camera. Nearly anywhere, scavenger birds are easy to approach when they're eating a carcass or other carrion.

Even if your longest lens is only 135mm, you can make good pictures at a bird feeding station. Set one up near enough to a window so that you can shoot from inside. It helps to have the feeder situated far from a distracting background, so that the birds you photograph will stand out quite clearly. You can also set up one or two electronic flash units near the feeder and trigger these from inside. This will illuminate the bird, making the background darker by comparison. Trees or bushes outside a window are also good locations for feeders; thick branches can make an excellent background.

You can reveal a lot about a bird's diet by showing its habitat, the structure of its beak (for instance, the serrated edge of a goose's bill, used for cropping grass), its feet (the talons of a hawk), and by locating the caches of food-storing species. Of course, you should also photograph plants and animals eaten by various birds – seeds, fungi, insects, frogs, mice, and other birds.

If you develop a keen interest in observing and photographing birds and their behaviour in a wide variety of situations, you will want to invest in a long telephoto lens (let's say a short-focus 300mm lens) and a bird blind. A short-focus lens will permit you to focus on nearby subjects, whereas a regular telephoto lens focuses much farther away. However, you can add extension tubes. In either case, you'll be able to fill the picture space with a nest of waxwings, make a close-up portrait of an owl, or even study the detail of a puffin's bill. However, a blind should go along with such a lens, especially if you want to make close-ups of birds nesting. Having one in place will allow you to make repeated trips to a nest or other sites that birds frequent. Some blinds are complicated structures, involving the erection of staging to achieve the height necessary for viewing, but a simple light-weight, portable blind can be immensely useful for many nesting sites.

To make a portable cube-shaped or pyramid-shaped blind, you'll need to have *1/* several pieces of small-diameter aluminum pipe or adjustable, collapsible tent poles that can be fitted together to form a frame; *2/* water-resistant canvas or heavy denim in dull or camouflage colours sufficient to cover the frame; *3/* a long plastic zipper or velcro to open and close the entrance slit; *4/* velcro to attach flaps over the openings cut in the canvas at various heights for photography (these flaps should be on the inside of the blind); *5/* ropes or pegs to secure the blind, if the pipes cannot be driven into the soil.

A blind need not be large, but should have space for your tripod, a seat, extra equipment, and you. A cube-shaped blind can be as small as one metre square at the base and one and one-half metres high, although you may prefer one slightly larger. A pyramid-shaped blind can have a base one and one-half metres long on each side, if the sides do not narrow rapidly as they rise to the top. Otherwise, two metres on each side of the base would be preferable.

If you are making close-ups of birds from a bird blind and you want to arrest their movements and illuminate them evenly, without shadows, you'll have to use flash. You'll need an electronic flash with a slave unit (and two sturdy, light-weight stands for them), one positioned near the camera but outside the blind, and the other aimed at the nest from one side or other from about the same distance as the first flash. It also helps to have a long extension cord, so you can keep the power source for the flash inside the blind and switch it off whenever you don't need it. (For more information on electronic flash see pages 166 and 167.)

Parent birds will often spot you approaching your blind, and many will flee, occasionally in such alarm that they will not return to the nest until you leave. This can be disastrous for the fledglings, as they must be fed frequently and regularly. Fortunately most birds can't count, so a good plan is for two photographers to approach the blind. One person will enter the blind to make pictures, the other will leave. Satisfied that the humans have all cleared out, the parents will return to feed their young. At a pre-determined time, the second person will return to the blind, and the first photographer will leave. Again, the birds will be happy and both photographers will have a chance to make pictures.

If you are thinking about using a bird blind, consider the birds first. Don't photograph nests with eggs or do anything else to disturb incubation, especially anything that attracts predators or keeps parent birds away. Wait until the fledglings are at least three or four days old before you make pictures. *Never* cut away branches or leaves that obscure a nest. You may intend to put the branches back, but withered leaves will not protect fledglings from hot sun and predators. If you must alter the position of a branch slightly, do it with rope, wire, or stout twine, and be sure to remove it when you have finished making pictures, so the branch will return to its original position. When you have finished, don't linger around to bother the birds or to attract predators through the commotion you might cause; use a rake or branch to straighten flattened grass near the nest; as you leave, walk around in random fashion (often criss-crossing your own path) to leave a scent trail so confusing that it will not lead predators, such as skunks, to the nest.

Always be concerned about the effect of every action you make when you are photographing natural things. If you have to choose between photographs and the safety of young birds, forget the pictures – even when you are alone at a nest site and nobody can see you. Preserve your integrity and the lives of the birds: then the photographs you don't make will be a greater contribution than those you do.

Insects

Insects play a broad and varied role in nature. They pollinate flowering plants. They serve as food for amphibians, fish, birds, mammals (including some people), and other insects. Some song birds eat virtually nothing else; a spell of cold weather that delays the hatching of insects can cause extensive starvation, and chemical insecticides may result in the devastation of bird populations by temporarily reducing the supply of insects. Insects also manufacture food – honey, for example – for the use of other creatures. Some insects control the population of other insects. Ants constantly aerate the soil and, along with other insects, aid in the important process of decomposition.

There are more insects and more species of insects than any other form of animal life, other than microscopic organisms. About one million species are known, but some estimates suggest that this is no more than 10 to 25 per cent of the total. Despite massive campaigns with poisons, radiation, and fire, human beings have never succeeded in exterminating a single species. Such tenacity deserves respect.

PHOTOGRAPHING INSECTS IN THE FIELD

A photographer can find insects, day or night, almost anywhere in and around the soil, in water, in the air, and on other living creatures. In winter it's possible to find insects in dormant stages – eggs and pupae. In March or April you may find snow fleas, which emerge to mate in large groups on old snow. However, you'll find insects most easily in spring, summer, and fall. Some are very easy to photograph at the beginning or end of the day, when they are less active. If you crawl around a meadow in the hour before sunset, you will be amazed at the number of insects resting. Many can be approached readily and photographed with a macro lens, such as the grasshopper on page 121. (A 100mm macro lens is probably better than a 50mm macro, since you won't need to approach quite as closely.) Similarly, chilly mornings are good times to look for insects, since they're less active in the cold. Perhaps you'll be rewarded with a dew- or frost-covered dragonfly or a sluggish, but very attractive butterfly, or the frothy covering of spittlebug eggs.

An excellent place to look for insects is on flowers, because flowers lure insects by their appearance and odour. The colour, shape, and lines of a flower are as informative to certain insects as airport markers are to pilots. They show the insect where to land and how far to taxi. If the insect follows instructions, it receives nectar for food; but it also involuntarily picks up a sticky load of pollen. All flowers have evolved methods to make sure than an insect does not leave until it has its cargo aboard. Some flowers stop insects for only a second, others keep them for hours.

If you want to show how plants attract insects, and you have some close-up equipment, you can start with nearly any common flowers. Note the colour, shape, and markings of a flower, and then watch to see where an insect lands and what it does afterward. It's a good idea to concentrate on one or two species until you learn how to observe well. Make pictures of the flower and its visual signals, and of an insect landing, if you can.

Some insects will return again and again to the same spot, which means that you can   1/ set up your tripod and your camera with a macro lens, extension tubes, or bellows,   2/ compose your image,   3/ pre-focus on the spot on which you expect the insect to land,   4/ determine the exposure by metering the flower or leaf, and   5/ wait. Monarch butterflies often have a favourite leaf, so focus on the leaf, and wait for the butterfly to return. Mosquitoes usually persist until they can spend a few moments on their victim. Bees make innumerable trips in and out of their nest or hive; simply focus on the entrance. You may be rewarded with photographs of cargo-laden bees.

When you photograph insects and their relatives (such as spiders), don't overlook examples of their constructions – from the protective cases built by caddis fly larvae, to termite hills, to spiders' webs. With almost any close-up lens or equipment, you can document webs as part of a story on a spider's activities, or approach them interpretively. Early morning is the best time, when dew drops outline each thread of a web. You may first want to show the structure of the entire web, using sufficient depth of field to ensure that all parts are sharp. Then, you may decide to lie underneath a web and shoot it against the sky, or go to one side and focus on the nearest edge to show its slender construction. You could explore the web using both maximum and minimum depth of field. With your close-up lens at its maximum aperture and its minimum focusing distance, inch toward a web until its threads and dew drops are transformed into shimmering bangles of line and colour.

Many insects are easier to photograph in captivity than in the field, and raising your own in glass jars or a terrarium can be an exciting project. A good way to begin is to gather immature forms (eggs, larvae, or pupae). The larvae of moths and butterflies may go through several caterpillar stages (instars) before they enter the pupa stage (chrysalis, cocoon), where they develop and change into a moth or butterfly. During the caterpillar stages they eat voraciously, and need to be supplied with fresh food daily. This is especially true of moth larvae, because once they become pupae, individuals of most species will never eat again. These moths have no feeding organs and, during their brief life span, exist on the strength they build up weeks or even months earlier in the larval stage. So, if you want moths, butterflies, and other insects to reach adulthood, you must provide their larvae with the proper food. For instance, the cabbage worm, or caterpillar, will thrive on cabbage leaves, broccoli, or mustard leaves, so there is little point in offering pea vines or oak leaves.

Let's say you have decided to raise a monarch butterfly. When you locate some eggs, take them, with the vegetation on which they were laid, to your terrarium. When you are ready to photograph them, keep them on their leaf so your pictures will include something of their natural habitat. The egg masses are usually large enough to photograph quite easily with a macro lens or other close-up equipment. For extreme close-ups you will need a bellows. After a few days or weeks, the caterpillars will emerge, eat voraciously for a few weeks, and then enter the pupal stage. The caterpillars and pupae, also, can be photographed with a macro lens or a bellows and a short-mount lens. When the adult emerges your photographic difficulties may increase, although your earlier practice should have built up your confidence.

Shortly before the butterfly emerges, you will be able to see its colours and markings growing progressively clearer through the pupal case. Make some pictures now, and more as the butterfly begins to emerge. The more of the transition you can capture on film, the better your photo essay is likely to be. Once the monarch is out of the chrysalis, you should have an hour or more to photograph it before it becomes very active.

The newly-emerged butterfly will cling to a firm twig or other object while it pumps fluid into its small, shrunken wings. These will expand gradually until they are fully developed. Then, as the fluid is reabsorbed into its body and the wings dry and harden, you will have several more minutes to make pictures. You may have longer with moths, because most moths are nocturnal and won't fly away if they emerge during the day. If your insect emerges during daylight hours, you may not require a flash, though in most cases a flash will enable you to make better pictures. The light from a nearby window may be sufficient for some shots, though it may not permit enough depth of field to get the entire insect in focus, or a fast enough shutter speed to arrest any movement. In that case try using flash.

Here are some suggestions about props and equipment for photographing insects in captivity.

1/ Once you have taken your insect model, for example, a monarch butterfly, out of its container, place a large piece of cardboard behind it. This should be lightly chalked or crayoned to look natural, but not so colourful that it competes with the butterfly for visual attention. Make sure the background is well behind your subject and any other material, such as twigs and leaves. If it isn't, strong black shadows will fall on it when you use flash, unless the flash is positioned well above the subject.

2/ Align the front of your lens carefully with the butterfly (parallel planes), if you want all parts of the insect to be in focus. With close-up equipment, depth of field is very limited, even at f/16 or f/22.

3/ Position your flash equipment carefully. For insects, it's better to use two flash units on tripods, as most insects will not tolerate a reflector close enough to them for good illumination. Place one flash unit above and to one side (at about a 45° angle) of the emerging insect, and point it at the subject. Place the other flash opposite to the first one, below and to the other side of the subject. The tripods will allow you to raise or lower the flash units to the best positions and to move them closer or farther away to get the proper distance for correct illumination. Set your film speed at 1/60 second (the usual speed for flash synchronization), add a colour-correcting filter if necessary, and calculate your exposure (see page 167 for determining exposure).

4/ Avoid using flood lights. They may cook your specimen or speed up the drying process and reduce the time you have for making pictures.

5/ Treat these suggestions as guidelines, and don't be limited by them. Many moths and butterflies have such beautiful colours and markings that you may be satisfied to document them as they are; however, don't rule out other ways of doing things that communicate something special about your subject matter. If your approach is interpretive, rather than documentary, you may not want the entire insect to be sharp. Or, you may want to include only the pattern on part of a wing. Or, you may decide to make a very dramatic image using only side lighting. You must adapt your props and equipment to suit the circumstances – and the insects.

All insects contribute in one way or another to their ecosystem and, ultimately, to life on Earth. If you study, explore, and photograph even one insect out of the millions of species, you will gain an appreciation of how valuable they are to the natural system.

My intention was not to describe these birds, but to document movement and convey an impression of flight. So, I chose a shutter speed of 1/15 second, which blurred the birds, rather than 1/250 or 1/500 second, which would have "frozen" them in the air. An alternative technique would have been to "pan" with the flock, that is to use a slow shutter speed as I followed the birds with my lens. This would have made the bodies of the birds sharp (though not their wings) and blurred the background, also giving a sense of flight.

The design of natural things enables them to function successfully in their habitat. That's why these aquatic plants have tiny air-filled sacs for flotation, and why starfish have suction cups on the underside of their "arms" for gripping rocks and other material. While an individual may vary in some significant way from the group to which it belongs, no plant or animal in the wild with a characteristic detrimental to its survival will be able to pass its variation along. Thus, common characteristics are those that have proven to be useful over a span of many generations.

This image and the facing one were made in the intertidal zone on the coast of Vancouver Island. When plant and animal life is wet, very bright highlights can be a visual distraction, even on cloudy days. Also, you may find that sky reflections in the water may interfere with your ability to photograph subjects below the surface. Both of these problems can be reduced, and often eliminated, by shading the picture area with your body or a dark umbrella. If possible, try to make some pictures showing the same subject at high and low tide – living in water, then in air.

A pond or small lake is a very different aquatic habitat from the intertidal seashore, but in both places water plants are often most abundant where light penetrates to the bottom. The yellow pond lily, common in the quiet water of rivers, lakes, and ponds across the continent, is an important food source for moose, beaver, and bear, which eat the large underground rhizomes, or stems. Insects, amphibians, and small birds use the leaves as floating platforms. The plants often form striking natural designs on the water surface, especially at sunrise or sunset, when the back-lighted leaves reflect the colour of the sky.

Where animal populations are large, and the water supply is concentrated in a few pools, the various species take turns in coming to drink. Photographing from a blind with a 300mm lens and an 80-200mm zoom (both cameras on a tripod), I was able to make pictures of a three-hour parade – zebras, wildebeest, impala, nyala, kudu, baboons, wart hogs, and guinea fowl. Early morning side lighting made the mammals stand out clearly against the background, and the quiet water mirrored them when they reached the edge of the pool.

The young fronds or croziers of the ostrich fern, called fiddleheads, are considered a delicacy when gently steamed and served with lemon and butter. Here you see them emerging through the dead stalks of last year's fronds. A nature photographer should resist the temptation to remove debris from around plants unless it is highly distracting, because it may provide important information about a plant's habitat or growing requirements, as well as aiding in composition.

The colour markings of many moths, butterflies, grasshoppers, and other insects have evolved as protective devices. For example, an insect may display an arrangement of spots that frightens some birds or, having found an insect unpalatable, a bird will be warned by its colour pattern not to try another one. While it's often easier to photograph insects under controlled conditions, good pictures can also be made in the field, especially early or late in the day when many insects are less active. However, I photographed this grasshopper at mid-day, with a 50mm macro lens.

A backyard, ditch, or patch of grass offers excellent opportunities to make nature close-ups – in every season and in all kinds of weather. Wherever you live, you can photograph the life cycle of plants and document important natural processes, such as decomposition and erosion. It's important to make pictures on a regular basis in order to feel at ease with your equipment and to improve your visual awareness.

In nature, beauty always has a purpose or function. It is never purely decorative. For example, because birds have good eyesight, many species have evolved stunning feather displays as eye-catchers in their courtship rituals. This peacock will face the hen to attract her with his colourful tail feathers. However, a male of a different species may turn his back to the female because the rear view of his feathers is more striking. Colours and markings can also serve as a warning to males that an area is the territory of another male of the same species.

Morning mist obscures detail and imparts an air of mystery to many nature scenes. Just before and just after sunrise it may take on the colour of the sun's rays, especially when back-lighted. You can retain the delicacy of tone and hue by slight overexposure, but you will reduce the mistiness if you underexpose. If you are photographing a similar situation for the first time, make several different exposures; then compare the results. You'll find your experiments to be valuable guides in future efforts.

Deliberate visual exercises can sharpen your ability to see and to produce fine images. On this autumn day I decided to explore the use of selective focus and shallow depth of field, especially in close-up and moderate close-up situations. So I set up my tripod and camera near a large clump of ferns. First, I opened my 100mm macro lens to the widest aperture and focused on background material, letting the foreground and middle ground go out of focus. Then, I focused on the middle ground, which blurred the front and back. Finally, I concentrated on foreground material, blending tones to enhance the delicacy of the ferns, and using gentle colour contrast to establish shapes.

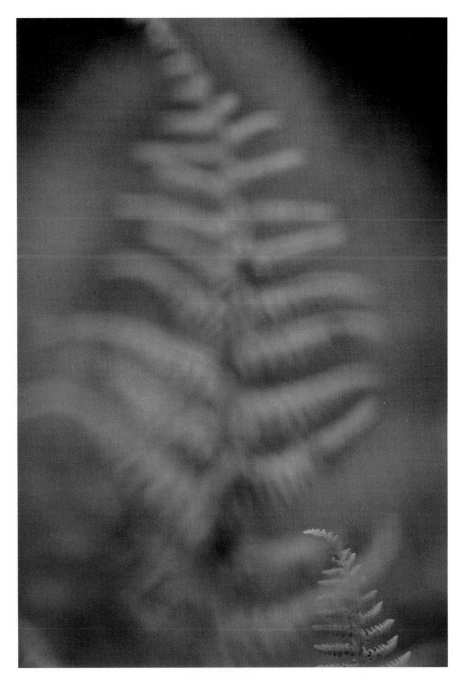

I find selective focus and shallow depth of field to be effective techniques for interpreting autumn. Sometimes the blending of tones and hues is inappropriate for the material and my feelings about it, but often it helps me to express a mood or a feeling that I cannot convey in any other way. Pictures like these can add dimension to a documentary photo essay or slide sequence, because they relieve the flow of information and allow viewers to respond on an emotional level.

A sense of open space frees one's spirit. In many images of the land and sky, this feeling of release may occur because of natural scale, perspective, or other visual features, but it can be heightened by careful design. In this case, I was able to increase the sense of space by using a 300mm lens. This lens has the effect of compressing distance and reducing perspective, but here it enabled me to eliminate foreground material and to suspend the line of autumn trees in the clouds.

The timing of an exposure often makes the difference between a good land-scape and a mediocre one, especially when clouds are changing shape or influencing the lighting. The rocks, the cloud, and the sky are the tangible subjects of this image, but they created a strong visual impression only when dark shadow fell across the foreground, balancing the sky above the cloud. Try to anticipate the best combinations of light and dark in a composition, then wait for them to occur and release the shutter at precisely the right moment.

Why do waterfalls have so much emotional appeal? Is it because we are unable to grasp the physical details of water in motion, and therefore are free to interpret it in fanciful terms? Some waterfalls evoke tremendous power and turbulence and are best photographed with fast shutter speeds, such as 1/250 or 1/500 second. Others suggest a gentler mood and may call for a slower speed, such as 1/8, 1/15, or 1/30 second. A time exposure made in low light can even give a misty aura. Try to make technical decisions that will convey your impression.

The dramatic sense of physical threat of an approaching storm can be mirrored in the human psyche. To convey the dark mood of a storm, you will need to underexpose. How much you deviate from the meter reading will depend on the tones in the stormy area and whether or not you want to intensify the sense of drama. If there is an area of very bright tone in the picture space, you will be able to underexpose by two or three f/stops and still retain sufficient contrast for a design strong enough to heighten the mood.

While colours and colour contrasts often exert powerful influences on our emotions, tones and tonal contrasts can have just as strong an impact. In images where colour is lacking or is restricted to one hue, composition depends entirely on the placement of tones. For this aerial abstract, I underexposed three f/stops to intensify the black of the earth and to define strongly the shape of the water. For me, the impression is of a primal landscape yet to be occupied by living things.

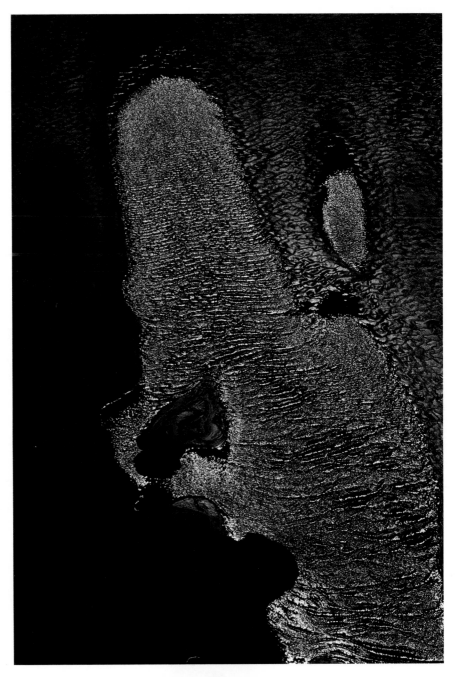

This small section of beach shows the force of moving water. The trails in the sand tell us that high waves or flooding carried the two small rocks to their present location. The smoothness of the rocks shows the effect of water erosion. The definition of shapes and texture is made possible by side lighting late in the afternoon and by the single colour. If I had included some nearby blue water in the composition, the second hue would have competed strongly for visual attention.

Natural processes and events occur everywhere, and an observant photographer will find myriad opportunities to document them. The negative and positive impact of the human species on these processes and events may be part of the visual story. All creatures die eventually, and many succumb to environmental conditions. While moths have a brief life span anyway, this one may have died a few hours before its time because the oil prevented its escape from the water. I kept the moth small in relation to the surroundings to suggest the fragility of life.

One November day when I was gathering the last vegetables from my garden, I noticed the leaf scars on a cabbage stalk, and stopped my work to examine my find. I was intrigued by the pattern of scars and the colours of the stalk and discarded leaves. While flowers are the most attractive visual feature of many plants, pictures of them tell only part of the story about how plants function. You can often tell more about them by photographing other parts, such as the seeds, leaves, stems, and the overall structure.

An expanse of snow and ice viewed from a hill at sunset may seem like an aerial view of clouds. Delicate variations of tone and hue create soft horizontal lines and spaces that contribute to the cloud-like appearance. The absence of any recognizable object that might function as a centre of interest – such as a tree – helps to create the illusion of distance and space. For me the image is both a document and an interpretation, because it does not falsify nature yet suggests something beyond the image itself.

These rocks and the skeleton of a tree tossed among them imply the power of wind and water to shape our planet and convert rocks and organic material into soil. Because of the implied power, I positioned my camera to show the tree as a strong oblique line, which adds a sense of the dynamic to the composition. Because of the texture in the boulders and the gradations of light on both the tree and rocks, I used maximum depth of field (f/22) to render everything in sharp focus.

Aquatic plants washed up on a beach form a natural still life. A casual observer might call it debris; but a nature photographer will see in it a variety of documentary and interpretive images. This is a good place to experiment with several lenses. You may want to start with a wide-angle lens to show the expanse of the plants and the beach, follow up with a 50mm lens for moderate close-up compositions, and then switch to a macro lens to feature details of the algae and other plants. You'll find that the soft light of a cloudy day eliminates shiny highlights and brings out the natural hues.

Northern and southern lights consist of colour displays and dances that seem choreographed by a celestial director. They leap and flow through vast spaces, often rising higher and higher in the night sky until they reach the zenith. To photograph this nocturnal display you'll need your camera on a tripod, a wide-angle lens set at maximum aperture (f/1.4, f/2.8), and an exposure of 15 to 40 seconds on ISO 64 film. Make several exposures in order to show the changing sweep of light.

Amphibians and reptiles

Like all animals, amphibians and reptiles need food, shelter, and the opportunity to reproduce. When you photograph their activities, you can employ most of the same equipment and techniques that you use for making pictures of mammals and birds. You may want to photograph some of these creatures in the wild, though you may prefer to go to a zoo to get close-ups of some reptiles.

AMPHIBIANS

In the spring, if you look in ditches or shallow ponds where water is likely to lie for a few weeks, you'll probably find frog, toad, or salamander eggs near the surface. Frogs lay their eggs in gelatinous masses; toads and salamanders produce gelatinous strings or single eggs. You can use a 50mm or 135mm lens to show the eggs in habitat, then switch to a macro lens or other close-up equipment for more detailed shots of an egg mass or string. For close-ups, you will probably need to shade the water with your body in order to eliminate sky reflections, or "milkiness," caused by ambient light. Later, after the eggs have hatched, you can go back to photograph the larvae. Tadpoles (which breathe through gills like the larvae of all amphibians) love to congregate in shallow parts of ditches where the water is warm, which makes them very easy to photograph. Or, you can take a few eggs home (in ditch water) and raise your own tadpoles. The young larvae will feed on the empty, gelatinous egg cases, and later on micro-organisms in the water. If you keep the eggs, and subsequently the tadpoles, in a small aquarium, you can make pictures whenever you want. Often the best way to light the container for photographs is to carry it outdoors or place it in a bright spot inside. If the glass is clean, you can focus easily on tadpoles in the container. To avoid picking up any detail in the glass itself, wear dark clothing while you photograph, focus beyond the glass *into* the container, and select a shallow or medium depth of field unless you are focusing very close up. You should return all your tadpoles to a pond after a few weeks, so they will have access to an adequate food supply and will mature properly.

You can photograph frogs day and night. During the day it's sometimes easy to approach them at the edge of a pond or in shallow water as they cling to vegetation. If you move slowly toward a frog, you can come near enough to fill the viewfinder, even with a 50mm macro lens. The trick is to approach head on, since frogs only see lateral movement. They will catch an insect flying past them, but not one moving toward them, unless it approaches from the side. However, while it is nice to get good close-ups, start shooting before you are really near, in order to show the frog in typical surroundings, as in the photograph on page 90.

Side lighting is excellent for making pictures of frogs, but just about any lighting conditions are acceptable. On one occasion when I needed fill-in light to illuminate the shaded side of a frog's head, I asked my sister to hold a large mirror. She was able to stand at least three metres away and still direct sunlight into the shaded area. You can try the same techniques with toads, as the common garden variety seems even more co-operative than frogs.

You may also want to photograph frogs at night. One of the best times is early spring, when the females are starting to lay eggs. You'll know where to go if you listen the night before. Take a powerful flashlight and an electronic flash unit for your camera. If you have battery-operated floodlights that can be positioned (during the day) to illuminate a section of the pond for general observation at night, by all means use them. The fixed floodlights will not bother the frogs, neither will a flashlight held fairly still, but your tramping about may. If so, pause until the chorus starts up again, and then move about cautiously. Obviously, it helps to have another person hold your flashlight, freeing you to use your camera and flash. If you are patient, chances are reasonably good that you can observe and photograph frogs singing, or a male fertilizing eggs as a female lays them.

Night is also the best time to look for salamanders, especially very cold nights in early spring when ditches are just beginning to thaw. Salamanders may be found by overturning rotting logs or piles of grass, but at night they go to shallow water. Salamanders, as well as other small, fast-moving amphibians, are tricky to photograph in the wild, so you may want to photograph them in a simulated natural habitat.

REPTILES

Several years ago I spent a day on a small boat cruising the Nile River in Uganda and, from time to time, passed crocodiles sunning themselves on the bank. The monsters of my childhood dreams were suddenly real. Their fierce demeanor and cold eyes make one feel rather uneasy approaching them for a portrait shot. The problems with crocodiles are usually caused by humans who don't respect their territories, and who become disturbed when a crocodile snatches domesticated animals and even people. However, crocodiles have an important role to play in the ecosystems in which they live. They stir up water and move nutrients around. Their burrows and channels become water reservoirs during dry periods – especially important in the everglades of Florida. (The American alligator is a crocodile.) The leftovers from a crocodile's meal are eagerly scavenged by turtles and fish. The spur-wing plover is also dependent on this reptile; it sits on the edge of a crocodile's open jaw and picks parasites from around its teeth.

To photograph crocodiles I used the same lenses (80-200mm zoom and 300mm) and lighting and exposure techniques as I did for photographing large terrestrial mammals (see pages 102 and 103). I experimented with a variety of compositions – habitat shots of several crocodiles sunning on the bank, a big crocodile splashing into the water, close-ups of a crocodile with its mouth agape while a plover picked its teeth, and so on. I made all my pictures from a small motor boat or from the safety of a permanent blind, as I had no desire to invade this territory on foot.

Snakes depend on a variety of senses in order to avoid predators and to seek food. They can determine how near you are to them in special ways. Some species have heat sensors near their lips, which enable them to tell not only that a mouse or other creature is nearby, but also its precise location. Hence the accuracy of a strike. A snake's forked tongue is also a sensor, carrying airborne particles to a chemical analyser in the roof of its mouth; so don't be alarmed if you see the tongue being rapidly thrust in and out.

Like other cold-blooded creatures, snakes sun themselves to raise their body temperature. With a long- or medium-range telephoto lens, you can make good close-ups of a snake if you approach gradually, but remember to shoot the entire snake in habitat as you approach. Garter snakes tend to move away quickly through grass, but they often pause to sense what you are doing, and because they rely on camouflage and keep still, occasionally you can come so close that you can make portraits with a 100mm macro lens. Last summer I turned over an old barrel and startled a garter snake just beginning to swallow a toad. The snake had hidden under the barrel because it would be quite helpless against predators during the time it would take to ingest its food. I ran for my camera and 100mm macro lens, and was able to shoot half a roll of close-ups as the toad slowly disappeared inside the snake. (See the photograph on page 91.)

Recently in the African veld, I photographed a puff adder, a large, bold, poisonous snake that is terrifying to encounter unexpectedly at close range. As

I ran up a rocky hillside, the puff adder warned me of its presence by raising its head and turning slightly toward me. It held this aggressive posture. Although I didn't think the snake could strike across the distance between us, I backed away a step or two to lessen its apprehension before I started to photograph. Even though I had only a 35-70mm zoom lens with me, I was able to capture satisfactory images of the snake and its surroundings.

If you are unfamiliar with any species of snake, watch for obvious warning signals, such as hisses, rattles, or rustling of leaves, and stay far enough away to avoid a quick strike. Local residents are usually the best source of information about snakes, but may discount possible danger because they are accustomed to having them around. On the other hand, remember that most snakes are not interested in attacking you – unless you threaten them somehow.

For portraits of snakes, especially of poisonous species, controlled conditions are usually best. The ideal situation is to make friends with somebody who works with snakes and other reptiles. Many biologists are not trained in photography and welcome a photographer who is interested in working with them.

Turtles and tortoises move slowly, so they would seem easy to photograph. However, once they are aware of your presence, they may withdraw into their shell. You can do two things. First, move in close and make pictures of their armour. If you don't know why the patterns vary from species to species, try to find out afterward – it will have something to do with the habitat. Second, sit down at a slight distance and be patient. After a while, your subject may peer out and decide to proceed on its way. Use a telephoto lens, if you don't want to interrupt its progress again.

Lizards are daytime creatures, and use their excellent vision to search for food, to evade predators, and to recognize both mates and rivals. Many species move very quickly and are not easy to photograph. Where there are lots of lizards around, try to spot a favourite rock or resting place, pre-focus your lens on the site, predetermine your exposure, and wait for a lizard to appear. One lizard, the chameleon, adapts its colour to its surroundings and is difficult to see, especially when it is motionless, but a photographer who spots one will probably be able to make pictures close up, because the chameleon doesn't want to ruin its camouflage by moving.

Whenever you photograph amphibians and reptiles, keep in mind that these creatures have the same basic needs as other animals. Don't treat them with contempt because they are more primitive than birds and mammals, and perhaps less easy for humans to understand. If you approach all amphibians and reptiles carefully – from frogs to crocodiles – and use common sense, you will be successful in making pictures of these creatures and their activities.

Fish and other water creatures

There are more species of fish than of birds, mammals, amphibians, and reptiles put together. While fish dominate the aquatic world, other forms of animal life also inhabit water, and so do many plants. Among the animals, all creatures with lungs (whales, for example) must come to the surface periodically for air. However, most aquatic animals – especially fish – are submerged for their entire lives or, in the case of many insects and amphibians, for their entire larval stage. So let's plunge beneath the surface of water to explore aquatic habitats and to photograph fish and other water creatures.

If you are making underwater photographs for the first time, you may be tempted to show things in isolation – a multicoloured fish, a striking branch of coral, or a meandering crab. But, the more time you spend observing, the more you will become aware of the intricate patterns and relationships in aquatic ecosystems. You may spot a very flat fish lying on the bottom and disguising itself as sand, and wonder whether it's hiding from predators or laying eggs. You may notice that some fish always swim in schools while others of the same size and similar appearance don't, and ask why. You may find a huge mop-like clump of eggs strung together, and determine to find out which species operates a communal nursery. As you explore and observe, you'll become aware that the fish realm resembles the bird world – individuals are often grouped into schools or flocks, courtship is highly ritualized and may involve elaborate displays of colour and movement, and so on.

To gain experience, you could commence your underwater photography fairly close to the surface, because the deeper you go, the darker it gets. At a depth of nine metres, 87 per cent of the light will be lost. Because even clear water is hundreds of times less transparent than air and full of particles of living and non-living material, light is scattered, which reduces contrast at all levels of illumination in much the same way that throwing any object out of focus blends colours, or mixes areas of light and dark. Shadows, which provide texture and definition, are reduced or virtually lost. To make matters more difficult, water absorbs colour. If it absorbed all hues equally, this wouldn't be so bad. However, it affects the wave lengths at the warm end of the spectrum – red, orange, and yellow – the most. This means that the farther down you go the more blue-green things look, especially on film. Another potential problem is light refraction. When light enters water, it travels more slowly. That has the effect of altering focal length and narrowing the field of view – a 35mm lens is suddenly a 50mm lens. However, most of these problems can be overcome.

MAKING UNDERWATER PICTURES FROM ABOVE WATER

There are at least three ways you can photograph underwater life from above water. The first is when you are working in a shallow tide pool or puddle, and your subject matter (a sea anemone or starfish, for example) is close to the surface. It is sufficiently illuminated to make exposure easy. All you have to do is set up your tripod and camera, and make your composition and exposure as if the subject matter were not under water. The main problems may be surface reflections from white clouds, a dull grey sky, or the sun itself, which interferes visually. In all these cases, you can position a large opaque umbrella to cover the area of your composition. If you are working close to frogs' eggs or insect larvae just below the surface of a puddle, the shadow of your body will eliminate reflections and allow you to see easily.

The second way to photograph under the surface of calm, shallow water is to put a diving mask on your camera. Simply place the window of the mask against the front of your lens, and you will be able to submerge the lens two or three centimetres. If water pressure does not hold the mask in place, try using the mask strap. A variation on this technique works better, but requires a little preparation. Cut the bottom out of a plastic tumbler and glue an ultra-violet or skylight filter on in its place. Be sure to use epoxy glue and seal any gaps. Then, pop the glass over your lens and poke the end under the water surface. (The water pressure will keep the tumbler around your lens.) You'll find this is a good device for exploring ponds.

The third way is to use a small aquarium, which will enable you to get spectacular results with a little practice. Try to obtain an aquarium or glass box that is quite narrow, so the fish, squid, crab, or other creatures you want to photograph can't move too close or too far away from the range in which you are focusing. If you already have an aquarium and pet fish, you can begin right away. If you don't, you can set one up, and start off by collecting specimens from natural aquatic habitats. Here's how you proceed once you have collected your specimen (with water, sand, stones, and/or plant life).

1/ Put the water and your subject matter into the aquarium and let the water settle. (Sometimes it will take a few days.)

2/ While it's settling, set up your camera and flash equipment. (See "Electronic flash" on page 167.) Your positions will vary depending on your subject matter. Because many marine creatures are translucent, they will show up best with side or back lighting. To place your flash units or a flash unit and reflector accurately, you may want to use studio lights (or other bright, portable lamps) for a test. There is no other way to check in advance where highlights or reflections may show up in the glass, unless you use your flash to pre-test with instant colour prints. However, you won't have to repeat this procedure every time you make a new composition, as you'll soon learn what flash positions to avoid. You can avoid problems by not pointing your flash at the glass surface from the camera position. Also wear dark clothing, so your own reflections will not appear in the glass, and in the final image.

3/ Press the depth-of-field preview button to make sure that the glass surface is completely out-of-focus. If it shows any detail, refocus. You may need to move closer, use a longer lens, or a wider lens opening for shallower depth of field. If moisture condenses on the outside of the aquarium, wipe it off, and have a fan or cloth nearby to keep it dry while you are photographing. (The warmer the room in relation to the water temperature, the greater the condensation.) If there is distracting material beyond the aquarium, you can use a dark cloth or cardboard for a background.

4/ Predetermine your exposure.

5/ Settle on a final composition, or watch for something to happen that you want to photograph, and press the shutter release when it does.

6/ Return your specimen to its natural habitat.

MAKING UNDERWATER PICTURES UNDER WATER

If you want to make photographs more than a short distance below the water surface, you will need to prepare properly. First, think of equipment for yourself – a face mask, scuba gear, wet suit, fins.

Second, consider the photographic equipment you'll require. You can purchase an automatic Nikonos rangefinder camera, which is waterproof to a depth of 50 metres; the Minolta Weathermatic is useful to about three and one-half metres. The range of the Nikonos, and the various lenses and close-up kit that are available for it, make it very useful for serious underwater photographers. (The close-up kit includes attachable viewfinders for correcting parallax when making extreme close-ups.) The alternative to a waterproof camera is an underwater housing for the equipment you already have. If you decide on this option, make certain that when the housing is on your equipment, you can manipulate all the camera controls easily – focusing ring, film advance lever, shutter release, and so on. If you can't, your underwater photography will be a very frustrating experience. Also, you must have an underwater electronic flash unit – several are available. In addition to noting these recommendations, try to go photographing with people who regularly photograph under water before you make specific purchases.

Photographing underwater objects that are more than three metres away from the camera is virtually impossible; this is a world of close-ups and semi-close-ups. So, if you want to show a wide expanse, you will need wide-angle lenses. (Remember that a 35mm lens becomes a 50mm lens under water, so you may want a 21mm lens, which will function as a 28mm one; or a 15mm lens which is like a 21mm). Flash is necessary for all shots eight metres or more beneath the surface, not only to provide illumination, but also to restore the natural colours. (Above that depth, warming filters or flash will help.) However, if you use the flash "head on," you may illuminate particles in the water, and have a picture that looks like a snow storm. Holding the flash to one side substantially reduces this possibility and also brings out the translucency of many underwater creatures. Because you are photographing in water, you will have to divide your flash guide number by four. You may find that dividing the flash GN by three is sufficient for distances of less than a metre. These are only recommendations; you must take into account how murky or clear the water is. Don't hesitate to bracket your exposures, and study your results carefully. Experience will be your best teacher.

When you are choosing film, remember that slow-speed film may give you less depth of field than you want. On the other hand, very fast films may not provide the resolution or colour quality you want. Ask for advice, but failing that, your favourite medium-speed film may be your best choice. If you want to make black-and-white images, also consider medium-speed films, which will provide sufficient contrast, especially when you use side or back lighting.

There's a unique excitement in photographing under water where subjects are suspended in apparent defiance of gravity, where creatures appear and disappear in the murky distances, and where people, by rights, don't belong. Sharing this strange world through your photographs can also be great fun, since most people are fascinated by it. When you are making pictures under water, don't overlook aspects of composition that you would carefully consider above water – the appearance of the background, the size of the main subject in relation to its surroundings, the pictorial effect of shooting toward the sun, and so on. Also, try for images that express your personal response to the environment. Identify what excites you most about a coral reef or the bottom of a rocky lake, and then consider how to use your equipment and techniques to convey silence, struggle, or peace.

The photography of natural things

Beside me sits a pot of hyacinths. Four days ago the emerging buds were barely visible among the leaves; now the blossoms are beginning to open. Within an hour their fragrance will fill the room. The process began three months ago when I planted the bulbs in soil, watered them, and placed the pot outdoors where the bulbs would get the cold they require for root development. In the transition from bulbs to flowers, the hyacinths have used all three life mediums – air, water, and soil – and the energy from the sun that makes life possible. Nature has worked perfectly.

However, leaves and flowers are not the culmination of the process. When the hyacinths wither and die, I will set the pot outdoors again, where insects, fungi, and bacteria will use the plants for food. The insects will nourish other creatures, and the fungi and bacteria will help to decompose the flowers and leaves until they are returned to the earth as organic material, enriching the soil. The plants will live on as bulbs, resting and gaining strength, until the cold weather again stimulates a new cycle of growth.

Next spring, when the hyacinths start to grow, they will not be starting from the same point they did last year. The bulbs will be larger, and the soil will have changed. Every spring is like the previous one, but every spring is unique. Plants, animals, and ecosystems evolve. Patterns of growth and development are more like spirals than circles. Nature moves in upward-moving cycles. The process is dynamic.

As a nature photographer, you will recognize in your own life the overall pattern of nature – one of steady, gradual development. You will probably be delighted by the reappearance of familiar things and be challenged by new situations – and grow as a person and a photographer because of them both.

To grow as a nature photographer you must be open and receptive to nature – in your home, the city, or the wilderness. Only an open flower can be fertilized and set seeds. Only an open flower can provide nectar. Just as a milkweed plant and a monarch butterfly depend on each other to ensure the future of their own kind, so a nature photographer must interact with other natural things for stimulation and growth. The milkweed plant produces seeds; the butterfly lays eggs. A nature photographer creates pictures. These images are like flowers, complete in themselves and worthy of attention; but they are also like seeds – ideas that will germinate when conditions are right for growth, giving rise to whole new generations of pictures. When you learn more about nature, pictorial design, and photographic techniques, your pictures will reflect the improvement. When you photograph the new spring, your pictures will show that you are growing in a spiral, like nature itself.

A good nature photographer will take direction from nature – as a person and as a photographer. You will recognize both nature's underlying order, or simplicity, and its basic dynamic of growth and change, and will also see that it maintains a balance between these two forces. Balance is nature's fundamental law, although sometimes it's not readily observable. But, if you care about natural things and observe them closely, you will recognize balance in every ecosystem from a vast forest to a puddle, and your pictures will reflect your caring.

There is a fundamental connection between the balanced design of natural things and the need for balance in pictorial composition. Every nature photograph begins with already-existing material – for example, an elm tree – which has a character independent of you and your reaction to it. The tree's shape is the result of both genetic and environmental factors. You will alter the appearance of its shape with every camera position or lens you use; so, try to make an accurate depiction of your subject that fulfills the demands of good visual presentation.

The awareness that subject matter is important in its own right is central to good nature photography. If you care for your subjects, you will make visual compositions that evolve from their intrinsic shapes, lines, texture, and perspective. When your pictorial arrangements of natural things harmonize with their natural designs, you will experience a sense of personal harmony with nature that is deeply satisfying, since that will put you more closely in tune with the system that created and supports you.

Every successful image, whether dominated by light tones or dark, is a strategic balancing of contrasting tones. The arrangement of tones in this image – the lines of bright aspens alternating with a background of shadows – results from the natural design of the subject matter, the way light is reflected or absorbed by it, and my choice of camera position and lens. I took advantage of both natural and pictorial design to document the subject matter in a manner that emphasizes its expressive features.

If you are sensitive to the role light plays in creating and maintaining life, you'll make better pictures of natural things. You will understand why most woodland plants grow, flower, and set their seeds during the spring, before the canopy of tree leaves grows and cuts the light. You will notice meadow plants slowly turning their blossoms as the sun arcs across the sky. As your sensitivity to the quality, brightness, and direction of light grows, your nature pictures will reflect your developing awareness.

Photographs of natural things often show communities – groups of individuals living together to meet common needs. Here rhododendron, bunchberries, and blueberries share the same habitat, each consuming the resources they need and contributing new ones. They help to support other communities of insects, birds, and mammals. Taken together, all these communities form an ecosystem developing toward maturity as a forest. The overall design of an ecosystem can best be photographed in a series of pictures made over a period of time.

Not long ago, this young forest was an abandoned pasture. Now its changed character evokes a whole new set of emotional responses, and a new set of photographic challenges. You could use scale both to document the size of trees and to convey the impression of height. By zeroing in on a line of fungi, or by using mist to isolate a clump of ferns, bushes, or flowers, you could express the sense of privacy of tiny habitats within the forest.

Because you are part of nature, you will frequently notice parallels between your own human characteristics and behaviour and those of other natural things. The delicacy of a tiny flower may symbolize your own fragility, so that when you photograph the flower you may be thinking of yourself, your own situation, or your hopes. By using your tools and techniques thoughtfully you can document the flower and, at the same time, express something of its meaning for you.

By observing the designs of natural things, you can read the story of their change and development. When you look at a river system from the air, you may decide to photograph the intricate network of arteries and veins created by the action of water on soil. Perhaps you'll want to reveal its similarity to the pattern of vessels that carry blood or sap to all parts of animals or plants. The more carefully you observe natural things, the better your pictures will be; and the more carefully you photograph nature, the more you'll learn about it.

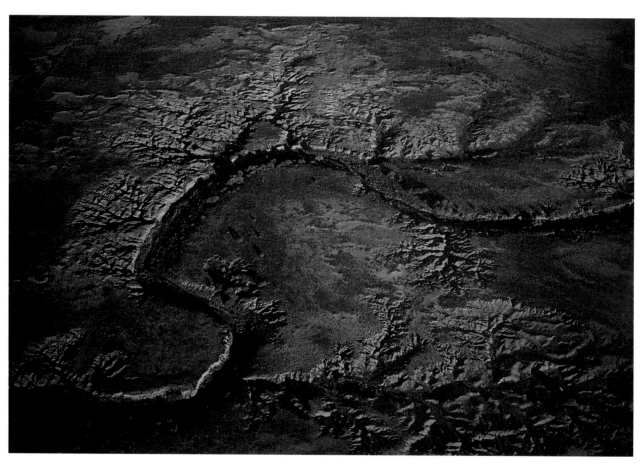

Photographing abstract designs in nature will make you aware of nature's fundamental principles. With abstracts, you can pull the labels off things and find new order in complex arrangements of lines and shapes. Through the use of oblique lines and rhythmic patterns, you can convey the dynamism of the natural world. In this way you can see more clearly that patterns of order and change in your own life are also expressions of how nature functions.

Photographing natural things is a way of being in touch with them and with yourself. Try to identify the essential character of your subject matter and to express it simply and clearly. If you can do that, your photographs will show your understanding of the material and your feeling for it. Also, you will convey something of your response to life itself. To me, life is a gift, and the opportunity to photograph the sweep of a sand dune is one of the privileges of being alive.

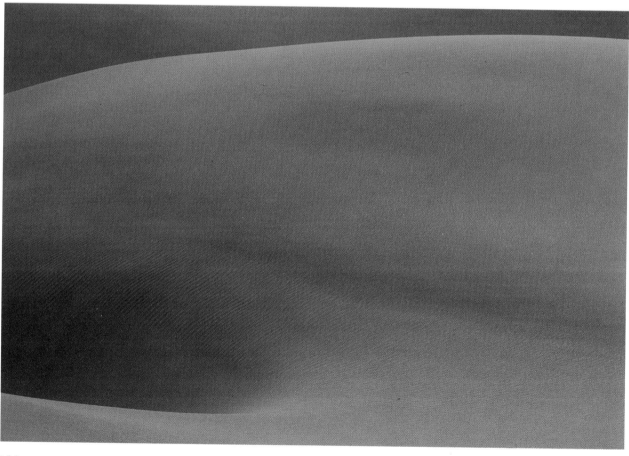

Preparing for a field trip

A field trip is an opportunity to explore, to observe, and to photograph another place. It is also a chance to enlarge your understanding of natural things. For a nature photographer, it implies canoeing, wading, walking, hiking, climbing, or puttering around in a particular area by yourself or with others. For these reasons, a field trip can be a special event, so it makes sense to prepare for it thoughtfully in order to enjoy it fully.

There are *three stages* to every field trip – *before, during, and after*. Your planning should take all three stages into account. This is as true for a half-day hike near your home as it is for a month spent in the great wildlife parks of Africa. In fact, apart from the special arrangements necessary for travelling long distances, a trip across the continent or overseas is not very different from a one-day field trip. Once you are in Africa or on the Amazon, you will no longer be preparing for the entire trip. Instead, you will be planning one day at a time, and you will have to consider what you need for that day in the way of equipment, films, food, and so on. So, let's think first about a one-day field trip.

PLANNING A ONE-DAY FIELD TRIP

When you are *planning a field trip*, you must consider *1/* what you will definitely need, *2/* what you may need, and *3/* what you can reasonably leave at home. What you *may* need is the tricky part. If you don't know very much about the place you are visiting or what you can expect to see and photograph there, you should question people who do know. The biggest mistake you can make is to take too much equipment or too many clothes, assuming that you *may* require them for one reason or another. It's better to travel light and miss some photographs than to miss pictures because you are overburdened and exhausted. So, decide on your minimum requirements and then add to them sparingly, unless you expect to be within easy walking distance of your car at all times.

During the trip, try to fulfill your photographic expectations, but also leave yourself wide open to the unexpected. As useful as planning a trip is, it can produce "mind sets" that will hamper your interest in exploring and your ability to see. If you set out to photograph hepaticas and bloodroot in a spring woods, but you have miscalculated the weather and no flowers are blooming yet, you have a perfect opportunity to do a story on the last vestiges of winter. Examine that remaining snowbank lying, unexpectedly, on the north side of a large boulder. Note beech leaves still clinging to branches. (Why haven't they fallen?) Observe the overall colour of the forest – you won't often see such lovely greys and browns. Take the time to examine lichens, bark, the signs of mammals and insects, and reflections in pools of water.

After the trip, once you are home, try to read about unfamiliar things you have seen or to answer questions about nature that never occurred to you before. (Why *do* those beech leaves cling all winter long?) Evaluate your negatives or slides as soon as you have processed them; try to assess where you succeeded or failed from a photographic standpoint – and *why*. Have you avoided the disorder of the forest, and made every scene or close-up into an overly tidy composition? Why are your exposures consistently accurate this time, when normally you might expect them to be less accurate? Which film reproduced the browns best? In short, reinforce the experience from a visual and a technical standpoint. Also, review your equipment. What did you take that you didn't use? What did you need that you didn't take?

Minimum photographic equipment

Unless I expect unusual weather or other circumstances, the following is my basic photographic equipment for a one-day field trip. I can easily carry all of these things in my hands, in large pockets, or looped over my shoulder or belt. In addition to this kit, I carry a bag of raisins and nuts.

1/ *A sturdy, medium-weight tripod with a ball-and-socket head.* Some people may question the value of carrying a tripod, but I consider it so important that, if I can't take it with me, I'll change my plans and go somewhere I can take it. If you don't have a tripod on most field trips, you will miss an enormous number of good pictures, and sacrifice quality in most of those you do make. The most useful tripod is one that extends to your normal eye level and can also be collapsed to ground level. There are a few good brands available. Besides providing the opportunity to make sharp, perfectly composed images, a tripod is the ideal place to rest your camera with the longer, heavier lens. A field trip is not a marathon: you pause a lot. Every time you do, you can leave the camera and tripod while you explore a little or examine subject matter.

2/ *Two camera bodies* (one on the tripod).

3/ *Two lenses* (on the cameras). If neither lens is my 100mm macro lens, I will also carry extension tubes for close-up work; but sometimes I'll break my two-lens rule and take along my macro lens in a pocket or in a case looped on my belt.

4/ *Skylight or ultraviolet filters* (on the lenses for protection).

5/ *Several 36-exposure films* (about two-thirds of them slow-speed and one-third medium-speed). To save space, I always remove them from their cardboard boxes.

6/ *Spare batteries* for my cameras.

7/ *A cable release.*

8/ *A folded piece of silver foil.*

9/ *Lens-cleaning tissue* or a small chamois.

Other equipment

Given a chance to enlarge my basic kit of photographic equipment, I will consider taking along the following items.

1/ *A right-angle adaptor* for the camera viewfinder. Only when I have absolutely no intention of making close-ups will I leave this behind, because it makes photography at ground level so much easier. Also, it's extremely easy to carry, because if I don't need it I simply keep it on whichever camera I'm not using.

2/ *A small backpack* for additional items, such as:

an extra lens

light-weight rain gear or a large plastic garbage bag

a small flash unit, with a tilting head and a cord

field guides to plants, animal tracks, birds

some more food, probably fruit for both nourishment and liquid content

insect repellant

a small first-aid kit

Because the following items add unnecessary weight and are unlikely to be used on a field trip, I never carry an umbrella, (except to shade tide pools or similar small water habitats), a separate light meter, a third camera, a thermos, or binoculars (unless I definitely am watching for birds or small distant objects). Generally, I resist the urge to cart along all the odds and ends of equipment that a photographer tends to accumulate.

Probably, your requirements will vary somewhat from mine. Also, you will alter your selection depending on the habitat you are visiting.

Preparations

When you are planning for a long trip, you should attend to a number of important matters long before you leave, and you should pack your equipment carefully, especially for a flight. Here are some specific suggestions.

1/ Keep your passport up-to-date, and allow ample time (a month or more) to obtain visas.

2/ Have your cameras and lenses cleaned and serviced. Purchase extra batteries for your cameras and flash, and test them while you are in the store.

3/ Type out a list of all your equipment, or just the equipment you expect to take (include serial numbers). At a convenient time take your equipment and list to a customs office, so the list (and a copy) can be validated. Or, fill out green customs forms and have them validated. Don't wait until you are boarding a flight or crossing an international boundary to do this.(The list will be valid indefinitely. If you add equipment later, you can have the additions validated.) Also, declare on a separate sheet the amount of film you are taking.

4/ Read what you can about the area(s) you expect to visit, making special note of everything that will affect nature photography, especially weather.

5/ Pack thoughtfully; remember that every day on the trip will be like a one-day field excursion. Here are important things to keep in mind, particularly for airplane flights.

a/ Choose a camera bag that doesn't look like a camera bag. (I prefer something with soft sides, so it will expand or collapse when I add or remove items.) Plan to carry it on the plane with you.

b/ Take all of your films out of their boxes and canisters. Put all of the Kodachrome 25 in one transparent plastic bag, all of the Ektachrome 64 in another, and all of the Fujichrome 400 in still another. Fasten each bag at the top with a "twist 'em." Then place all three transparent bags in another clear plastic bag and seal it. If you are carrying a lot of film, this will greatly reduce the amount of space required and, equally important, make it easy for customs and airport security officers to hand-inspect your film. (I've never had one even bother to open the bag, because the films are completely visible.)

c/ You should pack two or three camera bodies. Choose the lenses to suit your journey. I may leave anything longer than a 200mm lens at home, unless I'm going specifically to photograph animal life. Normally, I carry two zoom lenses (let's say, 28-50mm or 35-70mm, and an 80-200mm zoom) plus my 100mm macro lens. If I had only one zoom lens, for instance the longer one, then I'd take both a wide-angle and normal (50mm) lens to replace the shorter zoom. If your carrying case or camera bag is not fitted with foam rubber,

wrap your cameras and lenses in extra underclothing, shirts, or socks.
Put everything else – batteries, filters, extra lens caps, etc. into two or three small plastic bags, and seal them. Be sure to include a small jeweller's screwdriver; vibrations of jets can loosen camera screws.
d/ Take the ball-and-socket head off your tripod (to shorten the tripod) and pack both in your suitcase.
e/ Keep your validated list of equipment and film with your passport.

Travelling

When you arrive at an *airport security check*, remove the bag of film from
your camera bag or carrying case. Let the camera bag go through the X-ray machine, which will save you and the security officer a lot of bother, and ask for a hand inspection of your films only. X-rays affect fast films the most, but all films after repeated exposure. Metal detectors have no effect.

When you arrive at *customs*, present your validated list (if requested, or if a check of your equipment is begun). Usually a customs officer will select only two or three items at random to check against your list. Remember the list is more important when you are returning home. Just to be on the safe side, in case I should ever lose my list, I always leave a validated copy at home.
If your equipment is insured, as it should be, your insurance agent can also prove to customs officials that you own the equipment, although it's conceivable that you may have to leave it with customs and claim it later. However, better that than pay duty on what you own.

If you are *travelling by car*, you will have packed differently. However, keep in mind that your equipment should be protected from dust, heat, extreme cold, and vibration, as well as being easily accessible for examination when you cross an international boundary. I always keep my equipment in two foam-lined camera cases in the trunk of my car. I place an old woollen blanket underneath them, and another over top. The foam and the woollen blanket provide total protection, yet I can quickly retrieve anything I want. (If you don't have foam-lined cases, more blankets will be satisfactory.)

Photographing

When you have arrived at your destination and are photographing in new surroundings, plan one day at a time. For example, don't carry all your films every day, unless it's unsafe to leave them behind. Take only what you think you'll need, plus two or three more. Leave the rest, plus exposed films, in the coolest safe place available. Make similar decisions about your equipment. Every day make notes of information about plants, birds, weather, etc. that you may require when you return home, but are likely to forget. Pick up local pamphlets, booklets, and other printed information. Write down the gist of conversations with local people, especially those who are knowledgeable about your subject matter. Record names and addresses.

If you are returning to an area where you have photographed previously, take a *short* slide show (50 to 80 slides) of your previous visit. The local people will be pleased, and once they've seen your show, you may be deluged with offers of assistance, tips on where the best flowers are, and so on. If nobody else has a slide projector, the local school probably will, and school children are usually very receptive to a program about local nature. They (and others) will be excited about your coming so far to photograph the plants, animals, and other natural features of their region, and they may gain a new respect for what is all around them.

Whether you are planning a nature trip near your home or halfway around the world, remember that the photographs you make are a useful resource. If you edit them well and arrange them thoughtfully into slide or print presentations, you are contributing to a better understanding of nature and, very possibly, helping to protect the areas you visit.

Choosing equipment

Take your time in studying and acquiring equipment. It's better to have a little equipment that you know well than a lot that you don't. Here are some suggestions to help you.

BASIC EQUIPMENT

camera   All well-known brands of 35mm single-lens reflex cameras are well-constructed physically and optically, but not all models have the features a nature photographer requires. These are the essential features.
1/ *Lens interchangeability.*
2/ *A depth-of-field preview.*
3/ *Manual over-ride* of automatic exposure.
4/ *Capacity for time exposure.*

lenses   1/ *A standard 50mm or 55mm lens.* Most cameras are sold with this lens, which permits a wide variety of nature photographs.
2/ *A macro lens, a wide-angle lens, a zoom lens.* You should add lenses slowly and thoughtfully, according to your interests and what you can carry comfortably. You may want to consider a macro, a wide-angle, or a zoom lens as a second lens. Some lenses have both macro and zoom capacity and may be attractive; however, check carefully before you buy one, as some macro-zoom lenses are relatively heavy and/or do not focus as closely as a regular macro lens.

tripod   A sturdy, light- or medium-weight tripod is essential because it enables you to compose pictures carefully and holds your camera steady. Here's what to look for.
1/ *Sturdiness.* A tripod must support your largest lens, and not tremble in the wind.
2/ *Ball-and-socket head.* Most tripods come with a pan head, which is for a movie camera. Remove this in the store and buy a ball-and-socket head, such as the large-size Leitz.
3/ *Legs that spread flat.* This allows you to work at ground level. Test all features of the legs for ease of operation.
4/ *Standard or accessory short centre post.* You can attach your camera to this when the tripod legs are spread flat.
5/ *Size and weight.* For hikes and air travel, consider a tripod no larger than 56 cm in length and 9 cm in diameter, weighing about 2 kg.

other

1/ *Spare batteries* for your camera.

2/ *A cable release* with a locking mechanism for slow shutter speeds and time exposures.

3/ *An ultraviolet or skylight filter* for lens protection from rain and dirt.

4/ *A tiny jeweller's screwdriver* for tightening camera and lens screws.

5/ *A carrying bag* for your equipment and film. Use a small flight bag or similar satchel until you have acquired two or three lenses and other equipment; then you may want to invest in a foam-lined light-weight metal case, with holes cut in the foam to accept each specific lens or other items.

6/ *An electronic flash.*

film

For both colour and black-and-white photography, you'll probably want to settle on a *slow- or medium-speed film* of ISO 25 to 125 for most shooting, and a *higher-speed film* of ISO 200 to 400 for situations that require hand-holding your camera in low light. Generally, slower-speed films appear sharper (have less granular structure), produce more saturated hues, are more tolerant of overexposure and underexposure, and provide the best contrast in tones. Because manufacturers improve films, test various films from time to time. You'll find that your preferences change.

EQUIPMENT FOR SPECIFIC SITUATIONS

landscape and habitat shots (one metre to infinity)

1/ *A range of lenses from wide-angle to telephoto.* A good combination is either a 24mm, a 28mm, or a 35mm wide-angle, a standard 50mm lens, an 80-200mm zoom, or variations on this range. One longer lens, say 300mm, can often be useful for very distant scenes.

2/ *A sturdy tripod.*

close-ups (plants, insects, dew drops)

1/ *One or more close-up attachments.* Consider a macro lens (a 100mm macro enables you to make the same close-ups as a 50mm macro, but at twice the distance from your subject), extension tubes and/or supplementary lenses to attach to your regular lenses, an adaptor ring for reversing lenses, a double-track bellows with a short-mount lens and a focusing rail (for both close-ups and magnification).

2/ *A wide-angle lens* for making close-ups that also show habitat.

3/ *A tripod* that collapses to ground level for the camera; a second tripod for off-camera flash (optional).

4/ *A right-angle attachment* for the camera viewfinder for making close-ups easier near ground level.

5/ *Kitchen foil* to reflect light into dark areas and/or an *electronic flash.*

mammals, amphibians, reptiles

1/ *A range of fixed-focal-length lenses or zoom lenses.* Consider lenses from 50mm to 400mm or, perhaps, a 35-70mm zoom, an 80-200mm zoom, and a longer lens.

2/ *A sturdy tripod* that will hold your heaviest lens.

3/ *A pistol grip* for lenses longer than 200mm (optional).

4/ *A motor drive* for rapid shooting and advancing of film (optional).

5/ *An electronic flash* for controlled situations indoors and for some close-ups of small creatures.

birds

1/ *A range of fixed-focal-length lenses or zoom lenses.* For portraits, such as photographs of small birds at nest, you should have a short-focus 300mm telephoto lens or close-up attachments for a 300mm telephoto lens or longer.

2/ *A tripod* for your camera and another for holding off-camera flash.

3/ *An electronic flash* for difficult lighting situations.

4/ *An inexpensive light-weight blind* for photographing birds' activities.

164

under water   See pages 143 to 146.

field trips   See pages 157 to 162.

FILTERS

Filters for colour

You can purchase filters of varying hue and saturation to use on a camera lens or on a flash head. Good filter charts with specific information about each type of filter are available in photographic stores.

yellowish or amber   Produces warmer hues. A pale amber filter, such as 81A, can take the chill off a sunny mid-day scene or the blue cast out of a mammal's fur. An 85B warming filter is useful for shooting tungsten film in daylight or with electronic flash.

bluish   Produces cooler hues. For example, an 80A cooling filter enables you to use daylight film in tungsten light. An 82A or 82B filter produces more satisfactory hues in blue flowers, which colour films often do not record accurately.

Filters for black-and-white

yellow   Darkens a blue sky, enhances clouds, and lightens green foliage. A dark yellow filter intensifies these effects, lightens yellow and red, and adds some contrast to sunlit scenes.

red   Lightens yellow and red, darkens blue sky and water substantially, reduces haze, and increases contrast in sunlit scenes. A dark red filter renders a blue sky almost black and makes clouds appear almost white.

green   Darkens a blue sky and lightens foliage.

blue   Increases haze and mist and lightens blue.

Other filters

polarizing screen   Helps to reduce glare and reflections, especially when used more-or-less at right angles to the sun's rays, thus making skies darker, clouds lighter, and water clearer.

skylight   Reduces bluishness and is useful for open shade on sunny days with colour films.

ultraviolet   Reduces haze. Many photographers keep either a skylight or ultraviolet filter on their lens at all times for protection against dust and moisture.

neutral density   Reduces the amount of light passing through the lens and is useful when light is very intense and you have high-speed film in your camera. It has no effect on colour.

CARING FOR EQUIPMENT

To protect your camera and lens against

rain	Cover camera with clear plastic bag with hole for lens; keep cap on lens when not shooting.
humidity	Store with small packs of silica gel.
fogging	Move gradually from warm-to-cold or cold-to-warm situations; allow time for moisture to evaporate; or, use gentle air flow from hair dryer or heater set at low.
heat	Store in cool, shaded place; insulate with woollen blankets or any material that traps large amounts of air, like foam.
cold	Have camera winterized by a service department for extreme cold; keep inside coat until ready to use; advance film carefully; have a good supply of new batteries handy, especially for automatic cameras.
dust, sand	Carry in airtight case, or wrap well with cloth; when shooting in dry, windy areas, shelter with your body or plastic bag.
jarring	Carry in foam-lined case; wrap in foam or thick layers of cloth.
deterioration	Have camera and lenses checked and cleaned professionally every year or two; handle with reasonable care.

If your camera and lens become

wet from rain or fog	Remove film and lens, dry with gentle air flow of hair dryer; use soft chamois for wiping, if necessary, but never touch shutter, mirror, or rear lens element.
wet from salt water	For exterior wetting only, wipe outside immediately several times with very damp soft cloth or chamois, then dry; if camera or lens is immersed in water, especially salt water, contact your insurance agent.
sandy	Shake gently, use camel's hair brush or air blower; avoid manipulating moving parts as much as possible; if serious, have cleaned professionally.
jammed	Avoid forcing jammed mechanism; try gentle flow of warm air to alter humidity level; check battery; return to manufacturer for service.
lost	List make, model, and serial number of all equipment at time of purchase; insure; keep documents in safe place, but take copies on trips.

ELECTRONIC FLASH

What to look for in an electronic flash unit.

    1/ Variable-position head.
    2/ Wide-angle to telephoto zoom feature.

3/ Variable power output.

4/ Capacity for manual and automatic operation (manual operation is essential for most close-up photography).

5/ Sensor that can be connected to an extension cord for precise exposure reading.

6/ Batteries. A flash unit with a nickel-cadmium battery is good for general use, because it is rechargeable. A flash unit with small replaceable batteries is useful when travelling abroad.

7/ Built-in filter holder (most flash units are colour-balanced for flesh tones, which may make slight colour correction necessary when photographing flowers).

8/ Size. If you expect to use a flash only for close-ups, a small unit is easy to carry and is powerful enough.

Using the flash guide number (GN) to determine exposure.

1/ Set your camera at 1/125 or 1/60 second or slower for electronic flash. (The *X* setting on the shutter speed dial is the highest shutter speed you can use.)

2/ Choose a subject and decide on the depth of field you want, say a lens opening of f/16.

3/ Divide 16 into the GN of the flash for the film you are using. For example, if you are using ISO 100 film, and the flash has a metric GN of 32 for that film, divide 16 into 32, which comes to 2. Then, position the flash 2 metres from the subject. (Or, conversely, if you have the flash positioned 2 metres from the subject, divide the GN of 32 by 2, and the answer of 16 will tell you f/16 is the correct lens setting.)

Making an exposure chart for close-ups.

The recommended guide number (GN) can be used to determine exposure when using flash with any lens, but not with close-up equipment. For making close-ups, you'll need to establish your own GN and an exposure chart for each film you use. Here's what you do.

1/ Load a film into your camera and get ready to make two or three exposures each of several close-up subjects.

2/ Make photographs at various apertures using the film's recommended GN, as outlined in the previous section.

3/ Make photographs using a GN of two-thirds of the recommended GN, for example, a GN of 20 instead of the recommended GN of 30.

4/ Try a GN between these two, say 24.

5/ Examine the resulting pictures to determine which GN settings consistently gave the best exposures.

6/ Prepare a simple exposure chart to record the type of film, the GN you prefer to use with it, and the distance the flash unit should be from the subject at each f/stop. Tape the chart to the back of your camera for handy reference when making flash close-ups with that film. (If you have a powerful flash or if you want to use a flash unit close to a subject, reduce the power output to 1/2, 1/4, or 1/8 power. Then, base your exposure chart on a reduced power output.)

Other equipment for use with flash

1/ Filters on the flash head or the camera lens to "correct" colours.

2/ A tripod to support an off-camera flash.

3/ A foil reflector for use with bounce flash. (Paste foil on pieces of cardboard that are hinged or taped together, so that it folds up for storage.)

4/ A piece of foil like an envelope around the flash head that directs or concentrates flash in a particular area.

Freeman Patterson's interest in photography began in childhood, even though he was twenty before he could afford his first camera. That was in 1958. Since then his involvement with photography has grown steadily.

Freeman was born at Long Reach, New Brunswick, graduated with a B.A. in philosophy from Acadia University in Nova Scotia in 1959, and received a master's degree in divinity from Union Theological Seminary at Columbia University in New York in 1962. The title of his master's thesis was "Still Photography as a Medium of Religious Expression." During his three years in New York he studied photography with Dr. Helen Manzer. In 1965 after teaching religious studies for three years at Alberta College in Edmonton, he resigned his teaching position to devote full time to photography.

Since 1965 his photographs have been published in numerous books, magazines, journals, newspapers, and advertisements, and have been exhibited around the world. Many of his photographs were selected for the National Film Board of Canada's three award-winning books, *Canada: A Year of the Land*, *Canada*, and *Between Friends/Entre Amis*. He is the author of the best-selling books, *Photography for the Joy of It* and *Photography and the Art of Seeing*.

Freeman has given innumerable slide presentations, lectures, and workshops, to both amateur and professional groups in Canada, the United States, and southern Africa. He is a past president of the Toronto Guild of Colour Photography, and for ten years was the editor of *Camera Canada*, a magazine published by the National Association for Photographic Art. From 1973 to 1977, with Dennis Mills, he operated a school of photography at Shampers' Bluff, New Brunswick.

In 1967 Freeman was awarded the National Film Board's Gold Medal for Photographic Excellence, one of the first two photographers to receive the award. In 1971 he was honoured with an Associateship in the Photographic Society of America for his contribution to amateur photography at the individual, national, and international levels. In 1975 he received the highest award (Hon EFIAP) of the Fédération Internationale de l'Art Photographique (Berne, Switzerland), an honour restricted to 200 living persons, and was elected to the Royal Canadian Academy of Art. In 1976 he became an Honorary Fellow of the Photographic Society of Southern Africa. In 1980 he became a Fellow of the Photographic Society of America for his writing and lecturing about photography, and received a Doctorate of Letters from the University of New Brunswick.